The Primary Encyclopedia

'Do you know your diphthongs from your digraphs? Are you au fait with all the main reading programmes published in the UK? And can you really tell the difference between a legend, a myth and a fable? If you have any doubt about saying yes to any of these questions, fear not; the answers are all in "The Primary English Encyclopedia". This fantastic resource contains such a comprehensive coverage of literacy topics that it will undoubtedly become one of the most regularly consulted titles on your bookshelf'
Literacy Time Plus

This newly updated, user-friendly encyclopedia addresses all aspects of the primary English curriculum and is an invaluable reference for all training and practising teachers. Now in its fourth edition, entries have been updated to take account of new research and thinking. The approach is supportive of the reflective practitioner in meeting UK requirements and in developing sound subject knowledge and good classroom practice. While the book is scholarly, the author writes in a conversational style and includes reproductions of covers of recommended children's books and examples of children's writing and drawing to add interest. The encyclopedia includes:

- over 500 entries, many expanded in this new edition, and some new ones, for example on dialogic teaching, multimedia texts and reading on screen;
- short definitions of key concepts;

- input on the initial teaching of reading including the teaching of phonics and the other cue-systems;
- extended entries on major topics such as speaking and listening, reading, writing, drama, poetry, non-fiction, bilingualism and children's literature;
- information on new literacies and new kinds of texts for children;
- discussion of current issues and input on the history of English teaching in the primary years;
- gender and literacy;
- important references for each topic, advice on further reading and accounts of recent research findings; and
- a who's who in primary English and lists of essential texts, updated for this new edition.

This encyclopedia will be ideal for student teachers, on courses preparing them for work in primary schools, and for primary school teachers. It is hoped that anyone concerned with bringing about the informed and imaginative teaching of primary school English will find the book helpful and interesting.

Margaret Mallett has taught primary school children, student teachers and teachers on MA Language and Literature courses. She is a team member of the editorial board of *English 4–11*, a fellow of the English Association and a regular reviewer of children's books and resources.

The Primary English Encyclopedia

The heart of the curriculum

Fourth edition

Margaret Mallett
with a Foreword by Sue Palmer

Routledge
Taylor & Francis Group

LONDON AND NEW YORK

First published 2002
by David Fulton Publishers
Second edition 2005
Third edition 2008
This fourth edition published 2012
by Routledge
2 Park Square, Milton Park, Abingdon, Oxon OX14 4RN

Simultaneously published in the USA and Canada
by Routledge
711 Third Avenue, New York, NY 10017

Routledge is an imprint of the Taylor & Francis Group, an informa business

British Library Cataloguing in Publication Data
A catalogue record for this book is available from the British Library

Library of Congress Cataloging in Publication Data
Mallett, Margaret.
The primary English encyclopedia / Margaret Mallett. – 4th ed.
p. cm.
Includes index.
Summary: "This newly updated, user friendly encyclopedia explains concepts, aims and current requirements in all aspects of the primary English curriculum and is an invaluable reference for all training and practising teachers. Now in its fourth edition, entries have been updated to take account of new research and thinking and now reflect the requirements of the new Primary National Curriculum and particularly The Communication, Language and Literacy Development element. The approach is critical but constructive and supportive of the reflective practitioner in developing sound subject knowledge and good classroom practice. The encyclopedia includes: – over 600 entries , including new entries on English in the Early Years, bilingualism, SEN, the use of the internet, synthetic phonics and many more – short definitions of key concepts – succinct explanations of current UK requirements – extended entries on major topics such as speaking and listening, reading, writing, drama, poetry, bilingualism and children's literature - input on new literacies and new kinds of texts for children - discussion of current issues and some input on the history of English teaching in the primary years - gender and literacy - important references for each topic , advice on further reading and accounts of recent research findings – a Who's Who of Primary English and lists of essential texts, updated for this new edition. This encyclopedia will be ideal for student teachers on BA and PGCE courses preparing for work in primary schools and primary school teachers"– Provided by publisher.
1. Language arts (Elementary)–Great Britain–Handbooks, manuals, etc. I. Title.
LB1576.M3626 2011
372.6'044–dc22
2011013491

ISBN: 978-0-415-58951-2 (hbk)
ISBN: 978-0-415-58952-9 (pbk)
ISBN: 978-0-203-80315-8 (ebk)

Typeset in Galliard
by Taylor & Francis Books

Printed and bound in Great Britain by
TJ International Ltd, Padstow, Cornwall

Contents

Foreword

In a *Times Educational Supplement* review, I once wrote that no one book could cover every aspect of primary English teaching today. The subject is so vast, so integral to everything that happens in the primary classroom, and so intensely controversial that a single volume – especially by one author – could never hope to do it justice. I was wrong. In her *Primary English Encyclopedia*, Margaret Mallett manages to accomplish this. It was therefore a great honour to write the foreword to the second and third editions and now this fourth, even more comprehensive edition.

From 'Abbreviation' on page 1 to 'Zone of proximal development' 474 pages later, Margaret tackles everything anyone could want to know about the teaching of English language, literacy and literature in the primary years, and she does so with clarity, practicality and considerable panache. To do justice to complex or controversial areas such as early years language and literacy, speaking and listening and history of English teaching, her 'extended entries' take the form of mini essays combining passionate concern with balanced, rational argument. This fourth edition includes several new entries, such as dialogic teaching, multimedia texts and classic texts: contemporary approaches to teaching them, as well as additions to many of the existing entries, for example on the atlas, popular culture and new media, and Information and Communications Technology (ICT) and English, ensuring that the encyclopedia is thoroughly up to date in terms of new technology and 'new literacies'.

Margaret originally planned this book at the request of her students, who wanted a starting point for learning about language and literacy. However, she also set herself the aim of writing a book that 'soars above the requirements of the day to capture some things of enduring importance about the primary English classroom' (after all, as her subtitle points out, English *is* the heart of the curriculum). She fulfils that aim admirably, reminding us through the breadth of her knowledge that obsession with tests, targets and objectives is not what English teaching is about.

The English language, and the uses of literacy that spring from it, are part of our heritage and, more importantly, ourselves. Everything about the way we teach English profoundly affects children's development and learning. The thoroughness and scholarship with which Margaret Mallett has compiled this encyclopedia is matched by the wisdom and humanity of her writing. Students and teachers can consult its pages confident that the author is both an expert on primary English and a passionate advocate for the sensitive teaching of the subject that is at the heart of the curriculum.

Sue Palmer

Acknowledgements

I would like to thank all the children, teachers and student teachers with whom I have worked and who have made me feel that teaching English in the primary years is exciting and satisfying. I would specially like to recognise all that I learnt during my twenty years as a governor at Castlecombe Primary School in Kent. Colleagues during my time in the Education department of Goldsmiths College added considerably to my understanding of children's development and learning in the early and primary years. I have also benefited over the years from the insights of the other members of the editorial team of the English Association's journal *English 4–11*. A highlight of my year continues to be the April meeting when we choose the prize winners of the Association's Illustrated Book competition.

The generosity of the authors, illustrators and publishers who allowed me to illustrate some entries with pictures from their work is very much appreciated. Full acknowledgement is given on the pages where the work appears.

I am grateful to the staff and children of Castlecombe Primary School in Mottingham, Kent, for allowing me to use the writing samples with the entries on alliteration and poetry. My thanks go also to Elaine Shiel and the children of Primary 3, Corstorphire Primary School, Edinburgh, for the writing about Cocoa the Brown Bear which appears with the entry on shared writing. Sele First School allowed me to include two poems about the Angel of the North and I thank the children and teachers involved. Michelle Coles and Abbie and Rowan kindly contributed Abbie's 'Edward the Lion' poem (play and language and literacy) and Rowan's writing and drawing (recount). Yasmine and her parents, Pouneh and Morten, kindly allowed me to include Yasmine's poem 'Summing Up!' in the entry on poetry. Gill Robins of Sun Hill Junior School in Hampshire allowed me to draw on her innovative work with children on using contemporary approaches to classic texts and to reproduce some of the children's multimodal creations. I thank Gill, Sun Hill Primary School and Year 5, and the English Association for giving me permission to reproduce the examples of work first published in *English 4–11*, Spring 2010, Number 38.

Above all, though, I would like to thank my husband, David: this task would not have been accomplished without his encouragement and practical help.

About this Encyclopedia

As I worked on the fourth edition of this encyclopedia, I kept in mind the helpful comments about the first three editions made by reviewers, students, teachers and colleagues.

Readers rightly expect a work like this to be kept up to date. I have done my best with ever-changing websites and new editions of key books – but I'm sure you will catch me out the odd time! All websites mentioned in the text were correct at the time of publication.

Teachers and student teachers can visit government sites for the latest requirements and guidance, but will benefit from reading more widely. So the entries draw attention to new books and research but sometimes refer to works which although written some years ago contain profound insights – these are the timeless classics of educational writing. Some of these are listed under 'My top ten texts'. Any books that were out of print at the time of publication of this Encyclopedia are marked O/P.

Teachers in the United Kingdom work within government-imposed frameworks and we welcome books that help us to do so creatively. It is important that reflective practitioners ponder on and evaluate lessons and activities. As Professor Alexander remarked when the independent Cambridge project *Primary Review* was launched, he and his team aimed to 'ask questions about the quality of the education children receive without fear or favour'.

There are some new entries for this fourth edition including those on author studies, dialogic teaching, multimedia texts, the history of children's non-fiction literature and reading on screen. New literacies are transforming how children think, learn and imagine, and I have augmented the existing entries on these, exploring new modes and media. I have also worked further on those topics of interest that might not be found readily elsewhere, for example lyrical non-fiction, children as authors, and the history of children's radio and television programmes.

Of course, no one author can be an expert on every aspect of so complex and important an area as primary English and readers are constantly referred to other books, resources and websites to expand their knowledge and understanding. Support is given over planning, evaluating and working creatively within current frameworks, but teachers have wider intentions and interests than these and the main aim of this encyclopedia is to support the reflective practitioner by equipping them to address the issues that matter profoundly to primary English in a constructive but critical manner.

The alphabetical format means that key words and concepts can be easily found. However, I have been concerned that this should not fragment the English curriculum and appear to avoid the complexities and the interconnections of the bigger picture. So I have written what I hope is a unifying introduction – *Primary English: the heart of the curriculum*. This gives an overview of the enduring principles on which excellence in the primary English classroom is properly based and draws out the significance of the relationship between the four language processes.

THE AUDIENCE

My audience includes student teachers on BA (Ed), PGCE and other courses, new teachers and teachers returning to the classroom after a career break. However, I hope the encyclopedia will be a valued reference book for all who are interested in and concerned about primary English. I have tried to encompass as much as possible of what someone, wherever in the world they work, would want to know (or want to know where to find out) when setting out to teach English in an exciting and well-informed way to children in the first eleven years of their lives.

THE ENTRIES

In selecting the entries I have kept in mind the great amount of subject knowledge teachers need. There are times when we like to check our understanding of key concepts and the entries contain some succinct definitions of grammatical and literary terms. Sometimes what seemed straightforward at first is more complicated on further research and reflection, and I have not sought conformity in entry length. Thus the size of the entries varies according to my judgement of the space needed. Some entries – definitions of parts of speech, the preposition, the pronoun and explanations of technical terms like 'ellipsis' and 'onomatopoeia' – will aim to give information briefly and clearly.

Others, like 'cohesion', 'genre' and 'portfolios', will need more space. I have tried to give glimpses into the work of the many scholars, teachers and authors whose work has enriched my teaching. Sometimes a brief quotation or paraphrased insight will persuade you that it is worth seeking out a particular book to read more deeply about a topic. I have taken up a simple approach to cross-referencing: other relevant entries on each topic are set out under the 'See also' heading.

EXTENDED ENTRIES

Thirty-four of the entries – for example bilingualism, children's literature, creativity in English, early years language and literacy, Information and Communications Technology (ICT) and English, junior years language and literacy, reading, speaking and listening, Special Educational Needs (SEN) in language and literacy, visual literacy and writing – have a special status in terms of space and format because they are crucial to the understanding of good English teaching. Here issues are identified and explored. Where space allows, some 'vignettes' from the classroom are included as well as enriching background material. I have drawn on all I have learnt from the children, students, colleagues and teachers with whom I have worked over many years. I want to communicate the enjoyment as well as the hard work that accompanies children's development as talkers, listeners, readers and writers.

WHO'S WHO IN PRIMARY ENGLISH

Passing time and changing emphases can mean that we lose sight of those who have made a lasting contribution. Some of these teachers and scholars are included alongside today's influential 'voices'. The list is one person's selection with an eye on space – my apologies go to those not included in spite of their achievements. In making my choices I have concentrated on those who have contributed to the practice, knowledge and understanding of the classroom teacher. Children's writers are too numerous for inclusion in the who's who and are mentioned instead under entries like 'picture books', 'poetry' and 'novels'. I have, however, included some of those children's writers and illustrators, for example Quentin Blake and Michael Rosen, who have written also for an adult readership and particularly for teachers.

It cannot be said too often that however many official reports and books we have, lively and worthwhile English work can only be realised in the classroom by the imagination, planning and pedagogic skill of a creative and reflective practitioner. Good teachers will incorporate new tools and technologies into their practice, but the questions we need to ask about new resources, whether print or electronic, remain the same: how can their strengths be exploited and how will they extend and enrich teaching and learning? Do they offer the best way of achieving a particular purpose? How do we best evaluate their contribution? The Introduction to this book places English work at its most inspirational at the very heart of the curriculum. If it makes you feel even more enthusiastic about your important work, especially your role as children's guide to a wealth of literature and language experiences then I will feel I have succeeded.

Margaret Mallett
October 2011

Introduction

Primary English: the heart of the curriculum

This short introduction soars above the requirements of the day to capture some things of enduring importance about the primary English classroom. Successful schools – and we must be encouraged by this – interpret current requirements in terms of their fundamental beliefs about English, language and literacy in the primary years and their judgement about the needs and priorities of their pupils.

The first thing to remember is that becoming an enthusiastic speaker, listener, reader and writer is essentially a social and collaborative process: it needs the involvement of other human beings. Everything we know about young children shows they learn actively and with others. Think of children when they first come to school: they are generally competent users of spoken language and ready to learn and share their thoughts, feelings and ideas with others. They are active inquisitive creatures not rock-bound sponges. They question, wonder, laugh, object, enjoy and constantly try to make sense of a shared world. The good practitioner builds on the excitement and enthusiasm of the younger children to energise speaking and listening, to teach reading and to encourage writing through the primary years. A classroom that is alive and purposeful will be one where teachers and children collaborate and share activities.

Using both spoken and written language to think and learn is central to every lesson and helps organise nearly every experience, whether in or out of the classroom. What, then, is distinctive about English lessons? Let me say at this point that I am aware that some teachers, particularly of the very young, prefer to think in terms of 'language and learning' more broadly as covering all their activities. Nevertheless, even in the earliest stages we can detect an 'English' perspective. English is associated with those times when we consider, evaluate, savour and enjoy language as a phenomenon in its own right. We study our mother tongue – its structure and functions and the ways in which it varies. Texts are the materials that we use for all these things. They may be spoken or written and found in many different media; they may be one of the great variety of non-fiction texts now available. Above all, however, English is the special home of imaginative literature in all its forms – picture books, short stories, novels, poetry and play scripts – and all its modes and media.

Although English has a content – the study of language and literature – it is essentially to do with processes, about becoming able to talk insightfully about texts and issues, to read competently, thoughtfully and critically, and to write with purpose and coherence. We want children to become passionate about using their language. The more we can link language work to real tasks and real purposes the better – lists, letters, emails and posters for a school event are simple examples. Of course, there are some essential and challenging things to teach and learn about language as a symbolic system – about parts of speech, sentences, cohesion, word meanings and so on. Children have to be taught about and helped with the conventions of paragraphing, spelling and punctuation if the content of their work is to reach the audience it deserves. Routines are needed to ensure that children receive skilled and structured support on the journey to literacy, but there is everything to be gained from hanging on to a sense of playfulness in language study – round rhythm, rhyme and puns, for example.

The stories children read draw on experience, good and bad, of the real world, but they also draw on the inner world of the imagination to explore what could be, or might be, as well as what is. The best writing for children gets to the centre of the human situation. When they talk about a story, relate it to their own experience, think about behaviour, attitudes and views, they use all their faculties of thought and feeling. Fiction has a unique power to help children assimilate knowledge and understanding by drawing on their experience of life, enriched by the memory of all the other books they have read. Here, English has something in common with other subjects that help us represent and assimilate experience – drama, music and art. Teachers and children can be comforted in an uncertain world when they share what human beings have in common. Stories bring them in touch with people who have problems over relationships with friends and family, who have fears about growing up or who are feeling the confusion that occurs when a family is moving home or breaking up. Fiction allows us to reflect on all this at a distance from the rawness of our own circumstances. We should not expect children to like everything they read. In fact we want them to be critical readers, able to scrutinise texts and give

evidence for their opinions. The notion of the 'critical reader' now embraces the ability to evaluate information from electronic sources like the internet as well as print. Discussion about issues can lead to children's own writing – in which they can maintain, if they wish, this distance from direct experience. The teacher and the other children provide a natural and empathetic audience.

The spirit of English can permeate the whole curriculum. By this I mean more than that we use language to learn in every subject. The things we do in English lessons can help us bring a personal perspective to other areas of the curriculum. The creative exploration of fiction can sometimes infuse a special life and energy into history, science or geography lessons. For example, if an ethical issue, such as the use of the environment or use of the world's resources, arises in geography or science, teachers might inform the discussion by turning to texts like *If the World were a Village* by David Smith, *The Whales' Song* by Diana Sheldon or *Where the Forest Meets the Sea* by Jeannie Baker. Here the essentially human response and the interest in texts nurtured in English lessons can be drawn on. Thus the collaborative, community atmosphere of the best English lessons, where everyone's voice is valued, benefits all areas of the curriculum. Where the sharing of enjoyments, insights and observation exists, the bigger purposes of becoming literate shine out and the hard aspects, the chores of learning if you like, are seen as more worthwhile.

None of this would be possible without the vital role played by teachers. They create contexts for learning, choose resources, respond to children's achievements and assess and intervene to help children make progress. Good teachers are responsive to what works well and flexible in adapting to what needs to be changed. There is a cycle and a rhythm to good English teaching: planning and teaching is followed by evaluation and record keeping, and then the fruits of the evaluation feed into the next cycle of planning. A momentum builds. Current assessment requirements include summative testing – to provide snapshots of what a child knows and can do at a given time. Teachers know that we need a richer profile to complement these results with more formative judgements which pinpoint where special help may be needed and help us celebrate achievements.

Part of being a reflective practitioner involves enriching our professional understanding with research findings. This can be built on our own classroom evaluations or on the published research of others, where we are entitled to take a critical approach. The English Co-ordinator has a crucial role, providing leadership and encouragement and a cooperative approach to curriculum development so that all teachers are involved. Just as children enjoy collaborating over their learning, so teachers benefit from interaction with colleagues – sharing, reflecting and discussing issues together. Not everyone will agree all the time – there is stimulation in sharing different views – but there needs to be trust and understanding between colleagues and agreement on the most important aspects of policy and practice.

It is hard to imagine good English practice that does not have a constructive and imaginative approach to those learning English as a second or additional language. There will always be concern too for supporting the progress of children with special language and literacy needs. There must be a carefully structured programme with clear routines for helping children to be able to read well by the end of the primary years. Skilled help is needed to help less forward and reluctant young readers. Partnership with parents and families, an essential part of a school's culture, is particularly important in helping these young learners.

From all this you will gather that I believe that the best English lessons can have a special atmosphere. How is this atmosphere created? It seems to be to do with giving value to worthwhile activities. Teachers and children often have rituals that symbolise the sharing and enjoyment of reading and telling stories – in one classroom by a child holding the 'story wand', in another the 'story mouse'. Another class was joined by William the bear when children read their stories aloud. For older children a regular time for reading the class novel, for reading out their own writing or for silent reading is enough to give the activity status and value.

If you ask me what I think is the greatest challenge for teachers, I would say it is helping children become competent writers. Teachers have the task of helping children feel confident when faced with a blank page. It involves helping them with difficult things like finding a theme, developing and keeping control of a piece of writing, and turning ideas into a structured and coherent account or a satisfying story. Then there are the transcriptional elements to perfect spelling, punctuation, handwriting or touch-typing. Above all, it is about helping children find their 'voice' so that what they write is recognisably their own. There is no doubt that new technologies – email and texting, for example – are helping those children not normally engaged with traditional forms to find new fluency and value in the written form. Young learners are also inspired by reading and writing multimodally, combining in paper texts design, illustration and writing. Digital technology has extended multimodality to the screen so that texts can also communicate through multimedia, adding sound, music and animation.

While ideas about English lessons in the primary school will change, I believe that these fundamental features will survive even as each new generation of primary teachers interprets their work in new ways. Increasingly, the expectation is that teachers will have a high level of subject knowledge.

Resources will become richer and more diverse and ways of working will continue to change. Already computer software allows teachers to create word banks and writing supports. Interactive whiteboards are creating new ways of teaching and learning; they make shared reading and shared writing easier and offer new visual technologies which help the teacher bring illustrations into lessons. However, the good English classroom will always be a fertile ground for new ideas, have an energy about it, be a place where interesting things happen and where there is a creative and reflective approach. This is not to underestimate the sheer hard work involved for teachers and children during periods of change. We can have any number of lists of what ought to be achieved but it is the individual teacher in the classroom who motivates, interests and, above all, values and respects his or her pupils. Some aspects of teaching and learning may be transformed by technology but we will always need the skill and commitment of teachers who are good models of confident and articulate speakers, sympathetic listeners and enthusiastic readers and writers.

For me, nothing is closer to the heart of English than the sheer enjoyment of teacher and children talking deeply and intently about a book, poem or a play. They savour the highlights, muse on the characters, admire the author's skill in developing the plot and using just the right word, phrase or image. Often they return to the text to find the evidence to support a point, they respond to the views of others and perhaps move on to further activities – drama or writing – to help assimilate new insights and ideas. Every faculty is brought into play – heart as well as mind – and the very act of sharing helps organise thinking and all the language processes are brought together. Often children's insights surprise us and make us see a story in a new way. Of course children and teachers need quieter times as well – to perfect handwriting or to finish tasks – but we savour most those occasions when the sheer creative energy of children spills over into talk, writing and drama; times when minds imagine, ideas flow, pens skip across the page or fingers fly over the keyboard. We hope that children will remember these times.

A

ABBREVIATION

See also: acronym, apostrophe, ellipsis

This is the shortened or contracted form of a word or phrase. Frequently used abbreviations or contractions include don't (do not), can't (can not) and haven't (have not). Children need careful teaching about the difference between possessive apostrophes and those used to indicate contraction. Sometimes the abbreviation becomes a word in its own right, for example pub, plane or fridge, and in these cases the apostrophe has been dropped. Other abbreviations are acronyms like SAT (standard assessment test) and NATE (the National Association for the Teaching of English). Useful abbreviations of Latin terms include: e.g. for example (exempli gratia); i.e. that is (id est); etc. and so on (et cetera); N.B. note especially (nota bene). The best account of 'abbreviation' known to me is in McArthur's Oxford Companion.

McArthur, Tom (1992) *The Oxford Companion to the English Language* Oxford: Oxford University Press.

ABSTRACT NOUN

See also: clause, grammar, noun, parts of speech, sentence

This is a noun which names a state or condition (melancholy), a quality (mercy), a concept (feudalism) or an action (favouritism). Such nouns are 'abstract' because you cannot perceive the phenomena they denote with your senses.

ACCENT

See also: language variety, speaking and listening

This is the aspect of language variation to do with pronunciation. All spoken language, including standard English, is spoken with an accent. Pronunciation varies according to a speaker's geographical and social origin. For example, I come from the north of England and pronounce 'bath' and 'path' with a short 'a' while my husband, a southerner, pronounces them with a long 'a'. People speaking in a second or additional language often have a distinctive accent. 'Received' pronunciation refers to the accent historically associated with BBC announcers (although regional accents are heard increasingly) and the well educated. However, language is dynamic and pronunciation like other aspects – dialect and vocabulary – changes with each generation of users and many well-educated people speak with a regional accent and are proud to do so.

ACRONYM

See also: abbreviation

An acronym is made up of the initial letters of a related sequence of words and pronounced as one word. Examples include NATE (National Association for the Teaching of English) and UKLA (United Kingdom Literacy Association).

ACROSTIC

See also: poetry, verse

This describes a poem or puzzle where the first letter of each line, read sequentially down the page, spells out a word or phrase. In a double acrostic, the first and last letters of each line spell out a word or phrase.

ADJECTIVAL CLAUSE

See also: clause, grammar, parts of speech

An adjectival clause modifies a noun.

'The girl, *who was flushed with pride,* rose to receive the bouquet'.

ADJECTIVE

See also: adjectival clause, grammar, parts of speech

Adjectives are words that modify nouns or pronouns or complement verbs.

- the *yellow* dress
- it is *spacious*
- those gloves look *attractive*

'Simple' adjectives include words like 'large', 'small' and 'red', while what are termed 'derived adjectives' are created by adding a suffix (-able, -ful, -ish) to a noun or verb, for example, 'readable', 'restful' and 'foolish'.

Adjectives (and adverbs) have comparative and superlative forms. Comparative forms include:

- hard – harder
- challenging – more challenging

Superlative forms include:

- large – largest
- impressive – most impressive

ADVENTURE STORIES

See also: history of children's literature

In Victorian times, adventure stories tended to reflect the traditional world of men and boys. The action often centred on dangerous journeys and exciting events on land and at sea. John Rowe Townsend (1995) locates the roots of children's adventure stories both in Daniel Defoe's *Robinson Crusoe* and the historical novels of Sir Walter Scott. *Treasure Island* by Robert Louis Stevenson introduced a vivid new kind of adventure story for children which broke away from the moralistic flavour of earlier books. The action is exciting and the characters are fully rounded mixtures of good and bad qualities. *Treasure Island*, which Stevenson wrote in 1881 to amuse his stepson during a wet August in Scotland, is still in print. Another book, H. Rider Haggard's *King Solomon's Mines*, also written in the 1880s, had considerable influence on later writers of adventure stories. For more detail about the early history of adventure stories, I recommend John Rowe Townsend's *Written for Children*, Victor Watson's *Cambridge Guide to Children's Books in English*, and Peter Hunt's *Children's Literature: An Illustrated History*.

There are fashions in children's reading choices as in other things. At the beginning of the twenty-first century children seem to favour stories set in magical worlds of the imagination: R.L. Stine's Goosebumps series, Roald Dahl's fantasy tales and J.K. Rowling's Harry Potter books. Nevertheless, stories of young people facing up to physical danger – sometimes touching the improbable but staying within the confines of the physical world – are still enjoyed. Historical novels for children often contain the elements of hazard faced up to with courage and resourcefulness that we associate with the best adventure stories. Rosemary Sutcliff's novels still interest and excite young readers in the later primary years. *The Eagle of the Ninth* (Oxford University Press, 1954) tells the story of a dangerous venture, north of Hadrian's Wall, to find out the truth about the disappearance of the Ninth Legion and to recover its lost Eagle. Two other much-read historical stories, again for the ten to twelve year olds, are Marita Conlon-McKenna's *Under the Hawthorn Tree* (Puffin), the tale of the dangerous journey to find help made by three courageous children during the Irish famine of the 1840s, and Berlie Doherty's *Street Child* (HarperCollins, 1993), which tells the true story of a boy who escaped from a workhouse in the 1860s and whose circumstances inspired Dr Barnardo to set up his homes. Cynthia Harnett's ever-popular book, *The Wool Pack,* is set in an earlier period, fifteenth-century Winchester and the Cotswolds. (A new edition was published by Egmont Books in 2001.)

Not all adventure stories are historical novels. The impact on people of natural disasters are described in Andrew Salkey's books: *Hurricane* (1964), *Earthquake* (1965) and *Drought* (1966). Enid Blyton wrote adventure stories in the 1940s and 1950s – *The Famous Five* series, for example, which were formulaic but created a predictable world which some children still find reassuring whatever the reservations of some adults. Still in print is Arthur Ransome's *Swallows and Amazons* series, which has strong male and strong female characters and involves children from the town in sailing adventures in the Lake District during their summer holidays. Twelve books were published between 1930 and 1947. Unlike contemporary authors writing in the category often termed 'realistic', Ransome does not involve us in issues like the tensions between parents and children. Subtle nuances in developing relationships are explored in *Walkabout* (Penguin, 1963) – James Vance Marshall's powerful story of some children's survival after an aeroplane crash in the harsh physical environment of the Australian outback. *Walkabout* and other children's novels of the second half of the twentieth century, for example Anne Holm's *I am David* (Egmont Books, 1989) and Ian Serraillier's *The Silver Sword* (Penguin, 1983), are not just adventure stories but quality works which tell us profound things about the human condition. Another kind of survival story – Robert O'Brien's *Z for Zachariah* (Penguin, 1998) – relates the events in Ann's life in the form of a diary when she discovers she is the sole survivor of a nuclear holocaust.

The traditional adventure story is thrilling because the characters face life-threatening situations. In the later part of the twentieth century there were many books that included some element of fear and mishap but with a light touch. Teachers have their own favourites which they include in the book collection. Two examples are Beverly Cleary's amusing tale *Ramona Quimby Aged 8* (Oxford University Press, 2001) – which, not surprisingly, appeals to girls about age eight – and Willard Price's *Arctic Adventure* (Vintage Books, 1993), liked by girls and boys of about ten years. The latter is one of a series telling about the travels of young Hal and Roger to different countries. Their mission is to collect wild animals for their father's zoo and in the story about the Arctic visit the brothers face freezing temperatures and lack of food.

New writers of the kind of adventure stories often liked by boys are emerging. Some of these are in the tradition of Henty and Buchan.

Anthony Horowitz's Alex Rider series – which includes *Stormbreaker* (now also a film), *Eagle Strike* and *Ark Angel* – are fast-moving stories about the adventures of a young boy recruited into MI6. They are written in a crisp, accessible style which is almost Blyton-like at times. Charlie Higson's stories about the teenage years of James Bond – *Silverfin, Blood Fever, Double or Die* – are complex and exciting, but a good deal of the action is quite explicitly violent.

Changes in society are reflected in the modern adventure story. Girls are now more likely to be protagonists. Themes, too, change and tend to be in tune with modern preoccupations – racism and the environment, for example (Butts, 2004). Look out for the work of authors of adventure stories enjoyed by both boys and girls, for example Michael Morpurgo's *Kensuki's Kingdom* and Geraldine McCaughrean's *Gold Dust*.

Adventure stories can be read online. For example, the whole of *Treasure Island* can be found at www.ukoln.ac.uk/services/treasure.

Annotated booklists for different ages and abilities are available from Booktrust, Book House, 45 East Hill, London SW18 2QZ. www.booktrust. org.uk

Butts, Dennis (2004) 'Shaping Boyhood' in Peter Hunt (ed., second edition) *International Companion Encyclopedia of Children's Literature* London: Routledge.

Hunt, Peter (ed.) (1995) *Children's Literature: An Illustrated History* Oxford: Oxford University Press.

Townsend, John Rowe (1995, sixth edition) *Written for Children* London: The Bodley Head.

Watson, Victor (2001) *The Cambridge Guide to Children's Books in English* Cambridge: Cambridge University Press.

ADVERB

See also: adverbial clause, connective, grammar, parts of speech

These are words which modify or give extra meaning to other parts of speech – to verbs, another adverb or an adjective. So: an example of an adverb modifying a verb is – 'She ran *swiftly*', of another adverb – 'She ran *very* swiftly', and an adjective – 'Her shorts were *really* elegant'. What are termed 'sentence adverbs' – 'happily', 'regrettably' – modify the whole sentence as in '*Happily*, she came first in the race'.

Adverbs can be divided into groups:

Table 1

Time:	soon, tomorrow, immediately
Frequency:	occasionally, sometimes, often
Place:	inside, near, here
Manner:	effectively, skilfully, swiftly

ADVERBIAL CLAUSE

See also: adverb, clause, grammar

Like adverbs, adverbial clauses modify, elaborate or qualify verbs.

In the following sentence, 'after the children had put on their coats' modifies the verb 'ran'.

'*After the children had put on their coats* they ran into the playground'.

Similarly 'when we left the school' is an adverbial clause modifying 'There was a hail-storm' in the sentence below.

'There was a hail-storm *when we left the school*'.

Adverbial clauses, like other clauses, usually have a subject and verb, as in the examples above.

ADVERBIAL PHRASE

See also: adverb, adverbial clause, clause, grammar

An adverbial phrase is a group of words functioning in the same way as a single adverb.

So in the following sentence 'in an encouraging way' is an adverbial phrase.

'He looked at me *in an encouraging way*'.

However, in the next sentence 'encouragingly' is an adverb modifying the verb 'looked'.

'He looked at me *encouragingly*'.

An adverbial phrase, like other phrases, is a group of words acting as one unit. Unlike a clause, a phrase does not have a verb and subject.

ADVERTISEMENTS

See also: environmental print, genre, multimodal texts, National Curriculum, persuasive genre, visual literacy

Advertisements on billboards, in magazines and newspapers and on screen are a powerful part of the environmental print that surrounds us. Children notice pictures and format from an early age and soon become sensitive to their cultural associations: advertisements reflect what we most value, fear and desire. They transmit strong social meanings which we may absorb unconsciously. They can be for 'good' purposes – to draw our attention to the merits of worthwhile events, places of interest and institutions. While the profit motive seems a less worthy purpose, some advertisements recommend products in an honest and reasonable manner and the competitive spirit they encourage is an aspect of a free society. The anarchic nature of the internet raises particular ethical issues about the use of advertisements in this medium. Reading and reflecting on the visual impact of advertisements and on their linguistic devices – persuasive vocabulary, puns, alliteration – has long been part of the English programme for older primary school pupils, reinforced by official guidance. However, younger children are also interested in the effects of this kind of text. I remember seeing a teacher work with seven year olds making posters about caring for the environment. The work had arisen from a shared reading of Julia and Charles Snape's picture book, *The Giant*. Working in pairs, the children simply did not want to leave their work to go out to play, so absorbed were they in communicating their own environmental concerns to others. Another exciting project on advertising involving young children is written up in Carolyn White's chapter, 'Somebody makes a choice' in Jon Callow's *Visual Literacy* (White, 1999). The work took place in Australia and began with the teacher recording a selection of television advertisements aimed at children. After watching the commercials the children were given task cards and asked to work in pairs. The cards gave each pair one of four tasks: record the colours used; describe the music; describe the characters; record who speaks and what is said. Just beginning to write, the children either asked the teacher to scribe for them or used pictorial representations to record the information. The teacher wrote a summary of the findings in each of the four categories on large pieces of paper for display. White points out that the work was spread over four weeks and was quite challenging for her exuberant five year olds. After studying several commercials, including one advertising McDonald's, the children and their teacher produced a list (see box on p. 7) of what a children's commercial needs to be effective. White was interested that the children picked out 'magic and pretending things' as a key ingredient – the McDonald's advertisement was set in a fantasy land showing children following Ronald McDonald along a yellow brick

5

road to find something scrumptious to eat. I have referred to this project in some detail as it shows that there are ways of involving quite young children in understanding persuasive texts. Indeed, at the end of the work, one child revealed that what he had learnt was much more than superficial: 'when you advertise, somebody makes a choice' – hence White's chapter title.

Children in the later primary years are often asked to study the design, language and illustration of advertisements. When they are asked to create their own, they draw on all their experience of this kind of text, experience gleaned at home and school, and move forward in controlling persuasive writing. In their paper 'Children's advertisement writing' Andrew Burrell and Roger Beard present a case study showing how two Year 6 children are able to draw on all that they have observed and learnt when going on to create their own advertisements. The researchers show how Lata was able to 'realise the power of the text' in writing an advertisement for Toffee Tower. She begins dynamically with a question: 'Do you crave for large toffee filled desserts?' (Burrell and Beard, 2010: 86). Sharing and discussing this kind of work can lead to critical reading and evaluation. If children are to understand the impact of this kind of material we need to build up resources. These include collections of advertisements for the book corner – examples from magazines and newspapers and from the internet and television. The book corner computer is important when it comes to children's work on their own creations: software programs can help children make professional-looking posters of any size. Once the resources are in place we need imaginative projects and tasks to get the children thinking through the issues. The ideas in the list below would be suitable for guided reading or writing in Literacy Time or for work outside it. I find three things helpful. First,

learning about advertisements and commercials as kinds of persuasive text is something revisited at different stages through the primary years. Each 'revisit' takes the pupils' understanding further, so teachers adapt ideas for different age groups. Second, wherever possible, it is best for children to design publicity and advertising material for real use. Third, we can help focus children's work by providing task cards, carefully selected resources and helpful ways of presenting their findings.

English work round advertisements

- Using an interactive whiteboard for collaborative writing of advertisements.
- Analysing an advertisement from a newspaper or magazine as an example of persuasive text, attending to choices at text level (format), sentence level (syntax) and word level (vocabulary).
- Designing and writing advertisements to promote a school event or an imaginary product.
- Experimenting with language and design for advertisements for different media – screen, radio, magazine or billboard.
- Presenting print advertisements to the group showing how linguistic and visual features combine to make an impact on a targeted audience.
- Acting out advertisements designed for television.
- Improvisation round the making of an advertisement involving children taking up the roles of business people paying for the advertisement and of the producer, editor and actors. (A Year 6 class known to me carried out a project like this. Teacher and children greatly enjoyed researching what was involved in each role and the final presentation was shown to the school.)
- Examining ethical aspects of advertising (some of these became apparent in the Year 6 case study referred to above).

- Studying advertising aimed at children (see example from Australia described above in which five to six year olds studied commercials). Older primary children often enjoy analysing advertisements aimed at children younger than themselves. Whatever the age group, it is helpful for them to work out some categories to guide their analysis.
- Making advertisements for constructive and worthwhile reasons for the book corner or posters to advertise a school function.
- Market research using questionnaires and interviews might usefully precede making posters to publicise school events. What would encourage pupils to support the events and how might this be incorporated into the publicity material?
- Specific topics like looking at the use of verse in advertisements and comparing verse for profit and poetry for aesthetic purposes. Using advertisements in developing children's visual literacy and showing, for example, the effectiveness of visual images and how the visual and the linguistic aspects link (Bearne and Wolstencroft, 2007). Children could be shown a TV advertisement and, in pairs, write down what they notice about aspects like choice of colour, style and image, the appearance of the characters and the way the product is packaged. Then they could discuss how far the language – name and description of product and what people say – matches or extends the visual aspects.

Examining advertisements and commercials and writing their own helps children develop critical abilities in several ways. It certainly draws their attention to how writing can be used to manipulate the reader and change attitudes and behaviour – often purchasing behaviour. We encounter advertisements in every form of media and children should understand the negative as well as the more positive implications. This kind of work also shows them how purpose and sense of audience interact. The purpose of an advertisement is to affect the perception of a product or event of a target audience. It is a way of helping children imagine how they might reach and impact on 'the wider community' which is one of the audiences children are expected to write for in the later primary years. A start can be made in the school magazine.

Now that multimodal and multimedia texts are, more than ever, part of our daily experience this kind of work helps develop children's visual literacy and draws their attention to how text and pictures link.

> ### A children's commercial needs:
>
> - Bright colours
> - Magic and pretending things
> - A catchy song or music with a beat
>
> (Based on the list five year olds made with the teacher's help after a study of television advertisements used in the commercial breaks between children's television programmes (White, 1999: 45).)

Bearne, Eve and Wolstencroft, Helen (2007) *Visual Approaches to Teaching Writing: Multimodal Literacy* London: Paul Chapman. (Includes a CD of examples of children's multimodal work.)

Burrell, Andrew and Beard, Roger (2010) 'Children's advertisement writing' in *Literacy*, Vol.44, No. 2, July 2010: 83–90.

White, Carolyn (1999) 'Somebody makes a choice' in Jon Callow *Visual Literacy: Visual Texts in the Classroom* NSW, Australia: Primary English Teaching Association.

AFFIX

See also: morpheme, prefix, suffix

An affix is a morpheme attached to a word which may be a prefix (*dis*appear, *un*inspiring), or a suffix (read*ing*, like*ness*).

AGREEMENT (OR CONCORD)

Agreement is to do with the relationship between number, person and gender.

'That *dog seems* to be hungry' (number agreement).
'*I* bruised *myself*' (person agreement).
'*She* managed to prepare lunch *herself*' (gender agreement).

There is a more detailed explanation, under 'concord', with copious examples in McArthur, 1992: 254–55.

McArthur, Tom (1992) *The Oxford Companion to the English Language* Oxford: QPD and Oxford University Press.

ALLITERATION

See also: assonance

This refers to the repetition of sounds in a sequence in prose or poetry for emphasis or effect. The term refers to consonants and the repeated letters are often the initial letters of words or in the stressed syllable of a word. For example, in Shakespeare's *The Tempest* we have the stirring lines:

'Full fathom five thy father lies'.

The under eights love the alliteration in Adrian Henri's poem about hedgehogs in danger – *H25*. The first line is 'Hedgehogs hog the hedges' and the second verse begins 'With halts for hungry hedgehogs' (*The Ring of Words* edited by Roger McGough and illustrated by Satoshi

Figure 1 Vanessa and Jamie (Reception class at Castlecombe Primary School) heard the teacher read John Foster's alliterative poem 'Zoo Dream' before typing their own illustrated alliterative sentences.

Kitamura). As well as a device in literary texts, alliteration is used in tongue twisters – 'Peter Piper picked a peck of pickled peppers', similes – 'as good as gold', proverbs – 'waste not, want not', advertisements – 'super sizzling sausages' and newspaper headlines – 'Saucy Sue Soaks up the Sun'. The language of newspapers and advertisements has long been part of the English programme of older primary children.

ALPHABET

See also: consonant, dictionary, early learning goals, horn book, non-fiction reading and writing, phoneme, reading, vowel

An alphabet is the set of symbols used in a system of written language. In English, there are 26 letters in the alphabet of which five are vowels – 'a', 'e', 'i', 'o', 'u' – and 21 are consonants – 'b', 'c', 'd', 'f', 'g', 'h', 'j', 'k', 'l', 'm', 'n', 'p', 'q', 'r', 's', 't', 'v', 'w', 'x', 'y', 'z'. As there are 44 phonemes (units of sound) and only 26 letters of the alphabet, some sounds are represented by combining letters.

From medieval times up until the eighteenth century children learnt to read with the help of alphabet books. Many early primers consisted of a flat piece of wood with a sheet of paper covered by a layer of transparent horn – hence their name, horn books. The alphabet was accompanied by prayers as reading and religion were linked. By the nineteenth century illustrators were producing beautiful alphabet picture books, for example Kate Greenaway's *A Apple Pie* (1886).

The twentieth century brought some excellent alphabet books and friezes.

Figure 2 A is for Africa by Ifeoma Onyefulu and *W is for World* by Kathryn Cave, both published by Frances Lincoln, are photographic alphabets that also teach children about distinctive environments and the people who live in them. Reproduced with the permission of the publishers, Frances Lincoln, © 2007 and 1979.

Favourites for the nursery/Reception age group include John Burningham's *ABC* (Jonathan Cape, 1964), Dick Bruna's *b is for bear* (Methuen, 1971) and Brian Wildsmith's *ABC* (Oxford University Press, 1995). Some of the books are enjoyed as toys – Robert Crowthers' *The Most Amazing Hide-and-Seek Alphabet* (new edition, 2005) is delightfully playful as the child pulls a tag to find which animal is hiding behind each letter. Children up to about eight years enjoy two life-enhancing geography alphabet books: K. Cave's *W is for World* (Frances Lincoln with Oxfam, 2007 new edition) and I. Onyefulu's *A is for Africa* (Frances Lincoln, 1997). Both books teach about different environments in the strong context of photographic alphabets.

Alphabet books can be read on screen too; for a jolly one look out for *Dr Seuss ABC* (Softkey, CD-ROM).

The alphabet provides a major way of organising information and children need to be helped to find their way round dictionaries, encyclopedias, indexes and catalogues, whether in print or electronic.

ANALOGY

See also: metaphor, simile

Analogy is used to explain or describe the nature of something by comparing it to something else. Thus it often takes the form of a simile or metaphor. We might say to someone – 'Think of life as a journey through time: sometimes the way may be rocky and difficult, at other times we may pass through cool meadows and rest beneath shady trees'.

Children make use of analogy, bringing what is known to something new, when they try to spell or read words new to them. Sometimes analogy does not work when children try, for example, to make plurals in line with examples known to them – 'mouses' is not the plural of 'mouse'. Even so, the attempt to bring existing knowledge to new situations is a sign of genuine learning and experiment and should be encouraged.

ANAPHORIC REFERENCE

See also: cataphoric reference

We use 'anaphoric reference' when we look back to an earlier word or words in a sentence to discover the meaning of a word or phrase. So in the sentence – 'Although the children were tired after the morning's work they could still enjoy the afternoon story' – the second part of the sentence makes sense in the light of the first.

ANECDOTES

See also: narrative, speaking and listening, storytelling

These are short accounts, usually of an event or something that happened to the teller or writer or someone known to them. From the earliest stage young children enjoy telling others about significant events: what they did today; what happened when their pet or favourite toy was lost; what the squirrels were doing in the park last Saturday. Often what they relate is chronologically ordered and this helps them develop a sense of the narrative form (Mallett, 1997). Reading and listening to literature is a strong context for the sharing of pertinent anecdotes. We value all the connections children make in their talk and writing between what they read and events and situations in their lives. The teacher's skill lies in his or her constructive and imaginative response to children's anecdotes. A number of children in a Year 6 class were responding to the teacher's reading of Anthony Browne's picture book *The Tunnel* (Puffin, 1989) by sharing anecdotes about sibling relationships. The teacher

focused the discussion by asking the children how their experiences were similar to and different from those of the children in the book. This nudged the anecdotes into a higher gear and, as often happens, the anecdotes were developed into a satisfying written piece.

When children write journals or diaries in or out of school they draw on anecdotes. These 'vignettes' from real life are more interesting when writers include their own attitudes, opinions and response. Here we can hardly have a better model than the writing in *Anne Frank's Diary* (Puffin, 1997).

Mallett, Margaret (1997) *First Person Reading and Writing in the Primary Years* Sheffield: NATE.

ANIMALS (IN CHILDREN'S STORIES AND INFORMATION TEXTS)

See also: history of children's literature

Animals have been a favourite element in many children's stories and information books over the centuries. In *Aesop's Fables* (told to if not originally intended for children) the stories about animals which embody human characteristics of envy, greed, insensitivity and wickedness are used to bring about moral awareness (Flynn, 2004).

A landmark book is Anna Sewell's *Black Beauty*, first published in 1877, written to draw the attention of adults to the plight of cab horses. Sewell uses the device of telling the story in the form of an autobiography of a horse and it soon became evident that children had a strong empathetic attachment to the story.

Very different from *Black Beauty* but also loved by children are Rudyard Kipling's *Jungle Books* (1894–95) in which the animals speak to Mowgli (John Rowe Townsend thinks this is an acceptable convention which gives the animals a necessary dignity) and Kipling's *Just So Stories* first published in 1902. Children love to hear these mythic versions of how the camel got its hump, the leopard its spots and the rhinoceros its folded skin.

In her very interesting analysis of *The Wind in the Willows* by Kenneth Grahame, Julia Briggs remarks on the anthropomorphic approach to animals and while appreciating the exuberance of the characters also notes that 'women and lower classes are silently excluded from this Arcadia' (Hunt, 1995: Chapter 7, 181). If you are prepared to consider good retelling, Inga Moore has brought out a wonderfully illustrated abridged version in two volumes: *The River Bank* and *The Adventures of Mr Toad* (Walker Books). Older primary children might appreciate William Horwood's sequels to *Wind in the Willows* which illustrate more current issues. For example, *The Willows and Beyond* includes the same characters now faced by pollution of the River and the threat of housing development on the land of the Wild Wood.

Beatrix Potter's books, for example *The Tale of Peter Rabbit* (1902), and Alison Uttley's *The Squirrel, the Hare and the Little Grey Rabbit* (1929) create a world where animals talk, wear clothes and have a social life similar to human beings. Townsend and others believe Potter's work superior: her illustrations are based on the scientific drawings she made of animals (Townsend, 1995). However, I have a personal soft spot for the Little Grey Rabbit stories which I received regularly as welcome gifts when I was a child. I still recall the smell of the glue on the binding and the shiny smoothness of the little pages.

It is true that the humanised animal story can descend into cosiness and we can tend 'to distinguish between "good" animals – usually meaning nice furry ones – and "bad" animals which are slimy or snappy and generally uncuddleable' (Townsend, 1995: 95).

In seeking an explanation for animal fantasies being one of the most endearing and enduring categories of children's fiction, I turn again to Townsend: it may be because of the essential innocence of animals who only know how to be the animal they are (Townsend, 1995: 213). Of course, there are some deliciously evil animal characters – the weasels in the Grey Rabbit books, Manny Rat in Russell Hoban's *The Mouse and his Child* and General Woundwort in *Watership Down*.

One of the most original animal stories of the second half of the twentieth century is *Watership Down* – Richard Adams' extremely successful first book which is enjoyed by adults as well as children. Here we have a strong story about the dangers a community of rabbits meet in their search for a new warren. The rabbits have their own fascinating language and culture and the story is underlain by some profound ethical issues. The book explores issues about leadership, loyalty to friends and endurance for a cause. Two animal books concerning issues about animal welfare and its conflict with the interests of human beings (although not equalling the epic *Watership Down* in literary stature) are enjoyed by children of about nine years. The first, *Mrs Frisby and the Rats of NIMH* by Robert O'Brien, tells two intertwined tales of a field mouse whose home is at risk from a plough and of rats who have escaped from a laboratory. The issues are dealt with in a way children can understand. The second, *The Midnight Fox* by Betsy Byars, brings powerfully alive a young boy's conflict between loyalty to a vixen who trusts him enough to show him her young and the relatives – farmers who have given him hospitality and friendship. This entry can only mention a few of the animal stories that are such a big part of most school collections, but I would like to mention the books about farmyard and other animals by Dick King-Smith. *The Sheep-pig*, *Dodos are Forever*, *Daggie*

11

Dogfoot, The School Mouse and many others tell exciting stories with humour and compassion and are often about succeeding against the odds and making the best use of any talent you have.

The assumption that children enjoy factual books about animals has long been established: Thomas Boreman's *Description of Three Hundred Animals,* first published in 1730, went into seven editions and books like this have been published ever since.

Today software, CD-ROMs (using sound as well as visual effects and text to bring alive animal habitats), and the internet join the ever-popular large-print encyclopedias of animals and the traditional information books often concentrating on one species. The life cycles of creatures can be presented in narrative form and, with its similarity to story, is a sympathetic start to the world of information books for the very young. Quite a lot of books for the under sixes are structured by questions. *Are You a Snail?* in Kingfisher's Up the Garden Path series brings humour and excellent illustrations to the task of identifying a snail's characteristics. Animals that speak and dress are also used as a device to draw children into books imparting facts. For example, a mother and baby seagull have a conversation about the water cycle in Sam Godwin and Simone Abel's *The Drop Goes Plop.* 'Genre confusion!' warn the purists – but children seem to find the imaginary journey exhilarating and they remember the basic information well.

The growing feeling that we should respect animals is not only apparent in the hundreds of guides to caring for pets but also in books raising questions about our wider treatment of animals, like Miles Barton's *Why Do People Harm Animals* (Gloucester Press, 1994) with its thought provoking cover picture of the monkey in a dress, and the more recently published *Animal Cruelty* by Chris Mason (Wayland, 2009). Anna Sewell's concern for animal welfare lives on.

Flynn, Simon (2004) 'Animal stories' in Peter Hunt (ed., second edition) *International Companion Encyclopaedia of Children's Literature, Volume I* London and New York: Routledge.

Hunt, Peter (ed.) (1995) *Children's Literature: An Illustrated History* Oxford and New York: Oxford University Press. (Chapter 7, section on Animal Lands.)

Townsend, John Rowe (1995 edition) *Written for Children* London: The Bodley Head. (Chapter 10, Articulate Animals.)

ANTHOLOGY

See also: poetry, short stories

An anthology is a collection of poems, songs, short stories or prose extracts, often by different authors and published in one volume. Collections of poetry and short stories are a most important resource in the primary English lesson. Some poetry anthologies are tried and tested over time and still enjoyed – *The Oxford Book of Children's Verse* (Peter and Iona Opie); *Peacock Pie* (Walter de la Mare); *The Young Puffin Book of Verse* (Barbara Ireson) – while the many exciting newer ones – including *Sensational Poems* (Roger McGough); *Thawing Frozen Frogs* (Brian Patten); *Mind Your Own Business* (Michael Rosen) – cover every aspect of life at school and home and, of course, the inner world of the imagination. Short story collections often concentrate on a particular genre, like fairy stories – *The Faber Book of Favourite Fairy Tales* (Sara and Stephen Corrin) – myths and legends – *King Arthur and his Knights of the Round Table* (Roger Lancelyn Green) – and folk tales from different cultures – *Anancy – Spiderman* (James Berry).

Useful also are the anthologies that teachers make – collections of poems and extracts and annotated notes and book reviews gathered over the years to support their English work. Children make collections too – they like to handwrite and illustrate favourite poems on themes like animals, people and food and to place their anthology in the book corner.

ANTITHESIS

This is used as a more powerful alternative to the word 'opposite', as in the following sentence.

> 'This mechanistic approach to children's art is the antithesis of all I believe in'.

ANTONYM

An antonym is a word that is the opposite in meaning of another word. For example, mean is an antonym of generous, fast of slow and tall of short.

APOSTROPHE

See also: punctuation

The apostrophe is used in three ways:

- to mark the omission or elision of letters and sounds, as in *don't* (do not)
- to mark possession in nouns, as in *the boy's hat; the teachers' notebooks*
- to indicate a plural form where adding just an 's' would introduce ambiguity, as in *mind your p's and q's*. An apostrophe also can be used to mark plurals of acronyms or some abbreviations, as in *NQT's*; however, usage is changing and it would be perhaps more common now to see *NQTs*.

Note that *it's* comes under the first of these uses, being short for *it is* or *it has*: 'it is time to leave for school' can thus become 'it's time to leave for school'; 'it has been a lovely day' can become 'it's been a lovely day'.

Its (with no apostrophe) shows possession:

> 'You can recognise a tiger by its stripes.'

In the classroom, I suggest that children ask themselves if their sentence would make sense if they expanded *its* to 'it is', in which case they need the apostrophe.

APPOSITION

When a noun or noun phrase is in apposition to another, it comes next to it and explains or in some way modifies it. Usually either one can be missed out without changing the broad meaning of the sentence. *Mr Brown* and *the British Prime Minister* are in apposition in the following sentence: 'Mr Brown, the then British Prime Minister, sought re-election in 2010'. The terms 'partial apposition' or 'weak apposition' are sometimes used where only one of the nouns or noun phrases can be omitted. For example, in 'Mrs Wilson, until recently the acting deputy head teacher, left the school at the end of the summer term', *until recently the acting deputy head teacher* cannot stand alone without some modification.

APPRENTICESHIP APPROACH TO READING

See also: 'big shapes', metaphor, miscue analysis

The apprenticeship approach to the teaching of reading has been clearly explained in Liz Waterland's booklet published in 1988. Waterland's approach is based on the work of Frank Smith and Kenneth and Yetta Goodman. Kenneth Goodman famously referred to reading as a 'psycholinguistic guessing game' in which contextual clues are of great importance. Some critics of this approach, for example Marilyn Jager Adams (1990), consider that it underestimates the importance of word recognition skills and the development of strategies to understand large units of text in becoming a fluent reader.

13

The apprenticeship approach has gone out of favour in its more extreme form. Nevertheless, Frank Smith's insistence on the importance of the teacher as model reader continues to influence good practice, and Goodman's diagnostic reading test – miscue analysis – is still used, usually in modified form, in many classrooms.

Adams, Marilyn Jager (1990) *Beginning to Read: The New Phonics in Context* Oxford: Heinemann.

Waterland, Liz (1988, second edition) *Read With Me: An Apprenticeship Approach to Reading* Stroud: The Thimble Press.

APPROPRIATENESS IN LANGUAGE

See also: language variety, register

This is a linguistic term referring to the fact that language varies according to the situation in which it is used. Children soon learn that the way in which they talk to Granny at home is different to the way in which they talk to their friends in the playground. Likewise some forms that may be appropriate in speech are not appropriate in written texts.

ARGUMENT

See also: genre, persuasive genre

Argument is a text type setting out the case for or against something. In the later primary years children are encouraged to develop their writing by following a rational theme to support or refute a case. Examples include: case for and against school uniform, sports days or air travel. Not only do children have to set out one viewpoint, they also have to anticipate what might be said in opposition. For a most thought-provoking account of young children's use of argument, see Chapter 8 'Developing control of the argument' in Riley and Reedy, 2000. There are suggestions for using a range of children's texts, including stories, to support children's work on argument (persuasion and discussion) in the classroom in Mallett, 2010: chapter 32.

Mallett, Margaret (2010) *Choosing and Using Fiction and Non-fiction 3–11* London: Routledge.

Riley, Jeni and Reedy, David (2000) *Developing Writing for Different Purposes* London: Paul Chapman.

ART AND ENGLISH

See also: advertisements, Bible, book making, carnival (and literacy), comics, history and English, illustrations, picture books, sacred texts, visual literacy

Art activities are an excellent context for learning a vocabulary to talk about making and creating things, to evaluate visual and tactile qualities, to develop understanding of how the visual and the verbal relate and to make explicit children's ideas about how to make imaginative use of their experience. The 'How Artists Use' series helps children acquire a vocabulary about such visual concepts as shape, colour, pattern and texture and encourages them to talk about such concepts (see for example Flux, 2008).

There is much potential for linking art with literacy both during Literacy Time and outside it. The picture books that are widely used and enjoyed in the primary classroom provide many opportunities for children to begin to appreciate such artistic concerns as form, colour and composition alongside a written text. There is more about this under the 'picture books' entry. In their action research study, Sue Ellis and Kimberley Safford explored how the visual arts, as well as dance, film making and drama helped extend children's literacy (Ellis and Safford, 2009).

Books can help children begin to understand about artists from different times and cultures. In the case of younger children, the books are often narratives. The story of Van Gogh's life as a painter is told in Laurence Anholt's *Camille and the Sunflowers* (Frances Lincoln); the book is a starting point for experiments with colour using different media. However, it also leads to a search for words to describe the many different yellows and golds the artist used, and it invites the exploration of the characters' feelings about the paintings. By the later primary years children will begin to understand the social and cultural factors that can affect the work of an artist. The story of Faith Ringgold shows the struggle of a black, woman artist from Harlem to achieve recognition for her work. Her story is told in *Faith Ringgold* by Robyn Montana Turner (Little, Brown, & Co) and children will appreciate that Faith's images – which vary from pictures of her slave grandmother to paintings of figures like Michael Jackson – tell of the artist's personal history. A book like this can inspire children's own writing – biographical and autobiographical – and their own art work.

Poems are often good starting points for children's pictures and some literature links well with the creation of timelines or friezes with illustrations. I have often seen the journey of Edward Lear's 'jumblies' represented in a lively and humorous frieze (see 'The Jumblies' in *A Book of Nonsense*, Dragon's World Publishers). Another favourite poem for inspiring art work is Robert Browning's *The Pied Piper of Hamelin*. A student of mine, working with nine year olds, asked them to create their impression of the landscape in the place where the children were taken by the piper. To get them underway, she showed them how different illustrators had imagined the land. Other teachers prefer not to show children other illustrations until after they have completed their paintings. I am still wondering which is the most fruitful way round. Perhaps children need more help than we sometimes appreciate to find

ways of building illustrations from a poem or story and to understand that they are not limited to representational works but that an abstract picture might better capture mood and atmosphere.

Carnival is a context in which many media and many ways of celebrating blend – visual (costume making, dance, masks, masquerade), aural (music) and verbal (poetry, improvisation and story).

Book making also links English and art in an interesting way: the complementary roles of written text and illustration come into strong relief and children are usually eager that their book should be aesthetically pleasing as well as being a successful story or non-fiction text.

Ellis, Sue and Safford, Kimberley (2009) *Animating Literacy* London: Centre for Language in Primary Education.

Flux, Paul (2008, second edition) *Line and Tone; Colour; Shape; Perspective; Pattern and Texture* How Artists Use series London: Heinemann.

ARTICLE

See also: definite article, determiner, indefinite article

In English there are two articles: *the* – the definite article; *a/an* – the indefinite article.

The definite article can be used with any common noun – singular (the teacher) and plural (the teachers). It also forms part of some proper names – *The British Museum*.

The indefinite article 'a' is usually used before consonant sounds – *a cat*, and the indefinite article 'an' before vowels – *an apple*. See the separate entry on indefinite articles for exceptions.

ASSESSMENT

See also: miscue analysis, portfolios, Primary Language Record, reading, record keeping, SATs, speaking and listening, writing

Rather than viewing assessment as something that always takes place at the end of episodes of work, it is helpful to see it as part of the whole cycle of learning. Assessment is an umbrella term for all the ways in which we evaluate children's progress. Our assessment of the pupils, whether it is built up through cumulative observation or is the result of a more formal set of tests of specific attainments, should feed back into the next cycle of planning and teaching. There are a number of possible formats for recording the results of assessment evidence. In assessing the children's progress, we are of course also evaluating the effectiveness of our teaching strategies and results will indicate if and how we need to modify these. This dynamic approach informs the assessment sections of the extended entries on the four language processes: speaking and listening, reading and writing.

There are some useful terms to keep in mind when selecting ways of assessing children's progress in English and indeed in the other primary curriculum subjects. One important distinction is between formative and summative kinds of assessment. Teachers make formative assessments as part of the everyday work of the class. This kind of assessment concentrates on a child's developing abilities and often diagnoses where help is needed. Comments on what the teacher has observed inform the pupil's profile. A great strength of this kind of assessment is that it is integrated with teaching and learning and feeds easily back into planning. For example, after a focus on fairy tales as a genre we might ask the children to write their own modern fairy tale. Their writing would be helpful and satisfying as part of their work and would also help the teacher see how far each individual had understood and applied features of the genre.

Summative assessment comes at the close of a phase of work and in the United Kingdom, at the end of the Key Stages at seven years and eleven years. Records of summative assessments form the basis of reports for future teachers and for parents, and provide snapshots of what a child has achieved at a particular age or stage. The descriptions of levels of achievement in the UK National Curriculum guide teachers in making summative assessments, while standardised tests, for example the National Curriculum SATs in reading and writing, add information to the profile.

The fitness for purpose of the SATs is constantly reviewed. There has long been concern that the tests might distort the curriculum in Year 6. Many teachers have also felt that the use of test data in league tables was unfair as progress was measured by benchmark testing of KS2 children with summative teacher assessment at KS1. Another area of worry was the assessment of writing by a test. This might work for spelling, grammar and handwriting, but many consider that children's ability to compose, review and edit and to show their creativity in their writing was best assessed by formative methods. Strong feelings about these issues and a general dissatisfaction with the quality of marking led to the boycotting of the KS2 tests by a quarter of schools in Summer 2010. These concerns were addressed in Lord Bew's Independent Review of Key Stage 2 testing, assessment and accountability which was published in July 2011. Lord Bew and his team recommended a mixture of ongoing formative assessment and benchmark testing to ensure reliability and to provide a consistent national picture of progress and attainment (Bew, 2011).

Where teachers wish to compare children's results with the average attainment, in reading for example, of a large number of pupils of the same chronological age, they use a standardised test. Norm tests provide a reading age which may be higher or lower than a child's chronological age. If we want to know how far a child has progressed in acquiring particular skills we use a criterion referenced test. The National Curriculum Levels of Achievement are criterion referenced since they compare a particular child's performance against the descriptions of each level of attainment.

Diagnostic tests are carried out to identify a child's particular difficulties in, for example, reading and writing. Where a child is judged to be eligible for a statement of special educational need diagnostic tests are carried out by an educational psychologist. These formally administered tests guide teachers in preparing and implementing an appropriate remedial programme. The miscue analysis entry explains how teachers can carry out a useful diagnostic reading test less formally. As well as carrying out and recording formal assessments of progress in spoken and written language, teachers also take note of what they learn from informal observation. Such informal assessment might involve observing the use of language by children during role play or of how they go about their writing in the literacy corner. Some aspects of progress in reading are assessed through observation – of, for example, the child's skill in 'skimming', 'scanning' and the use of retrieval devices important in every lesson and required by the National Curriculum. Planning and teaching might also be informed by observing the range of reading children undertake. We need to consider whether a child's reading is sufficiently wide. We can learn how far children are able to concentrate by observing them in quiet reading times. In *Assessing Children's Learning*, Drummond provides a helpful review of developments in approaches to assessment over the last ten years (Drummond, 2007). Teachers' skilled and sensitive observations, combined with information from more formal assessments, help them set targets, give constructive feedback and plan 'next steps' for individual children (Blenkin and Kelly, 1992; Clark, 2003, 2008; Hall and Burke, 2004).

Teachers develop ways of recording their observations and there are a number of books that help here. There is an account of different kinds of record keeping in *Assessment for Learning and Teaching in Primary Schools* and suggested formats for recording time sample observations in *A Practical Guide to Child Observation and Assessment* (Briggs, 2008; Hobart and Frankel, 2009). The *Primary Language Record Handbook,* developed by the Centre for Literacy in Primary Education, encourages a rich sampling of what children have achieved and has influenced record keeping all over the world (Barrs *et al.,* 1988). There is also a collection of articles published in *The Primary Record in Use* with classroom case studies (O'Sullivan, 1995).

So far this entry has been concerned with teacher assessment and record keeping, but the contribution that parents, peers and the children themselves can make to monitoring progress is also important. Parents are invited to comment on, for example, children's reading at home and evidence from these discussions with the teacher finds a place in modern record keeping systems. Peers can help each other and develop, with the teacher's help, criteria for judging each other's work constructively. Peer assessment can give all the pupils a vocabulary for describing and talking about what a successful piece of work is like (Black *et al.,* 2003). Above all, though, children are now encouraged to talk about their enthusiasms, preferences and progress and, as the entry on portfolios explains, are also involved in the selection of work that is to be kept. Reviewing progress with the teacher helps children understand both their learning achievements and their learning needs. They are then more likely to have an informed view of their agreed learning goals and targets.

Barrs, Myra, Ellis, S., Hester, H. and Thomas, A. (1988) *The Primary Language Record*

Handbook London: Centre for Literacy in Primary Education.

Bew, Paul (2011) *Independent Review of Key Stage 2 testing, assessment and accountability* London: HMSO, July 2011.

Black, Paul, Harrison, Chris, Lee, Clare, Marshall, Bethan and Williams, Dylan (2003) *Assessment for Learning* Milton Keynes: Open University Press (based on the 'Assessment for learning' project funded by the Nuffield Research Foundation at King's College, London).

Blenkin, Geva and Kelly, Vic (eds) (1992) *Assessment in Early Childhood* London: Paul Chapman.

Briggs, Mary (2008, second edition) *Assessment for Learning and Teaching in Primary Schools (Achieving QTS)* London: Learning Matters.

Clark, Shirley (2003) *Enriching Feedback in the Primary Classroom* London: Hodder Arnold (see chapter on Literacy).

——(2008) *Active Learning Through Formative Assessment* London: Hodder.

Drummond, Mary Jane (2007, second edition) *Assessing Children's Learning* London: David Fulton.

Hall, Kathy and Burke, Winnifred (2004) *Making Formative Assessment Work: Effective Practice in the Primary Classroom* Milton Keynes: Open University Press.

Hobart, Christine and Frankel, Jill (2009, fourth edition) *A Practical Guide to Child Observation and Assessment* Cheltenham: Nelson Thornes.

O'Sullivan, Olivia (1995) *The Primary Language Record in Use* London: the Centre for Literacy in Primary Education.

ASSIMILATION AND ACCOMMODATION

See also: prior knowledge

Assimilation, the adaption of new material to an existing system, and accommodation, the adjustment of existing structures to new material, are complementary processes in Jean Piaget's adaptive model of learning.

To explain how an individual learns, Piaget uses the analogy of the digestive system. When we eat something it has to be assimilated – changed by gastric juices in the mouth and stomach to become capable of being used by the body. At the same time, the digestive organs have to make adjustments to receive the food and allow for its passage through the organs of digestion. So it is with new learning: we have to present it in the right way for the young learner and it has to be capable of being absorbed into the young learner's existing frameworks of knowledge. The 'presenting new information in the right way' is crucial and at the heart of the teacher's professional skills.

One thing to take account of is the prior knowledge a learner brings to a new topic. Skilled teachers are able to help children organise their prior knowledge, often by inviting carefully orchestrated discussion. What we sometimes find is that children have concepts and understandings but do not yet control the formal vocabulary to refer to them. Part of the teacher's role is to help children move from what Piaget called 'spontaneous concepts' (those we acquire in the course of living – 'stone', 'food', 'water') to 'scientific concepts' (usually acquired in formal contexts – 'igneous rock', 'vitamins', 'water cycle'). Vygotsky took over Piaget's classification of concepts and suggested how they could be exploited in classroom learning (Vygotsky, 1986). For an account of how an understanding of 'spontaneous' and 'scientific' concepts can help us plan and reflect on lessons – in this case an interesting lesson about 'rocks' to ten year olds – see Chapter 2 'Systematic learning: what is involved?' in Mallett and Newsome, 1977. This reminds us (at a time when work in United Kingdom primary schools can be rather subject-orientated) that all good teaching has to begin with children's existing concepts – there is no other sensible place to start.

18

Educational theories come in and out of fashion but over a long teaching career I have found Piaget's adaptive model extremely helpful to keep in mind in my planning and teaching of both children and students. For a clear introduction to the work of Piaget, Bruner and Vygotsky and some helpful suggested applications to the classroom, I recommend David Wood's book *How Children Think and Learn*.

Mallett, Margaret and Newsome, Bernard (1977) *Talking, Writing and Learning, 8–13* Schools Council Working Paper 59. London: Evans/Methuen.

Vygotsky, L.S. (1986 edition with an introduction by A. Kozulin [1962]) *Thought and Language* Cambridge, Mass.: The MIT Press.

Wood, David (1988, second edition) *How Children Think and Learn* Oxford: Blackwell.

ASSONANCE

See also: alliteration

This is the term used to refer to the repeated use of a vowel phoneme in poetry or prose for aesthetic impact or to enhance meaning by drawing attention to particular words. Examples include: 'handstand', 'easy to please', 'plain Jane'.

ATLAS

See also: geography and English, non-fiction reading and writing

An atlas is a book of maps and communicates visually. It is best to start with simple map making when children are very young. They can begin to make maps of the classroom and the journey to school so that the principles of the representation of space and distance are established. Lani Yamamoto offers some inspiration here in her book *Albert*, which includes picture maps of the area where the little boy lives.

Representations of fairy tale journeys have often been used by early years teachers to provide an interesting context to talk about time and distance. Wayland's *Big Book of Mapwork 1,* which began delightfully with a map of Red Riding Hood's journey, is sadly out of print, but the *Oxford Reading Tree Atlas,* which includes a CD-ROM, enthuses young learners by featuring characters like Biff and Kipper. There are a number of books with 'first atlas' in the title, including Patrick Wiegand's *Oxford First Atlas* which is accompanied by an e-atlas that can be shared with the whole class on an interactive whiteboard. Young users of the *Usborne Sticker Atlas of Great Britain and Ireland* would enjoy placing the stickers, but most under eights would need help in accessing the internet links and with understanding the information. Atlases, like other reference texts, tend these days to be the result of the work of a team of editors, writers, illustrators and designers. While this often results in a sound information source, it would be a pity if the more quirky kind of book was pushed out. I'm thinking here of books like Parrogon's *Gold Star Children's Atlas* which has colourful maps studded with pictures of places and animals.

In the later primary years children are ready to understand more sophisticated cartography and the quality of design and the supporting materials is important. CD-ROM and internet-linked atlases enable children to explore the world using multimedia interactive maps and film clips. Oxford, Collins, Usborne and Dorling Kindersley are amongst those publishers at the forefront of new media atlases. A visit to their websites (or to amazon.co.uk) informs about the latest editions. The Geographical Association website has a link to primary school geography with imaginative teaching ideas and reviews of the latest materials (www.geography.org.uk/eyprimary).

Teachers of older primary school children seek good screen material. The *Collins Primary World Whiteboard Atlas* is in CD-ROM format and includes printable blank outlines to support seven to eleven year olds' mapping activities. Patrick Wiegand is well respected for the quality of his print and e-reference books. His CD-ROM version of the *Oxford Primary Atlas,* the *Oxford Primary e-Atlas,* has maps and other geographical information for whole class work using an interactive whiteboard. Usborne was one of the first to develop internet-linked reference texts, for example *The Usborne Essential Atlas of the World.* Large atlases of this kind for older primary children and younger secondary children cover similar ground and are good resources for teaching study skills as well as geographical concepts. However, most, like this one, require considerable mediation from the teacher and here, of course, class-based work on the whiteboard has an important role.

The new technology can be motivating and empowering, but children need to be taught how to get the best out of it. For many purposes a simple print atlas suffices – *Philips Junior Atlas* for example. Whether print or electronic, the best atlases and map books for the under elevens have some clear characteristics. Particularly for the younger children it is wise not to have maps with too small a scale or too much density of information, as this makes it a reading challenge. It simply is not necessary to clutter maps with non-essential information. Teachers look for clear global organisation and an index that has a helpful way of differentiating the names of towns, rivers and mountains (Mallett, 1999, 2010). We also look for a good mix of colour maps, diagrams and statistics.

Mallett, Margaret (1999) *Young Researchers: Informational Reading and Writing in the Early and Primary Years* London: Routledge (pp. 135–36).

——(2010) *Choosing and Using Fiction and Non-fiction 3–11* London: Routledge (see chapter 33).

Scoffham, Stephen (ed.) (2010, revised edition) *Primary Geography Handbook* Sheffield: Geographical Association (see chapter 8 on mapwork).

For reviews of other geography books and materials visit the website www.geography.org.uk.

ATTAINMENT TARGETS

See also: assessment, criterion referenced assessment, National Curriculum, SATs

Attainment Targets describe the standards children are required to meet in English and in all other subjects as they follow The National Curriculum Programmes of Study.

In English there are three Attainment Targets: Speaking and Listening, Reading, and Writing. Primary children are normally placed at one of the first six National Curriculum English levels and it is hoped that as many children as possible will achieve a level 2 or above at the end of Key Stage 1 and at least a level 4 at the end of Key Stage 2. As each level in each Attainment Target is described in terms of criteria, this approach to assessment is described as 'criterion referenced'. It is also 'norm referenced' in the sense that expectations are linked to the likely achievements of other children of the same age.

AUDIO RESOURCES

See also: CDs, radio programmes for children, reading corner/area, speaking and listening

In the recent past audio books, tapes and cassettes, containing the taped version of a printed book, were used in school and at home. However, technology moves on and audio cassettes have been replaced by

CDs which, just as cassettes once were, are often bought together with the print version of a book. This enables young readers to follow in the print version of a story as the CD is being played.

Spoken word recordings have been of much higher quality in recent years so that the best deserve a place in the classroom collection and are worth considering for home listening. Improvements have been brought about partly by technology; computers have greatly helped producers achieve complicated editing and convincing sound effects at a relatively low cost. BBC Radio 7 has stories, dramatisations and readings for children which can be recorded digitally and used flexibly. Audio material, including that from archives, can be streamed and played through a personal computer. What then are some of the qualities we should look for in audio books and CDs? First and foremost, of course, the story has to be well read. There are some lively recordings of favourite books for very young children, for example *Goodnight Moon* read by Linda Terhayda (Line Oak Readalong) and *Where the Wild Things Are* read by Tommy Grimes. For older children there are such gems as the BBC audio CD of Rudyard Kipling's *Just So Stories* read by Johnny Morris, and Puffin's *Roald Dahl's Phizz Whizzing Audio Collection* brought to life by James Bolam, Geoffrey Palmer and Andrew Sachs. Ben Tibber, aged twelve years, reads the audio book of *The Curious Incident of the Dog in the Night-time* by Mark Haddon (Random House) in just the right monotonous tone to suggest a young autistic. Another example of an audio story being brought alive by a first-class narrator is Imelda Staunton's reading of *The Gruffalo* (Macmillan). The quality and suitability of sound effects and music in drawing in young listeners is another aspect we should consider. The recording of *Arthur, King of the Middle March* (Orion) features just the kind of music to suggest location. Where

appropriate, a cast of actors can greatly add to the impact of audio recordings and CDs. The CD of *Lyra's Oxford* (Random House) in which the author, Philip Pullman, is the storyteller brings in the voices of a cast of actors to make hearing the story a different experience to that of hearing a reading by a sole voice (Macpherson, 2004). Where one actor takes all the parts within the story we need to judge whether they keep up the pace successfully and differentiate the voices sufficiently, as happens in Philip Pullman's *The Ruby in the Smoke* (BBC Cover to Cover).

Although the best story recordings have much to offer all children in the primary years, they have a special role in drawing in young reluctant or dyslexic readers, who gain insight into what books can offer without the need to read them. For more suggestions about good audio books for different age groups I recommend Angela Macpherson's (2004) article 'Listening to a good book'.

It is worth mentioning a national scheme run by the Sonic Arts Network which aims to help children appreciate the aural environment (see www.sonicpostcards.org). In a visual world we should not overlook the importance of sound. Sound can provide a window into other people's worlds. Children at one primary school created 'sonic cards' using a digital media player to record the sounds of their village – the rustle of leaves, the peal of church bells and the rattle of a butcher's curtain (Bloom, 2005). The idea was to send these cards electronically to children in other primary schools. Of particular value was the talk to decide which sounds to use and how to order them to give the most authentic impression of their village.

The strategy should, of course, be used as well as and not instead of reading out loud to children. Sometimes audio resources are included in packages like the Story Sacks series for the very young produced by Child's Play. *The Old Lady Who*

21

Swallowed a Fly, which won an Alcuin Award from the European Parents' Association, is a typical story sack containing an audio version of the song and other favourites, a doll of the Old Lady into which bean-filled creatures like the spider and the fly can be stuffed and a board game bringing together words, pictures and memory.

As well as these commercial audio resources, teachers often build up resources by making their own recordings of favourite books. Older children sometimes make recordings for younger ones and sometimes parents will be prepared to translate stories into their children's home languages. There is a strong case for having a listening area with easily used recording and play back equipment and a good range of stories within the classroom, perhaps as part of the book corner.

Audio recordings of a child involved in shared reading can be added to their English portfolio to provide extra evidence of progress.

Finally, in a visual world, the oral tradition remains important and can be a direct link between schools, homes and communities. This was the focus of Marilyn Mottram's Story Spinner Project in which a Story Spinner DVD (with stories from around the world) was used to promote the listening enjoyment of children between ages five and eleven (Mottram, 2009).

Bloom, Adi (2005) 'Hear where they are coming from' in *Times Educational Supplement*, 7 January, p. 2.

Macpherson, Angela (2004) 'Listening to a good book' in *Books for Keeps*, No. 144, January.

Mottram, Marilyn (2009) 'The Story Spinners Project' in *English 4–11*, No. 45, Spring 2009, pp. 18–20.

AUDIT (OF PRIMARY ENGLISH)

See also: English/Literacy Co-ordinator, planning

English audits are carried out as part of a school's general cycle of curriculum improvement but are particularly needed when a new English/Literacy Co-ordinator takes over, after an OFSTED Inspection or when new statutory requirements have to be put in place. During an English audit every aspect of the English curriculum is reviewed including resources and the school library, teaching approaches, assessment and record keeping. The auditing process leads to an action plan and to setting literacy targets.

The Co-ordinator might well begin by examining the school's English policy and noting where it needs updating or improving. The next stage is to identify some key questions about what needs to be found out and to note ways in which the evidence will be obtained and then presented to others. The most effective way of gaining a picture of the state of the school's English work is by making careful observations during sensitively conducted visits to all the classrooms and talking to the teachers and the children. This helps show up any mismatches between what is written down in the policy and what actually happens. Sometimes teachers are asked to fill in questionnaires about their practice and views. This can generate a lot of work and the question sheet is best kept short!

The English/Literacy Co-ordinator needs to liaise with the head teacher, the Co-ordinators of the two Key Stages and the Special Needs Co-ordinator. In a very useful analysis of the whole auditing process, Merchant and Marsh point out that peer observation, in particular, can be 'unnerving' for teachers. It is justified as probably the most powerful way to bring about professional development but it needs to be carefully managed (Merchant and Marsh, 1998: Chapter 3).

Once evidence has been collected from observations, discussions, questionnaires, reports, SATs results and English portfolios, the next stage is to give feedback and work towards improvement of any areas shown to need attention. The Co-ordinator with energy and vision tries to create a good working atmosphere in the meetings and a sense of excitement about the changes – whether in teaching, assessment or improving the school library and in investing in new technology like software, CD-ROMs and the internet. Realistic literacy targets should be agreed and supported by an action plan to ensure the development of good English practice in the school. The secret is to make the implementation of improvements a combined effort involving all the teachers in a constructive way. Tyrrell and Gill include an interesting case study in *Co-ordinating English at Key Stage 1* in which a Co-ordinator gains respect by allowing others to observe her own practice in an area which has been shown through the audit to need support. Teachers needed some help with 'modelling' how books work and helping children to understand book language. We are shown the steps by which the Co-ordinator demonstrated in her own classroom how children could be helped to enjoy a story *and* learn about reading and print as the use of speech marks, commas and capital letters were 'modelled'. The big book used was Joy Cowley's *Mrs Wishy Washy* (Story Chest) which has a welcome touch of humour about it (Tyrrell and Gill, 2000: 17–19).

Merchant, Guy and Marsh, Jackie (1998) *Coordinating Primary Language and Literacy* London: Paul Chapman (Chapter 3).

Tyrrell, Jenny and Gill, Narinderjit (2000) *Coordinating English at Key Stage 1* London: Falmer Press (pp. 12–14 and 17–19).

AUTHORS OF CHILDREN'S BOOKS

See: history of children's literature

AUTHOR STUDIES

Older primary school children often undertake the study of one author's work, spreading their study over a few weeks. Writers of longer stories and children's novels tend to be chosen and favourites include David Almond, Cressida Cowell, Roald Dahl, Anne Fine, Dick King-Smith, Michael Morpurgo, Philippa Pearce, Louis Sachar, Marcia Williams and Jacqueline Wilson. However, there is no reason why children should not choose to look at the work of an illustrator (Quentin Blake, Anthony Browne) or poet (Brian Patten, Michael Rosen). Author studies, when supported carefully and imaginatively, create good opportunities for research, discussion, drama and presentations.

Some hints about making author studies valuable include:

- Suggesting that children keep the scope manageable by choosing just two or three works.
- Planning the work with the children rather than delivering a list of things to do.
- Allowing them to include negative as well as positive opinions as long as they can back them up with reference to the texts.
- Avoiding children copying chunks of material about authors from books or websites. Suggesting that they go into their research with some questions and use these to structure their account.
- Pointing out that most children's authors have helpful and sometimes interactive websites to give biographical details.
- Encouraging the young writers to find an intriguing anecdote about their author. Geoff Fox's book *Dear Mr Morpingo* starts thus: when Michael was a baby, his pram somehow became attached to a car which pulled off at great speed. Fortunately, when he was tipped out, he was only bruised and lived to create his wonderful stories.
- Making the work collaborative by having class discussions and asking

children to read out bits of their developing studies.

- Encouraging children to design their pages and include drawings, timelines and cartoon strips, perhaps, as well as writing.
- Recognising that children appreciate the opportunity to experience an author's stories in some different media – audio CDs and film as well as print.
- Setting up role play – that great energiser of this sort of project; inviting children to answer questions in the role of the author or as one of the characters in a book.
- Welcoming a variety of outcomes: a folder that is put on display for others to peruse, a short film, a web page, an annotated display or a PowerPoint presentation.

AUTOBIOGRAPHY

See also: anecdotes, biography, first person writing, genre, letters

An autobiography is a first person account written by the subject which may seek to justify, explain or excuse as well as to inform. The boundaries between fact and fiction can become blurred as a writer selects and shapes particular incidents. What we get is one person's version of what happened and how they felt about it. 'Some autobiographies come near to being works of fiction and many works of fiction have autobiographical aspects' (McArthur, 1992: 98).

There are not many full-length autobiographies for readers under eleven years but two good examples are Roald Dahl's *Boy: Tales of Childhood* (Puffin) and *Anne Frank's Diary*. A case study of Year 6 children using these is under the 'first person writing' entry.

Autobiography is sometimes used in information books on recent history. See,

for example, the *In Grandma's Day* series published by Evans in the late 1990s: each book is organised round the memories of one person's life in the 1930s and 1940s. Reading about the memories of a real person living through dramatic times (for example, as an evacuee in the Second World War) in the twentieth century gives children a different perspective on history. Such texts can also be used in English or in Literacy Time to compare the features of first and third person accounts. For the mature ten year old and older children, the autobiographical novel based on the diaries of Tatjana Wassiljewa, *A Hostage to War* (Collins), is a powerful account of a young girl's courage during the famine caused by the Nazi invasion of the Soviet Union. The first person voice of the diaries (translated by Anna Trenter) speaks movingly of hunger, fear and the ceaseless toil of Tatjana as she faces work on the farms and factories of the Third Reich.

Where we want children to compare autobiography with biography, Roald Dahl's autobiography, *Boy*, might be compared with Chris Powling's short biography of *Roald Dahl* in Evans' *Tell Me About Writers* series.

Fictional autobiographies use the first person 'voice' as a literary device. There are always reasons for the choice of 'voice'. It may suit the author's purpose to show a set of events very powerfully from one character's viewpoint or to give an impression of spontaneity. Far from being easy to write in the first person, it is in fact a very sophisticated kind of writing which has to be carefully crafted to succeed. In *The Midnight Fox*, for example, Betsy Byars wants the readers to share the intensity of the urban boy's experiences in the countryside. The use of Tyke's 'voice' in *The Turbulent Term of Tyke Tyler* by Gene Kemp gives the narrative energy and immediacy and draws the reader in more than a third person account might have done. Letters are an important kind of first person writing that can be a powerful literary device. They are used, to great effect, in Simon James' *Dear Greenpeace* for children of about six to eight years and, for older children, in Beverley Cleary's *Dear Mr Henshaw* and Harry Horse's *The Last Polar Bears*.

Letters, real or imagined, are also important in the work of Marcia Williams and of Mick Manning and Brita Granström. Marcia Williams uses diary entries and letters to bring alive the 'voice' of a young girl during the Second World War in *My Secret War Diary by Flossie Albright 1939–45*. Mick Manning and Brita Granström have brought new energy to both autobiographical and biographical writing for primary aged children. *Tail-end Charlie* tells of the experiences of a rear gunner in a Lancaster bomber during the Second

World War. This airman was Mick's father and the first person narrative draws on the many stories and anecdotes father shared with son. Their companion book *Taff in the WAAF* relates the wartime experiences of Mick's mother, and the narrative reads as if she was speaking. Williams and Manning and Granström bring immediacy to the lives of their subjects, not only through different kinds of writing but also through a range of illustrations showing artefacts, people and scenes.

Children whose roots are in countries far away from where they live often see letters as a way of bridging the distance between friends and relatives. For children of about nine plus, *Jazeera's Journey* by Lisa Bruce (Methuen, 1991) shows how letters can link lives, in this case the lives of Jazeera in England and her grandmother in Asia.

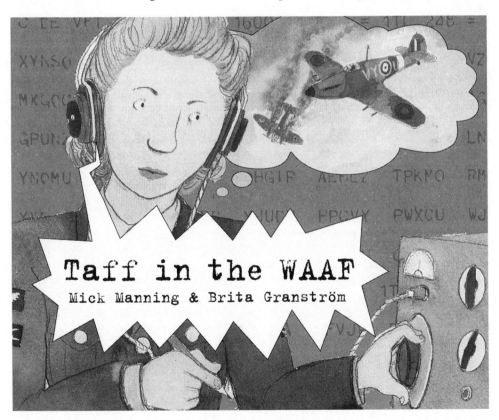

Figure 3 Front cover of *Taff in the WAAF* by Mick Manning and Brita Granström. Reproduced with the permission of the publishers, © Frances Lincoln, 2010.

Reading books like those mentioned above can be a helpful starting point for children's own writing (see more about this under 'first person writing'). Typing emails, texting and Facebook entries are increasingly popular forms of first person and autobiographical writing. This is bound to impinge on children's writing and improvised drama in school. Year 5 children in a London school wrote emails 'in role' when responding to Charles Causley's poem 'What Has Happened to Lulu' (Safford, O'Sullivan and Barrs, 2004).

McArthur, Tom (ed.) (1992) *The Oxford Companion to the English Language* Oxford: Oxford University Press.

Mallett, Margaret (1997) *First Person Reading and Writing in the Primary Years* Sheffield: NATE

——(2010) *Choosing and Using Fiction and Non-fiction 3–11* London: Routledge (chapter 26).

Safford, Kimberley, O'Sullivan, Olivia and Barrs, Myra (2004) *Boys on the Margin* CLPE: London.

AUTOCORRECT

See also: spelling

Autocorrect is a feature in Microsoft Word, found in the tools menu. The computer usually defaults to autocorrecting certain spellings and capitalising first words of sentences. These quick changes may not be noticed by a child user and for this reason teachers often switch off the facility. The young learner will then see wrong spellings underlined in red and can be encouraged to use the spelling facility themselves or a dictionary.

AUXILIARY VERB

See also: modal verb, parts of speech, verbs

An auxiliary verb adds meaning to another verb, as in the following:

'They *have* descended'.

'He *is* going'.

'*Can* you sing?'

In these examples 'have', 'is' and 'can' are auxiliary verbs and 'descended', 'going' and 'sing' are the main verbs. The most frequently used verbs that can function as auxiliaries are 'be', 'have' and 'do'.

B

BALLAD

See also: poetry, verse

A ballad is a long poem or song telling a
story. Traditionally, ballads were narrative
poems sung to a simple musical accompaniment, passed down through the
generations and adapted and changed by
different singers. The old ballads tell stories
about brave deeds or the momentous
events of a particular community. The
ballad was at its most popular in the
late Middle Ages, especially in the border
counties of Scotland and England. Sometimes a distinction is made between
'high' ballads about heroes like Sir Patrick
Spens and 'low' ballads reflecting popular culture. Growing up in the North-East,
I often heard dialect ballads like The
Lambton Worm – about a community
threatened by the emergence of a monster
from the Wear – sung at gatherings and
parties.

From the sixteenth century onwards
printed poems called 'broadside ballads'
about recent events became popular in
England. (It is probably from this tradition
that the folk songs of Bob Dylan and
modern pop songs come.) These coexisted
with the continuation of 'high' ballads
including the 'literary ballads' which were
narrative poems written by established
poets whose work took on some of
the form and spirit of the old ballads. The
ballads of the Romantic period include, for
example, Coleridge's literary ballad, 'The
Ancient Mariner' (*Lyrical Ballads,* 1798).
Scott's 'Proud Maisie' and Keats' haunting
'La Belle Dame sans Merci' are also well-
known ballad poems.

In the primary years children over about
eight years enjoy hearing ballads read out
loud because of the exciting (albeit often
ultimately sad) events, the strong rhythm
and the repetition of words for dramatic
effect. In Literacy Time children consider
the features of ballads and narrative
poems. Of course we want them to
respond to a good story most of all, but
children can also appreciate the short
regular verses and rhyme scheme of a ballad. The pattern can take many forms, but
traditionally the ballad stanza is a quatrain
in alternate four and three stress iambic
lines. Many of us can remember by heart
the first stanza of Sir Patrick Spens and
this is a good example of the classic ballad
form.

> 'The king sits in Dumferling towne,
> Drinking the blude-red wine:
> 'O whar will I get a guid sailor,
> To sail this schip of mine?'

Children can be helped to acquire a vocabulary to enable them to discuss the
characteristics of the poems. In his book
Young Readers and their Books Gervase

27

Phinn suggests that we talk about features like the mood, theme, metre and figures of speech. We can also consider why particular words are used and how the characters are brought to life. The first verse of Sir Patrick Spens shows us the typically abrupt start that ballads often have and the use of stark 'to the point' dialogue. Talking about all this will help children write their own ballads to read out loud and arrange in a book. A good place to start if you want to introduce a study of ballads is with a dramatic poem like, for example, 'The Highwayman' by Alfred Noyes. This and other stirring ballads, like 'The Pied Piper of Hamelin' by Robert Browning, are included in *The Oxford Book of Story Poems*. Some ballads are only found in general poetry collections and teachers often build up their own anthology over the years.

Of course the term 'ballad' is now often used to describe modern narrative poems that do not conform to the traditional stanza format. You will find help to extend interest and understanding of modern ballads with able, older primary children in Robert Catt's (2006) chapter in Fisher and Williams' *Unlocking Literacy*. He concentrates on ballads and narrative poems on animal themes by present-day poets, for example Charles Causley's 'I Saw a Jolly Hunter' and 'My Mother Saw a Dancing Bear'. Catt stresses the importance of careful reading of the poems out loud by teacher and children to communicate subtle meanings. His classroom examples indicate the importance of encouraging a 'community of enquiry' – a context in which children share with each other and the teacher their understandings and response to what are often heart-rending and disturbing themes. Looking again at Catt's analysis of his work reminded me that teachers themselves, including myself, need much more than a superficial knowledge of ballad poems to develop work of high calibre.

Enjoying ballads

(Based on Holly Anderson's 'Follow the Piper' TES Primary: 47. 22.1.1999.)

- Tell the children the story first.
- Share any interesting background (e.g. Pied Piper of Hamelin based by Browning on a fourteenth-century legend).
- Compare different editions and their illustrations (Browning's poem is in his complete works, in a colourfully illustrated version published by Ginn, in *The Everyman Children's Classic,* illustrated by Kate Greenaway).
- Discuss particular sections and suggest how they illuminate character.
- Draw attention to choice of word and phrase and their effect.
- Improvise parts of the story – in The Pied Piper of Hamelin the teacher in role as piper, perhaps.
- Script dialogues (e.g. between the children at different points in the story).
- Talk about deeper meaning/moral of the poem.

Catt, Robert (2006) '"Jolly good I said": using poetry with older children' in Fisher, Robert and Williams, Mary (eds) *Unlocking Literacy: A Guide for Teachers* London: David Fulton.

Phinn, Gervase (2000) *Young Readers and their Books: Suggestions and Strategies for Using Texts in the Literacy Hour* London: David Fulton (see p. 106 for Phinn's poem based on the northern legend – The Legend of the Lambton Worm).

BIAS (IN CHILDREN'S BOOKS)

See also: factual genres, history of children's literature, reading

All books have a bias in the sense that they draw on an author's distinctive view of the world in general and on the story or topic in particular, but when we say a book is 'biased' we usually mean that there is some unwelcome favouring of one perspective over another in a way that distorts 'the facts'. Of course general agreement on what 'the facts' are, particularly in the more controversial and sensitive topics, is sometimes problematic.

When it comes to children's texts, including books, ebooks and visual material on film and television, there are two main kinds of unwelcome bias. First, there might be a bias in the whole book collection towards texts by authors from one culture and where the characters and settings favour one approach to the world and human experience. Individually, such books may be excellent – they may meet important criteria like having powerful stories and convincing characters. Any book that is good of its kind and suitable for the age group is welcome. Rather, it is the possible omission of the work of authors from all parts of the globe, authors who can share with readers some different experiences and perspectives, that concerns us. This is why I support all those who feel teachers should be helped, in their college days and beyond, to acquire and continue to develop expert knowledge about the full range of books and resources for the age groups they teach.

The handbook that many teachers found particularly useful when developing library collections was *A Multicultural Guide to Children's Books 0–16+* edited by Rosemary Stones, sadly out of print. There may be a new edition at some point. Meanwhile, we have Deborah Hallford and Edgardo Zaghini's *Folk and Fairy Tales: A Book Guide*, which is based on the recognition that every country and culture has its own store of traditional tales (Hallford and Zaghini, 2004). However, more good books from different parts of the world

need to be published: this is the conclusion in Rosemary Stones' article following the 2006 Diversity Matters conference 'Multicultural publishing: what it took to get us where we are' (Stones, 2006). Shereen Pandit's article 'Diversity in publishing for children' also argues that there is some way to go before quality books from across the world are fairly represented in publishers' lists. Only when this improves will we have school collections that reach out to all the groups in our society (Pandit, 2006). Part of the problem has been to do with difficulties in finding gifted translators of books in languages other than English. Those who would like to learn more about this would find Hallford and Zaghini's *Children's Books in Translation* illuminating. This whole issue has been energised by the establishment of the Marsh Award for Children's Literature in Translation.

The second kind of bias is to do with the content and attitudes expressed in particular books and in film and television programmes (Schneeweil, 2009). I am thinking about stories or non-fiction texts that offer a stereotyped view – in language or illustration – of gender, race or social class. Many of us are uneasy with the notion of censorship but none of us would offer children books and resources – print or electronic – that were offensive to any of the groups that make up our society.

Hallford, Deborah and Zaghini, Edgardo (2004) *Folk and Fairy Tales: A Book Guide* London: Booktrust.

——(2005) *Children's Books in Translation* London: Milet Publishing.

Pandit, Shereen (2006) 'Diversity in publishing for children' in *Books for Keeps*, No. 160, September.

Schneeweil, Birgit (2009) *Pre-school Children and Language and Gender Stereotypes: Animated Features and Their Influence in Acquiring Gender Stereotypes and Gender Appropriate Language* Salzburg: VDM, Verlag.

Stones, Rosemary (1999) *A Multicultural Guide to Children's Books 0–16+* London: Books for Keeps (O/P).

——(2006) 'Diversity Matters – Multicultural publishing: what it took to get us where we are' in *Books for Keeps*, No. 161, November.

BIBLE (THE)

See also: parable, sacred texts

The Bible is a collection of sacred books divided by Christians into two parts – the Old Testament and the New Testament. It is studied not only because of its religious significance but also as literature – it contains writing of many kinds including prose, poetry, epistles and prophecy. So great has been the influence of the Bible on Western culture that knowledge of the scriptures is important in understanding the work of many authors and poets, for example George Eliot, John Milton and William Blake.

Since the times of these writers we have become a much more plural society and there are stories for children based on other holy books as well as the Bible (see 'sacred texts' entry). The stories from both the Old Testament and the New Testament are used in Religious Education but also have a place in English lessons as powerful tales and parables with profound insights about the human situation. The best versions manage to communicate the deeper meanings. In a thought-provoking article in *Books for Keeps*, Ralph Gower urges us to seek retellings of holy books that retain the significance of the stories and therefore the approval of Jewish, Christian and Muslim believers. He considers, for example, that John Ryan's *The Very Hungry Lions* (Lion Publishing, 1999) gets nearer to the importance of the Daniel story to Jewish people than some of the other retellings for the very young. We need to look at the details added by authors to the tales and also at the illustrations, and ask ourselves whether these are distractions or helpful aids to understanding and reflecting. Children under eight years would find some of Mary Auld's retellings of Old Testament stories appealing – *Noah's Ark* for example (Franklin Watts). Walker Books' 'Bible Stories' series includes the dramatic tales – *Jonah and the Whale, The Amazing Story of Noah's Ark* and *Joseph and his Magnificent Coat of Many Colours* – all well written and illustrated by Marcia Williams in a colourful cartoon style that works well. *The Usborne Children's Bible* (written by Heather Amery for Usborne) draws stories from both the Old Testament and the New Testament and would be good for reading out loud to five to seven year olds. The younger end of this age group would also enjoy sharing two traditional tellings of the Christmas story – Heather Amery's board book (illustrator Norman Young), *Christmas Story* (Usborne) and Georgie Adam's picture book (illustrator Anna Leplar), *The First Christmas* (Dolphin).

Older primary children (and children in the early secondary years) might find *The Lion Graphic Bible* scripted by Mike Maddox and illustrated by Jeff Anderson (Lion Publishing) a vigorous if startling retelling. In comic strip, different formats are used to separate parables and dreams from the main text – very useful if children and teacher are considering the language and imagery of parables. Some might not like the very up-to-date language in the speech bubbles. Perhaps, too, the comic strip form can sometimes miss the more subtle connotations of some stories. This version could be used alongside a scholarly work like *The New Encyclopedia of the Bible* which is edited by John Drane and provides comprehensive coverage of Bible history. I was encouraged, by Ralph Gower's recommendation in his *Books for Keeps* article, to look at two collections (both from Macdonald Young Books) which take us beyond Bible stories. These are Sybil

Sheridan's *Stories from the Jewish World* (which includes recent historical experience in the Holocaust) and David Self's *Stories from the Christian World* which tells of the life of Francis of Assisi and of later important figures, including Adjai Crowther, the first black African bishop. Apart from their merit as powerful tales which illuminate aspects of human experience, the use of biographical material makes these source books helpful texts for nine to eleven year olds.

Gower, Ralph (1999) 'Biblical books for children' in *Books for Keeps*, No.115, March.

McArthur, Tom (1992) *The Oxford Companion to English Literature* London: QPD with Oxford University Press (pp. 116–24).

BIBLIOGRAPHIC CUE-SYSTEM

See also: cue-systems, phonics, reading, spelling

The bibliographic cue-system is less universally acknowledged than the other three cue-systems, which are semantic, syntactic and grapho-phonic (see separate entries). It comes into play when children use their existing knowledge of different written texts to identify the text they are reading. After tuning into whether it is fiction or non-fiction they might decide on assigning the text to a narrower category – for example, a short story or a biography.

The bibliographic cue-system begins to be used at an early age. Very young children use their developing experience of books to understand features of the cover title and author and the relationship between pictures and text.

BIG BOOKS

For many years big books, about 50cm × 36cm, have been used to develop young children's literacy. The 1998 and 2006 UK Literacy Frameworks brought renewed interest in big books as resources for shared reading, that is reading with a whole class or large group. Even now that the Framework is abandoned, big books are still used and enjoyed in Literacy Time and English lessons. In a careful and inspiring account of how to plan and carry out shared reading, Judith Graham and Alison Kelly advise against doing too much all at once and remind us that, above all, a teacher is showing the pleasure and rewards to be gained from reading an entire text (Graham and Kelly, 2007). Some books are written specially in large format. Others are enlarged versions of smaller format books and many of these have proved successful resources for class-based work, for example Jeannie Baker's rain forest book *Where the Forest Meets the Sea* (Walker Books), Manning and Granström's *What's Under the Bed* (Franklin Watts) and a number of Walker's Read and Wonder titles – *Big Blue Whale* and *Spider Watch*. However, books with a lot of print on each page, with tiny labelled diagrams or many small, detailed and delicately coloured pictures may not survive the expansion so well. Children have to be able to see the print and pictures easily and to read headings, labels and diagrams if they are to benefit from the teacher's demonstration.

Big books come in all genres – stories, poetry, reference and information books. Publishers with strong big book lists include Frances Lincoln, Walker Books, Oxford University Press, Pearson and Heinemann Library. They come in ebook and CD-ROM format to use with an interactive whiteboard as well as in more traditional print form. You can see the BBC Active non-fiction CD-ROM list on the Pearson website: www.pearsonschoolsand fecolleges.co.uk/Primary and the Pelican Interactive Big Book CD-ROM list at www.schoolsresourcesonline.com. For details about Oxford University Press's Reading Tree big books and big cards, visit

31

ukcatalogue.oup.com/category/education/ primary.do. Information about Walker books, including their big books, is available at www.walker.co.uk. Frances Lincoln big books are listed on www.franceslincoln. co.uk/en-gb/C/1/Subject/20/Big_books. McGraw Hill/Kingscourt show details of some of the much liked Story Chest big books as well as big books on CD-ROM on their website, for example Myth and Fable for older primary children: www. mcgrawhill.co.uk/kingscourt/bigbooks.

The important thing to check is that they are good examples of their kind with clear inviting language and illustrations that link well with the written text. Children learn about the features of each kind of book, often joining with the teacher in reading out loud. Teachers will draw attention to text-level aspects – the setting, characters and plot in fiction and the distinctive global organisation – headings, information boxes, retrieval devices – of the different kinds of non-fiction text. In both fiction and non-fiction there will be a focus on the links between illustration and written text, on the author's choice of vocabulary and on helping children use their knowledge of context and sentence structure to make meaning from print.

A selection of big books from different publishing houses and for different ages is shown in the box 'recommended big books'. Teachers also like to work with children to make their own big books. At Goldsmiths College in South London Carol Eagleton, a primary specialist in art, helped student teachers over a number of years to make big book resources inspired by the approach in Don Holdaway's (1979) influential book *The Foundations of Literacy*.

Figure 4 Front cover of big book edition of *Where the Forest Meets the Sea* by Jeannie Baker. Reproduced by permission of Walker Books Ltd. London SE 11 5HS, 1987. This often inspires lively discussion about environmental issues and encourages children's writing and art work.

Recommended big books

For under fives

- *That's Mine!* by Jennifer Northway. Frances Lincoln.
- *Baby Goz* by Steve Weatherill, lift-the-flap big book. Frances Lincoln.

For Key Stage 1

- *Splish, Splash, Splosh* by Mick Manning and Brita Granström. Franklin Watts, about the water cycle.
- *What Babies Used to Wear* by Anne Witherington and Bobbie Neate. Longman. Pelican Big Books.
- *Jamela's Dress* by Niki Daly. Frances Lincoln.
- *Owl Babies* by Martin Waddell and Patrick Benson. Walker Books.
- *The Story of Toys: Toys Big Book* by Monica Hughes. Raintree.
- *I Want a Pet* by Lauren Child. Frances Lincoln Big Books.

For Key Stage 2

- *An Encyclopedia of Greek and Roman Gods* by Brian Moses.

Pelican Interactive big book CD-ROM. (These CD-ROM big books are available in packs of six for age groups from Reception to Year 6. This title is for Year 5 together with *Theseus and the Minotaur*; *Story Poems*; *A Collection of Similes and Metaphors*; *Water, a point of view*; *World Weather*).

- *Words Borrowed from Other Languages* by Sue Palmer and Eugenio Low. Pelican Big Books.
- *History from Photographs* by Kath Cox and Pat Hughes. Wayland.
- *Aesop's Fables* retold by Geraldine McCaughrean. Pelican Big Books (Print and CD-ROM).
- *Reduce, Reuse, Recycling Big Book* by Alexandra Fix. Heinemann Library.

Graham, J. and Kelly, A. (2007, third edition) *Reading Under Control* London: David Fulton.

Holdaway, Donald (1979) *The Foundations of Literacy* Sydney: Ashton Scholastic.

'BIG SHAPES'

See also: 'bottom-up' reading approaches, 'interactive' reading model, reading, 'top-down' approaches to reading

'Big shapes' refers to the larger textual structures which provide a framework for the reading process; the term tends to be associated with 'top-down' approaches and the search for meaning. Barrs and Thomas explain the term in *The Reading Book*, as follows: 'These large over-arching textual structures – such as different kinds of narrative structures, and the structures that relate to different genres – and the way these are reflected in the rhythms and tunes of written language, are a most important source of knowledge which readers have to draw on, in addition to their sense of the unfolding meaning of a text, to support their reading' (Barrs and Thomas, 1991: 6). The importance of recognising 'the tune on the page' suggested by these writers has had great influence on good practice.

However, important as sensitivity to these 'big shapes' is, there are, as Barrs and Thomas make clear, other important aspects of reading. There needs to be careful teaching of the 'smaller shapes' as well: letter- and word-level work, phonetic information and letter-sound correspondence. Good initial teaching of reading manages to orchestrate strategies to develop the different aspects of reading and to integrate the best of both 'top-down' and 'bottom-up' approaches. For clear, practical advice about combining the different aspects in classroom routines, I recommend Graham and Kelly's analysis in Chapter 3 of their book *Reading Under Control*. They emphasise the role of storytelling and reading stories out loud in drawing children's attention to the bigger shapes of literacy – developing their contextual and semantic understanding – while showing also how graphic and phonic work fits into the programme.

The term 'big shapes' can be used more generally to refer to larger structures in bodies of knowledge. Margaret Meek uses it in *Information and Book Learning* when considering the challenge of learning history in school and making sense of history texts: 'The problem for readers begins with the writers' difficulties in relating the "big shapes" of historical time to the minutiae of any given event' (Meek, 1996: Chapter 7). Although we have more information sources than ever and the printing techniques to reproduce original documents, she fears we may still lack enough 'interpretative text' to fit bits of information together to achieve some overall coherence.

Barrs, Myra and Thomas, Anne (eds) (1991) *The Reading Book* London: Centre for Literacy in Primary Education.

Graham, Judith and Kelly, Alison (2009, fourth edition) *Reading Under Control* London: David Fulton.

Meek, Margaret (1996) *Information and Book Learning* Stroud: The Thimble Press.

BILINGUALISM

See also: dual-language texts, equal opportunities, language variety, mother tongue, multiculturalism, multilingualism

People who are bilingual can operate in two languages. While in Britain and the United States operating in one language, monolingualism, is the norm, about half the world's population is bilingual 'and kinds of bilingualism will be present in every country of the world' (McArthur, 1992: 126).

Definitions of bilingualism vary from equal competence in both languages as speakers, readers and writers, to much greater competence in one language or incomplete competence in either. Skutnabb-Kangas offers the following definition of being bilingual as able to 'function in two (or more) languages, either in monolingual or bilingual communities, in accordance with the sociocultural demands made on an individual's communicative and cognitive competence by these communities and by the individual herself, at the same level as native speakers, and being able positively to identify with both (or all) language groups (and cultures) or parts of them' (Skutnabb-Kangas, 1984: 90). This very full definition reinforces the notion that taking on a language involves taking on a culture. The high level of linguistic and cultural competence described in Skutnabb-Kangas' definition is our ultimate aim for young children entering our schools as learners of English as an additional language. There are, however, a number of important and quite complicated issues here. Even the terminology is problematic and the terms themselves change: 'English second language learners' (ESL), and 'bilingual children' became in the 1990s 'children with English as an additional language'. In her book *Making Sense of a New World* Eve Gregory points out that teachers in some countries avoid using the term 'bilingual' because it might deflect attention from the fact that children need help as they go about learning in a new language (Gregory, 2008). Gregory suggests that the term 'emergent bilinguals' is appropriate to refer to children who are at the very beginning of the journey that will take them to the level of competence in Skutnabb-Kangas' definition. Such children may come from very different cultural and linguistic backgrounds but have in common that they are usually the first in their family to receive formal education in their new country and do not speak the language of the host country at home.

There are issues about how far official requirements for a prescribed curriculum and frequent testing in Britain are helpful to emergent bilinguals. The official attitude is that children should control their new language as speakers and listeners, readers and writers as soon as possible. The intention is good – that these children should maximise their opportunities in their new society. However, if they are to maintain the very real linguistic and cultural advantages of being bilingual, they need also to be encouraged and enabled to continue to use and develop their competence in their mother tongue (Issa and Öztürk, 2008). These are complex issues – for example, some parents want the emphasis to be very much on their children's swift acquisition of the language of their 'host' country. The books mentioned below explore these issues further, often like Gregory (2008) and Drury (2007) sharing case studies of the progress of particular children. Drawing on them, I now offer some pointers to good practice in supporting emergent bilinguals at school and classroom level.

- *Positive attitudes.* A young bilingual benefits from a school culture that recognises becoming bilingual as positive – as leading to increased linguistic awareness and cultural sensitivity (Bialystok, 2001). The whole school community can benefit from the knowledge and expertise of emergent bilinguals and their parents. Nevertheless, the teacher plays an important role in helping children to become bilingual and helps co-ordinate formal and informal learning (Gregory, 2008). For a most interesting ethnographic study which shows how we might understand and support young bilingual children as individuals, see Drury (2007). The individual strategies used by four children as they cope with nursery school show how each child reflects on their experience. A socio-cultural perspective creates a strong theoretical framework in which to learn from the individual 'voices' of the children.

- *Knowledge and understanding.* Educators need to have as much knowledge as possible about the spoken and written forms of the languages represented in the communities whose children they teach and about the cultural context. Whitehead (2010) acknowledges that we are unlikely to have the linguistic skills and cultural experiences to meet all language needs. The knowledge we need is the kind which supports our professional expertise, see for example Baker (2007) and Cunningham-Andersson and Andersson (2004) for advice for parents and teachers. We can also encourage the participation of parents, grandparents, older siblings and members of local linguistic groups. Indeed to be effective practitioners we

need to know about the children's literacy experiences at nursery schools, play groups and in religious settings in their communities.

- *Interaction with peers.* Emergent bilinguals benefit greatly from learning alongside their monolingual peers and the benefits are mutual. The recent trend has been away from setting up withdrawal units where children tended to learn English through de-contextualised exercises. One encouraging thing is that what seems beneficial to emergent bilinguals is also good practice for all children: conversation round practical tasks in science, mathematics and technology (children link language and meaning through a general sense of the context); games where instructions and activities are linked and repeated; stories in a shared and interactive context; and writing for real audiences and purposes. For a more detailed analysis of these issues see Wiles, 1985.

- *Storytelling and listening.* The telling of stories with dramatic expression, gesture and story boards, and other props like dolls, boxes and hats, helps children learn their new language in an enjoyable way. The very young also learn well through the rhythms of rhymes, songs and verse.

- *Reading and listening to stories.* When they have stories read to them children experience structured language as opposed to the relatively unstructured language of everyday conversation. This structure – which basically consists of a beginning (providing a setting for a story and an introduction to characters), a middle (where things happen and a plot develops) and an end (at which point conflicts and problems are resolved) – is sometimes termed a 'story grammar'. The text children hear is stored as a resource for retelling their own stories. Fox (1993) has contributed to our understanding about

35

this. The language resource that written stories provide is valuable to all children and not least to emergent bilinguals (Gregory, 2008).

- *Learning to read.* Young children learning to read in a second or additional language need careful help over co-ordinating the cueing systems (Harding-Esch and Riley, 2003). We have to remember that contextual cues may not be as available to them as to other children – even now that we have universal supermarkets and global news programmes. Monolingual children are more secure in the idiom of their language and quickly grasp 'knife and fork' and 'fish and chips'. Children whose first language is in another script have to learn a new set of symbols. Word order in a language also relies on culturally acquired knowledge. As Gregory (2008) shows, young readers in a second language usually catch up quickly, but we still need to be aware of their needs.

- *Dual-language texts.* These are often traditional stories and criteria for selections are discussed under the entry of this name. The best are a helpful resource but we need to check the quality of the language and illustration. There are a number of publishers committed to producing quality dual-language books including Frances Lincoln, Milet Publishers and Mantra Lingua. Dual-language labels and signs are sometimes helpful, but other languages can also be brought into high status curriculum areas like mathematics and geography. Children, parents and teachers can write their own bilingual texts using all the available technology of computers, printers and photocopiers, laminating machines and cameras. As well as producing dual-language versions of stories, poems and songs, we can extend our enterprise to anecdotes about the children's lives,

games, birthday cards and letters. Such collaborations could also lead to helpful multilingual materials for real purposes and audiences. Among valuable teaching and learning ideas, Whitehead suggests all children, whatever their first language, listen to nursery rhymes and poems on a recording, spoken in different dialects and accents (Whitehead, 2010).

- *Multicultural resources.* All children deserve the very best books and resources from across the world. If we have in our class children whose roots are in a particular country we may seek out stories of quality from that place. Here teachers have been helped over the years by the work of Viv Edwards (2009) and by Rosemary Stones' book *A Multicultural Guide to Children's Books 0–16+*. This is out of print at present, but there is guidance in Booktrust's *Folk and Fairy Tales* (Hallford and Zaghini, 2004).

Baker, C. (2007) *A Parents' and Teachers' Guide to Bilingualism* Clevedon: Multilingual Matters.

Bialystok, Ellen (2001) *Bilingualism in Development: Language, Literacy and Cognition* Cambridge: Cambridge University Press. (This provides a valuable review of studies suggesting that bilingualism accelerates children's ability to attend selectively to relevant information.)

Cunningham-Andersson, Una and Andersson, Steffan (2004, second edition) *Growing up with Two Languages: A Practical Guide* London: Routledge.

Drury, R. (2007) *Young Bilingual Learners at Home and School: Researching Multilingual Voices* Stoke-on-Trent: Trentham Books.

Edwards, V. (1998) *The Power of Babel: Teaching and Learning in Multilingual Classrooms* Stoke-on-Trent: Trentham Books.

——(2009) *Learning to be Literature: Multilingual Perspectives* London: Multilingual Matters.

Fox, C. (1993) *At the Very Edge of the Forest: The Influence of Literature on Storytelling by Children* London: Cassell.

Gregory, Eve (2008) *Learning to Read in a New Language: Making Sense of Words and World* London: Paul Chapman.

Hallford, Deborah and Zaghini, Edgardo (2004) *Folk and Fairy Tales: A Book Guide* London: Booktrust.

Harding-Esch, Edith and Riley, Philip (2003, second edition) *The Bilingual Family: A Handbook for Parents* Cambridge: Cambridge University Press. (Covers such important issues as bi-literacy.)

Issa, Tözün and Öztürk, Alayne (2008) *Practical Bilingual Strategies for Multilingual classrooms* Leicester: UKLA, Minibook 27.

McArthur, Tom (1992) *The Oxford Companion to the English Language* London: OPD for Oxford University Press.

Skutnabb-Kangas, T. (1984) 'Multilingualism and the education of minority children' in Skutnabb-Kangas, T. and Cummins, J. (eds) *Minority Education* Clevedon: Multilingual Matters.

Stones, Rosemary (ed.) (1999) *A Multicultural Guide to Children's Books 0–16+* London: Books for Keeps (O/P).

Whitehead, Marian (2010, fourth edition) *Language and Literacy in the Early Years* London: Sage.

Wiles, S. (1985) 'Language and learning in multi-ethnic classrooms: strategies for supporting bilingual students' in Wells, G. and Nicholls, J. (eds) *Language and Learning: An Interactive Perspective* London: The Falmer Press.

Wyse, Dominic and Jones, Russell (2007) *Teaching English, Language and Literacy* London: Routledge.

BIOGRAPHY

See also: factual genres, genre, non-fiction reading and writing

The author of a biography usually writes about the life story of another individual in the third person. Along with auto-biography, biography is one of the more literary kinds of non-fiction. At best, as Margaret Meek argues, it is ' … an encounter with a life and ideas' (Meek, 1996).

Children can appreciate this kind of writing from an early age and often encounter short biographical accounts in history and religious studies texts. Publishers that have promoted biographies for children include Evans, Franklin Watts, Heinemann, Frances Lincoln, Orion Books, Oxford University Press and Walker Books. Written for children aged about seven or eight years, the titles in Oxford Reading Tree's True Stories are clearly written and visually alive. There is also an effort to include just the sort of information which appeals to young readers. For example, in *The Life of Alex Brychta*, some of the subject's insect drawings, done when he was a child, are included. If you are looking for writers and illustrators of children's books for the over eights, then you might find useful Evans Brothers' Tell Me About series which includes biographies of writers for children such as Enid Blyton, Anne Fine, Roger Hargreaves, Beatrix Potter and Roald Dahl. The author of the last of these, Chris Powling, does not hide the more eccentric aspects of Dahl's nature, describing him as an outsider and someone who never behaved as other people expected him to. The sad events in his life – the illness of one of his children and his wife – are included as well as his achievements. Children above about eight years would manage most of the books in this series. Nine to eleven year olds would find much to interest them in *Dear Mr Morpingo: Inside the World of Michael Morpurgo* (illustrated by Michael Foreman, Wizard) by Geoff Fox. First comes a biography in which insightful links are made between some of Morpurgo's childhood experiences and his later life as a writer. Then there are the author's comments about his work including about the story 'The Story that Wrote Itself', which he includes as an example. The strength of the later chapters, on Morpurgo's beliefs about writing and his personal preferences, is that they introduce us to notions of how children can begin to read critically.

Biography can link history and English, helping us to see the private as well as the public person (Hoodless, 1996). Some biography-type books for children introduce us to the lives of famous people through story, for example *Clever Cleo: The Story of Queen Cleopatra* by Stuart Ross and *The Story of Sir Francis Drake* by Rob Childs, which are titles in Wayland's Historical Stories series which often suit children who would not wish to be faced by large blocks of written text.

Picture books can also introduce children to the notion of biography and the events and texture of a life. Josephine Poole's beautiful subtle picture book *Joan of Arc*, illustrated by Angela Barrett, would be enjoyed from about eight upwards (Hutchinson). Older primary children will be ready for more conventional biographies, for example Leon Ashworth's *Queen Victoria* and Neill Tongue's *I Have a Dream: the Story of Martin Luther King* (Franklin Watts). History books tell of the deeds and policies of prominent people but biography can help show how their lives and more ordinary lives were lived at different times. For children over ten years, Raymond Briggs' comic strip biography *Ethel and Ernest: A True Story* (Jonathan Cape) shows the ups and downs of domestic life in the period leading up to the 1930s. Briggs captures how his parents are affected by the impending war and by the changes it will bring for people like them. Children appreciate the background detail and the moving story of the main characters. Mick Manning and Brita Granström are two author illustrators who have created a number of fine biographies for

children including some about famous folk – *What Mr Darwin Saw* and *Charles Dickens: Scenes from an Extraordinary Life*, and others about more ordinary people, for example *Tail-end Charlie, Taff in the WAAF* (Frances Lincoln) and *My Uncle's Dunkirk* (Franklin Watts). Teachers and children like the lively writing combined with a highly visual element so distinctive in their work. Asked about their approach to illustrating their books, these authors commented:

'From our early days of working together we discovered the alchemy of binding word and image to layer information. We like to use different sorts of images, main images, of course, but also explanatory illustrations, sequential "strips", collage and sometimes ephemera. We also use fact boxes, hand-lettering, speech and thought bubbles, perhaps a snatch of music hall song as in our book on Charles Dickens or a sing-along round the piano in *Tail-end Charlie* … all in the space of a few page turns. These elements enrich the experience and act like different sorts of voices, whispering quietly or chattering loudly in the child's ear, making the subject unforgettable by embedding different kinds of information and sparking off connections'.

(Mallett, 2010a)

Another innovator in the field of biographical writing for children is Vivian French whose book, illustrated by Paul Howard, *Chocolate: the Bean that Conquered the World* (Walker Books) is a fascinating 'biography of chocolate'. Children are informed about the history of chocolate from the Aztecs to modern times, but in an imagination-stretching way. Facts are combined with recipes, speculations and memories in a way likely to connect with young readers. The appeal of the works of Manning and Granström and Vivian

French has a lot to do with the lively design if their books. Orion Books in their Brilliant Brits series, which includes subjects drawn from popular culture like *David Beckham* and *The Beatles*, as well as well-known historical characters like Shakespeare and Henry VIII, use colourful strip cartoon and speech bubbles to capture children's interest. Another writer for children, Marcia Williams, also uses strip cartoon to good effect in her biographical books, for example *Bravo Mr William Shakespeare!* and *Charles Dickens and Friends*.

Film and televisual texts can spark an interest in the lives of both famous and ordinary people at different times. It is worth checking to see what is available. Channel 4 often has online historical information, for example about the lives of Victorian children (www.channel4learning.com) and BBC Schools has a 'life through images' series showing such things as the routines of a Victorian governess: www.bbc.co.uk/schools/primaryhistory.

Sites providing online information about texts, including biographies for children, are available on www.booktrustchildrensbooks.org.uk, www.childrenslaureate.org.uk and www.booksforkeeps.co.uk.

Letters, photographs, timelines, maps, posters and theatre programmes are all used in biographies and autobiographies to complement, illuminate and extend the written text. Children can be helped to see all of these as identifying typical features of the genre and learn to use them in their attempts at biographical writing.

Hoodless, Pat (ed.) (1996) *History and English: Exploiting the Links* London: Routledge.

Mallett, Margaret (2010a) 'Interview with Mick Manning and Brita Granström online', the English Association website: www.le.ac.uk/engassoc/fellows/SIG/clmb.html.

——(2010b) *Choosing and Using Fiction and Non-fiction 3–11* London: Routledge.

Meek, Margaret (1996) *Information and Book Learning* Stroud: The Thimble Press.

BLANK VERSE

See also: free verse, poetry

Blank verse is a form of poetry that has rhythm and metre but not rhyme. It is often in iambic pentameter – lines of ten syllables with an unstressed/stressed syllable pattern. This pattern is evident in the following lines from Shakespeare's *A Midsummer Night's Dream* spoken by Oberon, Act IV, Scene I.

'I did then ask of her her changeling child:
Which straight she gave me, and her fairy sent
To bear him to my bower in fairy-land.'

Children are unlikely to write in blank verse in the primary years, but by age ten or eleven they may encounter it in their first forays into Shakespeare's work and in some classic poetry.

BLEND

See also: cluster, phoneme, phonics

The noun 'blend' is a synonym for a cluster of sounds, while the verb 'blend' refers to the process of merging phonemes by someone decoding a word.

BLURB

See also: modelling (of language processes), reading

The 'blurb' is the writing on the back and flaps of the book cover which tells potential readers about the content and style of the book and often provides bibliographic detail about the author. We can help children to scan the 'blurb' to find out if they want to read a particular book. Information about the kind of book they have picked up, and whether they have read some of the author's other works is useful and makes them active selectors of what they read. However, children must also realise that the 'blurb' will not mention weaknesses as well as strengths as reviews do since authors and publishers want us to buy their books and are likely only to include the positive. We need to remember this when we read 'This is the best book on … ' or 'Highly acclaimed, this book will … '.

BOOK CORNER/AREA

See: reading corner/area

BOOK MAKING

See also: art and English, blurb, writing

Making books is an enjoyable and meaningful way for children to learn about reading and writing and has an important place across the curriculum. The actual making, decorating and illustration of the books links English to art and to craft, design and technology. Book making has long been considered to be of great value and students and children can make exciting books of all shapes and sizes and on all possible topics. Stories of all kinds, poetry books, big books and the full range of non-fiction texts appear again and again in book making workshops. More recently electronic books are part of the repertoire. Many of the principles discussed in this entry apply to making both print and electronic books. Commercial programmes can support electronic book making or teachers and children can use Word or PowerPoint's hyperlinking feature. For some thoughts on creating electronic texts see entries entitled CDs, CD-ROM and ebooks.

Covers of print books can be varied and inviting, in the shape of animals, real and fantastic – dragons, unicorns, bears, lions and foxes – or made to look like houses, castles, footballs, birthday cakes, pizzas and household objects like disks, telephones, plates, rubbish bins and chairs. Students and children can be helped to use a range of fabrics – wallpaper, silver foil, cloth, sandpaper and fur to make the illustrations arresting. I have found children and students are most inventive and love making little doors, wheels that turn, unusual games and pop-ups to add fun and interest. Very young children need direct teaching about folding and cutting and, of course, safety rules should be observed by everyone and perhaps displayed in the form of a chart. From time to time teachers and children enjoy making hard-covered books that are bound, glued or stitched, but it is less time consuming to make simple concertina and origami books (see Paul Johnson's books on book making, for example *Get Writing! Creative Book-making Projects for Children 7–12*).

As well as individual children making books with the help of an adult, other contexts include children working in pairs or groups and even as a whole class where the different tasks will be shared out. Older primary children making class magazines or newspapers enjoy taking up roles as editors, feature writers, illustrators and proof readers.

Book making, whether the text is hand-written or word processed, is hugely motivating and satisfying, but there are a number of other important reasons to encourage children in this activity.

Most importantly, making their own books involves children in the kind of talk and reflection that help them understand how books work – bringing into conscious focus the nature and conventions of written language. They take on the role of author which involves them in important choices. When writing a story, for instance, they need to decide on the setting, plot and characters and whether to tell the tale from the point of view of one character or in the third person. If the latter, might they include direct speech? Often this brings energy to the tale and helps with characterisation as well as providing the teacher with an excellent opportunity to reinforce paragraphing and speech marks. Indeed, book making is a good context in which to attend to transcriptional aspects of writing as children usually care enough about their book to want it to be above reproach in spelling, punctuation and general presentation.

Book making can make an important contribution to a young writer's understanding of genre. Stories and non-fiction texts are organised differently because they have different purposes. While a story follows a time sequence and builds momentum as it proceeds, a non-fiction book is usually non-narrative and is organised according to the dictates of the subject. Children learn to divide the main topic into smaller topics and aspects and to use sub-headings to indicate this. They learn also about the retrieval devices – contents page, index and glossary – which help the reader find their way round the book. The kind of illustrations a book has identify it with a genre and book making helps children understand what is appropriate and how illustrations complement and sometimes extend the written text. Thus actually writing a non-fiction book teaches a child more about the distinctive genre features than anything else can do. On those occasions where a hardback book is created with a dust jacket, children have the opportunity to use a different kind of writing – the 'blurb' – to promote their work and some brief biographic details.

Because it is a relatively sustained task, book making is an excellent context in which to encourage children to plan their writing, make a rough draft and then re-read and refine the draft into the final copy. The word processor has made this much easier and discussion round the computer with other children or the teacher about how to improve the draft is particularly valuable.

I have already mentioned that the attention of a child making a book can be drawn to the fact that the purpose of a piece of writing is linked to certain genre features: a story, for example about a journey, might be to thrill, move or just simply enjoy, while a non-fiction book, on boats and ships perhaps, would need to provide accurate and interesting ideas and information. The other fundamental aspect of any piece of writing is the intended audience since the interests, age and ability of the likely readers also has a considerable effect on how the book is written and illustrated. Older primary children often enjoy producing books for the younger children in the school. Sometimes teachers arrange for the older and younger children to meet up before the book making starts to agree on the sort of book that is wanted and then again at the end of the project to share the work.

Every writing task has the potential to involve the other three language processes – reading, talking and listening – but the sustained nature of the book making activity and the high level of interest that usually accompanies it makes this a particularly rich context for language development. Child and supporting adult (or other members of the group) discuss each decision, listening carefully to each other's views and the writing is constantly reviewed by being read back to each other. Once the book is made, children often like to read it to the class or a group and again this gives rise to further talk and questions.

For advice about non-fiction book making and a detailed account of a child working with her teacher and her mother (who took the photographs) on a pizza recipe book – see my *Young Researchers*. A lively, information-filled and entertaining book for children aged about nine to eleven is Powling and Anderson's *The Book about Books*. As well as good sections on whether electronic books will replace paper ones and what makes a classic, there is a helpful attempt to explain how an author creates a book. It is important to help children to share the books they have made with their class, with other classes in assembly and with a wider audience by displaying them on open evenings. The computer, printer and photocopier all make it easier for children to make more than one copy of their book so that they can take it home as well as enjoy having it in school. In one school I know two children made such an interesting book on dragons that six copies were made for group reading. Books made by children are often placed in the classroom collection in the reading corner. Sometimes they are included in the library.

Johnson, Paul (2008) *Get Writing! Creative Book-making Projects for Children 7–12* London: A&C Black.

Mallett, Margaret (1999) *Young Researchers: Informational Reading and Writing in the Early and Primary Years* London: Routledge (see Chapter 4).

Powling, Chris and Anderson, Scoular (2001) *The Book about Books* London: A&C Black.

BOOK REVIEW

See also: author studies, portfolios, reading diaries, writing, writing corner/area

A book review is a written evaluation of a text. It usually gives a brief outline of the events in a story or novel (or an indication of the scope and coverage of a non-fiction work) and goes on to comment on strengths and possible weaknesses.

Reviews of children's books, software, CD-ROMs and websites – both fiction and non-fiction – appear in journals, for example *English 4–11* (The English Association), *The School Librarian* and *NATE Classroom* (National Association for the Teaching of English). National newspapers including *The Times* and *The Guardian* have reviews by well-regarded critics.

There are also a number of websites featuring reviews including those by classroom teachers: www.booksforkeeps. co.uk; www.booktrustchildrensbooks.org. uk; www.clpe.co.uk/library/recommended-reads; www.justimaginestorycentre.co.uk.

For reviews of both fiction and non-fiction texts for children aged three to eleven, see Mallett, 2010.

Teachers ask children to write reviews of books and resources, sometimes in a reading diary (see separate entry) and sometimes they ask for a longer review for display or for a class book. Always being expected to write a review after reading a book or using a resource becomes tedious. On the other hand, we do want children to reflect on what they read and to develop some criteria to judge quality.

There should be a list on file of the main reading each child does each term, but I would be inclined to ask for a full-length review only from time to time and to try to vary the tasks and set them up in interesting ways.

Suggestions for reviews of books and resources

- Very young children like writing their short reviews inside the shape of an animal or object in the story. I have seen a colourful display of such reviews of Eric Carle's *Bad-tempered Ladybird* written in the ladybird shapes the children had drawn themselves.
- Children very much appreciate it when a teacher or student teacher does some writing specially for them. Where the whole class has enjoyed a shared reading of a novel or story the teacher could join the children in writing a review and make a display with the story, novel or picture book in the centre. If the book has been

written recently and reviews are available older children might appreciate a published review on display as well. Sometimes publishers or book shops will be prepared to send a poster or other publicity material to enliven the display.

- Choose an author the children like and display children's reviews of all or some of his or her books. Ask the children to say why they prefer one particular book by this author. I have seen this done with the work of Dick King-Smith, Roald Dahl, Anne Fine and Michael Rosen.

- Ask the children if they have a favourite kind of story, for example – animal stories/poems, horror stories, amusing tales, fairy tales or traditional stories from different cultures. Choose a different kind of story for review every few weeks and ask the children to read out their work.

- Have a focus on a particular aspect of stories – plots, settings, characters – and ask older children to compare this aspect in books by different authors. After reading out the reviews there could be a class discussion.

- Formats for writing reviews – including headings for setting, plot, characterisation, illustrations, language, would you recommend this to a friend? and so on – can help some children get started but can become rather mechanistic if the same one is used too often. Rather than always presenting children with a given format, they might enjoy planning their own with sub-headings to organise their writing. One child asked to do this suggested giving each book a star rating from one star to five 'on

excitement'. Reviews set out as an interview with a teacher or another child add variety. As well as writing, reviews can include sketches and drawings, lists and cartoon strip.

So far, I have had reviews of fiction in mind but I find both boys and girls enjoy evaluating non-fiction texts – both print and CD-ROMs – if the task is set up in an interesting way. For example, I asked children from a Year 5 class (nine year olds) to read and make notes on two non-fiction picture books based on the same theme. Each of the books was based on the true tale of Mary Anning, a young girl who discovered a dinosaur skeleton at Lyme Regis: *Stone Girl, Bone Girl* by Laurence Anholt, illustrated by Sheila Moxley and *The Fossil Girl: Mary Anning's Dinosaur*

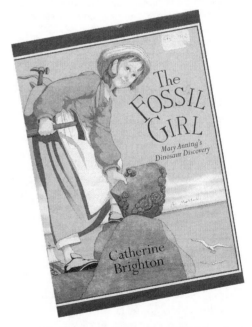

Figure 5a Front cover of *The Fossil Girl: Mary Anning's Dinosaur Discovery* by Katherine Brighton. Reproduced with the permission of the publisher, Frances Lincoln, © 1987; 2006. The book tells the story of the discovery of the first complete Ichthyosaur fossil in lively comic strip.

43

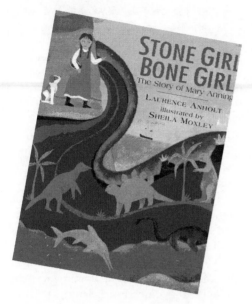

Figure 5b Front cover of *Stone Girl, Bone Girl: The Story of Mary Anning* by Laurence Anholt and illustrated by Sheila Moxley. Reproduced with the permission of the publishers, Frances Lincoln, © 2006. This tells the same story as that in *The Fossil Girl* but emphasises Mary's family relationships and the influence of the other 'curiosity' collectors on her hobby. Children of about eight or nine enjoy the challenge of comparing the two tellings.

Discovery by Catherine Brighton, presented in cartoon format.

The children noted:

- that although each writer had gone to the same sources, each had chosen to emphasise different parts of the story;
- the style of illustration was matched by the language used to tell the story.

The books were displayed together with the children's reviews on a table in the literacy corner. The books and then the reviews were read out loud and led to a class discussion about fact and opinion and the advantages and possible disadvantages of using a cartoon format.

We often invite authors of poetry and fiction for children to visit our schools, but it is worth asking good non-fiction authors if they would tell the children about their work.

Mallett, Margaret (2010) *Choosing and Using Fiction and Non-fiction 3–11* London: Routledge.

BOOKS FOR KEEPS ONLINE

'The best scholars, reviewers, authors and critics write for *Books for Keeps*. We hold a mirror up to the children's book world and it reflects back its output, issues and preoccupations'.

(Rosemary Stones, 2010)

This is an international children's book magazine that provides reviews of books and other materials, fiction and non-fiction from preschool to twelve years and up. Contents also include author interviews, articles on all aspects of writing for children and a useful briefing page covering news, letters and book prizes. In 2010 the print journal ceased publication but the magazine's reviews, articles, strong editorials and news briefings continue its strong independent voice in the online version (Mallett, 2010).

Books for Keeps: www.booksforkeeps.co.uk
Mallett, Margaret (2010) 'In Praise of Books for Keeps' in *English 4–11*, Autumn.

BOOKSTART

See also: Booktrust, family literacy projects, siblings (and literacy)

Bookstart, launched in 1992, is administered by Booktrust and aims to give a pack of books to every baby in the United Kingdom. The 'Bookstart Bag' contains two quality books and some guidance material about sharing books with babies. The aim? To inspire 'a love of books in every child'.

BOOKTRUST

Booktrust's expressed aim is to encourage 'people of all ages and cultures to enjoy books'. An independent UK-wide charity, Booktrust informs about and celebrates storytelling and writing to satisfy curiosity and to help 'provide escape into an imaginative world'. The website also shows a recognition that rapid changes in technology increasingly affect the way texts are produced and read. As well as being a valuable source of information about all aspects of literacy, Booktrust also promotes books as gifts for children, sponsors research and organises campaigns. Television advertising was used to inform viewers about their campaign to encourage dads to read to their children. Social networking sites like Twitter and Facebook are used by the Trust as well as more traditional methods of communication. Its website has links to other sites of interest, for example to Books for All, which aims to connect with a variety of cultures and countries. The Children's Books part of Booktrust's website is a resource and information centre which houses a large number of children's books. Its priority is 'bringing books and readers together'. Members receive regularly updated and helpfully annotated book lists for specific age groups and abilities. The age categories are: five years and under, five to eight years, nine to twelve years and teenage. Booktrust also awards book prizes and supports research into children's reading and literature. One major recent initiative was a five-year pilot called Bookstart, which pioneered the provision of books for the very young. Parents were encouraged to read with their children.

Booktrust: www.booktrust.org.uk
Booktrust's Children's Books: www.booktrust
    childrensbooks.org.uk
Booktime: www.booktime.org.uk

'BOTTOM-UP' READING APPROACHES

See also: 'big shapes', 'interactive' reading model, 'top-down' approaches to reading

'Bottom-up' approaches are based on the assumption that reading is initially learned by manipulating the smallest units of language – letters and words. Traditional phonics teaching was based on this approach. In contrast, what are often called 'top-down' approaches concentrate on prediction and guessing and on young learners searching for meaning rather than just decoding words.

For a clear explanation of how 'bottom-up' and 'top-down' approaches can be combined to promote an 'interactive' model of reading, see Chapter 2 in Jeni Riley's book *The Teaching of Reading*.

Riley, Jeni (1996) *The Teaching of Reading* London: Paul Chapman Publishing.

BOYS AND ENGLISH

See: boys' literacy and gender and language development

BOYS' LITERACY

See also: adventure stories, equal opportunities, gender and language development, girls' literacy

It has long been known that when it comes to literacy at the nursery and primary stages, generally speaking boys mature more slowly than girls. Sue Palmer reminds us of the importance of this developmental issue, remarking that small boys are often simply not ready to 'sit still, listen for individual sounds in language, relate these sounds to abstract symbols, and then manipulate a pencil to draw the symbols' (Palmer, 2004).

The relatively slow pace of some boys to learn to read and their less positive attitudes to writing became more starkly evident when SATs were brought in in the early 1990s to assess performance in relation to the objectives of the National Curriculum. The mismatch in boys' and girls' achievement in literacy became the subject of many papers and books, including those by OFSTED – *Boys and English, The Gender Divide* and *Yes He Can: Schools where boys write well.* These publications marked a considerable change of emphasis in how language and gender issues were viewed. Students, and those starting their teaching careers after the mid-1990s, may not remember that gender issues used to centre on girls' tendency to be dominated by boys in group and class discussion. There was also concern about the less enthusiastic approach of girls to the computer and multimedia texts and the disadvantages to which this might lead. The entry on 'girls' literacy' explores these issues further. Gender differences in language and literacy are complicated and rather than concentrate on the needs of either boys or girls, the more constructive approaches see the two genders as 'differently literate' and needing different kinds of teaching and support to make good progress (Millard, 1997; Baxter, 2001; Bearne, 2002). Having said that, this entry directs you to some of the latest thinking and research on how we can support boys and turn them on to literacy.

Just before we turn to the school context, revealing work has been done on boys' literacy at home. Sally Rundell found that boys are often interested in the 'work literacies' – typing invoices, reports and minutes of meetings – that they observe when their parents are engaged in work at home (Rundell, 2001).

For an entirely constructive approach to developing boys' literacy in school we do well to turn to the work of the Centre for Literacy in Primary Education (CLPE) team, who have conducted classroom-based research into boys' literacy over a number of years. Their publication *Boys and Writing* identified some of the main factors in successful initiatives for supporting boys' literacy. These include: reflective approaches which recognise the role of talk; a strong role for ICT in promoting literacy learning; a recognition of the value of graphic forms – drawing on mapping in planning writing (Foreword, Barrs and Pidgeon, 2002).

Reflective approaches which recognise the role of talk in developing literacy

A major finding of the CLPE team was that when teachers were given time to explore, through unhurried discussion, really involving texts and time to develop writing, boys who had often found English work difficult began to make progress. So, while there is evidence that reinforcing boys' interest in non-fiction texts leads to increased self-image and self-esteem (Moss, 2000) they can also be helped to connect with powerful and involving fiction.

Texts have to be well chosen to invite boys into the kind of 'booktalk' and 'social networking round texts' which seems to come more easily to girls. *There's a Boy in the Girls' Bathroom* by Louis Sachar got Year 6 boys in the CLPE study involved and the talk seemed to fuel their writing efforts. Talking about the poem 'What has happened to Lulu?' enabled the boys to interpret the themes of kidnap and murder in a contemporary way. Imaginative tasks inspired the boys to talk and think deeply about the poem. Sally Rundell discovered that boys found much to relate to in *Goodnight Mr Tom* when they were given time to talk through issues (Rundell, 2001). Talk as a means of reflection before writing was found to be effective in *Raising Boys' Achievement,* a research and intervention project commissioned by DfES (Warrington *et al.*, 2006). Anne Faundez argues that humour too can be a spur to discussion in her article 'Spud Murphy gets kids reading' (Faundez, 2005).

A strong role for ICT in promoting literacy learning

Interactive ICT is highlighted as a major motivating force for many boys (Bearne, 2002). The increasing inclusion of multimodal texts in English and literacy work is likely to help boys achieve. Help with resources is available from the education department of the British Film Institute, which offers advice on promoting learning through the use of the moving image. In their study of the English work of Year 6 boys in some urban, multiethnic classrooms, *Boys on the Margin*, the CLPE team incorporated imaginative use of ICT into the lessons. For example, they made it possible for the pupils to email their own questions about the fate of the girl in Charles Causley's poem 'What Has Happened to Lulu?' (Safford *et al.*, 2004). One of the project researchers answered in the role of Lulu.

However, we have to make sure software is pitched at the right level for the individual pupil. The software prepared by the research team to support the folk tale *Sea Woman* by Kevin Crossley Holland (and which provided links to websites of online readings of other Selkie stories) was found to be too difficult for some children (Safford *et al.*, 2004).

A recognition of the value of graphic forms in literacy

There has been a surge of interest in visual kinds of literacy and in the drawings done by very young children to make meaning of their world. Boys, in particular, like to illustrate their first writing, often completely integrating word and image in early list making. Pahl argues that we should regard boys' diagrams as texts to be read and valued just as we value written texts (Pahl, 1999).

One of the teachers working with *There's a Boy in the Girls' Bathroom* provided mini-journals with writing prompts and spaces for drawing, recognising that some boys like to map out their writing plans using sketches as well as words (Safford *et al.*, 2004). Other classroom research studies show there are imaginative ways of inspiring 'underachieving, uninterested boys' (Martin *et al.*, 2008).

The heightened motivation and involvement of the boys in the CLPE study and their successful talk and writing suggest that the strategies described above do indeed increase achievement. The team felt that the current summative assessment framework seems not to detect the small but very real gains by young readers and writers with literacy difficulties. To tap into these they suggest we need to look at teachers' records of their pupils' changing behaviour as readers and writers and at collections of their work over time.

Barrs, Myra and Cork, Valerie (2001) *The Reader in the Writer* London: CLPE.

Barrs, Myra and Pidgeon, Sue (eds) (1998) *Boys and Reading* London: CLPE.

——(eds) (2002) *Boys and Writing* London: CLPE.

Baxter, Judith (2001) *Making Gender Work* Reading: National Centre for Language and Literacy, University of Reading.

Bearne, E. (2002) 'Multimodal narratives' in Barrs, M. and Pidgeon, S. (eds) *Boys and Writing* London: Centre for Literacy in Education.

British Film Institute: www.bfi.org.uk/education

Causley, Charles (1996) 'What has happened to Lulu?' in *Collected Poems for Children* London: Macmillan.

Crossley-Holland, Kevin (2001) 'Sea-Woman' in *The Magic Lands* London: Orion.

Faundez, Anne (2005) 'Spud Murphy gets kids reading' in *Books for Keeps*, No. 150, January.

Magorian, Michelle (1981) *Goodnight Mister Tom* Harmondsworth: Penguin.

Martin, Tony, Lovat, Chira and Purnell, Glynis (2008) *The Really Useful Literacy Book*

London: Routledge (see Chapter 15 'We Made the story! Making whole stories with underachieving, uninterested boys').

Millard, E. (1997) *Differently Literate: Boys, Girls and the Schooling of Literacy* London: Falmer.

Moss, G. (2000) 'Raising boys' achievement in reading: some principles for intervention' *Reading*, 36:101–6.

OFSTED (1993) *Boys and English* London: OFSTED.

——(1996) *The Gender Divide – Performance Differences Between Boys and Girls at School* London: OFSTED.

——(2003) *Yes He Can. Schools Where Boys Write Well* London: OFSTED.

Pahl, K. (1999) *Transformations: Making Meaning in Nursery Education* Stoke on Trent: Trentham Books.

Palmer, Sue (2004) 'Primary View' in *Times Educational Supplement*, 18 October.

Rundell, Sally (2001) *Able Boys' Literacy Practices at Home and School* Suffolk: Suffolk Education Authority (there is a synopsis in *Literacy Today* number 28, September 2001).

Sachar, Louis (2001) *There's a Boy in the Girls' Bathroom* London: Bloomsbury.

Safford, Kimberly, O'Sullivan, Olivia and Barrs, Myra (2004) *Boys on the Margin: Promoting Boys' Literacy Learning at Key Stage 2* London: CLPE. www.clpe.co.uk.

Warrington, M.P., Younger, M., with Bearne, E. (2006) *Raising Boys' Achievement in Primary Schools: Towards a Holistic Approach* Maidenhead: Open University Press.

BRAINSTORMING

See: concept mapping

BREAKTHROUGH TO LITERACY

See also: reading, reading schemes

Breakthrough to Literacy, developed by David MacKay *et al.* for publication in 1970, is a reading programme based on children's own experiences and language. It consists of banks of words, letters and punctuation marks which are arranged in pockets and can be displayed on a wall at a height children can easily reach. The children have sentence makers – small stands in which they can build up sentences which become their first reading materials. Children compose sentences about their lives and the programme is therefore associated with what has been termed 'the language experience approach' to reading and writing. I remember teachers who liked the programme very much, but others found it difficult to keep track of all the word bank items and found organisation rather labour intensive. The small reading books are colour graded according to readability and while some retell traditional tales, many of them are on topics close to the children's experience like 'The Loose Tooth' and 'In the Park'. The developers of the programme visited primary schools and asked the children what they would like their reading books to be about.

Some teachers still use the word banks and sentence makers to help children understand the concept of a word and a sentence. However, the programme is unlikely to be used alone as it has too little emphasis on phonological aspects of reading to be in tune with current United Kingdom practice.

BRISTOL LANGUAGE AT HOME AND SCHOOL PROJECT

See also: early years language and literacy, research (into primary English, language and literacy)

Directed by Gordon Wells, this longitudinal study carried out during the 1970s and 1980s showed a strong link between young children's familiarity with story and their later success in reading and writing. Wells argues that having books read to them at an early age helps children understand about the de-contextualised nature of print, something that does not become evident in encounters with environmental print. Stories take us away from our immediate context and serve as a bridge to the abstract.

The analysis of a large number of recordings of preschool children and parents talking suggested that ordinary family activities often provided excellent contexts for literacy learning. Parents who use writing often during the day – notes, letters, shopping lists and so on – provide strong models of literacy and their children do particularly well as writers when they get to the later primary years.

The project generated many articles and books. *The Meaning Makers: Children Learning Language and Using Language to Learn* (Hodder and Stoughton, 1987 and in a revised edition in 2009) is particularly helpful and inspiring to teachers of the primary age range. It follows a representative sample of children from their first words to the end of the primary years. The transcripts of children, parents and teachers talking and the telling classroom vignettes make this a useful and enjoyable read.

BRITISH FILM INSTITUTE (BFI)

See also: film making, television and literacy, television programmes for children, video-film and DVDs, visual literacy

The education department of the British Film Institute provides information, resources and services to support teaching and learning about moving image media. The resources include video-films and DVDs to help different age groups use the moving image as part of their visual literacy education. *Starting Stories*, for three to seven year olds, consists of five short films: Baboon on the Moon; Laughing Moon; Little World; The Lucky Dip; and Otherwise. There are notes giving teachers suggestions for activities.

British Film Institute: www.bfi.org.uk/education

BRITISH LIBRARY (THE)

The British Library, based at St Pancras in London, is the official repository of the United Kingdom and a world-class research institution. It contains a huge store of the world's knowledge in its collection of both primary and secondary resources, so its value to teachers is enormous. Even if they live too far away to make a visit feasible, they can browse the catalogue for information to support work across the curriculum. To give some idea of the vast range of resources available, The British Library holds 13 million books, 920,000 journals and newspaper titles and 3 million sound recordings. The history of the written word is fully covered with examples of marks, symbols and signs used in different historical periods and in different cultural contexts. The Arts and Images section holds a huge collection of visual images (including, for example, Da Vinci's notebooks) and shows how these can communicate ideas. For those children in schools near enough to make a visit possible, there is a constantly developing programme of exciting workshops, activities and resources for all ages from the Foundation Stage upwards. Look on the website for details of current workshops and exhibitions, many of which help children learn how to find things out from a huge variety of resources including maps and paintings, archive material and electronic resources.

Teachers constantly seek ways of helping children develop their research and study skills and they will appreciate the advice in the Creative Research Ideas section. Good research, it is suggested, starts by finding a method which helps answer the main questions a young researcher has at the beginning of a project. At workshops children are shown how to make a preliminary research 'map' on a big piece of paper; this is a way of recording questions, ideas (in writing or illustration) and details of sources. These suggestions can also be read online.

The British Library: www.bl.uk

BULLET POINT

See also: paragraphing

This is a device used in text books and in word processed accounts to set out a related sequence of information or list. For example, here is nine year old Taylor's bullet pointed list when he was asked to summarise his learning about measuring forces:

- force is measured in newtons (n)
- simple devices made of a spring and a scale
- the greater the force the more the spring stretches

It is helpful for children to learn about bullet point format and to use it in some of their non-fiction writing. Overuse of the device, however, risks disorganising a piece of writing.

BULLOCK REPORT

See also: history of English teaching, language across the curriculum, LINC materials, subject knowledge

The Bullock Report, *A Language for Life*, was presented in 1975 by the Committee of Inquiry set up by the Secretary of State for Education and Science, Margaret Thatcher, in 1972. Chaired by the historian Sir Alan Bullock, the committee investigated all aspects of the teaching of English as a mother tongue, advised on how practice might be improved (and the role that initial and in-service training might play) and made recommendations about how children's levels of attainment might be monitored.

The tone of the report, which was over 600 pages in length, was optimistic and constructive. The committee recommended that teachers in both primary and secondary schools should have informed views on how children make progress in learning to talk, read and write, and work towards a whole-school language policy.

Although we now have in the United Kingdom a more prescribed approach to teaching English than the Bullock Committee envisaged, many of their recommendations continue to influence our thinking and practice. For example, the importance of talk in learning in every lesson, the contribution parents can make by taking an interest in children's reading and writing, and the recognition of language study and subject knowledge as important parts of English work all have their roots in the views underpinning the Bullock Report.

C

CAMBRIDGE READING

See also: reading schemes

During the 1990s and beyond this was a well-regarded reading programme with books of every genre for children from the nursery stage through to Year 6. The primary materials have been reorganised under a new heading: Cambridge University Press English Language Teaching (www.cambridge.org/gb/elt). Following the link to 'Readers' shows lists in two categories: Cambridge Factbooks and Cambridge Storybooks. Some of the storybooks are accompanied by audiocassettes/CDs and are designed to help young readers learning English as an additional language.

CAPITALISATION

See also: full stop, proper noun, punctuation, sentence

This term refers to the consistent use of capital letters to begin the first word of a sentence and the first letter of a proper name, for example of a person or city. However, are the rules for capitalisation in English clear cut? In his detailed account, Tom McArthur (1992) comments that while some people prefer to capitalise the first letter of the first word of a phrase following a colon others keep to lower case. Convention favours the latter option but the former is

not judged to be 'wrong'. Is it the 'Earl of Essex' or the 'earl of Essex'? Either is acceptable but more people feel easier with the former when designating an actual title.

While we need to understand that use of punctuation changes as do other aspects of language and that there are some areas of dispute, we can agree that by about seven children should have been taught the following:

- English is one of the languages that has two interlocking systems of letters – upper case and lower case.
- Sentences always begin with a capital letter and end with a full stop, question mark or exclamation mark.
- Names of people, cities, countries, titles, days, months, etc. begin with a capital letter.
- 'I', referring to the writer, is capitalised.

McArthur, Tom (1992) *The Oxford Companion to the English Language* Oxford: QPD with Oxford University Press.

CAPTION

This is usually a title or short explanation introducing a diagram or picture.

CARNIVAL (AND LITERACY)

See also: art and English, diary, non-fiction reading and writing

Carnival is a celebration which uses many art forms – dance, art, costume making, drama and masquerade. In Britain carnivals take place in towns and cities in the summer months and the largest is Notting Hill Carnival. Cultural influences from Africa, Asia, Europe, the Americas and the Caribbean are combined. Lambeth Schools Carnival Pack is an excellent starting point for a school carnival.

There are rich opportunities for channelling the excitement and enthusiasm Carnival generates into literacy activities – talking and improvised drama and stories and poems. Children could be encouraged to develop their autobiographical writing abilities in Carnival diaries as well as non-chronological reports.

CARTOON

See: comics

CASE STUDY APPROACH TO RESEARCH

See: research

CASSETTES

See: audio resources

CATALOGUE

A catalogue is a list of items, often in the form of a booklet, which sets out for example items for sale or for mail order. Bibliographic catalogues provide the contents of a library or libraries.

CATAPHORIC REFERENCE

See also: anaphoric reference

This is a forward reference in a text. So in – 'If he wanted to, Harry could concentrate for long periods' – 'he' is cataphoric.

CD-ROM (COMPACT DISC-READ ONLY MEMORY)

See also: fairy tales, fiction, information books, Information and Communications Technology (ICT) and English, non-fiction reading and writing, visual literacy

CD-ROMs are disks that are read by a computer system and usually combine a number of media – text, video and sound. They have 'hot-links' which allow the user to move from one piece of text to another by clicking on a word or phrase. Children need help in navigating successfully and retrieving information from a vast store. As Lydia Plowman (1998) puts it, 'The main navigational problem is knowing when all the relevant information on a given topic has been seen and how it relates to the structure of the multimedia document'. Visualising the mainly invisible structure of the text in its entirety requires some experience and sophistication.

Educational CD-ROMs need to achieve the right balance between educational and entertainment aspects. Some CD-ROMs have little educational content despite their title. CD-ROMs should not just be books on a screen but should allow users to explore pathways and make good use of sound, animation and video. Marian Whitehead urges us to be selective about the 'reading books' on CD-ROM we choose – they should not simply mask meaningless text with visual tricks and loud music (Whitehead, 2010). The team researching for *Reading on Screen* found that teachers' choices of CD-ROM did not always match well with children's level of expertise and preferences (Bearne *et al.*, 2007). Questions we might usefully ask when choosing CD-ROMs include:

Does the CD-ROM:

- Match with the needs of the age group for which it is intended?
- Engross and entertain the young learner?

- Make imaginative use of the technology?
- Prove a suitable medium for the subject?
- Enable the user to navigate easily?
- Provide quality search systems and bookmarks?
- Offer quality content – taking account of accuracy, comprehensiveness, creativity and interest?
- Offer quality images and audio experiences?

CD-ROMs are well established as resources for the primary curriculum. They are used for teaching reading – for example the Dr Seuss ABC ('Living Books' series) and Nursery Rhyme Time (Sherston) – and are part of the fiction collection in class and school libraries. However, perhaps their impact on children's research across the curriculum has been most significant. CD-ROMs make it possible to show an animal's life cycle – the laying of eggs and hatching of tadpoles perhaps – and the working of the digestive system or the functioning of a machine. The information in a set of space-consuming print encyclopedias can be placed instead on a disk for easy storage. Publishers of children's reference books – dictionaries, atlases, encyclopedias and thesauri – have been producing CD-ROM versions for some time. Patrick Wiegand's *Oxford Primary Atlas* is an interactive atlas based on *The Primary Oxford Atlas* and can be used with seven to eleven year olds on an interactive whiteboard. Like similar electronic reference texts, it offers video-film and animation to extend what is described in writing. Viewing a CD-ROM is highly motivating for many children, and a different sort of experience to reading print. Nevertheless, we should remember that reading books remains a distinct experience and electronic interactive media complement rather than replace books. In fact many publishers offer a CD-ROM together with a book as a package. Two-Can Publishing (Zenith Entertainment plc) have an exciting range

of combined resources in their Interfact series. The electronic extension activities link extremely well with each sub-topic. For example in *Water*, the double spread on 'Shipshape and Seaworthy' has a disk link which allows the young learner to control a fleet of cargo ships, to learn about how ships float and how you have to judge the right weight of cargo if the vessel is to be seaworthy.

Bearne, Eve, Clark, Chris, Johnson, Annette, Mottram, Marilyn and Wolstencroft, Helen (2007) *Reading on Screen* Leicester: UKLA.

The British Interactive Media Association (BIMA) supports the British digital industry and shares knowledge and best practice in schools: www.bima.co.uk

Plowman, Lydia (1998) 'Reading multimedia texts: Learning how CD-ROM texts work' in *Language Matters*, Spring.

Whitehead, Marian (2010, fourth edition) *Language and Literacy in the Early Years* London: Sage.

CDS (COMPACT DISCS)

See also: audio resources, CD-ROM, Information and Communications Technology (ICT) and English, living books, multiple literacies

CDs were once principally associated with music, but the new educational CDs often have a strong visual element. Younger children learn from the playful approach of Microsoft's Magic Bus CDs. Older children will appreciate learning through the illustrations and animations of the Dorling Kindersley 'Explorer' series.

Making a CD to explore a history or geography topic can be a highly creative project for children at Key Stages 1 and 2. I recently looked at a CD on Evacuees in the Second World War made by a Year 6 class to present their drawings, research findings and poems during a history project. There were dramatic moving images of the Blitz and there were plans to improve the CD by incorporating some drama episodes they had improvised on the experiences of evacuees. In this example a teacher was working with groups within the class which encouraged a great deal of talk and collaboration.

Perhaps the quality of information CDs is better than that of stories at present. Olivia O'Sullivan, Assistant Director of the Centre for Literacy in Primary Education (CLPE), remarks: 'There are very few electronic texts to which I could give a wholehearted 10 out of 10, in the way that I could recommend a host of picture books' (O'Sullivan, 2005). One of her own favourites is *Sheila Rae the Brave*; this is an account of the adventures of a resourceful female mouse told with such humour that it is still effective 'on multiple rereadings'. Many of my readers will know of Mantra, a publisher for many years of multilingual texts for children, which is now making an impact in CD production. The multilingual dictionaries in many languages are most helpful. A more recent initiative is their CD series of stories based on traditional tales (although they refer to them as ebooks.) These invite young readers to try their own versions of the tales.

Dorling Kindersley CDs: *Become a Human Body Explorer; Become a Science Explorer; Become a World Explorer*.

Mantra Multilingual dictionaries on CD and ebook, available from www.mantralingua. com.

Microsoft Magic School Bus CDs: *Bugs, Ocean, Dinosaurs* (all available from software suppliers, for example from www.amazon.co.uk).

O'Sullivan, Olivia (2005) 'ICT and early literacy' in *Books for Keeps*, September.

CENTRE FOR CHILDREN'S LITERATURE, UNIVERSITY OF CAMBRIDGE

As well as researching in the field of print books and materials, the team at this centre study the electronic texts that are so important in a multimedia society. The first director of the centre, Professor Nikolajeva, believes children's literature should be studied in a social context, so the centre will treat children's television programmes, video games and films as texts in their own right. Innovative print texts, for example graphic stories and novels, will also receive attention, as well as traditional tales and classic novels like *Peter Pan* and *Tom's Midnight Garden*. More information about the work of the centre, which is based in the university's Faculty of Education, is available at: www.educ.cam. ac.uk/centres/childrensliterature.

CENTRE FOR LITERACY IN PRIMARY EDUCATION (CLPE)

See also: Primary Language Record, record keeping

The Centre for Literacy in Primary Education, founded in 1971, is an educational centre in Webber Street, Southwark, London for teachers, parents, teaching assistants and other educators. It has had considerable influence on primary English, language and literacy and assessment and record keeping throughout London, more generally in the United Kingdom and in other countries, particularly the United States. It is well established in three areas. First, it has an excellent library of books and resources and is well known for the quality of its own publications, not least *The Primary Language Record Handbook* and *The Core Book: A Structured Approach to Using Books Within the Reading Curriculum*. Second, it links closely with schools and offers a wide range of consultancy services and professional courses. Third, the staff carry out classroom-based research, one recent initiative being a spelling project which is described and evaluated in *Understanding Spelling* by Olivia O'Sullivan and Anne Thomas (CLPE, 2000).

Another research study draws on research in Year 5 classrooms on the links between the study of literature and writing development and a main outcome was *The Reader in the Writer* by Myra Barrs and Valerie Cook (CLPE, 2001). There is information about many other research projects on the website. For example, from 2010, Myra Barrs and Kimberley Safford have been working on a school-based research project called 'The Imagined World' (Barrs & Safford, 2011). This investigation, taking place in ten schools, aims to illuminate the way in which stories and literature can lead to and enrich work in the creative arts.

The Centre team has made a considerable contribution to knowledge and understanding about gender and literacy. One outcome of their classroom-based research in this area is *Boys on the Margin*, which describes and analyses the work of six classes using three texts chosen to enthuse the pupils. As with all their work we find here a high level of scholarship combined with carefully organised classroom research. The Centre team never forgets that teachers have to work within statutory guidelines but helps them do so as creatively as possible.

The Centre is constantly taking on new projects and regularly produces exciting publications; look out for details on the Centre website about its annual Poetry Award. The first Award was made to John Agard and Grace Nichols for their anthology of Caribbean poems *Under the Moon and Over the Sea* (Walker Books).

The Power of Reading Project encourages enthusiasm for reading and involves over 100 schools. Also based at the Centre is the Parental Involvement in Creative Partnerships project, which is funded nationally by the Department for Culture, Media and Sport, and seeks to help parents understand how their children learn.

Formerly known as The Centre for Language in Education, the Centre's new title is a consequence of its change of status to a registered charity in 2002. Following the retirement of its distinguished director (and then co-director), Myra Barrs, the Centre's co-directors are Julia Eccleshare (children's book editor of *The Guardian*) and Sue Ellis.

Barrs, Myra and Safford, Kimberley (2011) *The Imagined World: Children's Language and Literacy Learning in the Creative Arts World* London: CLPE.
Centre for Literacy in Primary Education: www.clpe.co.uk

CHAPBOOKS

See also: history of children's literature

Chapbooks were inexpensive works of popular literature sold by itinerant pedlars from the sixteenth to the nineteenth centuries in Europe and America. They usually contained ballads, romantic stories, folk and fairy tales. Up until the start of the eighteenth century their often bawdy humour made them suitable reading only for adults, but by about 1800 children's chapbooks containing nursery rhymes, alphabets, prayers, riddles and stories were increasingly sold. By the end of the eighteenth century children's chapbooks were small – about 4 inches × 2½ inches (10cm by 6cm) – and about 16 pages in length. The leather covering of the earlier adult chapbooks was replaced with rough paper, rather like sugar paper. There is a detailed account of the form and history of children's chapbooks in Carpenter & Prichard, 1984. These authors comment that many chapbooks, whether for adults or children, were not only poorly printed and spelt but they were also sometimes written 'with little or no regard for the dramatic shape and highlights of the story' (ibid.: 107). Nevertheless, there were some important contributions made by the tradition of chapbooks. They were the only form of imaginative literature accessible to a large number of poor people. Their existence also ensured the tradition of nursery rhymes and fairy tales was continued into the nineteenth century. Some publishers, Rusher of Banbury in the nineteenth century for example, produced small children's books of some merit (*Jack the Giant Killer*) with woodblock illustrations, sometimes hand-coloured. Those seeking more information about the place of chapbooks in the history of children's publishing would enjoy Chapter 2 in Peter Hunt's *Children's Literature: An Illustrated History* which also includes a number of interesting illustrations showing the different formats of chapbooks at different times.

Carpenter, Humphrey and Prichard, Mari (1984) *The Oxford Companion to Children's Literature* Oxford and New York: Oxford University Press.

Hunt, Peter (1995) *Children's Literature: An Illustrated History* Oxford: Oxford University Press (Chapter 2).

CHART

A chart is a type of diagram or table often with a numerical element. Children learn that the kind of illustrations used in a book or resource help identify it with a particular genre. For example, charts in geography texts may show variations in temperature or population while in history they may take the form of timelines and family trees.

The verb form of chart as in 'The explorer's next task was to chart the island' means to make a map of an area or, more generally, to record and monitor as in 'We need to chart our progress over the next few weeks'.

CHILD-CENTRED LEARNING

See also: 'big shapes', creative writing, history of English teaching (in the primary school), hobbies and English

Child-centred or progressive models of learning, following the theories of Rousseau, Dewey and Froebel, afford experience and discovery a central position. At the heart of this philosophy, especially in its more extreme forms, we have a horticultural metaphor which views the adult's role mainly 'as provider of a rich soil in which to watch the child bloom' (Czerniewska, 1992). In the first half of the twentieth century, English teaching in the primary years leaned towards a 'basic skills' model and children spent much time on grammar and spelling exercises. In the 1960s, partly as a move away from what many saw as a mechanistic attitude to learning which regarded young children as 'sponges' soaking up teaching input, there was a shift towards recognising the needs, interests and preoccupations of the young learners. The 'personal growth' model of language development shows how a child-centred approach can be used in English. The teacher's role was to provide experiences in a motivating environment, to provide quality resources including story books and to be an audience to children's talk and writing. Rather than fit the child to the curriculum, child-centred teachers adjusted the programme to the needs of individual children. If you want to get a flavour of this approach I suggest you read John Dixon's book *Growth Through English*. The Plowden Report (1967) celebrated the talking and writing that came out of the best classrooms during this child-centred period. In *Child-Centred Education*, the authors set out the origins and history of the approach and explain its central beliefs and values (Hilton and Doddington, 2007).

Current approaches favour a more structured approach to the teaching of English in which teachers intervene to support children's progress in all aspects of language development. Most children need systematic help to become readers and writers and contexts for speaking and listening need to be carefully planned and set up.

It is worth retaining some things of value from a child-centred approach. A child's special interests, abilities and preoccupations are an important consideration. The spoken language reveals these and its role in learning is central in child-centred approaches; it has a very important role in any English programme and across the whole curriculum as a tool for learning. It is also wise and motivating for children to have choice about some of the writing they do in the classroom. Sometimes, it is helpful for them to concentrate on compositional aspects – the content and flow of their writing, attending to the transcriptional aspects in a later draft (Smith, 1982). 'Differentiation' in teachers' planning helps us take account of the needs of particular children and the current emphasis on involving them in monitoring their own progress in reading and writing is very much in the spirit of a child-centred approach.

Czerniewska, Pam (1992) *Learning About Writing* Oxford, UK and Cambridge, Mass.: Blackwell.
Dixon, John (1967) *Growth Through English* Oxford: Oxford University Press with NATE.
Hilton, Mary and Doddington, Christine (2007) *Child-Centred Education: Reviving the Creative* London: Sage.
Smith, Frank (1982) *Writing and the Writer* London: Heinemann.

CHILD LANGUAGE ACQUISITION

See: language acquisition

CHILDREN AS AUTHORS

See also: book making, creativity in English, illustrations: finding a vocabulary, picture books, visual literacy, writing

Making books, print or electronic, with the support of an adult, helps children understand some of the choices they need to make in their own writing and illustrating and to begin to understand how words and pictures interact (Johnson, 1991, 1997). There is more about these important choices and how we can support them under 'book making'. Here I want to look more broadly at whether children of primary age can function as authors – writing out of choice and on their own – and at what this tells us about the motivation to write and how it might be encouraged.

Adult authors often remember making their own little books as children; Anne Fine, for example, recalls how much she enjoyed writing as a child. There are fascinating historical examples of young children writing without any apparent help from adults. I refer to two such examples: first the Brontë children who lived in Haworth Parsonage, and second, Daisy Ashford, who wrote *The Young Visiters* when aged nine years.

The Brontë children

In the nineteenth century the Brontë children created an imaginary world at their home near the wild Yorkshire moors and wrote about it in copiously illustrated miniature books. These books, which contained poems, stories and plays, can be seen in the Brontë Parsonage Museum at Haworth. In her book for children of about eight to ten years, *The Brontës: Scenes from the Childhood of Charlotte, Branwell, Emily and Anne*, Catherine Brighton shows in vivid words and pictures the wild environment where the children grew up (Brighton, 2004). Children are often interested in the writing done by other children; seeing the small books and learning the story of the Brontë children can inspire children's work today.

A school example

Here I want to tell you about the work of Diana Hartley and her class of Year 5 and

Year 6 children inspired by seeing the Brontë children's 'small books'. This was part of a larger project on poems and stories about miniature worlds and, after finding out about the Brontës' small books from websites, they visited the Brontë Parsonage Museum where twelve out of the one hundred little books the Brontë children made are on display. They were designed to read to a set of toy soldiers Branwell had been given. These tiny manuscripts, crammed with minute, spidery writing and measuring just a few centimetres across created a fantasy world for the soldiers. The books were made of scraps of paper and had hand-sewn covers made of wallpaper and sugar bag paper. The Brontës made the books tiny because they were for the small soldiers, but there were two other reasons why the books were small scale. The teacher comments: 'My class were delighted to learn that the Brontë children saw the miniature size of the books as a way of keeping the content of their stories away from the prying eyes of adults – adults can only read the books easily with a magnifying glass. It was also a very economic way to produce books for a family whose financial situation was very insecure'. Of course the research led to the children learning a lot of social history and gaining a sense of what it might have been like to have been a child in that family at that time. They noted all the details at the museum; for example that the smallest book was just 5cm long and some tiny pages contained 1,500 words. A wooden soldier similar to the ones Branwell had as a boy and a copy of one of Charlotte Brontë's little six-page books were bought at the museum shop and brought back to display at school. The children were very excited about making their own little books and had noted that the Brontës used a marbling effect on their covers. By a happy chance, one of the children's parents was an antique bookbinder and he came into school to show the children how books were made at the time of the Brontës. Below is a simplified account of how the children made the miniature books. The children then took great pride in each writing their own story in the little book they had made.

Making little books

- Fold a plain piece of A4 paper into eight sections and cut to make four double pages;
- Cut and fold a piece of white card slightly larger than the paper pages to make a cover for the book;
- Take half of an A4 sheet of plain paper and place it in a tray of water to which marbling inks have been added;
- Allow the marbled paper to dry and then lay it down with the unmarbled side uppermost;
- Cut the marbled page so that it is a little bigger than the cover;
- Glue it to the cover folding over a margin of the paper neatly round the inside of the cover;
- Place one of the four double pages in the marbling tray and when it is dry glue to the inside of the cover to make marbled end pages;
- Using a strong needle and twine stitch the three remaining double pages into the cover to make a book.

Daisy Ashford

A child author who captured the public imagination was Daisy Ashford, whose novel *The Young Visiters*, written in 1890 when she was nine years old, is still in print. It gives insight into the social history of the late nineteenth century and relates an absurd romance with great verve and humour. It is worth reading – it will take about two hours and you will find everything is wonderfully wrapped up at the end – no conflicts left unresolved!

Daisy's grandchild, Terry Rose, writing on *The Young Visiters* Amazon site, tells us that Daisy wrote with her sisters purely for entertainment from the age of about four when she dictated 'The Life of Father McSwinley' to her father. Her last book, *The Hangman's Daughter,* was written when she was fourteen years old. She did not develop into an adult writer and nothing else she wrote had quite the same narrative drive as *The Young Visiters.* The book creates interesting characters like Mr Salteena and Ethel and offers a perceptive contribution to our understanding of social history and a unique insight into how a child understands the adult world. There is an intriguing story of how the book came to be published. Daisy and her sisters were clearing up their mother's house after her death and came across the manuscript of *The Young Visiters* and sent it to cheer up a friend who was ill. The friend passed the book to Frank Swinnerton, a novelist and reader for Chatto and Windus, which published the book with a witty introduction by J.M. Barrie.

Daisy Ashford was clearly exceptional both in her ability and in her circumstances. Nevertheless, this example tells us that children can have a huge urge to explore and reflect on their world by writing about it. Even though today writing at home has to compete with many other activities – not least the new technologies – some children, with encouragement, will be prepared to write with freedom and enthusiasm away from the formalities of school. Teachers can help by creating a space within the school week for children to write without the expectation that it will be subject to scrutiny and assessment. Let me just mention two classroom examples here. A teacher of nine year olds gave them

a writing journal which they decorated and wrote as a diary. They could share their work or not as they wished. For some of the children the time for journal writing, secured from the busy school week, became valued and helped them find a 'writing voice'. In an interesting report 'Writing journals: an investigation' it is made clear that different models of journal writing suit different teachers and different pupils. One teacher found 'dialogue journals' – a model where the teacher provides responses to what children write – enthused many children in her class. However, other teachers involved in the action research found written teacher responses hard to maintain with all children in busy classrooms (Graham, 2003).

In the second example ten year olds were given time each week to write a novel or at least a book in chapters. They could discuss their plans with the teacher and they could, if they wished, take their developing work home. The children in both examples were given experience of extended kinds of writing that demand much commitment.

Young authors today – adding electronic authoring

The Brontë children, Daisy Ashford and the children in the classroom examples mentioned here all felt very positive about their writing. This helps answer Nigel Hall's question in *Writing with Reason* in which he shares what he learnt from observing young writers aged from three to seven years. Can they, he asks, function as authors if given freedom and encouragement? (Hall, 1994). The children wrote non-fiction – letters and lists of rules as well as stories – and Hall observed the processes involved in their writing as well as considering the features of the final drafts.

Children will continue to enjoy making print books and there is more about this under the 'book making' entry. However, today's children can also use exciting new electronic authoring tools that broaden the choices. Multimedia authoring using Hyperstudio and PowerPoint bring additional options – to do with animation, transitions and the use of sound. Children find that making their own multimedia texts helps them acquire a deeper understanding of how these texts are put together. This contributes to their becoming more sophisticated readers of electronic texts. If you have used digital photographs and animations alongside text in the course of making your own information book you understand the choices authors of this kind of text have to make. Somehow making a multimedia story seems to encourage playfulness and creativity. As well as making their own stories children like the challenge of personalising favourites like *Owl Babies* and *Peepo!* A teacher collected pictures of her nursery class as babies from parents to incorporate in a multimedia retelling of the latter story. As with print book making, multimedia text making is valuable not only because a lively resource is produced, but also because of the talk and collaboration that accompanies it.

Acknowledgement. The author thanks Diana Hartley and her class at Askrigg VC Primary School, Yorkshire for allowing reference to be made to the miniature book project.

Ashford, Daisy (1984 edition, illustrated by Posy Simmonds) *The Young Visiters* London: Chatto and Windus.

Brighton, Catherine (2004) *The Brontës: Scenes from the Childhood of Charlotte, Branwell, Emily and Anne* London: Frances Lincoln.

Brontë Parsonage Museum: www.bronte.org.uk/museum

Graham, Lynda (2003) 'Writing journals: an investigation' in *Reading Literacy and Language* (the journal is now called *Literacy*), 37 (1), April.

Hall, Nigel (1994) *Writing with Reason: Emergence of Authorship in Young Children* London: Heinemann (O/P).

Johnson, Paul (1991) *A Book of One's Own: Developing Literacy Through Making Books* London: Greenwood Books.

——(1997) *Pictures and Words Together: Children Illustrating and Writing Their Own Books* London: Greenwood Press.

CHILDREN'S LAUREATE

See also: fiction: choosing and using, history of children's literature, illustrations: finding a vocabulary, picture books

The Children's Laureate is a lifetime achievement award granted to an outstanding children's writer or illustrator every two years. It is administered by Booktrust and sponsored by Waterstone's bookseller and a number of publishing houses, and carries a £15,000 bursary. Judges for new laureates consider nominations from organisations representing libraries, critics, writers and booksellers. Children can nominate their favourite writer or illustrator by filling in and sending a form online. The main tasks of the Children's Laureate are:

- to encourage children to read all kinds of books;
- to make sure as many people as possible value and celebrate books; and
- to publicise books and all they offer children through newspapers and magazines, television, radio and the internet.

Quentin Blake

(Illustrator of the books of other authors as well as of his own humorous, often profound picture books: www.quentinblake.com.)

The first Children's Laureate, Quentin Blake, the writer and illustrator, was appointed in 1999. His illustrations, with their quirky, distinctive spare line, are found in many storybooks, for example Roald Dahl's *James and the Giant Peach* and *The BFG*, in poetry books, for example Michael Rosen's *Wouldn't You Like to Know* and *You Can't Catch Me* and in his own life-enhancing picture books including *The Clown, Mister Magnolia, Zagazoo* and *The Green Ship*.

The choice of Quentin Blake as first Children's Laureate encouraged many of us to think more deeply about finding a critical language to discuss the visual element in children's books. At a one-day conference at the Learning Centre, Somerset House, in March 2004 on the theme 'Words about Pictures', organised jointly by Ghislaine Kenyon and *Books for Keeps*, Quentin Blake and other illustrators of children's books shared their insights with about thirty teachers, publishers and reviewers. Quentin explained that an illustrator has to keep a number of things in mind at the same time – mood and atmosphere, what can be gleaned from the written text and the appearance and gestures of the characters. His story *Zagazoo* needs little background detail while *The Green Ship* has richly wooded and colourful surroundings (Kenyon, 2004). Those who have seen him at work describe how swiftly his pen and ink images form on the page. While Blake's very recognisable line might seem to have been achieved effortlessly, it can express a range of emotions very skilfully: in *The Clown* human feelings are communicated through the gestures and the orientation of the character's body.

Anne Fine

(Writer of forty books who has won many awards, e.g. the Smarties Prize and the Carnegie Medal: www.annefine.co.uk.)

Anne Fine, an author who writes for all age groups, was the second Children's Laureate, in 2001–03. She has been a lifelong supporter of children's libraries and children's reading and seems to write equally successfully for the very young and for teenagers. The under eights like books like *How to Write Really Badly* and the terrifically funny *Diary of a Killer Cat* and *Return of the Killer Cat*. The eight to elevens will like a recent book *Frozen Billy*, an adventure set in the late Victorian world of the music hall, as well as old favourites like *The Tulip Touch, Bill's New Frock* and *Goggle Eyes* (made into the film 'Mrs Doubtfire' with Robin Williams in the lead). Anne is known for her convincing dialogue and for describing the realities of family life. Her ear for what people say has led to her writing some fine playscripts for children, often based on her books. Ginn have *Stranger Danger* as a big book playscript or in packs of six small books for five to seven year olds. *Celebrity Chicken* is a play for the over eights based on Anne's book *The Chicken Gave It to Me*.

One of the central planks of her laureateship was the Home Library Scheme. 'The home library project aims to encourage the assumption that owning books and having books in the home is normal' (Mallett, 2002: 10.) All children with the help of their parents and teachers were encouraged to have their own home bookshelf and to adorn their books with special bookplates by well-known children's illustrators, which could be downloaded from her excellent website (Mallett, 2002). Anne also did much to help support young readers of Braille. Her award-winning website continues to give many book suggestions for different age groups, helpful reviews and competitions.

Michael Morpurgo

(Writer of over ninety titles as well as screenplays, he is dedicated to creating the readers of tomorrow: www.michael morpurgo.com.)

61

From 2003 until May 2005 Michael Morpurgo brought a distinctive vision to the laureateship. He comments, 'I keep my eyes open, my heart fresh'. He says he gets ideas for books from places, people and stories he hears. His books include *Kensuke's Kingdom*, *The Butterfly Lion*, *The Dancing Bear*, *Farm Bear* and *War Horse* and two well-liked picture books *The Rainbow Bear* and *Wombat Goes Walkabout*. Michael was a friend of Ted Hughes, the late Poet Laureate, and the two were the first to think about the possibility of a Children's Laureate.

I recommend Geoff Fox's book *Dear Mr Morpingo: Inside the World of Michael Morpurgo* for older primary children who want to know more about how this author writes and thinks. Two books that Michael likes are Ted Hughes' *The Iron Man* and R.L. Stevenson's *Treasure Island*. During his many tours and talks during his time as Children's Laureate, Michael remembers particularly one letter, from Struan Wilson aged seven years. Struan writes:

> 'Reading is to me like music. To me, a shelf of books that I have not read is like gold to other people. My favourite place to read is lying on my bed when it is beginning to get light. I'm so engrossed in my book that I only hear the voices of the characters'.

Jacqueline Wilson

(Prolific author of children's novels, tapping into the realities of modern life: www.jacquelinewilson.co.uk.)

Her many books explore through story the lives of children facing difficulties. The story of *Tracy Beaker* (1991) and *The Dare Game* (2000) are about children living in residential care, and *Candy Floss* (2006) follows the lives of a single-parent family living in difficult circumstances. Appointed in May 2005, she was uniquely qualified to encourage children's reading. She has toured the country to meet young readers, and promoted reading aloud to children in school and as a bedtime routine for younger ones. Her book *Great Books to Read Aloud* shares her experience and insight (Wilson, 2006).

Michael Rosen

(Author, poet, charismatic lecturer and presenter of radio and television programmes: www.michaelrosen.co.uk.)

Appointed as Children's Laureate in 2007, Michael Rosen is well known for his poetry for children. Collections include *You Can't Catch Me!* and *Quick! Get Out of Here!* He also writes non-fiction, novels and picture books, and retells classics and stories from other cultures. His aim was to boost all children's reading for pleasure, and to give a special lift to 'the wonderful diverse world of poetry'.

Anthony Browne

(Author and illustrator of many acclaimed picture books who shares his expertise about visual literacy: www.childrenslaureate. org.uk/previous-laureate/anthony-browne.)

Anthony Browne, made Children's Laureate in 2009, is one of the most successful, imaginative and exciting picture book creators ever. Favourite Browne books include *Gorilla*, *Voices in the Park*, *The Tunnel* and *The Shape Game*. His autobiography, written with his son, Joe, gives an insight into his distinctive approach to combining image and word and suggests that when we write or draw we transform our experience into a story or picture (Browne & Browne, 2011). This author-illustrator's books have a strong narrative drive and illustrations that are full of colour and pattern. No one else combines the real and the surreal quite like Browne. His books have wide appeal – not least for the more sensitive child. At the centre of his laureateship has been the celebration of contemporary picture books and the promotion of understanding of wider aspects of visual literacy. Antony Browne has won many awards for his books including the prestigious Hans Andersen medal.

Julia Donaldson

(Author of 120 books for children of different ages, Julia Donaldson is one of the most entertaining and inventive picture book authors of recent times. She has a marvellous ear for words and rhymes and this is why her stories have such appeal for young children. www.juliadonaldson.co.uk.)

At her inauguration as seventh laureate in 2011, she promised to be 'an active laureate', encouraging children's enjoyment of music and drama alongside their reading and listening. She is passionate about the role of libraries in inspiring a love of books and intends to promote them across the UK. She promises to be a 'hands-on' laureate who wants to organise exciting events in libraries and schools. She has had much experience of sharing her books by reading them aloud, sometimes with a musical accompaniment. Everyone has a favourite Donaldson picture book – for example *The Gruffalo, The Snail and the Whale* and *Room on the Broom*. These three, as is the case with so many of her books, are brilliantly illustrated by Axel Scheffler.

Booktrust: www.booktrusted.co.uk/childrens laureate

Browne, Antony and Browne, Joe (2011) *Playing the Shape Game* London: Doubleday.

The Children's Laureate: www.childrens laureate.org

Kenyon, Ghislaine (2004) 'Beginning the conversation' in *Books for Keeps*, No. 146, May (see this article in the archive online: www. booksforkeeps.co.uk).

Mallett, M. (2002) 'Books for young readers: The Home Library Project' in *English 4–11*, the Primary Journal of the English Association, No. 16, Autumn.

Wilson, Jacqueline (2006) *Great Books to Read Aloud* London: Bloomsbury.

CHILDREN'S LITERATURE – A GUIDE TO THE ENTRIES, ETC.

See also: anthology, audio resources, big books, book review, Books for Keeps online, Bookstart, Booktrust, British Film Institute, CD-ROM, Centre for Literacy in Primary Education, chapbooks, children's literature awards, children's literature in translation, class reader, classics, core books, cultural diversity and resources, English Association, fantasy, fiction: choosing and using, fiction as a source of information, film making, history of children's literature, horn book, illustrations: finding a vocabulary, information books, internal rhyme, library skills, literary criticism, literature across the curriculum, living books, metaphor, metonymy, metre, multimodal texts, multiple literacies, narrative, National Association for the Teaching of English, onomatopoeia, oxymoron, pathetic fallacy, personification, prose, radio programmes for children, reading choices, reading diaries, reading environment, realism, response to reading, retrieval devices, rhyme, rhythm, scan, Shakespearian drama, skimming, stanza, story sacks, storyboxes, storytelling, structural guiders, study skills, talking books, television programmes for children, texts, transactional writing, United Kingdom Literacy Association, video-film and DVDs

(For entries on different genres of children's literature – picture books, novels, reports, etc. – see the text types in the section of this entry, *Categories of children's texts*.)

Children's literature is a vast subject which, as you would expect, receives considerable coverage in this encyclopedia over many entries, the most substantial of which is the extended entry 'History of children's literature'.

Children's publishing is a massive international industry from which comes a huge number of texts for children of every possible kind (both paper and electronic). There are also many publishers of texts about children's literature itself. As you probably will have found, 'children's literature resources' brings up a bewilderingly large number of sites on the web across literary, educational and social studies. This shows us that for academics the area of 'children's literature' offers an exciting mix of interdisciplinary study. So it is not surprising that the second edition of Peter Hunt's well-regarded *International Companion Encyclopedia of Children's Literature* includes contributions of interest to anyone concerned with 'literature, education, internationalism, childhood, or culture in general' (Hunt, 2004). The articles in Hunt's guide cover theory and critical approaches, forms and genres, publishing and reviewing, classroom use of texts and many essays on the current state of world children's literature. My encyclopedia can only begin to introduce you to some of these areas and suggest sources of further information. My priority has been to provide an introduction to what the classroom teacher needs to know about text types and for further support here I recommend *Exploring Children's Literature* (Gamble & Yates, 2008). These authors share their knowledge about language and literature in the belief that it is knowing about and understanding these things that gives practitioners the foundation for effective teaching. They also include lively ideas for practice which show that reading and discussing texts, whether fiction or non-fiction, can be one of the most rewarding parts of the curriculum. Other texts that support teachers' knowledge and understanding are Goodwin's *Understanding Children's Books*; Meek, Warlow

and Barton's *The Cool Web*; Whitehead's *Language and Literacy in the Early Years*; Watson's *Cambridge Guide to Children's Books in English*; and Mallett's *Choosing and Using Fiction and Non-fiction 3–11*.

First in this entry I set out, under *Categories of children's texts*, a classification of children's texts which complements the 'History of children's literature' entry and which works with the 'see also' list above to guide you to other entries contributing to coverage of this topic. Second, under *Support for reading diaries/ resource files on children's literature*, I try to help those creating such files as part of their initial training. Third, under *Some useful websites* I offer selective sources of information for those who wish to take their studies further.

Categories of children's texts

There is an entry for each of these text types – novels, recounts, etc. – in this encyclopedia.

Fiction

Picture books are illustrated books that tell a story through words and pictures or through pictures alone. The best are highly sophisticated works of art and many are valuable in the initial teaching of reading.

Novels are sustained fictional narratives; children's novels take up themes such as adventure, animal, domestic and family, fantasy, historical and school.

Stories – whether taking the form of print books, talking books, ebooks or living books – are often arranged in chapters and may be classified as humorous, horror, school, fantasy, domestic or animal.

Classics are short stories or novels that have stood the test of time and appeal across the generations.

Short stories are longer and more demanding of the reader than the 'stories' category described above. Here we would include the following: creation stories (about the origins of the earth, its people and creatures); parables (short stories including those in the New Testament which make a moral point); and fables (stories with a moral which becomes explicit at the end). Also there are traditional tales which include the following types: fairy, folk, myth and legend.

Playscripts are texts in prose or in verse written for performance.

Poetry is language with a distinctive form and pattern which often manifests literary devices like metaphor and personification. Kinds of poetry include: ballad, couplets, cinquain, epics, epitaphs, free verse, haiku, kenning, limericks, prayer, riddle, rhyming forms (see rhyme and nursery rhyme), songs (see chorus), sonnets and tanka.

Non-fiction

Non-book print includes captions, charts, diagrams, labels, lists, notices, posters and signs.

Illustrations, with or without annotation, help identify a text with a genre and include drawings, graphics, paintings and photographs.

Non-fiction text types (these can be classified in different ways; the categories used here will be familiar to UK teachers).

Recount – chronologically ordered retelling of events, observations, visits or news.

Report (exposition) – non-chronologically ordered accounts on every subject, starting with an introduction to the subject, moving on to main characteristics.

Instruction (procedural) tells us how to do something in chronological order: recipes, instructions showing how to do things and directions.

Explanation tells us about structures like a plant or processes like the digestive system.

Persuasion presents one viewpoint, as in advertisements, leaflets, newspaper articles, letters to newspapers, circulars, flyers and some kinds of journalistic writing.

Discussion expresses different viewpoints on a topic.

Literary kinds of non-fiction include autobiography (letters, journals, records of experiences), biography (also draws on letters and diary entries) and travel writing.

Reference texts (often alphabetically ordered, with glossaries and indexes) include atlases, catalogues, dictionaries, encyclopedias and thesauri.

Media texts include advertisements, internet sources, newspapers, magazines and flyers.

Support for reading diaries/resource files on children's literature

There are a number of entries (in addition to those to do with the classification of texts above) which aim to help those assembling a diary or file. I have in mind both student teachers concerned with the 'children's literature' part of their course and teachers developing a classroom collection. The entry on 'literary criticism' discusses how the term applies to children's literature and directs you to entries on stylistic aspects like 'imagery', 'metaphor' and 'alliteration'. The entry 'Illustrations: finding a vocabulary' suggests some terms for discussing the visual aspects of children's books, particularly picture books.

Whether your resource is paper or electronic you will need a format for recording information about the texts. A number of journals about children's texts have good formats, for example *Books for Keeps online* and *The School Librarian*. A simple format would be as shown below.

- Name of book and age for which it is intended
- Type of book (picture book, information text, novel ...)
- Author, illustrator, publisher
- ISBN and price, number of pages

Discussion might include something about the design and format, the content (synopsis of story theme or, if a non-fiction category, brief description of the scope of the topic treatment), the illustrations (drawings, paintings, photographs and diagrams) and the language. Not every resource will require long discussion, but some of the entries should be in some depth.

Discussion

You need to be aware of what children choose to read. The database of the Public Lending Right organisation indicates that the children's authors who have been most borrowed in recent years include Jacqueline Wilson (Tracy Beaker stories), J.K. Rowling (Harry Potter books) and Francesca Simon (Horrid Henry stories). Close competitors include Julia Donaldson, Mike Inkpen, Janet and Allan Ahlberg and Lauren Child. When it comes to non-fiction, Terry Deary's Horrible History books are amongst the most popular. The websites of the Public Lending Right organisation (www.plr.uk.com) and Booktrust (www.booktrustchildrensbooks.org.uk) give information about the most recent lists of the books most borrowed from public lending libraries.

Some useful websites

University courses

There are hundreds of courses and research websites. Here are a few I have found useful:

- Open University, course on children's literature EA300: www3.open.ac.uk/study/undergraduate/course/ea300.htm
- Centre for Children's Literature, University of Cambridge: www.educ.cam.ac.uk/centres/childrensliterature
- University of Reading: www.reading.ac.uk/Study/courses/taught/machildren.aspx

- University of Roehampton: www.roehampton.ac.uk/postgraduate-courses/childrens-literature/index.html

Organisations and journals

Again, what is offered is a selective list from a huge number of organisations.

- Questia: www.questia.com. There are links to many other sites and lists of journals and books here.
- Seven Stories Centre for Children's Books: www.sevenstories.org.uk. A charity that houses displays of the work of modern British writers and illustrators in a converted Victorian mill in Ouseburn, Newcastle-upon-Tyne. Taking up an historical perspective, one aim is to record the great diversity of culture, style and subject matter inherent in children's literature. The education programmes are impressive and students from colleges and universities are made welcome at workshops and on courses.
- The Federation of Children's Book Groups: www.fcbg.org.uk.
- The International Research Society for Children's Literature: www.irscl.com.
- International Board on Books for Young People (IBBY UK): www.ibby.org.uk. *IBBY LINK* is a UK journal published for IBBY members three times a year.
- *Children's Literature in Education*: www.springer.com/education+%26+language/linguistics/journal/10583. An international quarterly founded by Geoff Fox who is now editor emeritus.
- Children's Literature Special Interest Group (SIG): www.le.ac.uk/engassoc/fellows/children.html. The site features interviews with children's authors.

Gamble, Nikki and Yates, Sally (2008, second edition) *Exploring Children's Literature* London: Sage Publications.

Goodwin, Prue (ed.) (2008) *Understanding Children's Books: A Guide for Educational Professionals* London: Sage.

Hunt, Peter (2004, second edition) *International Companion Encyclopedia of Children's Literature* London: RoutledgeFalmer.

Mallett, Margaret (2010) *Choosing and Using Fiction and Non-fiction 3–11* London: Routledge.

Meek, Margaret, Warlow, Aidan and Barton, Griselda (eds) (1977) *The Cool Web* London: Bodley Head.

Watson, Victor (2001) *The Cambridge Guide to Children's Books in English* Cambridge: Cambridge University Press.

Whitehead, Marian (2010, fourth edition) *Language and Literacy in the Early Years* London: Paul Chapman (see Chapter 7, 'Books and the world of literature').

CHILDREN'S LITERATURE AWARDS

Awards and prizes tend to be for children's fiction rather than for their non-fiction literature. Sponsors of the prizes often give their support for a limited period and it is sometimes difficult to find individuals and organisations to take over when that time is over. So awards sometimes come to an end – the much-respected Smarties Prize, for example. However, new ones spring up too! Look out for the *Roald Dahl Funny Prize*. Shortlists and the latest information appear in print journals like *English 4–11* and *The School Librarian* and on websites, for example Booktrust (www.booktrust. org.uk), Books for Keeps online (www. booksforkeeps.co.uk) and Write Away (www.justimaginestorycentre.co.uk).

Awards for fiction include:

- *Blue Peter Book Awards* are in three categories: Best Book with Facts, The Book I Couldn't Put Down and Most Fun Story with Pictures.
- *Booktrust Early Years Awards* include: The Best Book for Babies (under a year); The Best Picture Book (up to five years);

Book by the Best Emerging Illustrator (for children up to five years).

- *Grinzane Junior Award* is an international children's book award. the first winner, in 2000, was Emma Chichester Clark for her picture book *I Love You, Blue Kangaroo*, Andersen Press.
- *NASEN Special Educational Needs Award* gives a prize to the book the panel consider most successfully provides a positive image of children with special needs.
- *Guardian Children's Fiction Award* selects the best children's novel.
- *The Carnegie Medal* is a Library Association Award (in memory of Andrew Carnegie, the great benefactor of libraries) for the author of what is judged to be the most outstanding book for children of the previous year.
- *The Kate Greenaway Medal*, from The Library Association, is awarded to a book with outstanding illustrations.
- *Hans Andersen Awards* recognise authors and illustrators whose complete works have made a lasting contribution to children's literature. Recent recipients include: Aidan Chambers, Peter Hunt, Quentin Blake and David Almond (UK); Anna Maria Machado (Brazil), Tomi Ungerer (France) and Jutta Bauer (Germany). It is presented at the Bologna Children's Book Fair by The International Board on Books for Young People (IBBY) www.ibby.org.
- *Red House Children's Book Award* is a national award sponsored by The Federation of Children's Book Groups. The books are voted for by children in two categories – younger readers and older readers.
- *Roald Dahl Funny Prize* was set up by Michael Rosen to recognise author/illustrators of humorous stories who might be overlooked by judges of other awards. Recently the prize for children was won by Louise Yates for her book *Dog Loves Books* (Jonathan Cape) and

the prize for seven to fourteen year olds was won by Louise Rennison for her book *Withering Tights* (HarperCollins).

Awards for non-fiction include:

- *Blue Peter* Best Book with Facts Award.
- *English 4–11* (The English Association) *Picture Book Award* given for an outstandingly good informational picture book for children aged four to seven years and one for children aged seven to eleven years, each May (www.le.ac.uk/engassoc).
- NCTE *Orbis Pictus Award* is sponsored by The Federation of Children's Books for 'excellence in non-fiction writing for children'. This very welcome non-fiction award commemorates the work of Johannes Amos Comenius and particularly his early encyclopedia *The World in Pictures* (1657). For more information visit the website: www.ncte.org/awards/orbispictus.

Finally, *The Eleanor Farjeon Award* is presented by The Children's Book Circle (www.childrensbookcircle.org.uk/farjeon.asp) for distinguished services to children's books.

CHILDREN'S LITERATURE IN TRANSLATION

See also: dual-language texts

Generations of children have benefited from reading translated literature; the fairy tales of the Brothers Grimm, Charles Perrault and Hans Christian Andersen at once spring to mind. More recently, English-reading children have enjoyed The Moomins, Pippi Longstocking, the Mrs Pepperpot books and Babar. However, as Joanne Owen pointed out in 2004, only 1 per cent of British children's books come from other countries (Owen, 2004). This is probably because it is more costly to translate and publish books from abroad and therefore less commercially viable. However, it is always worth going to some trouble to make available books with originality, interesting ideas and a fresh voice. Those who translate books into English widen our reading enjoyment and provide a window into different cultures and countries. When it comes to children's books we need translators of skill and sensitivity if young readers and listeners are to enjoy the qualities of the original text.

For some years the Marsh Award for Children's Literature in Translation has stimulated interest in and awareness of international children's literature. The award, sponsored by the Marsh Christian Trust and Arts Council England and administered by the National Centre for Research in Children's Literature at Roehampton University, is made every two years. The judging panel considers books from a short list. Recent short listed books include *Kamo's Escape* by Daniel Pennac (Walker Books), translated from French by Sarah Adams, and *The Thief Lord* by Cornelia Funke (The Chicken House), translated from German by Oliver Latsch. *The Thief Lord* is an exciting story for children of about nine or ten years. Set in Venice, it is about the adventures of two orphaned brothers who join a gang headed by the thief lord of the title.

The Marsh panel would like to see more books from countries outside Europe represented in the short list. Members are convinced there is a wealth of material waiting to be translated including picture books from Korea and Japan. Booktrust supports interest in books in translation by including them in the Children's Book Show which tours England each year and involves school children in workshops with authors.

Those wishing to increase their knowledge and understanding of international approaches to children's literature would find *The Routledge International Companion*

Encyclopedia of Children's Literature helpful. Publishers who seek out good children's stories from other countries include Walker Books, The Chicken House, Egmont Books, Bloomsbury Children's books and North South Publishers.

Booktrust: www.booktrust.org.uk

Hallford, Deborah and Zaghini, Edgardo (2005) *Outside In: Books in Translation* London: Milet Publishing.

Hunt, Peter (ed.) (2004, second edition) *The Routledge International Companion Encyclopedia of Children's Literature* London: Routledge.

Marsh Christian Trust: www.marshchristian trust.org

Owen, Joanne (2004) 'Children's Literature in Translation' in *The Bookseller, Children's Supplement,* 19 March.

CHOOSING BOOKS AND RESOURCES

See: audio resources, CD-ROM, CDs, core books, creation stories, fairy tales, fiction: choosing and using, folk tales, history of children's literature, Information and Communications Technology (ICT) and English, information stories, legend, myths, non-fiction reading and writing, picture books, reading range, traditional tales

CHORUS

See also: poetry, rhyme, rhythm, verse

The noun 'chorus' can refer either to a group of singers or to the part of a poem or song that is repeated after each verse. Its origin is in Ancient Greece where a 'chorus' (khoros) of actors or singers gave the commentary in plays. A similar role is found in Elizabethan drama – the chorus in Shakespeare's *Henry V* draws us into the action. Used as a verb, if people 'chorus' something they say it together.

Children usually learn about the function of a chorus by singing songs in music lessons

and reading and writing poems with this feature. Poems with a chorus that children enjoy performing are *The Pied Piper of Hamelin* by Robert Browning (1842) and *Goblin Market* by Christina Rossetti (1862). T.S. Eliot's *Old Possum's Book of Practical Cats,* published by Faber Paperbacks in 1974, includes several poems where the chorus contributes to the energy and message – *Macavity: the Mystery Cat, The Old Gumble Cat* and *The Rum Tum Tugger.*

CHRONOLOGICAL NON-FICTION

See also: factual genres, information stories, narrative, non-fiction reading and writing

Chronological non-fiction (or narrative non-fiction) is a term used to refer to any text that is organised mainly on a time sequence basis. The most commonly encountered kinds of chronological non-fiction in the primary and preschool years are 'information stories', 'procedural' kinds of writing (including recipes and instructions for experiments in science) and early autobiographical writing.

CIRCLE TIME

This refers to times when a whole class of young children at the nursery or Reception class stage sit with the teacher in a circle to share news, opinions and feelings. Sometimes, to help with understanding of 'turn-taking' conventions, the teacher will hand an object like a toy or ball to whoever is invited to speak. Where this is working well the atmosphere is relaxed and non-threatening and listening to others is praised as much as spoken contributions.

CLASS DISCUSSION

See: collaborative learning, discussion text, drama and English, plenary, speaking and listening

CLASS READER

See also: fiction: choosing and using, narrative, novels

The class reader is the novel or short story chosen by the teacher to read aloud to the class over a period of time. The children may or may not have their own copies of the text to follow the reading. There are important reasons for finding time to read a whole work to the class. Above all listening to and discussing a quality work of literature brings the class together as a community of readers and listeners and places the emphasis on enjoyment and sharing. I have often heard children make insightful comments about the boy's conflict of loyalty in Betsy Byars' *The Midnight Fox* – should he care most about his hospitable farming relatives or about the vixen who has trusted him with a glimpse of her young? Younger children love talking about dangers in the environment and about family relationships when hearing Dick King-Smith's *The Hodgeheg*.

The discussion that accompanies the reading is often of high quality – there are few better contexts for sharing thoughts, ideas and feelings. Just listening to a fine plot unfolding, interesting characters developing and savouring the setting in which the author places the story is educative. Less forward readers listen to language and imagery in books which they are not yet able to tackle independently. The shared context is also helpful to young learners for whom English is a second or additional language. Response can be deepened through carefully chosen writing and drama activities – for further suggestions see under 'fiction: choosing and using'. Sometimes just reading and talking about the story is enough but for further suggested activities see under 'fiction: choosing and using' in this book and in Bunting *et al.*; Graham, 1997; Graham and Kelly, 2007; Mallett, 2010; Whitehead, 2010.

Bunting, Jane, Ellis, Sue and Vernon, Jenny (updated every two years for each year group) *Book Power: Literacy Through Literature* London: CLPE.

Graham, Judith (1997) *Cracking Good Book* Sheffield: NATE.

Graham, Judith and Kelly, Alison (2007, third edition) *Reading Under Control* London: David Fulton.

Mallett, Margaret (2010) *Choosing and Using Fiction and Non-fiction 3–11* London: Routledge.

Whitehead, Marian (2010, fourth edition) *Language and Literacy in the Early Years* London: Sage (see Chapter 7, 'Books and the world of literature').

CLASSIC TEXTS: CONTEMPORARY APPROACHES TO TEACHING THEM

See also: creativity in English, drama and English, multimodal texts

Teachers and children have a large repertoire of fiction from which to choose, including graphic novels, contemporary picture books and moving image stories. However, classic texts in print form are still a valued part of children's reading experience. Often such texts take readers into another time or into an imaginary world. How do we help children to take the imaginative leap sometimes needed and become engaged with these stories? Improvised drama as a way of empathising with characters gained momentum after the pioneering work of Dorothy Heathcote and her students. Discussion on the lines of Aidan Chambers' 'booktalk' and writing in role help too. Gillian Robins uses these approaches in her innovative teaching and also brings in multimodal and multimedia ways of helping children respond to classic texts like Shakespeare's plays and the work of H.G. Wells. In the following case study we join Gill and her class as they engage with the story of Beowulf.

Case study: A Year 5 class explore the Anglo-Saxon epic *Beowulf*

The project started with exploratory talk about Anglo-Saxon images which the teacher had loosely categorised into work, materials, homes and lifestyle. Working in five groups, the children were encouraged to talk about what could be learnt from the pictures. Each group made notes on large pieces of sugar paper and then summaries were shared with the class. 'No easy feat', comments Gill, 'as by this time children's thoughts and questions were tumbling over each other as they talked themselves towards a conclusion'. Questions pepper their notes. Under 'work' one group commented that one occupation must be fighting. They add 'but were the fights to defend themselves or to attack others?' The images made of gold, iron, wood and bronze suggested the people were traders.

The next stage found the teacher taking up the role of Anglo-Saxon chief and, in a darkened room, the children were told they had travelled from Europe in boats between 700 and 1066 in search of good land to farm. The children were excited by the idea of the 'scop' and the storyteller's role in the community.

Here, as in all fruitful drama work, there was a problem to be solved.

The incomers had been given some land, but there were not enough of them to work towards a sustainable community. Options were to return home, to send for more people to join them or to work with the existing population. Ancient problems with a modern resonance!

The children now had some information and insight about an Anglo-Saxon community to take to their reading of the text. Julia Green's translation *Beowulf the Brave* was read to the children (A&C Black, 2008). Also available were Rosemary Sutcliff's *Beowulf-Dragon Slayer* and Michael Morpurgo's *Beowulf* which has atmospheric illustrations by Michael Foreman.

After talk about the three-part structure of the plot – the killing of Grendel, the revenge of Grendel's mother, and the dragon – the children chose one of the story's scenes and created a graphic version.

After hearing and reading Julia Green's story, the children watched the animated DVD, *Beowulf*, directed by Kulakov and with voiceovers by Derek Jacobi and Joseph Fiennes (Brightspark productions, 2007).

It is well worth tracking down Gill Robins' article to appreciate the richness of this work. It was an ideal context in which to learn about and appreciate the ingenuity of kennings and to create their own such as – 'talk maker' and 'star runner'. One of the most animated discussions was about monsters and how we enjoy narratives in different media, including Doctor Who episodes. The opportunity to create children's multimodal texts and to experience

Figure 6 Part of a storyboard created by Year 5 children at Sun Hill Primary School, Hampshire on creating monsters.

a story in different media also helped make this project exciting and successful.

This case study is based on a fuller account in *English in 4–11*, 38, Spring 2010.

CLASSICS (OF CHILDREN'S LITERATURE)

See also: fiction: choosing and using, history of children's literature, picture books

Classics are books with lasting appeal, but what qualities are needed to achieve this endurance in books for those under eleven years? It would be brave to set out criteria, not only because they might be challenged, but also because I believe works of undoubted value and originality would slip through them. So what follows is no more than some observations about what seems to help a book earn classic status.

Classics link the generations – parents often want to share what they enjoyed with their own children. Parents often instinctively choose to share powerful stories that are not 'time bound'. They may be set in a distinct period but their imaginative appeal seems to set them above a particular time so that children of different generations can enjoy and respond to them.

No-one would deny the importance of a gripping, page-turning story but classics, in addition, tell us something universal about the human situation – about conflict, confusion and loss, and about achievement against the odds, kindness and love – very often through the eyes of the growing child. This is what I think Julia Eccleshare (2001: 9) has in mind when she refers to a book capable of 'tapping into the constants of childhood and of parent/child relationships'.

The best books create a strong setting – a coherent world – for the events and characters they create. These imaginative worlds, sustained throughout a story, are valuable achievements in their own right but also create wonderful refuges for the young reader – an escape sometimes from the harshness of the real world. Of course the imaginary worlds created in books are often far from bland or cosy but often full of challenge and danger, as readers of *The Hobbit*, *The Borrowers* and the Harry Potter series know. Perhaps the point is that it is easier to face virtual dangers than real ones.

Of course a large number of books having these qualities have been written over the years, but those works that are consistently recognised as classics have some of them to an unusual degree.

There is debate about which children's books justify being called 'classic' and people disagree about the merits of particular works. Teachers, scholars of children's literature and children themselves would, if invited, produce different lists of the 'ten best classics', although I would expect the same three or four books to appear in most selections. My own list? *Black Beauty* by Anna Sewell, *Alice in Wonderland* by Lewis Carroll, *The Secret Garden* by Frances Hodgson Burnett, *The Wind in the Willows* by Kenneth Grahame, *The Tale of Peter Rabbit* by Beatrix Potter, *The Lion, the Witch and the Wardrobe* by C.S. Lewis, *The Silver Sword* by Ian Serraillier, *Carrie's War* by Nina Bawden, *Tom's Midnight Garden* by Philippa Pearce and *The Iron Man* by Ted Hughes. I found it difficult to stop at ten.

Publishers produce editions of established classics alongside more contemporary books which seem to have classic potential. It is interesting to see which titles are included in publishers' lists – Puffin Modern Classics (*The Borrowers* by Mary Norton, *Stig of the Dump* by Clive King) and Oxford University's Oxford Children's Modern Classics (*Flambards* by K.M. Peyton and *Eagle of the Ninth* by Rosemary Sutcliffe). If you want to learn more about the best contemporary books you would enjoy Watkins & Sutherland's (1995) chapter in Hunt's *Children's Literature: An Illustrated History*. For a most interesting analysis of the role of publishers in sustaining interest in the classics and helping establish newer classics, see Julia Eccleshare's (2001) article in *Books for Keeps*. While welcoming publishers' initiatives which keep outstanding books in print, she hopes this will never be at the expense of promoting good contemporary literature.

Eccleshare, Julia (2001) 'The proliferation of modern "classics"' in *Books for Keeps*, No.126, January.

Mallett, Margaret (2010) *Choosing and Using Fiction and Non-fiction 3–11* London: Routledge (see Chapters 7 and 18).

Watkins, Tony and Sutherland, Zena (1995) 'Contemporary children's literature, 1970–present' in Hunt, Peter (ed.) *Children's Literature: An Illustrated History* Oxford: Oxford University Press.

CLAUSE

See also: adjectival clause, adverbial clause, grammar, sentence, subject knowledge

A clause is a group of words containing a verb. It can sometimes stand on its own as a simple sentence or it can be a structure within a sentence as in 'because I wanted to' in 'I went to the party because I wanted to'. There can sometimes be two clauses, capable of existing independently, joined by a conjunction as in: 'I went to the party and I had a good time'. The clauses in this example could become short sentences: 'I went to the party'. 'I had a good time'.

Clause analysis involves breaking down a sentence into its constituent clauses. So let us consider how the following sentence – 'When they departed, they discovered that their coats had been left behind' – might be broken down. 'They discovered' is the main clause; 'when they departed' is an adverbial clause of time modifying the verb 'discovered'; 'that their coats had been left behind' is a subordinate noun clause, object of the verb 'discovered'.

Although there has been a move back towards the study of grammar as part of English work, few would advocate spending long hours on formal clause analysis in the primary years. One issue is whether studying clause analysis would have a beneficial effect on children's writing. There are some interesting tasks round clauses and sentences for children in *The Primary Grammar Book* by Bain and Bridgewood.

In the United Kingdom teachers are required to have knowledge about sentences, phrases and clauses as an underpinning to their teaching. For a clear account, see Chapter 7 in Angela Wilson and Julie Scanlon's book *Language Knowledge for Primary Teachers*.

Bain, Richard and Bridgewood, Marion (1998) *The Primary Grammar Book: Finding Patterns – Making Sense* Sheffield: NATE.

Wilson, Angela and Scanlon, Julie (2011, fourth edition) *Language Knowledge for Primary Teachers: A Guide to Textual, Grammatical and Lexical Study* London: David Fulton.

CLICHÉ

This is a phrase or idea that has lost its impact because it has been overused. Some metaphors – 'the apple of his eye' – and similes – 'as good as gold' – come into this category. However, the favourite sayings of a culture tell us much about values, beliefs and attitudes. Our shared knowledge of what they mean can be a quick route to communication and it is quite difficult to avoid clichés altogether. Indeed the sheer familiarity of some much-used phrases can sometimes serve a useful function – by helping us through upsetting or difficult situations. We find ourselves saying 'it may be for the best' or 'there are other fish in the sea' to comfort others. In written form, except for direct speech, clichés tend to be tedious ('In this day and age'; 'explore every avenue'; 'the bottom line'). I recently reviewed a book which aimed to help children write stories. It recommended that young writers used linking phrases like 'out of the blue' and 'suddenly I heard a loud noise ... ' This will help you control the adventure story genre, it claimed. I doubt it! Children are capable of thinking of phrases of their own which have more energy and originality than these exhausted notions.

CLOZE PROCEDURE

See also: cue-systems, grammar

'Cloze' stands for 'closure'. It refers to a reading task in which children 'guess' the words needed to fill the gaps deliberately omitted from a text. So the procedure is used not only to assess children's prediction abilities but also as a diagnostic tool showing where teachers can fruitfully intervene to give finely tuned help to a young reader (for example to help them understand how verbs and objects need to agree). Cloze procedures can also be used to measure readability of a text.

Sometimes in cloze procedures, the words to insert in the various gaps are given at the foot of the passage, while at other times young readers have a free choice of words. Teachers may choose to construct their own cloze exercises or use published examples. The words omitted may be a particular part of speech – adjectives or conjunctions perhaps. Or every nth word is missed out, but here the remaining text must provide enough semantic and syntactic support to enable its successful completion. During the task children use their knowledge of syntax and semantics to fill in the omitted words. Syntactic knowledge helps a young reader sense whether, for example, the word will be a verb or a noun and to tune in to subject-verb agreement when deciding whether nouns are singular or plural. Teachers often model the process for the children by thinking through the prediction task out loud – 'this word would make sense and sounds right'. Where children talk in a group about their decisions the task becomes a truly reflective activity.

Of course more than one word can often be appropriately placed in a gap. Older primary children can be asked how the meaning of a passage may be changed with each alternative. Consider the following sentence:

'The – entered the room and began to stroke the dog to quieten it'.

Our syntactic knowledge tells us that the space has to be filled with a subject, a noun likely to be a category of person – vicar, teacher or intruder – but consider how the context interpretation would vary depending on which one was chosen. As meaning develops during the reading of the passage, some of our earlier decisions might need to be altered.

Now that English work is often informed by a media education perspective, cloze procedure approaches can be extended in a number of interesting ways, for example to deconstruct visual texts. In an advertisement made up of a series of images, we might substitute one of them and discuss with the pupils what difference this makes to the meanings conveyed by the series (Potter, 1994).

Potter, Frank (1994) 'Media education, literacy and schooling' in Wray, David and Medwell, Jane (eds) *Teaching Primary English* London: Routledge.

CLUSTER

See also: blend, consonant, phoneme

Sometimes called a blend, a cluster is a group of sounds that run together, for example, spr (spread) or gr (greet).

CODE OF PRACTICE

See also: Special Educational Needs (SEN) in language and literacy

The 2001 Code of Practice

The 2001 Code of Practice arises from the Special Educational Needs and Disability Act (SENDA). The Code is in two parts: first it provides guidance to strengthen the rights of parents and children to access mainstream education; part two extends the Disability Discrimination Act 1995 to education so that the civil rights of children and adults are recognised in schools and colleges. For a detailed account of the implications of the code for the SENCo and its application to children in different categories of special need such as hearing impairment and visual impairment see *Supporting Special Needs* by Penny Tassoni.

The Code of Practice 1994

This followed the 1993 Education Act and required that children with Special Educational Needs should normally be educated in mainstream schools. It reinforced the principle established by *The Warnock Report* (1978) that, where appropriate, children should be given a statement of special educational needs. It insisted on the importance of early identification of children's difficulties and the drawing up of an Individual Education Plan (IEP). Primary schools have a Special Educational Needs co-ordinator (SENCo) who liaises with the class teacher and the English co-ordinator over formulating an IEP for children with special needs in reading and writing. Lady Warnock has called for a review of the Code and of special needs policy; the latest details will be on the Government website: www.education.gov.uk

Department of Education (2001) *Special Needs Code of Practice*, www.education.gov.uk

Tassoni, Penny (2003) *Supporting Special Needs: Understanding Inclusion in the Early Years* London: Heinemann.

COHESION

See also: register

Cohesion helps create what linguists call 'textuality' – the sense that what we have in front of us is a text rather than a random group of sentences. Angela Wilson describes how the careful writer ensures that 'each bit of their meaning is somehow bound into the whole so that readers or listeners can follow their drift, and can see the connections between one sentence or one part of the text and another' (Wilson & Scanlon, 2011). Cohesive links or ties can be achieved at sentence level by using conjunctions (and, but) and adverbs (soon, there). At text level, one way of achieving cohesion is by using pronouns (such as he, she, they) which help a reader make referential connections to earlier parts of the text. There is an abundance of connectives and cohesive ties which are used differently according to the particular kind of text. A procedural text, like a set of instructions to use machinery, might achieve cohesion by numbering or bullet pointing the steps. There is another kind of cohesion called lexical cohesion which in literary texts is sometimes achieved by using vocabulary creating images linked to a particular theme. An example of this kind of linkage is found in the repetition of hot, firey imagery in *The Firework-Maker's Daughter,* an exciting novel for children of about nine years upwards. When Lila entered the Grotto of the Fire-Fiend: 'red fire and flame licked and crackled at the rocky roof', 'a wide carpet of boiling lava spread' and 'mighty hammer and anvils rang with the rhythm of a great fire-dance' (by Philip Pullman, Corgi Yearling Books, 1996).

There are a number of ways in which teachers can help children understand more about cohesion so that they have the opportunity to bring that understanding to their own writing. For example, a text can be cut up, perhaps into paragraphs, and a pair or group of children asked to put the story together in the right order. Sometimes the end of the story is omitted and here children enjoy creating their own ending making it of a piece with the rest of the text. In their helpful resource book, *The Primary Grammar Book*, Bain and Bridgewood (1998) include interesting activities to help children learn how to create cohesion in a text, including using both co-ordinating connectives (where the clauses linked together are of equal status) and subordinating connectives (where one clause functions as part of another one). Many students also find *The Grammar Book* for secondary pupils useful to support their own understanding of grammatical terms (Bain and Bain, 1997).

As Key Stage 2 gets underway, cohesiveness in writing comes to the fore. Sentence and text level work in Literacy Time supports children's developing sense of cohesion. Towards the end of Year 4 sentence level work should include using connectives – adverbs and conjunctions – to structure an argument, reinforced at text level where children assemble and sequence points to convey a point of view. Using connectives both to link clauses in sentences and to link sentences in longer texts should be a sentence level objective and this meshes with writing tasks such as writing a letter of protest and constructing an argument at text level. By the final term of Year 6 children can be helped to divide whole informational texts into paragraphs and to comment on how the paragraphs are sequenced and how appropriate connectives are used to link one paragraph to the next.

Bain, R. and Bain, E. (1997) *The Grammar Book* Sheffield: The National Association for the Teaching of English.

Bain, Richard and Bridgewood, Marion (1998) *The Primary Grammar Book* Sheffield: The National Association for the Teaching of English.

Crystal, David (2010, third edition) *The Cambridge Encyclopedia of Language* Cambridge: Cambridge University Press.

McArthur, Tom (1992) *The Oxford Companion to the English Language* Oxford: Oxford University Press.

Wilson, Angela and Scanlon, Julie (2011, fourth edition) *Language Knowledge for Primary Teachers: A Guide to Textual, Grammatical and Lexical Study* London: David Fulton (Chapter 7).

COLLABORATIVE LEARNING

See also: book making, constructivism, critical discourse, dialogic teaching, discussion, discussion text, drama and English, Information and Communications Technology (ICT) and English, language and thought, metacognition, plenary, speaking and listening, zone of proximal development

The term 'collaborative learning' refers to any activity in which pupils or students work together, but it is particularly associated with pupil-led group talk. Using talk to plan, reflect on and evaluate learning was a favoured strategy in many classrooms in the 1970s and 1980s. While good practitioners have always included contexts for group discussion, before the publication of *Language, the Learner and the School* by Douglas Barnes, James Britton and Harold Rosen in 1969, talk exchanges in many classrooms consisted mainly of pupils' responses to the teacher's questions. This book created much excitement and there were many courses on language and learning which emphasised collaborative talk as a way of using language to learn across the whole curriculum. Douglas Barnes wrote the 'Language and Learning' unit for an Open University Education course which set out the principles underpinning the approach and provided examples of good practice. The well-known 'Role of Language in Learning' course (affectionately referred to as 'the role course') was established at The London Institute of Education. Where collaborative talk was well planned and organised the benefits were clear – not least that children became much more motivated and there was a new energy in many classrooms. Children are after all social beings who thrive on co-operation with others. However, there was sometimes a lack of a clear focus and some felt that children spent too much time over relatively unstructured conversations. There was also a growing appreciation of that part of Vygotsky's work which drew attention to the role of the teacher in directing children's work and 'modelling' certain kinds of thinking by talking through ideas and solutions to problems alongside the pupil.

Now, in the United Kingdom and in other parts of the world as well, there has been a move towards more structured contexts where the teacher is very firmly at the centre. There is some concern, particularly amongst early years practitioners, that our more prescriptive frameworks may not provide enough opportunity for collaborative talk round activities.

However, the thoughtful practitioner can fulfil current requirements and provide for children's talk. Indeed many of the purposes for talk to meet the requirements of the National Curriculum can only be met by pupils having the chance to contribute to small group talk. In an interesting research project, small groups of children were asked to draw up some ground rules for collaborative talk. Some sensible rules emerged, for example that you should think before you speak, respect the contributions of others and be prepared to change your mind (Mercer, 2000). In this research children's increasing awareness of their own learning and how it can be improved (metacognition) is valued and exploited. I end with some ways in which we can bring collaborative pupil-led talk fruitfully into English work. First, when we read to the whole class from a novel, short story or other literary text there is often an issue or aspect of characterisation of interest and importance. Where appropriate, the teacher can stop reading, divide the children into groups and ask them to discuss the issue. Often it is helpful for one child to act as scribe and to make some notes. Then the groups feed back comments, conclusions and questions to whole group discussion. The teacher's role in weaving together the different contributions is highly skilled. He or she also helps initiate pupils into a 'critical discourse' – a questioning, speculating kind of discussion. Terry Phillips puts it like this: '"Facts" are taken-for-granted hypotheses; they can be reflected upon in small group discussion, unpacked and turned into amazing new ideas' (Phillips, 1994). A second context is talk round the computer. Children can work jointly on cloze procedures and other language activities, but the teacher needs to monitor this carefully – just working together using the computer does not necessarily lead to useful talk and collaboration. For a very helpful analysis of how we can organise this see chapter 5 'Developing exploratory talk' in Grugeon *et al.* 2006. A third context arises when we ask children to write as a group. The computer may be used for group writing or the children can handwrite their work. Sometimes pupils benefit from working on a writing task with their peers in pairs or a small group. Book making and making class journals and magazines lend themselves to collaborative work. Under the 'drama and English' entry the many ways in which children can collaborate round improvisations and texts is covered.

Barnes, Douglas, Britton, James and Rosen, Harold (1969) *Language, the Learner and the School* Harmondsworth: Penguin.

Grugeon, Elizabeth, Hubbard, Lorraine, Smith, Carol and Davies, Lyn (2006, third edition) *Teaching Speaking and Listening in the Primary School* London: David Fulton.

Mercer, N. (2000) *Words and Minds: How We Use Language to Think Together* London: Routledge.

Mercer, N. and Hodgkinson, S. (2008) *Exploring Talk in School: Inspired by the Work of Douglas Barnes* London: Sage.

Phillips, Terry (1994) 'The dead spot in our struggle for meaning: learning and understanding through small group talk' in Wray, David and Medwell, Jane (eds) *Teaching Primary English: The State of the Art* London and New York: Routledge.

COLLECTIVE NOUN

See also: noun, parts of speech

A collective noun refers to a group of things or people – crowd, herd, flock or team. As this category of noun is singular, strictly speaking, it matches with a singular verb as in 'The crowd moves forward'. However, as we think of the collective noun as plural in meaning, many find it acceptable to use it with a plural verb – 'The crowd move forward'.

COLLOQUIALISM

This refers to any expression that is informal and non-standard – for example 'She ain't at home'.

COLON

See also: punctuation

The colon is a punctuation mark with four main uses:

- It can introduce a list of items. 'We need for the writing corner: a computer, lined paper, sugar paper, pens, pencils and crayons.'
- It may replace a comma when speech or a quotation is used. 'The school dentist told the children last week: "Clean your teeth morning and evening".'
- It indicates a semantic link between two parts of a sentence. 'The ants are all over the school yard: they must have a nest nearby.'
- It can replace a conjunction like 'and' or 'but' to create a crisp or even dramatic effect. 'I asked for your assignment: you did not hand it in'.

COLOUR CODING

See also: reading, reading corner/area

Colour coding is an organisational device used in class libraries or in the book or reading corner to indicate either type of book (fiction, poetry, information, reference) or what Cliff Moon calls 'the readability of texts'.

Moon, Cliff (published yearly) *Individualised Reading* Reading: Reading University Reading and Language Information Centre.

COMICS

See also: illustrations, popular culture and new media, visual literacy

Comics are a category of popular literature mainly, although not exclusively, for children. As well as weekly comics we have all seen the annuals that feature particular comic strip characters – these appear in book shops as Christmas approaches. I remember my sister and I eagerly awaiting the arrival of *The Rupert Bear Annual*. The comic strip cartoon format is well known: pictures show a series of events which may be humorous or tell a story. Often there are stock characters and young readers acquire a cumulative insight into how they are likely to behave and react. Although some comic strips only have pictures, there is usually a brief text at the bottom or top of each illustration and distinctive speech balloons coming from the characters' mouths. Noises – 'Boom!!',

'Smash!!', 'Crash!!' – are included with multiple exclamation marks and visual effects.

Comics became widely available reading matter in the first part of the twentieth century. Those that remained popular after the Second World War included *Beano*, *Buster* and *Dandy* – in which the events and characters are entertaining but one-dimensional – and the comics read by older boys, *Wizard*, *Hotspur* and *Rover*.

Some comics originally included quite long prose stories but by the end of the 1960s 'the comic across all age groups had demoted the word in favour of the picture' (Hunt, 1995). The dominance of the visual has intensified now that children watch more and more animated cartoons on television and use interactive texts on CD-ROMs (Pizzi, 2004; Bearne, 2009). A number of researchers are urging us to help children become critical readers of comics and other visual material. We are reminded in *Teaching Visual Literacy* that seeing comes before words (Fisher and Frey, 2008).

Worth a mention when considering the history of the comic are two 'quality' publications – *Eagle* and *Girl* – which came out in the early 1950s. Both comics aimed to include a balance of fact and fiction as well as comic strips and show that a cartoon strip format in itself does not imply trivial treatment of an issue or a story. (Modern picture books sometimes use a comic strip format to tell stories of some profundity – for example Briggs' *When the Wind Blows* about nuclear war, for older children and adults.) *Girl* was a particularly interesting case in the history of comics as the editor, the Reverend Marcus Morris, tried to 'blur gender boundaries and modernise the self image of girls' (Hunt, 1995). To this end there were stories about female pilots and detectives. However, when the original editor moved on *Girl* resorted to the more traditional themes in girls' magazines – school stories,

ponies and nurses. It was claimed that market research showed girls themselves wanted this change of emphasis. Another development was the emergence of the 'horror comic'. This came from America and led to much disquiet. Concern over the violent content of some of the comics led to a voluntary 'Comics Code' in America and to the Children and Young Persons (Harmful Publications) Act in Britain.

Of course comics, like other kinds of popular fiction, are culturally situated and tell us, amongst other things, something about how men and women, boys and girls are regarded in our society. If you want to learn more about the relationship between popular fiction, reading behaviour and gender you would find Jenny Daniels' (1994) 'Girl talk', Chapter 2 in Styles *et al.*'s *The Prose and the Passion*, of great interest. Once children leave the cosy world of *Postman Pat* and *Jack and Jill* – comics for the very young – the type of popular literature they choose is gender related. Boys tend to read comics for sheer entertainment and more than one generation has enjoyed characters like Dennis the Menace and Keyhole Kate. The stories in *Bunty* and *Judy* involve the girls who read them in moral dilemmas and relationship issues. Daniels believes the 'social realism' in girls' reading material leads to greater emotional maturity. So while the home reading of many boys locks them into the narrow genre of their comics, girls' reading is more likely to make them aware of human motivation. On the other hand, girls are more likely to be influenced by advertising and nudged too soon into the world of adult preoccupations. While children, like adults, are entitled to read for entertainment in their leisure time, it is important they understand the limitations of some reading material. There is also a problem with stereotyping of different groups in our society in some comics – parents and teachers would not want to condone the reading of violent and stereotyped material. It is all the more important, then, that we introduce children to as wide a range of reading as possible in school and encourage critical reading. Boys are perfectly capable of reflecting on their reading if given encouragement and opportunity. After reading some back copies of the now discontinued comic *Roy of the Rovers*, ten-year-old Tom remarked that although he found them entertaining 'You know Roy will always win and do brave things for the team'. The very features of familiarity and predictability of boys' comics which appeal to boys also make them a limited kind of reading. The suggestions below are activities that aim to help children to develop their critical thinking about comic strip texts.

Children can be asked to:

- Analyse use of character, setting, plot and language in comics brought from home. Or, if you feel some children might resent this invasion into their private reading choices, another idea is to suggest they examine critically comics for children younger than themselves – for example *Twinkle, Jack and Jill* or *Postman Pat*.
- Add text and speech bubbles to their own version of Raymond Briggs' wordless comic strip picture book – *The Snowman* (1979). Then they might discuss whether the narrative was best driven by pictures alone or with written text added. Other wordless books can give rise to interesting and quite profound discussion about how pictures alone can create a story, for example Shirley Hughes' wonderful wordless story of a little girl's flying fantasy *Up and Up* (1979). Another successful wordless book is Pat Hutchins' *Changes, Changes* (1970) in which a man and woman make a house out of building blocks and then change it to a fire engine, a boat, a truck, a train and then back to a house again.

- Look at some Rupert Bear cartoon strips with the prose story but without the rhyming couplets and then write their own verses. Later compared their efforts with what Alfred Bestall, one of the authors of the Rupert Books, wrote.
- Compare the impact of a print comic strip and a film cartoon. Examine story and picture books in comic strip format, for example – Catherine Brighton's lively comic strip version of the Mary Anning story *The Fossil Girl: Mary Anning's Dinosaur Discovery* (Frances Lincoln) for children of about eight years and above. A Year 5 teacher (nine to ten year olds) helped children to compare Brighton's version of the dinosaur find with Laurence Anholt's prose text in *Stone Girl, Bone Girl* (Doubleday-Transworld Publishers).
- Talk about books containing different kinds of text including comic strip. An outstandingly good example is *Chips and Jessie* (1985) which includes letters, prose and cartoon strips to tell five stories about two friends and their family and pets by Shirley Hughes. Other authors who use comic strip to good effect are Mick Manning and Brita Granström in their non-fiction books, Marcia Williams in her retellings of the classics and some creators of the postmodern picture book, for example the Ahlbergs, Raymond Briggs, Neil Gaiman and Anthony Browne.
- Look at the use of comic strip and cartoon characters in non-fiction – reference and information books. There are lots of examples. Snoopy and Charlie Brown from Schulz's cartoon *Peanuts* are used in *The Charlie Brown Dictionary* (Random House). The interesting thing here, pointed out by Tom McArthur (1992), is that the publishers rely on children knowing that life is perplexing for Charlie Brown. Only if they know this are they able to appreciate the humour. Children like the

colourful cartoon stories in the M.Y. Bees series (Macdonald Young Books) which explain the water cycle, the plant cycle and life cycles of animals. Sam Godwin's *The Case of the Missing Caterpillar* uses speech balloons when the ladybird characters tell the story of the butterfly's life cycle. Children might like to try this format for some of their writing and to discuss the impact of direct speech. When children begin to think about creating a comic strip, research suggests that at the pre-writing stage children enjoy planning their strip in a sketch book, drawing on everyday life and the mass media for themes (Nixon, 2011). They can also be supported as they acquire a discourse using terms like 'panel', 'layout' and 'gutter'.

Bearne, Eve (2009) 'Multimodality, literacy and texts: developing a discourse' *Journal of Early Childhood Literacy*. Special edition on Multimodality, London: Sage, August.

Daniels, Jenny (1994) '"Girl talk": the possibilities of popular fiction' in Styles, Morag, Bearne, Eve and Watson, Victor (eds) *The Prose and the Passion* London: Cassell.

Fisher, Douglas and Frey, Nan (2008) *Teaching Visual Literacy: Using Comic Books, Graphic Novels, Anime, Cartoons and More to Develop Comprehension and Thinking Skills* London: Corwin Press.

Hunt, Peter (ed.) (1995) *Children's Literature: An Illustrated History* Oxford, New York: Oxford University Press.

McArthur, Tom (1992) *The Oxford Companion to the English Language* London: QPD for Oxford: Oxford University Press. (See also *The Concise Oxford Companion to the English Language*, 1998, by the same author.)

Mallett, Margaret (1997) 'Gender and genre: reading and writing choices of older juniors' in *Reading*, UKRA, 31 (2), July.

Pizzi, K. (2004) 'Contemporary comics' in Hunt, P. (ed., second edition) *International Companion Encyclopedia of Children's Literature*, Volume 1 London and New York: Routledge.

Watson, Victor (2001) *The Cambridge Guide to Children's Books in English* Cambridge: Cambridge University Press.

Nixon, Rhonda (2011) 'Teaching narrative writing using comics: Delainey and Rasmussen, the creators of the comic strip Betty, share their composing strategies as rich literary resources for elementary teachers' *Literacy*, in press.

COMMA

See also: punctuation

A comma is a punctuation mark which is used to separate different parts of a sentence where this would be helpful in making meaning clear. So it is used:

- to mark off things in a list before the conjunction. 'I suggest you bring plums, apples, pears, strawberries and grapes'.
- to indicate an aside, instead of using dashes or brackets. 'The girls, sheltering underneath the tree, will begin the races just as soon as the rain stops'.
- to separate clauses in a sentence. 'As soon as we got into the car, which was waiting on a yellow line, she found the homework was missing'.
- to introduce direct speech instead of a colon. 'He pleaded, "I want to take the dog for a walk".'

If you are looking for a book on the use of commas for children from about age seven years which combines clear and witty explanations with lively cartoon illustrations, I recommend *Eats, Shoots and Leaves: Why, Commas Really Do Make a Difference* (Truss and Timmons 2006).

Truss, Lynne and Timmons, Bonnie (2006) *Eats, shoots and leaves: why, commas really do make a difference* London: Profile Books.

COMMAND

Sentences in the imperative mood express a command. 'Sit down!' Sometimes a pronoun is added. 'You sit down!' Commands often end in an exclamation mark to add impact.

COMMON NOUN

See also: abstract noun, grammar, noun, parts of speech, proper noun

A common noun refers to things and people as an example of what the word in question denotes – a village, a hamster or a teacher. (A proper noun, on the other hand, refers to particular identities and names and begins with a capital letter – James, Newcastle or July.) Common nouns can be abstract (love, beauty, joy) or concrete (pencil, rock, train). Some common nouns can be described as countable (having a singular and plural form like book and books), others as uncountable (mass nouns which are usually singular like relief, electricity and wool).

COMMUNICATION SKILLS

See: drama and English, speaking and listening, writing

COMMUNICATIVE COMPETENCE/ COMPETENCE AND PERFORMANCE

See also: appropriateness in language

This is the ability to adjust our use of language to particular social situations. We might say, 'Shut up' to a whining sibling but we are more likely to say, 'Please be quiet' to an adult talking in a library where we are trying to work. Both requests are grammatically sound but they are appropriate in different circumstances.

The linguist Noam Chomsky distinguished between 'competence' – knowing the rules of grammar – and 'performance' – knowing how to use the knowledge in actual

situations. (A similar sort of distinction was made by Ferdinand de Saussure between 'langue' and 'parole'.) The anthropologist Dell Hymes used the term 'communicative competence' to cover both knowledge and social use of language.

Crystal, David (2003, second edition [1987]) *The Cambridge Encyclopedia of the English Language* Cambridge: Cambridge University Press.

COMPETENCE

See: communicative competence/ competence and performance

COMPLEMENT

In its everyday sense 'complement' refers to things that go well together, as in 'The study of letters as evidence in history and the work on different types of letter in the English lesson complement each other'.

In language study, the word or words needed to complete the meaning of another word are the complements. Let us look at the following sentence which exemplifies the function of a complement.

'Jatinder is very strong'.

The subject is 'Jatinder' and 'is' is the verb, but there is no object. 'Very strong' is the complement. Usually complements tell us more about the subject. There are complements for each part of speech (see McArthur, 1992), but they very often occur after verbs like 'be' and after other linking verbs – 'become', 'seem' and 'get'.

In the following examples the complements are italicised.

'Leone seemed *confident*'.

'Jim became *faster at running*'.

'Sally is *an acquaintance of mine*'.

82

McArthur, Tom (1992) *The Oxford Companion to the English Language* London QPD for Oxford: Oxford University Press.

COMPOSITION

See also: grammar, writing

Compositional aspects of writing – getting ideas, selecting vocabulary and grammar – were distinguished from transcriptional aspects by Frank Smith (1982). Smith believed that there was a strong case for allowing young writers to take the risks involved in the creative aspects of writing and to organise their thoughts and ideas before tidying up the transcriptional or secretarial aspects – neat writing, spelling and so on – in a later draft.

Smith, Frank (1982) *Writing and the Writer* London: Heinemann.

COMPOUND SENTENCE

See also: sentence

This is a sentence consisting of two main clauses. The following compound sentences are punctuated in different ways to link the two clauses:

- using a conjunction – in the following sentence 'but' – together with a comma. 'Mr Smith pushed the notes through the door, but no one heard the package fall on the mat'.
- using a conjunct – in the following sentence 'however' – and semi-colon. 'I was concerned that Mary felt unwell on the morning of Sports Day; however, she had recovered by noon in time to enjoy the egg and spoon race'.

A compound sentence is capable of being presented as two simple sentences.

COMPOUND WORD

A compound word is formed by joining two words, as in sandpit, daytime and headache.

COMPREHENSION

See also: prior knowledge

To comprehend something is to understand it. When we read, our level of comprehension is dependent on a number of factors including our existing understanding or 'prior knowledge' of the subject and the level of attention to the passage we achieve. The noun 'comprehension' used in the context of the classroom often refers to an exercise in which pupils or students read a passage of prose or a poem and then write down the answers to questions about it. The issue here is – does answering questions about a text develop children's reading ability? This partly depends on the nature of the questions. If an opinion backed by evidence from the text is invited we could argue that it does. On the other hand, requests for fairly obvious information are unlikely to help a young reader make progress. One danger is that too much of children's time might be spent in answering rather mechanistic questions about a text and not enough time in sharing their thinking and response to literature with the teacher and children in lively discussion.

CONCEPT MAPPING

See also: assimilation and accommodation, metacognition, prior knowledge

This is a method of accessing and organising prior knowledge, often when a new topic is being introduced. The teacher might begin by placing headings on a chalkboard or computer whiteboard and then ask children to 'brainstorm' round

83

each heading. So if we wanted to start work on traditional tales, we might begin with headings like fairy tales, folk tales, creation stories and legends. Sub-headings under fairy tales might include 'oral tradition', 'written versions – Perrault, Grimm and Andersen', 'rags to riches theme', 'modern versions/postmodern tellings'. Or children themselves might make headings and make links between them with arrows. It is the discussion of what has been jotted down that is so helpful at the start of new work. This involves the young learners in the planning and development of the lessons or project. Amy Cassata-Widera (2009) accepts such benefits, but also assesses possible limitations of concept mapping for young children. Lewis and Wray consider the approach is helpful for older children; in their book *Literacy in the Secondary School* they suggest that concept maps and brainstorming have a place not only at the beginning of a topic, but also at the end when the fruits of thinking and reading will have modified the original map. In fact the comparison of the 'before' and 'after' maps can provide evidence for assessment purposes and can be used in the later primary as well as the secondary years. Pupils could add to their original maps what they have discovered in a different coloured pen. The advantage of this is that pupils get a sense of the development of their own thinking and knowledge (Lewis & Wray, 2000).

Cassata-Widera, Amy (2009) *Concept Mapping with Young Children: from Representation to Metacognition* VDM: Verlag.
Lewis, Maureen and Wray, David (2000) *Literacy in the Secondary School* London: David Fulton.

CONCEPTS

See: functions of language, language acquisition, language and thought, spontaneous and scientific concepts

CONCEPTS OF PRINT

Children need to understand some basic concepts about print before they can learn to read and write. Marie Clay, the New Zealand reading expert, devised a series of questions which a teacher can ask a young child to establish what they know. This structured assessment is called the 'Concepts about Print Test'.

However, as Graham and Kelly (2007) point out, Clay's books *Sand* and *Stones* make the assessment quite tight – there is a formal score sheet and children are asked to correct deliberate errors. So many teachers prefer to formulate their own questions and use a book of their own choice.

Marie Clay's work has had great influence and helped teachers identify what needs to be known about print before children can learn to read. Some of the principles underpinning her work have influenced UK reading tests and strategies. During this sort of test, amongst other things, children are asked to show the teacher which parts of a book we read, the pictures or writing, whether they understand the purpose of punctuation marks and have a concept of directionality.

Clay, Marie (1979) *Sand: Concepts About Print Test* London: Heinemann.
——(1979) *Stones: Concepts About Print Test* London: Heinemann.
——(1985) *The Early Detection of Reading Difficulties* Auckland: Heinemann.
Graham, Judith and Kelly, Alison (2007, third edition) *Reading Under Control* London: David Fulton (see Chapter 4 'Monitoring and assessing reading').

CONFERENCING

See also: process approach to writing, speaking and listening, writing

Conferencing refers to the conversations between teacher and pupil and between pupil and pupil to support children's writing. The notion is associated with Donald Graves and the 'process' approach. Conferences can take place before, during and after the writing is completed. At the planning stage children can be helped to make their aims explicit. First drafts – handwritten or word processed – can be discussed and improvements suggested as well as features praised. After the writing is completed a child can review the result with the teacher or another pupil. When choosing samples to include in a child's Language Portfolio there is an opportunity for a broader review of what has been achieved. Sometimes children will mention writing that has been done at home. It is useful to record which kinds of writing the child has enjoyed and to set targets for future progress. In 'Monitoring and assessing writing' Liz Laycock suggests that teachers might mention the writing they enjoy – letters or stories perhaps (Laycock, 2009). Sometimes a small group of children enjoy a shared reviewing of their writing over a period of time. *Using Talk to Support Writing* is an interesting research-based book which combines ideas and evidence on teaching writing with classroom examples (Fisher *et al.*, 2010).

Fisher, R., Jones, S. and Myhill, D. (2010) *Using Talk to Support Writing* London: Sage.

Graves, Donald (1983) *Writing: Teachers and Children at Work* New Hampshire: Heinemann.

Laycock, Liz (2009, third edition) 'Monitoring and assessing writing' in Graham, Judith and Kelly, Alison (eds) *Writing Under Control* London: David Fulton.

CONJUNCTION

See also: punctuation

A conjunction is a part of speech which connects words, phrases or clauses. There are two main kinds: co-ordinating conjunctions and subordinating conjunctions.

- Co-ordinating conjunctions (including and, but, or) connect units of equal status as in: 'Amanda was very tall for her age *but* she was not at all self-conscious'. Where adjectives are of equal status the last in the list can be preceded by 'and' as in: 'The apples were large, red and juicy'.
- Subordinating conjunctions (including if, because, although) connect a subordinate clause to the main clause as in: 'I am going to the open air theatre tomorrow if it does not rain'.

CONNECTIVE

See also: adverb, adverbial clause, adverbial phrase, cohesion, conjunction

A connective is a linking word or phrase that can be a conjunction – 'if', 'as' and 'but' – or an adverb – 'finally', 'however' and 'then'. Connectives that are adverbs or adverbial phrases or adverbial clauses help make texts cohesive. For example, they may indicate consequences – 'therefore'; explanation – 'in other words'; or opposition – 'however'.

While connecting conjunctions join clauses within a sentence, connecting adverbs make a meaning bond between clauses that remain separate sentences.

'I intended to go *if* it stopped raining' (conjunction). 'I had already seen the film. *Nevertheless* I decided to join her' (adverb).

Punctuation can also act as a connective sometimes, as the dashes do in the sentence:

'Helen – late as usual – gave the keynote lecture'.

For more examples, see DfEE (2000) *Grammar for Writing*, p. 187.

CONNOTATION AND DENOTATION

Connotation or affective meaning refers to the fact that some words or terms may bring about an emotional response in individuals or groups. For example, the connotation of the word 'examination' might be an optimistic one for high-achieving individuals and groups – a chance to show what they know and to excel – while for others the word may be associated with anxiety and stress.

Denotation is a contrasting term purely to do with cognitive meanings and refers in an emotionally neutral way to objects and ideas. We may denote the 'blueness' of an object precisely by describing the colour as 'sky blue'. (Of course particular colours may well have a personal and emotional connotation for individuals or for whole cultures, for example red for good fortune in China and white for mourning in India.)

CONSONANT

See also: cluster, digraph, phoneme

All the letters of the alphabet that are not vowels (a, e, i, o, u) are consonants and usually occur at the beginnings and ends of syllables. Note that the letter 'y' can function as both a vowel (ay, ey, oy) and a consonant. When forming a consonant, the speaker interrupts the air flow with lips and tongue.

CONSTRUCTIVISM

See also: assimilation and accommodation, language and thought

This is a theory of learning in which it is claimed that we form mental representations or 'constructions' from our experience of the world. Learning involves the continual building of these constructions so that our mental picture of the world becomes more complex and more coherent.

It is not just a matter of adding to our knowledge as new experience sometimes requires us to reshape or even abandon our existing ideas because they no longer fit with the evidence – human beings had to rethink the notion that the earth is flat. This links with Piaget's notion of 'accommodation' of new information by our existing structures. As Herne *et al.* (2000: 3) put it, 'Learning is about understanding things differently – not just remembering more information'.

The constructivists see learning as essentially active, as a constant making sense of experience in the world. So a school programme that made the pupils relatively passive would not provide the opportunities to interact, interrogate and collaborate which seem to follow as desirable from a constructivist point of view.

Herne, Steve, Jessel, John and Griffiths, Jenny (2000) *Study to Teach: A Guide to Studying in Teacher Education* London: Routledge.

CONTENTS PAGE

See: retrieval devices

CONTEXTUAL UNDERSTANDING

See: 'big shapes'

CO-ORDINATOR OF ENGLISH

See: English/Literacy Co-ordinator

COPYING

See also: handwriting, non-fiction reading and writing, writing

There are contexts in English in which children copy as a part of their learning. I want to look at the more positive aspects of copying before turning to some problems. In the early years children are often helped to trace or copy letters of the alphabet, and this not only helps them become familiar with the letters but also gives practice in holding and controlling a pencil or crayon. There is wide use of handwriting books which help children to practise the key movements of letter formation by either tracing over letters or copying them underneath the printed version. However, as Anne Washtell (2009) points out in 'Routines and resources', it is important to talk to the children about these activities and what they find easy and difficult so that it is not just a passive activity. As children move through the primary years they copy words from dictionaries and other reference sources and sometimes lists of tasks and titles from the board or screen to help organise their work. New technology is helping to save both teachers' and children's time. For example, in the primary school where I was a governor for many years the classrooms now have 'interactive whiteboards' and children can download what the teacher has written onto their personal laptops. The word processor makes editing and proof reading quicker. Nevertheless, there will always be a place for children sometimes making a handwritten fair copy of their most important work.

Now to the more troubling aspects of copying. The issue of passive copying, particularly from non-narratively organised information books, has long been recognised by teachers (Mallett and Newsome, 1977: 100), inspectors (OFSTED, *Annual Report*, 1993: 8) and researchers (Wray and Lewis, 1992; Mallett, 1999). Children carrying out research using secondary sources were often asked to put the information in their own words. However, once an author has organised information and chosen a structure and a vocabulary, it is very difficult to rewrite their work unless the information can be changed and enriched by new ideas and facts. Trying to make a synthesis from several different sources is extremely challenging, even for older students. Increasing use of the internet for

research purposes has added to the problem; children sometimes download pages of information and reproduce it with few changes. In their research for *Reading on Screen*, the team were concerned that 'the more sophisticated research skills of internet researching are not being widely taught' (Bearne *et al.*, 2007: 27).

What then might help? Here are some suggestions which my students and I have found useful for researching in print and electronic texts. (These are also discussed under the non-fiction reading and writing extended entry.)

Ask children to:

- Spend some time discussing what they already know about a new topic, with the teacher, as a class or in small groups, so that their 'prior knowledge' is organised into a framework to receive the new information actively.
- Take some of their own questions to secondary sources, including the internet and electronic texts (Mallett, 1999, 2010).
- Talk to the teacher and other pupils about all the new ideas and information.
- Make notes on the particular topic, if possible from several sources, and write the final account from the notes.
- Make notes on information from pictures and diagrams as well as from written text and construct their own diagrams from information in written sources.
- Write in a different genre to the source used – for example the source might be a report on Tudor food in an information book and the writing task could involve using the information to make a Tudor menu or recipe (Lewis and Wray, 1996, call this 'genre exchange').

Teachers can help by:

- Choosing, and where appropriate displaying, lively resources of different

87

readability levels – both print and electronic – to enthuse young learners.

- Including visual materials in book, poster and CD-ROM form, as a source of information.
- Feeding in new experience relevant to the topic – a video-film, a visit from an expert, an outing, classroom research – to sustain interest and so that the secondary materials are not the only inspiration for children's writing (see Mallett, 1999, end of Chapter 3, for an interesting challenge to the information in a book – six year olds found their classroom snails preferred a different diet to that recommended in the text they were using!).
- Making opportunities for talking about and sharing new ideas (Riley and Reedy, 2000).
- Making writing tasks interesting and, where appropriate, using 'scaffolding' techniques like 'conferencing' (planning and discussion between teacher and pupil or pupil with pupil partner) or writing frames (outline structures of different generic forms) to support young learners (Lewis and Wray, 1996).

Bearne, Eve, Clark, Chris, Johnson, Annette, Manford, Penny, Mottram, Marilyn and Wolstencroft, Helen (2007) *Reading on Screen* Leicester: UKLA.

Lewis, Maureen and Wray, David (1996) *Writing Frames: Scaffolding Children's Non-fiction Writing in a Range of Genres* Reading: Reading University Reading and Language Information Centre.

Mallett, Margaret (1999) *Young Researchers: Informational Reading and Writing in the Early and Primary Years* London: Routledge.

——(2010) *Choosing and Using Fiction and Non-fiction 3–11* London: Routledge (see Chapter 34).

Mallett, Margaret and Newsome, Bernard (1977) *Talking, Writing and Learning 8–13* Schools Council Working Paper 59. London: Evans/Methuen.

Riley, Jenni and Reedy, David (2000) *Developing Writing for Different Purposes: Teaching about Genre in the Early Years* London: Paul Chapman.

Washtell, Anne (2009) 'Routines and resources' in Graham, Judith and Kelly, Alison (eds) *Writing Under Control: Teaching Writing in the Primary School* London: David Fulton.

Wray, David and Lewis, Maureen (1992) 'Primary children's use of information books' *Reading*, Vol.26, No.3.

CORE BOOKS

See also: audio resources, CD-ROM, creation stories, fairy tales, fiction, folk tales, individualised reading, non-fiction reading and writing, novels, reading schemes, short stories, traditional tales

'Core books' refers to the heart of the collection of reading materials for each year group in the primary school. The collection in British schools includes books and materials covering the different kinds of fiction and non-fiction genres required by the National Curriculum English programmes. Sets of books from reading schemes and programmes may be included. The English Co-ordinator meets with classroom teachers to decide on how the core collections should be developed and the best new texts added. Experienced teachers have a sense of what children are likely to enjoy. There are many good publishers' collections of 'core books'. Often these have been chosen on sound principles and include many quality texts. However, choosing books for the children we teach is one of the great pleasures for most practitioners and it is satisfying for teachers to be active in creating their own collections. For many years, Cliff Moon's Individualised Reading Programme, which used colour coding to place large numbers of books into categories to match children's different reading stages, was a useful guide. However, the final guide came out in 2007.

Of course matching child and resource by 'readability' criteria is not a mechanistic procedure. Teachers take account of children's interests and sometimes their prior knowledge of a topic when helping them select texts. I remember a group of six year olds who had been enjoying some work on mini-beasts, talking with great interest about the cross-section of a spider in a book intended for nine year olds and above.

The Centre for Literacy in Primary Education team first set out the principles underpinning the creation and development of a core collection in *The Core Book*. These principles have been applied to the booklists in *The Core Booklist* which sets out quality texts under age ranges and in categories like traditional tales, picture books, stories and information books; it is updated every two years (Ellis *et al.*). Julia Eccleshare's *1,000 Children's Books You Must Read Before You Grow Up* is attractively illustrated and the recommended books are usefully divided into age groups (Eccleshare, 2009).

In their chapter 'Resources for reading', Graham and Kelly (2007) include an interesting section on core books, making it clear that these are the books that show children the pleasure of reading. They recommend that we include books with significant stories that will connect with children's feelings and interests (*The Patchwork Quilt* by V. Flourney and J. Pinkney), books with prediction opportunities (*All in One Piece* by Jill Murphy) and books with secrets (*The Very Hungry Caterpillar* by Eric Carle).

Eccleshare, Julia (ed.) (2009) *1,000 Children's Books You Must Read Before You Grow Up* London: Cassell.

Ellis, Sue (ed.), Lazim, Anne, Moss, Elaine and Nicholson, Deborah (updated every two years) *The Core Booklist* London: CLPE.

Graham, Judith and Kelly, Alison (2007) 'Resources for reading' in *Reading Under Control* London: David Fulton.

Mallett, Margaret (2010) *Choosing and Using Fiction and Non-fiction 3–11* London: Routledge.

Moon, Cliff (2007, final edition) *Individualised Reading* Reading, Berkshire: Reading and Language Information Centre.

COUNT NOUN (ALSO CALLED COUNTABLE NOUN AND UNIT NOUN)

See also: collective noun, common noun, grammar, noun, parts of speech

A countable noun can be singular or plural (for example, mother/mothers; dictionary/dictionaries), unlike a mass or uncountable noun which is usually only used in the singular (for example, health; furniture).

COUPLET

See also: onset and rime, poetry

This term refers to two consecutive lines of poetry or verse which rhyme and/or are of the same length. Sometimes couplets stand alone at the end of a poem, but they can be the form throughout the poem. The Rupert Bear books courageously tell whole stories in rhyming couplets with an alternative prose narrative.

'Next morning, Rupert wakes to hear
A strange sound come from somewhere near …
He peers outside the tent and blinks
"It's frogs! They're everywhere!" he thinks'.
('Rupert and the Raft', *Rupert, The Express Annual*, Exeter: Pedigree Books, No. 63, 1998: 47)

A teacher working with nine year olds provided some prose passages from one of the Rupert books and asked the children to write their own couplets. Then they compared their efforts with those in the book. The children took up a playful approach and produced some interesting results with the touch of humour this verse form can often encourage. This also proved a good context for reinforcing onset and rime patterns and punctuation knowledge.

In Shakespeare's plays, couplets are sometimes used to signal that a courtly character is in reflective mode, especially as a scene comes to an end.

> 'I will go tell him of fair Hermia's flight
> Then to the wood will he tomorrow
> night
> Pursue her: and for this intelligence
> If I have thanks, it is a dear expense;
> But herein mean I to enrich my pain
> To have his sight thither and back again'.
> (Helena speaking at the end of Scene i,
> Act I *A Midsummer Night's Dream*,
> William Shakespeare)

COX REPORT

See also: history of English teaching, Kingman Report, LINC materials, National Curriculum

At the time the National Curriculum was first set up, Professor Brian Cox chaired the committee which produced *English for Ages 5–16* (known as the Cox Report) for the Department of Education and Science in 1989. The committee was asked to focus on teaching English in England and Wales, but their remit did not extend to Scotland and Northern Ireland.

The recommendations had to take account of the model of English language teaching in the Kingman Report (1988) and the format of the assessment model required by the National Curriculum. Nevertheless, the report reflected many of the views of teachers, linguists and educationists who recognised the subtlety of the processes by which children acquire language. Teachers warmed to the report's acknowledgement that literature is central in successful English teaching and that

language is socially situated and used for a diversity of purposes. Further, the needs and contributions of those in British society having a mother tongue other than English were sympathetically analysed. However, the report also introduced systematic teaching and assessment of spelling and punctuation, teaching about the forms and functions of language and the expectation that children would be helped to acquire standard English in writing by the end of the primary years.

Because teachers needed considerable subject knowledge to carry out the recommendations in the 1989 Cox Report, a government-funded, in-service training project called *Language in the National Curriculum* or LINC was established and headed by Professor Ronald Carter. Professor Carter and his team produced 500 pages of in-service training materials designed to help teachers carry out appropriate language study with their pupils. About 400 training courses were set up, attended by about 10,000 teachers, but the Government at that time decided to suppress the materials, saying that they were not suitable for classroom use. Of course the materials were not for direct classroom use: they were to help teachers acquire the extensive knowledge about language they needed in order to fulfil the requirements of the National Curriculum. There was also a feeling, exploited in parts of the press, that the Government felt that the materials did not sufficiently privilege standard English. Yet, as Brian Cox argues in his book *Cox on the Battle for the English Curriculum*, the LINC materials 'adopted a balanced and moderate position towards controversial issues like the teaching of grammar and the place of standard English and dialects in the curriculum' (Cox, 1995: 18). No wonder that Peel and Bell use the metaphor of a volcano to suggest the devastating force with which language issues can break into the public domain. The LINC materials did not disappear into oblivion; they were commercially produced and are available from Nottingham University. Not only did the in-service materials flourish, but several LINC-related books emerged and the BBC produced LINC TV programmes. There was a political decision in the early 1990s to rewrite the 1989 English Curriculum and the revised version was finalised as part of a slimmed down National Curriculum in 1995. Cox regarded the new English orders as having an unfortunate tone and emphasis and making 'the teaching of English seem dull and mechanical'. Nevertheless he considered that teachers could still carry out good practice if they enriched the new curriculum with insights from the 1989 Cox Curriculum (Cox, 1995). Since Cox wrote this book the whole National Curriculum, including the English Curriculum, has been revised – in 2000. The English Curriculum has become even more slimmed down and at Key Stages 1 and 2 there has been a move towards teaching phonics as a major part of the reading programme. A National Literacy Strategy was put in place and set out objectives for each term of each year from Reception until Year 6 in a document called *The Framework for Teaching* (DfEE, 1998). The publication of guidance like that in, for example, *Grammar for Teaching* (DfEE, 2000) showed the trend towards a grammar-based approach to the teaching of writing. In 2006 a renewed *Framework* called the *Primary Framework for Literacy and Mathematics* was published. This promised the prospect of a more flexible and creative use of Literacy Time, but was abandoned in 2008. A revised National Curriculum was put in place in 2013.

Perhaps one of the main legacies of the Cox Curriculum for the Primary years is the emphasis on the power of story and narrative. To give something of the flavour of the Cox Report and to remind us of the role of narrative in becoming literate – something recognised in the current frameworks in which we work – I end this entry with a direct quotation.

'Young children hear stories either told or read from a very early age and, as soon as they have the skill they read themselves. In this way, they internalise the elements of story structure – the opening, the setting, character, events and resolution. Similarly, they come to realise that, in satisfying, well structured stories, things that are lost will be found, problems will be solved, and mysteries will be explained and so on'.
(Department of Education and Science, 1989: para. 17.28)

Cox, Brian (1995) *Cox on the Battle for the English Curriculum* London: Hodder & Stoughton.
Peel, Robin and Bell, Mary (1994) *The Primary Language Leader's Book* London: David Fulton.

CREATION STORIES

See also: Bible, myths, sacred texts, traditional tales

Creation stories are tales about the origin of the Earth and all its physical features, people and creatures. In that these stories deal with and try to explain a great human concern – how did we begin? – they can be broadly placed with myths. We learn much about a culture different from our own by reading its creation stories, but a sensitive approach is needed and indeed myths and legends which carry a culture's religious beliefs will be handled and presented differently from a light-hearted folk tale.

If you want a beautifully illustrated story about why day follows night I recommend *The Coming of the Night: a Yoruba creation myth from West Africa* retold by James Riordan which Frances Lincoln has brought out in a big book edition. Creation stories are included in Anita Ganeri's collection for Macdonald *Out of the Ark: stories from the world's religions*. Ann Pilling keeps the flavour of the oral tradition in her retellings in Walker Books' *Creation: Stories from Around the World*. Elizabeth Laird's retellings in *When the World Began: Stories collected in Ethiopia* shows the strong storytelling tradition of that country.

Ted Hughes' *How the Whale Became and Other Stories* is a classic for younger children while older primary children enjoy the intriguing stories in print and on CD in his anthology *The Dream-fighter and Other Creation Tales* (Faber).

CREATIVE WRITING

See also: child-centred learning, process approach to writing, writing

'Creative writing' (sometimes termed imaginative, free, personal and intensive writing) is associated with the 'personal growth' model of English teaching of the 1970s and 1980s. To some extent this approach was a reaction to the emphasis on grammar exercises in the 1950s and 1960s. Often the starting point for creative writing was a story, music, drama, painting or poetry. More contrived 'stimuli', as they were often called, included lighted candles, displays of unusual objects and tape recordings of strange noises (Basil Maybury's book, *Creative Writing for Juniors* Batsford, 1967, describes some of the more bizarre approaches). In some classrooms children were helped to find a 'voice' to express feelings as well as thoughts and ideas, and writing was produced that was spontaneous and individual in character. In others, however, there was an approach welcoming 'free expression' without any profound engagement with ideas or very much concern about spelling, handwriting or punctuation. For an interesting account of the history of writing in the classroom before the 1980s see Pat Pinsent's (2009) chapter. We are invited to join Mary, an imaginary teacher in the 1960s and 1970s, as she copes with the changing approaches to supporting children's writing.

At the beginning of the twenty-first century unstructured approaches to writing are out of favour in the United Kingdom. Story writing is still an important and enjoyable part of the English curriculum but children are usually helped to plan, draft, edit and proof read their work. There has also been a move towards encouraging, in addition to story writing and personal writing, informational kinds of writing in Literacy Time and outside it.

Teachers interested in developing their own creative writing abilities enjoy the courses on writing poetry, stories and drama for radio and television at the Arvon Foundation which has houses in Devon and North Yorkshire.

Arvon Foundation, The Arts Council of England: www.arvonfoundation.org

Pinsent, Pat (2009, third edition) 'From copying to creation' in Graham, Judith and Kelly, Alison (eds) *Writing Under Control* London: David Fulton.

CREATIVITY IN ENGLISH

See also: book making, children as authors, classic texts: contemporary approaches to teaching them, drama and English, poetry, storyboxes, storytelling

When we think about 'creativity' we might think about the ability to invent something new or to develop an original idea. Certainly we would expect a creative person to go beyond received knowledge and beyond established solutions; such a person may find new ways of solving problems in technology or science or new ways of representing human experience in a work of art. However, there can also be creativity in the way in which we live in the world from day to day. What do we mean by this? Perhaps it is about having the confidence to think critically about the things we encounter and to make sense of them in our own way. There is official recognition of the need for teachers to think about the concept of creativity and to bring 'creativity' into their classrooms; see, for example, OFSTED's (2003) publication *Expecting the Unexpected*. There is overwhelming evidence that babies have the potential to explore the world in an active and inquiring manner (Gopnik *et al.*, 1999). If we believe a creative approach to the world is important we need to nurture this potential and ensure that all children, and not just an elite, have the opportunity to develop active kinds of intelligence from a young age.

This entry starts with a selective review of the work of those who illuminate the beginnings of creativity and advise on how it is best fostered in very young children. The importance of nurturing their creative capacity cannot be overestimated. Here are sown the seeds of those cultural activities to do with stories, poems and drama. Then I move on to thinking about what happens in English lessons through the nursery and primary years and how we can foster creative approaches to language and learning. You will find that I believe that 'creativity' cannot be bolted onto a tightly prescribed curriculum; rather it emerges when time and space are given for unhurried reflection and activity.

The beginnings of creativity

There are developmentalists whose work offers help to anyone wishing to understand more about creativity and how to foster it in children. At the heart of human creativity is our ability to use symbols to represent experience. For this kind of symbolic thinking, which seems to predate verbal language, children need to have reached the stage in their development at which they are able to form images in their minds. Educationists turn to the work of

developmentalists like Jean Piaget and Jerome Bruner to learn about the use of symbols in a very young child's thinking and playing (Piaget, 1952; Bruner, 1986; Bruner and Haste, 1987). When we use a symbol, we can make one thing stand for another thing and this helps us do more than simply experience the world in the here and now. To give an example: a child made anxious by the absence of a parent might be reassured by the sight of their teddy bear because this might conjure up images of being safe in their cot and of the absent parent telling them a story. By playing with the teddy bear the young child makes creative use of time until the parent returns. Having control over symbols allows us to represent aspects of our experience to ourselves and thus to think without the need to use words, that is in a pre-verbal way.

Of course we acquire symbols in a cultural and social context; thus in young children the wish, and the need, to relate to others and to communicate with them is the driving impetus to learning and thinking and of course to acquiring language (Trevarthen, 1998). In *Mind in Society* Vygotsky (1978) argues that the highest forms of thinking are rooted in social relationships.

Evidence about the importance of family and social relationships in the intellectual and emotional development of children has also come from child psychiatrists. Donald Winnicott has written insightfully on the beginnings of creativity which he locates in earliest babyhood. In *Playing and Reality* he illuminates a paradox: a baby's sense of being safe with loved ones who can be trusted and relied on makes it possible for that baby to 'be' and to play alone. It is, he writes, a sign of emotional maturity to be able to enjoy your own company (Winnicott, 1965). We can nurture this developing emotional maturity by letting babies play and enjoy personal space but – and this is important – with loved

93

ones near. We have all seen babies playing happily in such situations, often with intense concentration. If a baby experiences total absorption in play then this augers well for later learning. The feeling of being safe means a very young child can play in what Winnicott calls 'the third area' where cultural life begins. So a child's capacity to enjoy make-believe and story and to be creative in other areas too, including their everyday life, begins here (Winnicott, 1971).

Winnicott did not advise directly on classroom practice, but many teachers of young children familiar with his work have taken up his belief in the need to create a safe and familiar environment. We can see this in the nursery classroom where children are free from the sort of worry and anxiety that saps their energy. Tina Bruce, for instance, believes that the first seven years of a child's life are a crucial time in the development of a capacity for creativity. She argues that teachers and caregivers have an important role in making young children feel safe enough to take risks and be inventive (Bruce, 2004). After all, learning involves being free to make your own mistakes and free from being expected to get everything right first time. This is why early years teachers build an experimental approach into early writing and spelling, and this is why an overly prescribed curriculum in nursery and primary schools can hinder the creative merging of activities which comes from a more holistic approach to learning. One of the most powerful examples of truly creative teaching and learning, the result of an imaginative practitioner forging cross-curricular connections, is celebrated in Sybil Marshall's book *An Experiment in Education* (Marshall, 1963). The five to eleven year olds she taught in a village school in the 1940s and 1950s wrote with exceptional vitality when music, art and drama were combined. If you want to read about good creative practice with very young children, then I recommend Tina Bruce's book

Cultivating Creativity in Babies, Toddlers and Young Children. Young children's creativity, she suggests, takes in all their creative representations, their role play and 'pretending' (often based on stories) and their playfulness with rhyme and language (Bruce, 2004). An exciting collection of resources needs to be at hand, and sometimes we have to bring something into children's play to move it forward and energise it. This might be an item of clothing or an object like a box or bag. In *Foundations of Literacy* the authors give examples of exciting resources – prop boxes, feely bags, magic boxes and story bags – to nurture and extend children's imaginations (Palmer and Bayley, 2008).

What, then, might form a broad framework of factors favourable to developing a creative approach to life and learning? What about:

- a safe and reliable environment in which to think and learn creatively;
- warm and positive collaboration with both adults and other children;
- classrooms where making mistakes is part of creative learning;
- opportunities for cross-curricular approaches to teaching and learning; and
- lively resources including texts of all kinds, play objects, materials for writing and making things.

Creativity and the English programme

The English programme has its roots in those times when teachers and very young children enter the inner world of the imagination and enjoy stories, songs and poems and language play. Teachers of older children build on this early experience providing time and space for reading all kinds of literature and time for talk to reflect on, puzzle about and savour that reading. They support children in finding their own ways of writing about the world, turning away from merely seeing things through the lens of someone else's experience and opinion. Whenever we encourage deep reflection on human issues and inspire children's response to experience through drama or through writing, we are helping the children to be creative. There is nothing new about this, good teachers have always approached their work in this way and will always find a way of doing so. Role play, discussion, storytelling, reading and writing (including book making) interact in providing opportunities for good creative practice but here I gather my thoughts under the following heads:

- creative approaches to speaking and listening;
- supporting creative responses to reading literature;
- helping children bring a creative approach to their writing; and
- creativity and the new technology.

Creative approaches to speaking and listening

The English classroom is a rich environment for all kinds of talk but here I focus on two: play and improvisation and storytelling.

Play and improvisation

One of the earliest and best contexts for the creative use of spoken language is the role play built into everyday good practice in early years classrooms. The home corner becomes a 'café', 'shop', 'clinic', 'post office' linking with the themes of the term. An example of this good everyday practice from Tina Bruce helps us understand the imagination – stretching quality of good role play. Nursery children went on a visit to a local supermarket and on their return settled into the 'shopping area' of the classroom. The children had become very interested in the boxes and bags they had

seen people use to carry their shopping. One of the children had taken a great fancy to the rucksack used by a staff member and integrated this into the role play. The children made 'credit cards' and scrunched up paper to make 'fruit' and 'vegetables'. There are three things of special interest here. The children by improvising bags, fruit and vegetables were making 'their own personal symbols' out of their experience and observation, something that creative people do (Bruce, 2004). Second, the children engaged in a 'shared creativity' through action and through a great deal of talk 'in role'. Third, the nursery team showed skill and sensitivity by allowing the activities to flow and, when appropriate, helping the children extend and develop their play by providing artefacts and props and asking questions. Part of the satisfaction children get from role play is to do with their being able to control and manipulate the play world. This is why children like to make miniature worlds in dens, nooks and odd corners and pounce on themes to do with mini-beasts, dolls' houses or pirate ships. If you want to read more about children's play worlds you would appreciate Vivien Paley's work. She notes some interesting gender differences: girls will tend to put characters in safe places and use a bear or lion character to lead a child home while a boy might have a lion or monster eat someone for supper (Paley, 1984).

Another interesting thing I notice as I visit nursery and Reception classrooms is the creative way in which small children bring in the new tools of the culture into their play. We now see a lot of pretend mobile phone use and a great deal of pretend text messaging and we hear references to DVDs rather than to video-film.

Role play and improvisation continue to foster the development of children's creative and critical thinking as they move through the primary years (Cremin, 2009). Some important contexts for drama include acting out themes from literature and role playing around the human and sometimes controversial issues that come up in class discussion or as part of language study. Drama to explore literature needs to be structured and focused. The careful planning and organisation needed for successful drama work is evident in a detailed account of a series of drama sessions with a Year 2 class based on Maurice Sendak's picture book *Where the Wild Things Are* in Chapter 4 of *Unlocking Creativity*. I was reminded of two things as I read this case study. First, I noticed how a good teacher helps children to combine verbal, visual and kinaesthetic ways of thinking. At one point in the drama, half the class becomes the wild things and the other children take on the role of Max meeting them for the first time. The emphasis is on the visual when the wild things are asked to 'freeze', creating a picture of monsters with frightening claws and teeth. Then verbal and kinaesthetic elements extend the visual aspect when the children taking the role of Max feel their way through the 'woods' and exclaim when they see and touch the monsters – 'They are so big!', 'They are terrifying!' (Fisher and Williams, 2004). Second, I was reminded of how children, when deeply involved in drama, can come out of role and apply critical thinking and discussion to particular issues. In this case they wanted to act out the part of the story in which there is a journey by boat. The children brought all their knowledge about boats to their planning of this stage in the work. Their critical application of what they knew fits with Dorothy Heathcote's notion of taking on 'the mantle of the expert' (Heathcote and Bolton, 1995).

Another example of excellent work, this time with Year 5 children, came out of a reading of *The Green Children* by Kevin Crossley-Holland. The children observed in this research project were from urban schools and found it quite challenging to imagine life in the country and so the improvisation was carefully planned to help them feel their way imaginatively into village life. The researchers give us a valuable and detailed account of how several Year 5 classes were helped to come close to the environmental issues arising from the text through carefully organised drama (Barrs and Cork, 2001: 221–25).

Language study themes also have the potential for creative exploration through drama. I remember a student teacher setting up improvisation about the work of a newspaper office. The children took on the roles of editor, reporters and photographers and acted out a series of situations including a crisis in the office when copy was delayed. As they did this they paused during the improvisation to reflect with the teacher about how they adjusted their language in different circumstances and according to character and gender. There is nothing like role play and entering creatively into a character's situation to show different perspectives on an issue.

Storytelling

Retelling familiar stories and telling new stories to a small group helps children sustain concentration and develop their imaginative power. Young children find 'story props' a useful support in sustaining the momentum of a narrative as they tell the story. Often these props are drawings of the characters in the story backed with Velcro so they can be moved about on a fabric-covered board. Soft toys can also be useful props; as Marian Whitehead notes, the child will tell the story to the toy and get satisfaction from being dominant in this reading partnership (Whitehead, 2007). Other props – things like boxes, blankets and wooden bowls – can serve as important symbols in the story.

When it comes to older children, writing stories becomes more important but storytelling should still have a place. Dramatised readings of key parts of a book can keep the oral enjoyment of literature alive and recordings can be made of these dramatised readings and kept as a classroom resource. You and your class will know the parts of a story that deserve this special attention. I immediately think of the scene in Philippa Pearce's *Tom's Midnight Garden* when Tom realises the old lady living at the top of the house where he is staying is the companion he met in the garden and knew as Harriet, and the scene in *The Midnight Fox* where Tom confesses to his farming relatives that he has let the baby fox escape.

Supporting creative responses to reading literature

From the earliest years and through to the end of Key Stage 2 we want children to respond creatively to quality texts. Their first stories are often in picture book form where words and pictures combine to encourage young children to talk about the story and how it relates to their own experience. Part of reading development is to do with becoming able to read and respond to a range of literature including short stories, novels, playscripts and all kinds of poetry. A creative response occurs where pupils make sense of the different elements in a text and carry this into their own improvisations and writing. Drama and improvisation make powerful settings for extending pupils' responses to literature partly because children experience the situations and interactions between characters very intensely. I have covered this already under the 'Creative approaches to speaking and listening' heading, where I make reference to two classroom examples. In this section I take up two contexts in which children can be encouraged to respond creatively to texts: storyboxes and booktalk.

Storyboxes

Young children often respond to things that can be handled and manipulated and so props for stories, as we have seen earlier, often turn them on to books. Sometimes a simple idea works well. A teacher read Martin Waddell's *The Happy Hedgehog Band* to her Reception class. She brought to the class toy animals similar to those appearing in the book. One group of boys played with the animals every day and she found they were making up stories about them and including details about their habits that they had got from other books and from television. The teacher began to collect other small objects which related to the stories they were reading, putting them into 'storyboxes'. She decorated the insides of these simple cardboard boxes so that they could be used by the children in the retelling of the stories. The children's accounts were often quite unexpected: 'I once heard a wonderful tale about aliens made from the Humpty Dumpty box!' (Bromley, 2004). When we observe children playing with story objects, sharing ideas and making up stories the composing process becomes visible. It is also true that, in the case of the very young, the freedom from having to write allows children's imaginations free rein. The storybox idea can be adapted for older age groups. Seven to eleven year olds will have read more and their stories will be more complex and could make possible sustained story and script writing. I remember a teacher working with a Year 6 class who made atmospheric storyboxes showing ominous wooded environments after reading Anthony Browne's picture book *The Tunnel*.

Chambers' booktalk

One of the best accounts of how talk about books can help extend our response and understanding is Aidan Chambers' *Tell Me: Children Reading and Talk* (Chambers, 1993). Here three sharings are identified – sharing enthusiasms, sharing puzzles and sharing connections. Sharing enthusiasms involves telling each other what we liked and did not like about a book we have all read. Sharing puzzles happens when the conversation moves on to things we found difficult in a story. Hearing what others have to say can help us resolve troubling elements in the book. Sharing connections is to do with discovering patterns which connect different elements in the text – language, characters and symbols – and which can help throw light on the puzzles. Chambers thinks that children who have difficulty in understanding what is meant by 'patterns' might be helped by looking at conventions in fairy tales: three wishes, twelve princesses, three challenges, magic.

Then there is what critics call 'world to text' discussion during which we compare things in our own lives with what happens to the people in the book. Or we may compare what happens in one text with what happened in another book we have read.

If we find some of these elements when children talk about books, then we have evidence of creative engagement and response.

Helping children bring a creative approach to their writing

Children need help in acquiring their own 'voice' in their writing. This takes time and so it is best to think of writing as an evolving skill. On their journey towards finding that 'voice', they need to feel secure enough to take risks and experiment with words and structures and to 'push at the boundaries' (Green in Fisher and Williams, 2004: 53). In this section I consider first how we can provide imaginative contexts for factual kinds of writing in English, moving then to the stories, poems and playscripts which traditionally have their natural home in the English classroom. Reading and writing interact in children's learning and I consider what we know about this relationship and how we can exploit it. Finally I look at the advice of two creative writers who have thought deeply about how to support children's

writing. I discuss Ted Hughes' advice on how to learn to concentrate well enough for a poem to emerge and Philip Pullman's beliefs about creating the best conditions for children's writing.

Imaginative contexts for factual writing

There are particularly strong contexts for factual kinds of writing in early years classrooms (Mallett, 2003; Fisher and Williams, 2004). The home corner provides ample opportunities for labelling drawings and items, writing lists for 'cafés' and 'fire stations', writing instructions, early recounts and letters, perhaps to Cinderella or Postman Pat. This early factual writing by children usually has a clear purpose and a sense of audience, a sense of who the writing is for. Early years teachers ask questions which help the children to become aware of and articulate about their reasons and purposes for writing: 'How do you know that?' 'Is there another word for that?' This kind of metacognitive awareness is, argues Mary Williams, the beginnings of 'creative literacy' (Fisher and Williams, 2004). Of course, we want children to ask their own questions as they use books, the internet and CD-ROMs to find out all those things they want to know. The kinds of factual writing associated with English work for older primary children include writing advertisements and writing as a result of a discussion on say mobile phones, sports days or environmental issues. How can we help children to produce lively and original work which has their own ideas at its centre? Of course children should be directed to material which will help them come to an informed view, but we also need to help them become able to make the information serve their own purposes and argument. The secret is to think of imaginative contexts for their work. Writing 'letters to the editor' on an issue encourages children to express different viewpoints. Book making is well established in early years classrooms and has an important place throughout the primary years. Older children might make a shared print or electronic book about a topic of human interest like smoking, bullying or animal conservation. As well as drawing on information on the internet and in print books, children might base part of the analysis in their book on interviews they have conducted with other children and adults. Experimenting with different formats and graphics – large posters and advertisements, cartoon strips – seems to motivate reluctant boy writers. Using email and creating a website with information about a topic can also enliven and give purpose to their writing. All these activities involve creative thinking and finding creative solutions to a task.

Writing stories, poems and personal accounts

How can we encourage the sort of writing that is closest to the heart of English – personal anecdotes, stories, playscripts and poems? This is language created and enjoyed away from demands to act or participate in the practical events of the day. James Britton calls this 'language in the spectator role' and contrasts it with language to get things done in the world, the language of action or to aid action which he terms 'language in the participant role' (Britton, 1970). Language at the 'spectator role' end of the language continuum may be 'poetic' in that it has a distinctive pattern or form, or it may be 'expressive', the kind of language that allows us to ruminate on recent experience or preoccupations.

How do teachers help children at different stages in their journey through the primary years to find confidence, satisfaction and pleasure in this kind of writing?

Inspiration from literature

It is never too soon to be inspired by quality literature. Those books and poems that tap into children's feelings and preoccupations can prove a creative starting point for their own writing. After hearing the teacher read Kit Wright's 'The Magic Box' (from his anthology *Cat Among the Pigeons*) nursery school children were helped to write about the contents of their own 'magic boxes'. The poetic form and repetition of 'I will put in my box' provided a shape for their creativity (Jones and Mallett, 2005).

Mary Anne Wolpert, Alison Brown and Emma Chapman share their imaginative work with Year 2 children round Mini Grey's playful fantasy *Traction Man*. The children were fascinated by the idea of an imaginary world rooted in everyday things and experiences. They also responded positively to the multimodal nature of the text with its cartoon images and speech bubbles. Drama, talk, writing and art work followed and hearing the story was a rich enough experience to inspire the children to create and write about their own superheroes and household villains (Wolpert *et al.*, 2010).

Writing in role after hearing a story seems to work well with children of different ages and abilities. Nine year old Sophie's teacher felt she achieved a 'stronger voice' in her writing after several opportunities to write 'in role' linked to reading a book. She writes, for example, as the green boy after reading Crossley-Holland's *The Green Children* (Barrs and Cork, 2001).

There is evidence that reading high-quality texts to the whole class and building imaginative writing tasks around their themes inspires reluctant writers. Such evidence can be found in the CLPE's *Boys on the Margin* classroom-based research (Safford *et al.*, 2004). One of the texts used in the research was Charles Causley's disturbing poem 'What Has Happened to Lulu?' Reading this led to a great deal of talk and a lot of writing including such things as notes from Lulu to her mother and emails to a teacher who took on the role of Lulu. Some of the children illustrated their writing with graphic drawings and decoration. What is clear from the analysis is that taking time to talk deeply about the themes in a text and then linking writing tasks to those themes unleashed the creativity of many of the more reluctant readers and writers, especially the boys in the class.

Learning to concentrate

There are different views about how to help children write poetry. Some teachers consider that they need to help them control its form, whether a haiku, a ballad or free verse. Ted Hughes thinks it is more a matter of concentrating on something with all your being and then carving out a poem. He wrote an enormously influential and inspiring book based on a radio series on poetry which he presented. In this book, *Poetry in the Making*, Hughes likens the quality of concentration needed for making a poem to that needed for fishing. He shows young writers what can be achieved when we really think about something, when we bring a high degree of concentration to perhaps one idea or to one object. This puts me in mind of the work of a primary school which makes an annual visit to The Angel of the North near Gateshead where they make notes, sketch, photograph and talk about this one, huge object. They then carve out their poems in the peace of the classroom over an extended period. No emphasis on quick results here.

Mystery, chance and silence

How do we encourage story writing? Philip Pullman, children's author and former teacher, believes that children's writing does not flourish under pressure. Obliging children to write to a strict time schedule is unlikely to result in a profound response.

He suggests three concepts worth bearing in mind if we want to nourish young writers: mystery, chance and silence. By 'mystery' Pullman means that we should not be 'pestering' the story to emerge or offer children a formula to speed them along. 'Chance' is 'unpredictable catching time' when we are given space to pounce on and use in our writing things from every area of our lives. 'Silence' provides 'the freedom to wander at will' and in your own space and, in the depths of the 'silence', ideas and words can unpredictably 'catch fire' and then the 'honey', the successful story, can be gathered.

How might this approach work in school where we have some pupils who are reluctant writers? How can we support them without the 'pestering' Philip Pullman dislikes? Let me try to answer this, partially at least, with reference to the work of a Year 6 class. I hope this example might provide a starting point for discussion. The pupils and the teacher were working on an English project on traditional tales. When they got to thinking about the 'fairy tale' as a genre the teacher asked them to keep in mind that he would be asking them to write a contemporary fairy tale in the form of a sequel to the Cinderella story. The 'mystery' time during this series of lessons was time spent reading and discussing fairy tales in traditional and modern versions. Teacher and pupils talked about the structures and patterns of fairy tales, the kind of language and imagery used and the way they were illustrated. As well as traditional tellings based on the work of Perrault, Grimm and Andersen, they read John Scieszka's *The Stinky Cheese Man and Other Fairly Stupid Tales*. They considered some of the differences between old and new fairy tales and searched for any elements common to both kinds. The children thought that to qualify as a fairy tale, a story had to have an element of magic and the main character had to experience some kind of transforming event. So without giving the children a formula the teacher had helped them find out enough about the genre to have a basis on which to write their own tale. Best of all – he had given the children time to think and read.

Moving to the 'chance' stage, when ideas from promising sources are garnered, we find the teacher providing writing journals. Children could draw on their lives inside and outside the classroom, writing down promising snippets of overheard conversation, jotting down ideas and sometimes doing annotated sketches. They also talked to each other and the teacher about their ideas for the story. I think this helped avoid the superficially competent but rather 'lifeless' writing Pullman dislikes.

Following Pullman to the 'silence' stage the children were given time for extended writing, for drafting their stories and writing out the final copy or word processing it. Nearly everyone illustrated their fairy tale. The final stories reflected a modern world with mobiles and texting, smoking and pop groups, hypermarkets and pop idol competitions. One boy made Cinderella a wrestler – 'the only work she could get'; her marriage to the prince has broken down and she has 'left prince, castle and sisters to start a new life'. The magic element pervades the stories – often in the form of a magic wand or a fairy godmother in modern dress. The main characters certainly had transforming experiences including travelling to a new country, meeting a new partner and adopting a different lifestyle.

Would Phillip Pullman approve? I'm not sure he would like such a strong emphasis on genre features. However, I think he would recognise that these children showed signs of beginning to enjoy writing and to feel they could make a fair effort and produce something with which they were quite pleased.

Creativity and the new technology

New inventions and tools often infuse work in school with energy, but the new technologies themselves will not necessarily make children creative. It is educators who can bring about the new forms of collaboration, the new social relationships and the new forms of educational practice that lift children's reflective powers into a higher gear (Buckingham, 2004). To take just one example, digital video has made it easier for older primary children to be helped to make short films, perhaps in the form of a news review, an advertisement or a story. Experimenting with new media and meeting the challenge of integrating and editing sound, music and moving images to bring a narrative alive are highly creative activities, often bringing a surge of motivation and interest. This kind of project with its opportunities for collaboration and sharing often helps young learners achieve where often they would find sustained concentration difficult.

You will find interesting case studies of creative practice in *Classroom NATE* and in the English Association's primary journal *English 4–11*. Let's take a glimpse at a teacher and a Year 5 class using web-based technologies. First the children looked at an image of the eponymous figure in Shaun Tan's picture book *The Lost Thing* (they did not read the book at this stage). They recorded their first impressions on a Wiki page. You might say that using the web page was similar to making jottings in an exercise book, but the children, including those not normally enthusiastic writers, enjoyed the collaborative nature of the work and the opportunities for designing and illustrating to which it led (Stone, 2011).

When we think about creative approaches to teaching and learning we cannot overestimate the contribution of practitioners. They are the cultivators of children's creativity. It is their imaginative planning and teaching, their capacity to know when and how to intervene, and their ability to lead children further in their thinking and questioning that makes the difference. Teachers need to continue with their own learning and to be passionate about their own interests if they are to inspire the young. I believe they should be experts in children's literature and resources. Above all, they need to believe that creativity – confidence in our ability to learn and confidence to represent our experience – is at the heart of what it means to be an educated person.

Barrs, M. and Cork, V. (2001) *The Reader in the Writer* London: CLPE.

Britton, J.N. (1970) *Language and Learning* London: Allen Lane.

Bromley, Helen (2004) 'Storyboxes' in *The Primary English Magazine*, 9 (5), June.

Bruce, Tina (2004) *Cultivating Creativity in Babies, Toddlers and Young Children* London: Hodder & Stoughton.

Bruner, J.S. (1986) *Actual Minds, Possible Worlds* Cambridge, Mass.: Harvard University Press.

Bruner, J.S. and Haste, Helen (eds) (1987) *Making Sense: the Child's Construction of the World* London: Methuen.

Buckingham, David (2004) 'New media, new childhoods: children's changing cultural environment in the age of digital technology' in Kehily, Mary Jane (ed.) *An Introduction to Childhood Studies* Buckingham: Open University Press.

Chambers, A. (1993) *Tell Me: Children Reading and Talk*. Stroud: Thimble Press (available in a new edition with the companion book *The Reading Environment*, 2010).

Cremin, Teresa (ed.) (2009) *Teaching English Creatively: The Primary Years* London: Routledge.

Fisher, Robert and Williams, Mary (eds) (2004) *Unlocking Creativity: Teaching Across the Curriculum* London: David Fulton (see particularly Mary Eve's chapter on creative literacy in the foundation years, Colleen Johnson's chapter on drama and Andrew Green's chapter on writing).

Gopnik, A., Meltzoff, A. and Kuhl, P. (1999) *How Babies Think* Weidenfeld & Nicolson.

Harris, P. (2000) *The Work of the Imagination* Oxford: Blackwell.

Heathcote, Dorothy and Bolton, Gavin (1995) *Drama for Learning: an Account of Dorothy Heathcote's Mantle of the Expert Approach to Education* Portsmouth: Heinemann.

Hughes, T. (2008, second edition) *Poetry in the Making* London: Faber.

Jones, E. and Mallett, M. (2005) 'The magic box' in *English 4–11*, Spring.

Jones, Nicolette (2003) *Raymond Briggs: Blooming Books* London: The Bodley Head.

Jones, Russell and Wyse, Dominic (2004) *Creativity in the Primary Classroom* London: David Fulton.

Mallett, Margaret (2003) *Early Years Non-fiction: a Guide to Helping Young Researchers Use and Enjoy Information Texts* London: Routledge.

Marshall, Sybil (1963) *An Experiment in Education* Cambridge: Cambridge University Press.

OFSTED (2003) *Expecting the Unexpected: Developing Creativity in Primary and Secondary Schools* London: OFSTED.

Paley, Vivien G. (1984) *Boys and Girls: Superheroes in the Doll Corner* Chicago, Ill.: Chicago University Press.

Palmer, Sue and Bayley, Ros (2008, third edition) *Foundations of Literacy* Stafford, Cal.: Network Educational Press.

Piaget, Jean (1952) *Plays, Dreams and Imitation* London: Routledge & Kegan Paul.

Pullman, Philip (2002) 'A National Curriculum worth having' *The Times Educational Supplement*, 8 February.

Safford, K., O'Sullivan, O. and Barrs, M. (2004) *Boys on the Margin: Promoting Boys' Literacy at Key Stage 2* London: CLPE.

Stone, Glenn (2011) 'www:wikis, word clouds and web collaboration to support primary literacy' in *English 4–11*, No. 41, Spring.

Trevarthen, C. (1998) 'The child's need to learn a culture' in Woodhead, Martin, Faulkner, Dorothy and Littleton, K. (eds) *Cultural Worlds of Early Childhood* London: RoutledgeFalmer.

Vygotsky, L.S. (1978) *Mind in Society* London and Cambridge, Mass.: Harvard University Press.

Whitehead, M. (2007, second edition) *Developing Language and Literacy with Young Children 0–8* London: Sage.

Winnicott, D. (1965) 'The capacity to be alone' in *The Maturational Processes and the Facilitating Environment. Studies in the theory of emotional development* London: Hogarth Press.

——(1971) *Playing and Reality* Harmondsworth: Penguin.

Wolpert, Mary Anne, Brown, Alison and Chapman, Emma (2010) 'Superheroes in the Classroom' in *English 4–11,* No. 40, Spring.

CREOLES

See also: bilingualism, grammar, language acquisition, language variety

These are languages which have come about through contact between speakers of different languages. The first stage in the development of a Creole is a 'pidgin' – a means of communication with a much narrower range of functions than the two languages from which it has come. Pidgin speakers use the vocabulary of the new language, embedding it in the syntax of their original language. It is important that we recognise pidgins as creative solutions to a problem: new language varieties which have come into being to serve the human need to communicate in often difficult and changing circumstances. Most pidgins have arisen out of colonisation and are based on European languages like English, Portuguese and Spanish. Pidgins either die away because their function is no longer needed or, where they become the mother tongue of a community, they develop into Creoles. The stages by which a pidgin changes to a Creole – including the expansion in structural linguistic resources in grammar, vocabulary and style – are clearly described by Crystal, 2010.

There is likely to be some conflict between a Creole and the language from which it is derived. The original language often enjoys status through its association with wealth and education while the related Creole may have its roots in slavery.

There has been renewed interest in both pidgins and Creoles because of the light they shed on language acquisition and language change and indeed on issues to do with whether there is a universal grammar underpinning all languages. In an interesting analysis, Tom McArthur examines some current political issues, for example the role and function of pidgins and Creoles in the transition of some countries into post-colonial societies.

Crystal, David (2010, third edition) *The Cambridge Encyclopedia of Language* Cambridge: Cambridge University Press.

McArthur, Tom (1992) *The Oxford Companion to the English Language* Oxford: QPD and Oxford University Press.

CRITERION REFERENCED ASSESSMENT

See also: assessment, National Curriculum

Where an assessment involves setting a pupil's performance against explicit criteria we describe it as 'criteria referenced'. For example, the National Curriculum English levels of attainment in speaking and listening, reading and writing list descriptions for performance at each level, and assessment is therefore criteria referenced.

CRITICAL DISCOURSE

See also: advertisements, argument, collaborative learning, dialogic teaching, fiction, language and thought, metacognition, non-fiction reading and writing, persuasive genre, reading, reflective reading

When we help children to control 'critical discourse' we help them to think deeply and evaluatively about information and issues, whether they are speaking, listening, reading or writing. I believe a good place to begin is with group discussion. We can help raise the level of discussion by the way we focus it and by the way we intervene to comment on children's contributions – 'Why do you say that?' 'Could there be another way of looking at this?'

When we help children to evaluate information, from whatever source, we need to help them distinguish between what is a relatively objective 'fact' and what is an opinion. They need this ability to make progress in the distinctive kinds of reading and thinking appropriate to each academic subject. Helping them to evaluate will also make them less vulnerable to persuasion by advertising and the mass media. Under the 'advertisements' entry there are suggestions for work to extend children's knowledge and understanding of language to persuade.

Thinking now about reading – we do not always need to read in full critical gear. One sign of a mature reader is that they read flexibly according to the nature of the reading task. They may swiftly scan a text for a date or name, skim to get the main 'gist' of the content, but they need to be able to bring their intellectual faculties into full gear if the task demands the need to understand and evaluate information or an argument. One of the clearest accounts of the different kinds of reading is given by Lunzer and Gardner in *The Effective Use of Reading*. The quality of the texts affects how easy or difficult it is to get our thoughts round the information and arguments. Information books that lack coherence and present 'the world in bits' do not invite us into a critical discourse (Meek, 1996).

Children who have managed to employ a critical discourse in discussion and in reading may still find it difficult to find a critical 'voice' in their writing. One of the most useful series of research studies to help here was carried out by Bereiter and Scardamalia in Ontario in the 1980s. These researchers remind us that successful writers have to do two things: first they call up from memory the content of what they want to write and then they use their knowledge of discourse types to compose the text. No wonder all of us find writing so difficult! Bereiter and Scardamalia have suggested some ways to help young writers using what they call 'prompts'. These 'prompts' include brainstorming ideas before starting to write, making a plan of headings, listing key words and phrases to develop an argument and, interestingly, writing the last sentence early on to focus the rest of the writing. Some of these strategies may help move children on from just memorising content and setting it down to actually transforming the content into a coherent argument or discourse (Bereiter and Scardamalia, 1987). Of course an interest in and commitment to the subject of the writing helps a great deal. Using some of the 'prompts' suggested by Bereiter and Scardamalia, Reedy helped six year olds produce satisfying pieces of writing on the ethics of keeping animals in zoos (see Riley and Reedy, 2000: 147–60). I wholeheartedly recommend this account to anyone concerned with helping children enter into the discourse of reasoned argument.

My analysis so far is mostly relevant to informational kinds of language. There are also different levels of engagement with fiction. Sometimes children, like older students and adults, enjoy reading a highly predictable book by a popular author. Their critical faculties will move to a low gear – but even young children can notice the limitations of an undemanding text. How, then, do we help children enter into the discourse of demanding, quality literary texts? Two scholars and teachers have helped particularly here. Aidan Chambers in a number of his books, including *Tell Me*, shows the educative energy of conversation between developing readers and a mature reader who loves literature. By gentle encouragement and nudging, perhaps some questioning, the children learn how to read and think about different literary texts and the different layers of meaning in those texts. This is one of the books my students and I returned to again and again as it shows so powerfully how a teacher can initiate children into the critical literacy that enables them to enjoy more and more literary forms. Margaret Meek argues that the texts themselves can teach. She has considered how young children come to understand and use the language of books and concludes that the way an author tells a story teaches a young reader how to enjoy and respond. In her book *How Texts Teach What Readers Learn* Meek pinpoints 'intertextuality' as one of the devices picture book authors use to draw in and extend the abilities of the young reader. Intertextuality is the way a text draws on and refers to other texts. She shows how Janet and Allan Ahlberg's *The Jolly Postman* combines a number of texts with which children will be familiar – letters, fairy tales, post cards, invitations and recipes – and brings together a number of shared cultural understandings between author and young reader.

As children listen to or read more texts they have the opportunity to become sensitive readers of literature. They learn, for instance, to relate closely to the author, appreciating sometimes teasing humour and learning to fill the space between words and deducing meanings that are hinted at. The evaluative abilities that are developed enable them to share their insights and enjoyments with others by adopting the critical discourse of mature readers.

Bereiter, Carl and Scardamalia, Marlene (1987) *The Psychology of Written Composition* Hillsdale, N.J.: Lawrence Erlbaum.

Chambers, A. (1993) *Tell Me: Children Reading and Talk* Stroud: Thimble Press.

Gamble, Nikki and Yates, Sally (2008) *Exploring Children's Literature* London: Sage.

Mallett, Margaret (2010) *Choosing and Using Fiction and Nonfiction 3–11* London: Routledge.

Meek, Margaret (1988) *How Texts Teach What Readers Learn* Stroud: The Thimble Press.

——(1996) *Information and Book Learning* Stroud: The Thimble Press.

Mills, Colin (1994) 'Texts that teach' in Wray, David and Medwell, Jane (eds) *Teaching Primary English* London: Routledge.

Riley, Jeni and Reedy, David (2000) *Developing Writing for Different Purposes: Teaching About Genre in the Early Years* London: Paul Chapman.

CROSS-CURRICULAR PROJECTS

See also: art and English, child-centred learning, creative writing, English projects, geography and English, history and English, language across the curriculum, physical education, music and dance and English, religious education and English, science and English

Cross-curricular projects, topics or themes in which the boundaries between the different subjects blur, are particularly associated with the late 1960s, the 1970s and the 1980s in the United Kingdom. The Plowden Report, published in 1967, celebrated the richness of children's response in talk, writing and art work in the best primary project work. Favourite topics for younger children included the seasons, ourselves, food, growth, places and pets. For older children, work was often round topics like change, travel, predators, festivals, town and country, buildings and environmental issues. Each topic included English in the form of stories, personal writing, writing in role and drama and at least one other subject. The seasons would be likely, for example, to include a geographical and science aspect and the perceptions of poets and writers as well as the children's feelings about them. A topic like buildings might combine history with literature. The principles behind this way of organising teaching come from the work of educational philosophers like John Dewey who put first-hand experience at the heart of the educational process for young children. Although John Dewey did not himself deny the existence of separate subjects, many had the impression that the Plowden Report 'saw subjects as rather contrived ways of viewing the world' (Riley and Prentice, 1999).

The best primary project work was lively and imaginative and involved children in worthwhile first-hand experience and in careful research from secondary sources. If you want a flavour of the vitality of children's talk and writing from broad-based project work you might look at two books – both outcomes of Schools Council projects in the 1970s – Connie and Harold Rosen's *The Language of Primary School Children* and Mallett and Newsome's *Talking, Writing and Learning 8–13*. One of the 'contexts' in Chapter 2 of the second of these research studies was a description and evaluation of an exciting study of ships and the sea from historical, musical and literary perspectives. As Primary Research Officer on the project, I was involved in travelling round the country to collect evidence of good practice during this research. I particularly remember visiting a school in Kinver, Shropshire and finding that it was the myth and folklore of the sea – especially monsters, pirates and mermaids – that seemed to appeal most to the imaginations of these nine year olds. One of the images that I remember most is in the first few lines of one of the many poems, lyrics and stories the children wrote.

'Frolicsome are the waves that reach the far shore
The swift eye of a sailor scans the sea.
A strange and wondrous voice rings like a crystal bell-
A maiden fair on the azure sea'.

Another project involved a class of ten year olds in a two-day field trip to a village, Craster, on the north-eastern coast. A visit to the kipper factory, an examination of the landscape and seascape, and interviews with local people about perceptions of their current lifestyles and occupations gave a geographical perspective. An exploration of the ruins of nearby Dunstanborough Castle provided opportunities for historical research as well as poems and story writing.

I have included these two 'snapshots' of project work because they give some idea of the richness and vitality of the work in this earlier period when it was planned and carried out by excellent practitioners. There was a freedom to take advantage of special interests and extend the research of individual children. There was a welcome recognition that language was the medium for learning across the curriculum. Contexts for collaborative talk and writing and for sharing the fruits of investigation arose easily. Perhaps English work fared particularly well as the broad content of many projects gave much scope for writing stories and for improvised drama. History, science and drama often benefited from an English perspective – feelings as well as thinking were brought into play. For example, in the ships and the sea project the children wrote sympathetic pieces 'in role' which revealed their understanding of the hard routines and conditions of sailors through the centuries.

However, there was also work described as 'project work' which lacked a clear focus and did not give enough time to helping children with spelling and language study. Many teachers also felt that by the end of the primary years children should have made a start in acquiring the ways of thinking and ways of validating evidence associated with each of the main school subjects. As early as 1978 official surveys were expressing concern about the lack of coherence in some thematic approaches (Department of Education and Science,

1978) and in 1984 Alexander pointed to the danger of work being *ad hoc* and 'whimsical'. While there was often much scope for differentiation, teachers identified a core of work for everyone and then created programmes for different groups and individuals, matters to do with progression sometimes did not fare so well. While each project might have been well planned and evaluated, how each built on the last and moved the children forward was often less clear. The arrival of a subject-centred National Curriculum changed the emphasis of primary teachers' planning and at the beginning of the twenty-first century project work crossing subject barriers is less common. English is regarded as a separate subject and much of the teaching is prescribed and takes place during Literacy Time.

Nevertheless, there was official recognition of the benefits of linking subjects within the newer frameworks and educational philosophies. *The Primary Framework for Literacy and Mathematics* (2006) encouraged links between literacy teaching and other areas of the curriculum. The frameworks were abandoned in 2008, and the Rose Curriculum, which divided the primary curriculum into some broad areas of learning while keeping some discrete subjects like science and mathematics, was never implemented because of the change of government in 2010. There can be imaginative teaching and learning where lessons are placed under the familiar domains of knowledge, and there is a case for moving children towards a more subject-centred curriculum as children reach the later primary years.

Particularly in the case of early years work, however, whatever the lesson or activity, children need to be helped to get a personal foothold in the learning and their own grip on meaning. In an inspiring account, Riley and Reedy describe how a class of Year 1 children are helped to write about keeping animals in zoos as part of a bigger science topic on living things. A shared reading of Anthony Browne's picture book *Zoo* (1992) had led to some passionate discussion about whether animals were 'happy' in zoos. Because the children's sympathetic imaginations had been put into full gear they were able to write with some energy about their viewpoints. The uniting of science and English in this was most successful in developing children's thinking and writing. At a time when we are trying to improve children's writing and make opportunities for extended writing, an English perspective can put warmth and commitment into some kinds of writing across the curriculum (Beere, 2010). Let me end by recommending an account of a special project carried out with older primary children in 2001 which brought together science, art and creative writing. In their inspirational book *Let Our Children Learn*, Brown, Foot and Holt describe how children's intellectual curiosity about natural objects they had chosen resulted in some life-enhancing writing, drawing and book making (Brown *et al.*, 2001). Projects like this one show that the spirit of cross-curricular work lives on even though the educational context in which we teach and learn has changed.

Alexander, R. (1988 [1984]) *Primary Teaching* London: Cassell.

Beere, Jackie (2010) *The Primary Learner's Toolkit* London: Crown House (accompanied by a CD-ROM which, like the book, explores social and emotional aspects of learning).

Brown, Tony, Foot, Michael and Holt, Peter (2001) *Let Our Children Learn* Nottingham: Education Now Publishing Co-operative.

Department of Education and Science (1978) *Primary Education in England* London: HM Stationery Office.

Dewey, John (1938) *Experience and Education* New York: Collier-Macmillan.

Mallett, Margaret and Newsome, Bernard (1977) *Talking, Writing and Learning 8–13*

107

Schools Council Working Paper 59. London: Evans/Methuen.

Riley, Jeni and Prentice, Roy (1999) *The Curriculum for 7–11 Year Olds* London: Paul Chapman.

Riley, J. and Reedy, D. (2000) *Developing Writing for Different Purposes* London: Paul Chapman.

Rosen, C. and Rosen, H. (1974) *The Language of Primary School Children* Harmondsworth: Penguin Books.

CROSS-SECTIONS

See: diagrams

CUE-SYSTEMS

See also: 'big shapes', grammar, miscue analysis, phonics, reading

The use of a number of cue-systems in making sense of print is associated with the psycholinguistic models of reading of Kenneth Goodman and Frank Smith. They reacted against the mechanistic decoding methods of the first part of the twentieth century, and while they did recognise that understanding of grapho-phonic correspondence played a part, they put the search for meaning at the centre of the reading process. In *The Reading Book*, Barrs and Thomas illuminate the psycholinguistic approach and show how it can inform classroom practice.

There are three generally accepted cue-systems important in learning to read – semantic (or context), syntactic and grapho-phonic. Some teachers and linguists add a fourth – the bibliographic cue-system.

The semantic cue-system helps the young reader to tune into what makes sense, drawing on their knowledge of the text, any illustrations and their wider experience of the topic.

The syntactic cue-system brings into gear a child's sensitivity to what sounds right grammatically and what is likely to come next.

The grapho-phonic cue-system keys into the young reader's knowledge of sound–symbol correspondences, visual understanding of letter combination and sight vocabulary. In spite of many exceptions there are quite a lot of times when this cue-system will help a child work out a new word.

The bibliographic cue-system draws on all that we know about texts, including the concepts about print – directionality of print, distinguishing between illustrations and text and so on – assessed in Marie Clay's well-known test. Our cumulative experience of fairy tales takes us into an imaginary world where the laws of science are not obeyed, where numbers like three and twelve are significant and where wishes are granted. The kind of language used and the illustrations are distinctive and help us link the text to the fairy tale genre. We develop a different set of expectations about information books, which have a particular global structure with sub-headings, retrieval devices and labelled diagrams.

Information from these cue-systems is successfully blended in fluent reading. Bussis *at al.* (1985) use the metaphor of an orchestra to stress that all must be in harmony although different instruments may be dominant at particular times. In the same way, one cue-system might come into prominence because it is the best one to tackle a particular word or phrase. The 'searchlight' model of the National Literacy Strategy (1998) suggested that we think of cue-systems as searchlights beamed on the text.

In 2006 the *Primary Framework for Literacy and Mathematics* based its model of learning to read on Professor Rose's 'simple view of reading'. This approach is founded on the belief that the initial teaching of reading should use the phonological cue-system exclusively for the first few months. The frameworks were abandoned in 2008, but the privileging of the phonic cue-system continues.

108

Miscue analysis is a diagnostic reading test which assesses how well young readers are using each cue-system.

Barrs, Myra and Thomas, Anne (eds) (1991) *The Reading Book* London: Centre for Literacy in Primary Education.

Bussis, Anne M., Chittenden, Edward A., Amarel, Marianne and Klausner, Edith (1985) *Inquiry into Meaning: An Investigation in Learning to Read* Hillsdale, N.J.: Lawrence Erlbaum Associates.

CULTURAL DIVERSITY AND RESOURCES

See also: bilingualism, carnival, dual-language texts, language variety, multiculturalism

The children in British classrooms now reflect the diversity of cultures, religions and languages in our world. The wide range of literacy experience in which many children from minority communities engage has been researched by scholars like Eve Gregory and Clare Kelly (Gregory, 2008; Kelly, 2010). Global travel and media coverage of events across the world make children more aware than ever before of the different environments in which human beings live. It would be surprising if all this did not affect work in English lessons. For it is in English lessons, above all, that children's whole experience inside and outside the classroom is the rich material on which we work. Books and other materials are a starting point for discussion, art work and writing, and writers and illustrators of children's books have begun to reflect this wide diversity of experience (Hallford and Zaghini, 2005). Children whose roots are in different parts of the world sometimes need to see themselves reflected in both stories and information books. Rosemary Stones assesses progress in providing diversity in children's publishing and believes there is some way to go before all groups are fairly represented in what is available (Stones, 2006). There are some fine picture books representing children's experiences across the world and those of newcomers to the United Kingdom. Frances Lincoln is a particularly well-known publisher of these. Mantra publish dual-language versions of outstanding picture books including *Amazing Grace, Badger's Parting Gifts, Owl Babies* and *Can't You Sleep, Little Bear?*

Gillian Lathey (2008) has recommended books for children in her chapter entitled 'Books in translation'.

Of course we do not want recipe-written books, but rather as Graham and Kelly put it, 'good stories which naturally and in an unforced way give our children a sense of themselves having a place in a diverse world' (Graham and Kelly, 2007).

Graham, Judith and Kelly, Alison (2007, third edition) *Reading Under Control* London: David Fulton.

Gregory, Eve (2008) *Learning to Read in a New Language: Making Sense of Words and Worlds* London: Paul Chapman.

Hallford, Deborah and Zaghini, Edgardo (2005) *Folk and Fairy Tales* London: Booktrust.

Kelly, Clare (2010) *Hidden Worlds: Young Children Learning Literacy in Multicultural Contexts* London: Trentham Books.

Lathey, Gillian (2008) 'Books in translation' in Goodwin, Prue (ed.) *Understanding Children's Books* London: Sage.

Mantra: www.mantrapublishing.com

Stones, Rosemary (2006) 'Diversity matters' in *Books for Keeps*, No. 161, November.

CURRICULUM DEVELOPMENT PLANS

See: audit

CURVE OF DISTRIBUTION

See: norm referencing

D

DASH

See also: compound word, hyphen, punctuation

This is a punctuation mark that signals either a pause or an aside or which separates dates. (The dash to link compound words like cross-curricular or cue-systems is called a hyphen.)

Considering pause first, in the following example the dash shortens the number of words needed. So we can write: 'The teacher went into the classroom – it was totally deserted' instead of something like 'The teacher went into the classroom and found it was totally deserted'.

We can show children that a dash can be used to create a more dramatic impact than a comma, as in:

'After so much rain there could only be one outcome – floods'.

Emphasis can also be achieved, as in:

'He wore scarlet robes – a very vibrant scarlet'.

When used as an aside, as in the following sentence, a pair of dashes provide an alternative to commas or brackets:

'Not one child sat waiting for her – every one of them had measles – so she returned to the staff room'.

Dashes can be inserted between dates '2001–2' or words 'The Paris–Dakar Rally' replacing the word 'to'.

Finally, a dash can be used where the writer chooses to miss out the middle letters of a swear word 'D–n!' or not to make fully explicit a well-known name as in 'D–d C–n'.

DEBATES

See: collaborative learning, dialogic teaching, discussion, discussion text, drama and English, plenary, prior knowledge, speaking and listening

DECODING SKILLS

See also: 'bottom-up' reading approaches, phonics, reading

Decoding skills are to do with the ability to translate letters into sounds. Phonic methods put this ability at the centre of the reading process.

The renewed *Framework* (now abandoned), following the Rose Report (2006), recommended that the phonic cue-system be used intensively with beginning readers. This requirement continues. There are a number of phonic programmes on the market, including the well-known Jolly Phonics books. Help in understanding the issues as well as supporting practice is provided in Goouch and

Lambirth (2008, 2010), Layton *et al.* (2002) and Lewis and Ellis (2006).

Goouch, Kathy and Lambirth, Andrew (2008) *Understanding Phonics and the Teaching of Reading: Critical Perspectives* Milton Keynes: The Open University.
——(2010) *Teaching Early Reading and Phonics: Creative Approaches to Early Literacy* Milton Keynes: The Open University.
Layton, Lyn, Deeny, Karen and Upton, Graham (2002) *Sound Practice: Phonological Awareness in the Classroom* London: David Fulton.
Lewis, M. and Ellis, Sue (2006) *Phonics: Practice, Research and Policy* London: Paul Chapman with UKLA.

DEEP STRUCTURE

See: transformational grammar

DEFINITE ARTICLE

See also: determiner

The definite article is the term used to describe the word 'the' which introduces a noun phrase. So in 'The term has begun well and everyone is full of energy', 'the' is the definite article linked to the noun 'term'.

'The' is also used to introduce comparative adverbs and comparative adjectives. In the following sentence – 'The longer the document the less likely I am to read it' – 'the' introduces the comparative adjective 'longer' and the comparative adverb 'less likely'.

DENOTATION

See: connotation and denotation

DESIGN AND TECHNOLOGY AND ENGLISH

See also: book making, language across the curriculum, procedural or instruction genre

We use language to teach and learn in every lesson – to plan, explain, question, discuss and evaluate. In a subject with a strong practical element it is important to communicate intentions and justify decisions. When it comes to reading and writing, a number of non-fiction genres are perfectly suited to use in the context of practical work. This range of material includes instruction manuals with procedural text. Dorling Kindersley's series *What's Inside?* shows how everyday things are made. An excellent book (in print and on CD-ROM) which seems to appeal to different age groups is David Macaulay's *The Way Things Work* (Dorling Kindersley). This explains the structure and function of a range of machines and implements using beautifully labelled and annotated diagrams. Then there are books that use technology to create pop-ups, windows and simple mechanisms linking technology with book making. Paul Johnson's books have been valued by teachers and children for many years, see for example *Get Writing: Creative Book-making Projects for Children* (Johnson, 2005).

However, an 'English' perspective, using story, poetry and make believe can sometimes enrich design and technology projects. Fiction can create an exciting context for making things that characters need. Teachers sometimes ask children to design a boat for Edward Lear's 'jumblies' which will be more effective than a sieve! ('The Jumblies' in *A Book of Nonsense,* Dragon's World Publishers). Countless classes have enjoyed making models of Ted Hughes' character in *The Iron Man*. Older children can be helped with technology to control the Iron Man's eyes. Picture books often inspire puppet making for improvised puppet plays. For example, children might help Mrs Armitage from Quentin Blake's *Mrs Armitage on Wheels* to improve her bike further.

English can humanise design and technology showing how things can be made to help people and make particular people happy. There is nothing like a work of fiction to help children feel empathy for characters and this can be exploited in making connections between hand, head and heart in work linking English and design and technology.

Johnson, Paul (2005) *Get Writing: Creative Book-making Projects for Children* London: A&C Black.

DESK-TOP PUBLISHING

See also: Information and Communications Technology (ICT) and English

This refers to the use of software installed in a personal computer and used for graphic design, editing and printing. Modern primary teaching areas have sophisticated electronic equipment, including desk-top computers, digital cameras, DVD recorders and an interactive whiteboard. The latter is a computerised screen which can be operated from a computer or by touching the screen. Children can present the findings of their investigations in English and in lessons across the curriculum using several different modes – writing, drawing and other visual material like photographs, charts and diagrams (Hayes, 2010). Basic software packages make it possible for children to design presentations which pay as close attention to clarity and to communicating meaning as to presentation. As well as varying the modes, software packages allow young writers and illustrators to vary the media they use to set out their findings – such as film, sound and animation. These can be used for children's electronic story making (Loveless, 2009).

Hayes, Denis (2010) *Encyclopedia of Primary Education* Abingdon: Routledge.
Loveless, A. (2009) *ICT in the Primary School* Maidenhead: Open University Press.

DETERMINER

A determiner is used with a noun or noun phrase and modifies the reference of that noun or noun phrase. Determiners include:

Table 2

articles	a drawing,	the dictionary
demonstratives	this packet,	these apples
possessives	my jacket,	their pockets
quantifiers	some sugar,	both hands
numbers	seven days,	fifty coins
question words	which car?,	which size?

DEVELOPMENTAL WRITING

See: early learning goals, emergent writing, writing

DEWEY SYSTEM

See also: libraries in primary schools

Most school libraries use a version of the Dewey system of categorising books. Children are taught from the earliest stages to look in the reference files, now often computerised, to find the allocated number of a particular book and then locate it on the shelf. Simplified Dewey systems often use colour to help children track down different subjects – history, geography and science. Older children can be asked to make task sheets or wall charts with simple instructions on finding a book to help younger children use the system.

DIAGNOSTIC ASSESSMENT

See: assessment, formative assessment, miscue analysis

DIAGRAMS

See also: CD-ROM, factual genres, illustrations, internet, multimodal texts, non-fiction reading and writing, visual literacy

113

While 'table' and 'chart' suggest a numerical element, 'diagram' raises the expectation of illustrations showing structures like parts of a machine or vehicle or processes like food chains or life cycles.

There are two things to remember about diagrams and other visual forms. First they are, like written texts, culturally situated – our cultural experiences affect how we view them. Second, visual kinds of literacy need to be taught – particularly the relatively new electronic forms.

Computer technology now provides the opportunity to see machines and parts of the body working, but will electronic forms make print texts redundant? I think not – for one thing reading a book is a distinct experience. So, rather than replacing books and print diagrams, new technology has energised book production and made possible highly effective computer-enhanced diagrams and illustrations, particularly in children's information and reference books.

What qualities make a good diagram, particularly for children? Apart from accuracy, clarity and attractiveness, good labelling like that in David Macaulay's book *The Way Things Work* (in print and on CD-ROM, Dorling Kindersley) is essential (Mallett, 2003). There also needs to be good linkage between diagrams and the accompanying written text. If children look at and talk about quality diagrams they are more likely to be inspired to construct their own in a clear manner. Cross-sections are a particular kind of diagram often encountered in texts written for primary school children. They are a feature of texts in several subject areas: history where the internal structure of the buildings of a period may be studied, for example a medieval castle or Tudor house; geography when soil layers or rock structures may need to be shown; science where the internal structure of part of the human or an animal body needs to be revealed (Mallett, 2010: 317). If you want to introduce cross-sections to the under eights in an entertaining way, I recommend Manning and Granström's *What's Under the Bed* (Franklin Watts, in small and big book format), a highly original story about the imaginary journey of two children and their cat through the layers of the earth right through to the burning centre. The big book version would be particularly helpful in showing how a key works – there is a splendid example of a key on the page showing the structure of an ant colony.

How much detail should a cross-section show? Of course it all depends on your purpose. One of my students worked with six year olds on a series of lessons on mini-beasts and noted that they found the simple, uncluttered cross-section of a spider in French and Wisenfield's *Spider Watching* (Walker Books) very helpful at the beginning of the work. However, when their questions about the spider's structure became more detailed, she brought in Ted Dewan's *Inside the Whale and Other Animals* (Dorling Kindersley, 1992 (O/P)). They needed a lot of help in understanding the enormously detailed cross-section of the spider but became deeply absorbed and asked the teacher to read the labels and annotations about the spider's tarsal claws and spinnerets. So, where children have got some foothold in a topic they can tackle difficult text and diagrams, with help of course, to feed their curiosity.

I find older primary children enjoy Stephen Biesty's work, in print or on CD-ROM, in which everything – pictures, labels, annotations and longer written accounts – is beautifully interrelated. A teacher using Biesty's *Incredible Cross Sections: Castle* in Year 6 history work praised the great attention to detail Biesty shows – for example on page 11 even a small corner of the cross-section shows how castles were built and the workers' authentic tools. Opposite the picture Biesty provides the fruits of his extremely conscientious research, telling us about the nature and origins of the materials used to build the castle, the structure and function of the different tools and even the procedures necessary to get permission to build the castle in the first place. The sheer fun and wit of the pictures draws the young readers in, but they find that the information both pictorial and written is far from superficial.

Bearne, E. and Wolstencroft, H. (2007) *Visual Approaches to Teaching Writing: Multimodal Literacy* London: Paul Chapman.

Mallett, Margaret (2003) 'Engaging heart and mind in reading to learn: the role of illustrations' in *The Best of Language Matters* London: Centre for Literacy in Primary Education.

——(2010) *Choosing and Using Fiction and Non-fiction 3–11* London: Routledge.

DIALECT

See also: language variety, standard English

(For issues to do with pronunciation see accent. What counts as a language rather than a dialect is a difficult issue to do with politics as well as linguistics – see Creoles for a discussion of languages that have developed under special circumstances.)

The term 'dialect' refers to a language variety that has a distinctive grammar and vocabulary. Regional dialects are part of an often rich home culture and identify speakers with a particular part of the country and a particular social group. Many children have done their first learning before coming to school in a non-standard but grammatically consistent dialect form. Standard English is a dialect which has acquired a special status for historical and cultural reasons.

The National Curriculum English Orders and the *Framework* (2006), now abandoned, required teachers to help children acquire standard forms in both speech and writing. The intention is that all children should learn to control the forms that enjoy a high status in our society and will help propel them through the gateway to better examination results and better occupational prospects. It is also true that speaking in standard English means that more people will understand – not because standard English is linguistically or grammatically better, but because, for historical and cultural reasons, it has acquired a high status here and abroad and is spoken and understood by a large number of people. There are important issues here. Many teachers feel concern about seeming to criticise the language of a child's home.

Some of these issues are explored in *Introducing Sociolinguistics* (Mesthrie *et al.*, 2009). A sensitive approach would be to explain to the children that it is a matter of adding to their language repertoire rather than replacing their first dialect, but how far does this notion of appropriateness help – particularly in the case of younger children who may still get the impression that there is something unacceptable about their speech? I am not going to pretend that there are any easy answers here, but I think the controversy is less troubling when it comes to written language. If I may bring in a personal observation here – I learnt as a child a wealth of Geordie songs, sayings and social history which remain part of my identity, but I am glad I was helped to control standard forms in writing quite early on in my school career.

Three areas where support may be needed to help children make their writing conform to standard English are as follows:

- Subject-verb agreement, particularly in the case of the verb 'to be' where 'we was' is nonstandard and 'we were' is standard.
- Special dialect words like 'canny' and 'bairn' (Geordie dialect words meaning 'sweet' and 'young child') are appropriate in direct speech where the speaker uses a dialect form, but not so appropriate in general prose passages.

- Use of double negatives in some non-standard dialects are appropriate in the direct speech of someone using a dialect form or in a dialect song, dramatic improvisation or poetry.

We can take a positive approach to language variety by on the one hand helping children to control standard forms and on the other making opportunities in drama and poetry writing for the enjoyment of their first dialect.

Older primary children enjoy studying their local dialect through song, drama and folk tale. They can look at other dialects in picture books, for example Allan and Janet Ahlberg's *Burglar Bill* and Antony Browne's different voices belonging to members of different families in his *A Walk in the Park*. In Chapter 2 of their book *Primary English: Knowledge and Understanding* Medwell *et al.* suggest that intending teachers look at the lexical and grammatical features that show Dickon, in Frances Hodgson Burnett's *The Secret Garden*, is speaking in a Yorkshire dialect. This kind of task can be adapted to use with older primary children and would give the message that regional dialects are worthy of study and interesting language forms in their own right.

Mesthrie, Rajend, Swann, Joan, Deument, Ana and Leap, William, L. (eds) (2009) *Introducing Sociolinguistics* Edinburgh: Edinburgh University Press.

Medwell, Jane, Wray, David, Moore, George and Griffiths, Viv (2011, ifth edition) *Primary English: Knowledge and Understanding*. London: Learning Matters.

DIALOGIC TEACHING

See also: collaborative learning, discussion, language and thought, speaking and listening

'The dialogue in dialogic teaching is not just between teacher and child, as the official "speaking and listening" formulation has it; it is also between

the individual and society. It is about cultural and civic interaction, not just classroom interaction'.

(Alexander, 2010: 105)

'Dialogic teaching' is associated with an approach to pedagogy recommended in the final report of the Cambridge Primary Review led by Professor Robin Alexander (2009). Classroom talk, when well conceived and organised, has long been recognised as a means of making learning interactive and effective, as the work of Jerome Bruner, Douglas Barnes, Courtney Cazden and others has shown. Alexander and his team take this notion further, arguing that classroom talk can and should be the way towards critical literacy and to 'connecting the language of learning with the language of democratic participation' (Alexander, 2010: 111). So what begins in the primary school can lead to the learner becoming able to make connections between the different kinds of knowledge they acquire and also becoming part of a reflective community beyond the classroom. The hope would be that children's experience of deep, meaningful conversation about information and ideas in lessons would actually lead to the kind of critical literacy and political awareness that enables them to have well thought out moral values and the creation of a responsible society and a fairer world. The kind of talk that links critical literacy with democracy has been termed 'accountable talk' and is not a new idea (Michaels *et al.*, 2008). It continues to be, however, an exciting notion that the imagination-stretching power of the best classroom talk could be harnessed to the idea of a truly democratic education and what a 'good society' might be. This was the theme at the 2009 UKLA conference 'Making Connections and Building Literature Communities' at which Professor Alexander gave the keynote speech.

While teachers and educational professionals have mostly welcomed the Alexander

Review, policy-makers have not always been so supportive. The Review was based on carefully collected evidence over a long period and careful analysis of that evidence, so it is hard to see how, as some have said, it is a strike against the teaching of the '3Rs'. In fact, Professor Alexander accepts the need for structure in teaching and learning and believes that whether teachers accept a dialogic approach or the traditional transmission one, children need to be taught about the 'domain of knowledge' of a lesson so that they have enough grasp to participate effectively.

Alexander, Robin, J. (ed.) (2009) *Children, their World, their Education: Final Report and Recommendations of the Cambridge Primary Review* Abingdon: Routledge.
——(2010) 'Speaking but not listening? Accountable talk in an unaccountable context' in *Literacy*, Vol. 44, No. 3, November. Oxford: Wiley-Blackwell Publishing.
Michaels, S., O'Connor, C. and Resnick, L.B. (2008) 'Deliberate discourse idealized and realized: accountable talk in the classroom and civic life' in *Studies in Philosophy and Education*, 27.4: 283–97.

DIALOGUE BOOKS/JOURNALS

See also: diary

These are booklets that accompany the books children take home, to read either on their own or with an adult or older child. Teacher and the adults at home can keep in touch by making a comment when they want to about the child's preferences and progress. Dialogue books are best introduced as a school policy with an agreed format so that there is continuity as the child moves through the school. Children often appreciate feeling part of the dialogue (instead of just being written about!) and many teachers encourage them also to write in the dialogue book if they wish.

DIARY

See also: autobiography, carnival (and literacy), dialogue books/journals, first person writing, reading diaries

A diary or journal can just be a calendar of engagements or quite a detailed chronological record of the writer's experiences, observations, feelings and attitudes.

Such private writing is usually done at home but some teachers reserve a space when children write in a diary, perhaps once or twice each week. This reinforces the notion that some people write for themselves, perhaps to record and make sense of all the experiences a human being has. Children under seven years are often encouraged to write their news in a special book or jotter, but this kind of writing is usually shared with the rest of the class, often at the beginning of the school day. The more private diary writing of older children can be a refuge from a perplexing world and it may not be claiming too much to say that it may encourage the

Figure 7 Front cover of *Antarctic Journal: The Hidden Worlds of Antarctica's Animals* by Meredith Hooper, illustrated by Lucia deLeiris (Frances Lincoln, 2000). Introduces children from about eight to eleven to writing nature diaries and combines meticulous first person observations with superb illustrations and sketches done on site.

development of a strong inner life. Writing a diary in school must always be an option and not something imposed. It is important that the teacher keeps the diaries in a safe place. Occasionally children may express a wish to share a particular entry with the teacher or the class, or even to make the diary interactive by asking the teacher to write comments and reactions. Children sometimes like to give their diary a name – Anne Frank called her diary 'Kitty' – and enjoy choosing a title like *My Secret Journal* or *The Life and Thought of* … The content is up to the children, who may like to include photographs, cartoons and drawings. It could be pointed out that the pictorial aspects should not make the diary look too much like a scrapbook.

How can we help children who want to write a journal but find it difficult to start? It might help to think of what an imaginary pen friend would like to know – about pets, hobbies and special places. Steiner and Phillips (1991) remind us that details about names and why they were chosen can make an interesting beginning. For those who need further help, they go on to suggest a sort of writing frame under headings like: Today I did; Today I felt; Today I felt sad/happy about; What I liked best about today. I have known of small groups of children who have enjoyed diary writing in the literacy corner and have produced their own agreed format. A small group of ten year olds in one school known to me decided they wanted to write their autobiographies. These turned out to consist of several chapters and the children were quite keen to read out particular parts of their books to the class. There are further practical suggestions for personal diary keeping in Mallett 1997 and Graham and Johnson, 2003.

So far the more private kind of diary has been considered. There are more open diaries and journals, the most usual being the reading diaries children keep to record their reading choices (see separate entry). However, some teachers of older primary children encourage the keeping of current affairs diaries and nature diaries. Current affairs diaries are usually written up once a week by nine to eleven year olds. Each child selects an item from a newspaper from home or from a collection in the literacy corner, writes up a summary and includes a personal response. Time is found for them to read out their work and to start a discussion with others. This is an excellent way to develop aspects of children's literacy since it encourages children to look closely at particular models of writing with a clear purpose in mind. Nature diaries provide a context where English and science perspectives can be mutually enriching, as the response of pupils to natural phenomena is encouraged. Younger children enjoy writing entries about the development of tadpoles, caterpillars or birds visiting the school bird table. Several schools have a website to share children's observations. If the diaries are a home project teachers need to inform the parents about what is required and gain their co-operation. A simple format needs to be agreed, but children need to be conscientious in recording the date and time of observations and labelling drawings. Younger nature diarists may find helpful Angela Wilkes' advice about keeping nature logs in *The Amazing Outdoor Activity Book* (Dorling Kindersley, 1996). Finally, the diary format can be used as a literary device by authors of both books for children and books for adults. Marcia Williams helps her young readers imagine what it might have been like to have been a child during the years of the Second World War by using the first person voice in her book *My Secret War Diary by Flossie Albright*. The diary approach is also used to good effect by Jamie Rix in *The Revenge Files of Alistair Fury*.

Graham, L. and Johnson, A. (2003) *Children's Writing Journals* London: UKLA.

Mallett, Margaret (1997) *First Person Writing in the Primary School: Enjoying and Reflect-*

ing on Diaries, Letters, Autobiographies and First Person Fiction Sheffield: NATE.

Steiner, Barbara and Phillips, Kathleen (1991) *Journal Keeping with Young People* USA Teacher Ideas Press, Libraries Unlimited.

DICTIONARY

See also: alphabet, non-fiction reading and writing

A dictionary is an alphabetically organised reference text which defines and gives the meaning or meanings of words. Some dictionaries provide further information, for example about the root and origin of the word and a guide to its pronunciation. The main purposes of a dictionary are to find the meaning of a word which is new to you, to check spelling and to confirm that a word is being used appropriately or to find a synonym.

There is a wide variety of print and electronic dictionaries for children of different ages. Sue Unstead presents an analysis of the thinking behind the making of dictionaries for children. The major role of a dictionary, she suggests, is to be a ' tool for the classroom' prioritising those words that are most needed (Unstead 2009: 8). When dictionaries are revised for new editions some words have to be discarded to make room for other words, perhaps to do with ever developing technology. Some people lament the loss of words that they feel are part of our heritage. There was quite a fuss when a new edition of *Oxford Junior Dictionary* sacrificed such words as 'monastery', 'psalm' and 'bishop'. Another thing to keep in mind when deciding on headwords is that children are writers as well as readers and need their vocabularies to be nourished by encountering not just nouns but interesting words that describe people and feelings – 'enchanting', 'ponderous' and 'joyful'. As Robert Hull argues, dictionaries should sometimes 'invite and enable leisurely wanderings' (Hull, 2009: 8).

Word books for the very young are not, strictly speaking, dictionaries as they are often organised thematically rather than alphabetically. However, they do foster an early interest in words and ideas – see Janet and Allan Ahlberg's *The Baby's Catalogue*. They also help children see how illustration and written text link to make meaning. Young children find Richard Scarry's colourful and detailed word books most entertaining – for example *Cars and Trucks and Things That Go* (Collins). *Collins First Word Book* provides bright double spreads of objects in familiar settings like the kitchen, garden and bathroom, surrounded by appropriate vocabulary. Words are helpfully embedded in phrases in *My Oxford Picture Word Book* – and there is now *My Oxford Word Box*, a CD-ROM combining stories with games, rhymes and word families. Alphabet books are an early introduction to alphabetic organisation (see under separate entry 'alphabet') and therefore are natural forerunners to first dictionaries. Many first dictionaries display the alphabet in upper and lower case round each page; *Ladybird First Picture Dictionary* highlights the letters dealt with on each double spread. A selection of early dictionaries has an important place in the early years classroom and might include Dorling Kindersley's *My First Dictionary*, *The Usborne First Dictionary*, *Oxford Very First Dictionary* and Irene Yates and Chris Fisher's *My ABC Dictionary*. There are some dictionaries that are in big as well as in small book format to help with class-based word level work with the under sevens. These include *Oxford Very First Dictionary big book* and *The Oxford Reading Tree Dictionary big book*. Confused by all the dictionaries with 'First' in the title? I do not blame you: dictionaries with similar titles often vary in the number of headwords and in the general level of challenge they present to young readers. As you might assume, *Oxford Very First Dictionary* is one of the simpler ones with just

300 head words, uncluttered pages and attractive illustrated opening letters which make for a bit of character. Teachers of the under sevens are familiar with the detailed and advanced questions young children sometimes ask. Dictionaries and encyclopedias intended for the younger age range sometimes do not give adequate coverage and explanation. Therefore it is wise to provide also a good dictionary intended for an older age group which teacher and child can use together when appropriate. *Oxford First Dictionary* would serve this purpose well.

In the middle primary years, from about age seven to nine, there are good print dictionaries by the main publishers of children's reference books and an increasing number of electronic versions. Good print dictionaries for this age range include *The Usborne First Dictionary* which includes puzzles and some excellent spelling tips. There are many splendid illustrated dictionaries for children up to the end of the primary years and some children will continue to feel more comfortable with these. *The Oxford Young Readers' Dictionary*, which has over 6,000 entries, is a good non-illustrated dictionary for the over sevens. Most children's dictionaries for the over sevens have 'bold print' head words, phrases and parts of speech, but this one is particularly clear, partly because of the choice of bold print on cream coloured paper. The 'using this dictionary page' is lucid and inviting.

As children reach the later primary years, their grip on certain genre features of dictionaries – the use of phrases as well as sentences, the provision of several, often numbered, meanings and abbreviations – strengthens. As we would expect, in general illustrations become fewer and written entries becomes longer. However, some children, and not only those with special learning needs, continue to benefit from carefully chosen illustrations. I have found children like using *Usborne Illustrated Dictionary* which looks inviting and has a particularly helpful user's guide to parts of speech, and hints and guidelines on forming plurals and using apostrophes. *Collins School Dictionary* suits abler eleven year olds and gives good guidance on grammar and pronunciation. I like the generous spacing in this dictionary; each 'sense' is given on a new line. Another good dictionary for the last year of the primary school and into the secondary years is the *Oxford School Dictionary*, which has over 40,000 head words, with plurals, tenses, nouns as appropriate and word origins for all root words. The format is plain and clear and new vocabulary, including words like 'internet' and 'virtual reality', are clearly explained. For Key Stage 2, *Dictosaurus* (Oxford University Press, 2008) is a multimedia resource combining a dictionary and thesaurus. Quite a few resources have a print and an electronic element – for example John Butterworth and Andrew Delahunty's *Primary Dictionary* is accompanied by a Primary Activities CD for the seven to eleven year olds (this is an edition of *The Oxford Primary Dictionary*). Usborne is well known for its internet-linked dictionaries which include *The Usborne Illustrated Dictionary* and *The Usborne Illustrated Dictionary and Thesaurus* for children in the later primary years.

Specialist dictionaries – for example Dorling Kindersley's *Dictionary of Science* – often provide a good browse, but the lack of A–Z organisation in some of them makes them seem more like encyclopedias.

Teachers and librarians develop criteria for choosing print and electronic dictionaries for particular age groups. Some of the general criteria are similar to those we use for information texts and I have indicated something about what to look for in referring to particular texts above. The best print dictionaries are easy to use and in a clear and inviting format while electronic books, in addition, need to communicate information which may not be linear in a helpful way. If there are illustrations and diagrams these need to be appropriate, clear and well labelled. Written explanations need to be lucid and the words contextualised (Mallett, 2010). It is worth checking that a new purchase covers the vocabulary children are likely to want to check across the curriculum. Clear explanations of words to describe new technological concepts like 'homepage', 'image map' and 'hypertext links' are now required. I would also ask myself if the print or electronic dictionary was likely to encourage browsing and an interest in words. This means including some unusual and interesting words. You just need to look in children's picture books to find some fascinating words which have a strong imaginative appeal, for example 'rumpus' in Maurice Sendak's *Where the Wild Things Are* (The Bodley Head), 'exultation' (of larks) in Patricia MacCarthy's *Herds of Words* (Pan MacMillan) and 'migration' in Karen Wallace's *Think of an Eel* (Walker Books).

New dictionaries in different media and formats, and for all age groups, are published constantly. I have given some examples in the analysis above, but anyone updating their dictionary selection would find it helpful to look at the titles from some of the main publishers of children's reference books which include: Collins, Dorling Kindersley, Global Software Publishing, Kingfisher, Oxford University Press and Usborne.

Hull, R. (2009) 'Wandering worth encouraging' in *Books for Keeps*, No. 176, May.

Mallett, Margaret (2010) *Choosing and Using Fiction and Non-fiction 3–11* London: Routledge (see Chapter 33).

Unstead, Sue (2009) 'A question of words' in *Books for Keeps*, No. 175, March.

DIGITAL LITERACIES

See: British Film Institute, CD-ROM, Information and Communications Technology (ICT) and English, reading on screen, video-film and DVDs

DIGRAPH

See also: phoneme, phonics

Digraphs are two letters that make one sound or phoneme in a word. There are two kinds: consonant digraphs (ch, ph, sh, wh) and vowel digraphs (ai, ay, ie, au).

DIPHTHONG

See also: phoneme, phonics

This describes two vowel sounds which create a new sound within a syllable. The tongue moves to change the pronunciation of one vowel sound to another as, for example, in hear, height and rain.

DIRECT AND INDIRECT SPEECH (OR DIRECT AND REPORTED SPEECH)

See also: dialect, punctuation, quotation marks, speech marks

Direct speech is the written down utterance of a person and speech marks are used to indicate what was actually said – '"Please put the science equipment back in the cupboard as soon as the lesson is over," he said to the classroom assistant'. Tom McArthur indicates how we can vary the reporting verbs – 'said, commented, cried, enquired, observed, replied, retorted, screamed, whined and yelled'. Adverbs can help convey something about the speaker's manner – 'demurely, happily, mysteriously' and so on (McArthur, 1992: 314). We can help children vary their choice of vocabulary by pointing out the possibilities. Reading interesting conversations in stories can be an inspiration to children in their own attempts at writing direct speech. We can explain that what people actually say is often an indication of character and attitude.

Indirect speech provides an account of what someone has said, written or thought and is written in the third person – 'He asked the classroom assistant if she would please put the science equipment back in the cupboard as soon as the lesson was over'.

McArthur, Tom (1992) *The Oxford Companion to the English Language* Oxford: Oxford University Press.

DIRECTED ACTIVITIES ROUND TEXTS (DARTS)

See also: cloze procedure, EXIT model, study skills, summary

DARTs help children learn about the structure of texts and the features of print, particularly if they are carried out in a supportive context. The under sixes enjoy simple sequencing games made by photocopying and cutting up sections of a suitable text and asking children to put the story together again. Of course it is the talk round the task that is so valuable. Favourite books for this activity include *Little Rabbit Foo Foo* by Michael Rosen (Walker Books, reissued 1999), *Oi! Get Off Our Train* by John Burningham (Walker, reissued 2000) and *The Jumblies* by Edward Lear (Orchard, reissued 1998). Bain and Bridgewood present sequencing tasks of increasing complexity in their book *The Primary Grammar Book*. The emphasis is very much on children becoming able to give reasons, both spoken and written, for the way they order the paragraphs making up a text.

One important activity that helps children use their predictive abilities is 'cloze procedure' which requires one or a pair of young learners to complete texts where words have been deliberately removed. Sometimes the words that have been missed out and are to be inserted are given at the bottom of the page. Alternatively, children can be given a text where more than one word would be semantically and grammatically acceptable to fill the gap. Again, talking with the teacher or another child about why some words fit and others do not makes this a highly reflective activity whether done using a print passage or on the computer.

If you want a book providing suggestions for meaningful games round children's books, particularly for five to seven year olds and inexperienced older readers, you cannot do better than look at Helen Bromley's *Book-based Reading Games*. There is advice about dice games based on cumulative texts, track games on journeys in stories and sequencing games. The children in the case studies returned to the texts independently 'with renewed confidence and interest'. There are suggestions for using the games with children with special needs, young bilingual learners and reluctant boy readers. Teachers will find the section on using the games helpful in energising shared and group literacy work. The EXIT model (Extending Interactions with Texts), developed by David Wray and Maureen Lewis, has given rise to activities round non-fiction texts. This approach aims to get children interacting with texts rather than closely paraphrasing them in their writing. Activities include activating prior knowledge, formulating questions to take to texts and communicating information.

Bain, Richard and Bridgewood, Marion (1998) *The Primary Grammar Book: Finding Patterns – Making Sense* Sheffield: NATE (National Association for the Teaching of English).

Bromley, Helen (2000) *Book-based Reading Games* London: A Language Matters Publication, Centre for Literacy in Primary Education.

Wray, David and Lewis, Maureen (1997) *Extending Literacy: Reading and Writing Non-Fiction* London: Routledge.

DIRECTIONALITY

See also: concepts of print, reading

Directionality refers to the reader's understanding of where one starts to read and the direction to go in. This is one of the basic concepts about print assessed by Marie Clay's Early Concepts of Print procedure.

Clay, Marie (1979, second edition) *The Early Assessment of Reading Difficulties* Auckland: Heinemann.

DISCOURSE ANALYSIS

See also: collaborative learning, dialogic teaching, field of discourse, mode, speaking and listening, speech act, tenor

Discourse analysis refers to the systematic categorisation of naturally occurring speech. A highly influential scheme for illuminating classroom discourse or conversation was devised by the linguists Sinclair and Coulthard in 1975. They divided spoken exchanges into three main categories:

- initiation: the teacher might ask: 'What are words called that tell us more about a noun?'
- response: a child might answer: 'An adjective?'
- feedback: the teacher assesses what the child has said: 'That's right. Good!'

This category system helped us understand roles and functions rather than intentions and meanings and it is important to bear in mind that the way the utterances are categorised depends, to some extent, on individual interpretation. (For a helpful review of the history of discourse analysis see Bunting, 2000: Chapter 3.)

Another great influence on language analysis, both spoken and written, in the United Kingdom was the functional approach of M.A.K. Halliday. The 'functions' are essentially social in Halliday's work. He stresses the situational restraints on language in terms of field (topic of the communication), tenor (relationship of participants – relative status, age and roles) and mode (medium for the communication). This functional model led to the 'Language in Use' approach to language study in some secondary schools. Children worked with spoken and written texts arising out of 'real' situations.

In the late 1980s, Edwards and Mercer carried out work on the creation of what they termed 'common knowledge' between teachers and children (Edwards and Mercer, 1987). They were interested in how this 'common knowledge' was constructed and the role of context in its creation. Two kinds of knowledge were identified: 'ritual knowledge' and 'principled knowledge'. Teachers initiate children into the conventions for expressing 'ritual knowledge' which consists of giving a 'right' answer expressed appropriately. 'Principled knowledge' is more to do with carving out an explanation which depends on a well thought out understanding of information and issues. The 'rules' of discourse were, according to Edwards and Mercer, learnt mainly in the classroom. Many teacher researchers were encouraged by the work of discourse analysts to tape-record classroom talk in an attempt to make explicit the dynamics of learning. As well as noting the findings of Edwards and Mercer, teachers were also inspired by earlier work on classroom conversations carried out in the 1960s by Douglas Barnes *et al.* These latter researchers suggested that a continuum of questions that teachers and children might ask ranged from those that were closed and required a 'right' answer and those that were 'open' and invited an opinion. The analysis was energised by lively transcripts from different classrooms (Barnes *et al.*, 1969). This approach to reflecting on classroom discourse reinforced the notion that even knowledge passed on by the teacher or a book has to be constructed anew by the learner. So, while children take on the cultural resources of their society, passed on partly by the school, there should be room for their own creative solution to problems and challenges.

An interest in classroom talk and how it illuminated gender issues was reflected in a number of studies in the 1970s and 1980s. The way teachers – often unconsciously through gesture and facial expression as well as what they actually say – shape the responses of particular children to the possible disadvantage of girls has been studied by researchers like Swann and Graddol (1989).

In the 1970s and 1980s there was an interest in the talk of preschool children in natural settings as well as talk in nursery and Reception classrooms. Gordon Wells and his researchers on the Bristol University project *Language at Home and School* recorded children's everyday conversations with their parents, caregivers and siblings to try to identify what kinds of language experience led to literacy success later on. The books which were an outcome of the longitudinal project, *The Meaning Makers* (1987) for example, emphasise the power of spoken language in bringing about learning. The importance of stories, read or told to children, as precursors of literacy is established by this research. The value of talk round written texts, particularly fiction, has been demonstrated by the classroom examples insightfully evaluated in Aidan Chambers' (1993) book *Tell Me: Children, Reading and Talk*. The role of talk in developing writing has been explored in a most interesting study which was an outcome of HEI and practitioner collaboration. Talk as a generator of ideas, the potential of 'oral rehearsal' and the value of metacognition in thinking and talking about writing are all areas covered in this thoughtful account (Fisher *et al.*, 2010).

Teachers continue to be interested in classroom talk but more as a way of learning and evidence of learning than as a way of analysing teacher and pupil roles. Talk episodes may be recorded to show children's progress in social aspects of speaking and listening, like turn taking and responding to the contributions of others, and as evidence of progress in planning, hypothesising and presenting an argument.

Barnes, Douglas, Britton, James and Rosen, Harold (1969) *Language, the Learner and the School* Harmondsworth: Penguin.

Bunting, Rebecca (2000, second edition) *Teaching About Language in the Primary Years* London: David Fulton.

Chambers, Aidan (1993) *Tell Me: Children, Reading and Talk* Stroud: The Thimble Press.

Edwards, D. and Mercer, N. (1987) *Common Knowledge: The Development of Understanding in the Classroom* London: Methuen.

Fisher, Ros, Myhill, Debra, Jones, Susan and Larkin, Shirley (2010) *Using Talk to Support Writing* London: Sage Publications.

Sinclair, J. and Coulthard, R. (1975) *Towards an Analysis of Discourse* London: Oxford University Press.

Swann, J. and Graddol, D. (1989) 'Gender inequalities in classroom talk' in *Gnosis*, Issue 14, London: LDA.

Wells, Gordon (1987) *The Meaning Makers: Children Learning Language and Using Language to Learn* London, Sydney, Auckland and Toronto: Hodder & Stoughton.

DISCUSSION

See also: collaborative learning, dialogic teaching, discussion text, drama and English, plenary, prior knowledge, speaking and listening

This implies an exchange of viewpoints and posing of open rather than closed questions. At every stage, discussion in class and group settings is a major way of making sense of all kinds of information, often derived from reading, in every lesson. It can also be a potent evaluative tool: for example children assess their learning – discussing perhaps the quality of resources used and the success of an episode of improvised drama. In English, fiction is an important starting point for the exchange of views on for example plot, characters, motivation, language use and ethical issues. One of the most useful and exciting books about this is Aidan Chambers' *Tell Me: Children Reading and Talk*.

Chambers, Aidan (1993) *Tell Me: Children Reading and Talk* Stroud: The Thimble Press.

DISCUSSION TEXT

See also: collaborative learning, dialogic teaching, genre, non-fiction reading and writing

This kind of text, one of the six non-fiction genres in the United Kingdom National Literacy Strategy *Framework*, presents different viewpoints on a topic. Children can talk about which argument they find most convincing and produce their own discussion texts to present to others. Although the Literacy Strategy *Framework* has been dropped, discussion text is still accepted as a category within the 'argument' genre.

Children are more likely to write with some passion and commitment if they have interest invested in a topic. So controversial local issues – should the new sports ground be built?; or school issues – should mobile telephones be allowed in school? are promising sources of topic. Children can then become convinced that if you want to argue a case it is a good idea to anticipate what might be said against the cause. In writing a discussion text, children are encouraged to write both sides of an argument in as fair a manner as possible and then, at the end, they can say why, on balance, they favour one viewpoint over the other.

Many lively discussions arise out of reading books or watching serialisation on television or film. After reading Michael Morpurgo's *Kensuke's Kingdom* ten year olds discussed both the benefits and possible disadvantages of families sailing round the world. The children had strong feelings of engagement with the themes of the book because they had spent time discussing them with the teacher. This meant they had a more than superficial grasp of the issues. After writing lists of benefits and disadvantages to guide their accounts, they were able to transfer the liveliness of their talk to their writing.

Topics for children's own 'discussion' writing might include the advantages and disadvantages of sports days, school uniform, dogs in parks, mobile phones and keeping pets.

DISPLAYS

See also: libraries in primary schools, reading environment, writing, writing corner/area

Good displays of books and resources and related children's work in the school entrance hall, the library and the classrooms encourage interest in reading and writing. They also invite comment and are a special way of communicating and sharing our knowledge about enjoying reading. All the books we select should of course be good of their kind. The following list brings together what I have seen and read over the years, which might usefully be held in mind when displays are set up to promote English work.

Finding a focus

It is best to present something coherent and not overcomplicated:

- Books/resources by one author/illustrator/publisher; on one theme – adventure, science fiction, spiders; or a

125

particular kind of book – for example poetry anthologies, short stories or non-fiction.

- Different versions of the same traditional tale. (I remember an excellent display made by a Year 5 class and their teacher on different tellings of *Red Riding Hood*. Some of the children's modern versions of the story were included.)
- One book in the centre of the display and reviews by the class and the teacher surrounding it.
- The ten favourite books of one class together with children's short reviews. (Tyrrell and Gill (2000) suggest we call such a display 'A Really Good Book'.)
- Favourite books from the childhoods of teachers and other adults in the school.
- Year 5 or Year 6 display for younger children of their favourite early books with annotation on stand up cards.
- New books and books short listed for a prize like the Carnegie Medal, Kate Greenaway Award or Orbus Pictus Information Book Award.
- Books on a particular country or culture or on a topical event or festival; dual-language books.
- Books related to film or television.
- Books children have made.
- Children's writing of a particular kind, attractively mounted.

Creating visual appeal

If you remember displays that impressed you, they tend to be uncluttered, fresh looking and with a focal point:

- An eye-catching book cover or an object like a box or vase that fits with the theme of a story might intrigue.
- We can get ideas from shop windows and museums about the grouping of items. Some imaginative teachers use boxes, packing cases, easels and coloured paper or a curtain as a back drop, but we do need to avoid a cluttered effect.

- On the whole, well-selected books attractively displayed can be enough. If we make displays too elaborate we might not change them as frequently as is wise. As Chambers (1991: 24) remarks 'every display has a natural life-span'.

Involving children in the display

- Copies of books should be readily available once children have been tempted by the display.
- A lively talk about the displayed resources in assembly can excite children's interest.
- Teachers can take the children to visit a display, read snippets from the books and talk to the children about them. There is much helpful advice about how to interest children in book displays in Bakewell, 2010.
- As well as regular small-scale displays, once or twice a year schools often make a large-scale set of displays involving parents, teachers and friends of the school in the preparation.

Bakewell, Lucy (2010) *Off the Shelf: How to Run a Successful Primary School Library and Promote Reading* London: Carel Press (has some downloadable resources).

Chambers, Aidan (1991) *The Reading Environment: How Adults Help Children Enjoy Books* Stroud: The Thimble Press (Chapter 5). (The Thimble Press have brought out a new edition which combines *The Reading Environment* with the companion book *Tell Me: Children, Reading, and Talk* Stroud: The Thimble Press, 2011.)

Tyrrell, Jenny and Gill, Narinderjit (2000) *Coordinating English at Key Stage 1* London: Falmer Press (Chapter 2).

DOMESTIC AND FAMILY NOVELS

See also: classics, fiction, history of children's literature, realism

Domestic and family novels, as we would expect, explore life in the familiar settings of the home, garden, local school and neighbourhood. Two books by Frances Hodgson Burnett – *The Secret Garden* (1910) and *The Little Princess* (1905) – which explore, amongst other things, relationships with family and friends, still have a continuing appeal for children in the primary years. The *William* stories, written by Richmal Crompton from the 1920s right up until her death in 1969, are about a socially privileged little boy, but he seems to have a universal appeal – perhaps it is his pitting himself against his parents and other adults that attracts young readers. Another enduring example of this genre is about people at the other end of the social scale – *The Family from One-End Street* by Eve Garnett (1937). It follows the everyday happenings in the household of a dustman and his washerwoman wife. Some have criticised it for being condescending. John Rowe Townsend comments, 'People from higher up the social scale are terribly nice to the Ruggleses; and the Ruggleses know their place' (Townsend, 1995: 150). In spite of such reservations the book remains in print and many children seem to enjoy the stable, supportive family world portrayed and the amusing things that happen – Rose burning a petticoat when she does the ironing and Kate losing her hat. As Peter Hunt points out, 'the period flavour is so strong that it is very difficult to judge how far the Ruggles family are being patronised' (Hunt, 1995: 218).

Perhaps we think of Arthur Ransome's *Swallows and Amazons*, set in the 1920s and 1930s, as adventure stories – but while making the children independent during their holiday activities, Ransome also sets them in a secure middle-class world. So while the books are about an escape from everyday family life, the domestic environment remains in the background.

Just because events take place in a homely setting does not preclude the occurrence of dramatic or even fantasy events. The story in Philippa Pearce's *Tom's Midnight Garden* (1958) takes place in a family home and young readers learn about the difficulties of a childless couple when they agree to look after a young relative. The novel explores in a profound way the nature of friendship. However, it is also a story about a series of journeys back to another time. Pearce's story for younger children *The Battle of Bubble and Squeak* also has lively events based round home: two messy gerbils infuriate the adults in the family.

The stories in Nina Bawden's novels are often in domestic and family settings. *Carrie's War* (1973) shows us how evacuees cope with separation from their parents and adjustment to strange domestic circumstances. *The Peppermint Pig* (1975) takes us through a year in the life of the Greengrass family after the father of the household leaves to seek his fortune in America. Bawden's novels support Victor Watson's assertion that family stories need not be cosy (Watson, 2001).

Two contemporary writers take on such unsettling themes as family tensions and breakdowns, inadequate parenting, changes of circumstances and poverty: Anne Fine and Jacqueline Wilson. In *The Granny Project* Anne Fine takes on the painful issue of a family trying to cope with an elderly and rather irritating relative. No easy answers here. Jacqueline Wilson has created an endearing but sometimes infuriating heroine, Tracy Beaker, who has to survive in a care home. To help us reflect on how authors deal with these contemporary issues in fiction, I recommend *Family Fictions: Contemporary Classics of Children's Fiction* (Tucker and Gamble, 2001).

Hunt, Peter (ed.) (1995) *Children's Literature: An Illustrated History* Oxford: Oxford University Press.

Townsend, John Rowe (1995) *Written for Children: An Outline of English Language*

Children's Literature London: The Bodley Head.

Tucker, Nicholas and Gamble, Nikki (2001) *Family Fictions: Contemporary Classics of Children's Fiction* London: Continuum.

Watson, Victor (2001) *The Cambridge Guide to Children's Books in English* Cambridge: Cambridge University Press.

DRAFTING

See also: composition, conferencing, editing, process approach to writing, proof reading, transcriptional aspects of writing, writing

Drafting involves taking ideas from a plan and developing them into written text. The work of both Donald Graves (1983) and Frank Smith (1982) has illuminated the role of drafting in the process of children's writing. Graves in particular argues that writing, at any rate that which is likely to go beyond the superficial, involves several different stages from the 'pre-composition' to 'publication' of the fair copy. In the United Kingdom the sequence was often: plan, draft, revise, proof read and present. Shared writing has been a good context in which to model how the writer moves through the stages. The plan can be oral or written down and then, using this, the writer shapes his or her thoughts in a draft either on paper or on the computer. The revision stage offers a chance to reshape ideas and thoughts to better effect and to add in anything missed. Proof reading concentrates on secretarial errors and it sometimes helps to have proof reading partners as it may be easier to spot someone else's mistakes. Finally, children present their work in fair copy. Two things have a considerable effect on the content, organisation and style of writing. First, the writer needs to have a clear idea of the purpose of the writing task and, second, they need to have a sense of the audience for their work. Bearing these two things in mind is helpful in following the sequence outlined above and bringing writing to final draft.

As children move through the school years require 'first draft' responses, children need some practice in planning 'in their heads' and writing a single draft.

There is also an issue over how often we should ask children to take a piece of writing through all the drafting stages. Here we need to have a sense of proportion. While it certainly gives value to writing if some of the work children do is taken through the stages discussed above – plan, draft, revise, proof read and present – there are occasions when a first draft is all that is required. I have found that struggling young writers find too much redrafting de-motivating.

Graves, Donald (1983) *Writing: Teachers and Children at Work* Portsmouth, N.H.: Heinemann Educational Books.

Smith, Frank (1982) *Writing and the Writer*. Portsmouth, N.H.: Heinemann Educational Books.

DRAMA AND ENGLISH

See also: creativity in English, genre, play and language and literacy, speaking and listening, writing

In this entry the use of drama and role play as powerful approaches to teaching aspects of English are considered. Drama and role play are important agents for learning in every lesson. Indeed, where drama has its own place in the weekly programme, teachers may use a drama lesson to develop a theme from history, geography, science or other curriculum areas. Where English is concerned, drama and role play have a special value: to develop spoken language in a range of contexts; to explore themes arising from children's experiences, anecdotes and from texts of all kinds; and to encourage reading and writing for different purposes and audiences. In doing all this we must remember that language is socially situated and the different kinds and usages have developed to serve different societal purposes. This complexity can be explored through drama. While the benefits of drama and role play to children's language and learning are undisputed, it is also valuable experience in its own right; it is the intense involvement in the created situations which leads to worthwhile and varied use of language. Feelings as well as thoughts are important in English and improvisation allows the exploration of many human situations that are part of growing up and often include painful episodes like separation from loved ones and difficulties with friends. Drama can also help children explore interesting aspects of cultural diversity where a story or information book might be a starting point.

Good primary practitioners have always used drama to energise English work. It was encouraging to find drama brought firmly into the 1995 National Curriculum orders and its place has been made even more secure in later revisions. To some extent there has been a softening of the old conflict between drama as a learning process and drama as a product to be presented. It is more helpful to regard these as two complementary aspects, each coming into strong focus at particular times for particular purposes. For example, teachers and pupils studying a play might explore a situation or issue through improvisation. Teachers may also help children to script an improvisation which has stabilised. A scripted improvisation could be the basis for a performance for parents, friends of the school and other children.

Role play in the early years (three to six years)

Children enjoy spontaneous role play from an early age; it allows the expression of feelings, attitudes and opinions in a relatively secure context. Early years teachers build opportunities for role play into their long-term planning and thereby achieve some of the language and literacy objectives in the early learning goals. In the context of imaginative play children can take on different roles. This creates opportunities for using spoken and written language for different purposes and thus makes a considerable contribution to language development.

Young children need space and time for role play. Changing the location of the activity and adding appropriate props increases the range of possibilities. The teacher and nursery team can intervene to link the play with literacy experiences and other learning. They can develop situations out of stories and anecdotes children bring to the classroom. Areas available for role play can be transformed into, for example, a café, office of a fire station, builder's yard, post office, shop, train station, clinic or garden centre.

With encouragement, young children will attempt writing linked to the theme of the role play. Five year olds learning about fire fighters might have an office with the duty rotas, posters about fire and safety, forms to fill in, records of fires extinguished, advertisements for fire equipment, instructions for use of fire fighting aids and some cards and letters of thanks from people they had helped. In fact, writing appropriate labels, posters and so on is part of helping the children understand the context for their role play.

A home corner also provides a non-threatening context for all kinds of writing to support role play activities like writing stories to read to dolls, menus for the toys' meals, greetings cards, shopping lists and letters to build into play situations. An outstanding project in which six year olds built much of their talk and writing for a term round the life of Mr Togs (a life-sized doll in charge of the classroom shop) is described and evaluated in *Mr Togs the Tailor* published by the Scottish Consultative

Council on the Curriculum in 1987. This book is now out of print, but the case study is one of the most interesting examples of good practice I have ever come across.

Early years teams become skilled in observing children's role play and judging where to intervene to help the children extend their activity. Four year olds who had listened to a reading of Allan and Janet Ahlberg's picture book *Burglar Bill* built aspects of the story into their play. To extend the children's reflection on the key issues – do ex-burglars make good parents? – one of the nursery teachers dressed up as Burglar Betty and, holding a doll, answered the children's questions in role. This is an example of 'hot seating' which is a technique useful for any age group when a teacher or child 'in role' is questioned by others. A student teacher working in the nursery said she will never forget the children's excitement and the profundity of their questions. For other examples of good imaginative drama work with this age group, see Ackroyd and Bolton, 2005.

Improvisation and drama at Key Stages 1 and 2

Contexts for speaking and listening

One challenge for teachers is to find ways of helping children become competent in the range of speech situations they will encounter as adults. Some of these are unlikely to arise naturally in the course of classroom work or to be part of the day-to-day experience of the child. Providing opportunities for dramatic improvisation, which is a development from the role play of younger children, is a valuable way of encouraging children to use different kinds of spoken language for different audiences and purposes. Examples include: persuading local councillors that provision of a park for the village community is a priority;

asking the police to help find a lost bicycle; children and adults in conflict over having a family pet. Often inspiration for these comes from a story. For example, one of my students helped children base an improvisation on the theme in James Simon's book *Dear Greenpeace* about a child who is convinced she has a whale in her garden pond. Particularly if you work with older primary children you will find inspiration in Jenny Griffiths' book *An Early Start to Drama*. I have seen a number of very successful series of lessons based on the waste dump idea. For example, people oppose the council's plan to have a chemical waste dump on the boundaries of a small town.

To extend their work and make it worthwhile, sensitive intervention by the teacher is necessary. This can be done by direct support and advice or by the teacher stepping into a role – perhaps as a key figure like a monarch or as a discordant voice such as a dissident peasant. Dorothy Heathcote, a great teacher of drama to all age groups and people of widely varying abilities and needs, showed how a teacher can energise children's improvisation by taking up a role.

Drama is essentially a co-operative activity and helps children listen, collaborate and learn from each other and to be aware of each other's needs. The discussion to plan an improvisation, the improvisation itself and its evaluation all help children to become more confident users of the spoken language. Drama benefits from having space and some basic resources like an overhead projector, musical instruments, a tape recorder, wooden blocks to create structures and some simple props. However, it can sometimes take place in the classroom. Issues arising from books can be explored in pairs, each child taking up a different role. While the emphasis is on the value of the process, I find children love to show their work to the class. Duologue work can lead to scripting.

Contexts for reading and writing

In English, texts can lead to dramatic improvisation which in turn inspires closer involvement with the story and to lively writing (Ackroyd and Bolton, 2005). Picture books, for example David McKee's *Not Now Bernard*, Maurice Sendak's *Where the Wild Things Are*, T.T. Khing's *Where is the Cake?* (and *Where is the Cake Now?*) and Mini Grey's *Traction Man* all have much potential for younger children's reflection, drama and writing. Colleen Johnson worked with children on Maurice Sendak's *Where the Wild Things Are*. The series of lessons round Max's journey involved the children in episodes of dramatic improvisation which were truly imagination-stretching experiences and led to constant revisiting of the book (Johnson, 2005). Many picture books make possible older children's involvement in dilemmas and issues. Anthony Browne's *The Tunnel* with its theme of sibling rivalry and Carol Ann Duffy's engaging modern fairy tale *The Tear Thief* can both be enjoyed by children of different age groups, including older primary school children. Other picture books which lend themselves to older children's drama and writing include some of Shaun Tan's enigmatic books – *Lost Thing*, for example, which starts with a boy playing on the beach, 'That's when I first saw the thing', and Helen Ward's books, some of which take up environmental issues in an oblique way as does *Varmints* which explores unwelcome changes. Contemporary picture books can be both intriguing and puzzling but we should not underestimate children's ability to find their own meanings from reading them and, importantly, from looking at the illustrations. Have you come across some of the new wordless picture books available now? Rodriguez's *The Chicken Thief* is a wordless, surrealist tale about a most unexpected friendship. Information picture books can also be good starting points for improvisation and writing. Marcia Williams' *Archie's War* has rich material which teacher and children could draw on to create some scenes to do with the privations of living through the First World War. This kind of drama work can lead to involved writing in role. Traditional tales, short stories and novels all provide powerful stories to extend and reflect on through drama. Television and film as well as books, newspaper articles and letters are good sources of themes and issues too. Where the issues in literature are explored through improvisation, children bring a new depth to their reading. Discussion of the plot, characterisation and use of language help children benefit from each other's insights. The planning of how episodes will be acted out and their evaluation contributes to children becoming careful and reflective readers (Clipson-Boyles, 2010, 2011). Improvisation can also awaken an interest in writing and help children find their writing 'voice'. Year 5 children, working on improvisations inspired by Barbara Jeffers' retelling of *Brother Eagle Sister Sky*, explored environmental concepts like 'conservation' and 'habitats' and wrote about issues of complexity like the reconciling of the needs of different groups. So, in conclusion, drama and improvisation have an important role in energising English and developing children's language in ways difficult to achieve by any other means. Above all, drama nearly always enthuses children and seems to bring about a spirit of co-operation which leads to much hard work and concentration.

Ackroyd, Judith and Bolton, Jo (2005) *The Teddy Bears' Picnic and Other Stories: Role Play in the Early Years 3–7* London: David Fulton.

Clipson-Boyles, Suzi (2010, second edition) 'The role of drama in the literate classroom' in Goodwin, Prue (ed.) *The Literate Classroom* London: David Fulton (this has an excellent annotated list of drama techniques with literacy examples).

——(2011, second edition) *Drama in Primary English Teaching* London: David Fulton.

Cremin, Teresa and Pickard, Angela (2009, second edition) *Drama: Reading Writing Speaking Our Way Forward* Leicester: UKLA Minibook 29.

Griffiths, Jenny (2000) *An Early Start to Drama* Hemel Hempstead: Simon & Schuster Education (practical ideas for building drama round issues).

Johnson, Colleen (2005) 'Creative drama: thinking from within' in *Unlocking Creativity: A Teacher's Guide to Creativity Across the Curriculum* London/Abingdon: Routledge.

Neelands, Jonathan (1992) *Learning Through Imagined Experience* London: Hodder & Stoughton.

DUAL-LANGUAGE TEXTS

See also: bilingualism, cultural diversity and resources, multiculturalism, multilingualism

Dual-language books or resources have a text written in English and another language. As well as helping bilingual young learners, having dual-language texts in the classroom increases the awareness of monolingual children of different languages and cultures.

The quality of dual-language texts is as important as in any other book. The story must meet criteria of exciting plot, good characterisation, convincing setting and successful illustrations. Format is also important and the two languages should have equal status.

Figure 8 Tortoise and the Hare: An Aesop's Fable, retold by Angela McAllister and illustrated by Jonathan Heale. Reproduced with the permission of the publishers, © Frances Lincoln, 2001, 2009.

The main problem with dual-language books is that we may find it difficult to judge the quality of the translation. Other problems have been high origination costs and relatively small print runs. However, there has been a trend to take good-quality picture books in English and to publish dual-language versions. Magi Publishing, for example, has dual-language versions of established picture books like, for example, *Amazing Grace*, *The Whales' Song*, *Owl Babies* and *Badger's Parting Gifts*. Other good publishers and suppliers of dual-language books include Milet (www.milet.com), Frances Lincoln (www.franceslincoln.com) and Mantra (www.mantralingua.com). Two centres amongst those that have good dual-language resources and an interest in research are: The Centre for Literacy in Education (www.clpe.co.uk) and The National Centre for Language and Literacy at the University of Reading (www.ncll.org.uk).

DYSLEXIA

See also: Special Educational Needs (SEN) in language and literacy

This term means literally word blindness or difficulty with words. It has been extended to refer to a syndrome which includes other symptoms like memory problems, clumsiness and spatial difficulties. Reid and Anderson pinpoint patterns of difficulties relating to the processing of information as the key symptom (Reid, 2009; Anderson, 2008). For a helpful account of the phonological processing difficulties of dyslexics, see Goswami (1999).

Sometimes dyslexia is developmental and therefore temporary – children just beginning to write often write words in reverse – 'saw' for 'was' or put the wrong beginning consonant – 'doy' for 'boy'.

Children are tested for dyslexia if they are of normal intelligence and general linguistic ability but have severe problems with written language – with reading, writing and spelling. The use of the term 'dyslexia' is controversial and some teachers and educational psychologists prefer to refer to 'specific learning disability'. There are two main positions on 'dyslexia'. First, we have the medical explanation where neurological factors to do with vision and hand-eye co-ordination are deemed important. Second, we have an explanation in terms of social and psychological factors including memory difficulties. What is not in doubt is that some children have considerable problems with learning to read and write and need carefully thought out support. Judith Graham and Alison Kelly have a useful section on specialised reading difficulties including dyslexia in their book *Reading Under Control* (Graham and Kelly, 2007).

Multi-sensory approaches seem to have helped children with dyslexia. These include drama in which children make letter shapes as part of the story, handwriting patterns that support spelling memory, and making the shapes of letters of the alphabet in paint, sand and clay. As computers provide a multi-sensory and multimodal forum for the exchange of information they are also helpful and, in Anita Keates' words, 'become (for dyslexic learners) a non-critical friend for life' (Keates, 2002: 84). All kinds of ICT, including tape recorders and hand-held spell-checkers, are likely to help dyslexic children of all ages.

Books written from a child's point of view include Ella Hudson's *Hudson Hates School* (Frances Lincoln) which manages to be both troubling and entertaining, and the upbeat *It's Called Dyslexia* by Jennifer Moore-Mallinos and Marta Fabrega (O'Brien Books).

The British Dyslexia Association is a national charity which co-ordinates over one hundred independent local dyslexia associations, organises conferences and sells publications. The help line telephone number is: 0845 2519002. www.bdadyslexia.org.uk

Figure 9 Front cover of *Hudson Hates School* by Ella Hudson. Reproduced with permission from the publishers, © Frances Lincoln, 2010.

Dyslexia Action carries out assessments for children and adults and aims to help by using skilled specialist help and teaching materials. It also conducts research. www.dyslexiaaction.org.uk

Anderson, Rosemary (2008) *Dyslexia and Inclusion: Supporting Classroom Reading with 7–11 Year Olds* Leicester: UKLA, Minibook 26.

Goswami, U. (1999) 'Speech coding and dyslexia: the phonological representations hypothesis' *Dyslexia Review*, 11 (2): 4–7.

Graham, Judith and Kelly, Alison (2007) *Reading Under Control* London/Abingdon: Routledge.

Keates, Anita (2002) *Dyslexia and Information Communications Technology: A Guide for Teachers and Parents* London: David Fulton.

Reid, Gavin (2007) *100 Ideas for Supporting Children with Dyslexia* London: Continuum.

——(2009, second edition) *Dyslexia: A Practitioner's Handbook* Chichester: Wiley.

Reid, G., Elbeheri, G., Knight, D., Everett, J. and Wearmouth, J. (eds) (2009) *The Routledge Companion to Dyslexia* London: Routledge.

Riddict, Barbara, Wolfe, Judith and Lumsdon, David (2004) *A Practical Guide for Teachers and Parents* London: David Fulton (covers age groups from early years to secondary).

E

EARLY LEARNING GOALS

See also: early years language and literacy, emergent writing, Foundation Stage, Foundation Stage profile, reading, speaking and listening, writing

These are the learning objectives for children to aim for by the age of six at the end of the Early Years Foundation Stage (EYFS). Since September 2000, early years practitioners have worked within the framework of these early learning goals. If you are a student you may find it helpful to look at the 'early years language and literacy' entry to read about some of the issues around how very young children are provided for in nursery and Reception classes. Government requirements are constantly modified and so it is with the early learning goals. The list of objectives from the Communication, language and literacy goals was long and detailed. By the end of the EYFS, most children were expected to be able, for example, to link sounds to letters, show an understanding of the elements of stories and attempt writing for different purposes. It has generally been felt that the early learning goals, including those to do with language and communication, could usefully be slimmed down. Following Dame Clare Tickell's review of the EYFS in July 2011, it was recommended that simplified goals should be organised under three main

areas of development: personal, social and emotional; physical; communication and language.

The website to consult for the latest statutory requirements and advice is www. education.gov.uk.

EARLY YEARS LANGUAGE AND LITERACY

See also: creativity in English, drama and English, early learning goals, emergent writing, enabling adult, Foundation Stage, Foundation Stage profile, junior years language and literacy, parents and families, play and language and literacy, reading, siblings (and literacy), speaking and listening, writing

The term 'early years' has often been used to refer to children up to eight years old. This is still the case in many countries, but in the United Kingdom the term is now applied mainly to children between birth and age five years in the Early Years Foundation Stage (EYFS). The experiences of a child in the preschool and early school years are likely to affect later development and there has been a lot of debate about how much structured learning there should be. Traditionally much of the learning during these years was through rich experience in play and discovery with little formal instruction. Recent initiatives affecting the under sixes include the formulation of 'early learning goals' for children entering school (thus creating a foundation pre-National Curriculum for children in under fives settings), the putting in place of baseline assessment shortly after children enter compulsory schooling, and an increase in the range of providers of early years education.

The main issue is whether children aged three to six benefit from the kind of structured learning environments and direct teaching OFSTED recommend in their publication *The Quality of Nursery Education*. Many respected practitioners and early years educationists believe that play-based and child-directed learning are more appropriate for the age group. Their concern is that direct teaching at too young an age might lead to a lack of self-confidence and create anxiety. Mary Jane Drummond has a vision for Reception class children in which children's learning – through play, first-hand experience and talk – is prized above teaching plans and targets. We need to ask the philosophical question: what is a good childhood and how can our provision support this (Drummond, 2003; Bruce, 2009)?

It is always helpful to know something about the approach in other countries when thinking about these issues. There is a trend in the French *écoles maternelles* and in Japanese private nurseries towards some literacy teaching, and New Zealand, Trinidad and the Republic of Ireland teach reading early as in Britain. However, many other countries favour play-based programmes for children under six or seven. In Norway, Denmark, Sweden and Finland children learn through play and discovery at nursery, learning to read and write formally only when they start school at seven years. Hungary, Austria and Switzerland favour an oral approach to teaching nursery-aged children and musical activities are integrated into the daily programme.

Early years practitioners in the United Kingdom hope the early learning goals can be interpreted in a way that will ensure a rich learning environment for the under sixes. I think this means achieving these within the 'big shapes' of learning (Miller and Pound, 2010). What are the 'big shapes' or priorities for language and literacy? First of all we should recognise that children bring to school many achievements and ways of dealing successfully with new experiences. This is where we begin. We need also to see becoming literate as part of a bigger picture of making meaning, through activities like role play, art and craft and talking and listening in a range of contexts. The nursery or early years team like to plan activities round a theme like ourselves, journeys, growing and so on. This gives a vitality and coherence to all the activities, including language activities. I remember a Reception class who helped the teacher make the home corner into a fire station and who were keen to write the work rotas for the notice board and to tell and write stories about rescuing people from fires (Dalton-Vinters & Mallett, 1995).

Language work is nourished by books and resources. Often the adult will take up an opportunity to enrich and inform children's play with a story or information book. Children enjoying play round the idea of journeys asked for a book that would tell them about how train doors shut and how you make tickets. This project and others are case studies in *Young Researchers* (Mallett, 1999: Chapters 2 and 3) and in *Early Years Non-fiction* (Mallett, 2003). Sharing stories is a particularly enjoyable and important activity: children listen, talk about the characters and link their own experiences with what happens. Early enjoyment of story is the foundation for later literary experience where children need to have sympathetic insight into the circumstances and feelings of others. Sometimes it is enough just to hear the story read and talk about it, but at other times it can lead to role play, early writing and art work.

Good partnerships between schools and parents and families is helpful for every aspect of learning, including literacy development. Teachers benefit from knowing about a child's literacy practices and experiences at home. There is more about this under the entries on 'parents and families' and on 'siblings (and literacy)'. Parents are often extremely supportive and willing to do practical things like displaying books and translating stories into home languages. I remember a student being delighted when the parents of her nursery class sent in photographs of the children as babies so that she could help them to make their own book based on the Ahlbergs' *Peepo!* When it comes to young children's first attempts to write, they like to draw as well as write words. In *Desirable Literacies* Jackie Marsh and Elaine Hallett explore this multimodality as a main way of communicating in the early years (Marsh and Hallett, 2009).

If you are a teacher of older children there are several reasons why you should make yourself knowledgeable about early years education. First, some of the most interesting research about how human beings learn, not least how they learn to speak and develop their language abilities, has been carried out with very young children. From birth to about six years there is 'unparalleled speed and complexity of growth in children's thinking, language, social and cultural awareness and physical skills' (Whitehead, 2009: 1). Second, the essentially active way in which children learn has implications for a model of learning to serve beyond the very early years. Third, later learning builds on the earliest stages. To take just one example, if teachers of older children are familiar with the kind of programme in good nurseries that emphasises young children's enjoyment and participation in storytelling, saying and singing nursery rhymes and sharing picture books of vitality and merit, they can build on this. Finally, the good

early years practitioner is a helpful model for the role of the teacher at all stages. We can learn much about how to observe children, how to relate these observations to our planning, how to intervene sensitively and how to evaluate progress. Not all of the books listed below are referred to directly in this entry, but they would all help extend your understanding of children's language and literacy needs at this crucial early stage.

Browne, Ann (2009, revised edition) *Developing Language and Literacy 3–8* London: Paul Chapman.

Bruce, Tina & Spratt, Jenny (2010) *A whole-Child Approach to Communication, Language and Literacy* London: Sage.

Bruce, Tina (2004) *Cultivating Creativity in Babies, Toddlers and Young Children* London: Hodder & Stoughton.

——(2009) *Early Childhood: A Guide for Students* London: Sage.

Campbell, Robin (1996) *Literacy in Nursery Education* Stoke on Trent: Trentham Books.

Dalton-Vinters, Julia and Mallett, Margaret (1995) 'Six year olds read about fire fighters' in *Reading* UKRA, April, 29 (1).

De Boo, Max (ed.) (2004) *The Early Years Handbook: Support for Practitioners in the Foundation Stage* London: The Curriculum Partnership (covers English, science, design and technology, geography and maths).

Drummond, Mary J. (2003) 'Breathe life into childhood' in *The Times Educational Supplement,* 28 November.

Glazzard, Jonathan, Chadwick, Denise, Percival, Julie and Webster, Anne (2010) *Assessment of Learning for the Early Years Foundation Stage* London: Sage (theories of development are clearly explained, including the approaches of Montessori, Steiner, Reggio Emilia and L.V. Vygotsky (social constructivist); also there are practical case studies).

Mallett, Margaret (1999) *Young Researchers: Informational Reading and Writing in the Early and Primary Years* London: Routledge.

137

——(2003) *Early Years Non-Fiction* London: Routledge.

Marsh, Linda and Hallett, Elaine (2009, second edition) *Desirable Literacies: Approaches to Language and Literacy in the Early Years, 0–8* Leicester: UKLA.

Miller, Linda and Pound, Linda (eds) (2010) *Theories and Approaches to Learning in the Early Years* London: Sage.

Nutbrown, C. (1997) *Recognising Early Literacy Development: Assessing Children's Achievements* London: Paul Chapman.

OFSTED: www.ofsted.gov.uk

Palmer, Sue and Bayley, Ros (2008, third edition) *Foundations of Literacy* London: Network Educational Press (shows how a structured, oral-based curriculum can be followed and suggests many lively activities in the areas of music, story and early writing).

Sylva, Kathy, Siraj-Blatchford, Iram and Taggart, Brenda (2003) *Assessing Quality in the Early Years: Early Childhood Environment Rating Scale Extension: Four Curricular Subscales* London: Trentham Books (these researchers have provided scales to measure quality in literacy, numeracy, etc., as observable in preschool settings. These scales are described in this book and while they are research tools it is hoped they will have a more general use in helping early years practitioners provide a quality environment in which children can flourish).

Whitehead, Marian R. (2010, fourth edition) *Language and Literacy in the Early Years* London: Paul Chapman.

——(2009, second edition) *Supporting Language and Literacy Development in the Early Years* Buckingham and Philadelphia, Penn,: Open University Press.

——(2007, third edition) *Developing Language and Literacy, 0–8* London: Paul Chapman.

EBOOKS

These are books in electronic form held on a computer's database or a dedicated hand-held device such as a Kindle, and stored like any other document. To read the text a 'reader' application is used, which displays the text page by page on screen. While more and more people are downloading ebooks, they are unlikely to entirely replace print books. However, they have advantages, particularly for students and researchers who need rapid access to published, copyright information. They can be searched in the same way as a CD-ROM and information can be bookmarked.

Where pay-per-view facilities are available selected pages can be downloaded, viewed and printed, as is the case with a CD-ROM.

EDINBURGH READING TESTS

See also: reading age, Standardised Reading Tests

This group, timed, written series of tests (in four age phases) published by Hodder and Stoughton (2002, revised edition) covers the age range from seven to twelve years. The materials are arranged in sentences and paragraphs. Reading behaviour as well as a number of aspects of reading, for example ability to sequence, use of syntax and comprehension, are assessed, resulting in a profile of the child's abilities. Therefore, as well as providing a summative measure the test has a diagnostic value. There are details at www.hoddertests.co.uk. It is, of course, more time-consuming to carry out than a simple word test like the *Schonell Graded Word Test*.

EDITING

See also: composition, drafting, transcriptional aspects of writing, writing

Editing a draft can involve reordering words and phrases, adding or removing text. The aim may be to reduce the number of words, to improve the flow or to sharpen up the argument. Proof reading for transcriptional errors can often be combined with editing.

By the end of the primary years, most children have learnt to check through their 'first drafts' for spelling or punctuation errors, but find it much more difficult to improve the compositional aspects of their writing once they have shaped their text.

By constantly reviewing their work as they write, editing can become a more dynamic activity, embedded into the whole process rather than just something that happens at its end. Teachers can help by modelling the editing process – perhaps on the whiteboard.

EFFECTIVE READING TESTS

See also: reading age, Standardised Reading Tests

Untimed, group and in the form of reading booklets, this four-level set of tests (Macmillan, 1986) has a total age range of 7.3–12.8 years. These tests emphasise comprehension – children answer questions on different sections of text.

ELABORATED AND RESTRICTED CODES

See also: language and thought, language variety

In the 1960s the sociologist Basil Bernstein identified two codes or ways of using language which he suggested were part of a general theory of social rules. The elaborated code, as the name suggests, was used in formal or educational settings where a range of linguistic forms made meaning entirely explicit. This kind of language was characterised by the use of subordinate clauses, the pronoun 'I' and the passive tense.

The restricted code was a form of language which was appropriate in less formal settings and in contexts where speakers were members of the same group and

therefore did not need to 'spell everything out' to get their meaning across. Features of this use of language were tag questions, liberal use of pronouns and gestures and intonation conveying meaning rather than flexible and creative linguistic forms.

Nobody had much trouble in accepting that language changes according to the formality of the context. The difficulty occurred because the codes became associated with social class. While middle-class and educated people were thought to be able to switch codes as appropriate, the poorly educated and lower working-class individual controlled only the 'restricted' code. At its crudest, one argument was that as lower working-class children spoke a 'restricted language' they were unable to learn properly at school. Terms like 'language disadvantage', 'language deprivation' and 'language deficit' came to be used and Bernstein distanced himself from arguments and conclusions which he considered were distortions of his theory. These issues are discussed in chapter 3 of *Gender, Race and Class in Schooling* by Chris Gaine and Rosalyn George. Today the notion that some children arrive at school 'linguistically disadvantaged' is thankfully unacceptable and we believe all but the most severely mentally handicapped children can be taught. Nevertheless, teachers try to help children become as competent and flexible as possible in their use of language to aid their learning.

Gaine, Chris and George, Rosalyn (1999) *Gender, Race and Class in Schooling: A New Introduction* London: Falmer Press.

ELECTRONIC BOOKS

See: CD-ROM, ebooks, factual genres, fairy tales, fiction, Information books, Information and Communications Technology (ICT) and English, non-fiction reading and writing

ELEMENTARY SCHOOLS

See also: history of English teaching

Elementary schools provided free education for children between five and twelve years from 1870, when they were established by the Elementary Education Act.

The curriculum was limited and there was much learning by heart, copying texts and writing to dictation. The government exercised control by the 'payment by results' system in which teachers were paid only if the children passed tests in the 'three Rs' – reading, writing and arithmetic.

The 1944 Education Act brought in age-phased organisation of schooling and established primary schools which catered for children from five to eleven years. Children then went on to secondary schools and so the all-age elementary schools began to close. The kind of secondary school that children attended was now decided by the 11+ examination which often had a narrowing effect on the English curriculum of the later primary years.

ELISION

See also: apostrophe

Elision occurs when a speaker slurs or a writer omits a vowel, consonant or syllable. In writing, elision is often indicated by an apostrophe – 'you shouldn't' and 'won't you?'

ELLIPSIS

See also: cataphoric reference, cohesion

An ellipsis refers to missing out part of a sentence in speech or in writing, where the omitted words are implied from the context. In conversation, we often rely on the context to communicate what we mean. A typical exchange might be:

> 'Where are the umbrellas?'
> 'At the door'.

The second speaker does not need to say 'The umbrellas are at the door' or even 'They are at the door'.

In writing ellipsis is less frequent because, in the absence of immediate feedback, we need to be more explicit. Even so, ellipsis can help avoid repetition and yet maintain cohesion. It helps the reader focus on the most important information. So we might have:

> 'The post was advertised for several weeks and eventually seven people applied. Two were invited for interview'.

We do not need to make the second sentence longer by repeating information – 'Two of the seven people who applied were invited for interview'.

In punctuation, ellipsis is indicated by three points and used to indicate part of a quotation that has been missed out. So 'Sunday newspapers, the last genre to emerge, have become a significant institution in Britain' (McArthur, 1992: 691) in a shortened version might become 'Sunday newspapers ... have become a significant institution in Britain'.

Sometimes the three ellipsis points can have a dramatic effect, as in 'The water came nearer and nearer ... ' Then the reader is left to draw their own conclusions and a new paragraph begins. For more examples and further information about 'ellipsis' you might consult Medwell *et al.* (2009) and McArthur (1992).

McArthur, Tom (1992) *The Oxford Companion to the English Language* London: QPD, and Oxford: Oxford University Press (a shorter, revised edition was published in 2005, *The Concise Oxford Companion to the English Language*).

Medwell, Jane, Moore, George, Wray, David and Griffiths, Vivienne (2009) *Primary English: Knowledge and Understanding* Exeter: Learning Matters.

EMAIL

See also: Information and Communications Technology (ICT) and English

Email (electronic mail) are messages and documents prepared on personal computers and delivered electronically – that is, using fixed-line or satellite communication links. The messages can be read and responded to 'on screen' without the need to prepare a hard copy or to print them out, and they can be merged into existing documents and productions. Increasingly children are using email as a way of communicating within the school or with children in other schools.

As we might expect with a new way of communicating, email is developing its own conventions and language style which are sometimes at odds with the ordinary rules of grammar and punctuation. Teachers need to remind pupils that while certain simplifications may be appropriate while using email, other writing tasks need to conform to standard forms of grammar and punctuation.

EMERGENT WRITING

See also: early learning goals, early years language and literacy, enabling adult, writing

'Emergent', also referred to as 'developmental' or 'early' writing, is a term for how a young child begins to control the process of writing from making their very first marks to beginning to use the conventions of writing to make meaning. At first children have little knowledge about words and sounds and how these are represented by letters. They experiment, imitating the flow and speed of the mature writer and play with the shape and orientation of letters and with punctuation marks like full stops. These early stages are explored by a number of writers including Bissex (1985)

who charts her own child's progress towards writing, Hall (1987) who stresses the young child's urge to experiment with different written forms, and Temple *et al.* (1992) who identify some stages in the journey towards becoming a writer. Marian Whitehead describes in detail the interplay between the young child as an active meaning maker and learner, and their personal and cultural environment in the journey towards becoming a writer. Here they are helped by the sensitive adult who takes the ideas and feelings that children are shaping into narrative forms and acts as scribe – setting the message down in a conventional form (Whitehead, 2010: Chapter 8). Then the child acquires the confidence to write himself or herself.

Alison Kelly is concerned that terms like 'emergent' and 'developmental' might suggest that writing abilities just happen without specific teaching (Graham and Kelly, 2009). However, early years educators are more likely to argue against mature forms being pressed on young children before they can cope with them. The important thing is that children should build confidence in their ability to write and feel positive about the enjoyment writing can bring.

Bissex, Glenda (1985 edition) *GNYS AT WRK: A Child Learns to Read and Write* Cambridge, Mass.: Harvard University Press.

Graham, Judith and Kelly, Alison (2009, third edition) *Writing Under Control* London: David Fulton.

Hall, Nigel (1987) *The Emergence of Literacy* Sevenoaks: Hodder & Stoughton.

Temple, C., Nathan, R.G., Burris, N.A. and Temple, F. (1992, third edition) *The Beginnings of Writing* Boston, Mass.: Allyn & Bacon (new edition in press).

Whitehead, Marian (2010, fourth edition) *Language and Literacy in the Early Years* London: Paul Chapman (see Chapter 8, 'Early representation and emerging writing').

141

EMOTIONAL LITERACY

See also: response to reading

This refers to a human being's understanding of how to relate to others in a constructive and sensitive way. It also has to do with consciousness of our own needs and the effects on others of our behaviour and attitudes. Many factors are likely to affect the level of emotional literacy an individual develops. One of these factors may be the special insights children develop from cumulative exposure to quality fiction: developing sensitivity to the subtle messages in texts may play a part in helping them grow and develop as responsive human beings. Of course, we must be wary of simple linking of cause and effect here – there is no evidence that students of literature and the arts are morally superior beings!

Let me give an example of how I think fiction may help, though. A student teacher read *Grace and her Family* to her eight year old class (Hoffman and Binch, 2007 edition, Frances Lincoln). This wonderful picture book tells the story of Grace's journey to meet her father's new partner and their children and in doing so explores her ambivalent feelings about this second family. The children particularly liked Grace's image of herself 'like gum stretched out all thin in a bubble' as she struggles to find the emotional resources to be part of two families. It showed them how it was possible to reconcile conflicting feelings and tolerate situations they would not have chosen. There are some subtle messages: we see an illustration of Grace reading fairy stories as her stepmother offers her food. The children came to understand that Grace's reading gave her insights into other people's dilemmas and challenges and this helped her with her own problems.

ENABLING ADULT

See also: Bristol Language at Home and School Project, reading environment, zone of proximal development

Perhaps it is Vygotsky who most powerfully brought the notion of the enabling adult to a form which made sense to the teacher in the classroom (Vygotsky, 1986). Listening to a more mature person thinking through some information or an issue provides a scaffold for the young learner in any subject or area of expertise. This intellectual companionship stretches the possibilities for the young learner. Some parents and caregivers are particularly gifted at encouraging the kind of conversations which help young children to develop and extend their interest in the world around them and to grow intellectually. Gordon Wells and his team of researchers on the *Language at Home and School* project found that these life-enhancing conversations occurred in all social groups (Wells, 1987: Chapter 1).

For a detailed and inspiring account of the role of the early years educator in supporting children's literacy progress see Marian Whitehead's analysis in *Language and Literacy in the Early Years*, chapter 9. Whitehead argues that teaching and demonstrating are important but the good early years educator should also provide 'mothering' support. By this she means that the good educator wishes for the success and achievements of the children and surrounds them with the incitement to succeed (Whitehead, 2010).

In English, the teacher is a model for children's discussion and for their reading and writing. Aidan Chambers, writing specifically about reading, argues that all the other obstacles in the way of learner readers can be overcome if they have the help and example of a trusted, experienced adult reader (Chambers, 1991: 15).

Chambers, Aidan (1991) *The Reading Environment: How Adults Help Children Enjoy Books* Stroud: Thimble Press (see particularly chapter 17).

Vygotsky, L.S. (1986 edition) *Thought and Language* Cambridge, Mass.: MIT.

Wells, Gordon (1987) 'The children and their families' in *The Meaning Makers: Children Learning Language and Using Language to Learn* London: Hodder & Stoughton.

Whitehead, Marian (2010, fourth edition) *Language and Literacy in the Early Years* London: Paul Chapman.

ENCYCLOPEDIA

See also: CD-ROM, factual genres, library skills, non-fiction reading and writing, study skills

An encyclopedia is a reference text in print or electronic form and is normally organised alphabetically (some encyclopedias for young children are organised thematically). General encyclopedias for adults (*The Encyclopedia Britannica* for example) can be huge, scholarly works with a large number of entries spanning every possible subject, written by leading experts and arranged in many volumes or on huge computer databases. Here we are concerned with encyclopedias for children – how we choose encyclopedias from the many on the market and how we help children of different ages use them.

General criteria for choosing an encyclopedia would include being up to date and accurate, well written and illustrated and with a content of interest and use to a particular age group; however, the very best encyclopedias have some other qualities. They manage to put across the idea that knowledge is not static but expands: astronomers discover new stars and palaeontologists find new kinds of dinosaurs. Often such discoveries are more than a superficial addition to what we know: one dinosaur fossil recently unearthed suggested that some of these creatures, far from being the green or brown we usually picture, were bright red and orange. Not only does this lead us to picturing the creatures differently, but it makes us think in a new way about camouflage and predators. Further, our attitudes to what is known change. Stephanie Harvey notes that the great contribution of native peoples to the development of the American West has transformed encyclopedia entries on this topic (Harvey, 1998). So a good encyclopedia explains knowledge that seems fairly secure while giving the impression that there is still much to be discovered and considered. This welcome speculative approach can be a feature of encyclopedias for the very young. Angela Wilkes, in *Your World: A First Encyclopedia* (Kingfisher), shares some theories about how dinosaurs became extinct with her young readers and makes it clear that 'no one knows exactly why'. In the Dorling Kindersley 2009 edition of *DK Dinosaur Encyclopedia*, Caroline Bingham explains to young readers how palaeontologists build up evidence and revise their understanding through time.

Another quality we look for is a capacity to draw a young learner, whether browsing or researching, easily into a particular field of knowledge. Good illustrations are most important. Some 60 per cent of the 175 seven to eleven year olds taking part in the Exeter Encyclopedia project said they looked at photographs, maps and drawings first, mentioning particularly entries on muscles, places, plants, lakes, events, sharks, the Second World War and Henry VIII. CD-ROM encyclopedias have strong potential for developing children's visual literacy. The *Britannica 2007 Children's Encyclopaedia* is in CD-ROM (PC/Mac) form, which reviewers found easy to navigate and to have amusing and informative graphics and film. Older primary children also find the visual aspect of both *DK's Children's Illustrated Encyclopedia* (2010 edition) and *Earth Quest* (an initiative by Dorling Kindersley with the National History Museum) appealing. The second of these explains and demonstrates the movement of tectonic plates, erupting volcanoes and destroying earthquakes. The written text in both print and electronic encyclopedias also has to inspire. The first part of a lively entry on 'storms' in Dorling Kindersley's *Children's Illustrated Encyclopedia* puts the phenomena in an interesting perspective:

> 'About 2,000 thunderstorms are raging throughout the world at this very moment, and lightning has struck about 500 times since you began reading this page. Storms have enormous power: the energy in a hurricane could illuminate more light bulbs than there are in the United States'.

This is a long way from the impersonal language of older encyclopedias, whether for adults or children. We know an encyclopedia has succeeded if children want to carry their research into other books. A visit to the websites of publishers specialising in reference books including children's encyclopedias – Dorling Kindersley, Kingfisher, Oxford, Paragon and Usborne (internet-linked) – shows the latest innovations and reveals details of the latest editions. Many publishers offer CD-ROM editions of their print books, often with multimedia features like sound and animation. There is innovation in print publishing, too. *Pick Me Up: Stuff You Need to Know* by David Roberts and Jeremy Leslie has a fascinating 3D-effect front cover and poses many questions, some quite unsettling, to the young readers. I should mention it has an American flavour, as do some other encyclopedias for a global market.

Valuable as browsing is – savouring the illustrations and dipping into the text – children also use encyclopedias to find specific information or as a first port of call when beginning a new topic. There are important issues about how we support children's use of reference books. Getting the best out of an encyclopedia can be a complicated matter. Even the older primary children in the Exeter Encyclopedia Project had difficulty with the index

volume of a multi-volume set of children's encyclopedias (Wragg, 2000), so some direct teaching about retrieval devices is needed. Teachers can best help very young children understand about head words and indexes in the context of an interesting task. Five year olds learning about whales were eager to consult reference books for a much older age group alongside their teacher to find the answers to their questions (Doyle and Mallett, 1994). The 'whale' work case study shows us that the desire to find out – children's sometimes passionate curiosity about something in particular – supplies the energy and will to learn about 'looking up' procedures. Older children often have timetabled sessions in the library to learn about library and study skills. However well intentioned, too many 'looking up' exercises outside a context to give them point and meaning can become dreary. This does not rule out times when teachers and librarians can help children understand the organisation of reference books and how to carry out searches in both print encyclopedias and electronic search systems (Mallett, 2010).

Whether children are using electronic or print encyclopedias, the important thing is how they use the information they find: perhaps to help them debate an issue in class discussion or to make notes towards a piece of writing which will be further enriched by what is found in other books. Margaret Meek reminds us that children are never too young to read critically and to have opinions about which texts have been most helpful (Meek, 1996).

Dorling Kindersley *Eyewitness Children's Encyclopedia* (this provides an array of multimedia navigation systems and links to DK's website; it has a talking dictionary and children can easily print screens).

Dorling Kindersley/Natural History Museum *Earth Quest* (CD-ROM) (goes beyond superficial information for children who love science).

Doyle, Kathleen and Mallett, Margaret (1994) 'Were dinosaurs bigger than whales?' *TACTYC Early Years Journal*, 14 (2) Spring.

Encyclopedia Britannica and *Encarta* (both comprehensive encyclopedias for teachers' use with good search functions).

Harvey, Stephanie (1998) *Non-fiction Matters: Reading, Writing and Research in Grades 3–8* York, Maine: Stenhouse Publishers (see Chapter 8).

Mallett, Margaret (1999) *Young Researchers* London: Routledge.

——(2010) *Choosing and Using Fiction and Non-fiction 3–11* London/Abingdon: Routledge (see Chapters 33 and 34).

Meek, Margaret (1996) 'The quick fix: reference books' in *Information and Book Learning* Stroud: The Thimble Press.

Wragg, Ted (2000) 'Obscure reference' in *Times Educational Supplement* (about The Exeter Encyclopedia project: funded by Encyclopedia Britannica, this study involved observing the strategies of 175 seven to eleven year olds, from five rural and five urban primary schools in the Midlands and South, as they carried out tasks using encyclopedias).

ENGLISH 21

This was an initiative from the Qualifications and Curriculum Authority (now abandoned) to help shape the future of English for all age groups. The plan was to revitalise English teaching by drawing on many planned debates and events and by benefiting from the comments of learners, teachers, parents and employers. There were four topic foci:

- English for all learners: here debate centred on issues to do with what language skills learners need; what we should teach about the spoken word; how our literary heritage should be defined given societal changes; and how we can nurture imagination and creativity.

- English and related subjects: this was mainly about flexibility and innovation for ages fourteen to nineteen.
- e-English – texts and technology: in what ways will new technology transform speaking and listening, reading and writing?
- Ways ahead in assessing English: what forms of assessment will best suit demands by 2015?

Although the Qualifications and Curriculum Authority is long gone, the debates round issues raised by English 21 will continue.

ENGLISH AS AN ADDITIONAL LANGUAGE (EAL)

See: bilingualism, dual-language texts, equal opportunities, language variety, multiculturalism, multilingualism

ENGLISH ASSOCIATION (THE)

Founded in 1906 and now based at the University of Leicester, this international body has branches, Fellows and members in Britain and throughout the world. The aim is 'to further knowledge, understanding and enjoyment of the English language and its literatures and to foster good practice in its teaching and learning at all levels'. It does this by arranging conferences and presenting awards and through its publications.

There are two committees concerned with the primary years: the Primary Education Committee and the English 4–11 Editorial Board which produces a thrice-yearly professional journal. The journal, first published in 1991, includes stimulating articles discussing current issues, materials for the classroom teacher and reviews of books, software and other resources. The editorial board contributes to the nomination of Fellows – those who have made an outstanding contribution to teaching, research or educational writing. The team, led by John Paine, the main editor until 2010, and now by Rob Sanderson, also help judge the English Association's annual awards for outstanding picture books published over the previous twelve months. A strong feature of the selection process is that teachers and children are involved in choosing books for the short-list. Prizes are in four categories – fiction and non-fiction for Key Stage 1 and fiction and non-fiction for Key Stage 2 – and are awarded at the Annual General Meeting.

The English Association: www.le.ac.uk/engassoc

ENGLISH DEVELOPMENT PLAN

See also: audit (of primary English), English/ Literacy Co-ordinator, English/literacy policy

This is a plan setting out the steps towards good practice often either after an 'audit' or an inspection which has identified strengths and weaknesses. The development plan will show the stages by which good practice in each aspect of English – planning, resourcing, teaching, record keeping – will be achieved and when. See Chapter 9, 'Producing a development plan' in Waters and Martin, 1999, for detailed lists of what should be included.

Waters, Mick and Martin, Tony (1999) *Co-ordinating English at Key Stage 2* London: Falmer.

ENGLISH/LITERACY CO-ORDINATOR (THE)

See also: art and English, assessment, audit (of primary English), core books, design and technology and English, displays, drama and English, early years language and literacy, enabling adult, English/literacy policy, equal opportunities, geography and English, history and English, Information

and Communications Technology (ICT) and English, junior years language and literacy, literacy hour, mathematics and English, National Curriculum, parents and families, phonics, physical education, music and dance and English, planning, Primary Language Record, reading, reading corner/area, record keeping, religious education and English, science and English, speaking and listening, writing, writing corner/area

The large number of 'see also' cross-references indicates that the responsibilities of the English Co-ordinator or Subject Manager take in every aspect of language, learning and literacy.

Co-ordinating English is a huge brief: not only are co-ordinators concerned with language and literature in English lessons, but they also reach out to the language activities – speaking and listening, reading and writing – which make possible learning across the whole curriculum.

There have always been positions of responsibility for subject areas in the primary school, often referred to as 'scale posts' in the past. Now the expectations resting on all subject co-ordinators have been formalised and their wide-ranging nature made explicit. The tasks involved are nearly always in addition to those of class teaching. For an account of the role of co-ordinators of subjects across the primary curriculum you may find Joan Dean's (2004) book *Subject Leadership in the Primary School* helpful, while the role of the SENCo is lucidly set out by Damien Fitzgerald (2007) in *Co-ordinating Special Needs.* The SENCo collaborates closely with the other co-ordinators, not least the English Co-ordinator. The English/Literacy Co-ordinator, Manager or Leader – the terminology changes frequently – would strengthen their own practice by reading the best books on the teaching of English at primary level, including Teresa Cremin's (2009) *Teaching English Creatively* and

Wyse and Jones' (2011) *Teaching English, Language and Literacy*. David Waugh's (2007) *English 3–11* is set out in textbook format and has helpful sections on popular culture and using multimedia. A hugely helpful book, one outcome of the United Kingdom Literacy Association's Teachers as Readers project is *Building Communities of Readers*. Not only does it help us to understand how to increase children's independent reading, but it aims to improve teachers' motivation and enthusiasm for their own reading. There is a clear role for the English Co-ordinator here – perhaps setting up occasional seminars to give colleagues the opportunity to share their reading enthusiasms (Cremin *et al.*, 2008).

Although it is a demanding one, the role of English Co-ordinator has many satisfactions: seeing children across the whole school develop as language users; convincing children of the pleasure of reading and producing their own stories and factual accounts; selecting a whole range of exciting resources, whether print or electronic; supporting students and probationer colleagues as well as collaborating with all the teachers to help them become excellent practitioners; and reaching out to parents and the wider community.

Four core areas of responsibility for subject co-ordinators can be identified: strategic direction and development of the subject; teaching and learning; leading and managing staff; efficient and effective deployment of staff and resources.

Each of these contains many familiar tasks and so here I have selected some which seem to me of particular importance. My account draws on the analysis of Waters and Martin (1999: Chapter 2, 'Being a co-ordinator').

Strategic direction and development of the subject

This aspect of the Co-ordinator's role is to do with putting in place policies and practices to promote good planning and resourcing, staff confidence in teaching the subject, regular analysis of data to monitor progress, set targets and achieve improvement. By creating a sound global framework, Co-ordinator and teachers can then turn with confidence to developing specific aspects of teaching and learning.

Teaching and learning

There needs to be good coverage, continuity and progression and this involves Co-ordinators and their colleagues knowing what the National Curriculum English programmes require. I believe the most successful Co-ordinators interpret and implement formal requirements in a way that serves the needs of the pupils and teachers in their school (Martin *et al.*, 2008; Cremin, 2009). Then there is the huge task of assessment and record keeping to attend to. This must be coherent and systematic, easily manageable and integrated into the teaching cycle. The Co-ordinator's task here also involves initiating and maintaining good communication with parents and the wider community, and encouraging their involvement.

Leading and managing staff

This includes communicating with senior management and other subject co-ordinators and supporting all teachers, not least newly appointed and student teachers, in their professional development. Co-ordinators are more likely to succeed if they build an atmosphere of co-operation and trust, and deal sensitively with cases where a teacher has to improve an aspect of their practice. The 'audit' entry gives an example of a co-ordinator showing how we meet the requirements for teaching reading while it still remains an enjoyable and life-enhancing experience for children and teacher (Tyrrell and Gill, 2000).

Efficient and effective deployment of staff and resources

Co-ordinators need to establish staffing and resource needs, including those to carry out the priorities in the development plan. These needs have to be costed and communicated to senior managers and a share of the school's overall budget negotiated.

Performing well in all of these areas requires organisational, management and motivational skills as well as a great deal of professional and subject knowledge about language and literature. I have formed my own view over the years of what characterises the above-average English Co-ordinator. Certainly those who command most respect are themselves excellent practitioners – models of how to plan, resource, organise and evaluate their lessons and to inspire their pupils (Myers and Burnett, 2004). We are more likely to take notice of what someone advises or demonstrates if we have been impressed by the fruits of their endeavours! I also find teachers are more eager and able to follow an English policy or strive to meet the demands of a development plan if they have been involved at every stage in its creation. Finally, and I have said this before, the Co-ordinator that can energise the other teachers by their enthusiasm, good humour and genuine concern for the progress of both colleagues and children is of great value to any primary school.

Cremin, Teresa (2009, second edition) *Teaching English Creatively* London and New York: Routledge.

Cremin, Teresa, Mottram, Marilyn, Collins, Fiona and Powell, Sacha (2008) *Building Communities of Readers* Leicester: UKLA.

Dean, Joan (2004) *Subject Leadership in the Primary School: A Practical Guide for Curriculum Coordinators* London: David Fulton.

Fitzgerald, Damien (2007) *Co-ordinating Special Needs* London: Continuum.

Martin, Tony, Lovat, Chira and Wood, Gynis (2008, second edition) *The Really Useful Literacy Book: Being Creative in the English Classroom* London and New York: Routledge.

Merchant, Guy and Marsh, Jackie (2000) *Co-ordinating Primary Language and Literacy* London: Paul Chapman.

Myers, J. and Burnett, C. (2004) *Teaching English 3–11* London: Continuum.

Tyrrell, Jenny and Gill, Narinderjit (2000) *Co-ordinating English at Key Stage 1* London: Falmer Press.

Waters, Mick and Martin, Tony (1999) *Co-ordinating English at Key Stage 2* London: Falmer Press.

Waugh, David (2007) *English 3–11: A Guide for Teachers* London: David Fulton.

Wyse, Dominic and Jones, Russell (2011, third edition) *Teaching English, Language and Literacy* London: Routledge.

ENGLISH/LITERACY POLICY

See also: English development plan, English/Literacy Co-ordinator

English policies are written plans setting out a whole-school policy on the teaching of all aspects of English and language and learning across the curriculum. Merchant and Marsh put it like this: 'A language policy is essentially a statement of the principles and practices which underpin the content and delivery of the English curriculum' (Merchant and Marsh, 1998: 52).

The policy needs to be written in accessible language so that the most important aspects are clearly communicated to anyone who might need to consult it. All the teachers should be given the opportunity to contribute to the formulation of the policy. Bear in mind it may be one of the first glimpses a new teacher, a new governor or an outside agency like an OFSTED inspection team has of the English and language work in the school. While the policy should do the work of teachers and children justice, it must be an honest reflection of what actually happens in the classroom. It therefore needs to be regularly updated. For a detailed account of how a policy document might be organised and the issues it should address, I recommend 'Developing and writing a language policy', Chapter 4 in Merchant and Marsh, 1998. Language policy documents are often written under headings which are likely to include: the school's aims and philosophy; resources and accommodation including the library; the organisation and methodology of the English programme; planning, assessment and record keeping; staffing and the role of the Co-ordinator; language in English lessons and across the curriculum; special educational needs; children learning English as an additional language; parents and the community; equal opportunities and children's entitlement; special achievements and initiatives.

Chapman, Myers, J. and Burnett, C. (2004) *Teaching English 3–11* London: Continuum.

Merchant, Guy and Marsh, Jackie (1998) *Co-ordinating Language and Literacy* London: Paul

ENGLISH PROJECTS (THEMES, TOPICS)

See also: advertisements, comics, cross-curricular projects, fairy tales, language variety, picture books

English projects provide an organising theme or topic for sustained work round an aspect of language or literature. Under 'cross-curricular projects' I observed that topics across the subject boundaries, once a favourite way of organising some primary school work, are out of favour in the subject-centred approach now prescribed by the government. English projects, fortunately, remain a good way of awakening and sustaining children's interest. Sometimes literature used in Literacy Time led to further work. For example, a class who had looked at a fairy tale enjoyed a deeper study of different kinds of the genre over several weeks. In the nursery and Reception

years a series of activities might take a story or picture book as the starting point. One nursery class of four year olds was helped to make their own book based on the Ahlbergs' picture book *Peepo!*

Older primary children might look at an aspect of language variety – the songs and sayings of the local dialect. Another linguistic topic is word meanings, starting perhaps with the street names and buildings in the area of the school. Language change is another possible focus for sustained work.

English work that is sustained over several lessons often achieves a momentum and goes beyond the superficial.

ENGLISH SCHEMES

See: planning

ENLARGED TEXTS

See: big books

ENVIRONMENTAL PRINT

This includes all the written language a child encounters including notices in parks, advertisements on billboards, shop and restaurant signs, writing on cereal packets and written language on the television and on CD-ROMs. Children often notice the letters that make up their own names and this interest in print needs to be reinforced. Early years teachers bring much of what the child sees in the way of print in the environment into the nursery and Reception classroom. The home corner might be a shop with all the labels and signs involved, or a café with menus, bills and newspapers. Graham and Kelly suggest we help children make notices based on those they have seen in the world outside the classroom (Graham and Kelly, 2007). So we might have 'Please keep the reading corner tidy' and 'Please wash your hands after feeding the tadpoles'. All this helps with the building of a sight vocabulary as children become readers and writers. Above all, it shows children the social purposes of writing and its importance in everyday life. For more about how environmental print helps children's understanding of literacy see Hall (1987) and Kirkland *et al.* (2007).

Graham, Judith and Kelly, Alison (2007) *Reading Under Control: Teaching Reading in the Primary School* London: David Fulton.

Hall, N. (1987) 'Environmental print' in *The Emergence of Literacy* Sevenoaks: Hodder & Stoughton.

Kirkland, Lynn, Aldridge, Jerry and Kuby, Patricia (2007) *Integrating Environmental Print across the Curriculum* London, Alabama: Corwin/Sage (by US researchers but there are many suggestions for practical activities round environmental print that would enrich the work of any primary classroom).

EPIC POETRY

Epic poems tell the story of some great person or event, generally bound up in myth or religion. Some have their origin in an oral tradition, and were handed down from generation to generation.

EPIPHANY

An epiphany is a special moment of insight when an idea or situation is seen with new clarity. Let me give an example: A teacher read Anthony Browne's picture book *Zoo* to six year olds who had not thought of keeping animals in cages as controversial. When the mother in the story comments 'poor thing' when the tiger is seen pacing up and down its cage they suddenly saw things in a new light. Perhaps, they said, it was cruel to enclose creatures who needed a lot of space (Riley and Reedy, 2000).

Riley, Jeni and Reedy, David (2000) *Developing Writing for Different Purposes: Teaching about Genre in the Early Years* London: Paul Chapman.

EQUAL OPPORTUNITIES

See also: bilingualism, boys' literacy, gender and language development, girls' literacy, multiculturalism, multilingualism

A school's English policy (and policies for other subjects) has a section which sets out how all children, whatever their gender, ethnicity or social group, will be given equal access to the curriculum. Having a whole-school policy helps make equality of opportunity consistent throughout the school. In her useful book *Making Gender Work* Judith Baxter shows how 'a planned cycle of observation, monitoring, and evaluation – of the differentiated needs of all pupils, plus a range of curricular provision' ensures no child is marginalised (Baxter, 2001). Such reflective practice is the key to benefiting all children whatever their age, ability, gender or cultural background. When this aspect of the English policy is monitored we might check some of the following:

- Resources – do the materials in the classroom and the school library reflect the needs and interests of children of both genders, children from ethnic minorities (including emergent bilinguals) and children from a range of different social backgrounds? Are there quality dual-language texts to show we value children's first languages and to encourage family involvement in literacy?
- Research – are the teachers aware of studies that indicate that girls may need encouragement to contribute fully in talk contexts and that some children, particularly boys, may need special help with literacy? For a background to language and equality issues see Gaine and George (1999: Chapter 3), OFSTED (1993) and Warrington and Younger (2006) for evidence of boys' literacy underachievement. Are teachers also aware of research into supporting young

emergent bilingual children, for example Gregory (2008)?

- Teaching strategies – is there evidence that teachers are putting into practice imaginative approaches, for example setting up drama work where the less confident children, often girls, take on leading roles and providing the more structured writing tasks that seem to motivate reluctant boy writers (see Baxter, 2001)?

Baxter, Judith (2001) *Making Gender Work* Reading: Reading and Language Information Centre.

Gaine, Chris and George, Rosalyn (1999) *Gender, 'Race' and Class in Schooling* London: Falmer Press.

Gregory, E. (2008, second edition) *Learning to Read in a New Language: Making Sense of Words and Worlds* London: Sage.

Myers, J. and Burnett, C. (2004) *Teaching English 3–11* London: Continuum (chapters 11 and 12).

OFSTED (1993) *Boys and English* London: OFSTED.

Warrington, Molly and Younger, Mike, with Eve Bearne (2006) *Raising Boys' Achievement in Primary School: Towards a Holistic Approach* Milton Keynes: Open University.

ERIC (EVERYONE READING IN CLASS)

ERIC is an acronym to refer to times when the whole class is enjoying sustained, quiet reading. You might also come across DEAR (Drop Everything and Read), USSR (Uninterrupted Sustained Silent Reading) and SQUIRT (Sustained Quiet Uninterrupted Independent Reading Time). Many teachers simply refer to it as 'reading time'. In Britain it was once fairly common practice to make available regular silent reading times, but this provision has diminished in recent times. There is, however, no reason – except for pressure of time – why teachers should not find time for this activity. There are several reasons why silent reading is worth preserving. Reading books at home now competes with time on the computer and watching television as well as outdoor pastimes, so if we want the clear message that reading is valuable for its own sake to come through we need to show it is worth making time for in school. Newly independent readers can be helped during reading time to make the transition from reading out loud to reading silently. Graham and Kelly observe that a gentle nudge to try reading in your head is all that is needed, but children must have peace and quiet for this to be viable (Graham and Kelly, 2007). Children of all ages benefit from the time and space to savour a book and read at their own pace. Sometimes the teacher reads as well to stress the importance of a class being a 'reading community' but there will also be times when it is helpful to observe particular children and to judge their level of concentration and choice of book. The most passionate argument for reading time in school is, for me, made by Aidan Chambers in his book *The Reading Environment*. He reminds us that 'a sacrosanct period is one of those rituals that condition our set of mind' (Chambers, 1991: 38). It is the teacher who can encourage and provide the willpower for children to enjoy sustained reading. This more than anything else is likely to make a child a committed reader for life.

Chambers, Aidan (1991) *The Reading Environment* Stroud: The Thimble Press.

Graham, Judith and Kelly, Alison (2007) *Reading Under Control* London: David Fulton.

EXCLAMATION

See also: punctuation

An exclamation is a sentence that communicates surprise, delight, shock, distress and other strong emotions. For example, 'I have passed all my examinations with high marks!' Sometimes an exclamatory phrase functions as a verbless 'sentence'. For example 'How wonderful!'

Exclamatory sentences and phrases, as is evident from the examples above, end with an exclamation mark.

EXEL PROJECT

See also: EXIT model, genre, genre exchange, non-fiction reading and writing, research (into primary English, language and literacy), writing frames

The Exeter University Extending Literacy (EXEL) Project was funded by the Nuffield Foundation and headed by David Wray and Maureen Lewis. They worked with teachers throughout the country during the 1990s to find ways of supporting children's non-fiction reading and writing. See under EXIT model for their process stages to extend interaction with texts.

They looked for essentially practical answers to questions such as: how can we support children's informational reading and writing so that they are less likely to copy wholesale from books and resources? Although writing frames (skeleton frameworks to help organise a piece of writing) and genre exchange (using information gained from one genre, for example an information book to write in another, for example, a diary entry, menu or advertisement) are not original ideas, Wray and Lewis brought them to a practical level for use in the classroom. Their six categories of non-fiction – recount, report, procedure (instruction), explanation, persuasion (exposition) and discussion – were used in the now abandoned National Literacy Strategy *Framework for Teaching* (DfEE, 1998, 2006) and have informed the National Curriculum English orders. Their work with Key Stage 2, seven to eleven year olds, is known best but they have also considered younger children's progress in

this area of literacy, and in the late 1990s and the early 2000s the project has turned to children in the secondary years. Many teachers feel the strategies are particularly helpful to children with writing difficulties.

Views about how often to use the frames differ and some teachers prefer alternative forms of scaffolding, for example helping children plan their writing verbally (see 'conferencing'). Used without thought and too often, writing frames can bring about a mechanistic response from young writers. Wray and Lewis themselves consider the frames to be a temporary prop which children eventually give up, and have written in depth about how best to use them.

The directors of the project and many of the teachers with whom they worked have given lectures and workshops to teacher conferences and seminars and a large number of books and articles have been published (for example Lewis and Wray, 1995; Wray and Lewis, 1997).

Lewis, Maureen and Wray, David (1995) *Developing Children's Non-fiction Writing: Working with Writing Frames* Leamington Spa: Scholastic.

Wray, David and Lewis, Maureen (1997) *Extending Literacy: Children Reading and Writing Non-fiction* London: Routledge (Kindle edition 2009).

EXIT MODEL

See also: Directed Activities Round Texts (DARTs), EXEL Project, non-fiction reading and writing, writing frames

The EXIT model (Extending Interactions with Texts) was an outcome of the Exeter Extending Literacy Project funded by Nuffield and carried out during the 1990s. The model identifies ten process stages, some of which are preliminary, like the 'activation of prior knowledge' and the 'establishing purposes', some of which are to do with learning from secondary sources like 'interacting with the text' and 'monitoring understanding', and others of which involve reconstructing what has been learnt 'communicating information' (Wray and Lewis, 1997).

This model informed the National Literacy Strategy training materials to help teachers carry out the non-fiction part of the literacy programme. Although the Literacy Framework has been dropped, the impact of the approach of Wray and Lewis to the teaching of non-fiction kinds of literacy is still evident in UK classrooms. There is no doubt that the activities recommended in this model would help children interact with texts rather than remaining relatively passive readers and writers, but for me there is something missing from the model: there is no explicit recognition of how first-hand experience might be integrated with the secondary source input, although it could be part of the 'establishing purposes' category. In my own model of non-fiction reading and writing, 'offering new experience' – which may take the form of an activity as in a science experiment, story (told or read), a visit or field trip or a contribution from a visitor – comes after 'organising prior experience' (Mallett, 1992: 61 and Chapter 8; Mallett, 2007). In a very interesting analysis of a series of lessons on zoos with a Year 1 class, David Reedy uses Anthony Browne's story *Zoo* to offer a new perspective to the children. The children had never thought that keeping animals in cages might be controversial until the picture book was read to them. A turning point came when they saw the tiger pacing up and down in its cage. This brought the children new energy and commitment to finding out more. Reedy comments: 'If we are to motivate children to want to go through the research process, then we must ensure their curiosity is stimulated, by exposing them to new information and ideas that cause them to want to know more' (Riley and Reedy, 2000: 145).

Mallett, Margaret (1992) *Making Facts Matter* London: Paul Chapman.
——(2007) *Active Encounters: Inspiring Young Readers of Non-fiction 4–11* Leicester: UKLA Minibook 24.
Riley, Jeni and Reedy, David (2000) *Developing Writing for Different Purposes: Teaching about Genre in the Early Years* London: Paul Chapman.
Wray, David and Lewis, Maureen (1997) *Extending Literacy: Children Reading and Writing Non-fiction* London: Routledge.

EXPLANATION TEXT

See also: genre, non-fiction reading and writing

An explanation text explains structures like those of a plant, an animal or a machine, or explains a process like a bird flying, the human digestive system or the workings of a car engine. It was one of the six non-fiction text types that informed the National Curriculum English orders and the now abandoned UK Literacy Framework, but it remains one of the genres that teachers want children to be able to control. Some see explanation text as part of the 'report' category (see Medwell *et al.*, 2009). David Macaulay's book *The New Way Things Work*, which has clear, well-annotated diagrams of wheels, levers and all sorts of moving parts, shows both structure and function and is one of those inspirational explanation texts that appeal to a wide age range. The CD-ROM version shows all the moving parts in action.

There is a detailed account of 'explanation' text for children in *Choosing and Using Fiction and Non-fiction 3–11*, which suggests good texts to use with different age groups. The titles in the Amazing Machine series for the very young, by Tony Mitton and Ant Parker, are about different vehicles and how they work. For example, *Amazing Aeroplanes* explains, using simple text and colourful, energetic

153

pictures, how a plane flies. Moonlight Publishing, in their First Discovery series, use transparent overlays to explain changes and processes, for example *Light* by Gilbert Houbre *et al.* uses cleverly designed overlays to illuminate the secrets of shadows, rainbows and how the world is lit after dark. Kate Petty and Jenny Maizels have designed imaginative books for older primary children which explain such natural phenomena as earthquakes, see for example their *Amazing Pop-up Geography Book*, published by Dorling Kindersley.

Mallett, Margaret (2010) *Choosing and Using Fiction and Non-fiction 3–11* London and New York: Routledge (see Chapter 30).
Medwell, J., Moore, G., Wray, D. and Griffiths, V. (2009, revised edition) *Primary English: Knowledge and Understanding* Exeter: Learning Matters.

EXPOSITORY TEXT

See also: discussion, explanation text, persuasive genre, report

'Expository' kinds of writing explain, describe or argue a case. Exposition is an impersonal form and the third rather than the first person tends to be used. Writer and reader are sometimes distanced from one another and an impression of objectivity is given by use of the passive voice.

EXPRESSIVE TALK AND WRITING

See also: speaking and listening, writing

'Expressive' talk and writing was one of the function categories in the model of language developed by Professor James Britton and his team of researchers during the Schools Council 'Development of Writing Abilities' project in the 1970s. Britton observed that most of us use a spontaneous, fairly unstructured kind of speech when formulating action plans or new ways of construing our experience of the world. This he termed 'expressive' language which helped us make a start on organising our ideas. The sort of conversations people have in their homes and in the pub about political initiatives are often like this. Young children's talk is full of their immediate interests, preoccupations and recent activities, and not surprisingly their first writing tends to resemble 'written down' speech in its spontaneity and openness about the mood of the moment. Often the child is not thinking about the needs of an audience but is eager to relate his or her immediate concerns – the visit to see the ducks in the park, the outing to swim in the local baths or the frog spawn on the nature table. Britton argues that children's writing development begins from this 'expressive' centre, moving on the one hand towards 'poetic' writing (with a form or pattern characteristic of different kinds of fiction) and on the other towards 'transactional' writing (which included all the factual genres). We recognise that a child's writing is moving towards the poetic end of the 'writing continuum' when there are signs of 'the deliberate organisation of sounds, words, images, ideas, events, feelings' (Britton, 1970: 177). When a child's writing moves from the expressive towards meeting the demands of the factual, it becomes more explicit. Britton explains that: ' … some features that might be omitted from the expressive version because they are implied when we write for someone of similar interests and experiences to our own, have now to be brought into the writing' (ibid.: 177). So for Britton writing development was at least partly to do with differentiation and increasing control over a greater number of writing types.

'Expressive' writing is not mentioned in current government orders or guidance material. As early as 1980 there were fears that too much 'expressive' writing might take time that could be spent on helping children develop other more disciplined kinds of writing (Allen, 1980). Thinking in Britain was influenced by teachers and scholars in Australia who became known as the 'genre theorists' and who felt that narrative genres, and particularly stories and writing with an 'expressive' function, dominated too much in primary schools. They argued that children should be helped to use a much wider range of reading and writing, not least non-fiction kinds. There is no doubt that some kinds of non-fiction writing were often neglected, or at least unsupported, in the primary school before the 1990s. However, expressive kinds of language have an important role in children's development of language and thinking. We should welcome the expressive touches in children's early writing that show they are trying to make sense of all their experience. Early years teachers are rightly concerned that children are not nudged too early into mature forms of writing. I believe that children are more likely to become successful talkers and writers if they have the opportunity to explore their experience and ideas in an expressive way.

Allen, D. (1980) *English Teaching Since 1965: How Much Growth?* London: Heinemann Educational Books (O/P, but worth mentioning as it contributes to our understanding of the history of English teaching).

Britton, James (1970 [1992]) *Language and Learning* London: Allen Lane, The Penguin Press.

EYFS (EARLY YEARS FOUNDATION STAGE)

See: early learning goals, early years language and literacy, Foundation Stage, Foundation Stage profile

F

FABLE

See also: history of children's literature, parable

A fable is a story with a moral that becomes explicit at its end. The characters are often animals showing unattractive human traits like pride, selfishness and greed. One of the best known collections is *Aesop's Fables*, often enjoyed by both children and adults. Aspects of the natures of the animal characters, for example the cunning of the fox, have become absorbed into our culture. Sayings like 'sour grapes' also originate from these tales, thought to have been written about the sixth century BC by a Greek slave. Jerry Pinkney's straightforward telling of the tales (published by Seastar Books) with superb illustrations came thirty-fourth in Booktrust's 2008 survey 'The Best Children's Books of All Time'. Under eights like the entertaining illustrations by Korky Paul in Vivian French's *Aesop's Funky Fables* told in a combination of rap-like verse and prose (Hamish Hamilton).

Fables are still well-liked forms of children's literature and there are many retellings of single fables in picture book format, for example Beatrix Potter's *The Tale of Johnny Town-Mouse*, Brian Wildsmith's *The Lion and the Rat* (La Fontaine version) and Geoff Patterson's *The Goose that Laid the Golden Egg*. There is an interesting history of fables and an account of their link with illustrations in Watson's (2001) guide. Some of the features of fables are found in print comic strips (for example in Beryl the Peril) and in animated cartoons (*Wallace and Gromit*, *Thomas the Tank Engine*).

Watson, Victor (2001) *The Cambridge Guide to Children's Books in English* Cambridge: Cambridge University Press.

FACTION

See also: transitional genre

A new term referring to texts, usually for children under eight, which combine features of both story and non-fiction. So we might have a story about the life of a dog or horse together with some panels and information boxes giving information about diet and breeding. Sometimes storybook characters and talking animals appear in these texts and many young readers enjoy the playful approach. Language must change, of course, and we need new words to clinch new concepts but some people, including the present writer, find 'faction' a charmless addition. The books to which the term refers vary in quality, but the best in this transitional genre are enjoyed by young readers and listeners who can learn within the familiar story framework. It is now a category under which new children's books are reviewed in well-thought of children's literature journals such as *Books for Keeps*, wherein recent examples include the books mentioned below.

Hooper, Meredith (illustrator), Curless, Allan and Burgess, Mark (2000) *Dogs' Night* London: Frances Lincoln (dogs climb out of their paintings at the National Gallery).

Lia, Simone (1999) *Billy Bean's Dream* London: David & Charles Children's Books (a numbers and colours book woven round an exciting story).

FACTUAL GENRES

See also: atlas, chronological non-fiction, diary, dictionary, discussion text, encyclopedia, EXEL Project, genre, information books, Information and Communications Technology (ICT) and English, information stories, internet, literacy hour, non-fiction reading and writing, persuasive genre, procedural or instructional genre, reading, recount, referencing, report, transitional genre, writing

Features of the many genres called factual, information or non-fiction are discussed under separate entries. Supporting children's reading and writing of non-fiction is covered under the entry 'non-fiction reading and writing'. This section considers the nature of factual kinds of material in general and their relevance to primary English.

Factual genres describe, explain, organise and explore aspects of the real world we all inhabit. This contrasts with fiction that is less tied to the actual, exploring the possible and the inner world of the human imagination. The differences can be quite difficult to pin down, though generally we can tell to which general category – fact or fiction – a particular piece of written material belongs. Good factual writing often demands imaginative power and the ability to think laterally. Some experts can write

speculatively about their field and show the same wonder and curiosity as a young child. Nearly every factual topic carries ethical issues which demand the sort of discussion we often associate with the best work in English lessons. The information explosion brought about by human endeavour and progress together with the technological revolution, the use of powerful computers and the internet, has transformed the sheer amount and variety of information available to us – a veritable explosion. This has made it all the more necessary to have strategies for selecting, accessing, making sense of and critically assessing all the information now available.

Fiction in all its forms and children's response to it is the beating heart of English and so we can think of factual kinds of reading and writing mainly informing other lessons, but we all know this division is too stark. Just as stories and poems can infuse life and meaning into work across the curriculum, some factual genres have an important place in the English lesson. In the introduction to this encyclopedia it is argued that feelings about issues and events as well as thought and reflection are central to learning in English. Teachers draw on all kinds of text in a classroom where there is informed discussion about all the issues that concern human beings. Newspapers and magazines are worth rifling for features and readers' letters on themes like homework, hunting and waste disposal. These can serve as models for children's own letters and oral arguments. Children now often share these reflections using email and the internet to link with children in other schools.

Factual books and the internet can often enrich reading stories and novels involving interesting issues. Children reading Dick King-Smith's *The Sheep-pig* asked for information about pigs to do with their breeding, life span and intelligence. Information books were sought on all these aspects and energised the children's response to the story (Mallett, 1992). I observed work in a Year 6 class where factual texts were used fruitfully alongside Ted Hughes' *The Iron Woman* to illuminate environmental issues.

The now abandoned *Framework* encouraged teachers to widen the range of texts used in the primary classroom; the six categories of non-fiction included in the *Framework* – recount, report, explanation, discussion, persuasion and instruction (procedural) – still inform teachers' thinking and practice. Medwell *et al.* suggest a slight revision of the text type list, placing 'explanation' under the 'report' category and adding 'reference' and 'records' (Medwell *et al.*, 2009). There are also some literary non-fiction genres, for example autobiography, biography and travel books. In the later primary years, children make progress in the more challenging kinds of factual genres, such as persuasive and journalistic kinds of reading and writing (Wilson and Scanlon, 2011). The discussion text gives more than one viewpoint which children can then talk about, perhaps justifying their own opinion.

Mallett, Margaret (1992) 'How long does a pig live?' in Kimberley, K., Meek, M. and Miller, J. *New Readings: contributions to an understanding of literacy* London: A&C Black.
——(2010) *Choosing and Using Fiction and Non-fiction 3–11* London and New York: Routledge (see part 2).
Medwell, J., Moore, G., Wray, D. and Griffiths, V. (2009, fourth edition) *Primary English: Knowledge and Understanding* Exeter: Continuum.
Wilson, Angela and Scanlon, Julie (2011, fourth edition) *Language Knowledge for Primary Teachers* London: David Fulton.

FAIRY TALES

See also: history of children's literature, fiction: choosing and using, folk tales, traditional tales

We term 'fairy tales' the kind of traditional tales that tell of magic and talking animals, of elves, sprites and other 'little people', but the boundary between fairy tales and folk tales, which also sometimes have supernatural elements, is thin. Some experts on children's literature believe that fairy tales are a category of folk tale. John Rowe Townsend argues that 'folk' refers to the origin of a tale while 'fairy' indicates the nature of the story (Townsend, 1995: 67). Very generally, the characters in folk tales tend to be ordinary people – farm workers, cobblers, seamstresses and woodcutters, for example – while fairy tales are usually about kings and queens, princes and princesses and others of noble birth.

Of course, it is well known that fairy tales began as oral tales to amuse adults, but by the middle of the nineteenth century, fairy tale collections by Perrault, Grimm and Hans Andersen had been published. The published versions were for child readers and the more shocking elements were toned down.

Primary teachers seeking to strengthen their understanding of the history and genre features of fairy tales would find illuminating Bruno Bettelheim's (1988) classic book *The Uses of Enchantment*. Jack Zipes' (2002) groundbreaking books, for example *Breaking the Magic Spell: Radical Theories of Folk Tales and Fairy Tales*, examine the main European traditions. For scholarship with a light touch, I recommend the entertaining chapter on fairy tales in *Written for Children* (Townsend, 1995). Guidance on further reading about traditional tales is set out in *Exploring Children's Literature* (Gamble and Yates, 2008) and *Choosing and Using Fiction and Non-fiction 3–11* (Mallett, 2010). While thinking about further reading suggestions, I should mention one of the most illuminating essays on fairy tales – the introduction by the Opies to their beautifully illustrated book *The Classic Fairy Tales*. For the Opies the defining feature is that a fairy tale 'contains an enchantment or other supernatural element that is clearly imaginary' (Opie and Opie, 1974: 15). We search out anthologies or books on a single tale where the telling makes a powerful appeal to the young imagination. The illustrations too must intrigue and please. *The Pea and the Princess* by Mini Grey is a delightful retelling of Hans Andersen's fairy story from the point of view of the pea! Sometimes the teller of a tale and their illustrator work together to produce an outstanding creation. Catherine Hyde's luminous pictures match perfectly Carol Ann Duffy's modern fairy tale *The Princess Blankets* (Templar). It begins thus: 'A princess once lived who was always cold'.

Two anthologies recommended for the under eights are *The Walker Book of Fairy Tales* told by Amy Ehrlich (Walker Books) and *First Fairy Tales* re-told by Margaret Mayo in rhyme and with much repetition. Vivian French's retelling of seven traditional fairy tales ('Jack and the Beanstalk', 'Hansel and Gretel', 'The Fisherman and his Wife', 'Beauty and the Beast', 'The Elves and the Shoemaker', 'Rumpelstiltskin' and 'Cinderella') is illustrated by Peter Malone with exceptionally fine paintings. French's gift for memorable language makes her creation of the magical worlds well worth reading out loud. Good primary school collections will include fairy stories from different lands. Reading or listening to them tells us about the culture from which they arose – its customs, values and beliefs. The Puffin *Classic Fairy Tales* has a good mix of English, Irish, Scottish and Welsh stories. Barbara K. Wilson tells a rather Cinderella-like tale from China about some magic fish bones in *Wishbones: A Folktale from China*. Yeh Hsien finds a wonderful golden fish and feeds it until it grows enormous but her jealous stepmother kills and eats the fish. *Tales from India* retold by Sanjeevini, Navjeet and Misti (illustrated by Daksha and Manju

Gregory) is a collection of Indian folk tales adapted for young readers. Mantra Lingua materials in both print and electronic form include fairy tales from different cultures. They are presented in English together with another language, including, for example, Gujarati, Punjabi, Hindi and Polish. Cambridge University Press publish packages for Key Stages 1 and 2 containing stories in print and CD-ROM versions; the latter enable the teacher to work with the whole class using an interactive whiteboard. The talkingPEN included in each pack allows a child to hear the story narrated in English or another language. More details are available on the Cambridge University Press website: www.cambridge.org/gb/education/primary.

Modern fairy tales often challenge traditional gender roles in an entertaining way, for example *Princess Smartypants* (1986) by Babette Cole, *The Paper Bag Princess* by Robert Munsch (1980) and William Jay's *The Practical Princess and Other Liberating Fairy Tales* (Nelson/Hippo) are enjoyed. Children of about eight years (when they will have a grip on the features and conventions of traditional tales) love the idea of dragons saving princes from princesses, and princesses wearing paper bags instead of gowns. Older children would appreciate the alternative tellings of well-known tales in Alison Lurie's *Clever Gretchen and Other Forgotten Fairy Tales*, now in an edition by iUniverse.com (2005). For a most entertaining postmodern picture book presenting playful stories around traditional fairy tale characters see John Scieszka's *The Stinky Cheese Man and Other Fairly Stupid Tales* (Puffin, 1992) and by the same author *The True Story of the Three Little Pigs*. Judith Graham has some helpful suggestions for follow-up activities after ten to eleven year olds have heard *The Stinky Cheese Man and Other Fairly Stupid Tales* – comparing the traditional and revised versions of the fairy tales and later on carrying out their own subversive adaptations to other traditional tales (see Graham, 1997: 68–9). It is worth checking on children's television and radio websites for the availability of online fairy stories. For example, teachers and parents welcome the return of Jackanory on BBC children's programmes. The programme has been redesigned for young viewers in the twenty-first century and includes narrations of fairy and folk tales (www.bbc.co.uk/cbeebies/jackanory).

Bettelheim, Bruno (1988) *The Uses of Enchantment: The Meaning and Importance of Fairy Tales* London: Penguin.

Gamble, Nikki and Yates, Sally (2008, second edition) *Exploring Children's Literature* London: Sage.

Graham, Judith (1997) *Cracking Good Books: Teaching Literature at Key Stage 2* Sheffield: NATE.

Hallford, D. and Zaghini, E. (2004) *Folk and Fairy Tales: A Book Guide* London: Booktrust.

Mallett, Margaret (2010) *Choosing and Using Fiction and Non-fiction 3–11* London and New York: Routledge.

Opie, Iona and Opie, Peter (1974) *The Classic Fairy Tales* Oxford: Oxford University Press.

Townsend, John Rowe (1995 edition) *Written for Children* Harmondsworth: Penguin.

Zipes, Jack (2002, revised edition) *Breaking the Magic Spell: Radical Theories of Folk and Fairy Tales* Kentucky: University of Kentucky.

FAMILY LITERACY PROJECTS

See also: parents and families, siblings (and literacy)

Family literacy initiatives involve teams working through parents to help their children to make progress in reading and writing and, at the same time, helping the parents' literacy. There have been many initiatives both at national and local level. Often a librarian with expertise in family reading provides collections of books and other reading material for children to take home. The 'story' of one such project, *The Raising of Early Achievement Literacy Project* based in Sheffield, involved a research team using families' existing knowledge as a starting point (Nutbrown *et al.*, 2005). The interesting thing about this and similar projects is that the collections contained books for different age groups and interests so that when the child took home a selection, there was something for each member of the family.

These initiatives and others like them work on the principle that parents and children can help each other in becoming more literate. The signs are that they can make a difference. However, family literacy initiatives raise complex issues, not least how you help maintain the interest and commitment of families when the initial project ends. We should not underestimate the challenge of helping those who do not usually feel comfortable in a library environment to acquire long-term interest in books and other materials.

The Centre for Literacy in Primary Education, The National Literacy Association and Booktrust are amongst those organisations that have shown commitment to the principles of family literacy. The Centre for Literacy in Primary Education has arranged storytelling events for parents, caregivers and children and has contributed to initiatives like Sure Start. An interesting contribution has been made by Carolyn Swain in *Reading Magazines with a Critical Eye in the Primary School*. She argues that carefully selected magazines deserve to be part of the reading repertoire and help emphasise that reading is for pleasure, and she suggests that magazines can also help bridge the gap between home and school reading (Swain, 2009). *Improving Primary Literacy* also sets out practical ideas, for example setting up home school folders and diaries (Teller *et al.*, 2007).

161

Cathy Nutbrown has written much of value about the important role of parents in children's literacy development, by setting out principles and theories alongside practical examples and case studies (Nutbrown *et al.*, 2005; Nutbrown, 2011).

Finally, I would like to draw your attention to a project exploring how teachers can become well informed about the literacy experiences children have at home and in the communities they serve and to utilize this knowledge in the classroom. The research project, Building Communities: Researching Literacy Lives, is led by Teresa Cremin and Rose Drury of the Open University and Marilyn Mottram of Birmingham LA and funded by the Esmee Fairbairn foundation and UKLA. The eighteen teachers from the ten schools involved were active researchers who had meaningful conversations with families during a series of home visits. These teachers said that their visits had led to them reflecting on their own attitudes and assumptions about parents and children. At their presentation at the UKLA International conference in Chester, July 16th 2011, the team mentioned how they found siblings helping each other with homework by sharing library books and mothers who had read great literature from around the world, for example one had studied Tolstoy's novels. (Visit the UKLA website for information about developments and publications: www.ukla.org)

Booktrust: www.booktrust.org.uk

Centre for Literacy in Primary Education: www.clpe.co.uk

National Literacy Trust: www.literacytrust.org.uk

Nutbrown, Cathy (2011) *New Concepts in Early Childhood Education and Care* London: Sage.

Nutbrown, C., Hannon, P. and Morgan, E. (2005) *Early Literacy Work with Families: Policy, Practice and Research* London: Sage.

Swain, Carolyn (2009) *Reading Magazines with a Critical Eye in the Primary School* Leicester: UKLA Minibook 39.

Teller, Anthony, Andrews, Jane, Greenhough, Pamela, Hughes, Martin, Scanlan, May and Wan Ching Yee (2007) *Improving Primary Literacy: Linking Home and School* London and New York: Routledge.

FANTASY

See also: faction, fairy tales, fiction: choosing and using, history of children's literature

A fantasy is something created out of the imagination and may be a daydream, painting, a story or a poem. James Britton, in his article on the role of fantasy, suggests it is located in 'a third area' between external reality and the inner world of necessity. The child who can inhabit this 'third area' can handle images as play. You need to read this rewarding but quite challenging article yourself; it is worth the effort – not least because it argues for the value of children's play. It suggests that a very young child who can live creatively through play is likely later to be able to enjoy and take part in all the richness of the cultural world including literature, music and art (Britton, 1971).

One of the activities that provides the space for playing with images in school is of course the enjoyment of books and the stories children tell and write. In children's literature, 'fantasy' is a category often contrasted with 'realism' which is to do with what has happened or what at least could happen without coming into conflict with the laws of nature.

Some of the finest children's books from the middle of the nineteenth century onwards belong to the literary genre called 'fantasy'. Charles Kingsley's *The Water Babies* (1863), Lewis Carroll's *Alice* stories (1865), J.R.R. Tolkien's *The Hobbit* (1937), C.S. Lewis' *Narnia* books (1950), Philippa Pearce's *Tom's Midnight Garden* (1958) and, more recently, J.K. Rowling's *Harry Potter* books of the 1990s and early 2000s, and David Almond's *Skellig*. Writing about the

Alice books, Victor Watson considers they established new possibilities for children's books by creating an imaginative space for writing about the dynamics between adults and children – 'dynamics that might be complex, loving, intimate or problematical, but were no longer just authoritarian' (Styles *et al.*, 1992: 18). I recommend John Rowe Townsend's book *Written for Children* if you want to find out more about fantasy literature for children through history: chapters on fantasy thread through the book under chapter titles like 'The neverlands', 'Fantasy between the wars' and 'Modern fantasy' (Townsend, 1995).

Fantasy can transform the everyday world, as in Philippa Pearce's classic, *Tom's Midnight Garden* (Smith, 2004). Perhaps other fantasies also create the space to think about ideas in an uninhibited way and allow us to experiment with notions unrestrained by the normal rules of time and space. Some books seem to invite the question, 'What would happen if – I was very small, very large, I could fly or if I had a magic finger?' I have found children are intrigued by Roald Dahl's short story *The Magic Finger* (Puffin, 1979). The girl in the story uses her magic finger to punish those who annoy her. Children, often powerless in real life, find this satisfying.

The modern picture book is an ideal vehicle for fantasy as the illustrations can provide a second narrative which may complement, extend or even contradict the written text. The idea of a magic implement comes into some of Anthony Browne's books. In *Bear Hunt* (1979), Bear escapes from hunters in the jungle by drawing himself out of trouble with his magic pencil. Children learn how to read a fantasy book by reading with an adult and interpreting the features of the genre. Use of certain symbols in the illustrations may have a special cultural meaning (Tyrrell, 2003).

Children, even those not normally eager to write, often enjoy writing their own stories about having a magic pencil or finger.

By inviting this kind of story we are giving children the opportunity to play with ideas in a highly satisfying way. If we want children's imaginative powers to grow we have to help them exercise them. Children's thoughts flow easily from fact to fiction and this is reflected by a category of books called, rather inelegantly, 'faction', the main function of which may be informational, but which may also feature storybook elements like talking animals. Many of these books, like the Macdonald Young Books Bees series, are for younger children, but there are books for older primary children of this type as well, for example Ted Dewan's *The Weatherbirds* (Viking, 2000) in which a stork, a parrot, a sparrow, a goose and a dodo undertake an exhilarating journey through the weather of the world. Different weather systems are clearly described and there are wonderful illustrations, including a panorama of New York at sunset. The fantasy elements will not be liked by everyone – some may think they risk 'genre confusion' – but I find that children enjoy the humour.

Britton, James (1971) 'The third area where we are more ourselves: the role of fantasy' *English in Education*, 5 (3) (reprinted in *The Cool Web* Meek, M. *et al.*).

Smith, L. (2004) 'Domestic fantasy: real gardens with imaginary toads' in Hunt, P. *International Companion Encyclopedia of Children's Literature*, Volume 1, London and New York: Routledge.

Styles, Morag, Bearne, Eve and Watson, Victor (eds) (1992) *After Alice: Exploring Children's Literature* London: Cassell.

Townsend, John Rowe (1995) *Written for Children* London: Cassell.

Tyrrell, J. (2003) *The Power of Fantasy in Early Learning* London: Routledge.

FICTION: CHOOSING AND USING

See also: adventure stories, animals, Booktrust, boys' literacy, class reader, emotional literacy, enabling adult, fable, fantasy, figurative language, girls' literacy, historical novel, history of children's literature, legend, novels, picture books, playscript, poetry, reading environment, reading range, response to reading, shared writing, short stories, subject knowledge

Fiction is literature drawing on invention and the inner world of the imagination, often using figurative language to get meaning across. The books listed below, and particularly *The Core Booklist*, give help in choosing good examples of children's picture books, novels, short stories, playscripts and poems, as well as recorded and electronic books (Ellis *et al.*, updated every two years). Mills and Webb (2004) clearly explain some of the elements in good texts for younger readers, for example familiarity and the possibility of growth and challenge. Journals that regularly review children's fiction include: *The School Librarian*, *English 4–11* and *Classroom NATE*. There are online reviews on a large number of websites, for example *Books for Keeps*, Write Away and Booktrust. Annotated and regularly updated book lists for different age groups and abilities are available from the Young Booktrust.

What is a quality fiction text for children? It might well have some of the following qualities: strong plot, interesting and convincing characters, language that is alive and powerful, layers of meaning, well-described settings providing virtual experience of other environments, relevance to a range of human issues, and engaging feelings as well as thoughts. The best books have something profound to say about the human condition and particularly the experience of the growing child, but not in a self-conscious way. In fact, children respond to humour, even if some darker issues are explored. Although nearly every possible topic has been explored in children's fiction, I cannot think of a book that is completely pessimistic – the ending

offers at least some hope. Looking at the whole fiction collection we would want to have books that appeal to both genders, include children who have their roots in every part of the world and avoid unwelcome bias.

By the end of the primary years we hope that children will have become confident and enthusiastic readers of fiction both at home and in school. We have succeeded if children read fiction independently and by choice. The entries on novels and on emotional literacy aim to explain the distinctive contribution that reading quality fiction makes to a child's intellectual and emotional development. New technologies are having an impact on the way fiction is taught in schools. Children are looking at the diversity of fictional narratives in film, picture books and DVD games. As Gamble (2004) points out, interactive gaming, role playing and story making are likely to be significant in the classrooms of the future.

When it comes to helping children deepen their response to fiction there are different levels to consider: whole text level, sentence level and word level (Wilson and Scanlon, 2011). At whole text level, there are some questions that can usefully be asked of each work: what kind of text is it; if appropriate, what is important about the plot, characterisation and setting; how is the resolution of central conflicts achieved; are any particular human issues considered in an illuminating way? Sentence-level study will involve drawing attention to kinds of syntactic structures used and use of literary devices like metaphor and simile, while word-level work will focus on the vocabulary used and its impact. Statutory requirements must be heeded, but one hopes that this will not prevent us from emphasising reading for meaning and pleasure in our daily practice. Response to fiction can be explored and enriched by carefully chosen activities. Benton and Fox (1986) consider that activities before, alongside or after hearing a story, play or poem should be those that lead children deeper into the layers of meaning. Sometimes just to listen or to read and reflect silently is enough, but often the children's response will be developed by a carefully thought out activity. Teachers know best which activities are most likely to interest the children in their class after they have enjoyed a particular piece of fiction. The ideas in books by Chambers (1993), Gamble and Yates (2008), Graham (1997, 2008), Lockwood (2009) and Mallett (2010) and in the list of suggestions below may be helpful, particularly to students and new teachers. This list is culled from many books and classroom examples. Girls are often thought to be more enthusiastic readers of fiction, but evidence from some studies suggest that the picture is more mixed – see for example the case studies in *Boys on the Margin* in which boys showed some stamina in reflecting on reading the Charles Causley poem 'What Has Happened to Lulu?' and the robust story by Louis Sachar *There's a Boy in the Girl's Bathroom*. Both boys and girls respond when fiction is well chosen and activities imaginative. I will never forget the power and passion of a discussion about what makes a good friend by a group of ten year old boys and girls after a teacher's lively reading of Gene Kemp's *The Turbulent Term of Tyke Tiler*. You need to decide at which point to introduce an activity – before, during or after the shared reading. Your choice will be affected by the nature of the actual text, the best ways of working in your particular classroom context, and the age, abilities and preferences of the individuals who make up your class. So adapt, extend and ring the changes.

Extending reading response

Speaking and listening

- retelling the story;
- reading favourite parts out loud;

- sharing predictions about how a story will develop;
- talking about the issues in a class or group setting;
- individuals presenting an opinion on an aspect of the text – characterisation, setting, plot or resolution – to encourage further discussion;
- if appropriate, talking about and interpreting illustrations;
- imagining the content of letters and conversations (could be written down later);
- talking about the writer's use of language and imagery for particular effects;
- dramatic improvisation around issues;
- recording a pretend radio book review programme;
- thinking aloud in role – revealing a character's motivations; and
- hot seating – one child takes up the role of a central character and answers questions from teacher and other children.

Writing

- 'reading journals' (see Judith Graham's photocopiable framework in *Cracking Good Books* or devise your own, consulting the children);
- preparing character dossiers with reports, letters and sketches;
- creating timelines – chronological charts of events in the story;
- scripting part of a story;
- sharing own anecdotes after reading an autobiography like Roald Dahl's *Boy*;
- alternative fairy stories on the theme of a traditional tale or other kinds of genre exchange, for example making part of a story into a film script with posters advertising the film and a cast list;
- poems on a powerful theme in the text;
- the story from another character's perspective;
- letters between characters, perhaps emails or text writing in pairs;

- diary entries;
- newspaper reports based on an event in a story (favourites are *The Three Little Pigs* and *Red Riding Hood*);
- sequels – these are challenging but older children might enjoy writing a chapter about what happened a few years after the book ended;
- some fiction lends itself to the making of maps of the setting or a journey; and
- display one author's work together with reviews, cover flap 'blurb' and comments by teacher and children.

Benton, Michael and Fox, Geoff (1986) *Teaching Literature 9–14* Oxford: Oxford University Press.

Chambers, Aidan (1993) *Tell Me: Children, Reading, and Talk* Stroud: The Thimble Press.

Ellis, Sue (ed.), Lazim, Anne, Moss, Elaine and Nicholson, Deborah (updated every two years) *The Core Booklist* London: CLPE.

Gamble, Nikki (2004) 'Teaching fiction' in Hunt, P. *International Companion Encyclopedia of Children's Literature* London and New York: Routledge.

Gamble, Nikki and Yates, Sally (2008, second edition) *Understanding Children's Literature* London: Sage.

Graham, Judith (1997) *Cracking Good Books* Sheffield: The National Association for Literacy in Primary Education.

——(2008) 'Contemporary picturebooks' in Goodwin, Prue (ed.) *Understanding Children's Books* London: Sage.

Lockwood, Michael (2009) *Promoting Reading for Pleasure in the Primary School* London: Sage.

Mallett, Margaret (2010) *Choosing and Using Fiction and Non-fiction 3–11* London and New York: Routledge (see part one).

Mills, C. and Webb, J. (2004) 'Selecting books for younger readers' in Hunt, P. *International Companion Encyclopedia of Children's Literature* London and New York: Routledge.

Safford, Kimberley, O'Sullivan, Olivia and Barrs, Myra (2004) *Boys on the Margin: Promoting Boys' Literacy Learning at Key Stage 2* London: CLPE.

Townsend, John Rowe (1995) *Written for Children* London: The Bodley Head.

Wilson, Angela and Scanlon, Julie (2011, fourth edition) *Language Knowledge for Primary Teachers* London: David Fulton.

FICTION AS A SOURCE OF INFORMATION

See also: art and English, history and English, information stories, science and English

We learn much about life at different times and in different environments and about the human condition from fiction. In primary English, fiction and informational texts can sometimes work together to help children learn.

After enjoying Kenneth Grahame's *The Wind in the Willows*, children sometimes turn to information books about the creatures of the riverbank. I have known cases where older primary children have taken their explorations further – into books about the changes in the natural environment and how we can prevent more damage being done to our riverbanks. The celebration in *The Wind in the Willows* of the natural world is a powerful background to looking at environmental issues because it gives us a sense of the richness we have lost or might lose.

Experienced teachers often find fiction a powerful beginning for other kinds of learning. Just a few other examples known to me of children's interest being sparked by stories include eight year olds wanting to find out about spiders after reading E.B. White's *Charlotte's Web*; nine year olds investigating pigs and animal welfare after a shared reading of Dick King-Smith's *The Sheep-pig*; and ten year olds researching the facts on evacuees during the Second World War after enjoying Nina Bawden's *Carrie's War*.

Things can happen the other way round. Richard Adams' *Watership Down*, a fantasy that gives us a sense of the spirit of the countryside, could be a starting point for or complement informational research. However, in an interesting case study by Donald Fry in Chapter 2 of *Children Talk About Books*, this novel is a way into enjoying fiction for a seven year old who has a preference for factual texts. Seven year old Clayton identifies with the interests of his father who works on a farm and reads *Farmer's Weekly*. Father and son enjoy informational reading about animals, agriculture and wild flowers. The teacher praised this at parents' evening but suggested that father and son might also read some fiction together to broaden the range of Clayton's reading. In this case a story read by father to son extended an interest in agriculture and wildlife (Fry, 1985).

Illustration can sometimes link fact and fiction. Picture book illustrators, in particular, often take great care over detail and accuracy. Judith Graham (1996) explores the potential of Alexander and Lemoine's story, *Leila*, about a child searching for her lost brother in the desert, a starting point for research into desert life. Clothes, plant and lifestyle are all portrayed powerfully. Scrutiny of illustrations in two picture books was also important in five year olds' science work on 'light'. The wonderful picture of a night time landscape in *Peace at Last* led the children to talk about the different sources of light – the moon and stars and the lights in people's houses spilling onto the lawn. After looking at *Can't you Sleep Little Bear* the same children identified a light source that gives warmth: fire.

So, there can be some rich interplay between texts of different kinds, but we need a light touch here – mostly stories are worthwhile for their own sake and impart their lessons with gentleness and subtlety.

Fry, Donald (1985) *Children Talk about Books: Seeing Themselves as Readers* Milton Keynes: Open University Press.

Graham, Judith (1996) 'Using illustration as the bridge between fact and fiction' *English in Education* 30 (1).

Mallett, Margaret (2003) *Early Years Non-fiction* London: Routledge (see Chapter 11).

FIELD OF DISCOURSE

See also: concept mapping, register

The field of discourse is an aspect of its register and is concerned with the topic or content of a spoken or written text. There is a close link between the topic or content and the vocabulary used in a text. When easing children into the field of discourse of a new topic teachers often invite 'brainstorming'. Here the words and concepts associated with, for example, volcanoes, the Vikings or electricity are identified and made into a concept map or web.

FIGURATIVE LANGUAGE

See also: analogy, metaphor, simile

In literary texts, particularly in poetry, language is often used obliquely to the subject by using devices like metaphor and simile (imagery) and analogy.

FILM

See: television and literacy, video-film and DVDs, visual literacy

FILM MAKING

See also: British Film Institute, interactive whiteboard, television programmes for children, video-film and DVDs, visual literacy

The availability of digital video makes it easier for teachers to offer older primary children the opportunity to make short films. In English, these films can be in the form of news reports or advertisements, or

167

based on the novels, short stories, poems or plays the children have been reading. Filming narratives links with other literacy work and helps children reflect on the differences between telling a story on screen and in print. Children must find ways of using new technology to create a coherent narrative which adds sound effects, music and visual input to the spoken word. They also need to provide a convincing set – a backdrop to the story that the film will tell (Mallett, 2007).

This kind of work benefits from careful planning and sufficient time is needed for children to learn about the camera and its controls. Young film makers have also to acquire new concepts and a new vocabulary to refer to these concepts, such as 'long shots', 'close-ups' and, when it comes to editing, 'copy', 'crop' and 're-order'. These terms will be used in creating and editing the film script. Children will have to learn about what is required by the different personnel – actors, producer, director and camera operators. Above all, the children will need to reflect on the extract and on the motivations and emotions of the characters and how these will be realised in the film. What are the viewers to understand from the film sequences? How will the mood of the story be achieved in film?

A Year 6 class helped to make some short films using extracts from books they had recently read and enjoyed, and were supported through all these stages in the work (Burnett *et al.*, 2004). The children worked in groups and used a digital video and then an editing programme – iMovie – which is available on most Apple computers. One group faced the challenge of creating the impression of a penal setting in Texas to bring alive the environment of their book, *Holes* by Louis Sachar.

The teachers concluded that although the children had much experience of watching film on television, actually making the films had helped them look at the

moving image in new ways. Children commented on how much work was involved in creating a short sequence. Although the work generated much enthusiasm, the children in this case study had to adjust their ambitious plans to what was practical – both technically and within the time limit set.

Burnett, Cathy, Keating, Caroline and Merchant, Guy (2004) 'Shooting the story' in *The Primary English Magazine*, 9(5) June.

Mallett, M. (2007) *Active Encounters: Inspiring Young Readers and Writers of Non-fiction 4–11* UKLA minibook.

FIRST PERSON WRITING

See also: anecdotes, autobiography, diary, expressive talk and writing, letters, recount

This is writing from one person's viewpoint and it can take the form of a diary or journal entry, a letter, a factual narrative (recount) or a full-length autobiography. Writers of fiction sometimes use the first person 'voice' as a device to achieve certain effects – see under 'autobiography'.

First person recounts or narratives are a very important kind of writing in English work, where all a pupil's intellectual and imaginative faculties are often brought into play. How we react to and feel about events, people and ideas are relevant in a way they might not be in other subjects. The very first writing children do is often very like written down speech. James Britton called this 'expressive writing' and considered it to be close to the interests and preoccupations of the writer.

The advantages of writing in the first person include the sense of immediacy it gives, the detailed insight gained into one person's way of dealing with life and experience, with events and people, and its potential to 'invite the reader in'. Within these very strengths, though, lie some possible limitations. As ten year old Hayley remarked, 'everything is shown through only one person's eyes'. Mallett (1997) carried out a series of lessons with a Year 6 class to point out some of the differences between first and third person writing.

After reading parts of Roald Dahl's *Boy: Tales of Childhood* (Penguin, 1984), *Anne Frank's Diary* (Unicorn Books, 1960) and *The Shorter Pepys* (Bell and Hyman, 1985), these were some of the features of auto-biographical writing that children and teacher noted:

- A diary entry, letter or full-length autobiography is the writer's selection of events and although it is closely based on real experience, the writer chooses how to tell each event, what to emphasise and what to miss out.
- The 'voice' has a friendly, confiding tone, in some respects like speech.
- Enough detail is included to involve the reader with the situation.
- Events, both sad and humorous, and which illuminate aspects of the human situation, are skilfully described.
- The narrative does not just describe events, it assesses them and their impact on people. The writer's own behaviour and that of others is constantly commented on and evaluated, and thoughts and feelings are of great importance.
- Direct speech can add to the vitality of the writing.

(Mallett, 1997: 14)

When it comes to their own first person writing some children find it difficult to go beyond the rather monotonous listing of events in chronological sequence with over-use of the conjunction 'and'. Teachers can help by looking with the children at how skilled writers add interest. Both Roald Dahl and Anne Frank energise their accounts with a lot of direct speech. The writers we want to read do not stick to safe and bland topics and reactions. Anne

Frank's diary is fascinating partly because we hear about who fell out with whom. The children in the case study liked the chapter in *Boy* where Dahl describes having his tonsils out without anaesthetic on the kitchen table!

A book my students and I have found helpful in inspiring children of between about five and seven years is Martina Selway's *What Can I Write? Rosie Writes Again* (Red Fox, 1998). The children are shown, with a touch of humour, that their everyday experiences are worth writing about. The same age group nearly always respond to Simon James' delightful book *Dear Greenpeace* (Walker Books), which consists of the letters Emily wrote to and received from Greenpeace about the whale in her garden pond. Other writers of fiction who use the first person 'voice' as a device are Jacqueline Wilson – in her book *Secrets*, Treasure confides her problems and observations – and David Almond, whose character Mina in *My Name is Mina* finds that she can express her thoughts and feelings powerfully and poetically in her journal.

Britton, James (1970) *Language and Learning* London: Allen Lane: The Penguin Press.
Mallett, Margaret (1997) *First Person Reading and Writing in the Primary Years: Enjoying and Reflecting on Diaries, Letters, Autobiographies and First Person Fiction* Sheffield: National Association for the Teaching of English (NATE).

FLASH CARDS

See also: reading

Flash cards are pieces of card about 15 cm by 10 cm with 'key' words printed on them in large letters. This resource is associated with the 'Look and Say' method of teaching reading, in which children learn a 'key' vocabulary before meeting the same words in a reading book. The approach is class-based and children get used to routines in which they say the words when the cards are held up and then find reinforcement in the reading books. Unlike the phonic approaches which emphasise sounds, the Look and Say method stresses the learning of whole words.

In modern practice, the building up of a core vocabulary is maintained, but mechanistic drilling with the flash cards has fallen out of favour.

FLOW CHART

See also: diagrams, visual literacy

A flow chart is a type of diagram that shows the stages involved and the options to choose from in various courses of action.

FOLK TALES

See also: fairy tales, multiculturalism, traditional tales

Folk tales are a category of traditional tales which are over time and which communicate the social attitudes, beliefs and customs of a particular culture. Although their roots are in oral tradition, many have now been written down. As Mary Steele writes, '"folk tale" and "fairy tale" have been used interchangeably by editors, although "fairy tale" in the title generally indicates that the book is intended for children' (Steele, 1989: 5). I find it helpful to join Townsend in regarding 'folk' as referring to the origin of a tale, while 'fairy' refers to its nature (Townsend, 1995: 67). So 'folk tales' is the larger category and a particular folk tale may or may not be a fairy tale.

Folk tales come from many different countries and alongside a good story tell us something about the cultures in which they are set. Enjoyed from about the age of seven years upwards are Caroline Ness' tales from the Indian sub-continent, *The Ocean of Story: a Collection of Magical Folk Tales* (1995) and Berlie Doherty's collection

in which stories from Africa, Canada, Australia and Wales are included, *Tales of Wonder and Magic* (1997). Books go out of print quickly and it is always a good idea to check publishers' catalogues and sites such as Booktrust (www.booktrust.org.uk) for lists of what is currently available.

If you want both to increase your knowledge of folk tales as a genre and gain helpful advice about using them in English and across the curriculum, *Tales for the Telling* is a most stimulating and helpful resource. The annotated lists are well organised, often under intriguing headings, for example 'stories about a land in the sky', 'stories in which somebody has a secret name' and 'stories with an unusual mode of transport'. Another source of insight is Ruth Bottigheimer's account exploring the traditional tales of different countries (Bottigheimer, 2004).

Bottigheimer, R. (2004) 'Fairy tales and folk tales' in Hunt, P. *International Companion Encyclopedia of Children's Literature* London and New York: Routledge.

Hallford, D. and Zaghini, E. (2004) *Folk and Fairy Tales: A Book Guide* London: Booktrust.

Seven Stories (2000) *Tales for the Telling: a Journey Through the World of Folktales* Seven Stories: Centre for the Children's Book (www.sevenstories.org.uk) (this education pack is an exciting guide through the folk tale world which suggests many language activities round folk tales).

Steele, Mary (compiler) (1989) *Traditional Tales* Stroud: Signal Bookguide, ed. by Nancy Chambers.

Townsend, J.R. (1995) *Written for Children* London: The Bodley Head.

FORMATIVE ASSESSMENT

See also: assessment, miscue analysis, reading, speaking and listening, writing

This is a kind of assessment which records what a young learner has achieved and how they might be helped to make further progress. It can serve a diagnostic purpose: a miscue analysis provides a profile of a young reader's strengths and limitations. Formative assessments feed into a dynamic cycle of planning, teaching and learning. The results of formative evaluations can be used with test results to provide a summative assessment, a snapshot of where a pupil is at a particular time.

FOUNDATION STAGE, THE

See also: early learning goals, early years language and literacy, Foundation Stage profile

How very young children are helped to learn is controversial and so it is not surprising that Government requirements and advice about teaching them in schools and nurseries is often reviewed and changed.

The Curriculum Guidance for the Foundation Stage, covering the years from three to six, that is until just before the end of the Reception year, was introduced in England in 2000. This guidance related to another earlier and significant QCA/DfEE (1999) publication – *Early Learning Goals*. Both documents set out learning goals in six areas. Those to do with communication language and literacy include: 'using language to imagine and create roles and experience', 'knowing that print carries meaning' and becoming able to 'write their own names'.

Those working with very young children rightly resist any downward pressure from the National Curriculum to nudge young children towards preparing for the tests and targets of statutory schooling.

Teachers working in different early years settings have distinctive perceptions of their role and varying beliefs about literacy learning. This theme was explored by Linda Miller and Alice Paige Smith who are academics at the Open University's Centre for Curriculum Studies (Miller and

Smith, 2004). The examples of children's work make the article a highly enjoyable read. We see how a planned activity linked to an early learning goal of children writing their names developed into a play situation. Important in this example were the rich play and writing resources available to the children and the teacher's belief in the learning potential of play. Miller and Smith conclude that the Foundation Stage of the National Primary Strategy does embody some of the principles of good early years work but that some practitioners need the kind of training and support that would give them the confidence to interpret the guidance in creative ways. The Foundation Stage is now integrated with Early Years and known as the Early Years Foundation Stages (EYFS). Dame Clare Tickell's review of the EYFS was widely welcomed. She favours a simplification of the Early Learning Goals and an emphasis on learning through structured play (Tickell, 2011). As well as reading about official requirements and guidance, insight and inspiration is found in texts by researchers and scholars in the field. Texts that help give this support include *Language and Literacy in the Early Years* by Marian Whitehead, *Developing Language and Literacy 3–8* by Ann Browne, *Foundations of Literacy* by Sue Palmer and Ros Bayley, *The Early Years Handbook* edited by Max de Boo and *Threads of Thinking* by Cathy Nutbrown. You will also find stimulation and support in the journal published on behalf of Training, Advancement and Co-operation (TACTYC), entitled *Early Years: An International Journal of Research and Development*.

Browne, Ann (2009, third edition) *Developing Language and Literacy 3–8* London: Paul Chapman.

De Boo, Max (2004) *The Early Years Handbook* London: The Curriculum Partnership.

Miller, Linda and Smith, Alice P. (2004) 'Practitioners' beliefs and children's experiences of literacy in four early years settings' *Early Years: An International Journal of Research and Development*, 24(2), September.

Nutbrown, Cathy (1999) *Threads of Thinking: Young Children Learning and the Role of Education* London: Paul Chapman.

Palmer, Sue and Bayley, Ros (2004) *Foundations of Literacy* London: Network Educational Press.

TACTYC: www.tactyc.org.uk

Tickell, Clare (2011) *The Tickell Review of the Early Years Foundation Stage* London: HMSO.

Whitehead, Marian R. (2010, fourth edition) *Language and Literacy in the Early Years* London: Paul Chapman.

FOUNDATION STAGE PROFILE

See also: assessment, early learning goals, Foundation Stage

This profile is a summing-up of a child's progress and learning needs at the end of the Early Years Foundation Stage.

There are no imposed tests, tasks or activities to carry out. The profile is based on teacher observation and assessment. The teacher keeps a record of each child's development and achievement on assessment scales based on the stepping stones and the early learning goals. Four weeks before the end of the summer term the teacher completes a profile summary. There is an electronic version of the scales booklet called eProfile.

If they wish, practitioners can use all or part of the completed profile as the basis for their annual report to parents.

For the purposes of national data collection, all the profiles are submitted to the LEA. This provides evidence for research into, for example, the pattern of children's attainment and the relative achievements of boys and girls.

FREE VERSE

See also: poetry

172

This is verse without a regular metrical pattern and rhyming system but featuring some conventions of poetry like imagery. Many modern poets favour a form that makes meaning, rather than a fixed rhyme or metre, paramount. Teachers often encourage children to write poetry in this form as it frees them from sacrificing meaning to achieve rhyme. It is important not to give the impression that free verse is just cut-up prose.

FULL STOP

See also: drafting, proof reading, punctuation, sentence, transcriptional aspects of writing

A full stop is used to show the end of a sentence, but for a young child the concept of what a sentence is takes time to acquire. We do not speak as we write, and may not always pause at the end of sentences. In a very interesting article, 'Developing concepts of sentence structure and punctuation', David Hutchinson worked with a child on a piece of writing which was a retelling of John Burningham's picture book *Come Away from the Water, Shirley*. The child seemed to be using his speech to develop his account and he used conjunctions where more mature writers would place full stops: 'shirley and her mum and dad were going to the seaside and her dad … '. When researcher and child looked again at the writing the next day, however, the child spontaneously decided to put a full stop after the title and with gentle nudging was able to add other full stops to the account. This seems to support the idea of separating compositional aspects (content) and transcriptional aspects (spelling and punctuation) and encouraging proof reading, even for the very young (Hutchinson, 1987).

In setting out principles for the teaching of punctuation, Nigel Hall urges us to see punctuation as a means of enhancing the meaning of writing. Hall's research reinforced the approach in Hutchinson's case study which placed the teaching of punctuation in the context of lively writing experiences (Hall, 1998). This is helpful for teachers to keep in mind when working with Year 1 children (six to seven year olds), who need to be able to recognise full stops and capital letters and become able to use full stops in their writing.

Hall, Nigel (1998) *Punctuation in the Primary School* Reading University: The National Centre for Language and Literacy.

Hutchinson, David (1987) 'Developing concepts of sentence structure and punctuation' *Curriculum*, 8 (3): 13–16.

FUNCTIONAL LITERACY

If someone is said to have achieved 'functional literacy' it means that they have sufficient competence in reading and writing to live and work in their society. It implies, for example, that they will be able to understand print in the environment – notices, labels, road signs – and manage to read well enough to do a job. The term is sometimes used pejoratively as it emphasises the utilitarian aspects of language. Notions of what is needed for 'functional literacy' will change as society and the job culture changes, for example competence on a word processor is now a basic requirement while up to about the late 1980s it was not.

FUNCTIONS OF LANGUAGE

See also: accent, communicative competence/competence and performance, dialect, field of discourse, language acquisition, language and thought, language change, language variety, mode, register, standard English, tenor, transformational grammar

The functions of language are to do with the purposes for which an individual uses it

at a given time and in a particular context. While structural linguists, like Saussure and Chomsky, emphasised language as an autonomous system made up of words, sentences and longer pieces of text, functional linguists, notably M.A.K. Halliday, saw the structures in a language very much as being derived from its functions (Halliday, 1978). So the form language takes is affected by the purpose of the user. We might be encouraging friends to take a holiday, giving a closely argued formal lecture or trying to persuade someone to vote for us: each purpose affects the form our language will take.

The context of the situation in which a language episode takes place also has a considerable effect on the form of what we say. Halliday describes the different aspects of the context. The 'field' is what is written and spoken about, for example children might be talking about the appearance and habits of the classroom snails. The 'mode' refers to the kind of language used (it will be different in a telephone call, an email or a lesson); the children in the example conducted a conversation in which they were beginning to use some scientific terms like 'habitat' and 'tentacles'. Finally, the 'tenor' is to do with the attitudes of participants towards each other – the children looking at the snails were sharing their observations.

There is more about how functional linguists view language variety and language change under these entries. Halliday's model of functions of language in the young child is covered under 'language acquisition'. It is important to mention here that for older children and adults Halliday suggests we make a distinction between two main functions of language: ideational and interpersonal. The ideational aspect is to do with the content, with what we express. The interpersonal aspect refers to the relationship between participants – our language choices are affected by the relative age and status of the language users and the gender of each and the attitudes they might have towards each other based on past encounters.

The functional approach to language has much to offer in the primary years. In the United Kingdom and other countries like Australia there is recognition that children need to learn about and use different kinds of text, spoken and written. A large part of learning about genre is understanding the different social purposes and the effect of different contexts on language forms. In her book *Teaching About Language in the Primary Years*, Rebecca Bunting goes into further detail about the application of the functional model to the classroom (Bunting, 2000: 21–4).

Bunting, Rebecca (2000 edition) *Teaching About Language in the Primary Years* London: David Fulton.

Halliday, M.A.K. (1978) *Language as Social Semiotic* London: Edward Arnold.

G

GENDER AND LANGUAGE DEVELOPMENT

See also: boys' literacy, equal opportunities, girls' literacy, language variety, video-film and DVDs

Debates about gender and language development are associated with other large issues like the implications of 'sex roles' in society and linguistic differences between women and men.

Proponents of feminist philosophies have tended to argue that it is the male-dominated use of language that has kept women in a subordinate position in society. In the current climate, with the very understandable concern about boys' literacy needs, we must not forget that women continue to be disadvantaged in the workplace, earning less than men for similar work and still sometimes battering at the glass ceiling when it comes to being appointed to some senior positions.

Here we are concerned with gender and language issues as they affect schooling. The picture is both interesting and complex. In the 1970s and 1980s, influenced by feminist analyses, teachers were preoccupied with the disadvantages girls might encounter in school. The emphasis was firmly on inclusion and equal opportunities. As one who lived and taught during these times two things stand out in my memory. First, while not wanting to act as

censors, teachers were concerned that classroom and school library book collections should not only reflect the traditional roles of girls and women in written text and illustration. Reading schemes in particular were scrutinised for sexual, racial and class stereotyping and publishers responded to criticisms made at this time, as the improved resources of today show. Second, there was considerable awareness of girls' disadvantage in talk contexts following the results of research studies, for example that of Swann and Graddol. These two researchers provided evidence, not only of the tendency of boys to dominate class and group discussion, but also of how teachers sometimes unwittingly encouraged it (Swann and Graddol, 1988).

By the 1990s the focus had shifted to boys and their underachievement, particularly in literacy. Of course, it had been known for a long time that boys are in general slower to develop their reading and writing abilities than girls, but why did this change from a preoccupation with girls' disadvantages to concern about boys' needs come about at this time? One reason seems to be to do with the increasing need in the United Kingdom for schools to meet demanding targets which brought the relative lack of success of boys in literacy to the fore. Both the National Curriculum and the National Literacy Strategy were based on inclusion – on the principle that all pupils, regardless of gender, class, ability or culture, should participate in every part of the curriculum. Also built into the requirements was the need to differentiate – to provide for an individual's particular needs and abilities in planning and teaching. Rather than concentrate on the needs of one gender to the possible disadvantage of the other, there is increasing recognition that boys and girls have different learning needs. Baxter, for example, in *Making Gender Work* suggests that if both girls and boys are to flourish we need to employ carefully thought out 'differentiated learning strategies and experiences' (Baxter, 2001: 3) A team from the Centre for Literacy in Primary Education working with teachers showed that all children, and particularly older primary school boys, were encouraged to enjoy reading and writing more when teaching approaches centred on discussion, drama and interactive ICT (Safford *et al.*, 2005).

When it comes to speaking and listening contexts, teachers need to be aware of their own use of language and their non-verbal communication like eye contact and gesture which could affect how children learn and contribute. Both Browne (2009) and Baxter (2001) suggest that allowing another teacher to observe our lessons and to report on boys' and girls' responses and our own teaching style might help us reflect on how we can promote a gender-fair speaking and listening programme. In her very interesting analysis of talk and learning, Browne observes that when they start school many children already show signs of gender identity in the way that they speak and listen to others. Although these are general trends – not all individuals will conform to the pattern – boys often already dominate and expect to be listened to while girls seem more likely to listen to others rather than participating. In planning our oracy work we can bear these tendencies in mind and extend the language experiences of both genders. For example, we can support and encourage

girls when they make contributions to discussions and praise boys when they listen and make supportive comments about the ideas of others. We need also to be fair in choosing topics to appeal to both genders for discussion. Boys and girls can be invited to take turns at being 'leaders' and 'scribes' in group work and giving presentations to the whole class.

Gender differences in reading are also evident early in a child's school life. Children tend to model their reading behaviour and attitudes on the same-sex, older members in their families. Very generally, women read fiction and men non-fiction. The emphasis is still on story in the early years and nursery and Reception classes tend to experience a mainly female culture, possibly reinforcing boys' impression that reading is for girls (Millard, 1997), but both boys and girls need to become able to read a range of texts as they grow older – for their own enjoyment and interest, it is hoped, but also as a way of making progress in school. Information texts as well as stories are important from the earliest stages. (The National Literacy Strategy helped by formalising the inclusion of a range of text types.) Even after the abandonment of the Literacy Strategy the greater value given to the best information texts continued and helped improve the attitude of many boys towards reading as an appropriate activity for both genders. Girls who read only stories had the opportunity to appreciate how quality information texts can satisfy their curiosity and create new interests. Reading out loud to children helps them experience a greater range of texts than if all had been left to independent reading. It is in this sort of context that teachers can model the critical, reflective kind of reading children need to develop to expand their thinking. Even older primary children greatly enjoy and learn from the teacher reading a novel or short story out loud – above all, it brings the whole class together, boys and

176

girls, as a community of young listeners and readers.

Gender differences are just as strong if not more so when it comes to writing as in reading. To some extent, the same preference for fiction is shown by girls and for non-fiction in the case of boys. Teachers can help by creating a balance between writing tasks, ensuring that both boys and girls have the opportunity for story writing and for the different kinds of non-fiction writing. It can be made clear that all aspects of writing are valued so that boys as well as girls take time over presentational aspects as well as the content and style of their work. Shared writing allows the teacher to draw on the strengths of both boys and girls. I was interested to read in Baxter's *Making Gender Work* that boys often prefer writing where there is some structure built into the task. I have also found this is the case. For example, in my own small-scale research study of one Year 6 class's reading and writing choices, two ten-year-old boys commented as follows:

DAN: I like writing the end of a story when the teacher has read out the first part. It gives you a good start ... you don't have to think of a beginning.

TOM: Yes and it gives you an idea of the sort of thing you can write, like *The Secret Tunnel* was a mystery.

Tom seems to be saying that there are conventions in a particular genre and you feel more confident about controlling them if you have been given some idea of how to proceed (Mallett, 1997: 55).

When there is a free choice of what to write teachers find boys and girls tend to choose very different stories in setting plot and characterisation. Girls often like to create fantasy situations and are interested in people's and animals' feelings and reactions. As all teachers know, boys on the other hand very often choose to write horror stories, sometimes showing the influence of their computer games and the television programmes they watch. Although we are glad that some children are prepared to attempt a story at all, there have to be some guidelines about what is acceptable. We must protest if a child consistently writes of violent events and weapons. On the whole, a constructive approach is best – one that encourages children to think about what they are writing and why they have chosen a particular storyline and particular words and phrases. In the entry on 'boys' literacy' there is information about the initiatives of the Centre for Language in Primary Education, initiatives that show that inviting work which includes drama and ICT texts can lead to boys reading and writing lively fiction.

The new media have made an impact on all children's literacy development. See the entry on 'popular culture and new media' for information about use of the internet, electronic texts and blogging, which are positive forces in encouraging many kinds of reading and writing. Popular culture does bring some gender issues. In 'Superhero stories: literacy, gender and popular culture' Jackie Marsh raises these (Marsh, 2003). Nevertheless, a great plus is that the new media can enthuse even reluctant writers. Schools creating blogging platforms on their websites have found both boys and girls enjoy the collaborative nature of these initiatives. There are some interesting case studies of lessons and activities in our digital age in the English Association's primary journal *English 4–11*. There are practical suggestions also in *Digital Literacies* to help teachers get to grips with digital literacy in the classroom (Carrington and Robinson, 2009). Boys and girls need to become familiar with the landscape of digital literacy and even the social uses of literacy – Facebook, blogs, texting, tweeting and computer games – will have an increasing impact on lessons in the classroom.

177

Baxter, Judith (2001) *Making Gender Work* Reading: Reading and Language Information Centre.

Browne, Ann (2009, third edition) *Developing Language and Literacy 3–8* London: Paul Chapman (see Chapter 7).

Carrington, Victoria and Robinson, Muriel (eds) (2009) *Digital Literacies: Social Learning and Classroom Practice* London: Sage with UKLA.

Mallett, Margaret (1997) 'Gender and genre: reading and writing choices of older juniors' in *Reading* UKRA 31(2), July.

Marsh, Jackie (2003) 'Superhero stories: literacy, gender and popular culture' in Skelton, Christine and Francis, Becky (eds) *Boys and Girls in the Primary Classroom* Milton Keynes: Open University Press.

Millard, Elaine (1997) *Differently Literate: Boys, Girls and the Schooling of Literacy* London: Falmer Press.

National Centre for Language and Literacy, University of Reading: www.ncll.org.uk.

Safford, Kimberly, O'Sullivan, Olivia and Barrs, Myra (2005) *Boys on the Margin* London: CLPE.

Swann, J. and Graddol, D. (1988) 'Gender inequalities in classroom talk' *English in Education*, 22(1): 48–65.

GENRE

See also: autobiography, biography, discussion text, explanation text, expressive talk and writing, faction, factual genres, fantasy, fiction: choosing and using, film making, history of children's literature, novels, persuasive genre, poetry (and sub-categories like epic poetry, ballad, haiku and free verse), procedural and instructional genre, realism, recount, report, television and literacy, text-level work, transactional writing, transitional genre, visual literacy

For particular kinds of children's books see under entries like adventure stories, animals, fairy tales, parable, school stories and traditional tales.

Genres are types or kinds of text. The form of a text varies according to its purpose. At one time the term 'genre' was used to refer mainly to kinds of literature – novels, poems and playscripts and their sub-categories; now it tends to refer to any type of text, whether written, spoken or pictorial.

The National Curriculum English programmes and objectives are partly genre based; the assumption is that development in literacy is partly to do with controlling, as readers and writers, the kinds of texts valued in our society. Included are all kinds of fiction and non-fiction in a wider range of media than ever before – in addition to print (books, articles, newspapers, letters, flyers, transcripts and posters), we have software, the internet, CD-ROMs, ebooks, film and DVDs.

Underpinning the National Curriculum emphasis on genre is the work of a group of Australian academics and teachers who are referred to as 'genre theorists'. Their classroom-based research studies found that teachers encouraged the writing of narratives much more than, for example, persuasive and explanatory kinds of writing. For essays by different genre theorists see Reid (1987) and for a critical analysis of the work of J.R. Martin, F. Christie and J. Rothery I recommend Wyse and Grant (2007).

Critics of the genre theorists often express concern about the formal teaching of genre to which their work has sometimes led. It is also felt that genre is presented as too static a phenomenon. While the characteristic elements of a genre may be organised fairly predictably, we must remember that language is socially situated and dynamic – it changes as a culture changes. Think of the impact on writing forms of the new technologies – the email is a developing form reflecting changes in our working procedures and resources. This more flexible approach to genre is found in the work of Wilson and Scanlon (2011) and Derewianka (1996).

Derewianka, Beverley (1996) *Exploring the Writing of Genres* UKRA Minibook series.

Reid, I. (ed.) (1987) *The Place of Genre in Learning* Victoria: Deacon University.

Wilson, Angela and Scanlon, Julie (2011, fourth edition) *Language Knowledge for Primary Teachers* London: David Fulton.

Wyse, Dominic and Grant, Russell (2007) *Teaching English, Language and Literacy* London: Routledge-Falmer.

GENRE EXCHANGE

See also: EXEL Project

This term is used to refer to transforming information read in one form into another. A child might read a non-narrative text about the food eaten by the Saxons and be asked to use the information to create a menu. It is a strategy that helps children draw on information in their writing rather than copying or closely paraphrasing.

GENRE THEORY

See: genre

GEOGRAPHY AND ENGLISH

See also: atlas, factual genres, information stories, narrative, non-fiction reading and writing, visual literacy

In geography lessons the things children learn about include the physical features and climate of the Earth, the places where people live and the environmental challenges that they face. An 'English' perspective helps children get a personal foothold in these topics. Geography, like other subjects, can be linked with English in literacy lessons; the same text can be used in either context but in different ways. The Geographical Association has an excellent early years and primary page with annotated lists of recommended resources. It has story competitions from time to time

to encourage children to develop their own response to places they visit. Some early geography books encourage personal response to environments. Meredith Hooper's *River Story* would help under sevens explore geographical concepts of time, place and change as the river makes its journey from its source to the sea. In English, the emphasis would be on how the visual and the verbal interact to tell an exciting narrative. Children could talk about the dynamic words to describe the water's movement – 'bubbling', trickling', 'bouncing' and 'slipping' – and how Bee Willey's pictures extend our understanding.

Resources for geography include books and print atlases, posters and publicity material from travel agents, maps and leaflets about local amenities from local authorities, newspaper articles and letters on environmental issues, CD-ROMs and websites. All this links the written word with social purposes children can understand. In the case of younger children, especially, we can use fact and fiction flexibly. Indeed many of the books written for them are 'transitional' in the sense that they only have some of the features of the mature genre they are leading towards. For instance, when it comes to 'map books' and early atlases there is everything to be gained from selecting those that relate to children's existing knowledge and experience (see under 'atlas'). The enjoyment of Pat Hutchins' story, *Rosie's Walk*, is often extended by asking children to make a map of Rosie's journey across the farmyard, pursued by a fox. The story can be a starting point for helping children understand directional language. Poetry can also inspire making maps. Teachers sometimes ask children to make a map of the village where Robert Browning's *The Pied Piper of Hamelin* is set, with its town hall, River Weser and Koppelberg Hill. A number of my students have praised Eljay Yildirim's *Aunty Dot's Incredible Adventure Atlas*, which uses letters to involve children in

179

a journey round the world. These are illustrated with clear maps, pictures and photographs that give insight into different cultures. This entertaining book can be the starting point for children's own letters and travel diaries which allow appreciation of personal response and evaluation of places (Mallett, 1999).

There is a long tradition of books that try to help children understand life in another country by following a day or week in the life of a child about their own age. Frances Lincoln's *Child's Day* series is a recent addition to this tradition and covers days in the lives of children in India, Russia, Ghana, Brazil and China. Some of the photographs give the flavour of subtle cultural differences; there is a picture of a class of young children in a Russian school in *Pollina's Day* which communicates powerfully what a serious business learning can be. Two other books, each with an alphabetic organisation, also tell us about our shared world in a warm and sympathetic way: Ifeoma Onyefulu's *A is for Africa* and Kathryn Cave's *W is for World*, both published by Frances Lincoln, introduce interesting vocabulary and ideas with involving photographs. The issues round having connections with two different cultures is a theme often explored in children's picture books and novels. The subtle feelings about both the people and the environments are explored in Hoffman and Binches' *Grace and her Family*. Children are also helped to imagine the feelings and perspectives of others through the device of a small bear in the Barnaby Bear resource packs (www.barnabybear.co.uk). Geography is concerned with large concepts like time and space, often difficult to explain to children. *Out There Somewhere, it's time to ...* by Manning and Granström (Franklin Watts) has an imaginative approach to understanding time differences across the world, by creating contrasts through text and exhilarating illustrations of different environments which include Guilin (in China), New York, Moscow and Newcastle upon Tyne. The book has two levels of text: the main text is bold and conversational, while the smaller text is more like that of a conventional information book.

Most of the texts mentioned so far linking geography and literacy have been suitable for the under eights, but older primary children also need the encouragement provided by powerful photographs and diagrams and interesting texts, and those found in the media and on the internet become increasingly valuable as children get older. For an interesting account of geography's contribution to environmental education, often through children's involvement with matters of local concern, see John Cook's (1999) chapter, 'Geography: a sense of place'.

Poems and novels also link English and geography. John Agard's poem 'What the teacher said when we asked, "What Er We Avin for Geography, Miss"' entertains but can also invite deep reflection on the subject of geography (in *Can I Buy a Slice of Sky?*, edited by Grace Nichols, Blackie Publishers). Then there are poems about volcanoes and earthquakes that show us the human side of natural disasters. 'Hurricane' from *A Caribbean Dozen* (Walker Books) gives an insight into what it feels like to be caught up in the 'big wind'. Novels and short stories that take us into a distinctive setting or environment very memorably or give us the texture and personal detail of a journey perhaps give the most powerful links between English and geography. Here we would all have our own favourites, which might include Anita Desai's *The Village by the Sea: An Indian Family Story*, Beverley Naidoo's *Journey to Jo'burg: A South African Story* and Ian Serraillier's *The Silver Sword*.

Cook, John (1999) 'Geography: a sense of place' in Riley, Jeni and Prentice, Roy (eds)

The Curriculum for 7–11 Year Olds London: Paul Chapman.

Geographical Association: www.geography.org. uk – see EY & Primary page for resource lists, maps and curriculum information.

Mallett, Margaret (1999) *Young Researchers: Informational Reading and Writing in the Early and Primary Years* London: Routledge.

GIFTED AND TALENTED CHILDREN

See also: Special Educational Needs (SEN) in language and literacy

Roughly 2 per cent of the children in this country are regarded as 'gifted' and this number includes boys and girls from all social and ethnic backgrounds. They may be outstandingly able (or potentially so) in one or more areas of intelligence: logical/ mathematical, verbal/ linguistic, spatial/ design, musical, kinaesthetic or inter-personal/intrapersonal. Many are creative and observant. However, of course, even within this group the range and depth of their abilities varies as does how well or otherwise they cope with the challenges of being gifted. They have to find a way to manage a likely mismatch between their intellectual age and their emotional/social age, and it is hardly surprising that many become bored and even disruptive if they encounter teaching that is too routine and unimaginative to stretch and challenge them. We must also keep in mind the needs of those gifted children at special risk of underachievement because of learning difficulties such as dyslexia, autism or a sensory impairment. Providing for these children as well as for other gifted children is required on grounds of 'equal opportunity'. This involves offering such variety of instruction and training needed to match their different ages, abilities and aptitudes.

When it comes to reading and writing, both in and out of the English classroom, we find that able children need the challenge of more difficult fiction and non-fiction texts. They are especially able to rise to the challenge of the layers of meaning and intriguing illustrations in more complex works. For example, Mini Grey's picture books which show unusual and interesting ways of looking at the world are liked by very young forward readers: *Egg Drop* (Red Fox) and *The Pea and the Princess* (Red Fox) seem to be particular favourites. Jeanne Willis' *Tadpole's Promise* is another intriguing story with a twist that advanced young readers are likely to savour. By eight or nine verbally and linguistically gifted children often respond well to the work of quality children's authors ahead of their contemporaries. They are able to grapple, for example, with the perplexing treatment of aspects of childhood and the wisdom of adults portrayed in a sinister and perplexing picture book *The Wolves in the Walls* by Neil Gaiman and Dave McKean (Bloomsbury) and are ready sooner for the books of major children's authors like David Almond (*My Name is Mina*), Phillip Pullman (His Dark Materials trilogy), Geraldine McCaughrean (*The Stones are Hatching*), Michelle Parver (*Wolf Brother*), Michael Morpurgo (*War Horse*) and Philippa Pearce (*Tom's Midnight Garden*). By Key Stage 2 gifted children are ready for more advanced non-fiction, for example full-length auto-biographies, biographies and travel books. This is the time to encourage increased use of other media – the internet of course, ebooks, video texts, newspapers and magazines. We need to ensure that in all these media they find coverage of the sort of controversial topics to do with social issues and the environment that the very able like to reflect on and discuss. All children need to encounter these texts but the linguistically advanced child often needs to be provided with them sooner. These are just a few suggestions and you would find further help from Booktrust and Young Booktrust: www.booktrust.org.uk.

Of great help to schools, parents and local authorities making provision for gifted children is the work of the National Association for Gifted Children (NAGC): www.nagcbritain.org.uk. This organisation has a government grant but is a charity financed by members' subscriptions and donations. Although they are represented on the Government Advisory Group for Gifted and Talented Pupils and other government committees, they have an independent voice and claim to 'have a good record of successful government lobbying'. Their website lists their publications and describes their philosophy and work. They aim to advise on the identification of the gifted, encourage partnership between home, school and community, and to share and spread best practice. NAGC encourages schools to build in the kind of flexibility and richness of opportunity that will foster the development of not only the gifted but of every child.

Clark, Catherine and Callow, Ralph (2002) *Educating the Gifted and Talented: Resource Issues and Processes for Teachers* London: David Fulton.

GIRLS AND ENGLISH

See: girls' literacy, gender and language development

GIRLS' LITERACY

See also: boys' literacy, equal opportunities, gender and language development

In the interests of improving gender equality, the 1970s and 1980s saw the stereotyping of girls and women in children's literature challenged. It was thought that the perception that girls had of themselves and of the opportunities open to them was influenced by their too often seeing themselves portrayed in domestic settings and in traditionally female jobs and professions.

Publishers took note and both reading scheme books and trade books began to reflect a more plural and gender-equal society. Research and thinking on gender issues was preoccupied with the evidence that boys often dominated discussion in mixed classes, sometimes with the teacher's unwitting connivance (Swann and Graddol, 1988). Then, as the 1990s got underway, there was a change of emphasis to a concern about boys' relative lack of success in literacy. It was already known that, in general, girls learn to read more quickly, say they enjoy reading more, read more widely than boys and perform better on reading tests (Baxter, 2001), so why did this issue come to the fore at this time? Part of the explanation is that the SATs, to assess children's learning from the National Curriculum and National Literacy Strategy, revealed rather starkly that boys were behind their female peers when it came to literacy, or at any rate in the kind of literacy abilities measured by summative tests. Part of this mismatch is to do with the tendency of girls to mature sooner than boys and therefore to forge ahead in their literacy development. Boys may well catch up later on. Schools, though, were pressed to 'raise standards' and the publication of league tables was a further spur to pushing all the children to achieve higher grades. Gender priorities at school changed to an emphasis on how to turn boys on to literacy. Two things are worth remembering when we try our best to see that both girls and boys develop all kinds of literacy and competence in language use. First, children are individuals with their own preferences, interests and strengths. Not all boys are behind in literacy development and some girls contribute confidently in group and class discussion.

Second, a concern to help boys to improve their reading and writing competence in areas where they lag behind girls must not make us neglect 'the continuing needs of girls' (Baxter, 2001: 3). The observations of Swann and Graddol and others who have carried out studies on classroom interaction should still inform our practice. Elaine Millard (2001), Eve Bearne (2002) and Judith Baxter (2001) are all concerned that we should not approach gender issues in a competitive way but regard them as different aspects of 'the same social and educational questions'. We are coming to realise that just as the principle of 'inclusion' requires schools to stress similarities and the ability of all pupils to participate fully within the curriculum, so we must nevertheless understand the implications of the principle of 'differentiation' – that we need to respond to the individual differences and the differing needs of particular pupils. There is a core of books and a range of activities likely to be enjoyed by both boys and girls, but, very generally, girls and boys may have some different needs when it comes to developing their literacy. Therefore, just as the entry on 'boys' literacy' concentrates on boys' needs, the present entry looks particularly at what we need to bear in mind when promoting the literacy of girls.

Supporting girls' literacy

Some girls need active encouragement to contribute confidently to discussion

Spoken and written language work together in children's language learning; discussion, as well as contributing to learning, often precedes writing. So in the interests of developing both girls' speaking abilities and their competence in related kinds of literacy we must make sure that silent girls are encouraged to speak out. One strategy is sometimes to have an all-female group for discussion. When groups are mixed the teacher can help by appointing girls as 'chair' or 'spokesperson' to move them away from being 'scribes' and 'helpers'. Girls also seem to appreciate time to prepare a contribution before the discussion

group comes together. Some teachers find it helpful to ask a colleague to observe them teaching with some specific questions in mind. For example, we might ask whether the colleague thinks we have a fair way of appointing roles and responsibilities or how sensitively we select children to contribute.

Girls may need support in using some ICT texts and with some computer activities

When new technologies came in towards the last quartile of the twentieth century, girls' relative lack of interest in multimedia texts and activities was noticed and it was feared by some that this risked them being disadvantaged in a technological world where familiarity and competence with these tools was becoming essential. There are some areas where, very generally, girls still lag behind. In their article 'How important is the digital divide?' the authors found some gender differences linked to a gender gap in spatial ability to the disadvantage of women and girls (Terlecki and Newcombe, 2005). However, the signs are that girls are catching up and enjoying the more social digital activities – texting, Facebook and blogs, for example. The story making potential of Web 2.0, including possibilities like wikis and the creation of virtual worlds, also appeal to girls as much as boys. A good source of help in developing digital literacies in the classroom, for both girls and boys, is *Digital Literacies* (Carrington and Robinson, 2009).

Girls need to learn from non-fiction

It is often observed that girls, given a choice, will choose to read fiction rather than information texts. Does this matter? I think it does because girls who do not read non-fiction hinder their acquisition of knowledge and understanding in English and other lessons across the curriculum.

183

Girls can be tempted into non-fiction reading by offering them narrative non-fiction (Myers and Burnett, 2004), so it may be worth suggesting they read texts that have a natural narrative organisation – life cycles, journeys and 'day in the life of' texts – although my own observations suggest that younger boys and younger girls both benefit from this 'information story' approach to learning. I have also noticed that girls and boys, but especially girls, like non-fiction texts that tap into their preoccupations and feelings as well as 'the facts' and deal with controversial topics like endangered species, risks from mobile phones and the responsibilities of keeping a pet. Girls' interest in relationships is exploited by elements in the mass media. By the later primary years many girls read magazines that offer advice about diet, make-up, relationships with boys and, of course, they include advertisements. It is important that girls develop a critical approach so that they are less likely to be manipulated by this kind of reading material.

To increase writing range, we must convince girls that wide reading is important

Teachers find that where a 'free choice' of activity is given to young children, girls are much more likely to seek out the writing corner than boys (Herring, 1990). As they get older many girls show a mature understanding of the emotional preoccupations of characters and their relationships, often using narrative and dialogue to tell the story. Of course, the writing of both girls and boys reflects what they read (Bearne, 2002; Millard, 1997, 2001). There is evidence that boys draw on their experience of reading multimodal texts so that their writing and imagery is often full of movement and sound while girls' writing tends to use more static images. Accordingly, we need to encourage girls to read a wide range of texts in many media to

support their thinking and learning and to encourage a broader variety of writing styles.

Girls sometimes need to prioritise content over presentation

Learning about good presentation, whether the work is handwritten or word processed, is part of producing a worthwhile final version. However, Browne draws our attention to the tendency of some girls to spend too much time on the careful presentation of first drafts. She suggests that they need to be reminded that content is more important, particularly at the drafting stage (Browne, 2009).

Baxter, Judith (2001) *Making Gender Work* Reading: The National Centre for Language and Literacy, University of Reading.

Bearne, E. (2002) 'Multimodal narratives' in Barrs, M. and Pidgeon, S. (eds) *Boys and Writing* London: Centre for Literacy in Primary Education.

Browne, Ann (2009, fourth edition) *Developing Language and Literacy 3–8* London: Paul Chapman (see chapter 7).

Carrington, Victoria and Robinson, Muriel (eds) (2009) *Digital Literacies: Social Learning and Classroom Practices* London: Sage with UKLA.

Herring, A. (1990) *What Are Writers Made Of? Issues of Gender and Writing* London: National Writing Project with Nelson (O/P).

Millard, Elaine (1997) *Differently Literate: Boys, Girls and the Schooling of Literacy* London: Falmer.

——(2001) 'Aspects of gender: how boys' and girls' experiences of reading shape their writing' in Evans, J. (ed.) *The Writing Classroom: Aspects of Writing in the Primary Child 3–11* London: David Fulton.

Myers, Julia and Burnett, Cathy (2004) *Teaching English 3–13* London and New York: Continuum International.

Swann, J. and Graddol, D. (1988) 'Gender inequalities in classroom talk' *English in Education*, 22 (1): 48–65.

Terlecki, Melissa and Newcombe, Nora (2005) 'How important is the digital divide? The relation of computer and videogame usage to gender differences in mental rotation ability' in *Sex Roles, Journal of Research*, Vol. 53, Numbers 5–6.

GLOSSARY

This is a list of specialist or technical words with explanations usually found at the end of the text they support. When children make their own information books a glossary is often appropriate and helps them clinch some important concepts about the topic.

GRAMMAR

See also: adjectival clause, adjective, adverb, adverbial clause, auxiliary verb, clause, cohesion, conjunction, participle, parts of speech, phrase, preposition, pronoun, sentence, subject knowledge, verbs

David Crystal suggests the following simple definition of grammar: 'Grammar is the study of how we make sentences' (Crystal, 2010). Children will understand this concrete view – that we make sentences out of words just as a carpenter makes things out of wood. If we follow the conventions in putting the words together we can make them do a job. Words, phrases and sentences can be split up and reassembled or transformed into different patterns.

The explicit teaching of grammar in the United Kingdom went out of fashion from the 1960s until the National Literacy Strategy, launched in 1998 and revised in 2006, brought it back on the agenda. Although the Literacy Framework is no longer followed, teachers continue to talk about how parts of speech like nouns and verbs function in sentences. This way of teaching and learning grammar is likely to improve children's ability to spell and punctuate. Teachers and children control a metalanguage for talking about such matters and this encourages a special awareness of language and how we use it.

In an interesting article in the *Times Educational Supplement* (22 January 1999), Sue Palmer sympathised with teachers not educated to analyse sentences: ' ... complex sentences can be a grammatical minefield into which even the most experienced grammarian steps with caution'. She advises, too, against getting bogged down in terminology when teaching children, reminding us that knowing what a verb or complex sentence is, is not an end in itself but a way of improving literacy: ' ... whenever grammatical terminology begins to mystify rather than clarify, it's time to stop using it'.

Bain and Bridgewood distinguish 'teacher knowledge', which is placed under headings called 'reminders', from the teaching objectives, which specify what children are to learn. The loose-leaf file format of their book, which contains much useful photocopiable material, makes it flexible to use. It includes the means of making activity cards which help children to explore language at word, sentence and text level through games (Bain and Bridgewood, 1998).

There are a number of books that are helpful to support our own knowledge of grammar including Crystal (2010), McArthur (1992), Medwell *et al.* (2009) and Wilson and Scanlon (2011). John Seely's (2006) *Grammar for Teachers* takes us through units on words, then sentences, then paragraphs and texts. *The Grammar Guide*, also by John Seely, shows that linguistics can be put across in an interesting way. For a more challenging guide, *Collins Cobuild English Grammar* (2005) might suit.

My own breakthrough came when I realised that what we need to do when defining phrases and clauses is to ask, just as one would of a word, what is the function of this phrase or clause in the sentence? This entry is about grammar, but I include punctuation as part of wider knowledge about language in the suggestions below.

Children's knowledge of grammar and punctuation

Learning is not neatly sequential and so teachers and children will return often to elements in grammar and punctuation first encountered earlier. Reading helps children's developing concept of what a sentence is and their understanding of why the written word needs the help of punctuation marks. Some things can be demonstrated on the interactive whiteboard or paper chart, but games and drama (children taking the parts of verbs and nouns in a sentence) make it more interesting. Recommended are the activities in *The Primary Grammar Book*. The entertaining books *The Perfect Pop-up Punctuation Book* and *The Great Pop-up Grammar Book*, both by Kate Petty and Jenny Maizels, would make good additions to the class library. Another amusingly illustrated book is the children's *Eats, Shoots & Leaves* by Lynn Truss and Bonnie Timmons, which concentrates on use of commas. Louis Fidge's *Grammar and Punctuation*, one of the Collins Primary Focus series, has clear explanations and lively illustrations. How directly grammar and punctuation are taught and when is subject to continuing debate. I offer the following list under year groups as a starting point for discussion.

Foundation stage

Moving towards simple sentences, some punctuation – capital letters for their names on pieces of work and full stops on brief annotations of their drawings.

Year 1

Using simple sentences, capital letters and full stops.

Year 2

Beginning to use some compound sentences, using tense more consistently, using question marks, and using commas to separate items in a list. Lists are likely to come into procedural/instructional kinds of writing, for example recipes or making things.

Year 3

Moving towards showing relationships of time and cause by use of subordination and connectives; sometimes using adjectives as well as verbs and nouns in sentences; understanding and using exclamation marks and speech marks.

Year 4

Developing ability to vary sentence structures to create meaning; using commas to mark clauses; incorporating the possessive apostrophe into writing (this takes time for many children to control – see the children's version of *Eats, Shoots and Leaves* (Truss and Timmons, 2006)).

Year 5

Moving towards linking sentence structure to different text types; maturing use of speech marks and apostrophes (the latter perplexes some children).

Year 6

Increasing control over constructing sentences to convey understanding of hypothesis, speculation and supposition; punctuation to clarify meaning in complex sentences. We would expect to find some use of: direct/indirect speech; active and passive voice; paragraphs. Writing will show appropriate use of different parts of speech, including conjunctions, adverbs, pronouns. Punctuation might include use of asterisk, parentheses/brackets, dashes, semi-colons, colons, bullet points, hyphens.

Moving towards Year 7

Moving towards using complex sentences with subordinate clauses; punctuation to integrate speech into larger sequences; increasing confidence in using Standard English and in understanding some of the differences between spoken and written language. Understanding about mode – writing, illustrating, design and multi-modal combinations – and about media – texting, email and film – increasingly has implications for how we conceive of, teach and assess writing and other ways of communicating meaning.

Bain, Richard and Bain, Elspeth (1995) *The Grammar Book* Sheffield: NATE.

Bain, Richard and Bridgewood, Marion (1998) *The Primary Grammar Book* Sheffield: NATE.

Crystal, David (2010, third edition) *The Cambridge Encyclopedia of Language* Cambridge: Cambridge University Press.

McArthur, T. (1992) *The Oxford Companion to the English Language* Oxford: Oxford University Press.

Medwell, Jane, Moore, George, Wray, David and Griffiths, Vivienne (2009, fourth edition) *Primary English: Knowledge and Understanding* Exeter: Learning Matters.

Seely, J. (2006) *Grammar for Teachers* London: Oxpecker.

Sinclair, John (ed.) (2005, second edition) *Collins Cobuild English Grammar* London: Collins.

Truss, Lynne and Timmons, Bonnie (2006) *Eats, Shoots & Leaves. Why, Commas Really Do Make a Difference* Putnam.

Wilson, Angela and Scanlon, Julie (2011, fourth edition) *Language Knowledge for Primary Teachers.* London: Routledge.

GRAPHEME

See also: grapho-phonic cue-system

A grapheme is the smallest unit of sound in the form of a written symbol. All the twenty-six letters of the alphabet are graphemes, as are any group of letters that forms one sound, for example the 'ow' in swallow. In short, a grapheme is a written-down phoneme.

GRAPHOLOGY

This is the study of the written form of a language.

GRAPHO-PHONIC CUE-SYSTEM

See also: cue-systems, grapheme, phoneme, phonics, phonological awareness

This cue-system helps young readers combine phonic and graphic knowledge in decoding text. To help, teachers need to understand the principles. These include knowing that: sounds or phonemes are represented by letters; phonemes are represented by one or more letters; the same phoneme can be represented in different ways; the same spelling may represent more than one sound.

GROUP DISCUSSION

See: collaborative learning, discourse analysis, discussion text, drama and English, speaking and listening

GROUP READING SCALES

Designed by Denis Vincent and Mary Crumpler for Hodder Education in 2009, these scales are a standardised measure of the reading ability of children aged from six to sixteen. The tests use multiple choice sentence completion tasks and questions. Pupils are required to use semantic and grammatical cues.

Like other standardised sentence-reading tests, these assess improvement, monitoring year-by-year standards.

GROUP WORK

See: collaborative learning, guided reading/ writing

GUIDED READING/WRITING

See also: literacy hour

Placing children into groups for reading has a long history. Sometimes children of a similar ability or interest were placed together, sometimes more forward readers sat with struggling readers to help them. Children often remained in their reading groups for other literacy activities, including writing. However, there was also a tradition of the teacher hearing each child read as often as possible and OFSTED (1996) argued that this was not economic use of a teacher's time. It was felt that it was more efficient for a teacher to work with several children of about the same ability who could benefit from the same teaching.

Ability groups for guided reading and writing were built into the organisation of Literacy Time when the Literacy Framework was followed. Group reading usually involves up to six children all reading the same text. The teacher may be present and help is given appropriate to the whole group. Children can learn from the teacher about predicting what might happen next in a story, how the setting is brought alive and how the author uses images. Most importantly, they benefit from discussing their response to the story or poem. When it comes to non-fiction, using the retrieval devices, learning to summarise and to 'read' the diagrams can be demonstrated. Many children seem to enjoy the interactive nature of group reading.

There are sets of books for guided reading from all the main publishers (for example Rigby Star, Heinemann Storyworlds, Pelican, OUP: Web Guided Reading), but some teachers prefer to assemble sets of books themselves, choosing books that they know will be liked by their pupils. There are a number of books explaining the principles and practice of guided reading, including *Book Bands for Guided Reading* (Baker *et al.*, 2007) and *Guided Reading* (Gamble *et al.*, 2003). Prue Goodwin (2010) discusses guided reading and writing in the context of a full and rich literacy programme in *The Literate Classroom*.

Alison Kelly finds Reception class children enjoy Martin Waddell's amusing picture book *The Pig in the Pond*; the cover showing a gleeful pig diving into the water sending a panicky goose flapping off prompts children's speculations about the story. Ian Beck's *Five Little Ducks* and Ian Whybrow's *The Noisy Way to Bed* are also recommended for guided reading at Key Stage 1. For children ready to make the transition from picture books to more sustained text, Katie Daynes' retelling of *The Elves and the Shoemaker* is divided into chapters which offer natural pausing points for reflection and prediction (Kelly, 2005). Other books in chapters include old favourites such as Anne Fine's *Bill's New Frock*, Dan Pilkey's *The Adventures of Captain Underpants* and Jill Tomlinson's *The Owl who was Afraid of the Dark*. Two series also help here: Egmont Children's Books' *Yellow Bananas* and Usborne's *Young Readers*, and there are good online resources such as *Roy the Zebra*: www.roythezebra. com. Ideal for supporting grammatical and contextual awareness is *Tadpole's Promise* by Jeanne Willis, which has children spellbound when a tadpole promises a caterpillar that he will never change!

Guided group writing follows the same principles: all the children work on the same writing task, possibly arising from shared reading or writing, with the help of the teacher. Just as in the guided group reading context, the teacher can demonstrate planning, drafting and proof reading and point out some of the differences between, for example, writing fiction and non-fiction.

Baker, Suzanne, Bickler, Shirley and Bodman, Sue (2007, fourth edition) *Book Bands for Guided Reading* London: Kingscourt.

Gamble, Nikki, Hobsbaum, Angela and Reedy, David (2003) *Guided Reading: A Handbook for Teaching Guided Reading at Key Stage 2* London: Institute of Education.

Goodwin, Prue (2010) *The Literate Classroom* London: Routledge.

Hobsbaum, Angela (2003) *Book Bands for Guided Reading: Organising Key Stage One Texts for the Literacy Hour* London: Institute of Education

Kelly, Alison (2005) 'Putting the passion into learning to read' *Books for Keeps*, March.

OFSTED (1996) *The Teaching of English in 45 Inner London Primary Schools* London: OFSTED.

H

HAIKU

This is a Japanese poem of three lines with seventeen syllables. Traditionally the poem reveals the writer's impression of a scene or an object in a particular season or time.

'A pink orchid blooms
in solitary splendour
in a silent wood'.

Another kind of Japanese poem, the tanka, has five lines: the first and third have five syllables, the others have seven.

HANDWRITING

See also: early learning goals, early years language and literacy, National Curriculum, phonics, spelling

A school's English policy will have a section on their approach to the teaching of handwriting and we need to communicate the school's approach to parents so that they can help. What aims should guide our choice of a handwriting style and approach? Rosemary Sassoon, who has carried out research into all aspects of handwriting and has written many practical books on how best to teach it, suggests three main aims to guide us. She believes that children should be able to write legibly, speedily and with a developing individual style. Many primary schools in the United Kingdom favour the cursive style, which is simple and aesthetically pleasing.

The National Curriculum English programme for Key Stage 1 also emphasises the importance of well-formed and legible handwriting to help children communicate their meaning. At this stage children are to be taught such basics as how to hold a pen or pencil, form letters of regular size and shape, leave regular sized spaces between words, form lower- and upper-case letters, and learn how to join letters.

Activities such as sky writing (making letter shapes in the air), making letter shapes to music, making letters in sand and using language to describe shapes, referring perhaps to 'the curly caterpillar shape' are encouraged by early years teachers. These controlled movements of the whole body help children gain 'gross motor control' and therefore posture and balance. Children also need to develop 'fine motor control' which includes smaller movements of the hand and fingers. Activities here might include cutting out letter shapes or patterns, finger painting and structured play with sand and water.

Children need to be encouraged to sit comfortably in an upright position and to position and grip their pen or pencil well. Left-handers tend to push the writing implement rather than pulling it, which can lead to a less smooth action (Graham & Kelly, 2009: chapter 5). Very simple things can help and are appreciated by young learners – making sure a child's writing book is on the left (tilted to the right so that the writer can see their writing) and demonstrating letter shapes using the left hand. In a useful summary, Ann Browne reminds us to allow left-handers more time to become competent and to help them establish a firm pencil grip (Browne, 2009).

At what age should joined-up writing start? Most teachers would introduce it by seven years and some begin as soon as children can form the separate letters so that spelling patterns can be reinforced.

Handwriting can be linked to both phonics and spelling. When they hear consonant phonemes in the initial position – s, m, c, t, g, h – children will need to learn the letter shapes alongside the sounds. If we learn the pattern of a word, writing it using the correct letter strings can become conveniently automatic and for the same reason there is also a case for introducing the writing of digraphs (ay, au, ch, wh, etc.) as a unit of two letters joined together. Some published handwriting packages link spelling and handwriting. For example, *Collins Handwriting* by Peter Smith and Judith Williams, a structured handwriting programme in spiral bound photocopiable books, features lists of simple key words to practise particular letters and letter strings.

Medwell and Wray found that some boys in particular have difficulty with handwriting (Medwell and Wray, 2007). For a helpful account of how to help older primary children with weak handwriting see 'Handwriting' by Wyse and Jones (2007).

Perhaps the teaching of handwriting has been relatively neglected as touch typing and word processing become more common in the primary classroom. Jane Medwell and David Wray, who are based at Warwick University, have carried out research into all the issues around the teaching of handwriting and have set out clearly the case for giving handwriting explicit attention. Their review of research in different English-speaking countries suggests that good teaching not only helps with ease and legibility of children's writing, but also makes a positive impact on the extent and quality of what they write (Medwell and Wray, 2007). In their paper 'Handwriting – a forgotten language' they develop their argument that handwriting may be linked to children's thinking and organisation of information (Wray and Medwell, 2008a).

Even now that writing on screen has assumed such importance, the teaching of handwriting should be cherished for all the reasons discussed in this entry. Clear and well-formed writing has aesthetic appeal and children appreciate having their best handwritten stories, poems and factual accounts displayed.

Browne, Ann (2009) *Developing Language and Literacy 3–8* London: Sage (see Chapter 5, 'Spelling, handwriting and punctuation').

Graham, J. and Kelly, A. (2009, third edition) *Writing Under Control* London: David Fulton (see chapter 5).

Medwell, Jane and Wray, David (2007) 'Handwriting: what do we know and what do we need to know?' in *Literacy* 41(1), April.

Sassoon, Rosemary (1983) *The Practical Guide to Children's Handwriting* London: Thames & Hudson.

——(2003, second edition) *Handwriting: The Way to Teach it* London: Sage.

Wray, David and Medwell, Jane (2008a) 'Handwriting – a forgotten language' in *Language and Education*, 22 (1) 34–47. Multilingual Matters.

——(2008b) *Primary English: Extending Knowledge in Practice* Exeter: Learning Matters.

Wyse, Dominic and Jones, Russell (2007) *Teaching English, Language and Literacy* London: Falmer.

HEARING IMPAIRMENT

See also: Special Educational Needs (SEN) in language and literacy

Some children suffer from complete hearing loss, others from partial hearing loss, and special strategies need to be put in place to support their learning and development.

The trend in the United Kingdom has been to reduce the number of hearing-impaired children being provided for in special schools, particularly where the schools are 'out county'. Instead, the money is used to put in place support for teachers of hearing-impaired children in mainstream classes. This help is either in the form of support from an adviser in special needs at the local education authority who assesses and makes recommendations, or withdrawal from classes for special help.

National Deaf Children's Society: www.ndcs.org.uk

HISTORICAL NOVEL

See also: adventure stories, biography, history and English, history of children's literature, novels

Good historical fiction helps children develop sensitivity to the different textures of particular historical periods. If we are reading a novel to enrich the study of a period in history, it is best if the story is fixed in a particular time frame to give children a more than superficial understanding. *The Railway Children* by E. Nesbit informs us about food, housing, transport and the lives of people of different circumstances in Victorian times in the context of a story of adventure and human warmth. A detailed grasp on what life was like in one period helps children understand from what life has moved on and contributes to a sense of chronology (Hoodless, 1998).

As well as contributing to the history lesson, historical novels often raise issues about the kind of human dilemmas we discuss in English. D. Oakden's *The Discus Thrower* (Anglia Young Books, 1992), for example, tells us about living in Ancient Greece and raises, in a subtle way, questions about how certain groups, including women and slaves, were treated in that culture. Rosemary Sutcliff's *The Lantern Bearers* also brings different ways of living, attitudes and beliefs to a human level. History lessons need stories about events arising from the conditions and beliefs of a particular period rather than stories where the historical setting is a superficial backdrop to events that could be set at any time (Cox and Hughes in Hoodless, 1998). In his novel *The Silver Sword* (Puffin, 1956), Ian Serraillier shows us the price of war through the experiences of refugee children searching for their father. Another novel, for older primary children, *When Hitler Stole Pink Rabbit* (Judith Kerr, 1993, HarperCollins) provides insight into living in Nazi Germany and then in wartime Britain. Novels like these take us beyond wars, treaties and laws and bring the past alive through human dilemmas, attitudes and feelings. Other powerful and affecting stories based in wartime include Michael Morpurgo's *War Horse*, Robert Westall's *The Machine Gunners* and Michelle Magorian's *Goodnight Mr Tom*.

Younger children not ready for a novel-length read can get a sense of time and place from picture books and short stories. The Ahlbergs' *Peepo!*, set in the 1940s, pictures such period items as clothes horses and large perambulators, while Sarah Garland's *Seeing Red* sets the story of young Trewenna's resourceful action against the Napoleonic wars. Children need help to understand an historical context communicated through text and illustration. As Judith Graham argues so powerfully, the story needs to be engrossing and have emotional impact too. Of particular value are those approaches that 'open up a channel from our own lives lived now towards an understanding of those lives lived in the past' (Graham, 2001: 62). So, thinking along these lines, a picture book like *Peepo!* with its family setting would help a young child empathise with the baby in the story. Some picture books with an historical setting appeal to older children and may help the move towards reading full-length novels. Michael Foreman's illustrated historical books, including *War Boy* and *War Game*, bring the events of the world wars to a young readership. Again, though, the emotional impact of the stories is important: Foreman was struck by the absence of uncles in his family. This led him to research their stories and one outcome was *War Game* (Foreman, 2001). When it comes to the more demanding novels, older children can be helped to reflect on how the historical background has been woven into the narrative. Reading out loud some of these – Rosemary Sutcliff's Roman stories, for example, and Geraldine McCaughrean's *Gold Dust* about the adventures of two children during the South American gold rush – helps make their insights accessible to children who would find them hard to read on their own (Collins

Figure 10 Seeing Red by Sarah Garland and Tony Ross. Reproduced with the permission of the publishers, © Andersen Press, 1996.

and Graham, 2001). In *Young People's Reading at the End of the Century* it is observed that children are choosing history novels less frequently, showing a preference for novels based on contemporary themes and for fantasies like the Harry Potter stories (Reynolds, 1996). However, if teachers and parents help by showing interest and reading books aloud, children might come to appreciate the special appeal of the best historical novels. Ten year olds whose teacher was reading them Nina Bawden's *Carrie's War* told me how much the story of the evacuees had helped them enjoy and understand their history work on the Second World War.

Finally, that category of historical novel often called the 'time slip novel' is worth some mention. Here, someone living in the present slips back to a previous time. The best authors of this kind of book carry out meticulous research into the customs and beliefs of a particular historical period, but they also bring alive the thoughts, ideas, dilemmas, preoccupations and feelings of the characters and tell a gripping story. Worth tracking down are *A Traveller in Time* by Alison Uttley, *Charlotte Sometimes* by Penelope Farmer, *Tom's Midnight Garden* by Philippa Pearce and Kate Saunders' more recently written book, *Beswitched*, which is about Flora Fox who has to cope without her iPod, mobile and laptop when she is transported to St Winifreds back in 1935. Timeslips can also work the other way – bringing a person from a far gone age to our present world – as happens in Clive King's *Stig of the Dump*.

Collins, Fiona and Graham, Judith (eds) (2001) *Historical Fiction for Children: Capturing the Past* London: David Fulton.

Foreman, Michael (2001) 'Flesh on the bones' in Collins, Fiona and Graham, Judith (eds) *Historical Fiction for Children: Capturing the Past* London: David Fulton.

Graham, Judith (2001) 'The historical picture-book – is it a "good thing"?' in Collins,

Fiona and Graham, Judith (eds) *Historical Fiction for Children: Capturing the Past* London: David Fulton.

Hoodless, Pat (1998) 'Children's awareness of time in story and historical fiction' in Hoodless, Pat (ed.) *History and English: Exploring the Links* London: Routledge.

Reynolds, Kimberley (ed.) (1996) *Young People's Reading at the End of the Century* London: Booktrust (this can be tracked down in the collection of books and research papers at the National Centre for Research in Children's Literature, based at Roehampton University).

HISTORY AND ENGLISH

See also: autobiography, biography, diary, historical novel, history of children's literature, letters, narrative, picture books, storytelling

When thinking about where English and literacy can flow with other curriculum areas, for me the most fruitful and sympathetic possibilities lie with history. The first point to make is that history is essentially a literate activity which involves establishing evidence and communicating ideas. Thus it provides a natural context for particular kinds of discussion, reading and writing. This richness of textual material connects it to Literacy Time and to the National Curriculum English programmes. Second, an 'English' perspective, often achieved through the use of narrative or drama, can help children begin to understand about the circumstances and lives of people living in a particular period. This analysis starts by looking at non-fiction texts and then at story as a way of bringing the past 'alive' for young historians.

Non-fiction texts for history include primary sources like letters, diaries, documents, inventories and reports, and secondary sources like information and reference books, both print and electronic, autobiographies and biographies. (For a thorough guide to written sources for history see Blyth and Hughes, 1997.) The same non-fiction text might be used in history to increase historical understanding and in Literacy Time to learn about the linguistic features of a kind of writing.

There are fruitful connections in the other direction as well. For example, older primary children who have worked as readers and writers on journalistic kinds of writing in English are well placed to evaluate newspaper sources in history.

Autobiography and biography can be used in both English and history, and publishers have long been commissioning these genres for children. They help introduce children to literary kinds of non-fiction and sometimes, by using photographs and other illustrations, show the lifestyles, dress, artefacts and customs of people in the past (Mallett, 2010). For examples of stories about historical figures and about ordinary people, see the 'biography' entry.

When it comes to children's writing, we need to help them begin to control explanation and argument. Research in Australian schools during the 1980s and 1990s suggested that history teaching could be too reliant on recount genres with a narrative structure and urged that other genres should be encouraged, including explanation and argument (Martin *et al.*, 1987).

Nevertheless, story forms in all their variety are a powerful meeting place for history and English. Teachers have known for a long time that novels, short stories and picture books set in the past can help develop historical knowledge and understanding. When a story is carefully chosen and read out loud with vitality and conviction, it will appeal to young imaginations and draw the children into a sequence of events, encouraging curiosity and discussion. Some stories bring part of the past alive in different cultures and periods in a way children can understand (Fisher, 2004). The feelings and motivations of all kinds of people are revealed and children can also be helped to gain a vocabulary to talk about events and issues in history. Children can enjoy the historical aspects of stories from a very early age: nursery and Reception children are fascinated by the settings, objects and clothes in the Ahlbergs' picture book set in the 1940s – *Peepo!* (Penguin, 1981). Two stories, both by Martin Waddell, *The Toymaker* and *Grandma's Bill*, explore differences between the generations. For age seven and above some of the books in the many 'history through story' series that publishers produce give a strong sense of lives lived in particular situations and periods through narrative and illustration. For example, George Buchanan's *Kidnap on the Canal* tells the story of a boat boy in the nineteenth century and ends with factual notes (1999, Franklin Watts Sparks series). Older primary children both learn about history and enjoy the language and drama of powerful novels like Rosemary Sutcliff's *Dragonslayer*, *The Eagle of the Ninth* and the many novels by Leon Garfield, Joan Aiken and Robert Westall (see more about this under 'historical novel' and 'history of children's literature'). Then there are the stories of the past that children can be helped to create themselves. Gordon Wells describes and evaluates a project carried out by ten year olds who were celebrating the centenary of their school through historical research, drama, writing and painting. One of the most successful activities was making stories for dramatic presentation about life in a school in the late nineteenth century (Wells, 2009: 206). This same imaginative reconstruction of the past through careful historical research and storytelling is a major theme in the work of Kieran Egan (1986).

While history and English can combine to good effect, they are separate areas of knowledge and understanding. Some of the differences in emphasis when we use stories for history and stories for English are quite subtle and worth looking at in a little more detail. In the analysis that follows, I draw on the case study used by Kath Cox and Pat Hughes in their chapter 'History and children's fiction' in *History and English* (Hoodless, 1998). They share with us some work with Year 2 children round Sarah Garland's *Seeing Red*, a children's picture book set in the eighteenth century and based on a legend that may be partially true (Anderson Press, 1996). It tells the story of Trewenna, a Cornish girl, who saves her village from invasion by the French. She manages this by persuading the other women to join her in showing their red petticoats from the cliff tops to deceive the French soldiers into thinking that English redcoat soldiers are lying in ambush. The plan succeeds and Napoleon Bonaparte commands his invasion fleet to return to France.

A major contribution that stories make in history is to support children's developing understanding of chronology through sequencing. So, as is the case in *Seeing Red*, pictures and written text tell of a series of events with pace and energy. This story is set at an identifiable historical time but the teacher needs to reinforce its historical aspects. To understand the events in *Seeing Red*, children have to know that England was at war with France 200 years ago, that Napoleon Bonaparte was a real person and that people used objects like bellows and candlesticks and wore a particular style of clothing. If this story were being used in an English lesson, it would be the power of the story, the characterisation and the language choices made by the author that would be paramount.

What about the significance of the illustrations in picture books used for each subject area? In *Seeing Red* they are integrated into the telling of the events and are a source of insight into aspects of the historical period – landscapes, interiors, dress and distinctive objects. The children in the history case study were shown other pictures including a reproduction of a watercolour painting of soldiers in the red uniforms worn at the time. Talk about the illustrations in English would tend to centre on how the pictures added to the dramatic power of the plot and extended our understanding of the qualities of the characters revealed in the written text.

The language of a story or picture book is important in both history and English, but in different ways. In history children need to learn some of the language of the period: historical vocabulary like 'musket' and 'flintlock pistols' is used in *Seeing Red*.

When the children commented that 'Old Boney' was 'a skitting name', the teacher helped them see the motivation behind this use of a nickname: people try to make fun of their enemies to reduce their terror. In English we would be interested in the effect of choices the author made in vocabulary, syntax, use of direct and indirect speech and choice of 'person' and tense. We would also want to think about the use of language devices like alliteration and use of imagery like simile and metaphor. Think of the power of these images of the petticoats and socks in *Seeing Red* – 'as red as cocks' combs, as red as holly berries, as red as a robin's breast … as red as the jackets of redcoat soldiers'.

Blyth, Joan and Hughes, Pat (1997) *Using Written Sources in Primary History* London: Hodder & Stoughton.

Egan, Kieran (1986) *Teaching as Story Telling: an Alternative Approach to Teaching and Curriculum in the Elementary School* London, Ontario: The Althouse Press.

Fisher, J. (2004) 'Historical fiction' in Hunt, P. (ed.) *International Companion Encyclopedia of Children's Literature* London and New York: Routledge.

Hoodless, Pat (ed.) (1998) *History and English: Exploiting the Links* London: Routledge.

Mallett, Margaret (2010) *Choosing and Using Fiction and Non-fiction 3–11* London and New York: Routledge.

Martin, J., Christie, F. and Rothery, J. (1987) 'Social processes in education: a reply to Sawyer and Watson (and others)' in Reid, I. (ed.) *The Place of Genre in Learning* Victoria: Deakin University.

Wells, Gordon (2009, revised edition) 'Stories across the curriculum' in *The Meaning Makers: Children Learning Language and Using Language to Learn* London: Hodder & Stoughton.

HISTORY OF CHILDREN'S LITERATURE

See also: adventure stories, animals, autobiography, ballad, biography, chapbooks, children's literature – a guide to the entries, classics, comics, creation stories, ebooks, factual genres, fairy tales, fantasy, fiction: choosing and using, folk tales, haiku, historical novel, history of children's non-fiction literature, horn book, horror stories, legend, lyrical non-fiction, myths, novels, picture books, poetry, realism, short stories, traditional tales

In describing what children's literature has encompassed over the centuries, Peter Hunt writes that it is 'everything from a sixteenth-century chapbook to a twentieth-century computer-based interactive device – everything from a folk tale to the problem novel, from the picture-book to the classroom poem, from the tract to the penny dreadful, from the classic to the comic' (Hunt, 1995: ix). While when we refer to 'children's literature' we usually have in mind fiction rather than information texts, I would include, at the very least, literary forms of non-fiction like autobiography and biography and lyrical kinds of non-fiction (Mallett, 2010). Moreover, while historians of children's books have generally explored writing they considered to have some literary merit, many now reach out beyond the established classics to the more popular children's fiction including comics and graphic novels. The range of media has expanded, too, in our digital age. Fiction, and the response of children to it, will always be central in the English Curriculum, but the emphasis of former and current frameworks on genre, on understanding the features of the different types of text, affects priorities in initial teacher education courses so that the careful study of the history of children's literature may be nudged into a marginal position or ignored altogether. Does it matter? There are two main reasons why intending teachers benefit from such study. First, looking at the origins and development of children's literature puts current attitudes and approaches in perspective and reveals the stages in the journey that children's literature has made. Second, it helps us to explore concepts of childhood: our society changes, attitudes to children change and all this is reflected in books written for them.

The history of children's literature is a huge area of study: there is an immense number of texts for children and also a growing body of writing about them. This entry can only provide a starting point by identifying some landmarks in the story, some important children's books and key texts of criticism, and just some of the issues about which people feel passionately. It only touches on children's literature outside the United Kingdom, interesting and important as this is, given the limits on space, but readers will find help here in Townsend (1995), Hunt (1995, 2004) and Watson (2001). At this stage, I want to mention some general works of analysis – often rather large tomes. A book on my 'most accessible' bookshelf is *The Oxford Companion to Children's Literature*. I find the alphabetical organisation helpful, particularly when I need information quickly. There was a new printing in 1999, but of the unrevised 1983 edition and so it does not take up developments in the later years of the twentieth century. Brian Alderson has revised F.J. Harvey Dalton's *Children's Books in England* and

there is a new, fifth edition of *Twentieth Century Children's Writers* now called *The St James Guide to Children's Writers*. A further valued addition to my bookshelf is Victor Watson's *The Cambridge Guide to Children's Books in English*, which provides a critical and appreciative overview of children's books written in English across the world. I like John Rowe Townsend's *Written for Children* because of its distinctive, forceful and sometimes controversial 'voice'. He tells us, in the preface to the definitive 1995 edition, that the book is 'a study of children's literature and not children's reading material', so don't expect to find there an analysis of 'popular series books and other material of insignificant literary merit'. Townsend does, however, include a brief chapter on the impact of the multimedia revolution and recognises that the boundaries between fiction and games and between education and entertainment are becoming blurred. One of my most 'borrowed by students' books – Peter Hunt's *Children's Literature: An Illustrated History* – is good for browsing. As the title promises, it provides important visual images of book illustrations across the time span and has strong sections on comics and other kinds of popular children's literature. The chronology at the back is extremely useful for quick reference. Hunt's *Children's Literature* (2001) contains thought-provoking surveys of the work of forty authors including contemporary authors like Michael Rosen, Quentin Blake, Anne Fine and J.K. Rowling, and some short 'topic' chapters on censorship, gender, drama, film, media and fantasy. Looking further along my 'most accessible' bookshelf I see current and back copies of *Signal*, a journal that contains scholarly and exciting articles about children's books, covering in some cases both the early part of the twentieth century and as far back as the nineteenth century. Ask any teacher, critic, educationist or librarian to tell you about the history of children's literature and you will find different authors and different aspects of the story emphasised. I hope that you will look at the entries on fairy tales, picture books, realism in children's books, novels and so on in this book and seek out some of the valuable works to which I have referred to nourish and enrich your understanding of this fascinating subject. Now for my brief telling of the story of children's books.

The first books for children

Before Caxton printed the first book in England, *The History of Troy* in 1474, books were handwritten, rare and expensive. The only material for children was books of instruction about manners and behaviour called 'courtesy books'. There were no books for their entertainment. However, it is highly likely that children would hear and enjoy the stories intended for adults, passed down by word of mouth. These stories took the form of fables (including those of Aesop), ballads (of Robin Hood and other folk heroes) and folk tales.

Until the end of the seventeenth century, nearly all books for children were school texts, often for teaching the alphabet or books of prayers and religious tracts. Townsend reminds us that the Puritans viewed children 'as young souls to be saved' (Townsend, 1995: 6); they sought books for their children that combined learning to read with religious instruction. The most well known was *Divine Songs, Attempted in Easy Language for the Use of Children* by Isaac Watts, published in 1715.

What form did these early instruction texts take? From around the sixteenth to the eighteenth centuries 'horn books' provided an ABC in upper and lower case, an invocation to the Trinity and the Lord's Prayer and sometimes lists of spellings. Horn books were made by putting a printed page into a wooden frame (with a handle so that it could be held like a mirror) and covered by a thin layer of transparent horn. The 'battledore', which developed from the horn book, was an early primer. It was a folding piece of cardboard with an alphabet and woodcut illustrations of animals and objects. If you want to read more about early children's books and see some interesting illustrations you would appreciate Gillian Avery's chapter, 'The beginnings of children's reading to c.1700' in Hunt (1995). It ends with 'a glimmer of light amongst the Calvinist gloom', Bunyan's *A Book for Boys and Girls* (1686) – a book of verses with images of animals, activities and everyday objects. There were still religious messages, but given with a light touch. In an age when children were regarded as small adults here is the start of a recognition that they might like books with some hint of the visual image and playfulness.

The first commercial publishers of children's books

From about the mid-seventeenth century some London publisher-booksellers began to print and distribute large numbers of cheaply produced books of popular literature for ordinary people. These slim pamphlets were known as chapbooks and were taken round the country by pedlars. At first they were written for adults – romances, ballads and fairy tales like Tom Thumb. The paper was often coarse and the illustrations rough and ready. The tales often lacked literary merit, but this was not always the case and the work of writers of the quality of Bunyan was sometimes published in chapbook form. Margaret Kinnell tells how as a young boy Walter Scott was inspired by chapbook romances from Allan Ramsay's Edinburgh bookshop (Hunt, 1995: 27). Sometimes a few pages for children would be included in an adult's chapbook – an ABC or a rhyme with woodblock pictures. Then whole books began to be published for them. John Bunyan's *A Book for Boys and Girls* was produced as a chapbook under a new title – *Divine Emblems*. One of the benefits of the chapbook industry was that it made available children's versions of books intended for adults. By the end of the eighteenth century there were abridged versions of Jonathan Swift's *Gulliver's Travels* and Daniel Defoe's *Robinson Crusoe*. These books had great appeal and, as Townsend points out, themes from both – the imaginary miniature world of the former and the desert island in the latter – have been echoed in many later books.

One publisher was particularly important in establishing a tradition of publishing and marketing of children's books. This was John Newbery of London, who with his associates published the first children's version of Charles Perrault's fairy tales. In spite of some negative religious attitudes, the fairy tale had come to England from France in the early eighteenth century in the form of *Tales of Past Times Told by Mother Goose* (1729) – a translation of the tales set down by Charles Perrault. Newbery's edition for children soon followed. Chapbook versions became common and at last children had access to imaginative literature in print. This recognition that fairy tales and the inner world of the imagination were valid areas for children's books helped establish a tradition of fairy tales for children in the nineteenth and twentieth centuries. Newbery published school books, story books, fairy tales and poetry collections for children as well as a large number of books for adults. A person of extraordinary energy he also succeeded in other businesses – newspapers and patent medicines, for example. Of all his children's books *Goody Two Shoes* seems to have been particularly popular. Perhaps the tale of a girl triumphing in spite of early hardships – who becomes the principal of a dame-school and a benefactor to the

poor – accounts at least partly for its strong appeal. Helpful analyses of the contribution of Newbery to children's publishing are found in Chapter 2, 'Mr Locke and Mr Newbury', in Townsend, 1995, and 'A Business of Importance', Chapter 2 in Hunt, 1995. Both writers note Newbery's commercial instincts in making a success of his publishing business. He aimed to distribute widely and he advertised in provincial newspapers. I should mention that the huge contribution made by those who translated books in languages other than English has not always been recognised. Translation of children's books into English is not a mechanistic process. Gillian Lathey in her book *Invisible Story Tellers* explains how translators are subject to cultural influences as they abridge, adapt and even alter texts (Lathey, 2008).

Children's books in the nineteenth century

This century saw the development of existing genres, the fairy tale and the adventure story, and the emergence of new forms like the school story and the 'new' fantasy. It also saw the emergence of what are now referred to as 'classics' – books with long-term appeal like Charles Dickens' *Oliver Twist* (1838), Thomas Hughes' *Tom Brown's Schooldays* (1857), Charles Kingsley's *The Water Babies* (1861), Lewis Carroll's *Alice's Adventures in Wonderland* (1865), Mark Twain's *The Adventures of Tom Sawyer* (1876) and Johanna Spyri's *Heidi* (English translation in 1884).

From the beginnings of fairy tales in children's chapbooks in the previous century sprang many retellings not only of Perrault's stories, but also of the German stories of the Brothers Grimm (1823) and the Danish tales of Hans Christian Andersen (1846). Oscar Wilde's anthology of his original fairy tales, *The Happy Prince*, came out in 1888 and Andrew Lang's expanding series of fairy tale collections began with *The Blue Fairy Book* in 1889.

The century also saw books that are not easily placed in a category. Charles Kingsley's *The Water Babies* is a moral tale about the working conditions of child chimney sweeps but as soon as Tom enters the water and drowns we are in a world of fantasy. In 1865 one of the most enduring fantasies of all time came out – Lewis Carroll's *Alice's Adventures in Wonderland* and, soon after, its sequel *Alice Through the Looking Glass*.

Stories based on experience of the real world weave their way through the century. Here I am thinking of Dickens' *Oliver Twist*, Frances Hodgson Burnett's *Little Lord Fauntleroy* published in 1886 and an early version of *The Little Princess* under the title *Sara Crewe* in 1887. (Her most-loved book, *The Secret Garden*, about transformation and rebirth, was published in 1905.) Also under the 'realism' umbrella is that remarkable animal book *Black Beauty* (1887) about the cruelties to which horses were subjected by harsh masters and mistresses.

Adventure stories celebrated a male world of empire building and adventure on land and at sea, while girls' books reflected the female world in domestic settings. The writers of boys' adventure stories in the nineteenth century reflected the world of imperialism, approved of kinds of male behaviour and occupation and Christian values. They were particularly influenced by two earlier authors – Daniel Defoe and Sir Walter Scott. The adventure stories of Captain Marryat, including *Mr Midshipman Easy* (1836), celebrated life at sea. There were a number of other writers who developed the boys' adventure story in the second part of the nineteenth century. R. M. Ballantyne, for instance, wrote a number of stories including the popular *The Coral Island: A Tale of the Pacific Ocean* in 1858. However, perhaps G.A. Henty was the most successful writer in the genre, with titles that included *Cornet of Horse* (1881) and *With Clive in India* (1884).

Henty, a retired war correspondent when he began writing full time for children, sold about 150,000 books annually at the height of his popularity. Henty often prefaced his tales with a letter to 'My Dear Lads', in which he drew attention to the heroic exploits of the story that followed and which had 'helped to create the empire'. Briggs and Butts make an interesting link between the structure of, on the one hand, adventure stories, and on the other hand, of folk and fairy tales, pointing out that both use 'formulaic elements and stereotyped characters' (Hunt, 1995: 151). Robert Louis Stevenson's *Treasure Island* (serialised in the boys' paper *Young Folks* 1881–82) has a folk tale structure with a hero, a challenge/conflict and then a resolution. However, as Townsend observes, it manages to be an exceptionally exciting story and to have characters that combine good and evil qualities, like Long John Silver (not all villain) and Squire Trelawney (not all hero). This complexity of characterisation created a new model for children's writing (Townsend, 1995: 46).

Another important genre to emerge in the late nineteenth century was the school story. The best known is Thomas Hughes' *Tom Brown's Schooldays*. Its exploration of friendship and the tension between the different perspectives of children and adults in the school has had a considerable influence on the school stories written since.

This skim through the nineteenth century would not be complete without mentioning the developments in colour illustration in its later years, since here we find the origins of the modern-day children's picture book. At the beginning of the century illustrations were still coloured by hand, but as mechanical colour printing developed it was brought to a high standard by master colour-printers like Edmund Evans. A number of gifted illustrators benefited. Walter Crane illustrated picture books based on nursery rhymes and alphabets for

201

publishers like Routledge and Evans. In *Written for Children*, Crane's illustration of the nursery rhyme 'Dickory Dock' from *The Baby's Opera* 1877 is reproduced. It shows two alert little children turning round to look at the mouse running up the grandfather clock (Townsend, 1995: 120). Kate Greenaway's pictures in, for example, *The Pied Piper of Hamelin* (1888) and *Under the Window* (1879) established her as a fine illustrator with a distinctive style, even if some found her children rather too perfect and the settings too idealised. Another renowned illustrator, Randolph Caldecott, was particularly good at showing action in his illustrations. If you want an impression of the energy Caldecott brings to his images look at his drawing of John Gilpin clinging desperately to his horse's mane as the creature gallops off in his drawing for Cowper's poem *John Gilpin* (1878) (Townsend, 1995: 117).

The history of children's literature is always about perceptions of childhood at particular times. As the nineteenth century came to an end the importance of play, games, dressing up and make believe to children's development was becoming increasingly recognised. This was reflected in books showing the pleasures of imaginative games like dressing up, playing with soldiers and dolls' tea parties, all of which provided an opportunity to imitate adult behaviour (see Julia Briggs' Chapter 7, 'Transitions 1890–1914' in Hunt, 1995).

Children's books in the twentieth century

Historical events – particularly the two world wars – brought about great societal change which had a profound effect on children's literature. The emergence of the children's librarian, trends in the publishing and marketing of children's books, the growing recognition that children's literature was worthy of scholarly study and could facilitate learning to read, and the coming of television and multimedia as dominant cultural media, were all momentous developments. The analysis in this section takes account of all this and sometimes I have to step away from straightforward chronology.

However, at first there was little change and the years leading up to the First World War were a good time in the history of children's literature. Rudyard Kipling's *Just So Stories* – much-loved, mythical explanations of how the camel got a hump and how the elephant got its trunk and so on – was published in 1902. The recognition of the playful element in childhood, notable in books towards the end of the previous century, was found in J.M. Barrie's *Peter Pan* (1904), Kenneth Grahame's *The Wind in the Willows* (1908) and E. Nesbit's *The Railway Children* (1906).

The First World War broke into this period of relative calm and continuity and in the years after the war the most important children's books were mainly in poetry and in fantasy. In his chapter 'Fantasy between the wars', Townsend explores the work of Walter de la Mare and Eleanor Farjeon: known mainly as poets, both were also writers of short stories for children (Townsend, 1995). The books from the 1920s that have survived best in spite of their period flavour are A.A. Milne's *Winnie-the-Pooh* (1926) and *The House at Pooh Corner* (1928). Peter Hunt explains their enduring popularity thus: 'Pooh Bear is the optimist (or mystic) everyman, as well as the amiable child. The enchanted forest contains the whole of childhood (with a touch of Arcadian nostalgia), and there is a hierarchy of types of children to identify with – Piglet, Tigger, and Roo; the children are in conflict with the strange and pretentious adults – Rabbit, Owl, and the misanthropic Eeyore – but all is made safe by the presence of Christopher Robin' (Hunt, 1995: 202).

The other enduring fantasy published between the wars was J.R.R. Tolkien's *The Hobbit* (1937). Tolkien reached back into myth and legend in creating a unique imagined land in which the hobbits – creatures about half the size of a human being – live their lives. Critics of children's literature (for example Townsend, 1995: Chapter 21) recognise the influence of Tolkien's work on his friend C.S. Lewis' Narnia series which also creates an alternative world. The first story, *The Lion, the Witch and the Wardrobe*, was published in 1950 and while the books have many admirers and remain in print, some have found the religious allegory oppressive. One successor of these stories creating an imagined world is J.K. Rowling's Harry Potter series. I am an admirer of Ursula Le Guin's Earthsea quartet, which also follow the fortunes of a young wizard in a secondary world and help young readers reflect on moral dilemmas in everyday decisions. They are not easy books to read and understand, but would challenge and interest the ablest readers in the later primary years.

The school story tradition, begun in the previous century, continued and developed during the twentieth century. The Chalet School series by Elinor Brent-Dyer began in 1925 and the books are still in print. In the 1940s and 1950s Enid Blyton wrote the Malory Towers series. William Mayne's quartet of choir school stories beginning with *A Swarm in May* (1955) brings alive the daily life of children whose lives centre round singing and the cathedral. Another distinctive world was created in Anthony Buckeridge's *Jennings* books, which present a picture of prep school life in the tradition of other great comic writers. By the 1970s many school stories centred on the modern primary school, for example Gene Kemp's *The Turbulent Term of Tyke Tiler* (1977) and Jan Mark's *Thunder and Lightnings* (1974). The latter includes incidents in school, although it is not a school story in the conventional sense. For a reference work on the history of school stories for boys and girls see Auchmuty and Wotton, 2000.

The tradition of realistic works begun in the nineteenth century also continued. During the 1930s and 1940s Arthur Ransome wrote his twelve novels in the Swallows and Amazons series about the school holiday adventures of middle-class children spent on boats in the Lake District. Another very well-liked writer whose stories followed the real-life events and challenges of family life was Noel Streatfeild whose first book, *Ballet Shoes*, came out in 1936. Around the same time, in 1937, a book about a very different family came out. Eve Garnett wrote *The Family from One End Street* which was about an urban working-class family called the Ruggles. Many children enjoyed the humour in the everyday life of the family – Rose, the eldest of the seven children, tries to help her mother with her job as a washerwoman but burns a customer's petticoat – but some teachers and critics found it patronising. Townsend, for example, writes 'Mr and Mrs Ruggles are seen from above and outside' (Townsend, 1995: 149).

The Second World War, like the First, changed society and many of the old certainties no longer existed; this had an effect on children's literature. Some thought the cultural change brought about by the greater availability of television and other media would have a negative effect on reading, but the picture is far less clear cut. Children's television brought excellent serials of children's books and programmes like *Jackanory*, which generated interest in talking about and buying books. There were other developments which led to an increase in quality children's books. Significant forces here were two groups of professionals who became very important to the development of quality children's literature. First, knowledgeable and enthusiastic children's book editors were, from the late 1940s and the 1950s, being appointed by publishing houses, for example Frank Eyre, John Bell and Mabel George of Oxford University Press and

Eleanor Graham and then Kaye Webb at Puffin (Penguin). Seven Stories, The Centre for Children's Books in Newcastle on Tyne, had an exhibition in 2010 of the books published by Puffin/Penguin and the correspondence of these two distinguished publishers, drawing on their considerable archive material. Publishers continue to have considerable influence – they decide if and when to reissue the established classics and help create 'modern' classics by the way books are reprinted and marketed. Publishers took advantage of the new consumerism of the 1970s, publishing large numbers of children's books in paperback format. Second, children's librarians were becoming expert not only at making children's books accessible, but also at how particular authors and kinds of books were perceived. If you want to learn more about the development of books and libraries for children you would enjoy Eileen Colwell's autobiography, *Once Upon a Time*. She became a librarian in 1921, a time when children were rarely welcome in public libraries (Ray, 2001). Elkin and Kinnell's *A Place for Children* celebrates the achievements of librarians like Eileen Colwell, who have made children's library services so successful in promoting the enjoyment of reading and storytelling. *The School Librarian*, the Journal of the School Library Association, remains an excellent journal for all those who care deeply about children's literature. It provides reviews of all kinds of literature, some 'briefing' pages about relevant events – book prizes, exhibitions and so on – and a number of articles exploring current issues and issues of continuing importance.

The post-war years also saw children's literature recognised as both worthy of scholarly attention and as an important agent in helping children learn to read. Two critics and scholars, Margaret Meek and Aidan Chambers, have made a considerable contribution to our understanding of the links between children's literature and literacy. Aidan and Nancy Chambers founded The Thimble Press in 1970 and the journal *Signal*, which is now read all over the world and contains scholarly articles and reviews of the full range of children's literature. *Tell Me: Children, Reading and Talk* by Aidan Chambers explores the role of talking about books and creating enthusiastic readers. In the introduction to *The Cool Web*, the authors point out the strong links that exist between literature and literacy – between the way readers are made and the treasure store of children's books (Meek *et al.*, 1977).

One outcome of bringing children's literature under the scrutiny of literary theory was an increasing interest in and concern about social aspects: this was a major preoccupation for many teachers and librarians in the 1970s as they exercised choice over what to buy for primary-aged children. Were we right to take into account, when evaluating children's books, issues to do with sexism, racism and social class? Could a book succeed on aesthetic criteria but fail on social ones? Certainly the children in our schools came from a wider range of ethnic and cultural backgrounds and this was a stimulus to providing the best books from all over the world for all the children. *Books for Keeps* and its editors, for example Chris Powling and Rosemary Stones, deserve recognition for the constructive approach taken to multiculturalism both in the journal *Books for Keeps* and for the regularly updated publication *A Multicultural Guide to Children's Books 0–16*, now, sadly, out of print. The greater sensitivity to the social messages that books might send to young readers stimulated discussion of what is often called the 'Blyton phenomenon'. From the 1940s Enid Blyton wrote a huge number of books which included the 'realistic' series Famous Five and Secret Seven, the Malory Towers school stories, and short story collections of fairy tales. Children loved them all, unlike critics, librarians and some parents. The books were criticised for racial, gender and social class stereotyping. There was also disquiet about the predictability of the stories and the linguistic shortcomings of the books – narrowness of vocabulary and simplicity of syntax. Huge numbers of articles and books have been published about Blyton. David Rudd has written a critical analysis of Blyton's work and he helps illuminate the appeal it has for children (Rudd, 2000). Certainly the settings for many of the stories are predictable and reassuring. Children can also have the excitement of a fast-moving story told simply.

Some adults feel similar sorts of reservations about the work of Roald Dahl, another commercially successful writer for children. There is no doubt that the books, published from the 1960s until Dahl's death in 1990, have been, and indeed are, hugely enjoyed by almost all children. They like the sheer exhilaration of the stories which have a distinctive imaginative appeal. Their themes often involve adults being humiliated while children overcome obstacles and win through to success. Feeling in control, even if vicariously, must be satisfying for children who are usually powerless in an adult world. While teachers and librarians do not, as a few did with Blyton's work, refuse to stock the Dahl books, some prefer to leave children to seek out his work for themselves rather than actively promoting it. Townsend approves of the friendly giant *The BFG* (1982), but considers many of the other books appeal to 'the cruder end of childhood taste'. He calls *Charlie and the Chocolate Factory* (1964) 'a thick, rich, glutinous candy bar of a book' (Townsend, 1995: 249).

No account of children's literature in the twentieth century is complete without some mention of historical fiction – there is more about this under the 'historical novel' entry. Historical novels for primary-aged children fell out of favour towards the end of the twentieth century (Reynolds, 1996). This is unfortunate as a story set in the past can, like other narratives, help us reflect on human relationships and the human condition. The best books stretch the imagination by showing us the lives of people in different times and circumstances while illuminating life in our own times. Rosemary Sutcliff, for example, explores timeless themes of honour, courage, loyalty and determination both in her earlier books, which include *Eagle of the Ninth* (1954) in which a young Roman seeks the lost Eagle of his father's lost legion in the wilds of the north of Scotland, and her later books like *Song for a Dark Queen* (1978) which explores Boudicca's attempts to avenge her treatment from the Romans. The outstanding novel exploring the Second World War is Ian Serraillier's *The Silver Sword* (1956), which tells the story of the search by three children for their parents during Nazi oppression in Warsaw. Nina Bawden is another children's writer who has brought history alive: *The Peppermint Pig* (1975) tells about the everyday life of a family at the turn of the nineteenth century and *Carrie's War* (1973) explores the life of young evacuees struggling to cope with change and separation when they leave London for a Welsh town in the 1940s.

Some of the best novels of the twentieth century are organised round timeslips: an early example is Alison Uttley's *A Traveller in Time* (1939). Penelope Taberner slips in and out of her life in an ancient farmhouse in Derbyshire to Tudor times when Mary Queen of Scots was imprisoned. Accounting for its enduring popularity, Townsend writes that the book succeeds because 'of a profound and loving sense of place, and of the endurance of that place in time' (Townsend, 1995: 139). This same strong evocation of a particular place is found in other time travel novels – Lucy Boston's

The Children of Green Knowe (1954) and Philippa Pearce's *Tom's Midnight Garden* (1956). I find the cover picture by Peter Farmer for the 1970 paperback edition of the latter book especially evocative in showing the power of a particular place in the memory. Victor Watson gives a fine appreciation of this novel towards the end of his chapter, 'The possibilities of children's fiction' in *After Alice*. The book, he writes, 'defines a space in which two people caught up in Time can find each other. The final chapter is a triumph: the boy and the old woman Hattie has become greet each other almost like lovers, accepting age and change and incomprehensible mysteries' (Styles *et al.*, 1992: 22).

The last decades of the twentieth century saw the rise and development of the children's picture book. Its roots are found in the nineteenth-century illustrators like Crane, Greenaway and Caldecott. Edward Ardizzone was one of the first twentieth-century illustrators to make an impact with his action packed 'Tim' series, the first of which was *Little Tim and the Seafaring Captain* (1936). It is significant perhaps that an illustrator, Quentin Blake, was appointed the first Children's Laureate (in 1999). His book *Words and Pictures* includes illustrations from much of his best work over the last fifty years. From the 1960s there was a golden age of picture books including the works of Charles Keeping, Brian Wildsmith, Shirley Hughes, John Burningham, Janet and Allan Ahlberg, Anthony Browne and David McKee. The multi-layered meanings and the subtle ways in which written text and illustration relate are discussed under the 'picture books' entry.

Looking back to the years at the end of the twentieth century four things stand out for me: the establishment of the ebook alongside print books, each offering a distinct experience; the development of the children's picture book as a major art form dominating displays in book shops; the delight in fantasy reaching a climax in the publishing success of J.K. Rowling's Harry Potter books; and the recognition that children's non-fiction literature is worthy of critical attention (see the entry on the 'history of children's non-fiction literature').

Into the twenty-first century

The technological revolution, bringing ebooks and all the potential of a multimedia world, began in the twentieth century and is accelerating as the new century gets underway. These huge qualitative developments are bound to have an enormous effect on how childhood is experienced, on the nature of literacy and therefore on the kind of texts written for children. In *Modern Children's Literature*, some of these changes and the debates round them are considered (Reynolds, 2005; see also Rudd 2010). Peter Hollindale homes in on one societal change, observing that British parents 'have quietly withdrawn children from the freedom of the streets and replaced it by the freedom of the bedroom doubling as an IT temple, with unforeseeable future consequences for imagination, socialisation and physical health' (Hollindale, 2001: 31–2). There is no doubt that 'book time' will compete more and more with alternatives like television viewing, film and the computer as well as other hobbies and pursuits. All these changes will have an impact on the way children's literature develops in the future. It seems that adventure stories, whether realistic or in the form of fantasies like the Harry Potter novels, are now finding more favour with child readers than historical novels, but does not the great popularity of the Potter books show that some things have not changed? Children have the same eagerness for stories exploring challenges, conflicts and relationships with others, even if these are explored through a parallel fantasy world. Indeed, a student group of mine returned from teaching practice convinced that a fantasy world like that created by J.K. Rowling has a helpful 'distancing' effect, making it easier for some children to reflect on and talk over issues to do with relationships, personal behaviour and courage in the face of difficult circumstances.

Given the speed with which new technology is developing, will the print book survive at all? Is Townsend right in thinking the book is 'a tough old bird', likely to keep going? The 'definitive' edition of *Written for Children* (Townsend, 1995) ends with this thought: 'Perhaps it is not too wildly optimistic to hope that in the twenty-first century, when all the modern miracles, and some we have not yet dreamed of, have come to pass, a child will still be found here and there, lying face down on the hearthrug or whatever may have replaced the hearthrug, light years away from his or her surroundings, lost in the pages of a book'.

Centres for literacy and children's literature (some housing collections of contemporary and early books)

- Centre for Literacy in Primary Education: www.clpe.co.uk (research and study centre with a large collection of contemporary children's books).
- Children's Books History Society: a newsletter for members is available from Mrs Pat Garrett through cbhs@abcgarrett.demon. co.uk.
- The Bodleian Library: collections include that formed by Peter and Iona Opie and the archives of C.S. Lewis, J.R.R. Tolkien and Alan Garner, www.bodleian.ox.ac.uk.
- Harrogate Library Collection of Children's Books: mainly Victorian period, contact harrogate.library@ northyorks.gov.uk.

- Seven Stories, The Centre for Children's Books: www.seven stories.org.uk. This has a large archive of children's books from different historical periods, including material donated by children's authors and illustrators.
- The National Art Library at the Victoria and Albert Museum, London: mid-nineteenth-century children's books, www.vam.ac. uk/nal.
- The National Centre for Language and Literacy, based at Reading University: www.ncll.org.uk, with some 18,000 contemporary children's books.
- National Centre for Research in Children's Literature, Roehampton: www.roehampton.ac.uk/research centres/ncrcl. The British Library-funded study *Young People's Reading in the Twentieth Century* was based at this centre, which has several collections including the Richmal Crompton archive and early and contemporary books.
- The National Literacy Trust, London: www.literacytrust.org.uk.
- United Kingdom Reading Association (UKRA): www.ukra.org.
- The Wandsworth Collection of Early Children's Books: Housed in Putney Library basement. Contact for researchers and students: fhorden@wandsworth.gov.uk.
- The Young Book Trust: The children's division of Booktrust – the national charity to promote books and reading. Booklists available. www.booktrustchildrensbooks. org.uk.

Children's literature journals

- *Books for Keeps*: www.books forkeeps.co.uk.

- *Carousel*: The guide to children's books, www.carouselguide.co.uk.
- *Children's Books History Society Newsletter*: contact cbhs@abcgarrett.demon.co.uk.
- *Children's Literature in Education*: www.springer.com/education+%26+language/linguistics/journal/10583.
- *English in Education*: www.nate.org.uk.
- *English 4–11*: a journal produced jointly by The English Association (www.le.ac.uk/engassoc) and the United Kingdom Literacy Association (www.ukla.org).
- *Growing Point*: is no longer published but back copies are available. It has a helpful index system which allows researchers to track references to particular authors and illustrators from 1960 to 1990.
- *Blackbird*: the journal of IBBYUK, the International Board on Books for Young People, contact ibby@roehampton.ac.uk.
- *Literacy Trust*: provides booklists, practical resources and carries out literacy surveys. www.literacytrust.org.uk.
- *The Junior Bookshelf*: is no longer published but back copies are available from libraries.
- *The School Librarian*: www.sla.org.uk.
- *Signal*: no longer published, this was a thrice-yearly journal devoted to books and reading. Back copies are available along with publications such as *The Signal Companion* by Elaine Moss and Nancy Chambers.
- *Write Away*: www.justimaginestorycentre.co.uk. Aims to select the best books for home and school.

Auchmuty, Rosemary and Wotton, Joy (compilers) (2000 edition) *The Encyclopaedia of School Stories* Aldershot: Ashgate.

Blake, Quentin (2000) *Words and Pictures* London: Jonathan Cape.

Carpenter, Humphrey and Pritchard, Mari (1983, reprinted 1999) *The Oxford Companion to Children's Literature* Oxford: Oxford University Press.

Chambers, A. (1993) *Tell Me: Children, Reading and Talk* Stroud: Thimble Press (now available with *The Reading Environment* in a new edition, Thimble Press, 2011).

Colwell, Eileen (1998) *Once Upon a Time … Memories of an Edwardian Childhood* Privately printed.

Elkin, Judith and Kinnell, Margaret (2000) *A Place for Children: Public Libraries as a Major Force in Children's Reading* British Library Research and Innovation Report 117. LA Publishing.

Harvey Darton, E.J. (1999 edition, revised by Brian Alderson) *Children's Books in England* London: The British Library & Oak Knoll Press.

Hollindale, Peter (2001) 'Odysseys: the childness of journeying children' *Signal* 94, January.

Hunt, Peter (ed.) (1995) *Children's Literature: An Illustrated History* Oxford: Oxford University Press.

——(2001) *Children's Literature* Oxford: Blackwell Publishers.

——(ed.) (2004) *International Companion Encyclopaedia of Children's Literature, Vols I and II* London: Routledge.

Lathey, Gillian (2008) *Invisible Story Tellers: The Role of Translators in Children's Literature* London and New York: Routledge.

Mallett, Margaret (2010) *Choosing and Using Fiction and Non-fiction 3–11* London and New York: Routledge.

Meek, M., Warlow, G. and Barton, G. (eds) (1977) *The Cool Web: The Pattern of Children's Reading* London: The Bodley Head.

Prendergast, Sara and Prendergast, Tom (eds) (1999 edition) *The St James Guide to Children's Writers* (fifth edition of *Twentieth Century Children's Writers*) London: St James Press.

Ray, Sheila (2001) 'Books about children's books 2000' *Signal* 95, May.

Reynolds, Kimberley (ed.) (1996) *Young People's Reading at the End of the Century* London: Booktrust.

——(ed.) (2005) *Modern Children's Literature* London: Palgrave Macmillan.

Rudd, David (2000) *Enid Blyton and the Mystery of Children's Literature* London: Macmillan.

——(2010) *The Routledge Companion to Children's Literature* London and New York: Routledge.

Styles, Morag, Bearne, Eve and Watson, Victor (1992) *After Alice: Exploring Children's Literature* London: Cassell.

Townsend, J.R. (1995) *Written for Children* London: The Bodley Head.

Watson, Victor (2001) *The Cambridge Guide to Children's Books in English* Cambridge: Cambridge University Press.

HISTORY OF CHILDREN'S NON-FICTION LITERATURE

See also: autobiography, biography, chronological non-fiction, dictionary, encyclopedia, factual genres, history of children's literature, information books, lyrical non-fiction, non-fiction reading and writing

As far as I know, there is no text offering a comprehensive history of non-fiction for children. Yet informational kinds of reading are an important part of children's repertoire, perhaps more so today than ever before. As the entry on the history of children's literature shows, the very first texts intended for children were not stories but lesson books. Indeed until the end of the seventeenth century, most books for children were school texts. The first books specifically for children were 'horn books' which appeared in the sixteenth century or before and continued until the beginning of the eighteenth century. They were made by putting a printed page into a wooden frame and covering it with a thin layer of

transparent horn. They had a handle and so were held like a mirror. An ABC in upper and lower case was provided, an invocation to the Trinity, the Lord's Prayer and sometimes a spelling list. The aim was to combine learning to read with religious instruction. The 'battledore', which developed from the 'horn book', was an early primer consisting of a folding piece of cardboard, with an alphabet and sometimes woodcut illustrations of animals and objects. Both horn books and battledores helped children read by the alphabetic method. The sharing adult would encourage the young reader to say out loud the letters of the alphabet, singly and then in simple combinations. For more about these very early information books and notions about learning to read I recommend Gillian Avery's article 'The beginnings of children's reading to c.1700' (Avery, 1995). Although the phonics and 'look and say' methods of teaching reading eventually replaced the alphabetic method, learning the alphabet has continued to be thought important right up to the present day, when there is a rich and interesting choice of ABC picture books on the market. As is the case with fiction, developments in non-fiction are not neatly chronological over the centuries. There is some overlap, some leaps backwards to earlier styles and content as well as moves forward. This entry proceeds to the first illustrated non-fiction books for children and then to some non-fiction landmarks in the eighteenth and nineteenth centuries. Finally, it considers non-fiction in the twentieth and twenty-first centuries.

Not only is the history of non-fiction interesting in itself, it also illuminates perceptions of childhood at particular times as much as does fiction. It is a huge and, I think, fascinating topic. As I can only provide an introduction here, I have indicated where a particular source might help further.

Early illustrated books

Towards the end of the seventeenth century, perceptions of childhood and how children should be instructed were changing. One very important contemporary influence was the thought and writing of the philosopher John Locke; he believed that children deserved books that were playful as well as instructional. Even before Locke's influence, though, books that both instructed and entertained were being written for children. Several writers on the history of children's books pinpoint *Orbis Pictus* or *Visible World* by John Amos Comenius as the first picture book for children; it was translated from German into English in 1659 by John Hoole (Avery, 1995: 7; Townsend, 1995: 112; Watson, 2001: 530). The aim was instructional – to help children learn to read Latin – and there was both the Latin text and, placed alongside, the vernacular version. Learning about the world was also encouraged. Fine copperplate illustrations helped children appreciate the beauty and variety of the natural world and human achievement. However, Comenius showed life as it is, and included pictures of war and death (Avery, 1995: 7). This pictorial encyclopedia with its 150 illustrations aimed to be comprehensive by including every visual aspect of the world and it 'remains a milestone in the history of illustrated children's books' (Watson, 2001: 358). Picture books depicting the natural world were acceptable to the church because 'animal creation was seen as being in a sense God's picturebook from which lessons about faith could be drawn' (Townsend, 1995: 112). Readers who would like to see reproductions of illustrations in early books for children will find these in Gillian Avery's 'Beginnings of children's reading to c.1700' (Avery, 1995). Woodcuts were a main means of book illustration, alongside copper and steel plate engravings, until the end of the nineteenth century.

The eighteenth century

By the end of the seventeenth century children had became a more significant proportion of the population. Scholars, for example Margaret Kinnell, point out that improved health (partly because of the availability of inoculation) and the emergence in the 1740s of a middle class with time for reading, created a market for books, including children's books (Kinnell, 1995: 29). Children were coming into their own as readers and needed books written especially for them (Townsend, 1995: 14). These new attitudes towards the child reader were noted by publishers. Thomas Boreman brought out a set of illustrated miniature books called *The Gigantick Histories* between 1740 and 1743. In another Boreman book, *Curiosities in the Tower of London*, there is a woodcut of a fierce-looking porcupine. Books like *A Pretty Book of Pictures for Little Masters and Misses* by Thomas Bewick (1771) showing his distinctive woodcuts of animals and birds, were the forerunners of today's nature books. The best-known publisher of the time, John Newbery, opened a children's bookshop in St Paul's Churchyard in 1744. Many parents welcomed Newbery's instruction books with verses, number games and pictures. His *A New History of England from the Invasion of Julius Caesar to the Present Time* (1761) was one of the first of the kind of information book for children that became familiar in primary classrooms in later centuries. Geography and travel books for children were also appearing now.

The nineteenth century

Books written by, for example, William Godwin, Mrs Markham and Lady Maria Callcott followed the history book tradition pioneered by Newbery. A landmark was Charles Dickens' *A Child's History of England*. This came out in a new edition from Wizard in 2008, abridged by Kate Agnew with reproductions of the 1873 illustrations by Marcus Stone. In the introduction to this new edition, John Waller describes Dickens' book as a forerunner of the Horrible Histories series so much enjoyed by children today. In the mid and late nineteenth century, biographies like John Edgar's *Heroes of England* were intended to promote positive notions of their nation's achievements in young male minds. One of the most prevalent kinds of book was one that tried to both entertain and provide information about history or about foreign lands; the well-travelled war correspondent, G.A. Henty, was a master of this kind of book. The interesting thing here is that some of his stories were set round real events and often illustrated with detailed pull-out maps and battle plans so that the young reader could both enjoy a thrilling story and gain information.

These adventure books were the forerunners of the historical fiction of writers like Rosemary Sutcliff, Judith Kerr and Ian Serraillier, who push at the boundaries between fiction and non-fiction. Before leaving the 'information through story' genre Maria Edgeworth's storybooks with information for the very young should be mentioned. Her book *Harry and Lucy*, published in 1801 by Joseph Johnson, tells of three days in the life of two young children who learn about milk in the dairy, watch bricks being made and a blacksmith at work. She encouraged her young readers or listeners to ask questions and the books were meant to support learning to read.

The 'information story' has a high profile in children's publishing today and we value the work of, for example, Ruth Brown, Sarah Garland, Brita Granström, Sam Godwin, Shirley Hughes, Mick Manning and Jo Readman. Their books are less didactic, less inclined to push a particular set of principles than Maria Edgeworth's.

Nevertheless she is a worthy pioneer of the form (Carpenter and Pritchard, 1983: 163–4). Thinking still about the youngest children, Kate Greenaway's fine picture books have a place in the history of illustrated books. *A Apple Pie*, published by Frederick Warne in 1886, shows actions – 'P peeped at it', 'S sang for it' and so on. It played its part in inspiring the alphabet and concept books on number, shape, opposites and colour that filled children's bookshops in the twentieth century and beyond (read it online: www.childrenslibrary.org).

The twentieth century

The same energy and recognition of children's eagerness for information about the real world that we find in Maria Edgeworth's work underpinned the early encyclopedias and wonder books that started to appear in the mid-nineteenth century. From the American writer Nathaniel Hawthorne's *The Wonder Book for Boys and Girls*, first published in 1851, we can trace a line to Arthur Mee's acclaimed *The Children's Encyclopedia*, first published in 1908. Then, not long after, Ward Lock brought out a series of wonder books including *The Wonder Book of Railways* (1911). The number and diversity of encyclopedias and reference texts available today reflects their enduring place in the body of non-fiction for children, but current texts are a great deal more sensitive to wider social issues and show awareness of the changing nature of knowledge and our attitudes to it.

The range and quality of information texts grew enormously through the twentieth century, which saw changes in the design and coverage of print books and the arrival of multimedia ways of communicating.

Some developments were gradual. Histories for children continued to have their place at home and in the classroom. Geoffrey Trease's *Our Island Story* was published in 1910 and Clark Hutton's *A Picture History of Britain* came out in

211

1945. Hutton's book, which emerged in a new edition in 2007, tells of significant events through the ages, revealing changes in transport, fashion and architecture. Hutton used a new illustrative method whereby an artist's pictures could be prepared directly for printing, 'without photographic intrusion', as Brian Alderson put it in one of the articles in his Classics in Short series (Alderson, 2008: 28). It was the illustrated books of R.L. Unstead that were the most familiar to generations of children from the 1950s onwards, until they fell out of favour towards the end of the century.

Information or 'fact books' for children became a large part of many publishers' output by the middle of the century, but the texts varied considerably in quality. The series format became much liked by authors and publishers and this resulted in topics being squeezed, sometimes less than comfortably or logically, into a standard number of pages. Format, language and illustrations were rather predictable and unexciting in some cases, but other books benefited from the imaginative insight of outstanding illustrators. Many a history book in the middle years of the century gained imaginative appeal through Alan Sorrel's atmospheric black and white drawings of people, animals and landscapes. The author illustrators Mick Manning and Brita Granström commented in an interview that Sorrel's 'atmospheric scribbly history drawings, particularly when depicting scenes from prehistory, had influenced their own work, for example the art work in their book *Stone Age Bone Age!*' (Mallett, 2006a: 6). Charles Keeping was another innovator in black and white drawing; his 'hatching' – the use of parallel lines to darken part of a picture – is effective in his street scenes from particular historical periods.

The books that are, along with R.J. Unstead's illustrated history and geography books, most likely to be remembered by those at school in the 1950s and 1960s are the Ladybird Books, first published by Wills and Hepworth in 1915. Non-fiction titles were included from 1952. These pocket-sized books, on a huge number of different topics, were arranged in sets on nature, science, history, geography and so on, and were a familiar sight in the primary school classroom in the second half of the twentieth century. The books were published in sixty languages and in different formats including posters and project packs. The writing was straightforward and clear and the colour illustrations, notably those by C.J. Tunnicliffe, Stanley Badmin and Rowland Hilder, were wonderfully detailed. Take the nature books, for example: here they managed to cram in huge numbers of pictures of plants and birds onto small four- by six-inch pages. One of Tunnicliffe's paintings of a scene in *What to Look for in Autumn* shows a foregrounded roof top with beautifully drawn birds taking the eye down to a scene of trees and plants (Mallett, 2006a: 6). These well-written and -illustrated small books were, and are, good value for money.

Very broadly, there were two main developments in non-fiction print book publishing during the later part of the twentieth century. First, information books, including encyclopedias, were transformed by new technology; authors and illustrators took full advantage of the advanced photographic techniques as a means of producing clear, arresting design and colour photographs of high quality of, for example, weather conditions, space and water environments. The second development was the arrival of the lyrical non-fiction book: this borrowed, in the written text, devices like simile and metaphor associated with fiction and used drawings and watercolour paintings which appealed to hearts as well as to minds.

Looking first at the development of the children's encyclopedia, the prototype was Arthur Mee's *The Children's Encyclopedia* which was first published in magazine form in 1908. It developed into a multi-volume encyclopedia still in print in the 1950s. Mee was a journalist and editor and a great collector of newspaper cuttings of articles and news reports on which he drew constantly in his writing and editing of children's books. What was the flavour of his well-regarded and -loved encyclopedia? It was not alphabetically organised, but rather each volume was in divisions of knowledge like 'literature', 'countries' and 'plant life'. There were more practical sections, too, including one that instructed children on how to keep a hedgehog as a pet. The tone of the writing was very much of its time and the encyclopedia contained many patriotic articles about the achievements of inventors and military men. The same sort of approach found its way into Mee's *The Children's Newspaper*. This weekly was published in March 1923 – May 1965. There were jokes, stories and copious illustrations, but there was also a strong non-fiction element. The 'photo pages' in the newsletter had items like 'Painting the Forth Bridge', 'Spring time in the countryside' and world maps explaining time differences. Those wishing to know more about this energetic and painstaking writer and editor might be able to track down a copy of Sir James Hammerton's out-of-print biography entitled *Child of Wonder: An Intimate Biography of Arthur Mee* published by Hodder and Stoughton in 1946. Modern encyclopedias link with Mee's in their ambitious coverage and their celebration of the visual. We associate the modern children's encyclopedia with a number of publishers: Collins, Dorling Kindersley, Kingfisher, Oxford and Usborne. In the 1970s and 1980s Dorling Kindersley produced encyclopedias and other sumptuous information books illustrated with arresting photographs and making use of new technology and with fine annotated diagrams in history, geography and science books aimed at particular ages within the preschool and primary years. Publishers have brought out electronic versions of their encyclopedias and other information books on CD-ROM and online. The print encyclopedia has proved to be adaptive to new demands in approach and content and is often, as in the case of the Usborne books, linked to designated websites. Like other non-fiction, the children's encyclopedia now receives critical attention and publishers are responsive to comment and advice. The trend is towards having whole teams of designers, editors, experts, educationists as well as writers and illustrators, which has advantages, of comprehensiveness for example, but which can lead to an approved kind of text that becomes rather uniform (Mallett, 2004: 624). There must always be space for the unusual, boundary-breaking book, perhaps by a sole author and single illustrator, that has energy and imaginative power. At about the same time as Dorling Kindersley and others were setting new standards of excellence for information books in terms of clear format, brilliance of illustration and faultless retrieval devices, and also moving towards multimedia texts to be read on screen, there was another kind of development in non-fiction publishing. This was to do with the publishing of non-fiction print books that were lyrical in approach. Here, of course, the authors and illustrators of the books in Walker's boundary-breaking 'Read and Wonder' series were the pioneers. The designer Matthew Lilly and the editor Amanda McArdie had a vision of an information book that communicated quality information but did so partly by starting from a personal perspective (I want to share with you my interest in animal life cycles, spiders and so on) and which drew on poetic images in language and illustration. The authors, who include Nicola Davies, Vivian French and Karen Wallace, and the illustrators, including Mike Bostock, Brita Granström, Mick Manning,

213

Charlotte Voake and others, started from a personal viewpoint but combined this with quality information (Mallett, 2006b).

Into the twenty-first century

We entered the twenty-first century with an expectation that children and teachers will work with a greater repertoire of information texts than ever before. Materials with an informational function reflect cultural needs and social change just as much as fiction does. The global markets for information texts and the rise of 'popular culture' tastes affect what is produced and published. We have, of course, to be aware of the dangers of crude commercial interest and need to keep on our critical hats when selecting new kinds of text for the classroom, just as we would when reviewing more traditional resources. New technology has expanded definitions of what modern literacy entails and the new literacies bring new ways of thinking and of conceiving of reading and writing. A study by the National Foundation for Educational Research on the state of reading in the early years of the twenty-first century found, as we might expect, that children's sustained reading, whether of fiction or non-fiction, has to take its place with other activities like hobbies and sport, relaxing with friends, texting, emailing, surfing the web, keeping up with Facebook and Twitter, watching television and playing interactive games. Visual literacy is becoming increasingly valued and children respond enthusiastically to images including moving images and graphics (Twist et al., 2006). Will the print information text continue? The internet and reading on screen already dominate in some kinds of reading and writing, but the print book has shown itself able to adapt to new tastes and demands and it offers a distinctive kind of reading experience. I would say that those print books that are original, thought-provoking and aesthetically pleasing to touch, read and look at are most likely to survive.

Alderson, Brian (2008) 'Classics in short', No. 69, *Books for Keeps*, No. 170, May.

Avery, Gillian (1995) 'The beginnings of children's reading to c.1700' in Hunt, Peter (ed.) *Children's Literature: An Illustrated History* Oxford: Oxford University Press.

Carpenter, Humphrey and Pritchard, Mari (1983, reprinted 1999) *The Oxford Companion to Children's Literature* Oxford: Oxford University Press.

Hammerton, James (1946) *Child of Wonder: An Intimate Biography of Arthur Mee* London: Hodder & Stoughton (O/P).

Kinnell, Margaret (1995) 'Publishing for children (1700–1780)' in Hunt, Peter (ed.) *Children's Literature: An Illustrated History* Oxford: Oxford University Press.

Mallett, Margaret (2004) 'Children's information books' in Hunt, Peter (ed.) *International Companion Encyclopedia of Children's Literature* London and New York: Routledge.

——(2006a) 'Mick Manning and Brita Granström: creators of lyrical non-fiction for young learners' *English 4–11*, Summer, Number 27.

——(2006b) *The Lyrical Voice in Non-fiction, Think of an Eel* Bookmark series, Leicester: The English Association.

Townsend, J.R. (1995) *Written for Children* London: The Bodley Head.

Twist, L., Shagen, I. and Hodgson, C. (2006) *PIRLS: Progress in International Reading Literacy Study* Slough: NFER.

Watson, Victor (2001) *The Cambridge Guide to Children's Books in English* Cambridge: Cambridge University Press.

HISTORY OF THE ENGLISH LANGUAGE

See also: English projects, functions of language, language change, language variety, structuralist model of language

A study of this history is beyond the scope of this book but is considered to some extent under the 'see also' entries shown above. The books listed below will help those who wish to read more deeply.

Barber, C. (1993) *The English Language: A Historical Introduction* Cambridge: Cambridge University Press.

Bryson, B. (1990) *Mother Tongue: The English Language* London: Penguin.

Hogg, Richard and Denison, David (2008) *A History of the English Language* Cambridge: Cambridge University Press.

Pyles, T. and Algeo, J. (1993, fourth edition) *The Origins and Development of the English Language* London: Harcourt Brace Jovanovich.

Wyse, D. and Jones, R. (2007) *Teaching English, Language and Literacy* London: Routledge (see Chapter 1).

HISTORY OF ENGLISH TEACHING (IN THE PRIMARY SCHOOL)

See also: Bullock Report, Cox Report, creative writing, elementary schools, English projects, Kingman Report, language across the curriculum, LINC materials, National Curriculum, National Oracy Project, National Writing Project, process approach to writing

The long list above shows that the fascinating and continuing story of the history of English teaching in the primary school underlies many of the entries of this book. Change comes about for many reasons – social, economic and political, and as a result of research by teachers and academics looking intently at what happens in the classroom. My account will be structured by some key landmarks which include reports and other initiatives that have brought about changes in approaches to language and learning and to models of English teaching.

I begin the story with the 1870 Elementary Education Act, which led to free education for all children from five to twelve years. At this time the 'skills' model of English teaching held sway. Children were taught in large formal groups and their writing consisted of copying from the board or writing down dictated passages. There was a lot of reciting of poetry and religious texts and an emphasis on spelling, grammar and handwriting drills. The payment by results code – the requirement that children should pass frequent tests in reading, writing and arithmetic in order for teachers to be paid – led to a mechanical and routine-driven curriculum.

A landmark in the emergence of English as a curriculum subject, encouraging practice in which children's creative language skills were developed, was The Newbolt Report on 'The Teaching of English in England' (Board of Education, 1921). Protherough and Atkinson (1994) pinpoint four central concepts in the teaching of English at all levels identified by Newbolt. These were the need for literacy to be at the core of the curriculum, the need to develop children's 'self-expression', a belief in the importance of quality literature, and a concern for the development of mind and character. By 'self-expression' the writers of the report were thinking of a style of teaching where talk and writing drew on children's creativity rather than one where drills and exercises prevailed. As the 1920s got underway, more schools began to encourage silent reading and, to some extent, children's creative skills, but this was in addition to, not instead of, grammar teaching by copying models of appropriate language.

The thinking made explicit in the Hadow reports, published in 1931 and 1933, took the more flexible approach to English and language development favoured in the Newbolt report further. As Wyse and Jones note, they read as 'remarkably progressive documents for their time, and the principles of child-centred education that are explicit in their recommendations continued to inform thinking in primary language teaching for

215

the next 50 years' (Wyse and Jones, 2007: 9). Not only did the reports recognise the importance of imaginative play for young children, they also identified three approaches to reading: 'look and say', 'phonics' and 'sentence-based', the last of these being more meaning-based, and recommended that teachers should draw on all of these in their literacy programme.

By the time the 1944 Education Act was passed (recommending the replacing of 'all-age' elementary schools by separate primary and secondary schools), some of the progressive recommendations of the Hadow reports were finding their way into more classrooms. In the 1960s the Plowden committee investigated how far the Hadow recommendations had been put in place and its report, published in 1967, celebrated existing good practice as well as making recommendations for improvements. In the same year John Dixon published his book *Growth Through English*. This book captured the spirit of the times and the emphasis on creative, imaginative and personal kinds of writing. It explored models of English teaching: the 'skills' model of the elementary classroom, the 'cultural heritage' model typical of English teaching in grammar schools which was based on a canon of quality texts and the 'personal growth' model in which writing expresses what the writer feels is worth saying (Pinsent, 2009).

The Bullock Report reinforced Plowden's emphasis on the 'process' aspects of speaking and listening, reading and writing. Rather than working through exercises, Bullock urged that children be helped to use language for real purposes and audiences. The report's areas of concern covered, on the one hand, the kinds of language use associated with English lessons – to appreciate literature, to talk about issues of human concern, to write accounts from their experience – and, on the other hand, English and language as a way of learning in every lesson. The report

encouraged every school to have a language policy and a teacher with special responsibility for co-ordinating everything to do with language.

Then, as the 1970s got underway, beliefs about how children were taught English began to change. We must remember that attitudes towards and trends in education do not lie outside more general economic, social and political climates. In the 1970s economic difficulties and concerns about the amount of government spending led to a reduction in the amount of money available for education and a greater focus on the efficient use of resources.

In 1988 the Education Reform Act was passed; it established a National Curriculum in state primary and secondary schools and gave the government more power to intervene directly in how the curriculum was taught. The National Curriculum brought about considerable change in English and language work. First it took, from the earliest stages, a subject-centred approach to the curriculum. This may have been partly a reaction to Plowden's favouring of the 'integrated day' where a teacher monitors groups of children working on different subjects. The 'integrated day' approach was considered by some to be particularly unsuitable for children beyond the infant stage. They considered the over sevens required a more focused approach which did justice to each school subject (Beard, 1999). 'English lessons' replaced 'language activities' in the official documents. Second, it was genre-based, that is language development was seen at least partly to do with children, both as readers and writers, coming to control an increasing range of kinds of written material. Third, it identified levels of attainment and put in place an intensive assessment system. These three features have persisted through several versions of the National Curriculum.

The National Literacy Strategy *Framework for Teaching* (DfEE, 1998) built on the National Curriculum English programmes and prescribed English teaching in more detail, setting out objectives at word, sentence and text level for each term from Reception to Year 6. There were many helpful and imaginative suggestions, not least for non-fiction reading and writing – often neglected in the past – but the problem with a prescribed programme is that it can take away a practitioner's will to evaluate principles and practice and to deploy them to meet the particular needs of their class. It recommended an essentially teacher-centred approach: direct teaching of the whole class replaced the group and individual work favoured by progressive teachers and given voice in the Plowden Report. Even group work was to be guided by the teacher or, in the case of independent groups, structured by carefully formulated tasks. There is research evidence that structured work is sometimes more successful than 'looser' approaches in the later primary years (see for example the findings of Mortimore *et al.*, 1988). However, Mortimore *et al.* insisted they were not imposing a 'blueprint' for every classroom.

The 1998 *Framework* required that reading be taught by a mix of methods – as recommended as long ago as the 1930s in the Hadow reports – and informed by a model using the metaphor of cue-systems as 'searchlights'. The 'phonic' approach was given greatest emphasis in the guidance material. This emphasis on phonics intensified in the renewed *Framework* – the *Primary Framework for Literacy and Mathematics*, 2006. When the *Framework* was abandoned it was hoped that there would be encouragement for more flexible use of Literacy Time and for the integration of ICT technologies and resources in the English and Literacy programme. The emphasis on prioritising the phonic cueing system in the initial teaching of reading continues.

How will English teaching in the primary years develop in the future? One thing is certain, it will not remain the same:

what happens in school responds to changes in our wider society. In the interesting final chapter of her book *The English Curriculum in Schools*, Louise Poulson maintains that further developments in information technology will continue to transform schools and how we define literacy (Poulson, 1998). I believe three things – to some extent already evident – would help English and language teaching in the primary years to change and develop successfully: flexibility in how the Literacy Time and other national initiatives are implemented; respect for teachers as reflective practitioners whose views on how changes are formulated and implemented deserve recognition; and linking curriculum development to the findings of quality research.

Beard, Roger (1999) 'English: range, key skills and language study' in Riley, Jeni and Prentice, Roy *The Curriculum for 7–11 Year Olds* London: Paul Chapman.

Dixon, John (1967) *Growth Through English* Oxford: Oxford University Press for NATE.

Mortimore, Peter, Sammons, Pamela, Stoll, Louise, Lewis, David and Ecob, Russell (1988) *School Matters: The Junior Years* Wells: Open Books.

Pinsent, Pat (2009, third edition) 'From copying to creation: the teaching of writing before the 1980s' in Graham, Judith and Kelly, Alison (eds) *Writing Under Control* London: David Fulton.

Poulson, Louise (1998) *The English Curriculum in Schools* London: Cassell.

Protherough, R. and Atkinson, J. (1994) 'Shaping the image of an English teacher' in Brindley, S. (ed.) *Teaching English* London: Routledge.

Riley, Jeni and Prentice, Roy (1999) *The Curriculum for 7–11 Year Olds* London: Paul Chapman (see Chapter 4).

Wyse, Dominic and Jones, Russell (2007) *Teaching English, Language and Literacy* London: Routledge (see Chapter 1, 'The history of English, language and literacy').

217

HOBBIES AND ENGLISH

See also: motivation, newspapers and magazines, non-fiction reading and writing

The interests and activities children enjoy out of school can enrich classroom discussion as well as their reading and writing. Very young children enjoy talking about their 'news' and will sometimes be asked to write and draw about such things as going swimming, playing computer games and family outings. Sometimes sharing a book can awaken an interest – it is never too early to become an expert! One of my students was surprised at the range and depth of questions from five year olds when she shared Claire Llewellyn's *My Best Book of Creepy Crawlies* (Kingfisher) with them. I find that seven to nine year olds often have hobbies based round collections of items which they like to label and annotate: wild flowers, shells, fossils and stones. Parents and friends can acknowledge and develop these interests with gifts of books, DVDs and CD-ROMs. Children's hobbies and interests provide a route into non-fiction reading and serve as a springboard for enthusiastic writing. Two friends, one aged eight and the other nine, were able to enthuse others in their class when the teacher invited them to talk about their shared hobby – reading and learning about fossils and especially dinosaurs (Mallett, 1992). The generation of lively talk and thinking is also evident in a case study in which a ten year old demonstrates his care of a pet snake to the whole school (Mallett, 2007).

Angela Redfern (1994) writes about her success in helping an unenthusiastic young writer gain a sense of purpose when encouraged to write about his passionate interest in hens. When asked about his chickens, Redfern writes: 'it was like switching on a light bulb. Once he got started, it became clear that Owen, aged six, knew everything there is to know about keeping chickens and as he gathered momentum he positively glowed'. After much effort, Owen was helped to produce a book for the school library which had sections on 'kinds of chickens', 'food' and 'laying eggs'. Used with adult guidance, the internet can make a great contribution to children's research on their interests and hobbies.

Mallett, Margaret (1992) *Making Facts Matter: Reading Non-fiction 5–11* London: Paul Chapman.
——(2007) *Active Encounters: Inspiring Young Readers and Writers of Non-fiction, 4–11* UKLA minibook.
Redfern, Angela (1994) 'Introducing Owen, expert eggstraordinary: the launching of a young writer' TACTYC *Early Years Journal*, 14(2).

HOME CORNER

See: drama and English, play and language and literacy

HOME-SCHOOL CONTACTS

See: parents and families

HOMOGRAPHS

These are words that are spelt in the same way but the meaning of which depends on how they are pronounced. Examples often quoted are 'entrance' and 'tear' as in: 'The entrance to the stock cupboard is near the window' and 'The power of the story to entrance was evident in the children's faces'; and 'The tear in her school blazer was worse than she had thought' and 'The tear rolled down the boy's cheek'.

HOMONYMS

Homonyms are words pronounced and spelt the same way but which can have different meanings. Examples are 'grounds' and 'bear': 'The school grounds offer pleasing views' and 'The coffee grounds spilled from the upturned cup onto the new carpet'; and 'The bear came menacingly from between the trees' and 'Many were called to bear arms to defend their country'.

HOMOPHONES

These words sound the same when spoken, but differ in spelling and meaning. So we might have 'whales swimming together' or 'hearing a baby's wails'. Another example is 'The bear caught a fish' or 'Her bare arms risked sunburn at midday'.

HORN BOOK

This is a book made of wood, with a handle so it can be held like a racquet, on which a sheet of printed paper is mounted and protected by a layer of transparent horn. The horn is held in place with a strip of metal. Horn books were often quite small, about four inches by three inches plus the handle. The printed sheet changed little over the centuries and usually included the alphabet in upper and lower case, the ampersand, the five vowels and the Lord's Prayer. Horn books were used for teaching reading from the sixteenth to eighteenth centuries.

HORROR STORIES

See also: fantasy

Many older children like the controlled feelings of fear that horror stories provide. Mallett quotes ten year old Natasha's remark that 'horror stories are exciting and you get frightened but nothing actually happens to you' (Mallett, 1997). One of the most interesting and exciting analyses of horror stories for children known to me is 'Horror' by Victoria de Rijke. 'Long live

dangerous fiction and the playful spirit of horror', she writes – but the danger needs to be under the child's control (de Rijke, 2004: 516). R.L. Stines' Goosebumps series appeals because of the humour of the tales as well as the scariness. Mallett discusses things to keep in mind when reading 'scary books' to the under eights. For example, it seems best that the frightening elements should be overt and not vague, and that things should be more or less resolved by the end of the story. It is also best to be aware that different children find particular things disturbing (Mallett, 2010). Sarah Hayes' *This is the Bear and the Scary Night* deals well with a particular situation. An owl carries away a little boy's teddy bear and the bear has to be brave as it gets dark in the park as night time falls. This kind of story, where all is well in the end, helps children cope with their fears. A touch of humour also helps mitigate frightening elements in stories.

A recent addition to the genre for older children is Justin Samper's Vampirates series – for example, *Demons of the Ocean* and *Tide of Terror* – set in the year 2505, in which flesh-and-blood and vampire pirate crews ply their trade.

de Rijke, V. (2004) 'Horror' in Hunt, P. (ed.) *International Companion Encyclopedia of Children's Literature, Volume II* London and New York: Routledge.

Mallett, Margaret (1997) 'Gender and genre' in *Reading* UKRA, 31(2).

——(2010) *Choosing and Using Fiction and Non-fiction 3–11* London and New York: Routledge.

HOT SEATING

This is a strategy used in drama to help children think deeply about a character's motivations and feelings. One child, or a pair of children, answer questions from the rest of the class, usually in role.

HYPERBOLE

This refers to statements that are a deliberate exaggeration of the truth, used for effect and not, generally, meant to be taken seriously.

HYPERMEDIA

When 'hypertext' is combined with graphics, sound and video-film on a CD or the internet we have 'hypermedia'. Children find they can be playful as readers and authors of such multimedia texts.

HYPERSTUDIO

From TAG (www.taglearning.com), this is a multimedia authoring tool which enables teachers and children to create interactive books. TAG's aim is to empower learning through ICT. TAG Learning is a provider for the curriculum 'online' company, TAG Learning Ltd.

HYPERTEXT

This is a term used in computing to describe the facility to jump from one page of text to any one of a number of earlier or later pages.

HYPHEN

See also: dash

This is a punctuation mark used in two main ways. First, we might use a 'link hyphen' to join words or parts of words together to create a new word: 'spare-part', 'after-hours' or 'green-house'. Over time, as the new words become established, the hyphen may be dropped. The second use, a 'break hyphen', is used in a text where a word cannot fit onto a line and has to be carried onto the following line, as in: 'After many years of travelling she decided to settled down and raise a family in the hot and dusty outback of Australia'.

'Break hyphens' may also replace commas to separate two closely linked pieces of text as follows: 'Word processing is preferable – particularly for an important piece of course work – as it is usually more legible and professional looking than handwriting'.

A hyphen may also replace the break between two short sentences: 'I think I will travel by rail – there might be heavy traffic on the roads'.

Where break hyphens replace commas or provide an alternative to two short sentences they are often called 'dashes'.

I

ICONIC REPRESENTATION

See also: language acquisition, language and thought, visual literacy

This refers to the representation in someone's mind of experience through an image. In Bruner's theory of development the 'iconic' stage is reached when children can think by drawing on remembered images. The breakthrough comes when they can conjure up the image of an object that is not physically present, for example of teddy, upstairs. Experiments have suggested that other primates can think through iconic representation – see for example the introduction to *A First Language* by Roger Brown (1973). After the acquisition of speech we continue to do some of our thinking and representation of experience iconically.

Brown, Roger (1973) *A First Language* Harmondsworth: Penguin.
Bruner, Jerome (1983) *Child's Talk: Learning to Use Language* US: Norton & Co.

ILLUSTRATIONS: FINDING A VOCABULARY

See also: chart, comics, diagrams, intertextuality, multimodal texts, photographs, picture books, postmodernism and children's picture books, visual literacy

Art is a powerful way of communicating and children are drawn to illustrations in books as much as to the words. Many children's books are illustrated, but in this entry I am concentrating on picture books which depend on an interaction between picture and writing. The outpouring of children's picture books in this century and in the last means that young children meet this highly sophisticated cultural form early in their lives. The variety of media now available to illustrators, both traditional and digital, is evident at exhibitions like the annual Bologna Children's Book Fair. Those wanting an account of the history of children's book illustration will find inspiration in Joanna Carey's essay in Blake (2002).

Picture books are a hugely important part of the early years collections in schools but the narrative complexity of some makes them also exciting reading material for older children and adults. These older readers are helped to reflect on issues like violence, bereavement and the environment, and 'on powerful emotions such as anger, sibling rivalry and jealousy' (Jordan, 1992). The work of Quentin Blake, Raymond Briggs, Anthony Browne, John Burningham, Lauren Child, Shirley Hughes, Pat Hutchins, Judith Kerr, David McKee, Tony Ross, Maurice Sendak and many others shows how powerfully these issues and emotions can be shown and the different levels of meaning the best picture books are capable of communicating.

In picture books illustrations can complement, extend or explain the written text.

Sometimes there can be an ironic connection between text and illustration. Thus, for example, pictures can playfully contradict the words or, like those in John Burningham's *Granpa*, reveal the different perspectives on events and memories of each character. Both pictures and words are 'read' and as David Lewis puts it, 'they act upon each other so that, to a greater or lesser degree, we read the pictures through the words and the words through the pictures' (Lewis, 2001: 131).

Particularly exciting, inventive and sometimes unsettling illustrations are found in what is often termed the 'post-modern' or 'contemporary' picture book. The innovations in this kind of picture book are often linked to developments in printing technology and illustrators sometimes combine the digital with other media. Neil Gaiman and David McKean bring their cutting-edge graphics and artwork to the nightmarish theme in *The Wolves in the Walls*. Emily Gravett brings hugely effective fonts, pictures and paper engineering in her entertaining book *The Rabbit Problem*. Another adventurous illustrator, Lauren Child, creates wonderful collages; her rich pages combine words, photographs and cartoon figures to make for a rich layout that links with children's screen experience. Much admired, too, is Brian Selznick's challenging book *The Invention of Hugo Cabret*. For more about some of these illustrators see Judith Graham's analysis 'Reading contemporary picturebooks' (Graham, 2005: 209–21). Booktrust seek out new 'voices' with boundless imagination in selecting a shortlist for the new illustrators annual award.

A very early picture book, perhaps the first, was the splendid illustrated encyclopedia *Orbis Sensualium Pictus* (The Visible World in Pictures) by Johannes Amos Comenius. The modern information picture book is relatively neglected, yet some of these have lyrical illustrations that deserve critical attention. Mick Manning and Brita Granström have long been at the

forefront of children's non-fiction picture books. Look at the beautiful pictures of plants, flowers and animals in their book *Nature Adventures* and the lyrical landscapes in *Roman Fort* and *Greek Hero*. Vicki White draws members of the Ape family with great sensitivity in her book *Ape* created with author Martin Jenkins. In these large portraits the animals look out from the pages with soulful eyes. It is not surprising to learn that this illustrator was at one time a zoo keeper.

This entry concentrates now on how teachers and reviewers can develop a vocabulary to make critical judgements about the visual in children's story books and particularly picture books. It is hoped that this will help teachers and students to reflect and comment on the visual aspects of the resources they encounter. As Ghislaine Kenyon laments, the commonly used phrase 'beautifully illustrated' does not get us very far. In discussing how illustrators approach their task and how line, colour and composition are used to create atmosphere and feeling, I draw on what well-known illustrators of children's books, mainly picture books, have said and written and on what I learnt at the *Words About Pictures* workshop at the Quentin Blake Gallery of Illustration at Somerset House in March 2004. Two classic books are worth tracking down for those who wish to strengthen their knowledge: Perry Nodelman's *Words about Pictures* (1999) and Maria Nikolajeva and C. Scott's *How Picturebooks Work* (2001).

Illustrators and their task

In his introduction to the *Words About Pictures* workshop at Somerset House, Quentin Blake mentioned some of the things about which an illustrator has to make decisions. These decisions cover things like the portrayal of the characters and setting and only come after considerable reflection on the mood and atmosphere of the story. Then there are issues about what scale would be best, how the story and pictures are best sequenced and from whose viewpoint the story should be told. In his picture book *Cockatoos*, Blake lets the words tell the story from the point of view of the human beings while the pictures show the perspective on things of the animals.

Alongside all this the illustrator has to think about where the book is placed along 'the gamut of realism' ranging from a book like *Danny the Champion of the World* to a fantasy like *James and the Giant Peach*; both books are by Roald Dahl and illustrated by Blake. However, one of the first questions Quentin Blake asks is: how can I best make this book exciting and appropriate for a particular age group?

Line

The finest illustrators have an instantly recognisable 'line' – the way they draw people and things. It might be heavy and bold like John Lawrence's in *This Little Chick* or light and sensitive like John Burningham's in *Granpa*. This is how Joanna Carey describes John Burningham's drawing of Georgie in another of his books, *The Magic Bed*: 'Georgie is drawn with a submissive tilt to his head – the pen sidles round his face, and although he has a nose, and a tiny dot for an eye, he has no mouth to speak of – or *with*, come to that' (Carey, 2004: 8). So an illustrator's 'line' communicates emotion and feeling. Talking to Nicholas Tucker, Niki Daly explains how he uses line and the gestures and orientations of the body to suggest the changing emotions of Jamila, a lively young girl (Tucker, 2005). Acquiring a distinctive line is part of achieving a 'visual voice' together with colour and tone (Kenyon, 2004).

Colour and tone

Illustrators can choose from many different media and this choice affects the colours and tone that can be achieved and therefore the mood and atmosphere. In *The Snowman*, Raymond Briggs uses coloured crayon to show appealing, gentle pictures of a child in a familiar environment. Pen and ink, line and wash, watercolour and collage are traditional choices but many illustrators now find the computer can offer a particularly rich range of colours. It is always illuminating to learn how illustrators approach their work. In his article 'Windows into Illustration', Chris Wormell explains that in his book *George and the Dragon* he faced the challenge of getting broad watercolour washes of colour as well as achieving some tighter more detailed work, for example the dragon's spiky back had a lot of fiddly bits to get round (Wormell, 2005).

It is helpful to a reviewer when an artist notes which techniques have been employed. John Lawrence, for example, explains that he has brought together vinyl engravings, watercolour washes and printed wood textures by using computer technology in *This Little Chick*. Younger illustrators like Lauren Child use new technology in making their pictures – scanning and manipulating images on the computer. Others who have been working with a traditional medium for many years sometimes change to using computer techniques. Niki Daly, author of *Jamila's Dress* and other books in the *Jamila* series and known in the past for using gentle, atmospheric backgrounds in watercolour, has recently turned to experimenting with colour directly on the screen.

Children's interpretations of illustrations and their own pictures alongside writing

How do children interpret the visual imagery they encounter in picture books? In *Children Reading Pictures* (Arizpe and Styles, 2002) we find evidence that, given interesting and challenging works like *Zoo* and *The Tunnel* by Anthony Browne and

Lily Takes a Walk by Satoshi Kitamura, children can respond insightfully to the textual richness in pictures. One of the clearest findings in the research study on which the book is based, carried out with eighty-four children in seven primary schools, was the energising power of group talk to help children discover what they might not have done alone (Arizpe and Styles, 2002). Of course, this is not a new idea: the teacher and writer Jane Doonan (1992) talked with children about picture books and set out her findings in *Looking at Pictures in Picture Books*. Sally Wilkinson sets out a fascinating analysis of Anthony Browne's picture books and how they can be used with Key Stage 2 children to explore themes to do with relations between parents and children (*My Dad*; *Changes*; *The Shape Game*), relationships between children and children and adults and children (*A Walk in the Park*; *Voices in the Park*) and gender stereotyping (*The Tunnel*; *Piggybook*). The illustrations in Browne's *Into the Forest* are very detailed and worth careful study. The teacher of a Year 4 class incorporated pages of this book into an interactive whiteboard notebook. By revealing part of each page at a time the teacher challenged the children's perceptions of what the picture was (Wilkinson, 2005).

If you want to read further about children's illustrated books and picture books, and about images in poetry books, comics, paintings and sketch books, I recommend *Art, Narrative and Childhood* which is based on the international papers on this subject given at a symposium at Homerton College, 2000 (Styles and Bearne, 2003). The scope of this book is huge: it not only looks at children's layered encounters with visual texts and the influence on reading and writing of the great range of multimodal and multimedia texts now part of children's reading experience but actually moves, albeit tentatively, towards a new theory of text. Of particular interest to the

subject of this entry is the chapter on picture books and metaliteracy which suggests that children can sometimes have a sophisticated grasp of the choices that author and artist have made. Another chapter, exploring visual paths to literacy, written by Colin Grigg gives interesting examples of children's writing in response to art works during an arts education project at the Tate Gallery. *Words about Pictures* is a book about illustration including Blake's collaboration with Roald Dahl which can be appreciated by both children and adults (Blake, 2000). Janet Evans' *Talking Beyond the Page* has input by leaders in the field of understanding images in children's picture books and discusses picture books for different age groups (Evans, 2009).

There is increasing interest in drawings and paintings done by children to accompany their writing. A number of educationists have produced research evidence to suggest that children, when provided with resources and the opportunity to experiment, find picture making a powerful route into their intellectual development (Matthews, 2004; and Baynes' work at Loughborough University).

From babyhood children see pictures on advertisements and other print materials both in the home and outside and, of course, still and moving images on the screen. Their first books are copiously illustrated as we have discussed above. Yet we do not always seem to build on this visual experience and understanding in school by encouraging children to see how it can communicate alongside their writing. Too often, argue Millard and Marsh (2001), drawing is regarded as 'a dispensable embellishment'.

Annotation is often an important extension to labelling and listing; four and a half year old Tom integrated pictures and words in his list of favourite foods. Orla, at only three and a half, used drawing as a way of solving a puzzle: how do people get to heaven? She drew a picture of ladders reaching up to the sky and got her mother to help her write 'This is a map to get to the sky' (Mallett, 2004: Chapter 5).

Modelling ideas using pictures and diagrams is linked to non-fiction reading and writing. Ken Baynes, a Visiting Professor at Loughborough University, records children's work using an interactive whiteboard. Boys in particular are likely to think and communicate with pictures and to enjoy using computer tools to illustrate their writing.

A vocabulary to refer to illustrations

Reviewers of children's books tend to be 'word' rather than 'picture' people, but need to develop a vocabulary for discussing illustrations, particularly when considering picture books. Student teachers are often asked to compile a resource of children's texts with some annotation and the following glossary, drawing on Mallett (2004) and Lewis (2001), may help provide a basic vocabulary for thinking about the strengths and weaknesses of the illustrated books they have encountered. Of course, we are interested in illustrators' choice of media, colour and line because these choices help us think, feel and puzzle over the characters and incidents in the book.

Glossary of words to discuss illustrations

- *Bleeding (of pictures)* refers to the extension of pictures to the very edge of the page.
- *Composition* is to do with the way things and people are placed on the page.
- *Double spread* means a picture that covers two adjacent pages – a design choice much liked by publishers of children's information texts.
- *Endpapers* are the pages we first see when we open a book. The endpapers of picture books often have drawings to introduce the story.
- *Hatching* is a term used to describe the parallel lines used to darken an area of a picture.

- *Hues* are the colours used in pictures.
- *Landscape* is a format in which the pages of a book are a rectangle with the longer sides in a horizontal position.
- *Line* simply means drawing of people and things. The 'line' an artist uses becomes distinctive and recognisable. There are subtle differences in the 'line' each artist uses, but an obvious variation is whether a line is bold (John Lawrence's *This Little Chick*) or light (Quentin Blake's *Clown*).
- *Modulation* refers to an artist's achievement in varying colour and hue.
- *Movable* describes a book that has flaps to open or tabs that can be pulled.
- *Picture book* refers to a book that tells a story through words and pictures, or through pictures alone. Picture books have become an important cultural form not least because young readers often have to use their developing predictive abilities to fill the narrative spaces. The non-linear reading of pictures has to be related to a linear written text.
- *Point of view (position)* is to do with the way an image is presented to show the reader objects and happenings from a particular perspective. So the 'point of view' affects how the reader understands the story.
- *Portrait* is a format in which the long sides of a rectangle are placed vertically.
- *Restricted palette* describes the palette of a picture limited to a small number of hues.
- *Salience* is a term meaning the emphasis placed, perhaps by a bright colour, on a particular element in a picture.
- *Vignette* is a small picture to enhance or extend written text. Manning and Granström use vignettes in their work; a well-known example is their cross-section in *What's Under the Bed?*

Arizpe, Evelyn and Styles, Morag (2002) *Children Reading Pictures: Interpreting Visual Texts* London: Routledge-Falmer (for a helpful review by David Lewis, see *Literacy*, 38(1), April 2004).

Blake, Quentin (2000) *Words about Pictures* London: Jonathan Cape Children's Books.

——(2002) *The Magic Pencil: Children's Book Illustration* London: British Library Publishing Division.

Bologna Annual (2003) *Illustration of Children's Fiction Books* London: North-South Books.

Books for Keeps www.booksforkeeps.co.uk

Carey, Joanna (2004) 'Judging illustration' in *Books for Keeps* 146, May.

Doonan, Jane (1992) *Looking at Pictures in Picture Books* Stroud: Thimble Press.

Evans, Janet (2009) *Talking Beyond the Page* London and New York: Routledge.

Graham, Judith (1990) *Pictures on the Page* Sheffield: NATE (O/P at present, but still one of the most inspiring books on the topic).

——(2005) 'Reading contemporary picturebooks' in Reynolds, Kimberley (ed.) *Modern Children's Literature: an Introduction* London and New York: Palgrave Macmillan: 209–26.

Jordan, Barbara (1992) 'Good at any age' in Styles, Morag, Bearne, Eve and Watson, Victor (eds) *After Alice: Exploring Children's Literature* London: Cassell.

Kenyon, G. (2004) 'Beginning the conversation' in *Books for Keeps* 146, May.

Lewis, David (1990) 'The constructedness of texts: picturebooks and the metafictive' *Signal*, 62: 131–46.

——(2001) *Reading Contemporary Picture-books: Picturing Text* London: RoutledgeFalmer.

Mallett, Margaret (2004) 'Words about pictures' in *English 4–11*, 21, Summer.

Matthews, John (2004, revised edition) *Children and Visual Representation* London: Paul Chapman.

Millard, E. and Marsh, J. (2001) 'Words and pictures: the role of visual literacy in writing and its implications for schooling' *Reading, Literacy and Language*, UKLA, 23(2): 54–61.

Nikolajeva, M. and Scott, C. (2001) *How Picturebooks Work* London and New York: Garland Publishing.

Nodelman, P. (1999) *Words About Pictures: The Narrative Art of Children's Picturebooks* Athens, Ga. and London: University of Georgia Press.

Sainsbury, Martin (2004) *Illustrating Children's Books: Creating Pictures for Publication* London: Barron's Education Series (written by the Director of the MA programme in Children's Book Illustration at APU Cambridge School of Art, this is intended for those seeking advice on publication, but it also has much of value and interest about picture books for the teacher).

Styles, Morag and Bearne, Eve (eds) (2003) *Art, Narrative and Childhood* Stoke on Trent: Trentham.

Tucker, Nicholas (2005) 'Authorgraph: Niki Daly' *Books for Keeps* No. 150, January.

Wilkinson, Sally (2005) 'Exploring the work of Anthony Browne' *The English Magazine*, 1 (3): 11–14.

Words about Pictures. A seminar and workshop organised by The Quentin Blake Gallery of Illustration, the Joint Education Department at Somerset House and *Books for Keeps*, March 2004. See articles in *Books for Keeps*, 146, May 2004.

Wormell, Chris (2005) 'Windows into illustration' *Books for Keeps*, 150, January.

IMAGE

See: iconic representation, visual literacy

IMAGINATION (SECONDARY WORLDS)

See: fairy tales, fantasy

IMPERATIVE

Sentences with an imperative as their main verb require the person addressed to carry out some action as in 'Jump now!' In addition to giving a command, the mood of an imperative verb may be a request 'Please give me the racquet', a warning 'Look out!', an entreaty 'Save me!', or an offer 'Have some more!' Often imperatives are in the second person, even if the pronoun is missed out. In 'Look out!', 'you' is implied. Less frequently an imperative can be in the first person ('Let's start now') or the third person ('Someone tell him to be quiet').

IMPERSONAL LANGUAGE

This is the language of text books and official documents. Sometimes impersonal language is in the passive voice. Thus in a report of a scientific experiment we might find language like: 'The chemicals were heated in a test tube over a Bunsen burner until the liquid turned blue'. Impersonal language contrasts with the personal tone usual in a letter to a friend or a more informal 'chatty' account in a newspaper or magazine.

When would we expect children to control impersonal kinds of reading and writing? Children from about age seven or eight onwards are usually able to recognise some of the features of formal as opposed to personal letters. The National Curriculum views control over more impersonal kinds of language as an achievement of the later primary years. By the end of Year 6 it is hoped that children will understand some of the features of impersonal language, for example sustained use of the present tense and the passive voice, as both readers and writers. One issue here is to do with insisting on children using adult kinds of writing before they are ready to do so. The entry on 'expressive talk and writing' invites a consideration of this.

IMPROVISATION

See: drama and English

INDEFINITE ARTICLE

This is the 'a' or 'an' we use to introduce a noun phrase. 'A' usually precedes a consonant, as in 'a little lamb', while 'an' usually comes before a vowel: 'an able adversary'.

There are, though, a few exceptions. 'An' is not used before a word beginning with a vowel that has a consonant sound, as in 'a used car'. Equally, 'an' would be used before a consonant that would have a vowel sound when spoken aloud, as in 'an MP3 player' or 'enclose an SAE'.

'An' is also occasionally used before words beginning with 'h', either because the 'h' is not pronounced, as in 'an hour', or because historically it was not pronounced, as in 'an historian'.

INDEPENDENT GROUP READING AND WRITING

See also: literacy hour, reading, spelling

Independent group reading and writing was part of good primary school practice before there was a National Literacy Strategy, but it came into sharper focus as part of the Literacy Hour in the 1998 and 2006 *Framework*, abandoned in 2008. At those times when some children are working independently, once tasks are set, the teacher is able to work intensively with other groups and individuals. It is important that the tasks are pitched at just the right level for children to manage on their own while being interesting enough to challenge them. The degree of collaboration depends on the task. The activities set out below can be adapted for different ages and stages.

Where the emphasis is mainly on reading, activities might include:

- Following up class-based phonics work with activities and games. For example, if split digraphs – 'a-e', 'i-e' and 'o-e' – have been covered children might be asked to notice these in the words of a book (Oxford Reading Tree CD-ROM, *First Phonics*, Sherston Software).
- Predicting the ending of the story read in the shared reading.
- Reading fiction on screen and noting features of style and vocabulary (older children).

227

- Reading and noting features of format of factual material on screen (Bearne *et al.*, 2007).
- Playing word games reinforcing a recent focus, for example the tasks on Sherston's *Oxford Reading Tree Rhyme and Analogy* CD-ROM.
- Researching and making notes on the life of the author of the week and their work, using books or websites (most children's authors have lively websites).

Where the emphasis is mainly on writing, activities might include:

- Making a plan for writing linked to class-based work.
- Using software to encourage some different formats for writing.
- Spelling games using dictionaries and word-bank (Palmer and Sanderson, 2000).
- Making books on aspects of language like homonyms and homophones, the letters of the alphabet and etymology.
- Reading poems and writing their own: haiku, limericks and rhyming and non-rhyming poems (John Foster's *Collins Rhyming Dictionary* might be helpful).

Bearne, Eve, Clark, C., Johnston, A., Manford, P., Mottram, M. and Wolstencroft, H. (2007) *Reading on Screen* Leicester: UKRA.
Palmer, Sue and Sanderson, Rob (2000) *The Little Alphabet Book* Oxford: Oxford University Press.

INDEPENDENT GROUP WORK

See also: collaborative learning, discussion, independent group reading and writing, speaking and listening

There is a long tradition of organising children in non-teacher-led groups to carry out some of their English work. The structure of such lessons varies but usually there is some input from the teacher before the children start work on their own. The theme for the work might arise from the teacher reading a poem or piece of literature or from showing of a film or DVD – perhaps a dramatisation of a classic like Philippa Pearce's *Tom's Midnight Garden*. On other occasions, the teacher invites the children to discuss and evaluate non-literary materials – advertisements, publicity material or letters to a newspaper on a controversial topic. Although Benton and Fox's influential book *Teaching Literature Nine to Fourteen*, written in the mid-1980s, is out of print, it is worth searching out because their ideas for literature-based work in pairs and groups are still extremely helpful. Just a few of these are: making a book programme, recording it on a CD; using a digital camera to make a film, improvising events mentioned but not described in detail in a book; and making a front page of a newspaper featuring a dramatic event in a novel or story. The ideas still inspire lively work and can be brought up to date with the use of digital cameras, interactive whiteboards and computer software. For other ideas for interesting group work see *Choosing and Using Fiction and Non-fiction 3–11* (Mallett, 2010) and *BookPower* (Bunting *et al.*, 2010). For analysis of some screen-based activities see Bearne *et al.*, 2007.

Towards the end of a lesson where group work has predominated, the children are nearly always invited to feed back their thoughts and conclusions to the whole class. The best work of this kind provides the opportunity for children to learn how to work well collaboratively and to develop their spoken-language ability. Children can both put forward their own opinions and listen and respond to those of others. Independent group work in Literacy Time can be a context for good collaborative work.

Benton, Michael and Fox, Geoff (1985) *Teaching Literature Nine to Fourteen* Oxford: Oxford University Press.

Bearne, Eve, Clark, Chris, Johnson, Annette, Manfold, Penny, Mottram, Marilyn and Wolstencroft, Helen (2007) *Reading on Screen* Leicester: UKLA.

Bunting, Jane, Ellis, Sue and Vernon, Jenny (2010) *BookPower: Literacy through Literature. Year 2* London: CLPE (other books in the series have suggestions for other year groups).

Mallett, Margaret (2010) *Choosing and Using Fiction and Non-fiction 3–11* London: Routledge.

INDEPENDENT READER

See also: core books, ERIC, individualised reading, reading choices

A child is described as an 'independent reader' when he or she is able to read even a simple text unsupported by a more mature reader. Some newly independent readers continue to read out loud for some weeks; others quickly become able to read silently. This move to controlling the reading process is a considerable breakthrough for the young learner. He or she has a source of pleasure that can be turned to at any time and a means of gaining information without adult help. See entries under core books and individualised reading for information about resources arranged according to difficulty.

INDEX

See also: factual genres, information books, retrieval devices

An index is the 'key' to locating specific information and is an important element in children's non-narrative information books. Bakewell and Williams (2000) conducted a survey and made twenty-one recommendations for good indexing of children's books. For example, a good index is consistent, avoids passing references and sub-headings and deserves a separate page or pages. Much emphasis is now placed on electronic searching. Interestingly these researchers believe that if children think in indexing terms they are likely to search the web more effectively.

Bakewell, K.G.B. and Williams, Paula L. (2000) *Indexing Children's Books* Society of Indexers Occasional Papers on Indexing No. 5. www.indexers.org.uk.

INDIVIDUALISED READING

See also: core books, independent reader

Rather than follow one reading scheme or stick to one publisher's selection of books for each age group, many teachers adopt a system where all the books (including those from schemes) are organised into broad bands of difficulty. Following the suggestions in Cliff Moon's well-known book *Individualised Reading*, some schools colour code the books. In this system, young readers have a quick indication of which books they should be able to read independently. The teacher makes sure that children have read a good selection of books at one level before moving on to the next. Although the last guide by Cliff Moon came out in 2007, the principles on which he based his system continue to inform practice.

This system works well in many schools but not everyone is a fan. Some teachers feel that children might be prevented from trying books they would enjoy, because they have been limited to those marked at a particular level. Interest in a topic sometimes motivates a young reader to read above their normal level. There might also be some competition about which level children have reached (Browne, 2009).

Browne, Ann (2009, third edition) *Developing Language and Literacy 3–8* London: Paul Chapman.

229

Moon, Cliff (2007, final edition) *Individualised Reading: A Teacher's Guide to Readability Levels for Children aged 3–11* Reading: National Centre for Language and Literacy, Reading University.

INFERENCE

See also: critical discourse, language acquisition, language and thought, metacognition, metalanguage

This refers to the ability to draw a logical conclusion from two or more statements. For example:

> 'Human beings need to eat to survive. Dr Smith is a human being. Conclusion: Dr Smith, like all human beings, needs to eat to survive'.

This is an example of the 'analytical competence' which the psychologist and developmentalist Jerome Bruner believes is created in the young of literate societies (Bruner, 1966).

Bruner, Jerome (1966) *Towards a Theory of Instruction* New York: W.W. Norton.

(N.B. This interest in intellectual development was characteristic of Bruner's early work. Since then he has drawn attention to the power of story and the imagination to enhance making sense of the world – see, for example, his book *Actual Minds, Possible Worlds* Cambridge, Mass.: Harvard University Press, 1986.)

INFINITIVE

This is the 'base' form of a verb signalled by the word 'to', so we have: to be, to speak, to sleep, to intervene and so on. In English, sentences must contain a 'finite' verb and the 'infinite' can be made finite by adding the boundaries of person, tense and modality.

INFLECTION

See also: affix, prefix, suffix

Inflection refers to the parts of a word that are added before or after the root. The parts added vary according to the function of the word in a sentence. So the inflections 'ing' and 'ed' added to the stem word 'ask' would give us – 'I was asking' and 'I asked'. Inflection also refers to changes to the spelling of words to suit the need in a sentence. For example 'spoke' is an inflection of the stem word 'speak'.

INFORMATION BOOKS

See also: CD-ROM, diagrams, dictionary, discussion text, encyclopedia, explanation text, factual genres, genre, history of children's non-fiction literature, lyrical non-fiction, multimodal texts, non-fiction reading and writing, persuasive genre, procedural or instructional genre, recount, report, visual literacy

The typical children's information book is illustrated, usually on a single topic, like squirrels, ships, the Vikings or volcanoes, and organised non-chronologically. (There are transitional kinds of non-fiction, some of which follow a time sequence or mingle fact and fiction – see 'information stories', 'faction' and 'transitional genre'.) Some publishers are particularly well known for their information titles, including Dorling Kindersley, Franklin Watts, Kingfisher, Longman, Walker Books and Frances Lincoln. Publishers like to present series of books and, with some honourable exceptions, they tend to fit each topic firmly in the series format, each title having the same number of pages and the same style of diagrams. They also love colourful, double spreads! Even a good format can become tedious if encountered too often. This entry examines some of the main features of information books, considers some criteria for selecting them and offers some reflections on their future.

One of the most insightful studies of the structure of typical children's information books was by Christine Pappas (1986). This analysis identified what she terms the 'obligatory elements' of the genre – the things that will always be present in an information book. Teachers would recognise these elements if they looked at one of the information books in their classroom or in the library. The first is 'topic presentation' which introduces the subject matter – 'A squirrel is … '. The second is the 'representation of attributes' and describes the different parts of the subject – 'A squirrel's body is designed to help them move and eat; they have a long tail and sharp teeth which can bite into nuts'. The third element is the 'characteristic events' and, in the case of a squirrel, would include its life cycle, breeding and hibernation and perhaps information about diseases and predators. Pappas suggests that children develop expectations about the order and nature of these obligatory elements and this helps them develop competence in this sort of reading. There are two optional elements in Pappas' model: 'category comparison' – 'Red squirrels … while grey squirrels … ' – and a 'final summary'.

While Pappas has illuminated the global features of an information book, others, like Bobbie Neate, have drawn attention to the desirability of their having effective mechanical guiders like sub-headings and having retrieval devices such as content, pages and indexes (Neate, 1999). The importance of having illustrations aligned with, complementing and sometimes extending the written text is emphasised in Mallett (1999, 2007). There are also considerations to do with content. Obviously we need books that provide accurate and up-to-date information and this can mean that the life of an information book tends to be shorter than that of a story book.

Looking across the whole collection of books in the school, we need to ensure that we have books reflecting history, knowledge and understanding from across the whole world.

Apart from criteria based on sound overall structure, helpful guiders and retrieval devices, good linkage between writing and illustrations and useful and comprehensive collection of books, what else should influence our choice of information books?

Of great importance is how the book is written, the way in which language is used to inform and inspire young readers. In her helpful account 'Do the blackbirds sing all day?', Helen Arnold cautions that an information book might be superficially attractive but not relate strongly enough to children's own experience. She urges us to reject books with language so bland and impersonal that a computer might have written them! The authorial voice is most important. Arnold asks: 'Is it genuine, conveying real interest in the subject?' and 'Can it excite curiosity without indoctrinating? Does it respect rather than patronise the reader?' (Arnold, 1992: 131). Both Helen Arnold and Margaret Meek, particularly insightful writers about information books, acknowledge how difficult it is to write them well. You need, argues Meek, to keep the 'big shapes' in mind when writing a history book, not allowing the 'minutiae of any given event' to overwhelm the main ideas. Nor must we allow illustrations of contemporary artefacts, however good, to lessen the amount of interpretative text which is necessary to help young readers fit bits of information together to make a coherent understanding possible (Meek, 1996: 61).

The work of critics like Margaret Meek, Helen Arnold, Sue Unstead, Ted Percy, Margaret Mallett and others have, in their reviews of children's books for a number of journals, including *Books for Keeps*, *English 4–11* and *The School Librarian*, helped bring a recognition that children's non-fiction

231

texts, both print and electronic, are worthy of critical attention. Reviews of children's information books, DVDs, CD-ROMs and software are also available on websites, some of which include teachers' assessments of books and resources for the classroom. There are age group-related lists and reviews in Mallett's (2010) book *Choosing and Using Fiction and Non-fiction 3–11* and in *The Core Booklist* (Ellis & Barrs, updated every two years and including an information text section).

What is the likely future of the information book? There is no doubt that there is a vast increase in the number of electronic texts and a greater use of the internet as an information source, with inevitable consequences on the demand for print books. However, new technology has brought about noticeable improvements in the format and layout of children's information books and a much higher quality of illustration. Dorling Kindersley, in particular, have contributed to transforming their look and appeal. Publishers are also bringing together the world of books and the world of computers in interesting packages. However, we have to apply the same criteria to these as we would to any other information text – making sure that pure entertainment does not compromise their educational work. I like the Interfact series (Two-Can Publishing/Zenith Entertainment plc) for use with PC and Mac, which aims to link electronic extension activities, puzzles and games closely with a book. The contents page in the book tells us 'What's on the disk' and 'What's in the book'. The package on 'water' for seven to eleven year olds covers topics like the water cycle, weather, being water aware, floating and sinking and surface tension in double spreads in the book, while 'disk link' boxes briefly explain the electronic extension activities. Thus the text for 'being water aware' is matched with a computer game to reinforce the notion that 'every drop counts' and that we should save water at home. Some publishers – Dorling Kindersley and Usborne publishing, for example – have been amongst the swiftest to link print books to websites to extend children's learning. Examples of the latter are Dr Anne Millard's *Castles* and *The Internet-linked Children's Encyclopedia*. A&C Black have developed website links to provide extension activities for David Smith and Shelagh Armstrong's imaginative geography book *If All the World Were a Village*. Reading print and reading on the computer are distinct experiences and I believe they will continue to exist side by side, increasingly complementing each other. However, I do think this is not the time to write or publish B+ print information books. To compete with information in other media they need to be superbly designed, meticulously researched, well written and illustrated, and have a strong appeal to a young reader's imagination.

Arnold, Helen (1992) 'Do the blackbirds sing all day? Literature and information texts' in Styles, Morag, Bearne, Eve and Watson, Victor (eds) *After Alice: Exploring Children's Literature* London: Cassell.

Ellis, Sue and Barrs, Myra (updated every two years) *The Core Booklist* London: CLPE.

Mallett, Margaret (1999) *Young Researchers: Informational Reading and Writing in the Early and Primary Years* London: Routledge (see chapter 1).

——(2007) *Active Encounters: Inspiring Young Readers and Writers of Non-fiction 4–11* UKLA minibooks.

——(2010) *Choosing and Using Fiction and Non-fiction 3–11* London and New York: Routledge (see part 2).

Meek, Margaret (1996) *Information and Book Learning* Stroud: The Thimble Press.

Neate, Bobbie (1999, second edition) *Finding Out About Finding Out* London: Info Press.

Pappas, Christine (1986) 'Exploring the global structure of children's information books' Paper presented at the Annual Meeting of the National Reading Conference, Austin, Texas.

INFORMATION AND COMMUNICATIONS TECHNOLOGY (ICT) AND ENGLISH

See also: autocorrect, CD-ROM, email, EXIT model, integrated technologies, interactive whiteboard, interactivity, internet, multiple literacies, non-fiction reading and writing, popular culture and new media, reading on screen, visual literacy, websites and primary English

In the twenty-first century, being literate means having the same facility in the use of digital and screen-based texts as we have long expected to have in using other media. Computers have transformed our working lives and our leisure activities. In their book *Digital Literacies*, Carrington and Robinson show how strengthening our understanding of Facebook, blogs, texting, computer games and instant messaging helps us keep up with children's social learning (Carrington and Robinson, 2009). In their snapshot survey, a UKLA team found that, when given a choice, pupils of different ages tended to prefer screen-based texts, particularly popular children's websites, over paper-based texts. Multimodal texts in all media were liked for leisure reading more than those composed mainly of words. However, it is important to note that this team made it clear that their data 'did not suggest a lack of interest in sustained book reading, rather an awareness from the children surveyed that they could gain different satisfactions from different kinds of text' (Bearne *et al.*, 2007: 10). This entry concentrates on ICT in school, but we need to keep in mind that children come to school in many cases already computer literate and with some preferences (Selwyn *et al.*, 2010).

Not surprisingly, ICT is perceived as a powerful tool for teaching and learning and there has been a great deal of investment in developing and promoting educational applications. For some time in the United Kingdom primary teachers have been using ICT, particularly in teaching English, mathematics and science. Teachers need to become experts in using all the media and modes through which information, knowledge and understanding is communicated (Evans, 2004; Rudd and Tyldesley, 2006). Multimedia texts, including CD-ROMs, DVDs and those on websites, combine moving images, sound and music, helping children understand concepts they might find difficult if expressed only in writing.

This entry is concerned with how the computer and the internet (see also the 'internet' entry) can be harnessed to good practice in the English classroom. Although the four language processes are interwoven in all learning, for clarity this account first considers speaking and listening, second reading and third writing. In my analysis I will consider particularly how the teacher intervenes to maximise the learning achieved when children are using computers. (For a discussion of the impact on English teaching of the interactive whiteboard see the entry of this name.)

Speaking and listening

Work using the computer is often collaborative and group based and this provides a good context for speaking and listening. One of the first decisions the teacher will make is about the size and nature of the group because its composition affects the kind of interaction. Three or four children is a good number for most activities, apart from those round 'text manipulation software' where larger groups are possible and sometimes more stimulating. The teacher will take account of gender, friendships and ability when grouping children for particular tasks. For example, teachers have found some girls adopt a passive role when in mixed groups, but their competence is now growing.

Speaking and listening get underway when children can be asked to create or read a text. They may begin a piece of group writing by word processing the fruits of a 'brainstorming'. Building on this, with one child acting as 'scribe', the group can develop their account on the screen. It is the interaction of pupil with pupil, listening and responding to each other's thoughts and ideas, which is so educative. The teacher's visits to the group will help the children review progress and move them on by posing questions that challenge their understanding.

Another strong context in which to use discussion to support literacy is one with the umbrella term – 'DARTs' (Directed Activities Round Texts). A well-known example is 'cloze procedure' which involves making decisions about restoring words that have been deliberately removed from a text. Here children can be helped to acquire and use a metalanguage to refer to aspects of language like 'meaning', 'text', 'letter' and 'word'. Use of this metalanguage, encouraged by the teacher, leads to a heightened awareness of some of the features of spoken and written language which can transfer to other contexts, for example evaluating a story. A version of cloze procedure is available in what is known as 'text manipulation software'. Typically, children work with a 'text' from which every letter has been omitted and which only retains the punctuation and dashes to represent the missing letters. Pupils can 'buy' or call up all the instances of one particular letter, usually beginning with the more common vowels and consonants. When these begin to replace the dashes, a pattern starts to emerge. The task becomes an absorbing game in which inference, prediction and hypothesising all come into play. Above all, the children share their thinking and 'guessing' as they reconstruct the text and from observation it will become evident that they are drawing on their knowledge of how texts are written.

Children have long enjoyed and critically evaluated literature without needing a computer to help them. However, having a poem or short story on screen for joint attention helps concentration and allows the teacher moving between groups to tune in quickly to what the children are discussing. Valuable discussion can also arise from group work round software not directly linked to literacy. Searching for information from websites and CD-ROMs can lead to lively discussion on topics and issues arising from history and geography. Where the group reports back to the rest of the class on what they have found, there are further opportunities for reflection. Questions from the teacher and other children will help those reporting back to sharpen their arguments and explanations. They can also be encouraged by the teacher to analyse how they learnt using this particular medium. They might, for example, talk about how scrolled and nonlinear texts are structured and how animations and interactive diagrams help their learning.

Reading

Large quantities of software have been developed to help with the teaching of reading. This software needs careful assessment and we need to be clear about the contribution a specific product makes to literacy learning. Computer-based reading resources tend to fall into two groups: first those that help children with the 'smaller shapes' – reading skills related to initial sounds and sound-symbol relationships, and second those that support children's understanding of the 'big shapes' – the meaning and context-related aspects of reading, by focusing on whole texts. Software supporting the text-level aspects of reading, available from the early 1990s, takes the form of a story presented on screen using written text, speech and animation. These are often referred to as 'talking books'.

There has been criticism of both kinds of resource. Graham and Kelly point out that *Dr Seuss's ABC* (part of the Living Books series), which teaches initial sounds through a question and answer approach together with amusing animations, proceeds at a slow pace even for beginners. We also need to keep our critical hats on when selecting electronic stories: sometimes the entertainment element is at the expense of their educational value. Nevertheless, many are excellent. Here is Graham and Kelly's appreciative review of Sherston's much-praised *Nursery Rhyme Time*: 'In this delightful CD-ROM children can choose to sing along with, play with and hear read aloud any one of about a dozen nursery rhymes which they can select by clicking on an easily readable picture icon. Lively cartoon illustrations reflect a multi-cultural world and the English voice-over is easy on the ear' (Graham and Kelly, 2009: 50).

Research so far suggests that electronic talking books are best used alongside other teaching strategies. Medwell, for example, found that the greatest benefits were attained when the teacher first heard children read in a traditional way, and then set up small groups to use talking books (Medwell, 1998). In his summary of current views about talking books, Garvey stresses that it is the pleasure and liveliness of the electronic book context which seems to help children learn actively about features of text and particularly about some of the links between spoken and written language. To give one example, children come to understand the role of spaces and pauses 'which can be highlighted on the screen and related to the role of punctuation in clarifying meaning' (Garvey, 2000: 111). Thus the teacher can reinforce the ways in which a break in language is indicated in speech and writing – in speech we have a pause, in writing we have to put a comma or full stop.

So far I have been thinking about fiction when considering the software available to support reading, but the best informational CD-ROMs also have considerable potential for helping children's progress. The multimedia nature of CD-ROMs – their use of sound and animation as well as written text – make them highly motivating and thereby provide an excellent context in which children are reading to learn. We do, of course, have to appraise them as rigorously as we would a print information text. The strategies for interacting with non-fiction set out by Wray and Lewis in the EXIT model – establishing purposes, locating information and so on – can be applied to research using CD-ROMs and the internet. See more on this under the entries on CD-ROM, EXIT model, encyclopedias, internet and information books (Wray and Lewis, 1997). Mallett (2010) explores the use of screen-based texts alongside traditional media in the case studies in *Choosing and Using Fiction and Non-fiction 3–11*. The growth of the internet raises some issues. While books and media programmes are usually independently edited, most websites are not and we need to be careful about children having access to material meant for adults and information where the content or language is of low quality. Many primary schools are taking a constructive approach by developing a 'bookmarking' system of good websites.

Writing

The word processor and desk-top publishing software have transformed how we approach writing tasks. This evaluation is personal and heartfelt! After writing a doctorate by hand, having it typed, then laboriously editing it and bringing it to final draft, my own output and efficiency increased enormously once I became competent with Microsoft Word. Today's primary school children take word processing for granted and learn to type alongside learning to handwrite. The advantages of the word processor over handwriting are that:

- Children can start to make marks on screen (perhaps using overlay keyboards) from the earliest stages. They can make marks on paper of course – but where their marks are put on screen, the adult can scribe to the child's dictation and they can expand the account together. Thus a child can feel like a writer early on.

- Multiple copies can be printed out so that a child can have a personal copy of a piece of writing, one for the class library, one for a portfolio, one to take home and so on. This must be motivating as there is so much payoff from the initial effort.
- Shared writing tasks are much more manageable – children in a group of three or four can focus jointly on the developing text.
- Drafting is less time consuming as compositional and transcriptional changes can be made much more easily.
- Because so many different choices about format can be made – children can produce professional-looking posters, leaflets and reports using desk-top publishing software. Attention is drawn to genre features and to how content and presentation reflect purpose and audience.
- Multimedia authoring allows children to combine written text with graphics, video and animation to produce on-screen electronic books.
- The professional-looking presentation possible motivates children to see writing as a worthwhile and even exciting activity, the fruits of which can be shared with others.

Text manipulation software has been referred to earlier in terms of its contribution to reading progress. It can also help children's progress in writing since it can be adapted to supporting learning about grammar and spelling.

A hugely flexible and useful tool in supporting children's writing development is the interactive whiteboard (see entry). John Garvey writes about its potential for promoting all kinds of literacy in 'Interactive whiteboard for whole class reading and writing' (Garvey, 2006).

Three things press on me. First, when children work with computers all the language processes come into play: they read what is on the screen, talk about how texts are structured at word, sentence and text level, and listen to what each other has to say. Second, the contribution of the teacher is critical in designing and focusing activities, challenging, questioning and extending what they are doing and celebrating success. Teacher questioning can help to promote pupils' development of skills of inference, prediction and hypothesis testing. Third, I agree with Wyse and Jones (2007) that exciting as the new technology is, it is unlikely to replace books, pens and paper.

Bearne, Eve, Clark, Chris, Johnson, Annette, Manfold, Penny, Mottram, Marilyn and Wolstencroft, Helen (2007) *Reading on Screen* Leicester: United Kingdom Reading Association.

Carrington, Victoria and Robinson, Muriel (2009) *Digital Literacies: Social Learning and Classroom Practices* London: Sage.

Evans, J.C. (ed.) (2004) *Literacy Moves On: Using Popular Culture, New Technologies and Critical Literacy in the Primary Classroom* London: David Fulton.

Garvey, John (2000, first edition) 'Incredibly creative tools' in Fisher, Robert and Williams, Mary (eds) *Unlocking Literacy: A Guide for Teachers* London: David Fulton.

——(2006, second edition) 'Interactive whiteboard for whole class teaching of reading and writing' in Fisher, Robert and Williams, Mary (eds) *Unlocking Literacy: A Guide for Teachers* London: David Fulton.

Graham, Judith and Kelly, Alison (2009, third edition) *Reading Under Control: Teaching Reading in the Primary School* London: David Fulton.

Mallett, Margaret (2010) *Choosing and Using Fiction and Non-fiction 3–11* London and New York: Routledge.

Medwell, Jane (1998) 'The Talking Book Project: Some further insight into the use of talking books to develop reading' *Reading*, May.

Naace: www.naace.org.uk. This is the professional association for those concerned with advancing education through use of ICT. It provides advice for organisations (including schools) and produces publications that reflect developments in ICT in educational contexts.

O'Sullivan, Olivia (2005) 'ICT and early literacy' in *Books for Keeps*, September.

Rudd, A. and Tyldesley, A. (2006) *Literacy and ICT in the Primary Classroom* London: David Fulton.

Selwyn, Neil, Potter, John and Cranmer, Sue (2010) *Primary Schools and ICT: Learning from the Pupils' Perspective* London: Network Continuum Education.

Wray, David and Lewis, Maureen (1997) *Extending Literacy: Children Reading and Writing Non-fiction* London: Routledge (Kindle edition 2009).

Wyse, Dominic and Jones, Russell (2007, second edition) *Teaching English, Language and Literacy* London: Routledge.

INFORMATION STORIES

See also: biography, chronological non-fiction, factual genres, history and English, lyrical non-fiction, narrative, transitional genre

Teachers and children often refer to texts which follow a time sequence but which also impart facts and ideas as 'information stories'. The life cycles of plants and animals, journeys and historical events all have a natural chronology which is helpful to young readers and listeners who are familiar with the rhythms of story. This kind of genre is 'transitional' in that some of the features of the mature texts on which it is based are modified. For example, fantasy elements may be brought in even though the function of the text is informational. Some teachers wonder if mixing text types might cause genre confusion! However, in my experience children understand which elements of texts are 'true' and which are devices to entertain us. For example, in *The Drop Goes Plop* by Sam Godwin and Simone Abel young children love the talking mother and baby seagulls who take us on an exhilarating trip through the water cycle. Another favourite title in this series is *The Case of the Missing Caterpillar* which takes a first look at the life cycle of a butterfly within an intriguing detective story.

Not all information stories incorporate fantasy elements. Some have a number of features associated with children's non-narrative information books – fact pages at the end, carefully labelled diagrams and sometimes an index. J.V. Wilson and Adrienne Kennaway's *Bumblebee* is organised as a life cycle and has a clear text which is inviting and also transitional between a conversational style and more mature informational writing. You will get an impression of the lyrical illustrations from the image of the book's cover that accompanies this entry.

Perhaps the best information stories are written by authors and illustrators with a personal foothold in a subject so that we benefit from their memories and feelings as

Figure 11 Front cover of *Bumblebee* by J.V. Wilson and illustrated by Adrienne Kennaway. Reproduced with the permission of the publishers, © Frances Lincoln, 2011.

well as 'the facts'. The Read and Wonder series (Walker Books) covers topics like apple trees, pigs, caterpillars, beavers and so on bringing a human dimension that strikes a chord with young readers. So we have, for example, *Spider Watching* by Vivien French and Alison Wisenfield which is based on the author's memory of persuading some other children not keen on spiders just how interesting these creatures are. It is not easy to write an information story for children that will truly make the young readers reflect and wonder. Karen Wallace and Mike Bostock manage this in *Think of an Eel*, another book in the Read and Wonder series, by sharing right at the beginning of the book the secret about the Sargasso sea. 'For thousands of years a secret lay hidden: this salt, soupy sea is where eels are born'. Yet 'no one has ever seen a wild eel lay eggs or an eel egg hatch'. The book appeals directly to the young reader's imagination through words and pictures. So we have the verbal image of the elver 'like a willow leaf, clear as crystal' and with 'teeth like a sawblade' and the perfectly matching illustration of the transparent creature. A good example of the 'journey' kind of book is *River Story*, by Meredith Hooper and illustrated by Bee Willey, which takes us from the river's source high in the mountains, through valleys and fields, into the city and finally to the sea. A rhythmic text and wonderfully detailed illustrations impart much information about the river and the creatures and plants which inhabit it at each stage of the journey. Books like this often provide an inspirational start to a new topic before children use more conventional information books and resources: I cannot think of a more inspiring way to begin a study of rivers with children about six to eight years than to read this story out loud.

The story approach has a place across the curriculum and is particularly well established in history. Under the 'history and English' entry there is an analysis of *Seeing Red* by Sarah Garland. The legend on which the story is based may be at least partially true and children up to about eight years learn about the eighteenth century from the landscapes, clothes and artefacts in the pictures as well as from the text (Anderson Press). For older juniors, Dorling Kindersley's Discovery series incorporates a story approach: each book tells the story of an exciting event and then gives an analysis of its significance. For example, in *Pompeii: the Day a City was Buried* we hear first of a dramatic series of events and then the impact of those events is discussed. Mick Manning and Brita Granström's *Roman Fort* and *Viking Longship* (Frances Lincoln Fly on the Wall series) embed quality information within exciting stories.

'Facts through story' kinds of texts are likely to be represented in the class and school collections of primary schools. Of course, like other books, they vary in quality. Some can be banal, patronising to young readers and provide very little useful information in either text or illustration. When choosing, we should seek books that arouse curiosity and share, in a way young readers can appreciate, some careful observations, ideas and feelings about the phenomena involved.

INITIAL TEACHING ALPHABET

The Initial Teaching Alphabet, ITA, was an attempt to help children learn to read more easily by regularising the sound-symbol system. Twenty extra symbols were added to the twenty-six letters of the alphabet. While the initiative arose from good intentions it cut young readers off from environmental print – a very powerful stimulus to getting meaning from print. It was also difficult for some young readers to change back to the conventional alphabet.

INNER SPEECH

See also: language and thought, meta-cognition

This is a term used by L.S. Vygotsky to refer to thinking. To understand what Vygotsky means by the sort of thinking he called 'inner speech' we have to be clear about his notion of the two different functions of language. First, he believes a child has a strong urge to communicate with other human beings – so the first function of language is essentially social. Second, though, the very act of speaking and listening and in turn being addressed, informed and explained to by others allows language to become an instrument of thought and of self-regulation. What seems to happen is that the child internalises the ways of going about a dialogue with another person so that he or she can conduct such a dialogue with themselves as 'inner speech' or thinking. So what began as an urge to communicate becomes the means of a child developing their thinking and reasoning abilities.

INSTRUCTIONAL TEXTS

See: procedural or instructional genre

INTEGRATED TECHNOLOGIES

See also: interactive teaching programmes, interactive whiteboard, visual literacy

This term refers to bringing together a variety of resources to use in a lesson or series of lessons to support a theme or the study of a particular text. These resources can include digital images, film, sound and music and need to be carefully chosen to enhance the teaching and learning opportunities. The integration of these different resources is often achieved by using an interactive whiteboard.

'INTERACTIVE' READING MODEL

See also: 'big shapes', 'bottom-up' reading approaches, cue-systems, phonics, reading, 'top-down' approaches to reading

'Interactive' reading models combine 'top-down' (emphasis on meaning) and 'bottom-up' (emphasis on code-breaking) approaches. In *The Teaching of Reading*, Jeni Riley promotes an 'interactive' model of learning to read by both providing the theoretical underpinnings (Chapter 2) and then explaining classroom implications (Chapters 3–5).

Informed reading practice in many parts of the world now seeks balance between a focus on larger units of language, taking account of context and content, and work on phonics and other word-level skills (see for example Adams, 1993).

Adams, M.J. (1993) 'Beginning to read: an overview' in Beard, R. (ed.) *Teaching Literacy and Balancing Perspectives* London: Hodder & Stoughton.

Riley, Jeni (1996, 2007) *The Teaching of Reading* London: Paul Chapman.

INTERACTIVE TEACHING PROGRAMMES (ITPS)

See also: Information and Communications Technology (ICT) and English, interactive whiteboard

ITPs facilitate the use of ICT in whole-class teaching contexts and are best used with an interactive whiteboard.

INTERACTIVE WHITEBOARD

See also: Information and Communications Technology (ICT) and English, integrated technologies, interactive teaching programmes, internet, Primary National Strategy, video-film and DVDs, visual literacy

An interactive whiteboard is a touch-sensitive screen onto which information taken from a computer is projected. The material projected onto the screen can be controlled by touching the board as well as by

239

using a keyboard or mouse. The basic equipment, therefore, consists of a computer, a projector and a whiteboard onto which the computer screen image is displayed.

There is no doubt that this computer-linked tool is transforming teaching and learning in English and literacy lessons, and in other lessons across the curriculum. It is not so much that the whiteboard helps achieve something completely new, but rather it helps important things to be achieved more easily. Concentration is likely to be keen where 'joint attention' of teacher and class focuses on print and images displayed on a large screen, a screen that is both more flexible and more dynamic than a chalkboard or flip chart. Lessons can be made visually powerful when teachers use the whiteboard to integrate and co-ordinate material from many different media. They can project print diagrams and photographs, and moving images from film and the internet, and deploy music and sound effects. Well used, this visual and aural input energises lessons for all children, but it has special potential to inspire those reluctant young learners who respond positively to a multimedia approach. The teaching of reading and writing in every lesson is greatly assisted by facilities for the sophisticated manipulation of text on screen. Highlighting and annotating tools, for example, make the teaching of reading and writing dynamic. They offer a window into a teacher's thinking as they demonstrate how to read and interpret different texts and to structure, review and edit their writing. Learning about the use of ICT itself – about software applications such as highlighting, and cutting and pasting texts – can be taught effectively to the whole class in a time-economic way. Once they are accustomed to working with a whiteboard, busy teachers find they can organise a range of diverse resources for a lesson swiftly, and of course they can create and display their own resources effectively.

It is important to understand that good use of an ICT tool like the interactive whiteboard requires the same degree of careful and skilful preparation and presentation that competent teachers would bring to any lesson. It is still the teacher's pertinent questioning that ensures that pupils interact intellectually with the texts and allows the effective assessment of what has been learnt. As Mary Le Breuilly puts it, 'Without the questioning, the interactivity remains in the electronic wizardry on the white board' (Le Breuilly, 2004).

So far the benefits of the interactive whiteboard that have been discussed can apply to every lesson. What, then, are some of the potential benefits which are particularly pertinent to class-based English work whether in Literacy Time or outside it?

Benefits of the whiteboard to English and literacy teaching and learning

Speaking and listening

We tend to think that the interactive whiteboard mainly contributes to developing literacy but, well used, it also encourages lively and focused talk and intelligent listening. The annotation tool is particularly useful in making sure class teaching is interactive, whether teacher and children are talking about phonics and grammar or about the features of a story or poem. It helps make easier and more participative those lessons where teacher and class want to summarise together what has been learnt, for example about a character in a book or play. So, for example, the teacher may act as scribe by listing the children's suggestions, and then inviting them to annotate the list. Yes – you could do this on a chalkboard or flip chart, but the whiteboard is more flexible. For example, relevant parts of a text can be shown alongside the developing summary using the split screen facility.

When it comes to fiction, sites with hyperlinks which offer children the chance to choose how they want a story to develop are set to help children understand the sort of choices authors make. Bringing up the choices available on a whiteboard provides a focus for class discussion about their implications.

Reading

Whiteboard tools for moving text, changing layout, highlighting and annotating help the teaching of literacy processes, including the objectives at word, sentence and text level set out in Primary Strategy documents. Word-level work, including phonics, can be enlivened on screen by visual and sound input. Sentence-level work, the teaching of grammar, can also be made interesting and even playful by a multimedia approach.

When it comes to text-level work, a whiteboard provides another way of sharing enlarged texts. Where texts are to be compared, teachers find the split-screen facility helpful as it allows two texts to be displayed at the same time.

The different genres that have their special home in English lessons, poetry, story and playscripts, can be shown on a big screen and annotated as class and teacher read, talk about and interpret the text. Film and sound clips can be used to add atmosphere while reading a particular poem or story. Highlighting tools help as the text is scanned for images and telling phrases. The whiteboard brings, potentially at least, a greater range of reading experience. Easily accessed are the interactive texts where young learners can select the direction a story takes and websites like BBC Newsround which provides a daily newspaper (much more immediate than a print one). Other kinds of written material easily accessible from websites are biographies of favourite authors and reviews of books (some by children), CD-ROMs and websites.

The visual media which can be used so easily with a whiteboard enrich English lessons where illustrations are an important part of the texts. Pictures from paper picture books can be shared and interpreted on the big screen. The photographs and drawings associated with literary kinds of non-fiction – autobiography, biography and travel books – can also be scrutinised. Phrases can be written on or beside the images and both the annotated and unannotated pictures can be saved for comparison. Then, of course, English work around advertisements in different media benefits from all the illustrations and clips of moving images the whiteboard can provide.

The flexibility of the whiteboard helps link reading and writing because it is easy to move back and forth from a studied text to the children's own writing in progress.

Writing

Teaching about both compositional and transcriptional aspects of writing is well supported by use of the interactive whiteboard tools. Taking the transcriptional aspects first, the teaching of spelling, grammar and punctuation all benefit from the skilled use of highlighting and annotation tools. Teachers also find the whiteboard files to store spelling banks very convenient. PowerPoint, online dictionaries and thesauri all help children check transcriptional aspects of writing.

When it comes to compositional aspects of writing it is helpful for children to look at the choices made by other writers in a particular genre. In this 'reading as writers' context, the annotating and highlighting whiteboard tools are invaluable in showing the features of different kinds of text. The global features of a large stretch of writing can be shown as well as writing style and distinctive vocabulary. Features important in poems and stories – imagery, use of dialogue, beginnings and endings – can be easily tracked. Switching back and forth from a text under study to children's developing writing is made easier with a split screen and aids the transition from reading a text to writing about it.

There are imaginative ways of using email in English work and electronic messages can be displayed on the big screen to share and discuss. For example, children can email each other 'in role' when studying a character in a work of literature.

English lessons benefit by bringing into play the rich range of resources – both paper and electronic – possible when using a whiteboard. Many children find film clips, still pictures and evocative sounds create a mood that inspires their writing. Making electronic or paper books, newspapers or magazines benefit from the ease with which images made by the children using digital cameras can be downloaded and displayed on the screen.

Sharing a pupil's successful poem, story or script is simpler using the big screen as there is no need for everyone to crowd round a computer screen or desk. Children's writing on paper can be scanned into the computer and shown on the screen for discussion. As with other use of children's work in this way, discussion has to be sensitive and constructive.

Possible limitations of whiteboard approaches

Of course all tools and approaches to teaching and learning have some disadvantages. There are some health and safety implications of using projection equipment like an interactive whiteboard in the classroom. Children must be instructed not to look directly into the beam of the projector and they should be supervised when it is being operated. We must also remember to be aware of the key characteristics of good teaching using ICT – not least informed use of presentation technologies. This kind of teaching, like other kinds, needs to be well prepared, carried out and evaluated. A professional learning community to develop, collate, share, improve and disseminate best practice using ICT is needed. NAACE, the National Association for Advancing ICT in Primary Education, helps here. The best sort of guidance encourages the creative and flexible approach that fosters a teacher's confidence in their own judgement when planning and carrying out lessons.

Above all, teachers need to judge when a powerful ICT tool like an interactive whiteboard helps and when other approaches might suit the aims of a lesson better (Gage, 2006). Young children need to experience multi-sensory manipulation of letters, role play and to handle books. At any age, talking about books and sharing enthusiasms is always going to be best managed face to face.

Gage, Jenny (2006) *How to Use an Interactive Whiteboard Really Effectively in Your Primary Classroom* London: David Fulton (second edition due in 2012).

Le Breuilly, Mary (2004) 'Benefits of the interactive board' *The Primary English Magazine*, NATE, 9 (5), June.

NAACE: National Association for Advancing ICT in Primary Education, www.naace.org.uk.

INTERACTIVITY

This is a term applied to computer software which has been designed to allow the user to make choices about the information they want to access and in some cases to test their understanding as their learning proceeds. This may involve, for example, clicking on links to get a fuller explanation of something not completely understood, to get more detailed information or to open up a new line of enquiry. Children can work at their own pace and be helped to tackle increasingly challenging concepts.

INTERNAL RHYME

Most rhymes occur at the end of verse-lines but those that occur in the middle of a line are termed 'internal rhymes'. Abrams uses a line of Swinburne's poetry to demonstrate the internal rhyming of 'fleet' and 'sweet':

'Sister, my sister, O fleet sweet swallow'.

There is an interesting account of rhyme in Abrams, 2008: 163–65.

Abrams, M.H. (2008, revised edition) *A Glossary of Literary Terms* New York: Heinie Language.

INTERNET

See also: email, Information and Communications Technology (ICT) and English, interactive whiteboard, museums and English

The internet is a world wide web linking information sites electronically to provide users with a mammoth database. It provides great opportunities for teachers and children to use it as a powerful resource for finding out about all manner of information to support learning.

The internet provides much to enrich English lessons: reviews of children's fiction and non-fiction both print and electronic; biographies of children's authors and many activity sites including the excellent National Archives website. The British Library provides courses for teachers and workshops for school aged children (for details visit www.bl.uk/learning/index.html). There are also opportunities to share good practice. Primary National Strategy are piloting work with interactive whiteboards and other integrated technologies so that teachers can now use film, still pictures, sound and music from the internet to enliven learning.

The internet has the potential to be a rich and powerful whole-school, cross-curricular resource. However, children need help not only to access information competently and swiftly, but also to use the material effectively that they find there.

When it comes to search engines many children find kids.yahoo.com user-friendly. The children's version of the Ask Jeeves search engine – www.askkids.com – can deal with whole questions. Increasingly children are using the internet at home as well as at school (Burnett and Wilkinson, 2005). The UKLA team researching children's reading on screen found that in the pre-school settings they looked at, children's home digital experiences were built on. Children used mobile phones and games consoles in role play and almost all of these three to four year olds 'were familiar with using the interactive whiteboard independently using their home experience of control devices and computer screens' (Bearne *et al.*, 2007: 6). School practice sometimes lags behind what children are experiencing at home. However, while schools need to draw on the full panoply of twenty-first-century communication possibilities, we must remember that while technology can make possible some valuable learning experiences, children also need to learn from interaction with other human beings. We are still developing a set of principles to guide the design of educational sites. Wyse and Jones (2007) suggest that a high quality of interaction is a feature of a good site for children. The BBC Teletubbies site, for example, included visual images, sound and speech and encouraged young children to investigate: 'Who spilled the Tubby custard?'

Teachers and children can add to the net as well as gaining information from it by creating a school website. Some school websites serve the same purpose as a school prospectus while others offer web browser display boards showing children's work. The latter provide opportunities for sharing between schools and are often an incentive for children to write to others, perhaps in other parts of the country or in other lands. Schools are increasingly using networks like *European SchoolNet*.

Bearne, Eve, Clark, Chris, Johnson, Annette, Manfold, Penny, Mottram, Marilyn and Wolstencroft, Helen (2007) *Reading on Screen* Leicester: UKLA.

Burnett, C. and Wilkinson, J. (2005) 'Holy lemons! Learning from children's uses of the internet in out-of-school contexts' *Literacy*, 39 (2): 158–65.

European SchoolNet: www.eun.org

National Archives: www.nationalarchives.gov. uk/education

Scott, Elspeth (2000) *Managing the Internet* School Library Association and The National Centre for Language and Literacy, Reading University.

Wyse, Dominic and Jones, Russell (2007) *Teaching English, Language and Literacy* London: Routledge.

INTERTEXTUALITY

See also: picture books

Intertextuality refers to the strategy of including allusions in one text to other texts. In children's picture books this means drawing on children's cultural knowledge to link ideas in different texts. This kind of linking occurs often in contemporary picture books – like Lauren Child's *Beware of the Storybook Wolves* in which young Herb worries about the possibility that the wolves might spring out from the pages of his story book – and one night they do! Judith Graham gives an insightful and entertaining analysis of the intertextuality in another of Lauren Child's books – *Who's Afraid of the Big, Bad Book?* Characters from different fairytales – Goldilocks and Cinderella for instance – mingle alarmingly as the happenings deviate from the original stories in an entertaining but rather terrifying and completely out of control manner (Graham, 2005: 222). In his book *The Tunnel* Anthony Browne includes images of Red Riding Hood, for example in a picture on the wall of the girl's bedroom. This makes readers reflect on possible thematic connections between one story and another. Other masters of intertextuality are the Ahlbergs. In their *Each Peach Pear Plum* each rhyming couplet refers to a different nursery rhyme character and in their *The Jolly Postman* letters are sent to fairy tale characters like Cinderella.

Graham, Judith (2005) 'Reading contemporary picturebooks' in Reynolds, Kimberley *Modern Children's Literature: an Introduction* London: Palgrave Macmillan.

INTONATION

This refers to the stress or emphasis placed on consonants, vowels and syllables by a speaker to give colour to their words and help listeners better understand their meaning and significance.

INTRANSITIVE VERBS

An intransitive verb is a verb in a sentence which does not have a direct object, as in 'She ran as quickly as she could'.

INVERTED COMMAS

See also: quotation marks, speech marks

Inverted commas are commas placed to show where a quotation, a heading or a title begins and where they end. The marks may be either single, as in the example, or double.

> 'As a storyteller Edward Ardizzone had the ultimate freedom of being both author and artist: he knew instinctively how to balance these skills and how to integrate words and pictures on the page'.
> (*Books for Keeps* 125, Nov. 2000: 6)

For a fuller account, see under 'quotation marks'.

J

JARGON

Jargon is those words and phrases used by all trades and professions as a shorthand way to describe or refer to technical matters. It can be used to communicate quite complex concepts, conditions or actions swiftly in a work context. Of course it can be quite irritating to an outsider to discover that something quite simple has been dressed up as something to sound complicated and difficult!

The world of education has its fair share of jargon – some of it useful in a school context, for example 'modelling' reading and writing, 'scaffolding' children's learning and inviting 'genre exchange'.

JOLLY PHONICS

See also: 'big shapes', cue-systems, graphophonic cue-system, literacy hour, onset and rime, phonics, reading

'Jolly Phonics' is one of the structured reading programmes that uses synthetic phonics. (Phono-Graphix and Superphonics are reading programmes that also use synthetic phonics.) One of the best-known resources for a synthetics phonics reading programme is the *Jolly Phonics* series. So, for example, the *Jolly Phonics Word Book* is a handy reference book with sections like 'words with consonant blends', 'specific digraphs' and 'tricky words'. The programme supports teachers as they introduce the forty-two main letter sound correspondences. The aim is to do this over a relatively short time so that children quickly have control over a decoding method for phonically regular words. Many teachers believe that the kinaesthetic aspects of the programme – for example making the shapes of the letters through gesture and facial expression – appeal to young children. This linking of touch, sound and action is demonstrated on the Jolly Phonics video-films.

The results of a seven-year study in Scotland, which suggested that children intensively taught synthetic phonics along the lines of the Jolly Phonics programme made rapid progress when compared with children taught by the 'mixed methods' literacy strategy approach, hit the headlines in February 2005. The study was carried out in Clackmannanshire schools by Professor Rhona Johnston of Hull University and Joyce Watson of St Andrews University. This study led to a renewal of the long-term debate about how reading should be taught and particularly about the relative merits of synthetic and analytic approaches to teaching phonics and spelling. (For details of Johnston and Watson's project use the links from the Reading Reform Foundation website.) In a nutshell, synthetic phonics – the kind used in the Jolly Phonics programme – is to do with learning and sounding out all the phonemes in words – so for 'chat' children would sound out ch-a-t. Quite a lot of the time this approach to decoding works, but the decoding of irregular words is a problem if synthetic phonics are used exclusively. (With this thought in mind, you might be entertained to read Becky Bloom and Pascal Biet's amusing children's picture book *A Cultivated Wolf,* Siphano Picture Books). Wolf is rejected by the surprisingly literate farm animals until he learns to read. The newer kind of phonics, 'analytic' phonics is based on helping children to recognise the first part of a word which precedes the vowel – the 'onset' ('ch') and the second part containing the vowel and final sounds – 'the rime' ('at') – ch-at. The research of Goswami and Bryant published in 1990 claimed that the analytic approach with its link to songs and rhythmic language like that in nursery rhymes was motivating to beginning readers. Passionate discussion about which kind of phonics should dominate the initial teaching of reading and about wider issues like the role of the other cue-systems, and indeed about which is the most helpful model of learning to read, is likely to continue. However, following the publication of Professor Rose's report (2006), synthetic phonics has been built into the programme for beginning readers in the UK although the Rose Curriculum in its entirety was never put into practice.

Goswami, U. and Bryant, P. (1990) *Phonological Skills and Learning to Read* Hove: Lawrence Erlbaum Associates.

Lloyd, Sue and Wernham, Sara (2000 edition) *Jolly Phonics Word Book* London: Jolly Learning.

Reading Reform Foundation: www.rrf.org.uk. This organisation is dedicated to promoting synthetic phonics as the most effective approach to the initial teaching of reading.

JOURNAL

See: diary, first person writing, reading diaries

JOURNALISTIC WRITING

See: advertisements, persuasive genre, visual literacy

JUNIOR YEARS LANGUAGE AND LITERACY

See also: assimilation and accommodation, Bullock Report, child-centred learning, constructivism, creativity in English, early years language and literacy, English projects, gender and language development, history of English teaching, hobbies and English, Information and Communications Technology (ICT) and English, interactive whiteboard, internet, language and thought, metaphors in education, reading, speaking and listening, spontaneous and scientific concepts, writing

There has been a tradition in the United Kingdom to view the 'early years' – up to the age of seven or eight – and the 'junior years' – from seven to eleven – as two distinctive stages of development each with its implications for classroom practice. For some time now in the United Kingdom, three stages have been identified: a Foundation Stage from three to six years (now adapted to an Early Years Foundation Stage 0–5, EYFS), a Key Stage 1 from five to seven (see 'early years language and literacy' entry) and a Key Stage 2 from seven to eleven. Thus the stage once known as the 'junior years', and now as 'Key Stage 2', still refers to children aged between seven and eleven (Years 3–6). The introduction of a terminology referring to 'key stages' went alongside the decision in the late 1980s, when the National Curriculum was introduced, to organise teaching in the primary years around subjects – English, mathematics, science, history and so on. This led to an emphasis on children acquiring subject knowledge, on target setting and on summative kinds of assessment, and to less concern with child development and its implications for the classroom. This is now very evident in initial teacher education: what children have to achieve in the primary curriculum subjects and the teacher's own subject knowledge is at the centre of BA (Ed.) and Postgraduate Certificate in Education courses. This has led to a reduced emphasis on knowledge about child development. Yet many believe that it is as important to know about the stages of development from seven to eleven as it is from birth to five or six. Concepts about child development have an interesting history: Linda Pound and Cathy Hughes have written helpfully about the main theories, including those of Montessori, Bruner, Piaget and Vygotsky (Pound and Hughes, 2005). Development in language and literacy is embedded in all aspects of children's progress in these years. In her book *Child Development 6–16 Years* Penny Tassoni covers emotional, social, physical and cognitive aspects of development including the 'normal' patterns of the seven to eleven age group (Tassoni, 2007). Although each child makes progress in his or her own way teachers are able to make some general observations. From about age seven, friends become a big part of children's lives. Girls and boys tend to play separately and, particularly girls, often like to have a best friend. Parents and families are still very important, however. Children between these years enjoy their increasing competence at sports and in acquiring knowledge, skills and abilities in lessons across the curriculum. Knowing that they are making progress increases their self confidence. These years are the great years of collecting things – stamps, wild flowers, DVDs and fossils. The other source of children's confidence as they make their way through these years is their fluency in speech and their increasing control over reading and writing. The different areas of development are interrelated. Carolyn Meggitt notes that 'cultural elements – the ideas, language, ways of communicating feelings and relationships amongst which a child is brought up' all influence his or her development profoundly (Meggitt, 2006: Introduction). So if a child has special needs or is from a family where English has been learnt as an additional language, this will be reflected in their development. Another huge factor influencing teaching and learning at every age phase as the twenty-first century moves on is the ceaseless shaping and re-shaping of our lives and activities by constantly advancing technology. What have been called the 'new literacies' are not so new now and ever more sophisticated media are transforming what is possible, shaping and transforming how we can communicate. Some of the new technologies have the power to change how adults and children think. Reading on screen demands a different way of processing information than do print-based materials and resources. Another interesting thing is that technology has also made an impact on print texts and materials, for instance making print multimodal texts ever more innovative and inventive. Some innovations make things easier to achieve rather than changing what can be achieved. Interactive whiteboards, for example, if imaginatively used can bring children's concentration and thinking into top gear. Teacher and children achieve 'joint attention' when they can focus on images and texts on a large screen. The whiteboard is more flexible and dynamic than a chalk board or flip chart and can make a lesson visually powerful. In spite of all the new developments, though, the principles of good practice remain largely the same.

For many years dedicated early years practitioners and educationists have worked hard to maintain the long-established principles on which good practice in teaching the very young are based and they challenged innovations which, interpreted inflexibly, might threaten them (Hurst and Joseph, 1998; Whitehead, 2010). I believe teachers of children aged between seven and eleven should also proclaim and protect the principles at the heart of good practice. These principles draw on what we know about how children grow and develop physically, intellectually, socially and emotionally and it is important that they continue to inform practice within the prescribed frameworks. I have organised my thoughts about these principles under five headings, drawing out in particular some of the implications for English, language and literacy in the years seven to eleven. These headings are: learning is active; learning is social and collaborative; language, learning and literacy are cross-curricular; society's expectations can be met creatively; and the adult's role is crucial.

Learning is active

Children can learn and make meaning actively, flexibly and imaginatively if given a sympathetic environment (Bruner and Haste, 1987; Egan, 1992). Learning is not just about absorbing information but about individuals transforming it to knit with and to extend their existing understanding. (The entries on 'constructivism' and on 'assimilation and accommodation' expand on this.) When supporting children's learning we need to understand their intellectual progress alongside their physical, emotional and social development. For further discussion of cognitive development I recommend Wood (1997: Chapters 4–6) and Riley and Prentice (1999: Chapter 1) which discuss the theories of Piaget, Bruner and Vygotsky. English lessons – where we talk about fiction, improvise drama and write stories and poems – bring together actions, thoughts, feelings and collaborative effort in a particularly satisfying way. Drama and role play build on the play activities of the very young. Junior aged children still need to use language round practical and co-operative activities to remain absorbed and focused in their learning.

Learning is social and collaborative

Children learn best when they are working with others. It was Vygotsky and Bruner who drew our attention most powerfully to the impetus to learning provided by talk and co-operation. By seven, children have settled into school and have some friends. They should be enjoying not just their growing competence in both physical and intellectual activities, but also their ability to relate to other children and to adults in school. Judy Dunn explores the importance of sharing and experiencing both the delights and problems friendship can involve in *Children's Friendships* (Dunn, 2004). Teachers of seven to nine year olds often remark on their sheer energy and enthusiasm for life. All this vitality can be channelled into learning together through joint activities, not least language activities in which children share ideas and information and listen and respond to the points of others. In English, sharing ideas round books, especially stories and poems, is particularly enjoyable. We also need to reach out to parents and families as they play an important role in children's developing literacy – see the 'parents and families' and 'siblings (and literacy)' entries for the benefits of partnership with families.

Language, learning and literacy are cross-curricular

Some of the most stimulating contexts for talking, reading and writing occur in lessons across the curriculum. Indeed, speaking, listening, reading and writing are agents of learning in every lesson. Riley and Prentice (1999: Introduction) argue strongly for a rich and flexible curriculum in the junior years and voice their concern that arts and humanities may be marginalised in an approach that privileges the 'core' subjects of the National Curriculum. Their observations are relevant to our consideration of the 2013 National

248

Curriculum which continues a subject-centred approach.

Fiction – the stories and poems that are at the heart of English – can also bring a personal foothold to learning in other lessons. This is a major theme in the introduction to this encyclopedia and in the entries linking English to art, design and technology, drama, geography, history, mathematics, physical education (and music and dance), religious education and science. For case studies celebrating children as young researchers, thinking deeply about their learning across the curriculum, see Mallett (1999, 2007).

Society's expectations can be met creatively

Making progress involves meeting the expectations of the society in which a child is growing up. In her influential book *Children's Minds*, Margaret Donaldson emphasises the demands that developing a capacity for abstract reasoning, valued now in so many societies, make on young learners (Donaldson, 1986: chapter 11). As children move through the junior years, they are expected to deal with increasingly complex materials as readers and writers. More of their learning is based on secondary sources. Today the sheer range of information is overwhelming. As well as dealing with books and other print sources, children grapple with computer software and the internet. It is important that they are not pushed into a passive role by the sheer weight of information. We want them to approach their learning creatively and to achieve their own 'voice' in what they say and what they write. We hope that during the later primary years they move forward in becoming critical and reflective readers, and writers who are not over-reliant on any one source. This stands them in good stead to avoid being manipulated by advertising and propaganda in the mass media. The realisation that language is socially situated and that some forms enjoy

a higher status than others also puts them in control.

The adult's role is crucial

The teacher's careful intervention remains vital to children's learning throughout the primary years. Careful planning, skill in interpreting the requirements of official frameworks for a particular class, making lessons interesting and keeping careful records of progress are all the mark of a good practitioner. Selecting an exciting range of fiction is a particularly enjoyable responsibility. From about age seven or eight children are ready for longer, more complicated stories and poems. They can appreciate themes that reflect the complexity of many lives – to do with the disruption as well as the opportunities that change brings, coping with parents and families that are fallible and make mistakes and dealing with ambivalent feelings about friends and siblings. The texts themselves teach as Meek famously writes (Meek, 1988), but the teacher's sensitive intervention can help more than anything else to make enthusiastic readers (Mallett, 2010). It is the teacher whose comments and observations can inspire children's talk and thinking about literature, whether in a class or a group context, in Literacy Time or outside it. Sometimes a question like – 'what makes you think that?' – encourages a child to find evidence for their view in the text. However, I have noticed that good teachers, whether students or more experienced practitioners, often offer a pertinent anecdote to the discussion and this seems to be more encouraging to some children than a question. I remember a student joining a group of nine year olds talking about Betsy Byars' *The Midnight Fox* and telling the children of her own confused feelings when her family moved from town to country and how writing letters to a friend helped. (Now, of course, people are more likely to keep in touch by email, text messages or on Facebook.) This led to involved talk by the children about their own experiences and those of others known to them. The student teacher skilfully led them into comparing how their experiences were similar to and different from those of the boy in the story. Talking about reading is one of the most important aspects of English teaching. Once again I recommend Aidan Chambers' inspirational book *Tell Me* in which he so eloquently makes this point and shows how teachers intervene to promote more profound discussion (Chambers, 1993). The work of Vygotsky and Bruner consistently shows the importance of the role of the adult in accelerating children's progress in many learning contexts (Vygotsky, 1986; Bruner, 1986; Bruner and Haste, 1987).

Teachers model and support children's writing too, whether they are handwriting on paper or touch typing on screen. Becoming a confident writer is a lot to do with finding a 'voice' and finding your own way of making sense of experience and information. For a most stimulating account of how a class of ten year olds were helped over the course of a school year to link their writing in English lessons with the study of literature – leading to writing in role, poetry and first person accounts – it is well worth reading *The Reader in the Writer* by Barrs and Cork. A review copy arrived on my mat one morning and I read it through in one sitting feeling thoroughly nourished and excited by the insights about the power of literature. I can think of few more rewarding books for any teacher of children in the junior years. One conclusion which matched with all I have learnt myself was that emotionally powerful texts, read aloud well by the teacher, can inspire passionate discussions and satisfying written accounts (Barrs and Cork, 2001). Books that inspired this class included *The Green Children* by Kevin Crossley-Holland which explores cultural difference in an interesting way,

The Lion and the Unicorn by Shirley Hughes about the loneliness of a child evacuee in the Second World War, and *Fire, Bed and Bone* by Henrietta Branford which, through the device of a dog-narrator, explores social issues at the time of the Peasants' Revolt. Literature in the junior years needs to support children's expanding ability to think and feel. Teachers can keep up with new books by reading journals like *English 4–11*, *The School Librarian* and *Classroom NATE* and by looking at reviews by critics, teachers and children on websites – for example *Books for Keeps* (www.booksforkeeps.co.uk), Booktrust (www.booktrust.org.uk) and Write Away (www.justimaginestorycentre.co.uk).

Good practitioners must ensure that teaching and learning are rigorous in the junior years. There are interesting but complicated issues to discuss, worthwhile but difficult books to read in print or on screen, and some challenging writing tasks. The good teacher is able to show children that all this is worthwhile. As Mallett remarks, 'Above all, it is critically important to inspire, interest and foster that sense of wonder in the world and its phenomena that very young children bring naturally to their learning' (Mallett, 1999: 126).

Barrs, Myra and Cork, Valerie (2001) *The Reader in the Writer: The Links Between the Study of Literature and Writing Development at Key Stage 2* London: The Centre for Literacy in Primary Education.

Bearne, E., Johnson, A., Manford, P., Mottram, M. and Wolstencroft, H. (2007) *Reading on Screen* UKLA.

Bruner, J. (1986) *Actual Minds, Possible Worlds* Cambridge, Mass.: MIT Press.

Bruner, Jerome and Haste, Helen (1987) *Making Sense: The Child's Construction of the World* London: Methuen.

Chambers, Aidan (1993) *Tell Me* Stroud: The Thimble Press (available with *The Reading Environment* (2011) in a second edition in the Routledge Revivals series, London: Routledge).

Donaldson, Margaret (1986, second edition) *Children's Minds* London: Fontana/Collins.

Dunn, Judy (2004) *Children's Friendships: The Beginnings of Intimacy* Understanding Worlds series, London: Wiley Blackwell (Foreword by Jerome Bruner).

Egan, Kieran (1992) *Imagination in Teaching and Learning: The Middle School Years* Chicago, Ill.: Chicago University Press.

Fisher, Robert and Williams, Mary (2004) *Unlocking Creativity* London: David Fulton (see chapters on early years literacy, drama and writing).

Foot, Michael, Brown, Tony and Holt, Peter (2001) *Let Our Children Learn* Nottingham: Education Now Books.

Hurst, Victoria and Joseph, Jenny (1998) *Supporting Early Learning* Milton Keynes: Open University Press.

Mallett, Margaret (1999) *Young Researchers: Informational Reading and Writing in the Early and Primary Years* London: Routledge.

——(2007) *Active Encounters: Inspiring Young Readers and Writers of Non-fiction 4–11* UKLA minibook.

——(2010) *Choosing and Using Fiction and Non-fiction 3–11* London and New York: Routledge.

Meek, Margaret (1988) *How Texts Teach What Readers Learn* Stroud: The Thimble Press.

Meggitt, Carolyn (2006, second edition) *Child Development* London: Heinemann.

Pound, Linda and Hughes, Cathy (2005) *How Children Learn: From Montessori to Vygotsky, Educational Theories and Approaches Made Easy* London: Step Forward.

Riley, Jeni and Prentice, Roy (eds) (1999) *The Curriculum for 7–11 Year Olds* London: Paul Chapman.

Tassoni, Penny (2007) *Child Development 6–16 Years* London: Heinemann.

Vygotsky, L.S. (1986 edition with an introduction by A. Kozulin [1962]) *Thought and Language* Cambridge, Mass.: The MIT Press.

Whitehead, Marian (2010, fourth edition) *Language and Learning in the Early Years* London: Sage.

Wood, David (1997, second edition) *How Children Think and Learn* Oxford: Wiley-Blackwell.

K

KEY STAGES

See: early years language and literacy, junior years language and literacy, literacy hour, National Curriculum

KEY WORDS

See: look and say, reading

KINAESTHETIC STRATEGIES

See also: handwriting, Jolly Phonics

This refers to the memorising of physical actions to help the forming of words (Wyse and Jones, 2007: 149). Eve Bearne argues that we are helped to internalise things through repeated movements so that, for example, a series of handwriting movements, if frequently carried out, would help a child memorise spelling patterns (Bearne, 2000). Literacy-related tracing activities like writing over letters helps develop knowledge of shape and orientation.

Bearne, Eve (2000) *Making Progress in English* London: Routledge.
Wyse, Dominic and Jones, Richard (2007, second edition) *Teaching English, Language and Literacy* London: Routledge.

KINDS OF WRITING

See: genre

KINGMAN REPORT

See also: Cox Report, grammar, LINC materials

Published in 1988, the Kingman Report on the Teaching of English in England and Wales aimed to produce a model that would inform the teaching of English language. Approaches based on the teaching of a grammar derived from Latin teaching were rejected. However, the report did recommend explicit teaching about the forms and functions of language and recommended that children be taught to use standard English in appropriate contexts. The Kingman model has four sections: the forms of the language; communication and comprehension; acquisition and development; and historical and geographical variation.

The Cox Report, which followed this, set out how this approach could inform the English programmes in the National Curriculum which was being put in place for the first time.

While the Kingman Report did not please everyone – some felt the linguistic topics considered did not link into a coherent whole – it did encourage English teachers of all age groups to increase their knowledge about language and how best to teach language study. The debate continues.

DES (1988) *Report of the Committee of Inquiry into the Teaching of English Language* (Kingman Report) London: HMSO.

KNOWLEDGE ABOUT LANGUAGE

See: metacognition, metalanguage, subject knowledge

L

LANGUAGE ACQUISITION

See also: communicative competence/competence and performance, functions of language, language and thought, nativist approach to language acquisition

There are a number of theories to explain how the human infant acquires language. It is very much in the interests of teachers of all age groups to reflect on how children learn to represent their experience symbolically, above all through speech. How the very young child becomes a language user has important implications for teaching and learning in school. The usual pattern of learning to talk is generally agreed. In the first few weeks of life children 'babble' – they make sounds for the sheer pleasure of trying out their speech apparatus. The adults and older children around them respond to the sounds that most approximate to their mother tongue. Gradually the sounds that are most reinforced become organised. Children acquire a vocabulary of single words – naming the people and things important to them, and then as they approach two years they produce 'pivot' words which are the beginnings of sentences 'more milk', 'all gone', 'get book' and so on. From then on children will acquire more syntactic structures and a vocabulary of several thousand words by the time they start school at five years. If you want to read about the stages of acquiring the structures of language you would enjoy 'How do we do it? (Whitehead, 2010: Chapter 3), Roger Brown's (1973) book *A First Language* or Eve Clark's (2009) *First Language Acquisition*.

In this short introduction I have pulled out what seem to me some of the main approaches to this fascinating but very complicated area of study: behaviourist theory of language acquisition; Chomsky and the Language Acquisition Device; cognitive theories; social interactionist theories; and Halliday's sociolinguistic functionalist model.

Behaviourist theory of language acquisition

Behaviourists believe that all behaviours are learnt and they extend this notion even to sophisticated behaviours like language. In his book *Verbal Behaviour*, Skinner (1957) argued that language, like much early learning, was acquired by imitation. So the child might hear the word 'milk' said as their parent hands them a glass of milk. The word becomes associated with the context and the parent is likely to praise or 'reinforce' the child's appropriate utterance of the word. Of course imitation does account for some kinds of learning – we have to hear our mother tongue spoken in order to acquire a vocabulary – but the behaviourist theory is less convincing when we move on from content words like

255

'milk', 'ball' and 'Mummy' to words like 'yesterday', 'because' and 'when'.

Chomsky and the Language Acquisition Device (LAD)

One of the best-known linguists contributing to our understanding of early language acquisition is Noam Chomsky, who believed with other nativists that language ability was genetically inherited. In his book *Syntactic Structures*, Chomsky (2002) criticised the mechanistic approach to language acquisition of the behaviourists and pointed to the speed with which children acquire language without overt instruction. He suggested that children have an innate predisposition to make sense of the sounds they hear. This he termed a 'Language Acquisition Device' (LAD) – a grammar-generating 'device' which processed fragments of language into a coherent system. If you listen to the conversation of very young children you soon find that imitation is only one strategy for learning language. In fact, children seem to hypothesise and build up knowledge of syntactic rules. Interestingly it is the 'errors' that young children typically make that suggest they are following rules and sometimes overgeneralise them. For example, as the past tense of verbs is normally inflected with an 'ed', children sometimes say 'heared' for 'heard', and as nouns often add an 's' to become plural they say 'mans' instead of 'men'.

Cognitive theories

Chomsky's theory has had its critics. Margaret Donaldson, for instance, thinks the notion of a language acquisition device can be just as mechanical as the behaviourist stimulus response model. Where, she asks, is 'the warm blood in the veins?' (Donaldson, 1986: 39). She refers to the view of John Macnamara who suggests that children do not have something as specific as a

sensitivity to language, but rather they have a well-developed capacity for making sense of situations involving direct human interaction. Macnamara, Piaget and other developmentalists leaning towards the cognitive view believe that language acquisition is part of general intellectual development. Piaget, for instance, believed that sensorimotor kinds of thinking (where the child feels his or her way round the environment and knows it through perception, seeing, touching and tasting) need to be in place before verbal language can be acquired.

We have to be careful not to give the impression that all theorists under the cognitive umbrella think the same. Macnamara, for instance, gives much more emphasis than Piaget to the human element in situations in helping children make sense of them (Donaldson, 1986). In their book *How Babies Think* Alison Gopnik and her team of US researchers bring together what is known about evolutionary tendencies, pre-programmed skills and environmental influences in understanding how children learn. Chapter 4, 'What children learn about language', argues that children make sense of the world rather as scientists do: they constantly revise their understanding in the light of new experience (Gopnik *et al.*, 1999).

Social interactionist theories

These theories, which became influential in the late 1970s and 1980s, emphasise the social purposes of language. Although Vygotsky was no longer alive, the implications of much of his thinking were only now becoming assimilated. He believed that the impetus to learning language was essentially social. While Piaget had tended to stress the importance of learning from objects, Vygotsky saw the adult, whether parent or teacher, and other children as very much part of the social situation in which a child takes on both a culture and a language. Vygotsky's views on early thinking and concept formation and the implications for classroom learning are discussed in his best-known book *Thought and Language* (Vygotsky, 1986).

Jerome Bruner is sometimes placed with the cognitive theorists. Like Piaget he suggests a number of overlapping stages in a child's development beginning with the enactive stage when the child makes sense of the world by movement and perception, progressing to an iconic stage when the child can represent the world through images, and finally reaching the symbolic stage when speech makes it possible to organise the thinking of the previous stages. In Bruner's theory we continue to learn through all three ways of representing the world. However, while he seems to stand with the cognitive theorists in believing some learning uses non-verbal cognitive abilities, he also insists on the powerful role of language, from an early age, in organising experience and thinking and communicating with others. Bruner, like Vygotsky, believes that young children's minds grow when they are stimulated and challenged by other children and adults. In this sense he leans towards a more interactionist view than, for example, Piaget.

Halliday's sociolinguistic functionalist model

Theories of early language acquisition have not only come to us from psycholinguistics. Sociolinguists have also taken an interest and one of the most influential is M.A.K. Halliday. Halliday asked a different question to the psycholinguists. He was interested in the functions for which children began to use language. In fact, he began to study his own young child's attempts at communication long before he had words. Halliday suggests that the first six functions of language acquired by a young child are:

Table 3

Instrumental	makes needs known
Regulatory	influences and manipulates others
Interactional	keeps relationships developing
Personal	establishes a unique identity
Heuristic	sparks the will to learn
Imaginative	to do with playing games, role play and creating stories

The seventh function – the *informational* or 'I've got something to tell you' function – is evident after about twenty-two months. The notion of telling somebody something they do not know is an advanced one and is usually dependent on words.

The books listed below give fuller accounts of theories of early language acquisition. As Whitehead remarks, no one theorist has answered all the questions about how children achieve the amazing feat of learning their language so quickly. Each perspective offers some insight. The behaviourists remind us of the role of imitation, while the nativists show that children actively construct their language. The cognitive theorists draw our attention to ways of making sense other than by verbal language and the social interactionists indicate the social and cultural functions of language. Sociolinguists like Halliday draw attention to the importance of having purposes so that language can serve functions in our social world. All these insights – not least the picture of the child as essentially an active meaning maker – have implications for teaching and learning in the primary school.

Britton, James (1970) *Language and Learning* London: Allen Lane, The Penguin Press (see Chapter 2 'Learning to speak').

Brown, Roger (1973) *A First Language* Cambridge, Mass.: Harvard University Press.

Chomsky, Noam (2002, revised edition [1957]) *Syntactic Structures* The Hague: Mouton.

Clark, Eve. V. (2009, second edition) *First Language Acquisition* Cambridge: Cambridge University Press.

Donaldson, Margaret (1986, second edition [1973]) *Children's Minds* London: Harper Collins.

Gopnik, Alison, Meltzoff, Andrew and Kuhl, Patricia (1999) *How Babies Think* London: Weidenfeld & Nicolson.

Halliday, M.A.K. (1975) *Learning How to Mean* London: Edward Arnold.

Skinner, B.F. (1957) *Verbal Behavior* Appleton-Century-Crofts.

Vygotsky, L.S. (1986, second edition with preface by Alex Kozulin [1962]) *Thought and Language* Cambridge, Mass.: The MIT Press.

Whitehead, Marian R. (2010, fourth edition) *Language and Literacy in the Early Years* London: Paul Chapman.

LANGUAGE ACQUISITION DEVICE (LAD)

See: language acquisition

LANGUAGE ACROSS THE CURRICULUM

See also: art and English, creativity in English, factual genres, geography and English, history and English, information books, Information and Communications Technology (ICT) and English, library skills, mathematics and English, non-fiction reading and writing, reading, science and English, speaking and listening, study skills, writing

The Bullock Report in 1975 brought formal recognition of the role of language in learning in every lesson. Good practitioners had always acted on this insight but the Bullock Report energised teachers' efforts to create a language policy for their school. In primary and secondary schools teachers met to decide on resources and teaching approaches to spelling, handwriting and grammar and to library and study skills, including note taking and making summaries. In secondary schools all teachers were encouraged to see a positive role in promoting children's development in language as well as their development of knowledge and understanding in a subject.

In the United Kingdom a subject-centred national curriculum nudged away some language across the curriculum initiatives. However, primary teachers made links between the then literacy hour and lessons across the curriculum, recognising that history, geography and other lessons provide strong contexts for kinds of non-fiction writing. Story, too, has relevance and importance beyond the English curriculum.

The principles behind the language across the curriculum initiatives still inform good practice. They include recognising that:

- It is helpful for each school to agree on a language policy, on how subjects are resourced, how the four language processes – speaking and listening, reading and writing – can be used to learn. A consistent approach to using the library and to study skills like note taking and summarising can be achieved.
- Children's language development is promoted in every lesson. Part of learning history, geography, science and so on is learning to use and control the kinds of spoken and written language involved. It is also true that some English objectives can be realised through other lessons. History provides good contexts for distinguishing fact from opinion, for example.
- Listening and responding to what others say helps make learning social and collaborative and helps develop, change and extend a child's understanding of a topic.
- Talk helps children get their language round concepts and ideas in every lesson. It reveals children's level of thinking and understanding at a particular stage so that the teacher can plan ahead in an informed way. History, geography and science can all provide

the content to inspire meaningful and enthusiastic discussion of issues.

- Subjects across the curriculum are the most appropriate and interesting contexts for particular kinds of reading and writing – the recount, report, instruction, discussion, persuasive and explanation genres of the National Curriculum.
- Visual kinds of literacy are best developed in a cross-curricular way and a school language policy can help create a culture where teachers and pupils use language to illuminate the visual and the abstract.
- Just as informational kinds of writing have a place in English, fiction can provide a personal foothold in lessons across the curriculum.

Fisher, Robert and Williams, Mary (2004) *Unlocking Literacy: Teaching Across the Curriculum* London: David Fulton.
Hoodless, Pat (ed.) (1998) *History and English: Exploring the Links* London: Routledge.
Mallett, Margaret (2010) *Choosing and Using Fiction and Non-fiction, 3–11* London: Routledge (makes practical suggestions for activities to develop children's response to fiction and non-fiction texts in English and in lessons across the curriculum).

LANGUAGE AND CULTURE

See: bilingualism, multiculturalism, multilingualism

LANGUAGE AND SOCIETY

See also: accent, dialect, genre, jargon, language change, picture books, postmodernism and children's picture books, register

We use language and literacy to serve our needs and purposes in everyday life (Trudgill, 2000). Because it is embedded in other human activity, some scholars think of language and literacy use as 'social practice'. Taking this thought, Michael Halliday and his colleagues developed a theory of language as 'social semiotic' – meanings are made in a cultural context – and have shown how we learn to adopt different 'registers' according to the setting in which language is used (Halliday, 1978). Barton and Hamilton point out that different uses of language are found in different 'domains' of life (Barton and Hamilton, 1998). These 'domains' are contexts associated with a particular language use; we vary our spoken language according to whether we are speaking to say a pupil, friend, police officer, parent or employer. Our reading and writing varies according to the context too: think of how we might read or write for pleasure – in a letter to a friend perhaps as compared with the language use associated with our job where we might have to, for example, explain or read instructions. Our concept of 'purpose' and 'audience' makes us flexible users of language throughout the working day. Of course children acquire and use language in the context of our society and there are culturally specific conventions about different language encounters. Encounters between parents and teacher on parents' evenings follow a pattern, as do conversations with shop assistants or medical professionals. These patterns in spoken language vary from society to society, where there may be different values and different attitudes towards considerations like age, gender and social class. Becoming able to deploy language in the ways used and valued in your culture, i.e. acquiring 'communicative competence', is part of language development just as is learning the structure of your mother tongue. The Australian genre theorists have taken a particular interest in how written texts vary. Texts united by purpose and form are described as 'genres'. Non-fiction genres in particular come about because of social need – to instruct, inform, persuade or explain. These needs constantly change in all but the most static of societies and if you read the work of genre theorists like John Martin, Frances Christie and Joan Rothery, you will find that they conceive of genres as dynamic, indeed as social processes that help us achieve our purposes. Their paper on social processes in education and other articles on genre are included in Reid's book *The Place of Genre in Learning* (Martin *et al.*, 1987).

Barton, D. and Hamilton, M. (1998) *Local Literacies: A Study of Reading and Writing in One Community* London: Routledge.

Halliday, M.A.K. (1978) *Language as Social Semiotic: the Social Interpretation of Language and Meaning* London: Arnold.

Martin, John, Christie, Frances and Rothery, Joan (1987) 'Social processes in education' in Reid, I. (ed.) *The Place of Genre in Learning* Victoria: Deakin University.

Trudgill, P. (2000, fourth edition) *Sociolinguistics: An Introduction to Language and Society* Harmondsworth: Penguin.

LANGUAGE AND THOUGHT

See also: assimilation and accommodation, collaborative learning, constructivism, critical discourse, language acquisition, metacognition, nativist approach to language acquisition, reflective reading, speaking and listening, spontaneous and scientific concepts, zone of proximal awareness

This entry introduces the interesting and complicated issue of the relationship between language and thought by looking at the ideas of some key contributors to the field. (There are links between issues here and early language acquisition – see 'language acquisition'.) All the positions are of interest, but the work of Vygotsky, Bruner and Donaldson is particularly relevant to the classroom because of the importance these developmentalists give to the role of instruction and the language used by both teacher and children.

The Sapir-Whorf hypothesis

This hypothesis proposes that language, and indeed the particular language we speak, affects our perception of the world. Whorf studied the differences between European and non-European languages and formed the view that the vocabulary of a language has an impact on the way its speakers think. A language reflects what is important in a society – a hunter-gatherer society is likely to have a particularly rich vocabulary of words to do with animals and plants. In Western societies there is a developing vocabulary for the new technology – 'hyperlinks', 'email', 'web browser' and so on – in line with the increasing importance of these concepts in the culture. Whorf also noted that the syntax of languages varies: his work on the languages of Indian communities in North and South America revealed that the grammatical patterns for referring to concepts like time and home was distinctive. Some nomadic societies refer to a 'sheltering' rather than something permanent like a house. This led him to argue that the thinking of a child would be shaped by the language of their speech community.

Many take issue with the proposition that children are moulded by their language into a restricted way of seeing the world. (See under 'elaborated and restricted codes' for a consideration of variations within one language.) This does not fit with the experience of bilinguals or that of anyone who is able to communicate successfully with people from different cultures. Translation from one language into another is not mechanistic, but ways of expressing the full range of human experience can be found within the resources of every language. As Whitehead argues, while children are 'initiated into the language uses and the ways of thinking of their communities' this is far from a straitjacket and is best thought of as an open framework or supporting trellis (Whitehead, 2010: 65).

The cognitive theory of Jean Piaget

Piaget and other cognitive psychologists believe that there are kinds of thinking that are language-free, including those that children use before they can speak (see 'functions of language' for comment on Halliday's work suggesting children 'mean' before they have verbal language). This position is a long way from the linguistic determinism of the more extreme interpretations of the Sapir-Whorf hypothesis, and tends to view language as one of a number of ways of making sense of experience. Piaget's adaptive model of learning, where new material is assimilated into an existing framework of knowledge which accommodates to take in the new knowledge, is described under the 'assimilation and accommodation' entry. I find this a valuable way of describing the learning process. Not least, it indicates the importance of organising prior knowledge before we introduce new learning. What is missing from Piaget's work is the recognition of the powerful role of language in learning from the earliest stages. Piaget is also well known for his description of qualitative stages of development beginning with the sensory motor stage when the child knows the world through action and perception, the concrete operational stage characterised by practical thinking about what can be directly perceived (and which takes in most of the primary years), and the formal operations stage when children become able to hypothesise and deal with things that are not present. Piaget's theory of development has stimulated much discussion and further research. Donaldson (1978) questions his belief that children's reasoning abilities are limited before age eleven. She draws on Martin Hughes' reworking of one of Piaget's experiments to show that children's ability to problem solve is apparent if the task they are given makes sense in terms of their experience of the world. In her later work Donaldson modifies Piaget's stages of development, and her model allows for more flexible thinking during the primary years (Donaldson, 1992).

Social interactionist approaches of Bruner and Vygotsky

These developmentalists place much more importance than Piaget on the role of language in the development of thinking and in the social situation in which learning takes place. Bruner's stages refer to ways of representing or thinking about experience: first comes enactive thinking which takes place through action and perception; second, iconic thinking which draws on images (of phenomena which may not be present); and finally the symbolic thinking through symbols which includes above all the ability to use language. Once a child reaches the symbolic stage, all three modes of representing experience interact in his or her learning and thinking.

Vygotsky also believed that children's development passed through a number of stages. Although convinced that thought and language have different roots, he considered that the child's mental functioning and powers of communication were transformed once the two systems come together. For Vygotsky the impetus for learning to speak is to be able to make contact with others. Through talking and writing children clinch concepts and internalise them. The role of the adult in the development of children's thinking is dominant in Vygotsky's work. There is more about this under the entries 'spontaneous and scientific concepts' and the 'zone of proximal development', and comment about Bruner's recognition of the power of adult intervention in augmenting the child's thinking and reasoning abilities under 'scaffolding'.

Developmentalists recognise the importance of becoming able to use systems of symbolic representation particularly for the more abstract kinds of thinking. Donaldson consistently shows the power of the written word to extend children's reasoning. Reading and writing seem to encourage the mind to grow in particular ways, ways which are valued in Western societies and necessary to make headway in them. For an interesting analysis of the kinds of thinking needed across the primary curriculum I recommend Chapter 1 in Riley and Prentice, 1999. Under 'constructivism' I show how children learn actively – they do not pass through the developmental stages without effort or without guidance from parents and teachers.

Donaldson, Margaret (1978, second edition) *Children's Minds* London: Fontana (Chapters 1–3).
——(1992) *Human Minds: An Exploration* London: Penguin.
Riley, Jeni and Prentice, Roy (eds) (1999) *The Curriculum for 7–11 Year Olds* London: Paul Chapman Publishing (Chapter 1).
Whitehead, Marian R. (2010, fourth edition) *Language and Literacy in the Early Years* London: Paul Chapman (Chapter 3).
Wood, David (1988 and 1997, revised edition) *How Children Think and Learn* Oxford: Blackwell (Introduction and Chapter 1).

LANGUAGE CHANGE

See also: functions of language, language variety

This is the modification to language which takes place over time, referred to by functional linguists as 'diachronic variation'. Language is essentially dynamic and so there are changes in how we pronounce words, in grammar and in vocabulary.

Change in pronunciation is gradual. We can detect quite subtle changes by comparing how speakers from a particular group spoke on film, television or on the radio with the present-day speech of people from the same social group. The speech of upper middle-class people in films like, for example, *Brief Encounter* was more rarefied than that of socially comparable people today. Younger and older members of the royal family speak differently from one another too. Something that fascinates me is the way in which regional accents endure: increased exposure to mass media has not so far resulted in a move towards standard pronunciation. This seems to be to do with group solidarity and identification with those with whom we feel comfortable.

Changes in grammar include the increasing acceptability of the split infinitive and modifications in verb forms like 'got, gotten'.

There is often resistance to change when it comes to vocabulary or lexis, particularly where a distinction between words is lost. A good example here is the loss of the distinction between 'uninterested' (not absorbed in something or curious about it) and 'disinterested' (an unbiased view or research study). However, language changes relentlessly whether individuals approve or not. Changes in vocabulary include loan words from other languages (anorak, pizza), clipped words (like zoo), acronyms pronounced as words (UNICEF), cult words (like yuppie) and words that have changed their meaning (meat once meant any food but now means animal flesh). Changes in vocabulary often reflect cultural change – for example we have a richer vocabulary to talk or write about the new technology – microchip, multimedia authoring, digital animation and hot-links, but sometimes there are attempts to make swift changes – for example feminist sociologists encouraged the use of 'Ms' to make it possible for women, like men, not to be defined by their marital status.

For a more detailed analysis and many interesting examples of language change, I recommend Rebecca Bunting's account in chapter 1, 'Principles of language study', in her book *Teaching About Language Study in the Primary Years*.

Bunting, Rebecca (2000 edition) *Teaching About Language Study in the Primary Years* London: David Fulton.

LANGUAGE FUNCTIONS

See: functions of language

LANGUAGE VARIETY

See also: accent, bilingualism, Creoles, dialect, field of discourse, functions of language, language change, mode, multilingualism, register, standard English, tenor

Language varies according to how speakers and writers use it. Functional linguists, for example Michael Halliday, recognise three main kinds of variation: dialectal, diatypic and diachronic. Dialectal variation recognises that within one mother tongue an individual may use a particular form of language – standard English or a regional or class dialect, sometimes called a 'sociolect'. There may also be variation according to gender, ethnicity and class. While 'dialect' is to do with variation in grammatical structures, 'accent' refers only to pronunciation – and may be 'received pronunciation' (RP) or a kind of pronunciation associated with a particular region or social group. This is normally a useful distinction but can become blurred in particular cases: Rebecca Bunting asks whether 'innit' should be regarded as a dialect feature of London English or as a feature of accent, as a pronunciation of 'isn't it' (Bunting, 2000: 19). Angela Wilson draws our attention to emotional aspects of different accents and how advertisers exploit this on film and television – Dorset and Somerset accents being used to sell wholesome products and French accents to sell perfume (Wilson and Scanlon, 2011). Diatypic variation refers to the adaptations we make in our language according to context and purpose. The 'register' of our language differs according to the formality of the situation – we would use language differently in a court of law or university seminar than in a pub or at a football match. Other factors also affect the 'register' or kind of language we use – the immediate context and the relationship between participants for example.

Diachronic variation refers to changes in language over time in vocabulary, grammar and pronunciation and is covered under 'language change'.

Bunting, Rebecca (2000) *Teaching About Language in the Primary Years* London: David Fulton (Chapter 1).

Halliday, M.A.K. and Hasan, R. (1985) *Language, Context and Text: Aspects of Language in a Social-Semiotic Perspective* Oxford: Oxford University Press.

Wilson, Angela and Scanlon, Julie (2011, fourth edition) *Language Knowledge for Primary Teachers* London: David Fulton.

LEFT-HANDED CHILDREN

See: handwriting

LEGEND

See also: traditional tales

Legends are a category of traditional tale. McArthur tells us that legends are generally 'unverifiable, usually fabulous, stories passed down (often orally) in a community and widely accepted as in some sense true' (McArthur, 1992: 595). A traditional tale is a legend or 'hero tale' (rather than a fable or parable, for example) if it is about heroes and heroines like Boudicca, William Tell, Pochahontas, King Arthur or Robin Hood – 'supermen who inspire marvel and wonder' (Steele, 1989: 11). These powerful stories have been told and retold from generation to generation and new versions of the Robin Hood and King Arthur legends frequently appear as films or television series as well as in print form. Mary

263

Steele provides a helpful annotated list of print legends up to the late 1980s and includes enduring classics like Rosemary Sutcliff's *Dragon Slayer* (superbly illustrated by Charles Keeping in the Puffin edition) and *The Faber Book of Greek Legends* edited by Kathleen Lines (Steele, 1989). More recent recommendations are set out in Mallett, 2010: Chapter 5. Legends lend themselves well to audio recordings. For a theatrical reading of tales based on the legend of Robin Hood I recommend the audio version of Michael Morpurgo's book *Robin of Sherwood* (Hodder, 2000), which has a distinctive slant on the political and social fabric of the story; for example, Robin becomes committed to helping the poor after his mother dies of starvation.

Like Robin Hood, King Arthur is a recurring figure in English legends. Kevin Crossley-Holland has written a trilogy which weaves the stories of King Arthur round the tale of another Arthur – a young boy in the year 1199 who longs to grow up and become a knight. The first book of this trilogy, *The Seeing Stone*, won the Guardian Fiction Award and was on Booktrust's 2002 list of 100 all-time favourites. Older juniors would find this an exciting retelling which recreates the texture of life in the Middle Ages with its hardships, challenges and distinctive sights and sounds (Orion Children's Books, 2000).

Maurice Saxby's interesting account, 'Myths and legends', covers some of the history of legend retelling for children and young people. He also reminds us that legends, along with other traditional tales, are truly multicultural and 'introduce children to a diversity of temperaments and the different ways of confronting universal and ongoing questions about life and human natures' (Saxby, 2004: 250).

First encounters with legends tend to involve children with stories recounting journeys and homecomings. Familiarity with legends from different cultures will not only enhance children's ability to read and enjoy this distinctive form of storytelling, but will also enrich their language and their vocabulary. The best writers and illustrators of legends for younger children relate the darker side of the tales in ways with which they can cope.

Teachers and parents seek out retellings that are exciting and told with energy and at a brisk pace to make for reading aloud well. Good dialogue is important too. Geraldine McCaughrean has a good ear for conversation as is evident in her book with illustrator Bee Wiley, *Myths and Legends of the World*. Another good one to read aloud to younger children is Gill Doherty's *The Usborne Book of Myths and Legends*. *The Orchard Book of the Legends of King Arthur* by Andrew Matthews stands out as a beautifully designed book, dramatically illustrated by Peter Utton and with an inviting written text. The introduction explains that a legend may begin as a true story, but as it is told over and over again 'it gets mixed up with people's hopes and dreams'. Children as young as six or seven enjoy hearing it read aloud and there is enough detail in each chapter to engage older readers too. Another retelling of the Arthurian legends that appeals across the primary age range is Marcia Williams' *King Arthur and the Knights of the Round Table*. Her cartoon strip approach allows for comic devices like speech bubbles and picture series showing actions but, like her *The Adventures of Robin Hood*, the book also benefits from thorough research. Heather Amery's *Stories from Around the World*, illustrated by Linda Edwards (Usborne), retells different kinds of traditional story, including legends about Dick Whittington and Brave Hendrick, a tale from Holland. Younger readers and listeners will be drawn into these well-told stories.

McArthur, Tom (1992) *The Oxford Companion to the English Language* Oxford and London: QPD with Oxford University Press.

Mallett, Margaret (2010) *Choosing and Using Fiction and Non-fiction 3–11* London: Routledge.

Saxby, Maurice (2004, second edition) 'Myths and legends' in Hunt, Peter (ed.) *International Companion Encyclopedia of Children's Literature*, Volume 1, London: Routledge.

Steele, Mary (1989) *Traditional Tales A Signal Bookguide* Stroud: The Thimble Press (visit www.thimblepress.co.uk for information about Signal books).

LETTER–SOUND CORRESPONDENCE

See also: 'bottom-up' reading approaches, phonics, reading, spelling

When we teach phonics we teach children the relationship between letter symbols and sounds. To make progress, children need to acquire the skills of segmentation and blending, know the alphabetic code and how to use their knowledge of that code in reading and spelling. In this approach children are helped to hear individual vowel and consonant sounds which are called 'phonemes' and to recognise the written symbols for these sounds which are called 'graphemes'. While there are forty-four phonemes, however, there are only twenty-six letters of the alphabet. There are two ways of getting over this. First, letters can make more than one sound, for example the 's' sound in 'has' is different to the 's' sound in 'seal'. Second, letters can be combined to make certain phonemes – 'sh', 'au' and 'ph'.

One issue here is that teaching phonics can become rather abstract. 'It is important, and this applies to whatever teaching skill you are focusing on, that the child does not lose sight of the fact that reading is a purposeful and meaningful activity and that there are some small and large shapes to attend to' (Graham and Kelly, 2007).

Graham, Judith and Kelly, Alison (2007) *Reading Under Control* London: David Fulton.

LETTERLAND

Letterland is a reading programme developing phonological awareness and introducing letter shapes and sounds. It is published by Letterland International Ltd (www.letterland.com) for use with three to seven year olds. The letter sounds are characterised by pictograms and the multi-sensory, interactive approach is thought to be particularly beneficial for children with reading difficulties. There is a range of materials – work books, picture books, big books, software and games – as well as a Teacher's Guide. As the materials reflect the phonics-based nature of the programme, it is recommended that they are used alongside other reading materials.

LETTERS

See also: autobiography, email, first person writing, texting

For some time now and for many people, including quite young children, email and texting have replaced some functions of the letter. However, receiving or writing a letter is a different kind of experience to typing an email, particularly when it comes to more personal matters. Emails tend to be typed swiftly and have developed their own succinct vocabulary and style. There is also the question of permanence: emails are more ephemeral and often soon deleted. So despite the fact that letters demand time and commitment from the writer they still have a role in life and a place in literature. They are a kind of first person writing and lie on a continuum from the intensely personal to the strictly formal. Many literacy corners include a folder of examples of different types of letter, as well as printouts of emails and text messages, for use in English and in history lessons where letters can give vivid insights into past times and lives. As children move through the primary years they increasingly come to appreciate that a letter's audience and its purpose affect the degree of its formality. Letters are a helpful resource when talking to children about the different effect on the reader of first person writing – autobiography – and third person writing – biography (Mallett, 1997). Younger children can be helped to write letters to recount, explain, enquire, congratulate and complain. Some genuine contexts for letters arise in school: writing to invite parents and friends of the school to special events and thank you letters to guides who have taken them round a museum or art gallery.

Other contexts for reading and writing letters can be found in stories. Children enjoy writing letters in the role of one character they have encountered in a story to another character. The book that has helped greatly here is Janet and Alan Ahlberg's *The Jolly Postman and other People's Letters* (Puffin edition). Other books structured round letters for younger children include *Dear Greenpeace* by Simon James (Walker Books) in which Emily writes for advice about caring for the 'whale' in her garden pond, and *Dear Peter Rabbit* (Warne) which includes facsimiles of the letters written by Beatrix Potter in the role of Peter Rabbit to her young friends (Johnson, 1999). Older primary children would find *Letters from Alain*, translated by Simon Breden from the book by Enrique Perez Diaz, intriguing. Short-listed for the Marsh Award for books in translation, this is the moving story about a boy who loses his friend when that friend and his family embark on a perilous journey to America in a small boat. Letters play a crucial role in the story as Arturo starts to receive letters from Alain after the boat is lost and the family dog, ominously, arrives home alone.

When it comes to children's own writing, writing in role, perhaps in letter or diary form, has long been a device for exploring character in children's stories, poems and novels. Good examples here are found in the case studies of classroom research by a group of teachers and the CLPE team described in *Boys on the Margin*. In one classroom example, a Year 5 class used both letters and email in follow-up activities after reading Charles Causley's poem 'What Has Happened to Lulu?'. Many of the boys in the class found this way of exploring the relationship between the missing girl and her mother energised their response to the poem (Safford *et al.*, 2004: 42). Nine year old Sophie's letter to Petie in the role of Tom (the main character in Betsy Byars' *The Midnight Fox*) shows how powerful letter writing can be as a way of exploring character and themes (Barrs and Cork, 2001: 89). Drama, too, is a motivating context for many kinds of writing and an authentic setting for letter writing which can help move the narrative forward. Drama can also be a strong context for encouraging the writing of more factual kinds of letter and here older primary children can attempt letters to persuade, criticise or protest. An exciting and involving theme is essential to the success of such work. One of the most impressive drama projects I have seen, in which letters and notices played a strong role, was carried out by a student teacher and a Year 6 class. Together they created the idea of a village community who found that developers were planning to take over a park at the edge of the village to build a hotel. This led to children writing letters in the role of angry villagers and the teacher answering them in the role of a local authority official. Other starting points for 'factual' letters might be a discussion on a current issue leading to letters taking up a viewpoint for a newspaper's correspondence column.

Barrs, Myra and Cork, Valerie (2001) *The Reader in the Writer* London: CLPE.
Johnson, Jane (1999) *My Dear Noel: The Story of a Letter from Beatrix Potter* London: Macdonald Young Books (for children of about seven years and above, this picture

book shows how a friendship can be sustained through letters.)

Mallett, Margaret (1997) *First Person Reading and Writing in the Primary Years: Enjoying and Reflecting on Diaries, Letters, Autobiographies and First Person Fiction* Sheffield: National Association for the Teaching of English (NATE).

Safford, Kimberly, O'Sullivan, Olivia and Barrs, Myra (2004) *Boys on the Margin: Promoting Boys' Literacy Learning at Key Stage 2* London: CLPE.

LEVEL DESCRIPTIONS

See: criterion referenced assessment, National Curriculum

LEXICAL TIES

See: cohesion

LIBRARIES IN PRIMARY SCHOOLS

See also: *Books for Keeps* online, Dewey system, displays, library skills, reading corner/area, writing corner/area

'I believe with the right pointers and advice every school can have, and should have, an inspiring school library'.
(Bakewell, 2010)

Most primary schools have both a central stock of books and resources and some classroom collections. Resources in the central stock are catalogued by title, author and subject in a card index system or, increasingly, in computer form. School libraries mostly use the Dewey system of classification or a simplified form of it. The School Library Association has produced a package which includes a Subject Index and a simple database on a CD-ROM, together with a Practical Guide and a poster with classification numbers (School Library Association, 2004). Quite often each class has a designated weekly slot in

the library to carry out research for a lesson or to be taught library skills.

It is important that children also have more informal library use. So a good system ensures that the central library is accessible, open as often as possible to the children and that it creates an interesting reading environment with displays and areas where children can sit to take notes, browse and reflect. Today's children will also expect the library to be equipped with computers so that they can access the internet for browsing and research (Mallett, 2007: 23).

Of course human resources are important and often it is the English/Literacy Co-ordinator who orders books and resources, after consultation with other teachers, parents and most importantly the children. The skilled Co-ordinator involves all the teachers in deciding how the library should develop. He or she can set up a staff room collection of journals which offer insightful reviews of books and resources, for example *The School Librarian* and *English 4–11*. There are also useful online journals like *Books for Keeps*. It is helpful, too, to send round new acquisitions with some comments about the merits of the book and how it might be used. If there is a lively dialogue about books and resources and teachers are prepared to browse in local book shops, this is much better than just ordering books from catalogues. Nothing beats the hands-on approach!

There are also good strategies for involving children in caring for the library. In quite a number of schools I visit, older primary children enjoy undertaking some light duties – replacing returned books to the shelves and helping younger children find their way round the library. Involvement in looking after their library is likely to encourage children to give reading priority in their lives. Primary schools can draw on the expertise of the school library services when creating a balanced collection of fiction, information books, audio-visual materials, CD-ROMs and software. The

267

librarians will sometimes visit to give talks to particular classes and groups of children about authors and illustrators and what the public lending library can offer them.

The books and resources in the classroom collections are usually centrally catalogued. English/Literacy Co-ordinators consult with other teachers to agree a coherent approach to taking books into the classroom from the central library for special purposes. Each classroom in each year group needs a core of carefully chosen classroom books and resources, for example picture books, stories and poetry particularly appealing to the age range, and appropriate reference books – dictionaries, encyclopedias, thesauri and atlases both print and electronic, and other texts to which children and teachers need to refer constantly. Please turn to 'reading corner/ area' and 'writing corner/area' for suggestions about making the literacy area in the classroom inviting. Helpful advice about involving children with books and resources of all kinds is covered in Aidan Chambers' (1991) book *The Reading Environment* and Judith Graham and Alison Kelly's *Reading Under Control* (Graham and Kelly, 2009).

Bakewell, Lucy (2010) *Off the Shelf: How to Run a Successful Primary School Library and Promote Reading* London: Carel Press.

Booktrust provide information about library resources: www.booktrust.org.uk

Chambers, Aidan (1991) *The Reading Environment: How Adults Help Children Enjoy Books* Stroud: The Thimble Press.

Graham, Judith and Kelly, Alison (2009, fourth edition) *Reading Under Control: Teaching Reading in the Primary School* London: David Fulton.

Mallett, Margaret (2007) *Active Encounters: Inspiring Young Readers and Writers of Non-fiction 4–11* Minibook 24. Leicester: UKLA (see Chapter 4).

School Library Association (2004) *The Primary School Classification Scheme* CD-ROM. The School Librarian Association.

The School Library Association produces an excellent journal, *The School Librarian*, which includes reviews of all kinds of books and of multimedia resources as well as articles on all aspects of setting up and developing a school library. The website is useful too, with an excellent primary section that includes news of recent developments and initiatives, lists of quality children's resources and books and articles online, for example the Riveting Reads PDF files – www. sla.org.uk.

LIBRARY SKILLS

See also: factual genres, libraries in primary schools, reading corner/area, retrieval devices, structural guiders, study skills, writing corner/area

We should do all we can to encourage children to enjoy and be skilled at using the school library. When children are at work in the library it is an excellent opportunity for the teacher to observe children's reading behaviour. How are they getting on with finding books through the Dewey system? Do they know how to browse and how to swiftly sample a book by checking the cover and reading a page or two? These observations will inform how the teacher builds in helpful activities and teaching. So that we ensure that children progress in their ability to use the library the English/Literacy Co-ordinator, with input from other staff, usually draws up a broad plan of what should be achieved by most children in each year group and how teaching will support this. This then feeds into the school's English policy and long- and short-term planning.

Specific skills like selecting books and multimedia resources and browsing through what is available can be modelled by teachers and older pupils. With encouragement, some children will be prepared to make themselves experts in library skills and general care of the library. This kind of involvement can be reinforced by inviting children to contribute an assembly item about what they have been doing.

Children enjoy making charts and labels to help others find their way round the books and resources (Mallett, 2010: 368). Charts can set out advice about using the numbers on the shelves to locate the books, and go on to explain how to use retrieval devices to find exactly the aspect of a topic they need. Of course, booklets on how to use CD-ROMs, software and the internet are necessary as well. This kind of writing task has a very clear purpose and audience. Waters and Martin describe a most interesting case study in which older primary school children were systematically trained by teachers and classroom assistants in using library procedures consistent with an agreed approach. Adults took small groups for short teaching periods and trained them in putting books into alphabetic order according to author surname, dividing books into fiction and non-fiction and in social aspects of using the library. The social aspects included discussing what a pupil would do if they entered the library and found a plant knocked over, a book thrown on the floor or a group of children behaving in a silly way. Children often respond well to being asked to reflect in a mature manner. Short tests were built into the lessons and children who passed these were awarded a library licence which set out their competencies, which included: being able to use the Dewey system; following the library code; knowing what to do if you have a problem. Possession of the licence led to certain privileges like being allowed to enter the library alone and to supervise another pupil who had not yet achieved the licence (Waters and Martin, 1999: Chapter 8).

If children feel confident and comfortable using their school library it is much more likely that they will make use of all their local lending library offers, including the many holiday schemes and projects.

Mallett, Margaret (2010) *Choosing and Using Fiction and Non-fiction 3–11* London: Routledge (see Chapter 34).

Waters, Mick and Martin, Tony (1999) *Co-ordinating English at Key Stage 2* London: Routledge/Falmer.

LIMERICK

A limerick is an amusing verse often with an aabba rhyming pattern. Edward Lear (1812–88) made limericks popular with children with his entertaining rhymes with illustrations in *Book of Nonsense* (1877). Here is an example of one of his limericks:

Bored by a Bee

'There was an Old Man in a tree,
Who was horribly bored by a bee,
When they asked 'Does it buzz?'
He replied, 'Yes, it does!
It's a regular brute of a bee!'

A number of anthologies of nonsense verse include limericks, for example Quentin Blake's *The Puffin Book of Nonsense Verse* which includes limericks by Edward Gorey, Ogden Nash and Edward Lear, and John Foster's *My First Oxford Book of Nonsense Poems* in which you will find some amusing limericks by modern poets such as Willard Espy, Colin West and Frank Richards. To ring the changes teachers can use audio CDs with limericks and other nonsense verse. Alan Bennett reads some Edward Lear limericks on *The Owl and the Pussycat: And Other Nonsense Rhymes* (Cover to Cover Cassettes Ltd).

LINC MATERIALS

See also: Cox Report, Kingman Report

The LINC materials (Language in the National Curriculum) were a government-funded, in-service resource produced by Professor Ronald Carter and his team to help implement language study programmes in response to the implications of the Kingman Report (1989). The 500-page pack was not intended for direct use in the classroom but was to help increase teachers' own knowledge about language and language study so that they could plan, implement and evaluate appropriate lessons with the age groups they taught. There were about 400 training courses and about 10,000 teachers attended them.

Then one of the most dramatic decisions in the history of the teaching of English was made: the government of the day refused to publish the materials. In his book *Cox on the Battle for the English Curriculum*, Brian Cox (chair of the Working Group that created the first National Curriculum in English in 1989) sets out the background to this official censorship. Although most teachers, linguists and educationists considered the materials were based on a balanced view of issues like the teaching of grammar, standard English and dialects, some ministers and journalists in some parts of the press thought otherwise.

The language volcano, always simmering away in the background, had erupted! All this showed what an emotional issue how we teach children about their mother tongue can be and how much people care about it. The materials and several related books were eventually published by Nottingham University and the work of Professor Carter and his team continues to inform those concerned with language study in school.

Four principles underpin the LINC programme. First, teaching about language should build on children's implicit knowledge – on the rich linguistic resources they bring to the classroom. The next principle is to do with the relationship between reflecting on language and use of language. The LINC team noted that children use language before they begin to consciously reflect and analyse it in school. As they get older they can be helped to use appropriate terminology to consider how they and other people use language and these insights can feed back into their own use of language. Third, language is best analysed in purposeful settings rather than out of context. (This is where drama work with its wide potential for different kinds of language use can make a considerable contribution.) Finally, teaching children about attitudes to language, its uses and misuses, can help children see how it is used to communicate people's underlying attitudes and beliefs (Cox, 1995).

Nothing stays the same and teachers are obliged to meet new requirements but we can keep hold of the four principles enshrined in the LINC materials as a way of keeping our classroom work engaging and exciting.

Bain, Richard, Fitzgerald, Bernadette and Taylor, Mike (1992) *Looking into Language* London: Hodder & Stoughton.

Carter, Ronald (1992) *Knowledge about Language and the Curriculum: The LINC Reader* London: Hodder & Stoughton.

Cox, Brian (1995) *Cox on the Battle for the English Curriculum* London: Hodder & Stoughton.

LISTENING

See: National Curriculum, speaking and listening, storytelling

LISTS

See also: factual genres, writing

Lists have purposes which even the youngest children can understand. They can remind us of things we need to do: to feed the classroom snails or to bring to school the ingredients to make sweets or biscuits. When it comes to planning a piece of writing, a list can be the first step towards producing a longer account.

Children working on their own information books are often encouraged to list the questions they want to consider – see for example the list of snail questions in case study 3.1 (in Mallett, 1999) which, with some rearrangement, became the contents page. As Barrs points out, a list can be one of the first kinds of writing children do that moves away from chronological organisation (Barrs, 1987). Lists can bring order to our experience and our thinking.

Children can be supplied with a note book to jot down lists of things they want to include in their writing. There is a most interesting glimpse into a classroom where children are encouraged to have inquiring minds and to make lists in their 'wonder books' in Stephanie Harvey's book *Non-fiction Matters* (Harvey, 1998). Eight year old Jordan lists, with detailed illustrations, twenty-two topics he wants to research including 'volcanoes, dogs and cats, the human race, black holes and electricity'. Making lists of what they want to find out can be the first step for a young researcher, and lead to long-term commitment to favourite topics and interests.

Barrs, Myra (1987) 'Mapping the world' *English in Education* NATE, 21(3).

Harvey, Stephanie (1998) *Nonfiction Matters: Reading, Writing and Research Grades 3–8* York, Maine: Stenhouse Publishers.

Mallett, Margaret (1999) *Young Researchers: informational reading and writing in the early and primary years* London: Routledge.

LITERACY CORNER/AREA

See: reading corner/area, writing corner/area

LITERACY EVOLVE – PRIMARY LITERACY FOR KEY STAGE 1 AND KEY STAGE 2

See also: reading schemes

This is a reading programme created in association with Michael Rosen, using whole books. There is an adaptable online planning tool to personalise the programme for individual needs and to help assess progress (Pearson Education: pearson schoolsandfecolleges.co.uk).

LITERACY HOUR

The 1998 Literacy Strategy *Framework* recommended that teachers put in place a carefully structured hour each day devoted to literacy teaching. Although the literacy hour was non-statutory, most primary schools chose to work within it. The renewed *Framework* – the *Primary Framework for Literacy and Mathematics* (2006) guided teachers towards a more flexible approach. This, too, is abandoned but some of the elements in the literacy hour survive, for example class-based teaching of phonics, group-based guided and independent reading, and close attention to text types both print and electronic. Teachers tend now to refer to 'Literacy Time', 'literacy lessons' or to 'literacy'.

LITERACY LAND

Literacy Land is a reading programme that offers support to children's reading across the curriculum. It has three strands: story street, genre range and info-trail. Many of the books are by acclaimed authors. The materials were published by Longman and there is information about the resource on www.pearsonschoolsandfecolleges.co.uk.

LITERARY CRITICISM

See also: genre, history of children's literature, illustrations: finding a vocabulary, picture books, postmodernism and children's picture books, subject knowledge

Literary criticism is the study of literary texts. The term has usually been applied to the evaluation of texts for adults but, more recently, specialist critical theories and terminologies are being developed specifically in relation to children's literature (Hunt, 2001: 2). Teachers find it helpful to use a set of terms to discuss and think about the texts they use both in and outside Literacy Time. Not all the terms used will be appropriate to use with children but they will be helpful to teachers when discussing their work with each other. There is now a welcome trend to recognising children's information texts, particularly the more lyrical kind, as worthy of critical attention (Meek, 1996). Teachers find help with analysing texts, both fiction and non-fiction, in Angela Wilson and Julie Scanlon's book *Language Knowledge for Primary Teachers* (Wilson and Scanlon, 2011). Mallett provides glossaries of terms: some are traditional ones like those to assign a work to a category – novel, drama, epic, sonnet. Others are technical expressions – iambic pentameter or rhyming couplet, or stylistic ones – imagery, metaphor, simile, alliteration and onomatopoeia (Mallett, 2010). The twentieth century brought new criticisms including structuralism and feminist criticism with whole new terminologies and concepts – deconstruction, intertextuality, metafiction and postmodernism. Obviously teachers need to know the distinguishing features of traditional tales, novels and ballads in order to teach about them, but do these later developments in literary theory have relevance to the teacher in the classroom? Interestingly, many teachers have been drawn into this world of literary theory through their interest in the children's picture book. The best picture books are original and highly sophisticated works of art which make considerable demands on the reader. For one thing the reader has to relate nonlinear 'reading' of the picture to linear processing of words (Hunt, 2001: 288). In a story like Pat Hutchins' *Rosie's Walk* there is a thrilling mismatch between the blandness of the verbal and the threatened chaos of the visual. A new metalanguage for discussing children's picture books is springing up. Jane Doonan, for example, refers to pictures' 'schemes of colour', 'small and large patterning' and 'network of linear rhythms' (Doonan, 1993). David Lewis has produced a scholarly analysis of the postmodern elements in children's picture books (Lewis, 1990: 133) and, more recently, in *Reading Contemporary Picturebooks* (Lewis, 2001).

Doonan, Jane (1993) *Looking at Pictures in Picture Books* Stroud: The Thimble Press.

Hunt, Peter (2001) *Children's Literature* London: Blackwell.

Lewis, David (1990) 'The constructedness of text: picture books and the metafictive' *Signal*, 62: 131–46.

——(2001) *Reading Contemporary Picture-books: Picturing Text* London: Routledge.

Mallett, Margaret (2010) *Choosing and Using Fiction and Non-fiction 3–11* London: Routledge.

Meek, Margaret (1996) *Information and Book Learning* Stroud: The Thimble Press.

Wilson, Angela and Scanlon, Julie (2011, fourth edition) *Language Knowledge for Primary Teachers* London: David Fulton.

LITERATURE ACROSS THE CURRICULUM

See also: art and English, drama and English, fiction as a source of information, geography and English, history and English, Information and Communications Technology (ICT) and English, mathematics and English, physical education, music and dance and English, religious education and English, science and English

In the primary years part of learning history, science and so on is to do with learning to think, speak and write in particular ways and with taking on a specialist terminology. Each subject is resourced with information texts, both print and on screen. Particularly when we are beginning some new topic in one of the primary curriculum areas, it is important to help children gain a personal foothold. We do this when we help children to organise in discussion their existing knowledge and experience – what do you already know about magnets, volcanoes, the Vikings or patterns? Fiction can also help children get involved with a topic and it may help to read a book or poem at the start or finish of a topic or series of lessons or alongside the work. There are examples of fiction to awaken the imagination under the entries in the 'See also:' part of this entry. The very youngest children can learn about the past through story by looking at picture books like the Ahlbergs' *Peepo!* which shows the clothes and objects of an Edwardian childhood. Older children learning about the Second World War find inspiration in books about the impact of war on the young like Nina Bawden's *Carrie's War*, *Anne Frank's Diary* and Marcia Williams' *My Secret War Diary, by Flossie Albright*. Other stories invite the sort of map work that would link with geography, for example Beverley Naidoo's *Journey to Jo'burg*.

Stories of this sort are often also a sympathetic introduction to human and cultural geography. The potential of fiction for very young children as a way of learning about the world is covered in Chapter 11 of *Early Years Non-fiction* (Mallett, 2003).

Michael Morpurgo's novels and stories often stir children's interest in environmental and ethical issues which link with subjects across the curriculum (Mallett, 2010). In *Wreck of the Zanzibar*, for example, Laura has to decide whether or not it is right to hide a turtle she has been feeding with jellyfish when human beings are short of food. As well as reading fiction, children sometimes write stories in response to work on a topic across the curriculum. There can be an interesting interplay between different texts and different ways of looking at topics. For example, Eric Carle's *The Tiny Seed*, Ruth Brown's *Ten Seeds* or similar nature books could lead to younger children's own stories about plants and to more science-based writing about observations as new seeds grow. Some information books for older primary children also have the potential to inspire different kinds of writing. David Smith and Shelagh Armstrong's *If the World Were a Village* might lead to stories in the role of one of the villagers.

Mallett, M. (2003) *Early Years Non-fiction* London: Routledge (chapter 11, 'The role of fiction in informational learning, securing a personal foothold').

——(2010) *Choosing and Using Fiction and Non-fiction 3–11* London: Routledge (see Chapter 32).

LIVING BOOKS (AS RESOURCES FOR EARLY READING)

See also: CD-ROM, CDs, ebooks, Information and Communications Technology (ICT) and English

Living books are texts on CD mainly used to support the initial teaching of reading. Some of the best-known living books for children from about ages four to six are *Green Eggs and Ham, Sheila Rae, the Brave* and *The Tortoise and the Hare* published by Broderbund. They encourage the development of conventional reading skills and abilities as the reader moves from one page to the next in a linear way, but as there are 'hotspots' which can be activated on the screen, living books can help young children use their understanding of the ways in which printed texts work to grasp the nonlinear structure of electronic texts. This prepares them for the greater demands of information CD-ROMs and websites (O'Sullivan, 2005). Some of the characteristics of living books which help young readers include:

- the motivating presence of animations and sounds;

- the facility (in some) of enabling readers to click on an individual word to hear it read aloud, helping the matching of sound and written word;
- the opportunities for interaction – for example, discussion and making their own stories;
- the facility of highlighting text to heighten print awareness – for example, one might highlight all the adjectives in a passage;
- encouragement to make their own decisions to revisit particular pages; and
- opportunities to become familiar with texts on screen – features like icons and 'hotspots'.

Well-contextualised visual and audio support makes the best living books helpful to young learners just beginning to learn English. Traditional tales with a strong rhythmic text like those from Kingscourt 'Inside Stories' on CD help as well. Teachers on courses at the Centre for Literacy in Education have observed that some children, and particularly boys, seem more likely to engage with print texts if their interest has first been caught by experience of screen books. The screen books seem to help heighten children's early print awareness (O'Sullivan, 2005).

However, there are some criticisms of living books, or at least those available at present, to bear in mind. Some reviewers find many living books lack the quality of language and story found in the best print books. Let us hope this will be rectified in the future by the production of new and better versions. Then there are criticisms to do with how far a particular living book stimulates interaction and discussion or maybe stimulates creativity – for example by inviting the reader to tell or write their own ending to the story. Sometimes it is difficult for young readers to become truly involved in the events of the story because there are so many chances to click on animations. This risks interrupting the rhythm

of the child's reading of the central story. Of considerable help in choosing living books of quality is the TEEM website which offers reviews of both software and websites.

Cinderella, The Billy Goats Gruff and *The Gingerbread Man* – Inside Stories Kingscourt/ McGraw-Hill, mcgraw-hill.co.uk/kingscourt.

Green Eggs and Ham, The Tortoise and the Hare, Sheila Rae, the Brave – Broderbund Living Books, available from www.taglearning.com, www.amazon.co.uk.

O'Sullivan, Olivia (2005) 'ICT and early literacy' *Books for Keeps*, September.

TEEM (Teachers Evaluating Educational Multimedia): teemeducation.org.uk

LONDON READING TEST

See also: cloze procedure, reading age, Standardised Reading Tests

Published by the NFER in 1981 this group, written, untimed test with a score range of 6.0–12.0 years is for Year 6 (ten to eleven year olds). It is in the form of prose paragraphs and uses cloze procedure and comprehension questions.

LOOK AND SAY

See also: reading

'Look and say' is an approach to the teaching of reading which aims to build up a sight vocabulary. The stress is on the whole word and sometimes teachers using this method would hold up flash cards so that children could learn the pattern of the word. Often the 'look and say' and 'phonic' approaches were combined in a practice which was common up until the 1970s. Reading schemes, for example *Janet and John* and *Jane and Peter*, aimed to build up key words and to use a restricted vocabulary to reinforce them.

Traditional 'look and say' teaching tended to place children in a passive role and

274

reflected a behaviourist approach of stimulus and response – the stimulus was the word in book or on flash card and the response was the child's saying of the word. However, learning the patterns of words and what the letter strings look like has a place in current reading programmes.

LYRICAL NON-FICTION

In the 1990s Walker Books published a groundbreaking new series called 'Read and Wonder'. These titles, which are information picture books for the five to seven year old age range, communicate information of quality and depth. Each one is written from the personal perspective of the author and is unique in approach and design. *A Ruined House* by Mick Manning shares the author's childhood experience of finding an old house in the countryside and exploring the creatures and plants that have taken up residence within the decaying rooms and walls.

Think of an Eel, written by Karen Wallace and illustrated by Mike Bostock, tells the story of the creature from elver to mature eel using rich language and imagery. The young eel is described as 'like a shoelace made out of glass'.

Lyrical non-fiction has three qualities: the text and illustrations appeal to children's hearts as well as their minds; thoughts and feelings are sometimes communicated

Figure 12 Page 4 of *Nature Adventures* by Mick Manning and Brita Granström, reproduced with the permission of the publishers, Frances Lincoln, © 2011.

through poetic devices like rhythm, alliteration and imagery; and the illustrations embody the distinctive 'line', 'hue' and 'tone' more usually to be found in paintings or picture book illustrations (Mallett, 2006). The illustration shows a lyrical painting from Mick Manning and Brita Granström's book *Nature Adventures* which includes poetry as well as giving well-researched scientific information.

Mallett, M. (2006) *The Lyrical Voice in Non-Fiction* Bookmark series, Leicester: The English Association.

M

MAGAZINES

See: advertisements, comics, newspapers and magazines

MAGIC

See: fairy tales, fantasy, traditional tales

MAGIC E

This refers to the 'e' at the end of a word (after a consonant) which gives a long value to the vowel before the consonant, as in mope, make and site.

MANAGEMENT

See: English/Literacy Co-ordinator

MARKING

See also: assessment, composition, process approach to writing, proof reading, tick sheets, transcriptional aspects of writing, writing

Teachers make an oral response to children's writing whenever teacher and child look at a draft or fair copy together. This is a good context in which to intervene as teacher and child can see quickly whether they understand each other. In line with a 'process' approach, children can be helped to improve their work before it reaches final draft. Children also appreciate a written response on some of their work and this helps a child take an interest in which pieces of writing are placed in his or her portfolio to show progress. I have also found that parents are very interested in the teacher's comments when they look at work on parents' evening or open day. It gives them clear evidence of how the teacher is intervening to help their child make progress. Older primary children are likely to write quite a lot each week and, as Wyse and Jones point out, there needs to be a whole-school marking policy to make the job manageable (Wyse and Jones, 2007). First the policy might attend to how to select samples for careful marking and perhaps others for skim reading acknowledged by a tick or teacher's initials. Range might be one criterion: it might be decided that during half a term the teacher will mark at least one piece of writing in each of the different genres introduced during that period. Second, strategies might be agreed for marking a piece of writing. Many teachers like to make a difference between secretarial corrections and suggestions for redrafting which involve reorganising the content or compositional aspect of the work. In the 'proof reading' entry I suggested that children might like to learn some of the conventional symbols for spelling and punctuation errors and omissions. This would be helpful if the teacher set up writing partners to look at secretarial aspects of each other's work.

The final comments might include – praise for the strong aspects of the work, for example 'an inviting beginning' or 'good, convincing dialogue', then advice about a weak point 'you need to keep up the pace of the action' or 'vocabulary needs to be more varied', and finally one or two clear 'next step' suggestions. These could be to do with global aspects of the writing 'let us work on paragraphing together on your next draft' or with elements like characterisation or setting the scene. In *Writing Under Control* (Graham and Kelly, 2009) Liz Laycock mentions the practice of a teacher who asked the children to do some of their writing in a book, leaving one page blank for redrafting suggestions and attempts. This fits with Laycock's suggestion that we think less in terms of 'marking' and 'correction' and more of 'feedback' and 'response'.

Graham, Judith and Kelly, Alison (eds) (2009, third edition) *Writing Under Control* London: David Fulton.

Wyse, Dominic and Jones, Russell (2007, second edition) *Teaching English, Language and Literacy* London: Routledge/Falmer.

MASS NOUN (UNCOUNTABLE NOUN)

See also: count noun, grammar, noun, parts of speech

When a noun is not normally used in the plural we term it a mass or uncountable noun. They are rarely if ever used with the indefinite article – 'a' or 'an'. Examples include: greed, salt, cotton.

MATHEMATICS AND ENGLISH

See also: diagrams, language across the curriculum, visual literacy

There are two considerations here: how language helps children learn mathematical concepts through speaking and listening, reading and writing; and how an 'English' approach to number and problem solving using stories, games and poems brings greater insight. Language used to discuss, question and speculate has an important role in mathematics as children learn about terms, concepts and the stages in solving problems. We want children to talk about mathematical ideas using their own language but there are important technical terms to learn which need good contextual support. We might praise a child for using the word 'oval' appropriately but add that mathematicians also use the word 'ellipse' to mean the same thing. Mathematical dictionaries or charts help to encourage children to check the meaning of words like 'mass', 'weight', 'tessellate' and 'estimate'. How mathematical texts – whether in print in the form of books, work sheets or work cards or on the screen – are written and presented is important. We want tasks that challenge and extend children's investigative abilities. We need to keep in mind that the children using them are at different stages in their reading development and will need different levels of mediation.

There was a time in the 1970s and 1980s when mathematics texts seemed to address children directly and this could be lonely for them because it reduced interaction with teacher and peers. Although there is a new emphasis on mental mathematics there is also recognition of the role of the teacher who intervenes to support, encourage and extend a child's thinking. Children enjoy working collaboratively to solve problems. So while there are non-verbal dimensions in mathematics, talk is a vital way of helping young children make sense of mathematics and relate it to real life experience. If you would like to read more about the role of talk in mathematics, particularly where children of six years and under are concerned, I recommend Janet Evans' (2001) article '"Four little dollies jumping on the bed" – learning about mathematics through talk'. Three important types of talk are teacher's talk to introduce new concepts, teacher-led discussion and children's task-focused talk with their peers. Mathematics texts may be used in Literacy Time to help children explore procedural and problem solving kinds of writing. Numbers, symbols, diagrams and verbal labelling all interact to make meaning and there are a number of very good big books to demonstrate all this. Where books show children engaging in mathematical activities we should ensure that girls and children from ethnic minorities see positive reflections of themselves as young mathematicians. Teachers and children often make their own mathematics materials – books and games – and add them to the classroom collection.

There is a creative, explorative side to mathematics which links it to the spirit of English and helps motivate children. For very young children there are imaginative number books which tell a story. For example, Simone Lia's *Billy Bean's Dream* (David and Charles) tells the story of the building of a rocket by Billy Bean and his friends and his friends' pets – there are so many things to count: the jellybeans, the work tools, the sandwiches and the stars as the rocket finally zooms into the sky. The book also shows how to work well in a team. In the school context, fiction (stories and poems) that includes vocabulary to do with size, measurement and money helps children secure mathematical kinds of thinking in an enjoyable way. For example teachers often use Browning's *The Pied Piper of Hamelin* in which there is much reference to size – the rats are lean, great and so on. Number songs like 'One Man Went to Mow' have much potential for singing and acting out. Each time another person enters 'the meadow' the children can pause and check the right number are there. These number songs can be reshaped by teacher and children to fit with current activities and preoccupations.

Evans worked with four to five year olds on Ted Arnold's story-song *Five Ugly Monsters* (Scholastic, 1988) and soon the monsters became 'five little dollies' as the children had to hand some dollies they had been using earlier for an attribute exercise. In this work English and mathematics were truly entwined in an exciting way. The children enjoyed singing and acting out their own version of a story-song which was made into their own big book for shared reading. Their mathematical experiences included using the language of sorting and sets in context, counting from nought to five, exploring mathematical patterns and talking about number values (Evans, 2001: 76). Alongside the role play and practical work, the teacher scribed the story and included the numbers patterns. Let me give an example here: in one verse, four of the dollies are jumping on the bed and one dolly is on the floor – so the teacher wrote: 4 and 1 = 5. Writing the symbols clinched all that had been learnt through talk. For a most interesting account of an interplay between practical activities and recording mathematical findings in symbols see Evans' book *Have Some Maths with Your Story* (Evans, 1995).

Children can be asked to estimate the number of days a fantasy journey in a book or poem might take. For example, working from Edward Lear's 'The Jumblies' (*A Book of Nonsense*, Dragon's World Publishers) they could estimate the amount of time the Jumblies were away, using different clues. Or they might create their own notion of what Jumblie time might be like. Perhaps they have a different number of hours in the day?

Evans, Janet (1995) *Have Some Maths with Your Story* Liverpool: Janev Publications.
——(2001) 'Four little dollies jumping on the bed – learning about mathematics through talk' in Goodwin, Prue (ed.) *The Articulate Classroom* London: David Fulton.

MEDIA STUDIES

See: advertisements, CD-ROM, Information and Communications Technology (ICT) and English, newspapers and magazines, television and literacy, video-film and DVDs, visual literacy

MEDIUM-TERM PLANS

See: English/Literacy Co-ordinator, planning

METACOGNITION

See also: constructivism, critical discourse, language and thought, non-fiction reading and writing

Metacognition is the awareness an individual has of how he or she has come to know something. Knowing oneself as a learner can lead to adopting more effective strategies and acting on them. For example, I find I need first to mark out a global structure, an overall plan, of the articles and reviews I write. Then I start working under each sub-heading. Being in control of our learning often involves some self-checking. As Riley and Prentice put it, 'being able to highlight for oneself those aspects of a learning task yet to be accomplished is emerging as one of the most valuable skills through which intellectual functioning can be enhanced' (Riley and Prentice, 1999: 8–9). This active involvement in one's own learning strategies is close to the spirit of the constructivist model (see constructivism).

How do we help children develop the ability to monitor their own learning progress? Children are more likely to become 'metacognitively wise' when performance is not over-emphasised (Galton, 2007). Discussion with children about their reading and writing over a period of time creates a context for talking about what they find easy and what they find difficult and what might help. To give a focus for such discussions it is helpful to have to hand perhaps the child's annotated reading journal or a selection of writing samples from which some are to be chosen, jointly, by teacher and child for their English portfolio. Children learn how to develop good strategies by observing the teacher and other children and from the feedback teachers provide. Searching for information is an area in which metacognitive abilities are particularly useful. It is not just a matter of hearing 'the facts' explained or reading them from one source. Teachers help children identify their purpose and then use all available resources – books, illustrations, CD-ROMs, the internet, visiting experts – and sometimes their own first-hand observation. Then there are strategies to control like note taking, summarising and sharing findings in a way that will interest others.

Galton, M. (2007) *Learning and Teaching in the Primary Classroom* London: Sage Publications (see Chapter 5, 'Making children metacognitively wise').

Riley, Jeni and Prentice, Roy (1999) *The Curriculum for 7–11 Year Olds* London: Paul Chapman.

METALANGUAGE

See also: functions of language, Information and Communications Technology (ICT) and English, reading, subject knowledge, visual literacy, writing

Metalanguage is a linguistic term which refers to language to talk about language.

The linguist M.A.K. Halliday proposed some functions for a young child's use of language (see under functions of language). One of these, the heuristic function, enables a child to discover much about the world and their experience. One of things they find out about is language itself (Halliday, 1982). They hear parents comment on their developing language use – 'new word', 'a lot of questions' and so on.

When a child learns to read and write he or she will hear and use words like 'letter', 'sound', 'page', 'spelling', 'vowel', 'consonant' and 'phoneme'. Through the primary years he or she will learn to talk about different language forms and their features – the 'plot', 'setting' and 'characters' of a novel or story, and the 'rhythm', 'rhyme' and 'metre' of poetry. The discussion of word meanings across the curriculum involves teachers and children in using a metalanguage to explain and discuss them. So in history we might talk about the concept of 'medieval', 'feudal' or 'chronology', in science about 'catalyst', 'chemical' or 'solution' and in geography about 'igneous' and 'sedimentary' rocks, 'environment' and 'boundaries'. Becoming more conscious of these terms and concepts also makes us more aware of our own learning processes and metalinguistic awareness therefore links with metacognition.

Changes in society bring about change in vocabulary as we need new terms to grapple with the new concepts. The need to acquire the ability to interpret and to create electronic texts has brought about new electronic literacies with their own concepts and terminology. Teachers use terms like 'computer literacy', 'network literacy' and 'online literacy' to refer to reading and writing using the new technology. Children now talk about 'hyperlinks' – a series of hot text links that enable users to navigate through a collection of screens or web pages – and to 'framing' – decisions about how much information is given to the viewer.

The need to explore the meaning of visual texts, still or moving, is giving rise to a vocabulary in which to discuss this kind of reading; for example we refer to 'composition' as the combination of the elements of an image into a whole text and to 'multimodal' to indicate a text that draws on a variety of communication modes – spoken, written, visual and spatial.

Halliday, M.A.K. (1982) 'Relevant models of language' in Wade, Barry (ed.) *Language Perspectives* London: Heinemann.

METAPHOR

See also: poetry, simile, subject knowledge

Metaphor permeates our use of language and it is difficult to imagine speaking or writing without this enrichment. While a simile makes the comparison between phenomena fully explicit – 'he fought like a lion' – a metaphor identifies two things with each other 'he was the lion of the team'. So, in a metaphor the qualities of the first thing carry over into the second.

In poetry metaphoric names for things are sometimes used. In a 'kenning', for example, compound words are used to name things. In Old English poetry we might come across 'bonehouse' meaning body.

Although metaphors occur in prose, they are more common in poetry and enjoying poems is a good context for introducing and learning about metaphor. While very young children tend to become locked into literal meanings by age seven or eight, most children's thinking has become sufficiently flexible to understand metaphors.

METAPHORS IN EDUCATION

See also: apprenticeship approach to reading, child-centred learning, reading, scaffolding

Educational writing is rich in metaphor. We have the behaviourist view of the child as a 'sponge' or 'vessel' to be filled, while the child-centred philosopher will often refer to the child as a 'plant' which will grow given certain necessary conditions.

More interactive models of teaching and learning will see the child as an 'apprentice'. Bruner's metaphor of the adult 'scaffolding' a child's learning so that the joint achievement is greater than what the less mature partner could have managed alone also presents learning as a partnership. The good teacher 'lends' essentially temporary structure and support which, like a scaffold during building, can eventually be removed.

The reading process has also had its share of metaphors. Bussis thought of the cueing systems – syntactic, grapho-phonic and semantic – as instruments in an orchestra. The model in the National Literacy Strategy Framework for Teaching (DfEE, 1998) took as its guiding metaphor the notion of the cueing systems as searchlights on the reading process. The Rose model of reading was known as 'the simple view of reading'.

Metaphors are a powerful way of referring to particular ways of seeing the educational process and the only certain thing is that each one will fall out of favour and be replaced by another or others.

Bussis, Anne M., Chittenden, Edward A., Amarel, Marianne and Klausner, Edith (1985) *Inquiry into Meaning: An Investigation of Learning to Read* Hillsdale, N.J.: Lawrence Erlbaum Associates.

METHODS OF ENGLISH TEACHING

See: history of English teaching

METONYMY

This is a figure of speech in which, rather like in a metaphor, something is brought to mind by mentioning something associated with it. Well-known uses of metonymy include 'crown' to suggest monarchy, 'bottle' to suggest alcohol and 'Number 10' for the prime minister.

METRE

This refers to the poetic rhythm of a text determined by the number of feet, or beats, to the line and the nature of the stress on syllables. For example, an iambic metre uses iambuses which each consist of a stressed and unstressed syllable, for example:

'Bobby Shaftoe went to sea'.

This consists of four iambuses when 'sea' is pronounced 'see-ee'.

MISCUE ANALYSIS

See also: assessment, reading, record keeping, running reading records

Miscue analysis is a diagnostic reading procedure useful in helping to pinpoint children's strengths and weaknesses. It was devised by Goodman (1973) who famously claimed it opened up a 'window onto the reading process'. There are a number of versions of miscue analysis, including a user-friendly one in Helen Arnold's book *Listening to Children Reading*. 'Running reading records' are a simple form of miscue analysis in which every word read correctly is marked with a stroke on a copy of the page. Rather than simply providing a stark score or reading age, miscue analysis – if conscientiously carried out – reveals which strategies the young reader controls well and where some support is needed. The use of the word 'miscue' rather than 'mistake' indicates a positive approach to a young reader's efforts to process the text drawing on different strategies.

Miscue analysis is usually carried out with newly independent readers or with older primary aged children who have a difficulty with reading. About 300 words of unfamiliar text, which makes some demands on the child without reaching frustration level, is usually chosen. You need a copy of the passage to mark in the miscues as the child reads out loud. Some teachers like to read with the child up to the selected passage so that he or she does not come to the task 'cold'. It is helpful to record the child reading and to explain you want to listen again so you can help them. Tell the child that you want them to try out any new words and that on this occasion you will not interrupt to help. (Of course it is best just to supply the word if children become confused and upset.) Teachers try to make the task as anxiety-free as possible and, when the analysis is complete, talk with the child about the meaning of the text, stressing the enjoyment element. Mark the photocopied text with symbols for omissions, substitutions, insertions, reversals, repetitions, hesitation and self-correction (see chart below).

Then you can show the results of a miscue analysis in a simple diagram similar to the one below.

Summary of a child's strengths and limitations

Next step comment

Although the conversation between the child and the teacher afterwards is not part of the formal procedure, the child's comments may be useful in confirming aspects of the diagnosis – that he or she was reading for meaning, for example.

If the miscue analysis is to be placed in a child's portfolio, a brief summary should accompany it explaining the significance of the results. Does the child, for example, show good use of self-correction strategies using visual and phonic cues? Does he or she use cues from the general context of the passage? How did the results inform the teacher's planning?

Symbols for marking miscues on photocopy of text read aloud by children

Omission	Circle the word/part of word which the child has missed out.
	e.g. 'Clara and Cliff(ord)get on very well'.
Substitution	Write in word/part of word child has substituted above appropriate part
	of the text.
	mustard
	e.g. 'and mushy peas'.
Insertion	Write added word above a caret ∧
	e.g. 'Clara Cliff takes ∧ Clifford Climber'. (*a* above caret)
Reversal Use	transpositional symbol
	e.g. 'Cats', Clara says.
Repetition	Draw a line from left to right under the portion of text repeated.
	e.g. 'Yum yum!' says Clifford.
Hesitation	Place an oblique stroke over or next to word or phrase over which child hesitates.
	e,g, ' /lawful wedded husband'.
Self correction	Write SC over word or phrase child self corrects
	e.g. 'Fish and chips'. (Child said 'first and chips' and then quickly self- (SC above Fish)
	corrected to 'fish and chips').
Assistance	Write 'T' above a word or phrase supplied by teacher.

(Examples are from six-year-old Charlie's reading of Alan Ahlberg's 'Ms Cliff the Climber'.)

Figure 13

```
Diagram to summarise miscues

Name and age:
Date:
Book details:
```

Miscue types	Symbol	Number	Comment
Omission	⬭		
Substitution	*write word*		
Insertion	∧		
Reversal	⤵		
Repetition	___		
Hesitation	/		
Self correction	SC		
Assistance	T		

Figure 14

Arnold, Helen (1982) *Listening to Children Reading* Sevenoaks: Hodder & Stoughton.

Campbell, Robin (2007, second edition) *Miscue Analysis in the Classroom* UKLA minibook.

Goodman, Kenneth (1973) 'Miscues: windows on the reading process' in Gollasch, F. (ed.) *Language and Literacy: The Selected Writings of Kenneth Goodman* Boston, Mass.: Routledge & Kegan Paul: 93–102 (Vol 1).

Graham, Judith and Kelly, Alison (2007, third edition) *Reading Under Control* London: David Fulton.

MNEMONICS

A mnemonic is a word, phrase or rhyme which helps you remember something. In spelling, for example, you might use the mnemonic – 'i' before 'e' except after 'c'; or an 'e' for envelope after the 'n' of 'stationery'.

MODAL VERB

See also: auxiliary verb, infinitive, parts of speech

A modal verb is a sub-category of the auxiliary verb class. See the list below:

can/could
will/would
must/ought
may/might
shall/should

Modal verbs are used to indicate prediction (Roger *will* be in Rome soon), speculation (I *may* decide to go out) and necessity (You *must* leave now). In these examples the modal verbs are 'will', 'may' and 'must', and the infinitives that follow each of them are 'be', 'decide' and 'leave'.

MODE

See also: register

Mode is part of the abstract linguistic concept known as 'register' and refers both to the pattern of the text and to the medium in which a spoken or written message is given. Patterns in a text are achieved by combinations of grammar and vocabulary – for example a story has a temporal pattern while a science text may have a cause and effect pattern instead of, or as well as, a sequence of events. Understanding the different text patterns helps children appreciate the purpose of a particular text. The medium for a written text might be a whiteboard, a print or electronic work sheet or a book.

MODELLING (OF LANGUAGE PROCESSES)

See also: reading, speaking and listening, writing

'Modelling' is a term used to describe the demonstration of a skill or means of going about something. It is often used in shared reading to show children how to understand and apply the cueing systems which help us to read and how to use skimming and scanning strategies in non-fiction reading. Enlarged texts are often used for this purpose. In shared writing, teachers demonstrate or 'model' how to plan, write and edit written texts, how to apply spelling strategies and how to proof read. When carried out well, it is in the spirit of Vygotsky's notion of the 'zone of proximal development' where the adult can, by the right kind of intervention, move young learners on further than they would manage alone. It is also compatible with Bruner's proposal that we 'scaffold' children's learning.

MODELS OF ENGLISH TEACHING

See: history of English teaching

MODELS OF LANGUAGE

See: communicative competence/competence and performance, functions of language, language acquisition, language and thought, nativist approach to language acquisition, transformational grammar

MOOD

In traditional English grammar there are three 'moods', expressed in clauses and sentences, which affect the meaning:

- the indicative mood which includes statements and questions as in 'He liked her' and 'He liked her?'
- the imperative mood expresses commands, requests, warnings or offers as in 'Sit down!', 'Please sit down', 'Look out!' and 'Have some more'.
- the subjunctive mood which expresses attitudes and wishes as in 'She preferred that it was not mentioned' or 'I wish my mother could have been here'.

MORPHEME

See also: reading

A morpheme is the smallest unit of meaning. A word might be one morpheme as in 'hand' or contain two or more morphemes as in 'handshake', 'handstands'. Prefixes (un, dis, in) and suffixes (ed, al, s) which can be added to change a word's meaning are morphemes.

MORPHOLOGY

This is a linguistic term referring to the structure of words, in contrast to 'syntax' which is the study of the order of words in the larger units of phrase, clause and sentence. The two kinds of morphology are: inflectional morphology which attends to how parts of speech are changed to indicate number, tense and so on, and lexical morphology which is the study of word-formation.

MOTHER TONGUE

See also: bilingualism, multilingualism

This usually refers to the language of a person's childhood home. Young emergent bilingual children need to go on developing their competence as speakers, readers and writers in their mother tongue while taking on their new language. If they do not, then they cease to be 'emergently bilingual' in a meaningful way. Researchers, like Mayor (1988), have linked children's intellectual development to their continuing progress in their home language. This progress may be sustained at home or at community schools at the weekend. However, home languages can still be respected and acknowledged in school – made visible in environmental print and in dual-language big books, CD-ROMs and bilingual books. Tapes of books or songs in children's home or mother tongue languages are also a useful resource whether they are commercial or made by parents or older children. Of huge help and inspiration is the Centre for Language in Primary Education Multilingual Book Collection which has a display of books in languages of different linguistic and cultural groups as well as many dual-language books. Main publishers include Milet and Mantra Lingua. Interestingly, recent research suggests that all children, not just emergent bilinguals, benefit from initiatives that value children's home languages (Thomas and Collier, 1998; Bialystok, 2001; Whitehead, 2010). Further reading would usefully include Ellen Bialystok's book *Bilingualism in Development: Language, Literacy and Cognition* which surveys research and values 'the story young bilinguals can tell us about human cognition and development' (Bialystok, 2001: xii). The analysis concludes, for example, that knowing more than one language accelerates the young learner's ability to concentrate on relevant information. Early years specialists and others will find much of value in Marian Whitehead's fourth edition of her book *Language and Literacy in the Early Years 0–7* in which she gives case studies of young children in early years settings, including those whose first language is not English.

Bialystok, Ellen (2001) *Bilingualism in Development: Language, Literacy and Cognition* Cambridge: Cambridge University Press.

Centre for Language in Primary Education: Multilingual Book Collection, for information see www.clpe.co.uk/library/multilingual-book-collection

Mayor, B. (1988) 'What does it mean to be bilingual?' in Mercer, N. (ed.) *Language and Literacy from an Educational Perspective Vol. 1* Milton Keynes: Open University Press (a classic collection, but O/P at present).

Thomas, W.P. and Collier, V.P. (1998) 'Two languages are better than one' *Educational Leadership*, 55: 23–6.

Whitehead, Marian (2010, fourth edition) *Language and Literacy in the Early Years, 0–7* London: Sage Publications.

MOTIVATION

See also: 'big shapes', book making, collaborative learning, constructivism, English/Literacy Co-ordinator, reading corner/area, shared writing, writing corner/area

'Motivation' is a psychological term to do with a person having the feeling that they want to do or achieve something, usually because they have a purpose or a need for doing so.

Speaking of curriculum reform, Wyse and Jones comment that if higher standards are to be achieved, it is essential to fully involve those who are going to be most affected by the changes, namely the children (Wyse and Jones, 2007).

There is a lot to cover in a modern primary English programme, including challenging work in gaining phonemic awareness in learning to read and understanding letter strings to improve spelling. These aspects are important, but if they are over-emphasised we risk a narrow view of the English curriculum and lessons that do not fully involve and interest young learners. The necessary language skills or 'smaller shapes' are best set in the framework of wider intentions and purposes, sometimes called the 'big shapes'. Let us take the 'big shape' of helping children understand how stories work as tellers, readers and writers. There is everything to be gained from making sure the classroom is an encouraging environment by having displays of books and children's work. Experienced teachers also know that children's enjoyment of learning is increased by sharing and collaborating with their peers. Speaking and listening and particularly talking about texts is a powerful context for language development. Here works like Aidan Chambers' *Tell Me* show convincing examples of children extending their understanding of stories through talk with both peers and adults. Improvisation and role play also contribute to the enthusiasm that children bring to their writing, especially where the context is meaningful for them. Shared reading provides the opportunity for the teacher to read stories in a way that will involve and excite the children. Retellings and discussion of the features of the stories and poems they are reading and later reading their own stories out loud help make work satisfying. Improvisation and language games are likely to enthuse children. When it comes to writing, we know that the 'process' approach of Donald Graves ensured high levels of motivation as children had some choice over what they wrote about and how they wrote it (Graves, 1983). If rich experiences precede children's writing, they are much more likely to have the will to write as well as they can, and to attend to the secretarial aspects that ensure their stories can be understood and enjoyed by others.

Teachers also need to feel interested and involved in their work and too much change and prescription can put their motivation at risk. Curriculum reformers need to involve them and consult them. It is the English/Literacy Co-ordinator who can make the difference when it comes to teachers feeling part of a well-motivated team who are dedicated to supporting children's enjoyment of the process of

becoming eager readers, writers and speakers.

Chambers, Aidan (1993) *Tell Me: Children Reading and Talk* Stroud: The Thimble Press.
Graves, Donald (1983) *Writing: Teachers and Children at Work* Portsmouth, NH: Heinemann Educational Books.
Wyse, Dominic and Jones, Russell (2007, second edition) *Teaching English: Language and Literacy* London: Routledge.

MOVING IMAGES AND LITERACY

See: television and literacy, video-film and DVDs, visual literacy

MULTICULTURALISM (OR CULTURAL PLURALISM)

See also: bilingualism, carnival, dual-language texts, equal opportunities, mother tongue, multilingualism, traditional tales

The term 'multiculturalism' can simply mean the co-existence of several different cultures in one place but it usually has a political connotation. It can be used to refer to a sociopolitical ideal which encourages cultural freedom and the development of different cultures in a plural society.

The term 'multicultural school' usually means a school which recognises in its curriculum and social policy making the diversity of cultures represented in its intake. This implies more than a few token gestures towards festivals across the world (although this might be part of it), and has to do first of all with attitudes, priorities and a belief that all the children and staff will benefit from strong links and activities involving the different communities. Themes like journeys, ourselves and traditional tales can have multicultural dimensions which can be explored. Schools following a multicultural approach, in

287

more than a superficial way, make parents and friends of the school welcome and value their contributions – perhaps in making dual-language versions of books and advising on customs like tea ceremonies. The 'carnival' entry shows the cultural sharing that is encouraged in this kind of initiative.

As well as these positive attitudes, a school wishing to take account of multicultural values will put much thought into the range of resources provided; the English/Literacy Co-ordinator nearly always has a key role to play. We want resources – both fiction and non-fiction – which reflect the different parts of the world where the children have their roots. However, all the children in the school deserve the very best texts from across the world. One of the most helpful guides to multicultural books was *A Multicultural Guide to Children's Books 0–12* edited by Rosemary Stones, sadly at present out of print. This work was helpfully annotated giving critical evaluations of the materials, including dual-language texts (which vary in quality of translation) and included interviews with the different authors. Many look forward to a new edition of this book or the publication of a new one with up-to-date lists of resources. Meanwhile, we can draw inspiration from the Multilingual Book Collection at the Centre for Language in Primary Education. This exhibition has books, many published by Milet and Mantra Lingua, in the languages of different linguistic and cultural communities as well as many dual-language books. For more information about the collection see library.clpe.co.uk/multilingual-book-collection.

Listening to, reading and telling stories from across the world crosses cultural boundaries and reinforces the value of a multicultural approach (see for example Gregory, 2008; MacLean, 1996). Shereen Pandit writes about initiatives to encourage the publishing of work by ethnic minority writers and illustrators in *Books for Keeps* (Pandit, 2006).

Societal attitudes are dynamic – always changing and reforming – and the whole notion of 'multiculturalism' was reconsidered in The Runnymede Trust's Commission – 'The Future of Multi-Ethnic Britain'. It was set up by Trevor Phillips the then Chairman of the Trust and now the Chairman of the Commission for Racial Equality (CRE). The report for the Trust reinforced the belief that Black and South Asian Britons should be treated no differently from their peers. However, it put less emphasis on 'difference' and more on a search to establish a core of 'shared values' to unite Britons whatever their roots. All of us have a number of identities that are important in how we see ourselves and we draw on all this in the best English work. The complexity of culture and identity is sensitively discussed in Chris Kearney's book *The Monkey's Mask* based on interviews with successful young Britons from countries and cultures other than the British mainstream. In her book *Hidden Worlds* Clare Kelly shows, through six interesting case studies of young children from different communities and attending the same nursery, how children draw on home experience and adult support to make a link with the new world of literacy (Kelly, 2010). I believe a school can foster 'shared values' and, at the same time, take account of children's origins and backgrounds, drawing on the culture and literature of all those nations which contribute positively to our communities.

Gregory, Eve (2008, second edition) *Learning to Read in a New Language: Making Sense of Words and Worlds* London: Paul Chapman, Sage.

Hallford, Deborah, Zaghini, Edgardo and Blake, Quentin (illustrator) (2005) *Folk and Fairy Tales*, a book guide, London: Booktrust.

Kearney, Chris (2001) *The Monkey's Mask: Identity, Memory, Narrative and Voice* London: Trentham Books.

Kelly, Clare (2010) *Hidden Worlds: Young Children Learning Literacy in Multicultural Contexts* London: Trentham Books.

MacLean, K. (1996) 'Supporting the literacy of bilingual learners: storytelling and bookmaking' *Multicultural Teaching*, 2: 26–9.

Pandit, S. (2006) 'Diversity matters' *Books for Keeps*, 160, September.

MULTI-LAYERED TEXTS

See: picture book

MULTILINGUALISM

See also: bilingualism, dual-language texts, equal opportunities, language variety, mother tongue, multiculturalism

If a person is described as being 'multilingual' it usually means they control three or more languages. The degree of competence required in each language to qualify for the description is more controversial; it ranges from high competence to enough knowledge to meet particular purposes. In countries like India it would be unusual to be unilingual (or monolingual), but individuals may have different degrees of knowledge and understanding in each language. They might, for example, use one language in the home and another at work, another spoken but not written and another just read.

In the school context we have many children in British schools who control, to some degree, three or more languages and therefore are likely to have considerable linguistic ability on which the teacher can build. While their parents will want them to become confident in English as speakers and as readers and writers, they may also want them to develop in their own first languages as well.

Wyse and Jones (2007) remind us that multilingual children are not a homogenous group. Some children will be newcomers while others will have been born in this country and be second or third generation. Communities differ in how far they want their children to embrace British language and customs and how far they wish them to maintain their cultural identity within their new 'host' community.

There are suggestions for good practice in supporting young bilingual children in taking on their new language and culture under the 'bilingualism' entry.

Wyse, Dominic and Jones, Russell (2007, second edition) 'Supporting black and multilingual children' in *Teaching English, Language and Literacy* London: Routledge.

MULTIMEDIA

See: advertisements, CD-ROM, Information and Communications Technology (ICT) and English, television and literacy, video-film and DVDs, visual literacy

MULTIMEDIA TEXTS

See also: British Film Institute, CD-ROM, film making, Information and Communications Technology (ICT) and English, interactive whiteboard, internet, reading on screen, schools' television programmes, television and literacy, television programmes for children

Multimedia texts combine a number of media including electronic elements such as sound, music and animation. Children grow up in a multimedia world and these texts create a link between literacy experiences in the 'real' world and at school (Bazalgette, 2010). Reading multimedia texts requires the young learner to listen and look as well as to read and so they encourage active and interactive kinds of learning. There is a danger of too much stimulating, and often noisy, input and too many links to operate, disorganising the reading process so other more traditional kinds of reading should continue to be encouraged. Of course much of children's experience of multimedia texts is to do with watching television programmes and films (see entries under these headings).

When it comes to children creating multimedia text on screen – short films, interactive books and presentations – such work often leads to much thought and collaborative planning. Teachers find that reluctant readers and writers, particularly boys, find new interest and point in literacy work when working with multimedia or ICT texts (Safford *et al.*, 2004; Warrington and Younger, 2006).

The interactive whiteboard with its potential for using media of different kinds has become a well-used teaching tool in many classrooms, but sometimes a book or flip chart can serve a purpose just as well as an on-screen text.

There are examples of teachers and children working with multimedia and digital texts in every lesson in the journal *NATE Classroom* (National Association of English Teaching) and in the Primary School journal of the English Association *English 4–11*. Here is an example of a project which generated much valuable collaborative talk and writing and considerable discussion about how sound and music might be used. Lindsey Apps of Hindsford Primary School describes how seven year olds, working with Sharon Swanton, made a film about electricity. They researched the possible dangers under three headings: electricity in the kitchen, outside substations or near pylons, and then scripted and filmed each section. The editing team linked the different sections together with music, transition and titles. Part of the soundtrack consisted of a chorus created by the children which they referred to as a 'rap'. It began:

'Keep safe in the kitchen,
When you use the cooker,
Remember it gets very hot!
Follow our advice and keep safe.
Follow our advice and keep safe'.

(Apps, 2007)

Apps, L. (2007) 'Making movies – stretching creativity in the under 11s' *English 4–11* 29, Spring.

Bazalgette, Cary (2010) *Teaching Media in the Primary School* London: Sage.

Safford, Kimberly, O'Sullivan, Olivia and Barrs, Myra (2004) *Boys on the Margin: Promoting Boys' Literacy at Key Stage 2* London: CLPE.

SLA, the journal of the School Librarian Association, appraises multimedia texts for children, as well as traditional print books and materials, see also their website: www.sla.org.uk.

Warrington, Molly and Younger, Mike, with Bearne, Eve (2006) *Raising Boys' Achievement in Primary Schools: Towards a Holistic Approach* Milton Keynes: The Open University.

MULTIMODAL TEXTS

See also: comics, illustrations: finding a vocabulary, visual literacy

Multimodal texts combine a number of different modes of communication. Paper multimodal texts combine writing, design and images while electronic multimodal texts may also include speech and music. At one time a text was thought of as something written down in a book or newspaper. The definition has widened to take in a conversation, a television advertisement, a photograph in a magazine, a text message or tweet (Evans, 2004). Children's experience of texts will continue to change as the wider social context changes. These changes in how we conceive of texts and literacy need to be reflected in the classroom (Bearne and Wolstencroft, 2007). There are a number of research studies into multimodality and how it can enrich lessons. A series of reports based on research by the United Kingdom Literacy Association have contributed considerably to our understanding of the range and worth of these texts. *More Than Words 1* and *More Than Words 2* explore the variety and value of children's multimodal texts with interesting examples and case studies. These publications show that children's multimodal texts may be informational or may create a story. Often they use devices like those found in a cartoon strip, for example picture series and speech bubbles. There are a number of children's authors who use multimodal text in their books. The modern picture book is often a small masterpiece of design. Mick Manning and Brita Granström show great inventiveness in creating their non-fiction texts for children, using illustrations and writing in interesting ways. For example, in their book *Charles Dickens: Scenes from an Extraordinary Life*, each page is rich with illustrations from landscapes to tiny vignettes and the writing differs in style and orientation to keep young readers interested. Marcia Williams' cartoon-style books retelling myths and legends are also multimodal: see, for example, how she designs the pages using size and orientation in print and pictures to tell the stories in *King Arthur and the Knights of the Round Table*.

Reading on Screen considers on-screen reading in different curriculum areas and indicates how assessment schemes can be applied to reading multimodal texts (Bearne *et al.*, 2007). In a very interesting journal paper entitled 'Multimodality, literacy and texts: developing a discourse', Eve Bearne clarifies recent thinking and research and provides a number of powerful examples of children's multimodal writing. Just as for all other texts, those multimodal texts children read and those they make themselves need to be critically appraised. Teachers are working towards embedding visual and interactive texts in the literacy programme. Exciting outcomes are possible when children are encouraged to work with combinations of different kinds of communication.

Bearne, Eve (2009) 'Multimodality, literacy and texts: developing a discourse' in *Journal of Early Childhood Literacy* London: Sage August 2009, Vol. 9, No. 2, pp. 156–187.

Bearne, E. *et al.* (2004) *More Than Words 1: Multimodal Texts in the Classroom* QCA/UKLA (concentrates on non-fiction).

——(2005) *More Than Words 2: Creating Stories on Page and Screen* QCA/UKLA (concentrates on stories and narrative).

Bearne, E., Johnson, A., Manford, P., Mottram, M., and Wolstencroft, H. (2007) *Reading on Screen* Leicester: UKLA.

Bearne, E. and Wolstencroft, H. (2007) *Visual Approaches to Teaching Writing: Multimodal Literacy 5–11* London: Paul Chapman (includes a CD of examples of children's multimodal work).

Evans, J. (2004) *Literacy Moves On: Using Popular Culture, New Technologies and Critical Literacy in the Primary Classroom* London: David Fulton.

The following organisations publish articles in their journals about using multimodal texts in the classroom and list publications on their websites:

The English Association (EA): www.le.ac.uk/engassoc

United Kingdom Literacy Association (UKLA): www.ukla.org

National Association of English Teaching (NATE): www.nate.org.uk

MULTIPLE LITERACIES

See also: CD-ROM, CD, Information and Communications Technology (ICT) and English, interactive whiteboards, internet, multimodal texts, video-film and DVDs, visual literacy

This has become part of the vocabulary we use to refer to the increasing range of media children encounter on the journey towards literacy. British children often have experience of computer use and the internet before they come to school.

At school they will use and make both ebooks and print books. Their multimedia presentations often integrate video-film and digital photographs and children's own pictures and their speech and writing can be included in exciting ways.

The continuing emergence of new ways of communicating changes our understanding of what literacy is or can become. Control over multiple literacies changes the way we conceive of the world and what we can achieve in it. As we might expect, we find increasing use of mobile phones, tweeting and text messaging in children's conversation, role play and improvised drama.

MULTI-SENSORY APPROACHES

Multi-sensory approaches to reading use all the senses – touch, hearing, movement and sight – to help young children to recognise letters of the alphabet. They can make the letter shapes in sand, feel textured letters or find the right letter in a bag of wooden or plastic letters. The feel of different kinds of cloth and paper can be exploited in the interactive alphabet books teachers and children make.

Hearing as well as seeing 'onsets' and 'rimes' reinforces the patterns and when it comes to writing, the actual handwriting movement can help children memorise spelling patterns.

Multisensory approaches are particularly helpful when teaching children with specific language disabilities.

MUSEUMS AND ENGLISH

See also: art and English, British Library

Museums – with their exciting displays of objects, costumes and paintings – are a major source of inspiration for children's talking, thinking, reading, writing and drawing. Most cities and large towns in the UK have their share of galleries and museums for schools nearby to choose from and good websites to help plan and focus a school visit, but if the museums with the items you want to see are too far away, children can view them on websites. The Tyne and Wear Museums website (www.twmuseums.org.uk) shows interesting objects and paintings from all their museums. Nothing is quite like a real visit or outing of course, and this group of museums cater particularly for the needs and interests of the early years age group. Another excellent site is the kids' section of the twenty-four-hour museum site: www.show.me.uk. It is easy to use, visually alive and essentially interactive. For example, children are invited to play a game from Roman times, design their own mosaic and to send in their own writing about journeys they have made. On this site, museums are shown to be alive to new finds and new ideas; for example you can see beautifully clear photographs of a Roman mural – illustrating a bunch of grapes that look fresh off the vine – just discovered in the centre of London.

Quality electronic resources have opened up the world of museums for people of all ages, but print books also have a part to play in showing what museums can offer. *The Museum Book* by Jan Mark for children from about eight years old is packed with pictures and photographs, but has a well-written text as well. Many children, however, would need some help from teacher or parent to sustain concentration. It raises interesting issues – the debate about the right location for the Elgin Marbles, for instance – to inspire the sort of discussions and persuasive kinds of talking and writing appropriate for older primary children. Tony Martin includes a valuable chapter on working with museums and galleries to encourage children's creative work (Martin *et al.*, 2008).

Martin, Tony, Loval, Chira and Purnell, Glynis (2008) *The Really Useful Literacy Book* London: Routledge.

MUSIC AND ENGLISH

See: physical education, music and dance and English

MYTHS

See also: creation stories, traditional tales

Myths are culturally significant traditional stories about gods and heroes and the best illuminate problems of human existence (Saxby, 2004). One important category of myth is the creation story which attempts, within a particular cultural setting, to explain how the world began.

The imaginative power of many of the retellings and the possibilities for art, drama, writing and discussion make them a strong part of the English programme. Because their origins are often in the oral tradition they can be modified and adapted for different audiences and purposes. For a delightful tale seeking to explain why different animal species are unable to live together see Francesca Martin's *The Honey Hunters: a Traditional African Tale* (Walker Books). If you want a collection for younger primary children or older children less forward with their reading, you might consider using *Zeus Conquers the Titans and Other Greek Myths* by Geraldine McCaughrean and illustrated by Tony Ross (Orchard). The Orchard First Myth series has stories told with drama and pace with appealing illustrations of people in traditional Greek dress, but with a modern touch. Marcia Williams' *Greek Myths* (Walker Books) presents the stories of Orpheus, Perseus and other Greek figures in amusing cartoon format. Teachers find

these a lively starting point for children's drama, storytelling and art work. A good classroom collection would need myths from a range of cultures represented. *Indian Myths* by Shahrukh Husain and illustrated by Bee Willey would suit five to eight year olds. *Tales From the Norse Legends* by Edward Ferrie is in CD as well as in print form. The double audio CD brings humour and excitement to the tales partly by using Gustav Mahler's atmospheric music, which appeals to young imaginations. Benjamin Soames uses different voices to add to the drama of the tellings.

Myths often have quite complicated narrative structures and many collections of retellings are most suitable for older primary school children. Even then, they are often best read out loud and shared. Examples include the story based on a Zulu myth retold by Margaret Wolfson and entitled *Marriage of the Rain Goddess: a South African myth* (Barefoot Books) and *Ishtar and Tammuz: a Babylonian*

Figure 15 Cover illustration © 1991, 2006 Marcia Williams. From *Greek Myths* retold and illustrated by Marcia Williams. Reproduced by permission of Walker Books Ltd, London SE11 5HJ.

293

myth of the seasons by Christopher Moore (Frances Lincoln) which explains the rhythm of the seasons. The Belitha Press collections of myths and legends include stories from Africa, China, South America and Celtic tales. Each collection has an introduction putting the tales in a helpful context. There are further annotated booklists in Phinn (2000: 29–32) and in Mallett (2010: 55–8).

Mallett, Margaret (2010) *Choosing and Using Fiction and Non-fiction 3–11* London: Routledge.

Phinn, Gervase (2000) *Young Readers and their Books* London: David Fulton.

Saxby, M. (2004, second edition) 'Myth and legend' in Hunt, P. (ed.) *International Companion Encyclopedia of Children's Literature, Volume I* London: Routledge.

N

NARRATIVE

See also: fiction: choosing and using, genre, history and English, novels, short stories, storytelling, text-level work, writing

A narrative usually tells of events using the past tense. When the events come from the imagination we tend to call the narrative 'a story', but of course even when we tell of real incidents, about our recent holiday to friends perhaps, we often reshape what happened to add interest! The recognition that narrative is a basic way of organising human experience through remembering, dreaming and planning is made in Barbara Hardy's 'Narrative as a primary act of mind' (Hardy, 1977). Since, as Hardy reminds us, our very lives unfold through time, it is not surprising that children respond with interest to the narration of stories, told and read, from an early age. Stories tell us about human behaviour, about how people respond to events and challenges. The drive of the narrative makes us want to hear or read more and this is why stories have had such an important role in learning to read and write. The shape of a story, sometimes called a 'story grammar', includes an introduction to the setting and characters, a middle section of events and challenges and finally a resolution. This basic pattern becomes familiar and helps children use the semantic or contextual cueing system.

Stories, whether read independently or in shared contexts, are above all a source of enjoyment. Angela Wilson and Julie Scanlon refer to the pleasure that children gain from making sense of a text (Wilson and Scanlon, 2011). There is, however, a balance to maintain between enjoying a story and analysing it. Wray and Medwell suggest a structure for analysing narratives like the fairy tale *Little Red Riding Hood* showing some of the elements necessary to give the story cohesion (Wray and Medwell, 2007). We have to be careful about assuming that any particular narrative structure can be universally applied. I recommend Nikki Gamble and Sally Yates' book *Exploring Children's Literature* for a clear and interesting account of narrative structure and its implications for character, setting and theme (Gamble and Yates, 2008).

The use of flashbacks and alternative tellings of familiar stories make classification problematic. It is also true that there are a number of ways of analysing texts. We might wish to examine the emotional impact of how the characters in the story respond to events and dilemmas. Or, as Wyse and Jones (2007) suggest, we may consider the social aspects of a story.

When it comes to children's writing they will certainly draw on the stories they have heard and read as well as on what they see on television and video-film and events in their own lives (Barrs and Cork, 2001), but there is an issue about expecting young children to conform to mature forms in their writing.

Barrs, Myra and Cork, Valerie (2001) *The Reader in the Writer* London: CLPE.

Gamble, Nikki and Yates, Sally (2008, second edition) *Exploring Children's Literature* London: Sage (see Chapters 3 and 4 on narrative).

Hardy, Barbara (1977) 'Narrative as a primary act of mind' in Meek, Margaret, Warlow, Aidan and Barton, Griselda (eds) *The Cool Web: The Patterns of Children's Reading* London: The Bodley Head.

Wilson, Angela and Scanlon, Julie (2011, fourth edition) *Language Knowledge for Primary Teachers* London: David Fulton.

Wray, David and Medwell, Jane (2007) *QTS English for Primary Teachers* London: Letts.

Wyse, Dominic and Jones, Russell (2007, edition) *Teaching English, Language and Literacy* London: Routledge-Falmer.

NARRATIVE NON-FICTION

See: autobiography, biography, chronological non-fiction, history and English, information stories, procedural or instructional genre

NATIONAL ASSOCIATION FOR THE TEACHING OF ENGLISH (NATE)

NATE is the association for those concerned with the teaching of all aspects of English, from preschool to university in the United Kingdom. As a member of the International Federation of the Teachers of English it both shares the experience of UK teachers and learns from teachers across the world. It aims to keep its members (about 5,000 in number) informed about new initiatives, and to provide them with a national voice. The association conducts research and welcomes involvement in curriculum development. It supports good practice in teaching and learning English through its annual conference, its journal *English in Education*, its newsletter and its many books and professional development materials.

Among its committees are two covering or overlapping with the primary years: The Primary Committee and the 9–14 Committee.

NATE: www.nate.org.uk

NATIONAL CENTRE FOR LANGUAGE AND LITERACY

Formerly called the Reading University Language and Information Centre, this research and teaching centre:

- Has a resource collection of 15,000 children's books in print, video-films, DVDs, cassettes, educational software and professional books and journals for teachers.
- Provides courses for teachers on all aspects of language and literacy.
- Carries out research on all aspects of language and literacy – initiatives include 'Literacy Learning in Chinese and Sikh communities', 'Multilingual word processing' and 'Interdisciplinary Perspectives on African Language Materials'.
- Produces fine publications for teachers, student teachers and parents about every aspect of English, language and literacy, including on speaking and listening, reading and writing, ICT and multicultural approaches.

National Centre for Language and Literacy: www.ncll.org.uk

NATIONAL CURRICULUM (THE)

See also: assessment, interactive whiteboard, literacy hour, Primary National Strategy, SATs

The case for a National Curriculum is that it tries to ensure that every child, whatever their social or ethnic origin, has the right to a certain standard of education. However, we must avoid making such a curriculum too complicated and labour intensive. Lessons were learnt about this and assessment, for example, has been simplified from the burdensome early requirements of UK versions of a National Curriculum.

Since a UK National Curriculum was first put in place in 1988 there have been several revisions, and in the nature of things, there will be changes in the future.

The National Curriculum until 2012

The National Curriculum (DfEE/QCA, 1999) for English, like the other Primary Curriculum subjects, sets out 'Programmes of Study' stipulating what must be taught, and then 'Attainment Targets' which describe levels of achievement.

English at both Key Stage 1 (five to seven years) and Key Stage 2 (seven to eleven years) is divided into En 1 Speaking and Listening, En 2 Reading and En 3 Writing. Each of these three elements is discussed under 'knowledge, skills and understanding' and 'breadth of study'. The 'breadth of study' paragraphs indicate the range of activities, contexts and purposes through which the knowledge, skills and understanding should be taught.

There follow some observations and comments:

- Although the language processes are dealt with separately it is made clear that speaking and listening, reading and writing should be integrated.
- Notes in the margin link the programmes with the early learning goals.
- Collaborative work is encouraged in En 1, and listening – often the neglected language process – is given consideration.

- Drama is given a welcome place in En 1. Many early years teachers would like more recognition of the value of play.
- Children are taught a range of strategies to learn to read but the phonological cue-system is emphasised for beginning readers.
- It is implicit that language development is partly to do with controlling a large number of genres. Non-fiction reading and writing is fully recognised as well as the full range of fiction, and both print and ICT forms of information texts are included.
- Children are to be taught about language variation, for example how language varies according to context and purpose and how talk and writing differ in form.
- Children must be taught about the structure of language and by Key Stage 2 (En 3) challenging concepts about grammar must be acquired.
- Children must acquire standard English forms in speaking and writing.
- There is recognition that the form of writing relates to the purpose and the audience.
- Teachers must help children plan and draft their writing. The SATs, however, require first draft accounts.
- Systematic teaching of spelling, punctuation and handwriting is required.

The National Curriculum from 2012/13

The 1999 National Curriculum has been reviewed and revised. During the consultation period respondents were encouraged to make clear what they felt was good about the previous orders as well as making suggestions for improvements. The curriculum will continue to be mainly subject centred and the phonic approach will be at the centre of the initial teaching of reading.

The latest requirements are available at www.education.gov.uk. Appraisal of the new curriculum as it effects the teaching of English, language and literacy is available on a number of websites, including those of the United Kingdom Literacy Association (UKLA): www.ukla.org and The English Association (EA): www.le.ac.uk/engassoc/

NATIONAL CURRICULUM FOR INITIAL TEACHER TRAINING

See: subject knowledge

NATIONAL LITERACY STRATEGY

See: literacy hour

NATIONAL ORACY PROJECT

This project was established in 1987 by the School Curriculum Development Committee and later administered by the National Curriculum Council.

Over the four years of its development many teachers in England and Wales were involved in establishing its priorities and direction. The work of the project and the belief in the centrality of talk in learning is explained and celebrated in *Thinking Voices* (Norman, 1992). The aims included:

- to enhance the role of speech in the learning process from age five to age sixteen by encouraging active learning;
- to develop methods of assessment through speech; and
- to promote recognition of the value of oral work in schools.

Norman, Kate (ed.) (1992) *Thinking Voices: The Work of the National Oracy Project* London: Hodder & Stoughton.

NATIONAL WRITING PROJECT

The National Writing Project (1985–89) involved many teachers across the country and brought to a practical level the notion of writing for different purposes and different audiences. One outcome was *Learning about Writing* by P. Czerniewska, director of the project. There was interest in writing across the curriculum as well as writing narratives and poems in English.

One of the strategies developed during the project was the idea of children acting as 'response partners' for each other's writing. The children usually needed some briefing from the teacher on how to comment on content and on spelling and punctuation in a constructive way. In *Responding to and Assessing Writing* (National Writing Project, 1989b) there is a case study of two very young children – Reception age – helping each other in this way.

Czerniewska, Pam (1992) *Learning about Writing* Oxford: Blackwell.
National Writing Project (1989a) *Becoming a Writer* Walton on Thames: Thomas Nelson.
——(1989b) *Responding to and Assessing Writing* Walton on Thames: Thomas Nelson.

NATIVIST APPROACH TO LANGUAGE ACQUISITION

See also: language acquisition, transformational grammar

Those taking a nativist approach to language acquisition argue that human beings are programmed to learn language as long as they have a speech community in which to use and learn their mother tongue. One of the most renowned linguists taking this view is Noam Chomsky. He found unconvincing the behaviourist position of language acquisition – that children respond to stimuli in the environment and learn chiefly by stimulus responses and imitation (Chomsky, 1957). This seemed not to fit with observations of children's creative early utterances which suggested they were actively trying to make sense of the rules of the speech system. For example, as Marian

Whitehead shows, children over-generalise, so that 'The mans are walking up the street' is a generalisation of how we usually make plurals. A child saying this is not imitating adult speech but actively trying to make rules which he or she will modify in the light of experience.

Chomsky's notion of an LAD, or Language Acquisition Device, was an internal capacity of the infant to process the language he or she hears and to generate their own meaningful utterance.

But the theory seems to underestimate the power of the social context and human interaction in making a child a communicator (Donaldson, 1978; Whitehead, 2010).

Chomsky, Noam (1957) *Syntactic Structures* Mouton: The Hague.

Donaldson, Margaret (1978) *Children's Minds* London: Fontana.

Whitehead, Marian R. (2010, fourth edition) *Language and Literacy in the Early Years* London: Paul Chapman (see Chapter 3, 'Psycholinguistics').

NEALE'S ANALYSIS OF READING

See also: assessment, reading age, Standardised Reading Tests

This is a standardised reading test used widely by teachers, psychologists and researchers in the United Kingdom. First standardised and printed in 1958, the story content and the format was updated in 1988. The test is individually administered and assesses reading ages from six to thirteen years. Advantages of this test include the presentation of words, not just in a list as in, for example, the Schonell test, but as part of a supportive context, and its appealing presentation with illustrations as well as prose text. The writers of the most recent manual show a broader notion of reading and point out that no test can sample all the components of the reading process. The revised test is based on a miscue analysis approach but rather than using it diagnostically a summative measure of the child's accuracy, comprehension and reading rate is provided. There have been some criticisms of the standardisation of the test but it remains popular for administering to very young readers as there are few other suitable individual tests available. In research where children are only to be compared with each other, as in Riley's case studies of children's progress during the first year of school, standardisation issues are of less importance (Riley, 1996: 104; Riley, 2006: 76).

Neale Analysis of Reading: Information and latest revisions about this test can be found at: www.gl-assessment.co.uk

Riley, Jeni (1996) *The Teaching of Reading: The Development of Literacy in the Early Years of School* London: Paul Chapman.

——(2006) *Language and Literacy 3–7: Creative Approaches to Teaching* London: Sage.

NEWS (WRITING OF)

See: diary

NEWSPAPERS AND MAGAZINES

See also: advertisements, literacy hour, persuasive genre, visual literacy

Newspapers are a useful resource for English and for lessons across the curriculum, and amongst other things can be used to help children make distinctions between fact and opinion. Of course, media texts in general need to be read critically. Carolyn Swain lists the magazines available for the primary age range and offers practical guidance on how they can be used in the classroom. She explores visual as well as verbal aspects of magazines and suggests we recognise some magazines as multimodal texts (Swain, 2010). Critical reading of both newspapers and magazines is helped if children learn to control a vocabulary to talk about newspapers, including 'head-lines', 'columns', 'features', 'front page' and 'captions'. All this helps when it comes to making their own magazine or newspaper. Microsoft Publisher and other desk-top packages have contributed greatly to children's sense of achievement in producing professional-looking texts. The easily managed changes that can be made in print size, insertions and so on leave children free to concentrate on the composition of their accounts. Activities using newspapers can be adapted for different age groups and include:

- Using newspaper reports as models for children's own writing for a class or school newspaper. Children can look, for example, at how headlines help the reader. For younger children, some teachers find it helpful in getting the format right if teachers provide column-sized strips of paper on which to write. These also help children edit their work to fit a limited space.
- Interviewing adults and children in school using a note book or tape recorder for an article in the class or school newspaper.
- Comparing the front pages of different newspapers and designing their own front pages using appropriate language and headlining, and attending to where to start new paragraphs.
- Looking at the purposes behind newspaper accounts – is a reporter trying to inform, persuade or make something sound sensational to sell more copies? How does the audience at which a newspaper is aimed affect its language and content?
- Considering how reporters use direct speech and quotation to add interest to an article. One of the books in Walker's News Series, for example Andrew Langley's *Roman News*, would help and inspire.
- Studying the visual aspects – to see how photographs, maps and drawings

communicate, explain, complement or extend the verbal element.

- Using old newspapers as a primary source and where both English and history perspectives can be brought to bear.
- Using reports, articles and letters about local or national matters of interest as a starting point for children's debates and persuasive kinds of writing (the Newswise website helps here).
- Improvising drama round what happens in a newspaper office: a teacher might be 'in role' as editor while children act as reporters and office staff.

First News is a newspaper for children aged seven to fourteen, produced in traditional tabloid format and with colour photographs and pictures. It aims to encourage children's interest in the world around them: www.firstnews.co.uk

Guardian newspaper has occasional pages for young readers, particularly during the summer vacation: www.guardian.co.uk

Langley, Andrew and De Souza, Philip (2009 edition) *Roman News* London: Walker Books.

Mallett, Margaret (2010) *Choosing and Using Fiction and Non-fiction 3–11* London: Routledge (Chapter 32).

Newswise: www.newswise.com

Swain, Carolyn (2010) *Using Magazines with a Critical Eye in the Primary School* Leicester: UKLA minibook.

Young Times: www.thetimes.co.uk/tto/education/youngtimes

NON-FICTION READING AND WRITING

See also: copying, diagrams, Directed Activities Round Texts, discussion text, EXEL Project, EXIT model, explanation text, factual genres, information books, information stories, language and thought, library skills, literacy hour, lyrical non-fiction, metacognition, motivation, persuasive genre, photographs, prior knowledge, procedural or instructional genre, recount, referencing, report, retrieval devices, spontaneous and scientific concepts, structural guiders, study skills, transitional genre, visual literacy, writing frames

The main functions of non-fiction reading and writing are to describe, inform, explain, persuade and instruct about aspects of the real world and all its phenomena. However, the best children's texts also often entertain and awaken a child's sense of wonder and curiosity. Learning to control the different kinds of non-fiction, whether print, software, CD-ROM or from the internet, is a most important part of becoming literate. This has been recognised in the different versions of the UK National Curriculum and in the now abandoned *Primary Framework for Literacy and Mathematics*, 2006. The six non-fiction genres referred to in these official documents – recount, report, discussion, instruction (procedural), explanation and persuasive – are still found to be useful ways of classifying the different kinds of non-fiction text. They match with the work of David Wray and Maureen Lewis on the EXEL Project and it is helpful to read one of their many books, for example *Extending Literacy: Children Reading and Writing Non-fiction* (1997). At text level, helpful questions to ask about a non-fiction text are: what type of text is it – report, persuasive text and so on; how is the text structured; what kind of authorial voice is adopted; and what are the graphic conventions used. Work at sentence and word level explores the syntax of the different non-fiction texts and their distinctive vocabulary. For a helpful analysis of how to go about studying non-fiction at text, sentence and word level I recommend the non-fiction chapters in Angela Wilson and Julie Scanlon's book *Language Knowledge for Primary Teachers* (Wilson and Scanlon, 2011).

I have considered the different kinds of non-fiction and criteria for judging their quality in some detail under the separate entries listed above under *see also*. Study skills and library skills and the work of the Exeter University Extending Literacy (EXEL) Project are all covered under the appropriate entries. Here I consider some ways of helping children make progress in this difficult aspect of literacy. In doing so I use the model of non-fiction reading and writing first set out in my book *Making Facts Matter* (Mallett, 1992) and discussed critically alongside the EXIT model in Riley and Reedy's (2000) book *Developing Writing for Different Purposes*.

Just before I do this, though, I want to mention some of the issues that arise when we start to think about which strategies best support this kind of reading and writing. Should the emphasis be on the teaching of study and library skills? Researchers of any age know these are essential tools to help us find out from secondary sources. The sheer amount of information that we can now access from print and electronic sources can be overwhelming and children certainly need skilful help to find what they need and then to use it and finally present it. The trouble is that too often this approach can lead to decontextualised 'finding out' exercises which can be extremely dreary. Too much time spent on identifying the genre features of different texts can also be mechanistic and joyless. Two very interesting and profound analyses help us get our minds round the issues here. First, Margaret Meek's (1996) *Information and Book Learning*, and second Helen Arnold's (1992) 'Do the blackbirds sing all day?'

An alternative approach starts from the young learners – their questions, comments, wonderings and curiosity about the topic in hand (Mallett, 2004). The desire to know is a powerful motivator and work organised round this is likely to arouse a high level of interest and commitment. We know that while much project work of

301

the 1970s and 1980s was excellent, some lacked a clear enough focus and neglected to include teaching about necessary research skills and strategies (see entry on 'cross-curricular projects'). The challenge is to combine the best of both these approaches by harnessing our teaching of study skills to children's concerns and purposes. The teachers and children in the classroom case studies in my books *Young Researchers* (Mallett, 1999) and *Choosing and Using Fiction and Non-fiction 3–11* (Mallett, 2010) try to achieve this balance.

This brings me to another issue. So often it is lessons across the curriculum that provide the most exciting contexts for research and yet a great deal of children's reading and writing now happens in Literacy Time. Fortunately, a flexible approach allows for some of the same texts that the children are using for research in history, geography and science to be explored from a language perspective in Literacy Time. There is a strong example of children using their history research – on child labour in Victorian times – to produce letters 'in role' as protesting Victorian citizens in the Centre for Literacy in Primary Education's video-film *Communities of Writers*. The teacher of the Year 5 class involved, Clare Warner, considered this writing task provided the children with a standpoint from which to select their material (CLPE, 1999). I now offer a model for non-fiction reading and writing, newly expanded and annotated, for discussion and for comparison with the EXIT model which is more detailed in the later stages. Although my model is presented as linear, the stages overlap. As Riley and Reedy point out, 'it may be the discovery of a new piece of information that makes us reflect on our previous knowledge and thus raise questions that need to be answered' (Riley and Reedy, 2000: 145). This model is shown in dynamic form in *Active Encounters* (Mallett, 2007).

A model for reading and writing non-fiction

Organising prior experience

Whenever a teacher begins a new topic it helps the children to organise what they already know by discussion and sharing. This is sometimes termed 'brainstorming' and making a topic web on a board or flip chart of all the ideas and issues may help. This involves the children in their own learning from the outset, but of course it is the teacher's skilful intervention that helps make the talk focused and valuable (Mallett, 2007).

Offering new experience

The younger the children, the less satisfactory it is to go straight to secondary sources.[1] Much better to offer an interesting experience which might be an outing, a talk by an expert, consideration of an artefact or reading a picture book or poem. I used a BBC video-film about a baby squirrel reared by a cat with her kittens as the 'new experience' for a study of squirrels within a 'living things' science project (Mallett, 1992).

Formulating questions

The new experience combined with the 'prior experience' talk usually gives rise to a large number of questions. These questions can be displayed in the literacy corner or written down in children's jotters. The important thing is that they put the children in the driving seat and make it much less likely that they will be overwhelmed by the texts they read. I find it also makes children take up a critical approach: do these texts answer *my* questions? Children learn that some of the most interesting questions (sometimes ethical ones) can be the most difficult to find answers to. I remember a six year old trying to find some insight on 'Is it wrong to kill a spider that gets into your bath?'

Discussion and planning

Once the children begin to search in books and on the internet it is important to keep meeting together as a class to share findings and puzzles and to clarify purposes and ways of representing their findings. Collaborating over 'finding out' makes it less lonely and often infuses energy into the learning. It also recognises the powerful role of the spoken language in getting our minds round new and sometimes challenging ideas.

Study skills and retrieval devices

By now the children have much commitment to their work. They are ready for some modelling and demonstration of both library and study skills. Finding their way round the library and understanding how to use retrieval devices in print and electronic text are most important. I have found encouraging children to share their experiences and frustrations in group discussion very valuable here.

Summarising, reformulating and reflecting

This stage includes oral summary and learning how to make notes and bullet points to provide material for extended writing later on. Copying and closely paraphrasing from books is less likely if children work from notes. Teachers can use scaffolding strategies to support children's efforts to make oral summaries – 'what three main things did you find most interesting?' and also offer support like the 'writing conference' of the process model and writing frames (see under entries on 'process approach to writing' and 'writing frames'). In the case of the squirrel work, the children's questions led to them creating contents pages which structured their findings.

Above all, children enjoy sharing all they have learnt both orally and in writing. The nine year olds in the squirrel project referred to above made books to share with the six year olds in the school. The time spent reading them aloud to the younger children and explaining the concepts was a highlight of the work.

Note

1 There are of course occasions when children carry out worthwhile Directed Activities Round Texts (DARTs), sometimes using text on the computer.

Arnold, Helen (1992) 'Do the blackbirds sing all day?' in Styles, Morag, Bearne, Eve and Watson, Victor (eds) *After Alice: Exploring Children's Literature* London: Cassell.

CLPE (1999) *Communities of Writers: Writing at Key Stage 2*, video-film from the Learning to be Literate series, London: CLPE.

Mallett, Margaret (1992) *Making Facts Matter: Reading Non-fiction 5–11* London: Paul Chapman.

——(1999) *Young Researchers: Informational Reading and Writing in the Early and Primary Years* London: Routledge.

——(2003) *Early Years Non-fiction: a Guide to Helping Young Researchers Use and Enjoy Information Texts* London: Routledge.

——(2004, second edition) 'Children's information books' in Hunt, P. (ed.) *International Companion Encyclopedia of Children's Literature* London: Routledge.

——(2007) *Active Encounters: Inspiring Young Readers and writers of non-fiction, 4–11* UKLA minibook 24.

——(2010) *Choosing and Using Fiction and Non-fiction 3–11* London: Routledge.

Meek, Margaret (1996) *Information and Book Learning* Stroud: The Thimble Press.

Riley, Jeni and Reedy, David (2000) *Developing Writing for Different Purposes* London: Paul Chapman.

Wilson, Angela and Scanlon, Julie (2011, fourth edition) *Language Knowledge for Primary Teachers* London: David Fulton.

Wray, David and Lewis, Maureen (1997) *Extending Literacy: Children Reading and Writing Non-fiction* London: Routledge.

NON-NARRATIVE TEXTS

See: information books

NON-STANDARD ENGLISH

See: dialect, language variety, Standard English

NORM REFERENCING

See also: assessment, Standardised Reading Tests

Unlike a criterion referenced test, norm tests do not serve a diagnostic purpose. Rather, as the results are set out in rank order, they make it possible to judge a person's performance compared with that of others. They work on the basis that in any assessment some individuals will do very well, some will have low scores, but most will be between the extremes. This expected pattern of results is called 'the normal curve of distribution'.

NOTE TAKING

See: study skills

NOUN

See also: abstract noun, collective noun, common noun, count noun, mass noun, noun clause, noun phrase, proper noun

A noun is a part of speech (or word class) which names a person, a thing or a concept. In the following sentence the nouns are in italics.

'When *Miranda* settled in the *country-side* away from the *crowd* in *London* she found *peace* at last'.

NOUN CLAUSE

See also: clause, grammar, parts of speech

A noun clause (or a nominal clause) works like a noun or pronoun. So while in the sentence – 'The claim was not justified' – we have a noun – 'claim … ', in the sentence – 'What he claimed was not justified' – we have a noun clause – 'What he claimed … '.

Noun clauses usually include some form of verb while noun phrases do not.

NOUN PHRASE

See also: grammar, parts of speech, phrase

A noun phrase, like a noun clause, functions as a noun in a sentence. Examples of noun phrases are: the largest cabbage; a red dress; my favourite nephew. A noun phrase differs from a noun clause in that the former does not normally include a verb while the latter does.

NOVELS

See also: adventure stories, animals, fantasy, fiction: choosing and using, historical novel, history of children's literature, narrative, realism, school stories

As they move through the primary years children become able to enjoy longer stories, or 'novels'. Like novels for adults, children's novels are sustained fictional narratives, long enough for the development of characters and for the reader to be taken through a series of events. There are suggestions for different age groups in *Choosing and Using Fiction and Non-fiction 3–11* (Mallett, 2010: 99–151) and in Nikki Gamble and Sally Yates' *Exploring Children's Literature* (Gamble and Yates, 2008: chapters 6–7). There is also information about children's novels on publishers' websites including Barn Owl books,

Bloomsbury, Frances Lincoln, Hodder, Oxford University Press, Penguin, Puffin, Red Fox, Scholastic and Templar. Print education journals, for example *The School Librarian*, *English 4–11* and websites including *Books for Keeps*, Write Away and Booktrust are also helpful sources of relevant reviews and articles.

Children's novels come in a great variety of theme, structure and style. There are classics like Philippa Pearce's *Tom's Midnight Garden*, historical novels like Rosemary Sutcliff's *The Eagle of the Ninth*, adventures like Nina Bawden's *The White Horse Gang*, 'realistic' stories like Jacqueline Wilson's *Tracy Beaker* and the rather surrealist and slightly disturbing fantasy, for instance *The Daydreamer* by Ian McEwan. Then there are graphic novels, for example David Almond's *The Savage*. Some children greatly enjoy reading novels independently, but a shared reading aloud of a novel is a deeply educative experience. Amongst the benefits are that children:

- share and enjoy an imaginary experience;
- learn from hearing the teacher's reading and their contribution to class discussion;
- experience interactive learning as they discuss and enjoy the text together;
- are exposed to different kinds of book language;
- are introduced to a wide range of fiction that they might not have read on their own – adventure, historical novels, fantasy, realism;
- develop empathy and understanding;
- are helped to make links made between text and life and vice versa;
- are helped to enjoy a building momentum and to develop cumulative insights over several sessions;
- have the others in the class to provide a good audience for drama and writing arising from the reading; and
- have their literacy developed in the widest sense.

In addition, teachers often find that children with special literacy needs can be encouraged to contribute and young learners of English as a second or additional language are placed in a supportive context.

Eight-year-old Cormac was not a bookish child but after hearing the teacher read Dick King-Smith's *The Sheep-pig* he remarked:

> I liked hearing the story because I could sit and listen and understand the story without having to read it myself. The teacher makes it sound funny and I can't wait for her to read the next chapter to find out what happens next. Sometimes I feel sad or scared for the character and sometimes I feel happy for them or they make me laugh. Hearing the story is one of my favourite things at school.

Books for Keeps: booksforkeeps.co.uk
Booktrust: booktrust.org.uk/Books/Booklists
Gamble, Nikki and Yates, Sally (2008, second edition) *Exploring Children's Literature* London: Paul Chapman.
Write Away: www.justimaginestorycentre.co.uk
Mallett, Margaret (2010) *Choosing and Using Fiction and Non-fiction 3–11* London: Routledge.
The School Librarian: www.sla.org.uk

NURSERY RHYME

See also: phonics, phonological awareness, play and language and literacy, poetry, reading, verse

This is a simple, traditional rhyming song or story. According to Townsend (1995: 105), the earliest known nursery rhyme collection was *Tommy Thumb's Song Book* published by Mrs Cooper of Paternoster Row in 1774. This collection included familiar rhymes like 'Sing a Song of Sixpence' and 'Hickory, Dickory Dock' as well as some rougher, cruder verses.

However, the Mother Goose anthologies – the first being *Mother Goose's Melody*, published, possibly by Newbery, in the 1780s – are the best known of the early collections.

The rhymes that survive in modern collections have their roots in different centuries and in different contexts (see Peter and Iona Opie's *The Oxford Book of Nursery Rhymes*, 1951). We must remember that the rhymes were often intended for the amusement of adults. Away from their original political and social settings they are often delightfully absurd.

This absurdity, and the subversion of the normal rules of the real world, seems to be one aspect that still appeals to the children of today. Nursery rhymes can create special worlds of the imagination and wonderful opportunities for language play. Margaret Meek writes: 'They are memorable as speech, they also form the bedrock of all play, the alternative world. Jack and Jill, Old Mother Hubbard, Simple Simon, Polly who put the kettle on are all there, ready to pop into stories, play-acting and a million children's books, generation after generation' (Meek, 1991: 84).

There is great variety in these short narratives we call nursery rhymes. Some tell of unpleasant events – Humpty Dumpty, Three Blind Mice and Jack and Jill all suffer grievous injury. In contrast, 'I had a little nut tree, Nothing would it bear, But a silver nut-meg, And a golden pear' is gentle and poetic. Whatever their theme they help prepare children for the imaginative world of fiction and for their own attempts at verse. You may know the landmark publication of the Opies – *The Lore and Language of School Children* – which celebrated the playground rhymes and culture of children in the 1940s and 1950s (Opie and Opie, 1959). Georgina Boyes has revisited the Opies' work and added evidence from her own research of the folklore of children brought up in a computer age. She shows how ancient rhymes are reworked and new ones added (Boyes, 1995).

As well as being hugely enjoyable for their own sake a number of research studies, notably those carried out by Bryant *et al.* (1989) and Goswami and Bryant (1990), link familiarity with nursery rhymes with success in learning to read. Children need to 'hear' separate sounds in the flow of spoken language around them if they are to learn to use the symbols of our alphabetic system to read and to write. Repetition of the nursery rhymes seems to help with a recognition of separate sounds which is called 'phonological awareness'. When children see the rhymes written down this brings to their attention some of the different ways in which sounds are spelt. It is splendid that something as enjoyable as listening to and saying nursery rhymes should also be helpful in learning to read. I heartily recommend *Rhyme, Reading and Writing* edited by Roger Beard: the contributors explain recent research on the central role of rhyme and alliteration in the process of learning literacy and celebrate children's sheer delight in the linguistic playfulness of nursery rhymes. Favourite collections for home and school include those where the children are in traditional dress, as for example in Zena Sutherland's *The Orchard Book of Nursery Rhymes*, which is illustrated with Faith Jacques' small bright pictures. Kathleen Lines' big book, *Lavender's Blue*, remains a favourite and has some contemporary rhymes – by Grace Nichols and Charles Causley – as well as traditional ones. If you want a generously spaced collection with imagination stretching contemporary illustrations you cannot do better than track down *The Orchard Book of Nursery Rhymes for Your Baby* compiled by Mary Ann Hoberman and illustrated by Penny Dann. Children love to sing and dance to rhymes and a jolly CD would add something to the nursery or home collection. *Oxford Baby Nursery Rhymes* has eighteen favourites, some accompanied by jazz and reggae music.

Of course the games and rhymes children enjoy in the modern playground are bound to be influenced by the new media as Professor Jackie Marsh found during her research project entitled 'Children's playground rhymes in a new media age' (Marsh, 2011). The British Library has a useful website on children's games and rhymes over the last century: http://www.bl.uk/learning/news/childrensgames.html

Avery, Gillian and Kinnell, Margaret (1995) 'Morality and levity' in Hunt, Peter (ed.) *An Illustrated History of Children's Literature* Oxford: Oxford University Press, 61–9.

Beard, Roger (ed.) (1995) *Rhyme, Reading and Writing* London: Hodder & Stoughton (Chapter 8).

Boyes, Georgina (1995) 'The legacy of the work of Iona and Peter Opie: the lore and language of today's children' in Beard, Roger (ed.) *Rhyme, Reading & Writing* London: Hodder & Stoughton: 131–45.

Bryant, P.E., Bradley, L., Maclean, M. and Crossland, J. (1989) 'Nursery rhymes, phonological skills and reading' *Journal of Child Language*, 16: 407–28.

Goswami, Ursula and Bryant, Peter (1990) *Phonological Skills and Learning to Read* Hove, East Sussex: Lawrence Erlbaum Associates.

Marsh, Jackie (2011) 'Britain's Got Talent in the Playground: empowerment through multimodal play in the new media age' unpublished presentation at the UKLA International Conference, July 16th 2011.

Meek, Margaret (1991) *On Being Literate* London: The Bodley Head.

Opie, Iona and Opie, Peter (eds) (1951) *The Oxford Dictionary of Nursery Rhymes* Oxford: Oxford University Press.

——(1959) *The Lore and Language of School Children* Oxford: Oxford University Press.

Townsend, John Rowe (1995, sixth edition) *Written for Children* London: The Bodley Head.

O

OBSERVATION

See: research (into primary English, language and literacy)

OFSTED (OFFICE FOR STANDARDS IN EDUCATION)

This is a government body set up in 1992 to carry out school inspections so that standards can be monitored. It reports directly to the Secretary of State for Education.

ONOMATOPOEIA

This is a figure of speech which refers to language where sound echoes sense, for example the 'squelch' of wet grass or the 'buzz' of a bee. Work round advertisements, strip cartoons and poetry introduces children to onomatopoeia.

ONSET AND RIME

See also: phoneme, phonics, phonological awareness

'Onset' is that part of the syllable that precedes the vowel while 'rime' refers to the vowel and final sounds. So in the word 'page', 'p' is the onset and 'age' is the rime. The research of Goswami and Bryant (1990) suggests that as children enjoy songs and rhythm, an approach to the

initial teaching of reading which exploits this enjoyment is likely to be successful. Nursery rhymes, for example, are a rich source of single syllable words that can be tackled by beginning readers as onsets and rimes.

Goswami, U. and Bryant, P. (1990) *Phonological Skills and Learning to Read* Hove: Lawrence Erlbaum Associates.

Riley, Jeni (1996) *The Teaching of Reading: The Development of Literacy in the Early Years of Schooling* London: Paul Chapman (Chapter 2).

ORACY

See: collaborative learning, drama and English, speaking and listening, storytelling

OXFORD READING TREE

This reading package for children aged four to eleven was first published by Oxford University Press in 1985 and new materials are still being added regularly. At its centre is the imaginative evocation of a tree with different branches for each aspect of reading and its associated materials.

The package includes a wide range of books including stories in small and big book format, poetry and non-fiction. Other materials include photocopiable worksheets, guided reading cards and a teacher's guide with many suggestions for activities. New additions include CD-ROMs and an online facility matching its reading scheme books (www.oup.com/oxed/primary/oxfordreadingtree). The clip art CD enables teachers to make their own material for interactive whiteboards; for example, they can sequence a story order.

Strong points include the attractiveness and variety of the materials and the support provided for the different aspects of reading.

Oxford Reading Web from the same publisher includes elements on phonics and grammar. It can stand on its own as a reading programme, or it can be used to supplement Oxford Reading Tree. Teachers of seven to eleven years olds welcome the addition of Treetops – top-quality books including Chris Powling's *The Million Pound Mascot* (about football and superstition) and Margaret McAllister's *My Guinea Pig is Innocent* (about bullying).

OXYMORON

This is a literary term applied to the juxtaposition of two apparently conflicting notions. You may be familiar with the following oxymorons: cheerful pessimist, wise fool, legal murder and bitter sweet. Writers seek new, exciting and unsettling oxymorons to energise their work.

P

PACT

See: parents and families

PALINDROME

This is a word or phrase which is the same whether read forwards or backwards, for example noon, peep, tat, Anna and madam.

PARABLE

See also: Bible, fable

A parable is a short story to make a moral point and is often associated with the teachings of Jesus in the New Testament. Well-known parables include the Good Samaritan, the Parable of the Talents and the Prodigal Son. A knowledge of parables is helpful in reading those books where some familiarity with them is assumed.

The term can also be used to describe some modern texts for adults and children. Perhaps Anthony Browne's *The Tunnel* can be read as a parable about sibling relationships. Another book, particularly enjoyed by six to seven year olds, which gives food for thought, is Mini Grey's *Three By the Sea* (Cape). A stranger joins Cat, Dog and Mouse. Disturbing things happen, but by the end the friends are able to live together harmoniously. Perhaps the best parables encourage conversation and questioning.

PARAGRAPHING

Paragraphing is a way of breaking up a text into topics and sub-topics. The beginning of a new paragraph is indicated by starting its first sentence on a new line and by indenting the first word.

Judging when to begin a new paragraph comes with experience. We get a sense as writers of when we have said enough about 'that' and need to move on to a new thought and therefore a new paragraph.

In direct speech, a new paragraph is often begun when a new speaker utters. Where a person speaks directly for several paragraphs opening speech marks are usually placed at the beginning of each paragraph but closing marks are only placed at the end of the paragraph with the last utterance.

PARENTS AND FAMILIES

See also: bilingualism, emotional literacy, English/Literacy Co-ordinator, family literacy projects, hobbies and English, multiculturalism, Primary Language Record

There is everything to be gained from schools and families keeping in close touch to support children's progress (Kelly, 2010). We tend to use the word 'parent' as a shorthand but this should be taken to include a wider family involvement. A term like 'partnership with families' might be appropriate in our ever-changing society in which family groupings are varied and not always stable. Contact best starts early and may take the form of home visits and liaison with the local play group or nursery. Continuity is achieved in these crucial early stages if members of a family are encouraged to visit the school in the child's 'settling in' period.

Good home–school partnership is particularly important for children developing language and literacy. Teachers benefit from extending their knowledge of children's literacy experiences at home and in the wider community. This is important for all the children and their families (Feiler *et al.*, 2007). When the school includes young 'emergent bilinguals' teachers benefit from some specific background knowledge. Eve Gregory lists some helpful initial questions; these include finding out in some depth about which languages the child speaks or writes and to what standard, and finding out about community-led classes and the pattern of tuition to which the child is accustomed. One very interesting aspect of Gregory's list is the emphasis given to the potential role of siblings in supporting each other's language development (Gregory, 2001, 2007, 2008). There are well-established ways of keeping in touch with families using letters, explanatory booklets about reading and English lessons, open days, meetings with staff and of course through the reading logs or diaries children take home. There is substantial research evidence about the value of children reading at home to parents, caregivers or siblings (see Wolfendale and Topping, 1995; Weinberger, 1996, 2006; Bastiani and Wolfendale, 2006). A parent or another member of the family may be asked to write some comments on progress in the reading log or mark the page they have reached in the book. The Centre for Literacy in Primary Education's Primary Language Record and other similar record-keeping formats include the opportunity for the parent to comment on their perception of the child's progress. This provides a good focus for discussion at meetings between parents and teachers. There is evidence that the interest of male family members in a boy's reading is helpful in encouraging positive attitudes towards literacy. Donald Fry (1985) describes the leap in seven year old Clayton's progress when his father read him Richard Adams' *Watership Down*.

The English/Literacy Co-ordinator is best placed to organise the valuable contributions of parent volunteers who may work in the library, make resources like story bags or kits,[1] bring particular expertise like computer skills or provide home-language text in book making and take part in storytelling in some of the children's first language. In the classroom, parents can hear children read and will appreciate some sympathetic briefing. In the early years classroom parents can act as 'literacy partners' who read print and scribe for young children (Whitehead, 2009). Much work goes into establishing and maintaining parent–teacher partnerships. Ann Browne provides good advice about the priorities and reminds us that, above all, we need to create openness and respect on both sides (Browne, 2009: Chapter 9).

Note

1 'Curiosity Kits', designed by Maureen Lewis and Ros Fisher, are a non-fiction version of a storysack or storybag. Find out more from the National Centre for Language and Literacy (NCLL, www.ncll.org.uk). Visit this site also for details of many research projects on families and home languages.

Bastiani, J. and Wolfendale, S. (2006) *Home-School Work in Britain* London: David Fulton.

Browne, Ann (2009, third edition) *Developing Language and Literacy 3–8* London: Paul Chapman (see Chapter 9, 'Involving parents').

Centre for Literacy in Primary Education (CLPE) run Family Learning programmes and provide courses for parent and caregivers: www.clpe.co.uk

Feiler, A., Andrews, A., Greenhough, P., Scanlan, M., Yee, Ching Wan, Johnson, D. and Hughes, M. (2007) *Improving Family Literacy* London: Routledge.

Fry, Donald (1985) *Children Talk About Books: Seeing Themselves as Readers* Milton Keynes: Open University Press (O/P at present, but it is a classic).

Gregory, Eve (2001) 'Sisters and brothers as language and literacy teachers: synergy between siblings playing and working together' *Journal of Early Childhood Literacy*, 1 (3): 301–22.

——(2007) 'What counts as reading inside and outside school and with whom, how and where?' in Bearne, E. and Marsh, J. (eds) *Literacy and Social Inclusion: Closing the Gap* Stoke on Trent: Trentham.

——(2008) *Learning to Read in a New Language: Making Sense of Words and Worlds* London: Paul Chapman.

Kelly, Clare (2010) *Hidden Worlds: Young children learning literacy in multicultural contexts* Stoke-on-Trent: Trentham Books (pages 87–95).

National Literacy Trust reports regularly on Parents as Partners in Literacy: www.literacytrust.org.uk

Teachers as Readers project concentrates on home-school reading relationships in its third phase (UK Literacy Association): www.ukla.org/research

Weinberger, Jo (1996) *Literacy Goes To School: The Parents' Role in Young Children's Literacy Learning* London: Paul Chapman.

——(2006) *Learning from Sure Start: Working with Young Children and their Families* Milton Keynes: Open University Press.

Whalley, Margy (2007) *Involving Parents in Their Children's Learning* London: Sage.

Whitehead, Marian R. (2009) *Supporting Language and Literacy Development in the Early Years* Buckingham and Philadelphia, Penn.: Open University Press.

Wolfendale, S. and Topping, K. (eds) (1995) *Parental Involvement in Literacy – Effective Partnerships in Education* London: Croom Helm.

PARTICIPLE

'Participle' is a term in English grammar to refer to two endings of non-finite verbs. These are 'ing', the present participle, and 'ed', 'd' or 't', the past participle. The 'ing' ending appears in a number of forms. Used with the verb 'to be' it becomes the progressive continuous as, for example, in 'she was *teaching*'. In a participle clause it is used as a verb as in 'After *talking* all through break, he was quiet when the teacher came into the classroom'. The 'ing' ending helps to form the future as in 'will be going' or the present, as in 'is talking'.

The past participle 'ed' is used in three ways. First it can be used with the verb 'to have' to form the perfect tense as in for example:

'The student has *produced* some excellent writing'.

Second, it can be used with the verb 'to be' to form the passive:

'He was *educated* at King's College'.

Third, it can be used as the verb in an 'ed' participle clause:

'*Questioned* for several hours, she still stuck to her story'.

For a particularly thorough explanation of participles, see Wilson and Scanlon, 2011, and McArthur, 1992.

McArthur, Tom (1992) *The Oxford Companion to the English Language* London and Oxford: QPD Paperbacks and Oxford University Press.

Wilson, Angela and Scanlon, Julie (2011 edition) *Language Knowledge for Primary Teachers* London: David Fulton.

PARTS OF SPEECH (OR WORD CLASSES)

See also: adjective, adverb, article, conjunction, noun, preposition, pronoun, verbs

Words are classified into categories which are known as 'parts of speech' or 'word classes'. The main parts of speech are named above and each is described under a separate entry. Words can belong to more than one category depending on their function in a sentence. For example, 'lift' can function as a verb in 'I lift the garage door each morning' or as a noun in 'I take the lift to the top floor'. The word 'that' can function as a determiner in 'I read that book last year', as a pronoun in 'what was that?' and as a conjunction in 'she claimed that she had written the book'. Another example of the flexibility in the use of words in English is 'love' which can be used in a sentence as a noun as in 'My love is like a red, red rose', as an adjective as in 'It was undoubtedly a love match' or as a verb as in 'I love you'.

The following websites may be helpful.

- The Internet Grammar of English: www. ucl.ac.uk/english-usage/resources/ige
- The Linguistics Association: this website provides further information including help over all aspects of language and linguistics, including grammar – www. lagb.org.uk

PASSIVE VOICE

See also: verbs

The passive voice is a grammatical term used to refer to the form of the verb in which the recipient of an action is the subject of the sentence: 'These teachers are being praised by the school governors for

their excellence'. This contrasts with a sentence in the active voice: 'The school governors praised the teachers for their excellence'.

Many consider it best for writers to use the immediate, active voice whenever possible. However, there are times when the passive is appropriate, for example in some scientific kinds of writing where a tone of detachment is required; in cases where the doer is unknown, as in 'We were burgled last night'; and where the recipient of an action is more important than the doer, as in 'The child managed to avoid being hit by the car'.

PATHETIC FALLACY

Like 'personification', 'pathetic fallacy' refers to the attribution of human feelings and characteristics to animals, plants and inanimate objects as a poetic device. 'Pathetic' refers not to pity, but to the awakening of emotional response to the comparisons. The term was used by Ruskin (*Modern Painters*, 1856) to criticise the falseness of imputing human characteristics to things in nature, even where personification adds to the literary quality of the language in a literary text. Sometimes 'pathetic fallacy' is applied pejoratively to the overblown or inappropriate use of personification. An example might be: 'The cruel stone landed on the suffering bluebell'.

PERSON

See also: first person writing

This is a term that applies to pronouns and verbs and tells the listener or reader about the 'person' concerned. Turning to pronouns first, in English only the third person singular has a distinct form – 'he', 'she' and 'it'. The first person singular 'I', the second person singular 'you', the first person plural 'we' and the third person plural 'they' all only have one form. Use of the first person gives an intimate flavour to a piece of writing. Use of the second person, too, can often give a friendly feel to a book for young children – 'Have you ever seen a squirrel crack a nut?' When it comes to using the third person we have to make sure children know that they have to look back in the text to find out who 'she' or 'he' or 'it' is. So we might have a series of sentences as follows. 'Leon gently lifted the mewing kitten from the tree. It was still trembling when he searched for its collar to find an address'. It is clear from the rhythm of the sentences and the context that 'it' is the kitten and Leon is the 'he' in the second sentence.

In some languages the 'person' is indicated in the verb, but in English only the third person singular of the present tense has a distinct form – 'he loves', 'she loves' and 'it loves'.

PERSONIFICATION

See also: pathetic fallacy

This is a device in written and spoken language which links human beings metaphorically with the non-human world of animals, plants and inanimate objects. It tends to be used in literary texts and particularly in poetry. Some uses of personification have become clichés – for example, 'the cruel hand of time'.

PERSUASIVE GENRE

See also: advertisements, argument, critical discourse, discussion text, literacy hour, newspapers and magazines, non-fiction reading and writing, visual literacy, writing frames

Persuasive kinds of language present the case for one viewpoint and include advertisements and political propaganda. Visual texts can also be powerful in pressing one way of looking at things. In the UK the

now abandoned *Framework* (2006) made a distinction between 'persuasive' texts which present one side of a case and 'discussion' texts which set out more than one viewpoint. Both of these kinds of writing involve argument, and we tend to consider that children may cope better with such challenging texts after about age ten. This reflects a general assumption that developmentally narrative precedes argument and that 'recounts' will be the main kind of non-fiction writing before about nine years.

There have been some convincing challenges to this view. Mallett and Doyle found five year olds were alert to the environmental issues when learning about whales. The picture book *The Whales' Song* by Sheldon and Blyth contrasts the view of Uncle Fred that whales are valuable for their blubber and oil with the belief of Lucy and her Grandmother that whales are unique and beautiful creatures which should be protected. It is never too soon to discuss issues! (Mallett, 1999: 164). Riley and Reedy also used a picture book, Anthony Browne's *Zoo* in this case, to help children organise the arguments for and against keeping animals in captivity. They conclude that there are good reasons for including 'argument' in our teaching from the earliest years. The kind of thinking used in spoken and written forms of argument and persuasion seems to develop much earlier than was once thought. Where children are deeply interested in a topic their enthusiasm can be harnessed to acquiring a form to express it (Riley and Reedy, 2000: Chapter 8).

There are some things to bear in mind in developing this kind of thinking, discussing and writing throughout the primary years. First of all we need to plan the work round something likely to engage the children's interest and arouse strong feelings. Riley and Reedy's zoo work came about within a bigger theme – 'living things'. Some kind of new experience can awaken a line of thinking – a letter, a picture or a story. In

315

the Riley and Reedy case study, a picture book was the trigger to thinking about some rather troubling issues. In Browne's book the mother thinks the lion looks 'sad' and children begin to reflect on why this may be so. The second thing to consider is how we support children's writing, how we direct all the excitement and feeling into an appropriate written form. Class or group discussion helps children consider the arguments and counter arguments of the issue. (Persuasive language presents one viewpoint but we do need to be aware of possible counter arguments in presenting the case powerfully.) Wilkinson got seven year olds to talk about the case for and against having playtime before asking them to write. The children were particularly encouraged to make a point and then elaborate it, and this structure was taken through to their written accounts later on (Wilkinson, 1990). Sometimes it is helpful to put a structure on discussion by linking it to headings on a board or flip chart. In Riley and Reedy's 'zoo' case study the teacher organised the children's discussion under two headings on a flip chart: 'good for animals' and 'bad for animals'. Of course we must remember that much early writing is transitional and we do not want to press young children too quickly into mature forms (Barrs, 1987; Mallett, 2010). The gentle shaping of thinking before writing used in the 'zoo' case study seems appropriate.

Are there some ways of helping older primary children to come closer to controlling the conventional ways of presenting argument? They still benefit from discussing the arguments first. When it comes to writing, they may need some help in creating a structure. Some children find the writing frames developed by Wray and Lewis helpful. These frames suggest that persuasive accounts setting out an argument begin with an opening statement defining the issue, go on to state the arguments using point and elaboration and end with a summary. A slightly different structure is suggested for discussion texts. These begin with a statement of the issue and also a brief preview of the main arguments. Then the arguments for the case are set out with supporting evidence, next the counter arguments get the same treatment and the writing concludes with a summary and recommendations (Wray and Lewis, 1997: 119).

The teaching challenge is, of course, to make sure the excitement and interest survives the writing tasks. It is well worth spending time on persuasive talking and writing, not least because understanding the ethical and controversial aspects of a topic takes children forward in becoming critical readers and writers.

Barrs, Myra (1987) 'Mapping the world' *English in Education* NATE, 21(3).

Mallett, Margaret (1999) *Young Researchers: Informational Reading and Writing in the Early and Primary Years* London: Routledge (Chapter 6, p.164).

——(2010) *Choosing and Using Fiction and Non-fiction* London: Routledge (see Chapter 32 'Argument').

Riley, Jeni and Reedy, David (2000) *Developing Writing for Different Purposes* London: Paul Chapman (see Chapter 8, 'Developing control of the argument/persuasive genre').

Wilkinson, A. (1990) 'Argument as a primary act of mind' *English in Education* NATE, 24(1).

Wilson, Angela and Scanlon, Julie (2011, fourth edition) *Language Knowledge for Primary Teachers* London: David Fulton (see Chapters 10 and 11).

Wray, David and Lewis, Maureen (1997) *Extending Literacy: Children Reading and Writing Non-fiction* London: Routledge.

PHATIC COMMUNICATION

See also: functions of language

This refers to comments and questions the function of which is more to do with reinforcing the relationship of the speakers than with conveying a meaning. Chat about the weather comes into this category as well as expressions like 'do you understand what I mean?'

Halliday, M.A.K. and Hasan, R. (1985) *Language Context and Text: Aspects of Language in a Social-Semiotic Perspective* Oxford: Oxford University Press.

PHILOSOPHY AND LITERACY

See also: constructivism, critical discourse, language and thought, metacognition, metalanguage

The study of philosophy develops our ability to think and therefore our literacy. The journey towards becoming a critical reader involves becoming able to get past the literal meaning in a text and thinking about it on an analytical or conceptual level. Other entries have emphasised the importance of encouraging children to bring their own questions to a text, to read critically and to think creatively. Introducing children to philosophical thinking is one way of helping them to enquire, reflect and to reach their own conclusions. One of the most interesting initiatives exploring the links between philosophy and children's literacy is the Philosophy in Primary Schools project led by Robert Fisher. The project team have developed an approach in which children are helped both to 'care' – to take responsibility for their own thinking – and to 'collaborate' – to connect with the thinking of others through discussion and working together.

The work of Jean Piaget, the Swiss developmentalist, suggested that children under the age of about eleven are unlikely to manage more abstract kinds of thinking. However, Fisher and his team found that stories provide a sympathetic starting point for young children to be helped to think philosophically. Fisher explains how a teacher, who was a participant in the research project, read six and seven year olds a story called *The Monkey and her Baby*; she encouraged them to go beyond the literal meaning of the story to a discussion of issues like what it means to be beautiful. Using a story allows a philosophical approach to enrich work in Literacy Time. However, the research team consider such an approach might have a place in lessons across the curriculum. Teachers would of course need to have some support in learning how to develop children's thinking skills. Feedback has been positive from both teachers and children who have put into practice programmes like 'Stories for Thinking'. Children seem to have improved their achievements across a range of measures, including literacy, and when asked have said they enjoy the approach.

If you want to read about some other approaches to developing thinking skills you could track down some of the relevant journals on philosophy for children. These include *Teaching Thinking: The Journal of Philosophy for Children* (P4C) and *Questions: Philosophy for Young People*.

Three issues occur to me. I get the impression that some approaches assume that reasoning skills developed through exercises will transfer to other situations. Is this really so, I wonder.

Second, might it be that children are moulded into a set way of thinking that might go against their own creativity? In fact, Fisher's approach tries to encourage children to open up new areas of inquiry. He gives two interesting examples of children taking the initiative. Tom, aged five, asked 'Where does time go when it is over?' A girl, after her father had finished a story with the words ' ... and they lived happily ever after', asked: 'What is happiness dad?' (Fisher, 2001: 72). So I think we can be assured that there is the possibility of children's thinking being expanded in a creative way.

317

Third, I think we need to remember that stories are not just for, or indeed mainly for, developing the intellect. Children, like adult readers, have an emotional and affective response to fiction and may sometimes want to read for sheer enjoyment. This is not to say that 'Stories for Thinking' is not an interesting way of developing literacy, but it is only one way of encouraging response to texts.

Fisher, Robert (2001) 'Philosophy in primary schools: fostering thinking skills and literacy' *Reading, Literacy and Language* UKRA, 35 (2), July (this article reports on the 'Stories for Thinking' approach).
——(2005, second edition) *Teaching Children to Think*. London: Nelson Thornes.
Teaching Thinking: The Journal of Philosophy for Children: www.teachthinking.com
Questions: Philosophy for Young People (P4C): secure.pdcnet.org

PHONEME

See also: cue-systems, digraph, phonics, phonological awareness

A phoneme is the smallest unit of meaningful sound. There are forty-four phonemes in English including the five vowels and twenty-one consonants of the alphabet.

'Phonemic awareness' is to do with hearing and recognising the different phonemes within a word.

PHONETIC

See also: Initial Teaching Alphabet, phonetic stage, spelling

If you spell phonetically, you consistently represent the same symbol for the same sound.

PHONETIC STAGE

See also: spelling

Children reach this stage in their approach to writing when they choose letters on the basis of sound and try to represent all the sounds in a word, for example 'cleen' for 'clean' and 'sesta' for 'sister'. Regional accent affects a child's pronunciation and therefore his or her attempts to spell phonetically.

PHONIC KNOWLEDGE

See also: blend, onset and rime, phoneme, phonics, phonological awareness, spelling

This refers to a reader's ability to segment a word into separate sounds and then to blend these sounds back together. This ability depends on knowing the alphabetic code and understanding the principles which inform the use of the code in reading and spelling. It is helpful when facing unfamiliar words and is the basis for word-level work in Literacy Time.

PHONICS

See also: cue-systems, grapheme, graphophonic cue-system, Jolly Phonics, onset and rime, phoneme, phonic knowledge, phonological awareness

Phonics is to do with the correspondence between sounds (phonemes) and letters (graphemes). Recent models of the reading process tend to separate the graphic and phonic strands. You will come across the terms 'synthetic' and 'analytic' phonics and it is important to know the difference between them. The traditional phonic approach begins at the level of the phoneme. Children are taught the sounds of the letters of the alphabet and the forty-four phonemes; they sounded out the phonemes in words – 'm-a-t', 'ch-a-t' and so on. There are only twenty-six letters of the alphabet to make forty-four phonemes. There are two ways in which all forty-four sounds in English are covered. First, some of the same letters represent different sounds: for example, the 'g' in 'gift' has a different sound to the 'g' in 'gentleman'. Second, letters are combined to represent sounds not covered by single letters, so we have, for example, the phonemes – 'th', 'ch' and 'ph'. The problem with a rigidly synthetic phonic approach came when children tried to decode irregular words. A newer approach to phonics, termed 'analytic phonics', encourages young readers to look at segments of words and at patterns in sounds and words: the identification of 'onset' and 'rime' in words is typical of this approach. The approach here is based partly on research by Goswami and Bryant (1991), which indicates that the key to reading is the ability to hear the separate phonemes in words.

The early part of phonic programmes requires children to recognise individual vowel and consonant sounds – in other words phonemes – and to match these with the written symbols we call graphemes. Learning to read and learning to spell are thus related. During what is often referred to as 'the phonetic stage' of spelling (Gentry, 1982) children spell words as they sound and this works well for a large number of words. However, English is not entirely a phonetically regular language, and this is reflected in early spelling of, for example, 'eny', 'lite' and 'werk'.

In a particularly clear analysis, Graham and Kelly (2007) explain that children need to grasp that not all sounds can be represented by a single letter of the alphabet. Sometimes two letters are combined to make a new sound. So while 'c' and 'h' are both phonemes, when combined in a word like 'chin' they form together a new phoneme 'ch'. When children become more secure in their understanding of this they become more confident spellers as well as readers (Lewis and Ellis, 2006; Bald, 2007). Dombey and Moustafa (1998) set out a phonics programme within a general philosophy of reading for meaning and purpose.

Phonics: three principles

- Phonemes are represented by one letter or more letters like 'sh' and 'th'.
- Phonemes represented by the same sound are not always written in the same way: for example, the 'oo' sound is written differently in 'to' and 'shoe'. In 'bed' and 'said' the rime sounds the same but is spelt differently.
- The same spelling can represent more than one phoneme: for example the 'ea' phoneme sounds different in 'mean' and 'deaf'. 'Said' and 'afraid' each have 'ai' when written down, but do not sound the same.

Phonic practice can be rather abstract so the approach through games in commercial handbooks like *Jolly Phonics* is helpful. Other cue-systems, tuning into the syntactic and contextual aspects of reading, are brought in after the first stage of learning to read in the 'simple view of reading'. Teachers in the UK are expected to teach synthetic phonics to beginning readers. However, all of us concerned with primary education are entitled to debate, research and react to what is required or recommended. Issues include the following:

- How confident are we entitled to feel about the results of the Clackmannanshire research into synthetic phonics? Wyse and Styles (2007) have concerns about the validity of the research design.
- Why have the findings of Goswami and Bryant (1991) about the role of analytic phonics been pushed aside?
- Does a prescribed programme limited, in the early stages, to the teaching of

one kind of phonics (synthetic) and only one cue-system do justice to the teaching of early reading?

Bald, J. (2007) *Using Phonics to Teach Reading and Spelling* London: Sage (includes a CD).

Dombey, H. and Moustafa, M. (1998) *Whole to Part Phonics: How Children Learn to Read and Spell* London: CLPE/Heinemann Educational Books.

Gentry, Richards (1982) 'An analysis of developmental spelling in GNYS AT WRK' *The Reading Teacher*, 36: 192–200.

Goswami, U. and Bryant, P. (1991) *Phonological Skills and Learning to Read* Hillsdale, N.J.: Lawrence Erlbaum Associates.

Graham, Judith and Kelly, Alison (2007, third edition) *Reading Under Control: Teaching Reading in the Primary School* London: David Fulton.

Lewis, M.D. and Ellis, S. (eds) (2006) *Phonics: Practice, Research and Policy* London: Paul Chapman Publishing.

Wyse, D. and Styles, M. (2007) 'Synthetic phonics and the teaching of reading: the debate surrounding England's "Rose Report"' *Literacy*, 41: 1.

PHONOLOGICAL AWARENESS

See also: cue-systems, nursery rhyme, onset and rime, phoneme, phonetic, phonetic stage, phonics, reading

This refers to the ability to hear differences in sounds and is broader than 'phonemic awareness'. Children need to be able to hear phonemes, syllables, onsets and rimes to help them with the phonological aspect of learning to read. Conscious awareness of the features of speech sounds develops over a period of time. Systematic teaching may accelerate this development. There is research evidence that sensitivity to phonemic structure of spoken words is linked with success in reading (Bryant and Bradley, 1985; Goswami and Bryant, 1991).

Bryant, P. and Bradley, L. (1985) *Children's Reading Problems* Oxford: Blackwell.

Goswami, U. and Bryant, P. (1991) *Phonological Skills and Learning to Read* Hillsdale, N.J.: Lawrence Erlbaum Associates.

Layton, Lyn, Deeny, Karen and Upton, Graham (1997) *Sound Practice: Phonological Awareness in the Classroom* London: David Fulton.

PHONOLOGY

See also: phoneme, phonics

Phonology is the study of the sound system of a language. There are texts that help with the implications of children's phonological awareness when reading in English, for example Layton *et al.*, 2002, and those that apply their analysis to different languages, for example Goswani, 2010.

Goswani, Usha (2010) 'Phonological development across different languages' in Wyse, Dominic, Andrews, Richard and Hoffman, James (eds) *The Routledge International Handbook of English, Language and Literacy Teaching* London: Routledge.

Layton, Lyn, Deeny, Karen and Upton, Graham (2002, second edition) *Sound Practice: Phonological Awareness in the Classroom* London: David Fulton (Chapter 1).

PHOTOGRAPHS

See also: advertisements, art and English, visual literacy

In school, children are most likely to come across photographs in the information and reference books and websites they use. Photographs are used to illustrate and make immediate and real phenomena that would otherwise take many words to explain. In successful books the visual and verbal link effectively. Illustrators are using new technology in exciting ways –

photographs can be taken in almost every situation, from space to within the body. As well as imparting information photographs can have a strong emotional impact. Of course, this is exploited in advertisements which is a good reason for helping children study or 'deconstruct' the social messages that may be imparted (Mallett, 1999a, 1999b). It is never too soon to learn that we can be manipulated by the visual as well as the verbal! However, this very power to move and affect is helpful in an educational context. There are a number of non-fiction authors who use photographs to illustrate their books. Many Dorling Kindersley authors use photographs in the Eyewitness series as their main type of illustration, as do Wayland and Frances Lincoln in some of their books. Examples of the latter's photographic books are those by Ifeoma Onyefulu showing the lifestyles, games and festivals of the people in an African village, for example *Ikenna Goes to Nigeria,* a title in the Children Return to their Roots series. In one of the books in Wayland's *History from Photographs* series, the photographs of children in their Edwardian classrooms give us imaginative insight into the lives of individuals. The power of the photograph to illuminate social history is also shown in Wayland's Migrations series. In Hakim Adi's *African Migrations* we see family photographs showing ten year old Yemisi in Nigeria and then photographs taken after 1967 in London, the capital of her new country. The photographs show the difference between the two environments and the human issues involved in a way that even a huge amount of writing could not. Of course a diagram or drawing is sometimes better for a particular purpose than a photograph, as we see in David Macaulay's drawing of the structure and function of machines in his book *The Way Things Work*. It is also true that photographs and other illustrations could not replace written contributions. Ten year olds

who had been moved by a photograph of a Tudor sailor's shoe taken from the *Mary Rose* observed that they needed to read about where and when the shoe was found and about Tudor shoe making to make full sense of the visual input.

If we give children the opportunity to take photographs to illustrate their own books, this takes them forward in understanding and appreciating the photographs from which they learn in information books. In making or 'constructing' images they learn about the choices open to the photographer and this helps them study or 'deconstruct' the work of others. This can be a worthwhile collaborative activity with children learning to use the language of image making – 'close-up', 'midshot' and 'long shot' – and talking about the social messages that can be communicated by the size and angle chosen to show people and objects (see Philip Hart's chapter in Callow, 1999: 82).

Callow, Jon (1999) *Visual Literacy: Visual Texts in the Classroom* New South Wales, Australia: PETA (see Chapter 7).

Mallett, Margaret (1999a) 'Engaging heart and mind in reading to learn: the role of illustrations' in *The Best of Language Matters* London: CLPE.

——(1999b) *Young Researchers: Informational Reading and Writing in the Early and Primary Years* London: Routledge.

PHRASE

A phrase comprises a number of linked words. As a unit of grammar it is more than a word but less than a clause. There are six forms of phrase:

- *noun phrases* have a noun as their headword as in 'famous people' ('people' is the headword).
- *adjective phrases* have an adjective as their headword as in 'very famous' ('famous' is the headword).

321

- *verb phrases* have a verb as their headword as in 'was acting' ('acting' is the headword).
- *adverb phrases* have an adverb as their headword as in 'very slowly' ('slowly' is the headword).
- *prepositional phrases* begin with a preposition. In the phrase 'of a cake' *of* is a preposition.
- *genitive phrases* include the participle 's' and usually modify noun phrases. In the following example – 'the girl's big dictionary' – 'the girl's' is a genitive phrase which is modifying (telling us more about) the noun phrase 'big dictionary'.

Students and children often ask how they can quickly tell a phrase from a clause. It is helpful to know that since a clause has a verb (while a phrase does not always have one), it is a more sentence-like structure than a phrase.

PHYSICAL EDUCATION, MUSIC AND DANCE AND ENGLISH

See also: junior years language and literacy, play and language and literacy

Physical education includes games, gymnastics, dance, swimming, athletic activities and outdoor and adventurous activities – all mentioned in the United Kingdom National Curriculum for the primary years. All this links with English in two main ways. First, as is the case with all learning, language is a crucial medium for teaching and learning. In physical education speaking and listening are used: to explain, 'narrate' a demonstration of a series of movements and to evaluate what children do. Because they need to plan and reflect on their performance, teachers and children develop a vocabulary to discuss movement and actions. In a useful taxonomy of language in physical education, Maude suggests we use vocabulary of body

awareness (stretching), of space (moving forwards and backwards), of time (accelerating, stopping) and of quality (gracefully, running lightly) (Maude, 1998). The uniting of physical activity and language make physical education a lesson where there is a lot of collaboration and co-operation. For safety reasons a teacher needs to use their voice as a means of control too. There are also some opportunities for developing literacy – children may read a story which is the basis of a dance drama and sometimes children are asked to write about their work.

Second, physical education links with English through play and the imaginative development of dance drama as a way of expressing human feeling. A dance drama round a story or poem creates the opportunity for many kinds of activity – language to plan, monitor and evaluate, physical activity shaped to tell the story and convey the emotions and aesthetic response to the music and the beauty of the movement. Costume and props may add to the visual impact. The roots of children's enjoyment of movement and music are in infancy. When we observe very young children we are struck by their urge to move from the earliest stages. As soon as they can stand, tiny children 'dance' and move to music. By the time they are nursery school age they choose physical activity as often as they can – skipping, running, climbing and riding little bikes and scooters. All this is highly enjoyable. Each new generation of children seems to recreate physical play for themselves and there may be some sort of 'play instinct' (Bailey, 1999: 32). This would explain both why children like their physical education lessons so much and why games and sport are so important in our society.

Bailey, Richard (1999) 'Physical education: action, play and movement' in Riley, Jenny and Prentice, Roy *The Curriculum for 7–11 Year Olds* London: Paul Chapman.

Maude, P. (1998) '"I like climbing, hopping and biking" – the language of physical education' in Bearne, Eve (ed.) *Use of Language Across the Primary Curriculum* London: Routledge.

PICTURE BOOKS

See also: art and English, fantasy, fiction: choosing and using, history of children's literature, visual literacy

Emerging during the last decades of the twentieth century and the early years of the twenty-first, the children's picture book has become an important cultural form. Each year new picture books, many of them excellent, pour out of the publishing houses. They have become the focus of academic study and there is a debate about whether it is the pictures that are central or whether we should be looking at the way in which the verbal and the visual interact to create meaning.

The best picture books have qualities that make them both hugely enjoyable and valuable in helping children learn to read. They are often narratives which encourage children to predict what might come next and sustain interest until the end.

However, the quality modern picture book is not just an illustrated story but a highly sophisticated work of art. When reading picture books we have to relate 'non-linear' reading of the picture to the linear processing of words (Hunt, 2001: 289). Perhaps children today are helped by their experience of computer software, CD-ROMs and the internet to be generally more visually competent 'readers' than earlier generations. Picture books can also be sophisticated reading material because they work at different levels. So a book like *Oi! Get Off Our Train* by John Burningham may seem at first to be an exhilarating story about different animals joining Mr Gumpy and his children on a toy train that has magically become full

size, but if we look more closely we see the animals are begging to get on the train because their habitats are being destroyed: as Townsend points out, the story can be read as a 'conservation fable' (Townsend, 1995: 335). Burningham's *Granpa* also works at deeper levels doing more than simply recounting a little girl's experiences and feelings during her grandfather's last months. The book is really telling us about the lack of communication between the generations because the experience of older people differs so much from that of the young. Burningham uses the visual to show us the mismatch between the grandfather's wishes and memories and the little girl. Anthony Browne's *Voices in the Park* contrasts the friendly playfulness of children with the snobbish attitudes of older people. Sometimes it is what the text does not say that matters. In Pat Hutchins' *Rosie's Walk*, for instance, the young reader is drawn into the humour of the situation by the illustrations. The hen is oblivious of anything other than her progress across the farmyard, but the pictures show the predatory, although ultimately thwarted, fox following her. Meek shows how the author invites the reader to share the joke. It is this kind of reader/author collaboration that helps make readers (Meek, 1988). There are, of course, picture books that tell the story through illustration alone. Examples here include Raymond Briggs' *The Snowman*, Pat Hutchins' *Changes* and Shirley Hughes' *Up and Up* – about a little girl's flying fantasy. The best wordless books have great imaginative appeal and provide rich opportunities for children to talk and speculate. Rodriguez's *The Chicken Thief* is a wordless adventure and rescue story which becomes surrealist when a most unusual friendship is discovered. Children make their own meanings from their scrutiny of the pictures.

Another quality of picture books is their ability to draw on, indeed sometimes rely on, the reader's cultural knowledge. The Ahlbergs' books do this particularly imaginatively. *Each Peach Pear Plum* tunes into a child's experience of nursery rhymes while *The Jolly Postman* brings in fairy tale characters as recipients of letters, postcards and catalogues. Anthony Browne also uses this 'intertexuality' with great success, for example in *The Tunnel* in which we see a picture of Little Red Riding Hood hanging in a young girl's bedroom. We see the same girl in a haunted wood later on.

Not only are picture books excellent reading material, but they can also help children see the choices a writer can make by including different kinds of text. Shirley Hughes' *Chips and Jessie*, for example, tells five stories of the adventures of two young friends through cartoons and letters as well as the main narrative. *The Jolly Postman* with its different genres and audiences is often used as the starting point for children's writing.

Picture books are not only for the very young. The same books can be enjoyed in different ways by different age groups. I have seen work based on Anthony Browne's *The Tunnel* with seven year olds and with ten year olds. The younger children concentrated on the story while the older ones used it to explore their experience of and feelings about sibling relationships. Some picture books like Michael Foreman's *War Boy* have appeal for older primary children: words and pictures are skilfully used to bring alive a young boy's village childhood during the Second World War.

Carol Ann Duffy's modern fairy tales in picture book format – *The Tear Thief* and *The Princess's Blankets* – intrigue older readers. Other picture book creators whose work stretches the imagination and understanding of older primary children include: Helen Ward (*Varmints*), Ben Morley (*The Silence Seeker*) and Shaun Tan (*Lost Thing*). The pictures and text in these picture books cover such themes as environmental issues, adapting to change and alienation.

To gain an historical perspective of the development of the picture book, I recommend 'The Picture Book' (Anstey & Bull, 2004). To extend your understanding of how picture books work, I recommend David Lewis' *Reading Contemporary Picturebooks*. This is a challenging read but it illuminates current thinking. It looks in depth at particular picture books – including favourites like Anthony Browne's *Gorilla* and Quentin Blake's *All Join In* and some interesting but slightly less well-known examples like Babette Cole's *Drop Dead* and David Pelham's *Say Cheese* – identifying their most important and interesting features. Lewis illuminates what is meant by 'the postmodern picture book' and identifies three important features. First, the best picture books are 'multilayered' and can be read at different semiotic levels. This is why children can return to picture books they first read when younger and gain new insights from them. Second, there is often 'intertextuality': the reference, often in subtle ways, in one text to other texts. Third, Lewis points out the 'metafictive' quality in some contemporary picture books. Take, for example, Lauren Child's *Beware of the Storybook Wolves*; young Herb worries that the wolves in his story book might come out of the pages – and one night they do! They burst forth with copious other fairy tale characters in a metafictive frenzy. Stories like these show young readers and listeners that fiction is created. The rules can be turned on their head and tidy beginnings, middles and ends abandoned (Mallett, 2010). You would also find helpful Margaret Meek's analysis in *How Texts Teach What Readers Learn* (Meek, 1988), John Rowe Townsend's chapter 'Picture books in bloom' (Townsend, 1995) and Peter Hunt's succinct chapter 'Picturebooks' (Hunt, 2001). Marian Whitehead gives a detailed account of the response of very young children to picture books (Whitehead, 2010: Chapter 7). *Talking*

Beyond the Page is another inspirational book of great value to teachers and student teachers about providing a rich range of activities that help children read and enjoy picture books. There is an insightful interview with Anthony Browne, 'A master in his time', in Chapter 10, about how he creates his imagination-stretching picture books (Evans, 2009). Finally, readers may like to take their study further by reading two illuminating essays both in Modern Children's Literature: 'Reading Contemporary Picturebooks' by Judith Graham and 'Politics and Philosophy in the Work of Raymond Briggs' by Lisa Sainsbury (Reynolds, 2004).

Anstey, Michelle and Bull, Geoff (2004, second edition) 'The picture book' in Hunt, P. (ed.) *International Companion Encyclopedia of Children's Literature, Volume 1* London: Routledge, pp. 328–39.

Evans, Janet (ed.) (2009) *Talking Beyond the Page* London: Routledge.

Hunt, Peter (2001) *Children's Literature* Oxford: Blackwell.

Lewis, David (2001) *Reading Contemporary Picturebooks: Picturing Text* London: RoutledgeFalmer.

Mallett, Margaret (2010) *Choosing and Using Fiction and Non-fiction 3–11* London Routledge (see Chapter 4).

Meek, Margaret (1988) *How Texts Teach What Readers Learn* Stroud: The Thimble Press.

Reynolds, Kimberley (ed.) (2004) *Modern Children's Literature: An Introduction* Hampshire and New York: Palgrave Macmillan, pp. 209–249.

Townsend, John Rowe (1995 edition) *Written for Children* London: The Bodley Head (see Chapter 29 'Picture books in bloom').

Whitehead, Marian (2010, fourth edition) *Language and Literacy in the Early Years* London: Paul Chapman (see Chapters 6–7).

PLAGIARISM

See also: quotation, referencing

Figure 16 Cover illustration © 2000 Gillian Tyler. From *The Snail House* by Allan Ahlberg and illustrated by Gillian Tyler. Reproduced by permission of Walker Books Ltd, London SE11 5HJ. www.walker.co.uk

This describes using someone else's work, and presenting it as your own. It usually refers to the unacknowledged use of another person's research, ideas or analysis in your own writing or in a lecture. It is entirely proper, and often desirable, to quote or paraphrase from both primary (original documents or research reports) and secondary sources (books and articles), provided you acknowledge them. Advice about this is under 'referencing'.

PLANNING

See also: English/Literacy Co-ordinator, English/literacy policy, literacy hour, National Curriculum

There are several levels of planning for primary English. Let us begin with the most global aspects and move towards the weekly and daily planning that guide everyday practice. The school's agreed policy on English sets out the general principles on which the English curriculum is based and specifies the speaking and listening, reading and writing routines and resources for specific age ranges. The school's long-term plan provides more details about the programme, again on a term-by-term basis for each year group. It is from this detailed document that a teacher's medium-term plans are developed (Myers & Burnett, 2004). Medium-term plans are sometimes called 'schemes of work'. Some teachers find it helpful to recognise three different aspects of medium-term plans – 'blocked', 'linked' and 'continuous'. 'Blocked' work refers to a series of lessons on one aspect of English, like discussing the role of imagery in poetry or learning about the linguistic features of persuasive writing as readers and writers. 'Linked' planning joins English work with other areas of the curriculum. Children might be learning about different kinds of first person writing in English and looking at the role of letters and diary entries as primary sources in history. Planning for aspects of English like learning to spell, handwrite and punctuate which need considerable practice may be termed 'continuous' planning.

Short-term plans for each week's work draw on medium-term plans. Teachers decide on a core of work together with appropriate resources for everyone and then plan for differentiation based on what they know about the capabilities of particular individuals.

In the United Kingdom first the 1998 *Literacy Framework* and then the 2006 renewed *Framework* have shaped literacy work in the primary years. Both are now abandoned but some of the good things about them survive in current good practice, for example the inclusion of non-fiction texts in planning the literature programme.

However, English is broader than literacy. Teachers of older primary children need to find time for extended reading and writing. Sometimes particular kinds of reading and writing that fulfil English aims are appropriate in lessons across the curriculum. For example, writing reports can flow from geography and history lessons and procedural writing is a major genre in science.

Planning frameworks from government for guidance can help ensure that children's experience in literacy follows a clearly defined, progressive and well-balanced sequence, particularly where it is followed with some flexibility. However, requirements that are tight and inflexible can inhibit a teacher from taking up learning opportunities that arise spontaneously and also from spending more time on lessons where real progress is being made or where extra help is needed before moving on (Washtell, 2009).

Myers, J. and Burnett, C. (2004) *Teaching English 3–11* London: Continuum.
Washtell, Anne (2009) 'Routines and resources', in Graham, Judith and Kelly, Alison (eds) *Writing Under Control* London: David Fulton.

PLAY AND LANGUAGE AND LITERACY

See also: drama and English

There is a strong link between play and early language and literacy. Imaginative play activities, drawing and games often provide the opportunity to explore and experiment with both spoken and written language (Browne, 2009).

A picture book, story or poem can be particularly powerful in encouraging role play and discussion. In her chapter on 'Books and the world of literature', Marian Whitehead explores children's playful exploration of pictures and written narratives (Whitehead, 2010). Let me give one example from my own experience of how a book can be the starting point for imaginative language and play. When asked to share with the seminar group the high points of her recent teaching practice a student who had been working with five year olds told us about her work round the Ahlbergs' picture book *Burglar Bill*. The home corner had been transformed into a room in the burglar couple's house and the children created their own role play round the story. Near the end of the practice, and with the class teacher's help, the student dressed as Burglar Betty and the children were invited to ask her about her behaviour, why she gave up being a burglar and what might happen in the future. It was a kind of 'hot seating' with the student teacher in the hot seat! The children were absorbed and their questions were interesting and profound. How, for example, would Burglar Betty stop Burglar Bill from slipping back into his old ways if money got short?

Children enjoy language play round nursery rhymes and other verses. A playful approach to sounds can also encourage phonological awareness which helps children learn to read.

Because role play encourages involvement often over a period of time and throws up

> *Edward the lion never comes out in the day,*
> *But when it gets all dark he goes out looking for his prey.*
> *Edward, Edward, Edward, Edward,*
> *He's a pretty lion,*
> *Edward, Edward, Edward, Edward,*
> *He's a lion you can rely on!*

Figure 17 Abbie experimented with words and rhymes on the computer at home and produced this poem when she was eight and a half. When it was read out at school, the other children liked the witty word play of 'lion' and 'rely on' in the last line.

motivating contexts, it can be an excellent way of extending the range and the purposes for children's writing. Mallett evaluates a case study where nursery age children have made a pretend train in the home corner and feel the need to write out tickets and notices for the station. They are becoming aware through play of the social purposes of writing (Mallett, 1999). Browne lists the varied kinds of writing that might result from setting up a post office: letters, postcards, invitations, notices, signs, posters, advertisements, stamp design, passports and writing addresses (Browne, 2009).

Children enjoy language play, games and improvisation in contexts outside the classroom as the Opies proclaimed in their pioneering book *The Lore and Language of School Children* (Opie and Opie, 1959). Readers may like to know that Steve Roud has extended and updated what the Opies began, making full use of modern communications and research tools, not least the internet. He uses photographs to show the history of playground rhymes and games from the 1890s up to 2010 and his book is rich with examples of children's rhymes and exuberant playground play throughout the United Kingdom (Roud, 2010).

There is now available a lot of software for the under sevens to encourage a playful, explorative approach to learning. For example the 'Max' series takes up a problem-solving approach. In *Max and the Secret Formula* children are invited to help Max find a hidden formula to save Auntie Lisa's leaning house. Of course, we would not want these programs to dominate – children can devise their own play situations – but the computer is part of our culture and we should exploit available software where it is helpful.

Older children also benefit from a playful approach to language. They still enjoy role play and improvisation – often round the themes in story books – and enjoy tongue-twisters, limericks and comic verse. Some of the poems from Edward Lear's *Book of Nonsense* – 'The Jumblies' for example – can encourage both oral and written responses. For helpful advice about how to include play opportunities in planning for English see 'Play and language' in Wyse and Jones (2007).

Finally, I would like to draw attention to an exciting research project entitled 'Children's playground games and rhymes in a new media age'. This project was carried out by Professor Jackie Marsh of Sheffield University and her team from 2009–2011 and partly funded by the AHRC Beyond Text programme. One outcome of this work was Jackie Marsh's lecture at the United Kingdom Literacy Association's International Conference in Chester, July 16th 2001. Using fascinating examples from primary school playground games and drama she showed how today's children are influenced, often in creative and constructive ways, by new media and popular culture. I found the dvd recording of the playfully mocking improvisation of older primary school girls, after they had watched the television show Britain's Got Talent, particularly telling.

Browne, Ann (2009, third edition) *Developing Language and Literacy 3–8* London: Paul Chapman.

Mallett, Margaret (1999) *Young Researchers: Informational Reading and Writing in the Early and Primary Years* London: Routledge.

Marsh, Jackie (2011) *Britain's Got Talent in the playground: empowerment through multimodal play in the new media age*, unpublished keynote lecture at the UKLA International Conference in Chester, 16th July 2011.

Opie, Peter and Opie, Iona (1959) *The Lore and Language of School Children* Oxford: Oxford University Press.

Roud, Steve (2010) *The Lore of the Playground: One Hundred Years of Children's Games, Rhymes and Traditions* London: Random House.

Whitehead, Marian (2010, third edition) *Language and Literacy in the Early Years* London: Paul Chapman (see Chapter 7).

Wyse, Dominic and Jones, Russell (2007) *English, Language and Literacy* London: Routledge.

PLAYSCRIPT

See also: drama and English, Shakespearian drama (in the primary years)

Playscripts are texts in prose or in verse written for performance. They include stage directions and sometimes notes about props. Improvised drama and role play, where the emphasis is on learning and co-operating rather than on performance, are more appropriate for younger children and continue to be important for older ones. However, writing and performing their own playscripts and using other people's is an important form of drama for children in the later primary years. Here they learn about the layout of a script on the page and about the strengths and the limitations of this kind of writing. They learn how everything is communicated through the words spoken by the actors and by gesture and facial expression. They can discover that playscripts differ from other kinds of fiction. A story or novel, for example, can provide some background and reasons why things have come about and people are as they seem in the play. However, we can explain that devices sometimes used by playwrights include a narrator or a soliloquy – a special kind of aside in which an actor confides his deepest thoughts to the audience. Medwell *et al.* (2009) provide a helpful account of the structure, layout and organisation of playscripts in their book *Primary English*. For some recommended playscripts and suggestions for using them, see Mallett, 2010: Chapter 14.

Mallett, Margaret (2010) *Choosing and Using Fiction and Non-fiction 3–11* London: Routledge.

Medwell, Jane, Moore, George, Wray, David and Griffiths, Vivienne (2009) *Primary English: Knowledge and Understanding* Exeter: Learning Matters.

PLENARY

This refers to a short period at the end of a lesson when children report back to the whole class on their achievements in group activities. This 'reporting back' might involve individuals in commenting on what their guided or independent group achieved or children may read aloud their writing. The teacher makes sure that, over time, each individual or group has their turn. The plenary provides a good opportunity for children to reflect on what they have been doing and to share what they have learnt. To give just one example: a group of ten year olds presented to the class a poster they had made which encouraged people to use the bins often placed at train or bus stations for glass, paper and cloth. The theme had been

'disposal of waste and rubbish' and the group were able to show how their work related to the larger topic.

P-LEVELS/P-SCALES

These are skill descriptors for pupils attaining below level 1 in National Curriculum subjects. P-levels 1–3 outline progress in basic skills and understanding while P-levels 4–8 indicate children's progress in specific subject skills in English and mathematics.

POETRY

See also: alliteration, anthology, ballad, creative writing, epic poetry, free verse, haiku, limerick, metaphor, nursery rhyme, onset and rime, personification, play and language and literacy, rhyme, rhythm, simile, sonnet, verse

Poetry is a most important part of children's language experience. It is language with a distinctive form and pattern which manifests certain literary devices like metaphor and personification. Sometimes poetry is the most appropriate form in which to express certain insights and feelings. Teachers need to know about the different forms poetry can take and these are discussed under the separate entries named above. If you wish to strengthen your own understanding of the features of and categories of poetry you will find support in Mallett's poetry Chapters, 15–19, in *Choosing and Using Fiction and Non-fiction 3–11* (Mallett, 2010).

Children start playing with language at the babbling stage when they repeat sounds for sheer pleasure. They are usually responsive to nursery rhymes and other verses which feature repetition and language play from the earliest stages. The shared experience of early verse and song, and the actions which often accompany it, is what makes it enjoyable in the home, play group and nursery. As Wyse and Jones point out, its brevity makes it manageable and memorable (Wyse and Jones, 2007).

Once at school children continue their interest in sound and rhyme in the playground where they sing or chant to skipping games. In the early years classroom children learn nursery rhymes, verses and songs and will attempt to write their own. As they move through the primary years they will work with riddles, limericks and the kind of verse that appeals through humour. (Anthologies like Yoland and Peter's *Here's a Little Poem* help here.) Nine year old Yasmine has achieved considerable competence and sophistication when writing her own playful poems. She writes a lot of poems at home and at school. Here, for example, is her witty rhyming poem 'Summing Up!', with the lovely image of words as 'prisoners' in the poet's head.

Summing Up! *by Yasmine*

A poet came to our school today
To earn his daily bread.
A real live poet,
With words in his head.
He told us to write a poem
Before the lunchtime bell.
We said we would,
If he would as well!
Some of ours were rather good.
But his face was rather red.
It's because he didn't do one,
His words were prisoners in his head.
He said there was no inspiration,
It's like me with sums,
I sit and stare at numbers
But inspiration never comes.

I am not sure if it happened in this case, but I find that children love reading their work aloud and other children enjoy hearing poems written by the others in the class or school.

Children will be introduced to longer poems too including traditional forms like

ballads and sonnets. As well as poetry with traditional forms and rhyming systems children will enjoy reading and hearing poems like those of Michael Rosen that have the natural cadences of conversation and everyday language. Successful teachers of poetry ensure they have the opportunity to experiment with free verse where they can concentrate on getting meaning across rather than on the form or pattern of the language. Teachers often read aloud to help children to enjoy a poem in its entirety whether it appeals to humour, tells a story or evokes memories of events and feelings. However, they also want to explore how the poet has used language and images to affect us. Jo Naylor of Heber Primary School helps a class of seven year olds to explore the language of *Where Go the Boats?* She manages to inspire the kind of discussion which encourages the children to enter imaginatively into the experience of the poem (*Becoming Independent*, CLPE, 1999).

When it comes to children writing poems there have been two main approaches in the primary school. The first is centred on the belief that children need strong experiences on which to base their own poems. Teachers often take children on visits to the countryside, seaside or pond, for example, or they bring in some objects like shells or fossils to inspire the children's writing. Sometimes the starting point might be a story or poem about a universal experience like a quarrel with a friend, loss of a relative or longing for a pet, and children are asked to write from their own experience. Teachers working in this way tended to feel that children would find the linguistic resources to express strong feelings without direct help over patterning their poems. The second approach privileged technique above experience: the important thing was to show control over a poetic form like a haiku, sonnet or ballad. Perhaps the best-known supporter of this way of approaching the writing of poetry

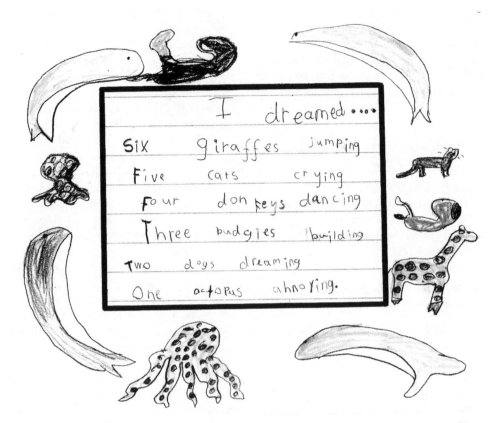

I dreamed ....

Six giraffes jumping
Five cats crying
Four donkeys dancing
Three budgies building
Two dogs dreaming
One octopus ahnoying.

Figure 18 Children sometimes find that a poem they hear or read gives them a framework for their own poetry writing. A six year old at Castlecombe Primary School, Mottingham, wrote her own alliterative poem 'I dreamed … ' after hearing John Forster's 'Zoo Dream'.

in school is Sandy Brownjohn. Her books, for example *Does it Have to Rhyme?*, are full of interesting and practical ideas, often in the form of games to help children acquire the techniques to write particular kinds of poetry. 'The Furniture Game', for example, invites children to choose an object and compare it to other things and then ask the other children to guess what it is. Does such an emphasis encourage children to structure genuinely felt ideas and emotions, however? One of the books that I have found most helpful in my poetry work is *Poetry in the Making* by Ted Hughes. He certainly thinks poetry is a disciplined activity but he also believes it has to shape strong feelings and ideas. Probably the best practice combines both

these approaches as the teachers in the following case study did.

Sele First School's Angel Poetry

For some years, Year 4 children at Sele First School have visited Anthony Gormley's *The Angel of the North*, a sculpture that towers above the motorway near Gateshead in the north-east. Teachers prepare the children by reading poems including Shelley's 'Ozymandias' and they talk about how poets used powerful images to communicate their thoughts and feelings. Clipboards are taken on the visit so that children can clothe their impressions of the sculpture in words. There is no rush to get to the final drafts and the children

331

are given time to reflect on the experience and to carve out a poem when back in school.

One year the children had the option of working in pairs and below are the poems of Emma and Sean and of Jessica and Hannah.

Angel of the North *by Emma Douthwaite and Sean Hanning*

The Angel casts its own shadow.
It is rich in colours, brown and rusty red,
Now it is clear to human eyes
The angel rotates to face the sun,
Feeling proud of itself.

The Angel *by Jessica Cusworth and Hannah Barrett*

The golden sun shines on the watching sentinel
Towering over lengths of grass and houses.
Its giant wings looking like a jet,
Rippling ribs running down its body,
A hard, cold, silent form.
Earth, blood and clay all moulded into a sharp, pointed shape –
The messenger of Gateshead.

I think you will agree the poems are vigorous and original. There is a strong metaphor in the second poem describing the Angel as a 'watching sentinel' and I very much like the personification of the sculpture in the line 'feeling proud of itself' in the first poem. Here are some observations – some aspects of the work that I think contributed to its success.

- There was helpful preparation for the visits including experience of how poets use images.
- The new experience – of a once controversial but now loved piece of artwork – was likely to lead to strong feelings and interesting thoughts.
- The children were encouraged to record their very first reactions to the dramatic sculpture so that their notes would serve as mnemonic when they were writing their poems back in school.
- Follow-up work included a display of the poems, photography and art work so that the children could share their work with the rest of the school – this raised their self-esteem as poets and encouraged younger children to feel confident about writing poetry.
- This work seems to combine something of the two approaches described earlier in this entry. It keeps children's responses to a striking, even moving experience, at the centre of the work while also providing opportunities for them to look at how other poets use language in particular ways to make their poems.

This is an example of a school's success in creating a culture of writing poetry and an atmosphere where it is valued. Another way of showing the value and enjoyment of reading and writing poetry is to provide awards for excellent anthologies. The Centre for Literacy in Primary Education awards an annual prize for the best anthology of poems of the previous year for children (www.clpe.co.uk). Since 2003, when the competition began, winners have included John Agard, Grace Nichols, Roger McGough and Carol Ann Duffy. The latter's prize-winning collection *New and Collected Poems for Children* brings together the best poetry from Duffy's four collections with some new poems included too. Teachers and children appreciate the humour and originality of poems like 'The Loch Ness Monster's Husband'. Those who wish to deepen their understanding of poetry for children and to learn about its history could not do better than read Morag Styles' (2004) chapter, 'Poetry'.

Becoming Independent: Reading at Key Stage 1 (1999) Video-film in the Learning to be Literate series. Centre for Literacy in Primary Education (for an inspiring glimpse into how a teacher in a Southwark primary school helps children explore the language of a poem and enter imaginatively into its theme).

Brownjohn, Sandy (2004, second edition) *Does it Have to Rhyme?* London: Hodder & Stoughton.

Hughes, Ted (2008, second edition) *Poetry in the Making* London: Faber & Faber.

Hull, Robert (2009) *Poetry – from Reading to Writing: A Classroom Guide for Ages 7–11* London: Routledge.

Mallett, Margaret (2010) *Choosing and Using Fiction and Non-fiction 3–11* London: Routledge.

The Poetry Library, Royal Festival Hall, London SE1 8XX. www.poetrylibrary.org.uk (houses a comprehensive twentieth-century poetry collection for children and young people and provides a national information service for all concerned with children and poetry).

The Poetry Society, 22 Betterton Street, London WC2H 9BU. www.poetrysoc.com (the education page of this organisation provides for members news about new publications, poetry posters and specialist advice on all aspects of poetry).

Rosen, Michael (1989) *Did I Hear You Write?* London: Andre Deutsch.

Styles, Morag (2004) 'Poetry' in Hunt, P. (ed.) *International Companion Encyclopedia of Children's Literature* London: Routledge.

Wyse, D. and Jones, R. (2007) *Teaching English, Language and Literacy* London: RoutledgeFalmer.

POP CULTURE

See: advertisements, CD-ROM, comics, television and literacy, video-film and DVDs, visual literacy

POLKA THEATRE FOR CHILDREN

Based in Wimbledon this theatre is a charity which puts on plays, music and activities for children from a few months old to the teenage years. The programme for each year includes plays based on picture books, stories and children's novels.

www.polkatheatre.com

POPULAR CULTURE AND NEW MEDIA

See also: audio resources, British Film Institute, CD-ROM, comics, ebooks, email, film making, hypermedia, hypertext, Information and Communications Technology (ICT) and English, integrated technologies, internet, multiple literacies, newspapers and magazines, photographs, radio programmes for children, television and literacy, television programmes for children, video-film and DVDs, visual literacy

Children growing up today use and learn from a wider range of media and we hear them referred to variously as 'the digital generation', 'the net generation' and the 'electronic generation'. For some years now teachers of all age groups have been giving more attention to the new media and the 'popular culture' it propagates because of their place in the lives of children. So they should: the time children spend with television and other media sources such as films, magazines, computer games, popular music and the internet takes up by far the most significant part of their leisure time (Buckingham, 2004). It is from these sources of a popular culture that children begin to develop attitudes, values, and preferences.

So the products of the mass media pervade children's lives, products where the main motivation can be the maximisation of profit rather than intrinsic quality and value. We worry with some cause about young people being exploited by programme makers and advertisers, and being introduced to unsavoury things like violence, extravagant celebrity lifestyles and what some would consider worthless activities.

333

However, many educators want us to accentuate the positive contribution of the new media to knowledge and understanding about the world. We can help here by encouraging young people to be critical and reflective about the information and influences coming from the new media and not to be merely passive consumers. One great appeal of the new and popular media lies in the communication between young people that it makes possible. Websites are usually interactive and many children enjoy surfing pop fan websites, playing computer games and seeking out information about hobbies and interests on the internet. Of course, emailing, texting and tweeting are extremely popular ways of keeping in touch. According to information on the Nesta website, children read books only for about fifteen minutes a day, watch TV, DVD or video-film for about 200 minutes a day and use the computer for about eighty minutes a day, although often some of these activities take place simultaneously, and while doing their homework! The following facts and figures show how far the new media have become embedded in the everyday lives of children.

Facts and figures based on David Buckingham's paper given at the 'Beyond the Blackboard' conference, 2004

The following percentages refer to children in the UK:

8 per cent have a home computer
70 per cent have internet access
80 per cent have a games console
55 per cent have cable or satellite TV
25 per cent [of households] have a video camera
4 per cent attend museums, art galleries or the theatre
46 per cent do not read books for leisure

Facts and figures from a ChildWise survey in which 2,500 children between ages five and sixteen were interviewed, 2011

The average age for first accessing the computer is eight years. Children between five and ten spend, on average, one hour and twenty minutes a day online, one-third of this time being in their bedroom. Some of this time is spent researching information for homework and on educational games on the CBeebies website, but even before they can have an account aged thirteen, many children visit Facebook and YouTube
(ChildWise, 2010/2011)

What is the significance of all this for the classroom? It is bound to be of concern to many of us that more than half of school-aged children say they do not read for leisure and only a tiny number seem to participate in traditional cultural activities such as going to the theatre. Some would say that the new media is rich and varied enough and, in some cases, of a quality to offer alternative satisfactions and benefits. There are quality websites and teachers and parents can visit www.thegoodwebguide.co.uk to direct their children to 'quality' websites. These include the following: mydrawings.me (children's drawings can be displayed and stored); a-z-animals.com (lots of information about animals); bbc.co.uk/schools/typing (games to help children touch type).

While accepting that the internet is a powerful source of information and entertainment, many – myself included – believe reading a book calls on the mind and its imaginative processes in a way that offers a unique experience. So there is a strong case for valuing the traditional cultural forms alongside the new. Nevertheless, as other entries suggest, teachers need to be aware of the aspects of the newer media that have captured the interest and imagination of children (Bromley, 2002; Lambirth, 2003; Marsh, 2004). They can bring into play the skills on the computer and the internet that children have acquired to enrich class activities and projects. Digital cameras can be used to create images to add to computer-produced stories and non-fiction accounts. There is every reason to hope that children's embracing of the new media will stimulate creative activities of all kinds, rather in the same way as has happened in the artistic community. There are encouraging signs that schools setting up blogging platforms for their pupils are finding even reluctant writers are taking part. For example, during a period of heavy snowfall when children could not get to school, Heathfield Primary School in Bolton set up a blog. The enthusiasm of the children was so marked, from Reception to Year 6, that the blogging was officially introduced into the curriculum. On visiting the school website I was most impressed by the range of writing children wanted to share: lists, advice on using the internet, reviews of books and films, requests for advice on writing topics, comments on political issues and stories in chapters. Illustrations added visual interest. Blogs set up by schools are successful because children think blogging is 'cool', because they know they have a wide audience for their writing and because it is a modern way of sharing their ideas, insights and feelings. It occurs to me also that blogging gives children the opportunity for talk and conversation which cannot be so readily provided in a busy and structured school day.

The *see also* lists entries that will help on particular media like television, radio, the internet and film.

Bromley, Helen (2002) 'Meet the Simpsons' *The Primary English Magazine* 7(4).

Buckingham, David (2004) *The Other Teachers* (based on a paper given at the 'Beyond the Blackboard' conference at Robinson College Cambridge, September 2004). David Buckingham is a Professor at the London Institute of Education. For details of his work visit www.ioe.ak/study/LKLB_7html.

ChildWise (2010/2011) *Digital Lives* A special report, see details at www.childwise.co.uk

Evans, J. (2004) *Literacy Moves On: Using Popular Culture, New Technologies and Critical Literacy in the Primary Classroom* London: David Fulton.

Lambirth, Andrew (2003) 'They get enough of that at home' *Literacy* 37(1).

Marsh, Jackie (ed.) (2004) *Popular Culture, Media and Digital Literacies* London: Routledge.

Marsh, Jackie and Millard, Elaine (2000) *Literacy and Popular Culture: Using Children's Culture in the Classroom* London: Sage.

PORTFOLIOS

See also: English/Literacy Co-ordinator, reading diaries, record keeping

Portfolios are folders or files in which representative samples of a child's work, the results of diagnostic tests and teachers' comments about progress, are kept. An English portfolio is likely to contain writing of different kinds, labelled diagrams and annotated illustrations and recordings of discussions showing the child's control over spoken language in different contexts. Running records or the results of miscue analysis are helpful in indicating reading progress. An annotated list of books read, perhaps in the form of a reading journal or log, and any dialogue book (a record of parents' and teachers' comments on reading at home or school during the year) are often included. Portfolios are valuable as a major way of showing a child's progress to future teachers, parents and the child himself or herself. Inspectors (for example OFSTED in the UK) also find portfolios a helpful source of evidence of coverage of the full range of work in the English curriculum including ICT and English. The English Co-ordinator will give guidance on the range of work which should be available in the children's portfolios. Inspectors will be looking for evidence of progression and continuity across the year group and will be interested in the quality of feedback given to children by the teacher. If you want to read more about the practical aspects of managing portfolios, I recommend Tyrrell and Gill's book *Co-ordinating English at Key Stage 1*. They emphasise that portfolios should reflect teaching and not drive it, and that children, however young, should be consulted about what is selected. If too much is kept, storage problems may arise. Many classrooms have a filing cabinet specially for the portfolios so that children and teacher have easy access. At the end of the year teacher and child usually discuss what should be sent up to the next class. As Tyrrell and Gill remark, if we are not selective 'portfolios could resemble suitcases by the time children reach primary six' (Tyrrell and Gill, 2000: 179). There is a trend towards using a networked computer system within the school to store data. The contents of portfolios can be scanned in and kept on disk, solving space problems.

However, portfolios are not just for children's work. Portfolios containing evidence of their classroom work are also kept by teachers sometimes because they wish to apply for accredited professional development courses. It is worth keeping evidence of children's work like writing samples and photographs of displays and reflections on the work. If you wish to read more about this, I recommend *Co-ordinating Primary Language and Literacy* by Merchant and Marsh (1998).

Merchant, Guy and Marsh, Jackie (1998) *Co-ordinating Primary Language and Literacy* London: Paul Chapman.

Tyrrell, Jenny and Gill, Narinderjit (2000) *Co-ordinating English at Key Stage 1* London: Falmer Press.

POSTMODERNISM AND CHILDREN'S PICTURE BOOKS

See also: illustrations: finding a vocabulary, language and society, picture books

This is a term applied to the art, literature and thinking which is in reaction to modernism. Modernism refers to the styles in art and literature which emerged in the early twentieth century and which were a rejection of more traditional forms and philosophies. It is not so much that postmodernism takes us back to pre-modernist thinking and traditions, but rather that it asserts the need for 'coherent rationales for definition, boundary, specific meaning and generalisation' (Hodkinson, 1998: 38). However, many consider that it fails to provide these rationales. So, this is a very difficult concept to grasp and is often used rather loosely, but it is something we have to grapple with because it is perceived to be a significant force in our contemporary world and is evident in the work of artists, writers and thinkers.

Primary teachers, pupils and parents are perhaps most likely to be confronted by postmodern influences when they read a picture book. A large number of today's picture books have been described as 'postmodern'. Here are four examples: David McKee's *I Hate My Teddy-bear*, Allan and Janet Ahlberg's *The Jolly Postman*, Anthony Browne's *Bear Hunt* and *Tadpole's Promise* by Tony Ross and Jeanne Willis. In the last of these a tadpole promises a caterpillar he will never change – so do not expect a happy ending! The writers, illustrators, designers and publishers of such picture books are part of the complex contemporary world we share and, as David Lewis points out, may respond to the tenor of the times by importing the approaches, techniques and sensibilities of postmodernism into their work (Lewis, 2001). The analysis in Lewis' chapter 6 is groundbreaking and too substantial to paraphrase here but I commend it heartily to anyone seriously interested in modern picture books and their cultural significance. Lewis suggests five loose categories into which he thinks both prose and picture books can fit: boundary breaking, excess, indeterminacy, parody and performance. All these devices allow picture book creators to push the form to the limits and 'unsettle readerly expectations' (Lewis, 2001: 99). The main insight I have taken from my reading of Lewis' work, however, is that the picture books we call 'postmodern' have one thing in common: they are metafictive – 'they comment upon, or direct attention to, the nature of fiction in the process of creating it' (Lewis, 2001: 93). This is linked to the playfulness we find in such picture books (Wilkie-Stibbs, 2004). Think of the teasing way the Ahlbergs take us in and out of different fairy tales in *The Jolly Postman* and how Neil Gaiman and Dave McKean mix homely details like Mum's homemade jam with the description of terrifying 'crinkling and cracking noises' in the walls of the family house in *The Wolves in the Walls*. At the end of the story we are left wondering – what happened?

Hodkinson, P. (ed.) (1998) *The Nature of Educational Research: Realism, Relativism or Postmodernism* Crewe School of Education: Manchester Metropolitan University.

Lewis, David (2001) *Reading Contemporary Picture-books: Picturing Text* London: Routledge.

Figure 19 Tadpole's Promise by Jeanne Willis and illustrated by Tony Ross. Reproduced with the permission of the publishers, © Andersen Press, Random House 2003.

337

Moss, G. (1992) '"My teddy bear can fly": postmodernising the picturebook' in Hunt, P. (ed.) *Literature for Children: Contemporary Criticism* London: Routledge.

Wilkie-Stibbs, C. (2004) 'Intertextuality and the child reader' in Hunt, P. (ed.) *International Companion Encyclopaedia of Children's Literature* London: Routledge.

PRE-COMMUNICATIVE STAGE

See also: spelling

This is the earliest of Richard Gentry's spelling stages; it refers to the period in a child's development when he or she does not yet make sound-symbol connections, but is beginning to recognise that symbols can be used to mean something. Children often write invented numbers and letters at this stage.

Gentry, Richard (1982) 'An analysis of developmental spelling in GYNS AT WRK' *The Reading Teacher*, 36(2).

PREDICATE

This is something said about the subject of a sentence. Thus in the sentence 'Janet has long, dark hair', the subject is 'Janet' and the predicate is 'has long, dark hair'.

PREFIX

A prefix is an affix which comes at the front of a word, for example *un*usual, *dis*appear.

PREPOSITION

A preposition is a part of speech (or word class) that comes before a noun or pronoun to show its relation to another word – over, between, beneath, in and on. In the following sentence 'under' is a preposition:

'The key is under the doormat'.

PRIMARY FRAMEWORKS FOR LITERACY AND MATHEMATICS (1998, 2006)

The Literacy element in the Primary *Frameworks* in both versions, 1998 and 2006, aimed to encourage creativity and flexibility within a coherent and clear structure. The 1998 version set out detailed weekly objectives for literacy lessons, which took place daily in a 'literacy hour'. The literacy hour was structured into shared and group reading and ended with a short plenary. Whole texts were examined, both fiction and non-fiction, and there was also work on reading and writing at sentence and word level. The 2006 version, referred to as 'The Renewed Framework', brought some flexibility into the tight organisation of its predecessor and took account of the principles of *Every Child Matters: Change for Children* (DfES, 2004) and *Excellence and Enjoyment: Learning and Teaching in the Primary Years* (DfES, 2004).

The Renewed Framework of 2006 drew on the Rose Report (DfES, 2006) which is remembered mainly because of a new conceptual model termed 'the simple view of reading', which replaced the 'searchlight' model. The new model favoured phonics as the main cue-system to be taught in the early stages of learning to read. Rose suggested that children start on systematic phonic work by the age of five but he favoured active, multi-sensory phonic practice when starting young children on the road to reading. Another strong recommendation from Professor Rose was that a rich curriculum was needed, fostering all four interdependent strands of language – speaking, listening, reading and writing. This emphasis aimed to encourage links between lessons across the curriculum. The Rose Curriculum was abandoned when a new government took over in 2010. Has the Literacy *Framework* had any lasting effect on practice in the classroom? For me, there are two main contributions that it has made. First, the guidance on government websites on using ICT texts and equipment has been innovative and useful. Genuinely creative approaches were encouraged and teachers were advised about how to provide children with interactive story frames, podcasts, hyperlinked digital texts, films and animations. There was recognition that texts can be multimedia and multimodal, combining words, sounds and images. Second, non-fiction texts were given equal status with fiction and the terminology of, for example, the different kinds of informational text – recount, report, instruction, persuasion and discussion – has sustained.

PRIMARY LANGUAGE RECORD

See also: Centre for Literacy in Primary Education, reading, record keeping

This is a format for recording children's progress and development in speaking and listening, reading and writing, developed by Myra Barrs and the staff at the Centre for Literacy in Primary Education. It is used by teachers in the United Kingdom and in the USA and has had considerable influence on record keeping in general since *The Primary Language Record Handbook* was published in 1988. The handbook provides a helpful theoretical chapter on language and literacy development from three to eleven and detailed examples of teachers' records to show how the framework is used in the classroom. Teachers find that using this kind of record-keeping system which gives a constructive picture of the child's progress indicates what is important in the whole area of language development. Thus planning, teaching, evaluation and then recording are combined in a coherent approach to the English programme. For example, if the record has space for using the spoken language for different purposes and audiences, this reminds us to reflect on and create opportunities for different kinds of talk. This comprehensive approach to record keeping notes the languages children use and whether English is being used as an additional language. It has also been praised for bringing the parent and the child into the assessment process. *The Primary Learning Record* is a cross-curricular development from the original *Primary Language Record* and sets out a systematic framework for the assessment of all the primary National Curriculum subjects and ways of collecting evidence of progress.

Barrs, Myra *et al.*, (1988) *The Primary Language Record Handbook* London: Centre for Literacy in Education.

Barrs, Myra, Ellis, Sue, Hester, Hilary and Thomas, Anne (1993) *Guide to the Primary Learning Record* London: Centre for Literacy in Education.

PRIMARY NATIONAL STRATEGY

See also: early years language and literacy, Early Learning Goals, Foundation Stage, Foundation Stage profile, junior years language and literacy, literacy hour, SATs

This was the combined successor to the Literacy and Numeracy strategies and 'supports teachers and schools to raise standards across the whole curriculum'. The Strategy deserves this short entry as a matter of historical interest.

When the Secretary of State for Education launched *Excellence and Enjoyment: a Strategy for Primary Schools* in May 2003 the following aims were included:

- to combine high standards with a rich, varied and exciting curriculum;
- to encourage teachers to be creative and innovative in how they teach;
- to support primary schools in taking control of the curriculum and for each to develop its own distinctive character;
- to put in place supported teacher assessment at Key Stage 1;

339

- to make possible school networks and encourage links with parents; and
- to encourage schools to put in place a wide range of learning experiences and to create links between subjects.

(*Excellence and Enjoyment: A Strategy for Primary School* DfEE/QCA 2003)

PRIMARY REVIEW: 'CHILDREN, THEIR WORLD, THEIR EDUCATION'

See also: dialogic teaching, history of English teaching (in the primary school)

The Primary Review, the biggest independent enquiry into primary education in England for almost forty years, was launched in October 2006. Based at the University of Cambridge, the two-year project was supported by the Esmee Fairburn Foundation. After two decades of government initiatives, an independent review was timely. The Director, Professor Robin Alexander, said at the launch that the independent nature of the review meant that he and his team were able 'to ask questions about the quality of the education children receive without fear or favour'. Evidence came from written submissions, oral soundings from leading figures in education and from parents, teachers and children. There were ten themes of enquiry, including: purposes and values; diversity and inclusion; curriculum and assessment; and parenting, caring and educating.

A key question under theme 3, 'curriculum and assessment', was: 'Do the current national curriculum and attendant foundation, literacy, numeracy and primary strategies provide the range and approach children of this age really need?' Since Professor Alexander wrote this, the literacy *Framework* has been abandoned and the Rose curriculum has not been adopted.

There is an entry under 'dialogic teaching' which explains the contribution of Professor Alexander and his team to the development of this kind of classroom dialogue.

www.primaryreview.org.uk

PRIOR KNOWLEDGE

See also: comprehension, concept mapping, non-fiction reading and writing

Prior knowledge is the existing understanding of a topic which we bring to learning about it. When teachers begin a new topic, they usually talk to the pupils to gain some insight into how much they already understand. This knowledge of where the pupils are conceptually at the start of the work helps the teacher plan and resource the lessons, taking into account the needs of different children.

PROCEDURAL OR INSTRUCTIONAL GENRE

See also: factual genres, genre, recipes

Procedural or 'instruction' texts tell us how to do something. The chronological organisation of procedural text makes it a sympathetic genre for the very young, particularly when step-by-step instructions are given. One of the best books on the kinds of genre children read as they move through the school years is Alison Littlefair's clearly written *Reading All Types of Writing*. As with other kinds of writing, she looks at the 'register' of procedural writing. Register has to do with three things: what is written about (field); who is being addressed (mode); and how the message is given (tenor). We would expect the tenor of procedural texts, both print and electronic, for early years children to be informal. An active form, using the second person, as in 'First you mix the flour and sugar together' is more inviting than the passive form – 'first the flour and sugar are mixed'. As well as the recipes children read and write for simple cooking activity, the kinds of procedural texts common in the early years classroom include: how to look after the classroom tadpoles, how to mix paints to make different colours and how to follow the stages in a science experiment. The notices we find in the classroom can also be a form of procedural writing, for example: 'Please wash your hands after using the paints'.

By the later primary years we would expect children to have progressed to more mature use of procedural texts. They may have the opportunity to read and write instructions for using computers, CD-ROMs, the internet and atlases, and to read and write stage directions and more sustained science experiments. Two examples of this kind of writing are Chris Oxlade's *Electronic Communication* and

Figure 20 Things to do with Dinosaurs by Mick Manning and Brita Granström. Reproduced by permission of the publisher, © Franklin Watts, 2000. This book includes lists, labelled diagrams and instructions about games, models and plays. Children learn about the different dinosaur types through interesting activities.

Catherine Chambers' *All About Maps*, both published by Watts. The latter explains clearly how to read a map and how to construct one yourself. By the end of the primary years children can usually cope with procedural text with more formal features, for example the use of the passive.

We do need to check that instructions are clear for children of all ages. In a small-scale research study Littlefair found that the complexity of instructions in science books for children in the later primary years required careful teacher mediation.

Littlefair, Alison (1991) *Reading All Types of Writing* Buckingham: Open University Press.
Mallett, Margaret (2010) *Choosing and Using Fiction and Non-fiction 3–11* London: Routledge (Chapter 27).

PROCESS APPROACH TO WRITING

See also: conferencing, writing, writing corner/area

In a process approach to writing or 'process writing' attention is paid to the stages a writer goes through rather than just the end product. Writing is viewed as involving much thinking and reflecting and the teacher has an important role in helping the young learner shape meaning. The conversations in which a teacher, or sometimes another pupil, help a young writer to choose a fruitful topic (perhaps through brainstorming) plan and carry out a first draft, then edit and proof read and later appreciate the writing, have been termed 'conferences' by Donald Graves, a teacher and researcher in the USA.

Graves, and others in favour of the process approach, emphasise the importance of the quality of the whole writing environment and the aim of making the children feel part of a writing community. In the spirit of this, teachers encourage a 'workshop' approach and often write for or with the children to model the writing process for them. Children may like to have writing partners for some of their work and to keep a writing journal of ideas and comments on their own progress. This notion of reflecting on their own writing and taking some responsibility for it is very much part of a process approach. Frank Smith, also associated with the process approach, urges us to help children to see themselves as writers so they feel confident and have a strong self-image. Sometimes we have to 'scaffold' their early attempts until they can manage on their own and young writers often need to concentrate on 'composition' (the content of their writing) first and then on 'transcription' (secretarial aspects) and presentation (Smith, 1982).

If children experience a constructive approach to what they write at each stage, they are more likely to feel like mature authors and to have considerable commitment to what they have achieved. In an interesting article entitled 'Renters and owners', Donald Graves suggests that we might usefully see process writing in terms of a metaphor of 'ownership'. If we own a property and tend it carefully we are likely to feel more commitment to it than if we just rent it. So the child who has been helped to become deeply involved in his or her work is likely to care about the quality of the final draft in terms of content and the secretarial and presentation aspects. This brings us to the 'publishing' aspects which are another feature of Graves' approach. The process approach brought a move towards 'publishing' some of children's work in hardback books with spines so that they were robust enough to join the school or class library – further reinforcement of the young writers' achievements. There was a commitment to writing for a clear purpose and a particular audience.

This dynamic approach to children's writing had great influence in the USA and Britain during the 1980s and into the 1990s. By the beginning of the twenty-first century Britain's National Literacy Strategy

had brought a greater emphasis on grammatical aspects of writing and the English Standard Assessment Tasks assess end products rather than processes like planning and drafting. The issue here is whether knowledge of grammatical constructions transfers into children's writing to bring about an improvement. There is also concern about motivating young writers where tasks may be more prescribed. However, concepts of purpose and audience, book making and the role of the teacher in supporting young learners as they write are all still recognised.

Graves, Donald (1981) 'Renters and owners: Donald Graves on writing' *English Magazine*, 8, Autumn.

——(1983) *Writing: Teachers and Children at Work* New Hampshire: Heinemann.

Smith, Frank (1982) *Writing and the Writer* London: Heinemann.

PROGRAMMES OF STUDY

See: National Curriculum

PROJECT X

Although Project X is a reading programme that aims to raise reading abilities in all pupils, its books and guidance materials have been designed particularly with boy readers in mind. There are electronic as well as print texts and some cartoon strip texts with an eye to 'turning boys into readers' (Lewis *et al.*, 2008).

Lewis, Maureen, Young, Karen, Doran, Pippa and Wilson, Gary (2008) *Project X: Let's Get Boys Reading and Writing: An Essential Guide to Raising Boys' Achievement* Oxford: Oxford University Press.

PROJECTS

See: cross-curricular projects, English projects

Table 4 Different categories of pronouns

Personal pronouns	I/me, he/him, she/her, we/us, they/them, it
Possessive pronouns	mine, yours, his, hers, ours, theirs, its
Reflexive pronouns	myself, himself, ourselves, themselves
Indefinite pronouns	someone, anything, nobody, everything
Interrogative pronouns	who/whom, whose, which, what
Relative pronouns	who/whom, whose, which, that
Reciprocal pronouns	each other, one another
Demonstrative pronouns	this, that, those, these
Determiners as pronouns	this, that, these, those

PRONOUN

See also: cohesion, punctuation

A pronoun is a class of word used to stand in for a noun, or for a noun phrase. Often repetition of the name of a person, place or object can be avoided by using a pronoun, for example:

'Mrs Brown entered the classroom after break and sat down to read a report. She read it until the class returned'.

The second reference to 'Mrs Brown' is by means of the pronoun 'she' and the second reference to the report is 'it'.

As pronouns require us to refer back to a previous unit, they contribute to the cohesion of an account.

McArthur, Tom (ed.) (1992) *The Oxford Companion to the English Language* Oxford and London: QPD Paperbacks direct and Oxford University Press.

PROOF READING

See also: drafting, editing, punctuation, spelling, writing

Table 5

Spelling error	cross through word and rewrite
Omission	$\wedge$
New paragraph	//
Punctuation	mark to be included

Proof reading is the stage in the process of producing a piece of writing where the secretarial errors are noted and corrected. Teachers can model the proof reading process in the context of shared writing. In many classrooms children help each other, perhaps by sometimes working in pairs, to pinpoint each other's errors. Punctuation is to do with communicating meaning, so it may mean reading parts of the draft out loud to decide what kind of punctuation would be helpful. When it comes to spelling errors, some children find it helpful to look through their personal dictionaries of words they find difficult to remind them what to check. Above all, though, it is good classroom practice to encourage children's genuine interest in and curiosity about words (Kelly, 2009).

Older primary children might like to learn some proof reading symbols used by professional proof readers.

Kelly, Alison (2009) 'Transcription, spelling, punctuation and handwriting' in Graham, J. and Kelly, A. (eds) *Writing Under Control* London: David Fulton.

PROPER NOUN

See also: common noun, grammar, noun, parts of speech

Easily recognisable because it begins with a capital letter, a proper noun refers to definite persons, places and periods of time (for example: Richard, Paris, Christmas).

PROSE

Prose is written language set out in sentences and in contrast to the stylised patterns of verse or poetry. For a detailed and most interesting account of different kinds of prose typical of different periods in history, for example Old and Middle English prose and Elizabethan and Jacobean prose, please see McArthur, 1992: 814–18. When he considers trends in the twentieth century and beyond, McArthur notes that while every kind of prose is still evident – technical, legal and literary – the general trend is towards shorter sentences and relatively simple vocabulary as far as the subject allows.

When it comes to teaching primary age children how to write, there is a current stress in official UK documentation on changing writing style and vocabulary according to purpose and audience. More controversially, the teaching of grammar has been placed at the centre of teaching sentence-level work on the assumption that making grammatical constructions explicit will build up knowledge that can be transferred to the young learner's writing.

McArthur, Tom (1992) *The Oxford Companion to the English Language* London: QPD Paperbacks and Oxford: Oxford University Press.

PSYCHOLINGUISTICS AND READING

See also: 'big shapes', cue-systems, miscue analysis, reading

Psycholinguistics is a discipline created by joining psychology and linguistics. It is associated with a broader view of reading than just decoding print. In this approach children predict as they read but check these predictions against the actual words and letters on the page. Children make use of a number of cue-systems – the semantic, the syntactic, the grapho-phonic and the

bibliographic. There is more under the separate entries on 'cue-systems' and 'miscue analysis'.

PUNCTUATION

See also: colon, comma, dash, exclamation, full stop, semi-colon, sentence, speech marks

Punctuation refers to those marks on the page or screen that serve as boundary markers in written text and which contribute to making meaning clear. Teachers in the United Kingdom have been required to teach punctuation systematically since the National Curriculum was first introduced. As part of their English and Literacy schemes, teachers decide on when the different punctuation marks should be introduced, from capital letters, full stops and question marks in Year 1, to the very demanding knowledge and understanding of colons, semi-colons, parenthetic commas, dashes and brackets usually covered in Years 5 and 6. Learning about punctuation is linked to children's developing understanding of some of the differences between speaking and writing and to their concept of what a sentence is. In writing, we need punctuation marks to serve the same function as stress, intonation, pause and gesture do in speech. For example, if we said 'You need some more pencils' we would indicate that this was a question and not a statement by using a rising tone. To make the same distinction in writing we would use a question mark: 'You need some more pencils?' Children are more likely to enjoy learning about punctuation and to see the point of it if we use examples from literature to teach it. Exclamation marks indicate how we should read a particular part of a text. In *The Giant Jam Sandwich* by John Vernon Lord and Janet Burroway, a favourite book for reading out loud with under sevens, exclamation marks are used a lot to show us when to raise our voice to bring out the full dramatic impact. After remembering that wasps love strawberry jam, Bap the Baker cries: 'Strawberry jam! Now wait a minute! If we made a giant sandwich we could trap them in it!'

Other punctuation marks indicate the boundaries of units like phrases, clauses, sentences and direct speech. Usage of colons, semi-colons, commas, full stops and speech marks is discussed under the separate entries. Children find some of these difficult to apply in their own writing. It helps if we are able to convince them that good punctuation helps them communicate their meaning to their audience, to those who read their work. I have also found that keeping their own notes with examples of using speech marks and apostrophes appropriately, perhaps at the back of their personal dictionary, gives a focus for discussing this aspect of their writing progress.

There are some issues to consider when thinking about teaching punctuation. As linguists like David Crystal point out, the conventions of punctuation have changed and will continue to change over time. Older primary children find it interesting to study this. We only have to look at how email has brought about its own punctuation – as well as new spelling and grammar forms – to appreciate how swiftly these changes can take place. Then there is the issue of whether punctuation, which has such an important contribution to make to the overall coherence of a written account, is a secretarial aspect of writing like spelling. For convenience, teachers usually plan and evaluate this aspect of children's writing development under the transcription or secretarial category and this seems sensible as long as the very real contribution punctuation makes to meaning is appreciated.

There had been relatively few research studies on this aspect of language to inform classroom practice until Nigel Hall and Anne Robinson began work on 'The Punctuation Project' in the Didsbury School of Education at Manchester Metropolitan University. They have published a number of books, some with insights from research into how children learn to punctuate as well as sharing the results of their own investigation. You might like to start with the shorter publication *Punctuation in the Primary School* (Hall, 1998). I recommend also Alison Kelly's chapter 'Transcription: spelling, punctuation and handwriting' in *Writing Under Control*, which helps us appreciate that punctuation is to do with meaning and part of writing as a whole. Teachers can add interest to activities to strengthen understanding of punctuation by asking children to change the speech in the bubbles of comic strips into punctuated text and vice versa. Finally, BBC Education feature, from time to time, amusing advice for children about grammar and punctuation showing how good usage can help avoid ambiguity.

Crystal, David (2010, third edition) *The Cambridge Encyclopedia of Language* Cambridge: Cambridge University Press.

Graham, Judith and Kelly, Alison (eds) (2009) *Writing Under Control: Teaching Writing in the Primary School* London: David Fulton (see Chapter 5).

Hall, Nigel (1998) *Punctuation in the Primary School* Reading: NCLL (information is available on the site of the National Centre for Language and Literacy, www.ncll.org.uk).

——(2009) 'Developing an understanding of punctuation' in Beard, Roger, Myhill, Debra, Riley, Jenny and Nystrand, Martin (eds) *The SAGE Handbook of Writing Development* London: Sage.

Q

QUALIFICATIONS AND CURRICULUM AUTHORITY (QCA)

See also: assessment, literacy hour, National Curriculum, SATs

This government agency has now been disbanded but deserves a mention as it has shaped how assessment has developed in the UK. It was responsible for:

- producing standard assessment tasks/ tests (SATs) and yearly handbooks for teachers on the administration of assessment procedures;
- research on and evaluation of pupil performance;
- guidance on target setting and meeting the requirements of the National Curriculum and the National Literacy Strategy; and
- advice on particular aspects of practice, for example speaking and listening.

QCA publications have been praised for their acknowledgement that assessment can inform classroom planning without the need to record every judgement. They also provided helpful suggestions on formats for observation and record keeping. QCA also funded research. For example, they have supported projects by UKLA including *Achieving Boys' Literacy* and *Reading on Screen*.

QUESTIONNAIRES

See: research

QUESTIONS

See: non-fiction reading and writing

QUOTATION

See also: direct and indirect speech, ellipsis, inverted commas, plagiarism, quotation marks, speech marks

I simply cannot do better than set down Tom McArthur's words: 'The concept of quotation depends on identifying (briefly or in detail) the source to which reference is made and from which words have been taken' (McArthur, 1992: 836).

In speech we say something like: as Iona and Peter Opie famously put it – a child who does not feel wonder is but an inlet for apple pie. If we are giving a formal talk rather than just relating the quoted words in conversation, we might add the name of the text from which the quotation comes and its date of publication.

In writing we use inverted commas to denote the beginning and end of the quotation. So the Opies' quotation would be set out thus: 'A child who does not feel wonder is but an inlet for apple pie' (*The Classic Fairy Tales*, Oxford University Press, 1974: 17).

Older primary children who wish to strengthen an argument in their persuasive writing or when writing a history account can be helped to use quotations. It is never too soon to learn how to acknowledge the source of a quotation and avoid accusations of plagiarism – the use of others' words without acknowledgement! Books of quotations have a place in the staff room and school libraries. Teachers use such classics as *The Oxford Dictionary of Quotations* (which includes quotations from major writers like Shakespeare and from texts like the Bible in alphabetical order) and the similarly organised *The Oxford Dictionary of Modern Quotations* to help children track down useful quotes. Children's history books are a good source of quotations. I remember a class of nine year olds being intrigued by quotations from Samuel Pepys' diary when they were reading about the Great Fire of London.

There are also many anthologies of quotations, proverbs and words that children can use on their own, including the well-liked Kingfisher publication, *The Children's Book of Words* by George Beal. Some children love the 'wise word' quotations in A. A. Milne's *Winnie-the-Pooh: The Book of Questions* (Egmont Books). E.H. Shepard's illustrations add greatly to the fun of the quotations. Books like these encourage browsing and sharing and an appreciation of the power of words.

McArthur, Tom (1992) *The Oxford Companion to the English Language* London and Oxford: QPD & Oxford University Press.

QUOTATION MARKS

See also: direct and indirect speech, inverted commas, quotation, speech marks

Quotation marks (also referred to as 'speech marks' or 'inverted commas') are punctuation marks which show the start and the end of direct speech or a quotation.

We teach the use of quotation marks as children make their way through the primary years. When direct and indirect speech is taught, teachers explain that the inverted commas are placed round what the speaker actually said. Even so, this seems difficult for some children. Sometimes taking a short playscript or scripted dialogue and turning it into direct and then indirect speech helps.

Children, particularly when they are using direct speech in their stories, often need suggestions for synonyms for 'he said/she said'. Below is an example of dialogue where an attempt has been made to vary the verb:

'Do you want to take the part?' demanded the teacher.

Leon paused and then asked, 'Will it mean regular evening rehearsals?'

'Yes. But I am going to see if we can use some lunch times as well so that we can keep the evening rehearsals to just once each week,' replied the teacher.

There are a few other ways in which quotation marks are used in addition to their use in direct speech and quotations from texts. They are often used to designate cited headings and book and article titles. Putting a foreign or unusual word in quotation marks can alert the reader to its special status. For example – she showed a lot of 'savoir faire' during the project. We also sometimes use quotation marks to show that a word has been used by someone else and we are not sure we approve, as in – these 'angels' seemed rather selective in the tasks they were prepared to take on.

I remember one very able eleven year old asking me how she could organise quotation marks where there was direct speech within direct speech. One way of coping with this is to use single commas for the main utterance and double commas for the quoted speech within it. For example – 'I heard Maria tell her little sister "You can eat the bun" and she did not need to be told twice,' insisted the girl.

Older children would also find it useful to know that where there are several paragraphs of direct speech, new paragraphs all begin with opening quotation marks, but closing marks are given only at the end of the last paragraph.

QWERTY

See also: alphabet, Information and Communications Technology (ICT) and English

In the standard keyboard configuration on computer keyboards and typewriters there are four rows. The first part of the second row, on most machines for speakers of English, produces the letter-name QWERTY – hence our reference to a 'QWERTY keyboard'.

R

RADIO PROGRAMMES FOR CHILDREN: A HISTORY

See also: schools' radio programmes, schools' television programmes, speaking and listening, television and literacy

This entry concerns those radio programmes for children the primary purpose of which has been to entertain. The entries relating to 'schools' radio programmes' and 'schools' television programmes' deal with programmes more directly to do with teaching and learning. More than any other medium, radio has had the capacity to make young imaginations work hard; as one child wrote in 1926, 'I like the wireless more than the theatre because the scenery is better' (quoted in Parker, 1977: 26). Radio programmes for children are, sadly, in decline, however, and this entry provides a glimpse of their fine contribution over the years.

The first programme for children was broadcast in December 1922. By 1924 a BBC station manager could write: 'There is no section of our programme work upon which more time and thought is spent than that termed Children's Hour' (Briggs, 1961–95: vol. I, 260). The richness and range of its programmes grew over the succeeding years which meant there was something to appeal to most children. There were stories, music, quizzes and documentary-style programmes as well as

original plays. A strong element was the quality adaptations of classic children's stories such as *Worzel Gummidge*, *The Wind in the Willows*, *Winnie the Pooh*, *The Eagle of the Ninth* and *Ballet Shoes*. However, there were also many memorable series created for the programme, such as 'Toytown', 'Norman and Henry Bones, the Boy Detectives' and 'Jennings at School'. Listening figures fell in the 1950s as television came into more homes and especially after commercial television was launched in 1955. Children's Hour was taken off the air in 1964 in spite of much opposition; one observer called it 'an unforgiveable slaughter' (Parker, 1977).

Although the heart had gone out of children's radio with the demise of Children's Hour, some programmes continued, for example the well-established programme of nursery rhymes and stories for preschool children, Listen with Mother. In her article 'Listen to the radio' Susan Stranks locates the beginning of the end for mainstream children's radio in 1982 at the time when this programme was ended by the BBC.

Why did children's leisure listening disappear? Clearly because our culture had changed because of the dominance of visual media, especially television, film and computer-driven interactive games. However, many felt, and feel, that we still need an established children's radio network. Radio more than any other medium encourages listening and concentration and the exercise of the imagination. Older children benefit from this special kind of cultural stimulation which offers a source of knowledge and understanding that may be different from that provided by school, parents and peers.

Efforts were made to bring the programmes on offer up to date; for example Radio 4 had a thirty-minute programme called *Go4it* for the pre-teens which included interviews with pop stars and factual input as well as stories. The arrival of digital radio provided space for children's programming. Little Toe on BBC Digital Radio 7 was for five to seven year olds, while Big Toe was for children up to eleven years. These programmes offered stories, competitions and quizzes and were an excellent way of introducing children to classic books as well as to modern writers like Anne Fine, Justin Somper and Jacqueline Wilson. Children were asked to participate by sending in their drawings of characters from the books which have been read. Another creative programme was abracaDABra!, which broadcast children's reading of their own poems, stories and their music making, enhanced with sound effects. Did you know that coconut shells can sound like unicorn hooves and Cellophane like a crackling fire?

A radio network to support the early and primary years is not to be, though. In February 2011 the BBC announced that it was going to completely abolish radio programmes for young children and reduce its overall output of children's radio by 75 per cent. This was after the BBC Trust noted that the output was 'performing very badly' in terms of listening figures and the age profile of listeners. So the 6.00 am–8.00 am CBeebies radio slot will be replaced by a twenty-minute daily CBeebies podcast available online only, so ending eighty-nine years of radio broadcasting for children which started with Children's Hour in 1922. There will, however, be one hour each day of 'family-friendly' radio aimed at older children and parents, which will include some topical content, stories, book readings, comedy compilations and entertaining quizzes.

Briggs, Asa (1961–95) *History of Broadcasting in the United Kingdom, Vols. I–V* London: Oxford University Press.

Parker, Derek (1977) *Radio: The Great Years* London: David Charles.

Stranks, Susan (2003) 'Listen to the radio' *Times Educational Supplement*, 24 October: 24.

READABILITY

See: individualised reading

READING

See also: CD-ROM, cue-systems, genre, internet, literacy hour, living books, multimodal texts, non-fiction reading and writing, phonics, phonological awareness, reading age, reading aloud, reading choices, reading conferences, reading corner/area, reading diaries, reading environment, reading on screen, reading recovery, reading schemes, research (into primary English, language and literacy), response to reading, visual literacy

A central aim of schooling is to help children become competent and thoughtful readers and writers. As a child becomes literate important kinds of thinking are developed and success in all parts of the curriculum becomes possible. Later, levels of literacy will affect job opportunities and contribute to competence in all areas of life. Literacy also enriches leisure whether a young learner's preference is for fiction or non-fiction.

Here we are looking at the reading rather than the writing side of the literacy coin. At its simplest, reading is to do with getting meaning from print. In the twenty-first century there are new kinds of literacy to control and children need strategies to read on-screen media texts (CD-ROMs, software and the internet) as well as print texts (books, newspapers and magazine articles). There is more attention paid to visual literacy too – and to multimodal texts which combine design, writing and illustration in inventive ways. New kinds of text and new technologies change what reading is and pose the challenge of how to assess these new texts and competences (Bearne, 2004).

There is no definitive theory about how children learn to read, nor one practical method of teaching reading which is generally agreed to be the only, or best, approach. Teachers and student teachers need to understand the reasoning which underpins their own practice so that they can evaluate any proposed changes in statutory requirements or guidance and assess the results of research. In a particularly lucid and comprehensive book Graham and Kelly describe principles and practice to help those who teach reading and want to be in control of the teaching and learning processes (Graham and Kelly, 2007).

This entry aims to give you a foothold in this vast area, but of course you will need to consult government websites, other books and to follow professional development courses on reading to keep up with the latest developments. Although there are many different theories and philosophies of reading and an array of programmes and resources, there are in essence only three methods of teaching reading.

Methods of teaching reading

First, there is the *alphabetic method*. Here the first step is for children to learn to name aloud the letters of the alphabet. Next they name the individual letters of syllables and simple words and then they learn and memorise the spoken form of written words. This method goes back to medieval times and survived into the seventeenth century. 'Horn books' used to teach reading by this method can be seen in museums. These are made of wood on which a layer of paper is placed and protected by a transparent horn film. They look rather like bats for ball games and feature religious texts and the letters of the alphabet. The alphabetic method is rarely used now, but the alphabet books and friezes found in modern primary classrooms reinforce the continuing importance of the alphabet in learning to read.

Second, we have the *phonic method* which replaced the letter-naming approach of the alphabetic method. Here, children are helped to decode words by using sounds. This method came to the fore in the mid-nineteenth century although it existed earlier. In its historic form children learnt carefully graded sequences of sounds and applied this phonemic knowledge to reading simple texts. As the English language is not phonically regular children's early reading books or primers were limited to a vocabulary of phonically regular words. I remember being taught to read using a story called 'Tig is a Pig'. While phonically viable, the tale was bizarre semantically – you need the magic of a Dr Seuss to make phonically restricted books exciting. In the UK, phonics has been given a new lease of life and current programmes are based on the results of recent research. Further issues here are covered under 'phonics' and 'phonological awareness'. The importance of the grapho-phonic cue-system in learning to read is well established but new approaches to developing phonemic awareness include games and activities rather than drills. There are a number of books which embed phonics teaching in the context of flexible reading programmes that provide carefully selected high-quality material (Gooach and Lambirth, 2010).

The third method, *look and say*, emphasises the visual aspect of learning to read. Children start by learning whole words, often from flash cards, before tackling them in a book. Reading books are graded to include an increasing number of key words. Just as phonic readers have a vocabulary carefully limited to sounds learnt so far, reading books based on key words have a controlled vocabulary with much repetition of key words. Aspects of the 'look and say' approach continue to inform current good practice. Since English is not phonically regular, some words have to be learnt by their shape, for example 'yacht' and 'salmon'. Children also benefit from having a sight vocabulary of key words to go alongside phonic and other strategies. Further, this method recognises that it is helpful to look at families of words, drawing attention to the change of shape in the stem word when inflexional endings are added.

Combinations of phonic and 'look and say' approaches were used during the twentieth century and, in reborn forms, are still used as part of reading programmes today. Those interested in an historical perspective will also want to know about two approaches which, while not actually reading methods, were manifestations of some philosophies and theories of reading dominant from about the late 1960s. These are called the 'language experience' approach and the 'whole language' approach. Both incorporated aspects of the phonic and 'look and say' methods but they were embedded in a different philosophy of learning to read. The 'language experience' approach is associated with the provision of large collections of reading materials and resources and the principles and practice are carefully explained in a teacher's manual called *Breakthrough to Literacy* (David MacKay, 1970). A key principle is that children's first reading materials are best based on their own oral language so that children's talk provided an impetus into decoding the written language. Using huge word banks, children and teacher built sentences together using plastic sentence-making stands. Just as phonic primers were limited to phonically regular vocabulary and 'look and say' materials to key words, reading books to accompany the *Breakthrough* materials were based on a particular kind of content – built from the research team's conversations with children on topics of everyday interest like 'The Loose Tooth' and 'The Lost Dog'. There were some fairy tales and adventure stories as well. Critics felt that while phonic kits were included in the materials, there was no class-based, systematic approach to teaching the grapho-phonic cue-system. However, its linking of reading and writing and its recognition of the value of talking about reading is enshrined in current good practice.

The 'whole language' approach, which is strongly associated with child-centred or progressive approaches to learning in general, was very much in evidence in some UK schools from the 1970s, but a similar approach was popular in the USA as early as the 1940s. All sorts of strategies were employed to help children to use all four language processes – speaking, listening, reading and writing – in their learning. There was emphasis on 'real books' rather than commercially produced reading schemes and children's own writing and book making was encouraged. Like the 'language experience' approach this one was criticised for undervaluing phonics. Its insistence on 'real' books is no longer such a great issue as the gap between reading scheme books and 'real' books has narrowed. The work of many 'real book' authors is now found in commercial reading programmes, and books used in learning to read are much more socially aware and linguistically interesting. The welcoming of parents as partners in learning, the benefits of paired reading and the importance of children's writing are all aspects of the 'whole language' approach that inform good current programmes.

So what is expected now of UK teachers helping children learn to read? They have to work within frameworks set out in a number of official documents, not least the latest version of the National Curriculum English orders. Following the Rose Report (2006), teachers were advised to use the synthetic phonic method to teach beginning readers, and while the Rose Curriculum was abandoned when the coalition government took over in 2010, the centrality of synthetic phonics in the reading programme continued to be statutory. Henrietta Dombey is in favour of a comprehensive, flexible and research-informed approach in line with the view of the United Kingdom Reading Association (Dombey, 2010).

The simple view of reading

This model of reading, which replaced the 'searchlight' model of the 1998 *Literacy Framework*, led to recommendations that children at the earliest stage of learning to read should be taught synthetic phonics discretely and daily, and in a multisensory way. Phonics programmes and materials usually meet the following criteria. They should help beginning readers:

- with grapheme-phoneme (letter-sound) correspondences (the alphabetic principle) in a clearly defined, incremental sequence;
- to apply the highly important skill of blending (synthesising) phonemes in order, all through a word, in order to read it;
- to apply the skills of segmenting words into their constituent phonemes to spell; and
- to understand that blending and segmenting are reversible processes.

Professor Rose's 'simple view of reading' was set in a conceptual framework that recognised two main dimensions of reading – decoding and comprehension. He made it clear that the first – learning to decode through phonics – is time-limited, while the second – the development of comprehension – progresses throughout life (Rose Report, 2006). While many welcomed the recognition of the role speaking and listening play in literacy learning and agree that phonics has a crucial role in learning to decode, some felt less sanguine about the marginalisation of the other cue-systems, particularly the semantic and syntactic in the first stage of learning to read.

Progression in reading over the primary years

Reading programmes often claim to help us to promote progression in children's reading abilities in several important respects, including progression in phonics and spelling. Reading development is also to do with becoming able to understand a range of different genres or kinds of reading material, both fiction and non-fiction and in a range of media. Of course, we would also expect there to be development within the main genres. For example, while a child in Year 1 would be able to enjoy a very simple fairy tale, by Year 6 an able reader would cope with a demanding fantasy like J.K. Rowling's *Harry Potter and the Philosopher's Stone*.

The quality of response to fiction develops so that by the upper primary years children can use inference to get at an author's more subtle meanings. We would also expect progress to be made in understanding and responding to more challenging kinds of non-fiction – texts featuring argument and persuasion. There is more about this under specific entries like 'response to reading' and the different kinds of texts – persuasive texts, argument and so on. The next section considers the importance of attitude in children's journey towards wide, enthusiastic and reflective reading.

Attitudes helpful in learning to read

As well as developing a range of strategies to help children decode print and get meaning from it, teachers try to reinforce certain positive attitudes towards reading. The findings of the Centre for Literacy's Power of Reading project suggest that teachers' knowledge about literature and own love of reading links with the attitudes the children they teach have towards reading. Above all, we must communicate the sheer enjoyment reading can bring (Lockwood, 2008). The team on the Teachers as Readers project set up by the United Kingdom Literacy Association found that where teachers' motivation and enthusiasm for their own reading was high, this increased children's interest in reading for pleasure (Cremin et al., 2008). Some kinds of reading are the means to an end – skimming through a train timetable or reading instructions to mend a fuse – but we need to convince children that many kinds of reading are deeply satisfying, from a favourite story or poem to an information book about an historical period or about a creature's life cycle. Children are helped to discover this satisfaction by teachers who read aloud to them for sheer shared delight.

It is also important to cultivate a child's sense of confidence in their ability to learn to read and to use reading to learn about the world. Anxiety can be reduced by teachers and parents responding positively to what children are doing well. Quite small achievements are worth commenting on – 'good – you stopped and tried again' or 'I like the way you broke that word up into chunks'.

Another useful attitude to cultivate in young readers is what we might term 'tentativeness' – a willingness to take risks and try things out and learn from mistakes. In the end, though, we have to direct a young reader to the words on the page and help them discover their meaning.

An attitude of openness to a range of reading experiences can be encouraged by creating a reading environment full of interesting and useful resources. Reading corners and displays exploiting the huge array of different kinds of text – in both electronic and printed form – support a breadth of reading experience. The resources work particularly well if used in a range of relevant contexts. For example, a display of work done in history lessons with reference books, artefacts and children's work supports both the learning of history and the achievement of literacy. When it comes to non-fiction reading and writing it is best to link these activities to real purposes rather than used as a vehicle for decontextualised exercises. This is not to say that DARTs (Directed Activities Round Texts) are not sometimes helpful and interesting.

Assessment and record keeping

Some reading assessments are summative and, like the National Curriculum SATs, take place at the end of an age phase (see entries on assessment, SATs and Standardised Reading Tests). However, for a fuller and richer picture of a child's developing reading abilities we need to integrate assessment and recording into the planning, teaching and learning cycle and to keep evidence of progress. Formative tests, those which have a diagnostic element, are useful in informing our next round of planning for particular children.

Most schools have a portfolio system, often electronic, to store samples of children's work (see entry under 'portfolios'). So – what would a good reading section of the English portfolio be likely to contain?

- A summary of the results of a miscue analysis. Many teachers carry out this procedure or the simpler version known as a 'running record' with each child about once a term to assess which cue-systems they are using well and where some support is needed (see details under miscue analysis and running reading records).

- Informal but systematic teachers' records of children's progress in a diary format. The teacher might make dated entries after observing children reading in different contexts. In the CLPE's *The Reading Book* (Section 10) there is an excellent matrix which can serve both as a planning tool and a record. It would help make a teacher's approach systematic as it covers all the reading contexts (choosing books, reading aloud, reading silently, developing print awareness, discussing texts, using information texts, reading in drama and storytelling) and the social contexts (reading alone, in pairs/small groups, child with adult, small group with adult and large group with adult) that we need to provide.

- Evidence of children's involvement in their progress. Sometimes children keep their own reading logs or journals, dating when they read books and adding some comments in a format agreed by teacher and children. Teachers might add a comment on the child's remarks, making the log interactive. The child's perspective is also often recorded when teachers write summaries of what are sometimes called, rather grandly, 'literacy conferences' – planned discussions between teacher and pupil covering their reading preferences, response, needs, opinions and agreeing an action plan to help further progress. The teacher will need to scribe for younger children while older ones may write up their own notes for the portfolio.

- Comments from the parent or caregiver. Children's reading books and reading diaries go from school to home and back and parents are usually invited to make comments on children's progress. What parents have observed is also shared on parents' evenings and recorded by the teacher.

- Teachers' notes on how children are doing in the different aspects of literacy. It saves time if comments can be swiftly written down in a simple format. For guided reading, for example, all that is needed is the name of the reading group, the date, the text and the teaching focus at the top of the page and a comment box for each child with a section at the bottom of the page to note aspects to consider for the next reading session.

From time to time all this evidence needs to be summarised and presented in a helpful and easy-to-use format, agreed by the English/Literacy subject manager or Co-ordinator with the other teachers. The format should be designed to make communication with parents and the next class teacher easy. One well-known and much-praised format is the Centre for Literacy in Primary Education Language Record, which provides space for the views of parents and the child and notes if English is being acquired as a second or additional language. The latest version, the Primary Learning Record (incorporating the Primary Language Record) is a welcome development for many teachers as it simplifies and unifies the whole record-keeping process across the curriculum (Barrs *et al.*, 1988). Although more than twenty years have passed since this record system was published, it is likely to remain a guide to good practice.

Some teachers find the National Curriculum reading levels in some respects rather schematic. To help here, the team at the Centre for Literacy in Primary Education has devised some reading scales to use alongside the official levels of reading attainment. Children from six to eight are placed on a criterion referenced continuum from the dependent beginner reader to the exceptionally fluent reader who 'has strong established tastes in fiction and non-fiction' and enjoys pursuing their own reading interests independently.

Another well-thought of reading profile which shows a child's progression at text level, making use of context and making meaning at word level is the First Steps Reading Development Continuum from Australia. This profile takes us through six phases – role play reading, experimental reading, early reading, transitional reading, independent reading and advanced reading. Information from both the CLPE Reading scales and the First Steps profile feed directly into good planning for individuals and can be summarised on a record-keeping format like the Primary Language Record at the end of the school year.

If you work with the foundation age group (three to six years) your records will take account of children's progress in the reading element of the Early Learning Goals. Objectives to do with reading include broad understandings like recognising the elements of stories and knowing how we use non-fiction texts as well as word-level skills like linking sounds to letters. You may also find the Croydon Early Years Development Record helpful in filling out the picture. It provides evidence for the entry profile and is designed to reflect competencies in the child's home language as well as in English. Devised by a working party of teachers from nursery and infant schools in Croydon and Lewisham, the Record has statements that can be highlighted, ticked and initialled. Statements are organised under attitude to books and stories, rhythm and rhyme, reading illustrations and print awareness (contact The Schools Advisory Services Croydon or Raising Standards, Lewisham Education).

Into the future

New literacies are created as society and technology moves on. How children are taught to read in the future may be influenced by the findings of educational researchers and on cultural developments including innovations in technology. It seems likely, though, that government philosophies and policies will also be a strong influence. What, one wonders, will be the effect in the classroom of innovations like voice recognition computers? Will screen types of reading soon dominate or even replace reading paper texts? I doubt it, as reading print and reading on screen are qualitatively different experiences.

Already we attend much more in the classroom to visual kinds of literacy from 'reading' diagrams and graphics of all kinds in print and electronic form to understanding purpose and meaning in photographs and images on video film and the internet. Effective ways of evaluating multimodal and multimedia texts and ways of improving children's ability to read on screen are sought and addressed by researchers, for example Bearne, 2004 and Bearne *et al.*, 2007. Language is dynamic and changes whether we wish it to or not.

Barrs, M., Ellis, S., Hester, H. and Thomas, A. (1988) *The Primary Language Record* London: Centre for Literacy in Primary Education.

Barrs, Myra and Thomas, Anne (eds) (1991) *The Reading Book* London: Centre for Literacy in Primary Education.

Bearne, E. (2004) 'Multimodal texts' in Evans, J. (ed.) *Literacy Moves On: Using Popular Culture, New Technologies and Critical Literacy in the Primary Classroom* London: David Fulton.

Bearne, Eve and Grainger, Teresa (2003) *Classroom Interactions in Literacy* Milton Keynes: Open University Press (foregrounds social and cultural issues and looks in depth at the nature of classroom discourse).

Bearne, E., Johnson, A., Manford, P., Mottram, M. and Wolstencroft, H. (2007) *Reading on Screen* Leicester: UKLA.

Cremin, Teresa, Mottram, Marilyn, Collins, Fiona and Powell, Sacha (2008) *Building Reading Communities of Readers* Leicester: UKLA.

DfEE/QCA (1999b) *Early Learning Goals* London: DfEE/QCA.

Dombey, Henrietta (2010) *Teaching Reading: What the Evidence Says* Leicester: UKLA.

Early Years Reading Development Record London: Schools Advisory Service, Croydon with Lewisham Education.

First Steps: Indicators for Reading Development Continuum (1994) Education Department of Western Australia. Published by Longman Australia.

Gooach, Kathleen and Lambirth, Andrew (2010) *Teaching Early Reading and Phonics* London: Sage.

Graham, Judith and Kelly, Alison (2007 edition) *Reading Under Control: Teaching Reading in the Primary School* London: David Fulton.

Grainger, Teresa (ed.) (2003) *The Routledge-Falmer Reader in Literacy* London: RoutledgeFalmer (the twenty-five contributors have a broad conception of literacy and contemporary literacy practices and cover the influence of popular culture, new technologies and multiple forms of text).

Hall, Kathy (2002) *Listening to Stephen Read: Multiple Perspectives on Literacy* Milton Keynes: Open University Press (reading experts each have their own view on how to help Stephen).

Lockwood, Michael (2008) *Promoting Reading for Pleasure in the Primary School* London: Sage.

READING AGE

This is established by a child taking one or more standardised reading tests which make it possible to compare individual performance with that of a large number of other children of the same chronological age. Thus a child's reading age found by that comparison may be above or below his or her chronological age. If a criterion referenced test is used a reading profile emerges, but where the test is norm referenced there is no diagnostic element. In either case, in addition to the test score more informal evidence of a young learner's reading strengths and limitations and reading behaviour is needed to give a balanced picture of progress.

READING ALOUD

See also: novels

Before children learn to read independently and silently they read aloud to the teacher who supports and monitors progress. Even when children become independent readers they continue to do some reading out loud. Contexts for reading aloud include guided reading sessions in literacy lessons, reading directly from the text to give evidence for an opinion about part of a poem, novel or other piece of literature, reading in assembly or at school concerts and as a way of communicating information from texts in every lesson.

The value of teachers reading to children from all kinds of texts has long been recognised. As a mature reader the teacher models important aspects of the reading process. Younger children enjoy hearing picture books, poems and stories read by the teacher. Teachers of older primary children often read a class novel for all the children to share and enjoy. Some children are by this means able to enjoy books they would not manage on their own. For suggestions for a range of books particularly suitable for reading out loud and some ideas for activities, see Goodwin and Redfern, 2000. Among the suggestions for Key Stage 1 are Quentin Blake's *Fantastic Daisy Artichoke* and Ahlberg and Amstutz's *Fast Fox/Slow Dog*. At Key Stage 2 recommended books include *Unusual Day* by Sandi Toksvig, and Brian Patten's *Beowulf and the Monster*. *Unusual Day* is described by Goodwin and Redfern as a 'bridging book' which has short chapters and a line drawing per page as an introduction to longer novels for children. You will also find interesting and useful suggestions in Jacqueline Wilson's book on reading aloud (Wilson, 2006) and in Olcott, 2009.

The present writer joins the many teachers who believe passionately that new demands and more prescription must not be allowed to threaten time allowed for this profoundly enjoyable and educative experience.

Goodwin, Prue and Redfern, Angela (2000) *Reading Aloud to Children* Reading: The Reading and Language Information Centre.

Olcott, Frances (2009) *Storytelling Poems Selected and Arranged for Storytelling and Reading Aloud for Children* London: BiblioBazaar.

Wilson, Jacqueline (2006) *Great Books to Read Aloud* London: Corgi.

READING CHOICES

See also: reading, reading on screen, reading range

Large-scale research into children's reading choices usually uses survey methodology; subjects are asked to fill in carefully constructed questionnaires. The data from these, assuming that subjects give accurate information, tells us what children are reading and how much time is spent on reading compared with other activities, but does not necessarily illuminate the reasons why. For this reason, a survey is often followed by qualitative approaches, for example, by setting up interviews with a sample of the children involved.

Surveys give us a snapshot of children's reading choices at a particular time. If they are carried out at intervals it makes it possible for us to note changes and trends in children's reading habits and choices. The data from Frank Whitehead's survey based at Sheffield University in the 1970s has been a starting point for comparing the results of more recent surveys.

After Whitehead, the next reasonably large survey of reading choices was undertaken by The Library Association in 1993 with 2,300 children between four and sixteen. It was found that Roald Dahl, Enid Blyton, Judy Blume and Dick King-Smith were amongst the most popular writers. Have these preferences sustained? On the whole the answer is yes: Blyton and Dahl continue to dominate the popularity tables as do the Harry Potter and C.S. Lewis books. The 1996/97 survey by the team at the National Centre for Research in Children's Literature at Roehampton University found a trend towards children preferring contemporary novels like those of Jacqueline Wilson and fantasies like the Harry Potter books to historical novels. Younger primary school children were not included in Martin Coles and Christine Hall's very thorough large-scale survey of the reading preferences of 8,000 ten to fourteen year olds in 1999, so there cannot be a direct comparison of data with some earlier and later studies. However, the project, based at Nottingham University and funded by W.H. Smith, did give a clear picture of the reading choices of large numbers of children in the last year of the primary school. Many liked fantasy books, including science fiction, confirming the trend in the Roehampton study, and there was interest in comics and magazines and some non-fiction preferences, for example for books about sport.

This brings me to Booktrust's 2007 survey of children's reading choices, which included information from children and parents. Best-loved characters included Harry Potter, Horrid Henry, Tracy Beaker, Biff, Chip and Kipper, Hannah Montana, Doctor Who, Winnie-the-Pooh, Captain Underpants and Charlie from *Charlie and the Chocolate Factory*. Picture books, including Eric Carle's *The Very Hungry Caterpillar*, remained well liked by children and parents. As was found in the earlier surveys mentioned in this entry, though, the pull of magical worlds and fantasy characters remained strong and the team found that the Harry Potter books and C.S. Lewis' Narnia tales remained popular choices in the primary school years. However, perhaps unsurprisingly, there were signs in Booktrust's research that DVDs of stories were taking up more space on the bookshelf. Some 57 per cent of parents and carers commented that children, particularly boys, were more likely to watch DVDs and play computer games than to read print books. Reading on screen and reading print books are each distinctive kinds of experience and children benefit from achieving a balance of reading material and media.

The appeal of Blyton's world of the 1940s and 1950s – The Famous Five, The Secret Seven – for modern children surrounded by television, computers and the world of technology puzzles many. The outdated language and attitudes of the Famous Five led to the rejection of the books by some teachers, parents and libraries in the 1980s, but editors made some changes – for example 'a nasty common voice' became 'a nasty mean voice'. Children seem to respond to the safe world Blyton creates and to some simple, fast-moving stories.

Finally, small-scale surveys carried out in school into children's reading preferences remain popular. Teachers sometimes use books like Judith Bell's *Doing Your Research Project* to help with the design of questionnaires. Older primary school pupils enjoy conducting them within their class or school. The findings can lead to lively annotated displays and book week activities, for example interviews with children about their best-liked books or question and answer sessions with a favourite author to visit the school.

Bell, Judith (2005) *Doing Your Research Project* Maidenhead: Open University Press.

Booktrust Survey in 2007: www.booktrust.org.uk

Coles, Martin and Hall, Christine (1999) *Children's Reading Choices* London: Routledge.

The National Centre for Research in Children's Literature (NCRCL), Roehampton University: www.roehampton.ac.uk/researchcentres/ncrcl

Reynolds, Kimberley (ed.) (1996) *Young People's Reading at the End of the Century* London: Booktrust.

READING CONFERENCES

Reading conferences are conversations between a teacher and child about the child's reading progress, reading choices and response to reading. These conversations need to be built into the programme and summarised in the reading record as they are an opportunity to find out about a child's out-of-school reading and use of information sources like the Internet, CD-ROMs and computer software. The value of 'conferences' with each child (and from time to time with their parents) about attitudes, reading preferences and reading progress has long been recognised in the philosophy of the staff at the Centre for Literacy in Primary Education. The conferences are an opportunity for children learning English as an additional language to make known to the teacher the wide range of literacy experience they may have outside the classroom (Gregory, 2008).

Now that 'guided reading' has to some extent replaced a child's one-to-one reading to the teacher, reading conferences are important contexts for helping to widen a child's reading repertoire.

Gregory, Eve (2008, second edition) *Learning to Read in a New Language: Making Sense of Words and Worlds* London: Sage.

READING CORNER/AREA

See also: displays, libraries in primary schools, reading, reading environment, writing corner/area

The reading corner is usually combined with a writing area and provides a quiet place for children to read, browse and work. The amount of space available varies but children need a literacy area in their classroom from the nursery years right through to Year 6. Bearing in mind the age group, teachers try to make the corner inviting by providing simple seating and display areas. There are many attractive books and materials for children of nursery age and we would expect there to be alphabet and word books, nursery rhymes, big books, picture books, folk and fairy stories and illustrated early non-fiction books. The 'starter list' at the end of chapter 3 in Marian Whitehead's book *Supporting Language and Literacy Development in the Early Years* provides many suggestions for enjoyable books for the Foundation Stage. The collections in each classroom include examples of the text types children are using in Literacy Time for that term or year. Children need to be helped to move from enjoying picture books, story books, short poems and simple non-fiction to classic fiction and poetry, full-length novels and more demanding kinds of non-fiction suitable for the later primary years. There is also a need for dual-language books and for books made by the children themselves. As well as books the corner should include video-films on cassette or DVD, CD-ROMs and computer software, posters, magazines, newspapers and collections of advertisements and letters. I recommend 'Resources for reading' in Graham and Kelly (2007) for a detailed discussion of the kinds of books and resources for each year group. They remind us what experienced teachers know – that if we want children to feel involved in the book corner it is necessary to involve them in setting it up. Discussions about how to house the books – on shelves or in simple plastic containers – and how to categorise and label them are valuable. If the teacher uses some reading scheme books these could be stored separately.

The reading area should be a resource that is built into the work of the class. The books and resources should be those used each day and there should be fair ways of making sure all the children have equal access.

Graham, Judith and Kelly, Alison (third edition, 2007) *Reading Under Control: Teaching Reading in the Primary School* London: David Fulton.

Whitehead, Marian (2009) *Supporting Language and Literacy Development in the Early Years* Buckingham: Open University Press.

READING DIARIES

See also: portfolios

Keeping reading diaries (sometimes called logs or journals) with the titles of the books they have read at school (and possibly also at home) during a particular period of time involves pupils in record keeping. The diaries have many different formats but entries are always dated and usually annotated. It becomes tedious to have to write about plot, characters and so on every time and often just a short comment is all that is needed – nine year old Adam put 'brilliant story, interesting characters and tells us about friends' about Gene Kemp's *The Turbulent Term of Tyke Tiler* (Penguin, 1979).

However, teachers sometimes require more detailed reviews of both fiction and non-fiction as a helpful indicator of how a pupil's critical faculties are developing. A selection of the longer reading entries could be photocopied, written out again or copied using the printer if the work has been word processed and placed in a child's English, language and literacy folder or portfolio. If you want detailed suggestions about a format for these longer reviews, I recommend Judith Graham's

(1997) response sheets. As the author herself makes clear, the six sheets are a starting point for teachers and pupils and not everything should be included in every review a child writes.

Other good ideas for book reviews are suggested in *Boys on the Margin*, in which the CLPE team describe and evaluate the use of mini-journals as a way of enthusing children's reading of Louis Sacher's *There's a Boy in the Girls' Bathroom*. Many of the Year 5 boys in the class, in particular, seemed to find this helpful in finding a writing 'voice' to explore and appraise the book. The teacher encouraged children to try different kinds of writing in the journals, including writing in the role of the different characters to show different points of view and to include sketches and drawings (Safford *et al.*, 2004: 68–9).

Children find it satisfying to present their reviews to the class and to lead discussion. This is an opportunity for the teacher to assess a child's progress in speaking and listening as well as reading and writing. It also encourages the children to think of themselves as a community of readers and writers.

Graham, Judith (1997) *Cracking Good Books: Teaching Literature at Key Stage 2* Sheffield: National Association for the Teaching of English (NATE).
Safford, Kimberly, O'Sullivan, Olivia and Barrs, Myra (2004) *Boys on the Margin* London: CLPE (see minibook idea on pages 68–9).

READING ENVIRONMENT

See also: displays, fiction: choosing and using, libraries in primary schools, reading corner/area, response to reading, USSR, writing corner/area

The 'reading environment' is to do with the social context of reading. Where we read is important as is having the reading materials we want. Our mood, the time we have, the reasons for reading and of course our more general attitude to it all affect the quality of our reading. These are the factors that decide how far we are willing, avid and, most important of all, thoughtful readers – factors explored by Aidan Chambers (1991, 2011) in one of the most inspiring books ever written on the reading environment.

At the heart of his book is the notion of the reading circle with the enabling adult at the middle, the selection of resources at the top and reading (reading time) and response (book talk) at each side.

Chambers, Aidan (1991) *The Reading Environment: How Adults Help Children Enjoy Books* Stroud: The Thimble Press.
——(2011) *Tell Me* and *The Reading Environment* Stroud: The Thimble Press (new edition combining two of Aidan Chambers' most well-regarded books).

READING ON SCREEN

See also: CD-ROM, multimedia texts, multiple literacies, popular culture and new media, schools' television programmes, television and literacy, reading

New technologies have led to an increasing array of choices, new reading strategies and new reading habits. Reading on screen is now a well-established part of a child's reading repertoire.

Eve Bearne and her large UKLA team carried out research into children's on-screen reading in different lessons. The researchers observed children reading different kinds of screen texts including interactive CD-ROMs, computer games, and information and narrative on websites. Children's views on their on-screen reading in and out of school were revealed through interviews carried out with children of different ages (Bearne *et al.*, 2007).

When children read on a computer screen, a smartphone or an ebook reader, different skills are brought into play than those required for reading paper materials. For example, on-screen reading involves non-linear navigating through texts. The sequence of reading is different to print reading as children need to use hyperlinks to jump between screens. (Of course, just as is the case with print texts, information texts and narratives make different demands.) Screen reading frequently involves the processing of more visual information (sometimes including moving images) than do print texts. Sound and music are often part of what is distinctive about on-screen reading. Children's experience of home use of the computer can include playing games that involve skills of touch and drag and being responsive to colour cues. They are also likely to see adults use the internet for all manner of purposes. All this means that they cope well with colour cues, hyperlinks and accessing the internet at school.

The benefits of on-screen kinds of reading include motivational ones. Children who are reluctant readers of print sometimes seem prepared to concentrate when looking things up on the internet and tend to stay with things that interest them. The motivating potential of screen texts is well borne out in some of the case studies in the UKLA study; ten year old Peter and Poppy were observed screen reading three different texts: an interactive CD-ROM, a computer game and websites. The children showed considerable interest in the last two of these (Bearne *et al.*, 2007: 14–16).

Is there a downside to the increased use of on-screen reading? There is some concern that sustained, critical reading is less likely to be encouraged because of the highly stimulating nature of some on-screen texts and the tendency to move speedily from one thing to another.

Teachers can help by creating their own interactive whiteboard presentations and designing them to encourage thoughtful, well-paced reading. It is also helpful to exploit the potential of on-screen texts on the whiteboard for shared reading and writing. The sharing is likely to lead to the exchange of insights and opinions and to critical, involved kinds of reading.

Bearne, Eve, Clark, Chris, Johnson, Annette, Manford, Penny & Wolstencroft, Helen, with Anderson, Rosemary and Gamble, Nikki (2007) *Reading on Screen* Leicester: UKLA.

READING RANGE

See also: discussion, explanation text, fiction: choosing and using, non-fiction reading and writing, novels, persuasive genre, playscript, poetry, procedural or instructional genre, recount, report, short stories, visual literacy

Good practitioners provide a collection of books and resources for children to read, listen and respond to, and children often add the books they have made themselves, both handwritten and using the computer. Schools reflect changes in culture and in addition to a wide selection of books we now include computer software, CD-ROMs, media texts and access to the internet. Teachers working in the United Kingdom build up resource boxes of materials including advertisements, articles and newspaper letters to fit with the requirement that journalistic and persuasive kinds of text should be made available to older primary children. Pages from texts are often presented on the interactive whiteboard to meet a particular requirement. Particularly in the case of fiction, it is best if children have a chance outside Literacy Time to read or hear the text in its entirety. It is recommended that there is free flow between texts used across the curriculum and texts or parts of text used in Literacy Time. Suggestions for texts for children of different ages are set out in Graham and Kelly, 2007; Lazin *et al.*; Mallett, 2007, 2010).

Graham, Judith and Kelly, Alison (2007, third
edition) *Reading Under Control* London:
David Fulton.
Lazin, Ann, Moss, Elaine and Nicholson,
Deborah (updated every two years) *The Core
Book* and *The Core Booklist* London: CLPE.
Mallett, M. (2007) *Active Encounters: Inspiring
Young Readers and Writers of Non-fiction*
UKLA minibook 24.
——(2010) *Choosing and Using Fiction and
Non-fiction 3–11* London: Routledge.

READING RECORDS

See: portfolios, reading, reading diaries,
record keeping

READING RECOVERY

See also: miscue analysis, reading

'Reading recovery' is an early intervention
programme to help children with reading
difficulties. It is associated with Marie Clay,
a reading expert working in New Zealand,
who has achieved international recognition
for her contribution to our understanding
of the teaching of reading and writing. Her
programme to help struggling readers,
how to diagnose children's difficulties and
how to put supportive teaching strategies
in place, is set out in her book *The Early
Detection of Reading Difficulties* (Clay,
1979). The European Centre for Reading
Recovery is based at the Institute of
Education, University of London.

Wyse and Jones admire the way in which
Marie Clay mixes down-to-earth practice
with rigorous research (Wyse and Jones,
2007). A reading recovery programme
based on Marie Clay's work was put in
place in the United Kingdom in 1992 but
funding was withdrawn in 1995 (see Qualifications and Curriculum Authority,
1998; Wright, 1998). It was expensive to
train teachers in the method and labour
intensive to run the programmes. Nevertheless, many of Clay's ideas are used by

schools and teachers in a modified form
(Wyse and Jones, 2007). In her book *The
Teaching of Reading*, Jeni Riley shows how
teachers can use Clay's approach to
observe the reading strategies of all the
beginning readers in the class (Riley, 1996).
Key elements in the 'reading recovery'
approach to struggling readers are:

• early identification of children who
would benefit (Clay's running record, a
modified version of miscue analysis,
helps diagnosis of reading difficulty);
• one-to-one teaching;
• using texts with natural language rather
than the controlled vocabulary of some
scheme books;
• encouraging children to make 'locating
responses' about the direction of text
and pages by pointing;
• looking carefully at print and carrying
out word analysis;
• hearing sounds in words;
• linking sound sequences with letter
sequences;
• engaging children in sequencing tasks –
reassembling a story cut into parts;
• encouraging children to write stories; and
• helping children to monitor their own
reading strategies by, for example,
asking 'how did you know that word?'
and reinforcing their successful strategies with a comment like 'I liked the
way you worked that out for yourself'.

Clay, Marie (1979) *The Early Detection of
Reading Difficulties* Auckland: Heinemann.
Institute of Education, University of London,
European Centre for Reading Recovery:
www.ioe.ac.uk
Qualifications and Curriculum Authority
(QCA) (1998) *The Long-term Effects of Two
Interventions for Children with Reading
Difficulties* London: QCA.
Riley, Jeni (1996) *The Teaching of Reading*
London: Paul Chapman.
Wright, A. (1998) *Evaluation of the First British
Reading Recovery Programme* NISS EBSCO

MasterFILE Service, *British Educational Research Journal* 18(4).

Wyse, Dominic and Jones, Russell (2007, second edition) *Teaching English, Language and Literacy* London: Routledge.

READING RESOURCES

See: displays, history of children's literature, reading environment, reading range, reading schemes, writing corner/area. Also see the many different text genres – fiction, information stories, transitional genre, etc.

READING SCHEMES

See also: big books, Cambridge Reading, core books, individualised reading, look and say, Oxford Reading Tree, Project X, Story Chest

Reading schemes consist of books and other materials arranged into difficulty levels for teaching reading from about age five to age ten or eleven. In the 1970s and 1980s there was much debate about whether children should be taught to read using a reading scheme, with its controlled vocabulary, or using what were termed 'real books'. The reading schemes available at the time often had a stilted text and were criticised on linguistic grounds. There were also objections to the social messages in some of the books which tended to show adults and children from one particular group in our society. Gender roles were shown as more fixed than in real life and children from some groups rarely saw themselves described or pictured in the books. This was all the more worrying as many schools insisted on the children making quite a lot of progress through the scheme before they were encouraged to read other books.

Publishers of reading schemes have responded positively to such criticisms and many of their books are now by quality authors so the old accusations of linguistic poverty in the books no longer apply. Characters and settings are more representative of all the groups that make up our society and both boys and girls are shown taking up a range of activities. They have also introduced other media – posters, audio resources, CD-ROMs and software. Increasingly, writing activities as well as reading activities are built in. Also of note is the introduction of non-fiction titles – this kind of literacy was given welcome recognition in both the 1998 and 2006 Literacy *Frameworks* which have now been abandoned.

More recently another factor, the emphasis in Literacy Time on shared rather than on individual reading, has shaped the design and content of reading schemes and reading packages. For example, many publishers now include big books, which are sometimes enlarged versions of existing books. Story Chest started to produce these many years ago but others – Cambridge Reading and Oxford Reading Tree – now have strong examples. There are also initiatives like Oxford Literacy Web, a programme with materials organised under 'letter sounds and rhymes' (phonological knowledge), 'fiction', 'non-fiction', 'poetry' and 'launch into literacy, grammatical skills in context'. This can stand on its own as a full literacy programme or fit alongside Oxford Reading Tree. Despite the improvement in the quality of reading schemes in the recent past, it remains essential for teachers to assess them carefully before committing the school to the considerable cost of a particular scheme. Another issue is the possible effect on teachers' professionalism and self-esteem of accepting ready selected and organised materials to meet detailed official requirements. Publishers have increasingly sought help from leading experts in explaining how their resources should be used and the advice for practitioners is often very sound. This and the sheer comprehensiveness of these schemes can both beguile and terrify! We need to remember that part of the satisfaction of being a teacher is to work with colleagues to select materials for literacy that meet the needs of the children in the school in which you work. Many schools prefer a flexible approach in which they use one or more schemes, or parts of schemes, together with books and resources chosen for different ages and stages by the teachers. In building resources for a reading programme there is guidance in Graham and Kelly, 2007, and Lazim *et al.*'s *The Core Booklist*, which is updated every two years.

Graham, Judith and Kelly, Alison (2007) *Reading Under Control* London: Routledge.

Lazim, Ann, Moss, Elaine and Nicholson, Deborah (updated every two years) *The Core Book* and *The Core Booklist* London: Centre for Literacy in Primary Education.

READING TESTS

See: under individual test entries, SATs

READING TIME

See: ERIC, independent reader

REALISM (IN CHILDREN'S FICTION)

See also: adventure stories, domestic and family novels, fiction: choosing and using, history of children's literature, school stories, short stories

'Realism' or 'social realism' in children's books refers to the use of themes and characters close to preoccupations in contemporary life and events which could happen. These cover almost every topic including sensitive ones like teenage pregnancy, drugs, assault, terminal illness and abandoned children. Peter Hunt traces the 'realism or fantasy' debate to the 1970s when the 'teenager' became a 'distinct cultural category' (Hunt, 1995: 298). Of course there were 'realistic' novels for young people before this – Salinger's *Catcher in the Rye* (1951) and Paul Zindel's bleak novel about children betraying their elderly friend – *The Pigman* (1968).

What about social realism in books for primary age children? These include some adventure, domestic and school stories, which are discussed in separate entries. The book that stands out as an early example of 'social realism' for the younger age group is Eve Garnett's *The Family from One-End Street* (1937). Children still find it highly entertaining but some teachers and critics have felt it patronises people from a particular social group. By the late 1970s there was much debate about whether social criteria as well as literacy criteria should be used to judge books for children. On the one hand some critics felt concern about sexual, racial or social bias in books for the young while on the other hand others feared this could lead to both censorship and recipe-written books portraying the world as it ought to be rather than as it is. I think it is also a question of looking at the whole book collection in a school library and checking that as a whole there are not too many books about children with nannies and ponies and too few reflecting children from different social groups and communities. This debate is taken up in the chapter on 'Contemporary children's literature' in Hunt (1995).

Perhaps the emphasis in Nina Bawden's books puts the raw side of life in perspective: social problems arising from divorce, cruelty and poverty are explored but these elements are firmly embedded in a fully realised story. So we have a theme of loneliness in a young child in *Squib* (1971) and how other children respond to it. Older primary children enjoy her book *The Peppermint Pig* (1975) which is about an Edwardian family left to cope without the father when he seeks his fortune in America. The story centres on a year in the life of Poll, the youngest of the four

Greengrass children. The year in question is also the life span of the piglet, Johnnie, who becomes a pet but meets his end, as pigs tend to, when the year finishes. The story is about a child becoming able to cope with the sad aspects of life. In another of her books, *Carrie's War* (1973), events and characters – neither of which are shown in a 'cosy' way – are seen very much from the point of view of two young evacuees. Philippa Pearce tackles the tension between what children want and what their parents find acceptable with a touch of humour in her book *The Battle of Bubble and Squeak* (1978). Two pet gerbils stretch the mother's patience to the limits. Another pet story is *A Dog So Small* (1962) in which Ben longs for a dog – but when dreams come true there is often a price to pay. The book also explores the impact of broken promises by people a child trusts.

Gene Kemp's book *The Turbulent Term of Tyke Tiler* (1977) is a humorous school story with a surprising end, but as one perceptive ten year old told me 'it is really about friendship and Tyke really caring about Danny and his learning difficulties'. Jan Mark is another distinctive voice in 'realism' for older primary children and her books appeal to boys in particular. *Thunder and Lightnings* (1976) is also about a friendship – between middle-class Andrew and the less advantaged Victor. As John Rowe Townsend points out, although we hear things from Andrew's viewpoint, 'the book is more about Victor, who is supposed to be backward but who has hidden depths' (Townsend, 1995: 264). Janni Howker has been writing stories about the north of England since the beginning of the 1980s. Older primary children enjoy the five short stories in *Badger on the Barge* (1984) which are partly about relationships between the old and the young.

There are a number of contemporary writers who have taken on some of the many difficulties that face families as a consequence of poverty, changing circumstances and inadequate parenting. These include Anne Fine and Jacqueline Wilson. In *Family Fictions* Nicholas Tucker notes Anne Fine's ability to take on difficult and painful issues in a way that older primary children can understand (Tucker and Gamble, 2001). *The Granny Project* takes on the difficult issue of how we best care for elderly dependent relatives. Fine's dialogue is convincing and alive and she creates rounded characters: granny is far from being a dear old lady and can be selfish and irritating. Jacqueline Wilson also takes on difficult social issues in her books. Her most endearing and often infuriating heroine is ten year old Tracy Beaker. In *The Story of Tracy Beaker*, which is written in diary format as if Tracy is speaking to us, the young girl faces the breakdown of her foster home placement and enters a care home to face a new set of problems.

Other contemporary writers show the humorous side of family life. Jamie Rix's character, Alistair Fury, meets life's challenges in a spirited way. In *The Revenge Files of Alistair Fury: Exam Fever* we find Alistair desperately trying to stop his mum and dad 'discovering I am the thickest in the family'. Another good writer for modern children is Louis Sachar. Bradley, in *There's a Boy in the Girls' Bathroom*, fights and bullies the other children in the school, which is in the USA. Can Bradley become a reformed character? Will the school counsellor change him? These questions keep the young reader turning the pages.

What about books reflecting our diverse society and what it might be like to join it? Lisa Bruce's series of books about Jazeera and her family, whose roots are in India, are sometimes set in London – *Jazeera's Journey* (1993) and *Nani's Holiday* (1994) – and sometimes in India – *Jazeera in the Sun* (1995) – and are enjoyed by independent readers of about eight to ten but can be read aloud to younger children.

A favourite collection of short stories, again about the impact of Indian culture in Britain, is *Grandpa Chatterji* by Jamila Gavin – for children from about five to eight years.

Mary Hoffman's picture books about Grace, *Amazing Grace* (1991) and *Grace and her Family* (1995), some of whose family are still living in the Gambia, have a life-enhancing message: that you can achieve things if you really set your mind to it. In *Grace and her Family*, Grace has to take on a new culture and cope with her ambivalent feelings about her father's new family.

There are a number of books by contemporary writers about living in a new culture or about living in other cultures and traditions. Elijah in *Safe at Home* by Sharon Richardson has to make a new life for himself when his father dies. Some books show children coping with the restrictions faced in a particular culture. In *Homeless Bird* by Gloria Whelan, Koly is caught up in a series of difficult events when her Indian family want her to have an arranged marriage, while in *Rickshaw Girl* by Mitali Perkins, Naima dresses as a boy to learn to drive her father's rickshaw in a village in Bangladesh. The best books are not recipe-written and they share profound things about human nature that transcend class, gender and ethnicity. As we move through the twenty-first century, though, children seem to prefer fantasy – the works of writers like Roald Dahl, R.L. Stine, C.S. Lewis and J.K. Rowling – and, particularly for boys, adventure stories like those of Charlie Higson and Anthony Horowitz (see results of the Booktrust survey, 2007). There will always be a place for those short stories and novels which we term 'realistic', however, the best of which take on those human issues that matter to children.

Booktrust survey (2007) www.booktrust.org.uk

Hunt, P. (ed.) (1995) *Children's Literature: An Illustrated History* Oxford: Oxford University Press.

——(ed.) (2004, second edition) *International Companion Encyclopedia of Children's Literature* Abingdon: Routledge (vol. 1, Chapters 34, 35 and 38).

Townsend, John Rowe (1995) *Written for Children* London: The Bodley Head.

Tucker, Nicholas and Gamble, Nikki (2001) *Family Fictions: Contemporary Classics of Children's Fiction* London: Continuum.

RECEIVED PRONUNCIATION

See also: accent, usage

Received pronunciation is a term used in linguistics and language teaching to describe the accent associated with educated British speakers. It is the form of pronunciation usually taught to those learning English as a second or additional language and, until recently, was the typical accent of readers of the news on BBC radio and television.

People speaking English with received pronunciation use standard English dialect, but not all users of standard English dialect use received pronunciation. It is possible to speak standard English with a regional accent and this is socially acceptable in all but the most rarefied stratum of society.

RECIPES

See also: genre, non-fiction reading and writing, procedural or instructional genre

Recipes are a sub-category of procedural writing which explain how to make or use something or how to carry out a science experiment. Cooking is a favourite activity for young children and they are often helped to follow simple recipes for biscuits and cakes in the nursery or Reception class. Recipes provide a list of ingredients and then provide instructions for making the dish, often written in the second person 'First you take one egg … '.

There are many good cook books for children, including Angela Wilkes' *Step-by-Step Cookbook* (Dorling Kindersley) and Fiona Patchett's *Children's Book of Baking* (Usborne, 2006).

RECORD KEEPING

See also: assessment, portfolios, reading, reading diaries, speaking and listening, writing

It is generally acknowledged that children's progress in English needs to be carefully monitored. In *The Reading Book* Barrs and Thomas pinpoint some characteristics of a good record-keeping system. They are thinking of reading, but the principles apply more generally.

A good record keeping system needs to:

- be based on sound educational principles;
- include the collection of different kinds of evidence;
- be a cumulative picture of a child's progress over time;
- communicate clearly to other teachers and to parents and the children themselves; and
- be a collaborative process involving teachers, parents and children.

The Centre for Literacy in Primary Education have carried out considerable research into record keeping. Visit their website to find details of their *Primary Language Record* – www.clpe.co.uk.

Barrs, M. and Thomas, Ann (1995) *The Reading Book* London: Centre for Literacy in Primary Education.

RECOUNT

See also: genre, non-fiction reading and writing

A recount is a chronologically ordered retelling of events. Children's early recounts

may be in the form of their 'news' writing, describing what they did at the seaside, at Grandma's house or in the park (Mallett, 2010). Recount is one of the six non-fiction genres in the National Curriculum English orders.

In looking at progress in recount writing, Liz Laycock assesses the work of eight year old Martin. His later recounts as he moves through Year 2 show greater control over chronology and the ability to link his sentences with connectives like 'first', 'then' and 'next' (see Laycock, 2009).

Laycock, Liz (2009) 'Monitoring and assessing writing' in Graham, Judith and Kelly, Alison (eds) *Writing Under Control* London: David Fulton.

Mallett, Margaret (2010) *Choosing and Using Fiction and Non-fiction 3–11* London: Routledge (see Chapter 26).

Figure 21 At just five years old Rowan is able to write a recount of a visit made to the school by a storyteller.

RECURRING PRINCIPLE

The idea that writing consists of the same shapes constantly repeated is known as the recurring principle. Many teachers and educationists have observed that very young children produce lines of recurring shapes which will later be used in their writing. Children understand and experiment with this feature of writing from an early age and soon detect the difference between drawing and writing (Clay, 1975; Browne, 2009).

Browne, Ann (2009) *Helping Children to Write* London: Paul Chapman.
Clay, Marie (1975) *What Did I Write?* London: Heinemann.

REFERENCING

See also: plagiarism, quotation, research (into primary English, language and literacy)

The most widely recommended reference style is called the Harvard system. In this system writers record the quoted author's surname, year of publication and, if a direct quotation is used, page number. For example: In discussing the results of her study of the literacy development of six young children from different cultural backgrounds who all attend the same nursery school, Clare Kelly finds that 'the emphasis is best put on respecting the experiences which children bring to school which is so important for relationships in which children feel valued, included and positive about themselves' (Kelly, 2010: 7). This style of referencing allows the reading to flow in the main text. Full details of all references are provided at the end of the essay, article or book in an alphabetically organised list or bibliography. There is a detailed account with many examples of how to reference academic work in Mallett and Mallett (2000).

You may need to seek the permission of author and publisher if you wish to quote more than about 200 words. A fee may be charged for work which will be published, but this is usually waived when the long quotation is needed for an academic essay or thesis.

Kelly, Clare (2010) *Hidden Worlds: Young Children Learning Literacy in Multicultural Contexts* Stoke on Trent: Trentham Books.
Mallett, Margaret and Mallett, Anna (2000) 'From starting point to fair copy: reading, writing and thinking' in Herne, Steve, Jessel, John and Griffiths, Jenny *Study to Teach: a guide to studying in teacher education* London: Routledge.

REFLECTIVE PRACTITIONER

See also: metacognition, research (into primary English, language and literacy)

A 'reflective practitioner' is someone in any professional field who thinks deeply about their practice rather than just delivering it to prescription (Schön, 2009).

When it comes to people preparing to teach, it is helpful for them to get to know themselves as learners. This knowledge of one's own learning strategies and processes is often termed 'metacognition'. A good way of organising one's thinking is to share it with others and to respond to their comments. So those who educate teachers – college and school tutors – need to provide opportunities for students to reflect on their developing practice and to encourage them to listen and respond to all the 'voices' involved (Kendall, 2000; Whitty, 1995; Paige-Smith and Craft, 2007; Elliott and Norris, 2011).

Once students qualify, they should continue to see themselves as learners. Lawrence Stenhouse urged teachers to take an active part in research and curriculum development (Stenhouse, 1975). More than ever, we need to evaluate the materials and teaching strategies we use and insist on being part of decisions on curriculum change. In the area of language and literacy, for example, it is only classroom teachers who will make Literacy Time a powerful means of developing children's reading and writing.

Elliott, John and Norris, Nigel (eds) (2011) *Curriculum, Pedagogy and Educational Research: The Work of Laurence Stenhouse* London: Routledge.

Kendall, Sue (2000) 'Professional working relationships' in Herne, Steve, Jessel, John and Griffiths, Jenny (eds) *Study to Teach* London: Routledge.

Paige-Smith, Alice and Craft, Anna (2007) *Reflective Practice in the Early Years* Milton Keynes: Open University Press.

Schön, D.A. (2009) *Educating the Reflective Practitioner: Towards a New Design for Teaching and Learning* San Francisco: Jossey-Bass

Stenhouse, Lawrence (1975) *An Introduction to Research and Development* London: Heinemann.

Whitty, Geoff (1995) 'Quality control in teacher education' in Kerry, T. and Shelton-Mayes, A. (eds) *Issues in Mentoring* London: Routledge.

REFLECTIVE READING

See also: critical discourse, language and thought, metacognition

We read in different ways and at different intensities, depending on the context and on our mood and purpose. Reflective kinds of reading, in contrast to the quick scanning of a passage of text for a date or name or skimming to get a rough 'gist' of the content and ideas, implies understanding and evaluating what we are reading in a deep way. The Bullock committee refer to 'interrogating the text', by which I think they mean challenging taken-for-granted facts and bringing all our critical faculties into play.

For a clear and interesting account of thinking and reading across the curriculum I recommend Lunzer and Gardner's (1979) book *The Effective Use of Reading*. When reading non-fiction children need to develop the judgement to understand the status of what they read. Is it fact or opinion?

Reading literature calls for a different kind of reflection. As well as enjoying the story or poem, the mature reader is also judging the behaviour of the characters by their own experience – does what this character thinks and does ring true? We also judge the quality of the language – the success of any dialogue in telling us about characters and situations, the author's ability to create a setting. Does the author make us think deeply about some aspect of the lives of human beings caught in particular dilemmas and circumstances? Children also learn to think and talk about the features of particular kinds of text – the first person voice of the autobiography or the distinctive structure of a traditional tale.

One thing does press on me – all my experience tells me that children do not learn to read and then to read reflectively. Through talk about books with adults and other children they enter into a discourse of critical thinking and transfer this to their reading.

Very young children sharing the picture book *The Whales' Song* were able to discuss the very different attitudes of the uncle and the grandmother towards non-human species. An older class were able to talk about the subtleties of sibling relationships after reading Anthony Browne's *The Tunnel*. The novels of a number of contemporary writers encourage the imaginative exploration of themes. David Almond's books, including *Skellig* about a young boy's discovery of an angel in the garden shed at a time when he and his family are experiencing some difficult problems, often result in deep discussion.

So to make possible reflective thinking about texts we need quality materials that themselves teach us (Meek, 1988) and the opportunity to think deeply and to share our thoughts with others.

Lunzer, Eric and Gardner, Kenneth (1979) *The Effective Use of Reading* London: Heinemann (O/P but a groundbreaking book).

Meek, Margaret (1988) *How Texts Teach What Readers Learn* Stroud: The Thimble Press.

REGISTER

See also: field of discourse, mode, tenor

Register is a linguistic term referring to the way in which language varies according to the situation in which it is used. There are three aspects of register. 'Field' is the topic, 'mode' is who is being spoken or written to, and 'tenor' refers to the way in which the message is given – how formal or informal it is. If you would like to read further about 'register' I recommend Alison Littlefair's book *Reading All Types of Writing* which shares new thinking about both register and genre and the educational implications. For a more challenging read you might try one of the books by the linguists M.A.K. Halliday and R. Hasan, for example *Language, Context and Text: Aspects of Language in a Social-Semiotic Perspective*, or *Language and Society: the Collected Works of M.A.K. Halliday* by M. A.K. Halliday and Jonathan Webster.

Halliday, M.A.K. and Hasan, R. (1985) *Language, Context and Text: Aspects of Language in a Social-Semiotic Perspective* Oxford: Oxford University Press.

Halliday, M.A.K. and Webster, Jonathan (2009) *Language and Society: the Collected Works of M.A.K. Halliday* Continuum International Publishing.

Littlefair, Alison (1988) *Reading All Types of Writing* Buckingham: Open University Press.

RELATIVE PRONOUN

A relative pronoun introduces a relative clause. Commonly used relative pronouns are 'who', 'whom' and 'which'. 'That' can also function as a relative pronoun.

In 'the teacher who came to lunch', *who* is a relative pronoun in the relative clause *who came to lunch*.

RELIGIOUS EDUCATION AND ENGLISH

See also: Bible, epiphany, literacy hour, sacred texts

As is the case in other lessons, children and teachers use language to understand information and ideas in religious education. However, English also links closely with religious studies because both subjects involve us in thinking deeply about our experience as human beings. Both fiction and non-fiction texts help here and we can link texts used in Literacy Time with those in religious studies. Factual texts about different religions and religious observances can be used in religious studies to inform children's developing understanding, while in Literacy Time the same texts could be looked at as examples of the different kinds of non-fiction genre. *Welcoming Babies* is recommended for children in Year 1, five to six year olds. This information book shows how babies are welcomed into Muslim, Jewish and Christian families and links with children's own experiences can be made both in Literacy Time and in religious studies. What about religious texts that are organised as stories, though? The texts used in Literacy Time are broadly divided into fiction (a text that is invented by a writer or speaker) or non-fiction. Many people would be offended at their sacred texts being described as 'invented', but there is a problem about automatically placing them with other non-fiction materials. We could replace the categories 'fiction' and 'non-fiction' with 'narrative 'and 'non-narrative'. Narrative describes the style rather than the status of a story and can cover a range of stories from historical to invented.

For children aged about eight to nine years, I recommend Penelope Harnett's

373

book *Lives and Times – St Francis.* There are imaginative suggestions for work both in Literacy Time, distinguishing between fiction and non-fiction for example, and in religious studies lessons – talk about what makes a 'good' person.

In both subjects we encourage pupils to make connections between the events and issues in stories and their own experience as growing human beings (Broadbent, 2004). It is the significance and meaning of religious stories that will be central in Literacy Time as well as in religious studies.

Broadbent, Lynne (2004) 'Creativity in religious education' in Fisher, R. and Williams, M. (eds) *Unlocking Creativity* London: David Fulton.

REPORT

See also: genre, information books, non-fiction reading and writing

While recount has a narrative organisation, report is organised non-narratively. Reports usually start with a general introduction, move on to the main features of the subject and often finish with a summary. The typical children's information book on one subject like 'spiders', 'rivers' or 'the Romans' is organised as a report. The features of report writing are discussed in Mallett (2007).

Mallett, M. (2007) *Active Encounters: Inspiring Young Readers and Writers of Non-fiction* UKLA minibook.

RESEARCH (INTO PRIMARY ENGLISH, LANGUAGE AND LITERACY)

See also: bilingualism, Bristol Language at Home and School Project, early years language and literacy, EXEL Project, EXIT model, history of children's literature (includes details of centres where research is carried out), National Oracy Project, National Writing Project, reflective practitioner, siblings (and literacy)

Educational research takes many forms including large-scale surveys and statistical analyses as well as qualitative studies based on classroom practice or in the home or the community. We must not forget that library-based studies can also be valuable, investigating as they do such areas as educational philosophy, the history of children's literature, the evaluation of official documentation and aspects of language, education and society.

There is a vast number of research studies into all aspects of primary English, not least into children's reading and writing. Much research is based in university departments, which receive funding from charitable bodies like the Esme Fairbairne Trust, the Paul Hamlyn Foundation and the Leverhulme Trust. There have also been a large number of government-sponsored and -funded research projects. Not everything can be described in depth here and what follows is selective. I mention examples of research projects carried out by different bodies and organisations together with the websites which will give more information. Research into children's literature and the Nuffield-funded EXEL Project of Exeter University into children's non-fiction reading are covered in separate entries. So here are some of the bodies that carry out research into aspects of primary English, language and literacy.

- Booktrust: www.booktrust.org.uk. The School Libraries Project is one of the research initiatives of this independent UK charity which is dedicated to encouraging people of all ages and cultures to enjoy books.
- Centre for Literacy in Primary Education: www.clpe.co.uk, has a fine record of research projects which directly support the work of the classroom teacher. The Power of Reading Project, funded

by the Arts Council, aims to raise children's achievement through developing teachers' knowledge of literature and its use in the primary classroom. Data analysed showed that as a result of the work of the project, children's attitudes to reading as well as their attainment improved.

- National Centre for Language and Literacy, Reading University: www.ncll. org.uk. Research projects include some on children's home and community languages.
- National Foundation for Educational Research: www.nfer.ac.uk/research. This is the largest independent educational and children's services resource organisation. It carries out large-scale surveys and undertakes many assessment-related projects, including informal trials and pre-tests of materials. Statistical analysis is often used to see what works well in practice. Progress in Reading Literacy Study (PIRLS) is NFER's international survey carried out every five years, comparing reading attainment and attitudes to reading of over 200,000 nine to ten year old children in forty-one countries.
- National Literacy Trust: www.literacytr ust.org.uk/research. Aims to carry out research that leads to improved literacy attitudes, habits and skills by informing policy and practice. Their project, Literacy: State of the Nation, found, amongst other things, that one-quarter of young people do not see a link between reading and success. It was also discovered that one in six people in the UK struggle with their literacy because they have not reached the level expected of an eleven year old.
- The United Kingdom Literacy Association: www.ukla.org/research. Has details on its website of the many research projects it has undertaken, into every aspect of literacy. Projects include work on multimodality and

how the multimodal texts that children read and those they create themselves can be assessed. A project with Sheffield University, Continuity and Progressions in Moving Image Education, has involved the evaluation of the BFI's training scheme for leading practitioners in moving image education. The Raising Boys' Achievement project was carried out with the help of three local authorities and found that using digital texts and drama helped make boys more enthusiastic writers. Teachers as Readers, funded by UKLA and the Esme Fairbairne Foundation, involved both quantitative and qualitative research approaches to investigate primary school teachers' personal reading habits and their knowledge of children's literature. Questionnaires were used to find out such things as teachers' favourite childhood books. The main aim was to support the development of children's reading for pleasure and to help create self-motivated and socially engaged readers. Articles about UKLA and other research studies appear in UKLA's journals and publications, including *Journal of Research in Reading*, *Literacy*, *UKLA Minibooks*, and *UKLA Research Reports*.

It is very much part of a teacher's professional role to keep in touch with research findings to inform their work in the classroom (Kershaw and Chaplain, 2006), but teachers themselves are well placed to carry out some kinds of educational research, including into language and literacy, and so I turn next to practitioner research in schools and classrooms.

The teacher as researcher

Here I am thinking of the small-scale, qualitative[1] studies of primary English, language and literacy which can be carried out by teachers and by student teachers writing dissertations. Any curriculum, including the language and literacy curriculum, develops and changes and it is important that teachers are part of the development process. Undertaking classroom research confirms the status of teachers as professionals and reflective practitioners and discourages a view of us as technicians delivering the requirements of others (Noffkes and Somekh, 2009). The kind of research known as 'action research' is particularly suited to the classroom for the following reasons. First, it is essentially practitioner-led, although there is no reason why teacher researchers should not involve others like college tutors and student teachers. Colleagues, too, can assess the findings to reduce subjectivity.[2]

Second, it can address those issues that have come up in everyday practice. Topics my students have investigated, often in collaboration with their teachers in partnership placements, include: how far exploring a text through drama can lead to improved range and quality in children's writing; the progress of groups of children in persuasive forms of writing with and without writing frames; the role of the computer in promoting group writing; teacher-led talk about particular fairy tales as a way of helping children control the genre as readers and writers; and strategies to promote confident storytelling. The team at the Centre for Literacy in Primary Education regularly carry out action research and classroom case studies in partnership with teachers in school. For example, the Centre carried out a year's research in Year 5 classrooms where pupils were introduced to challenging literature as part of their English and literacy lessons. The book that sets out and evaluates the study, *The Reader in the Writer*, pinpointed writing in role and the teacher's skilful reading aloud as important to children's progress (Barrs and Cork, 2000).

Third, action research, like teaching, is cyclical and can enrich practice as it goes

forward. There is the formulation of a question or hypothesis, planning, teaching and evaluation, and then the fruits of the research are taken into the next round of planning and so on. However, although it has much in common with good teaching, action research involves a more than usual amount of time at the planning and evaluation stages. When well planned, it should be as systematic as any other kind of research (Bearne *et al.*, 2006). Collection of data has to be meticulous and includes recordings and films of classroom work, producing transcripts of children's talk, collecting examples of writing, formulating and assessing questionnaires, recording interviews and making notes of observations in research diaries. There needs to be careful attention to the dates on which things happened, who was involved and the time spent on particular activities.

The next challenge is to write up the story of the research, the findings and conclusions in a rigorous and lucid way. This will involve a section, a literary review, which situates the study in the context of other relevant research and thinking. Support here can be found in Judith Bell's well-known book *Doing Your Research Project* (Bell, 2005). While the challenge of taking on these projects alongside all the other things a teacher has to do must be recognised, sharing the fruits of the work with others is usually satisfying and enjoyable.

Notes

1 Qualitative researchers use texts, written and spoken (questionnaires, interviews, writing samples and lesson transcripts), and observations of what people do as a basis for their conclusions. They are systematic in their gathering of data. In contrast, quantitative approaches 'collect facts and study the relationship of one set of facts to another' (Bell, 2005: 5). They often involve large-scale surveys with substantial samples to produce quantifiable conclusions which

can be generalised. Many researchers use both qualitative and quantitative approaches within one study.

2 This is known as 'triangulation'.

Barrs, Myra and Cork, Valerie (2000) *The Reader in the Writer: the Links Between the Study of Literature and Writing Development at Key Stage 2* London: CLPE.

Bearne, Eve, Graham, Lynda and Marsh, Jackie (2006) *Classroom Action Research in Literacy: A Guide to Practice* Leicester: UKLA, Minibook 23.

Bell, Judith (2005) *Doing Your Research Project* Maidenhead: Open University Press.

Kershaw, Ruth and Chaplain, Rowland (2006) *Understanding Special Educational Needs: A Teacher's Guide to Effective School-based Research* London: David Fulton.

Mallett, Margaret and Mallett, Anna (2000) 'From starting point to fair copy: reading, writing and thinking' in Herne, Steve, Jessel, John and Griffiths, Jenny (eds) *Study to Teach* London: Routledge.

Noffkes, Susan and Somekh, Bridget (2009) *The Sage Handbook of Educational Action Research* London: Sage.

RESOURCES FOR ENGLISH TEACHING

See: CD-ROM, displays, history of children's literature, individualised reading, reading, reading environment, reading schemes, writing corner/area. See also under the different text genres like advertisements, comics, recipes, recount, report

RESPONSE PARTNER

See also: collaborative learning, discussion, speaking and listening, speaking and listening frames

Pairing children for oral or written work can bring variety and energy to an English lesson. Children choose or are allocated a 'response partner' and asked to discuss something that will help move the lesson on – what they think of a character in a story or why a sentence is punctuated in a particular way. Younger children are sometimes asked to discuss and carry out a simple task with their partner, perhaps to do with organising spellings into groups or making a list of synonyms or antonyms, and then report back to the class.

There needs to be some guidance from the teacher to help children make their discussions truly part of learning. Children have to be encouraged to listen to what their partner says and to make a genuine response and not just to agree with them. Teachers also help by focusing the task, suggesting things that are important to cover, perhaps writing them down on a board, flip chart or whiteboard. Writing tasks can also be shared and discussed and resources in different media are increasingly used to add variety; for example, a video clip added to an on-screen story can create a special atmosphere or setting. Above all, teachers can help by example, by monitoring discussion in Literacy Time and by initiating conversations in 'guided' groups by talking to individuals about their choices. 'Why did you begin your account like that?' Or, with older children, 'the passive voice works well there, can you say why?' These conversations demonstrate to children how they might proceed with a response partner. The great benefit of making tasks collaborative is that children gain practice in making their thinking explicit and experience how to learn from each other.

RESPONSE TO READING

See also: enabling adult, fiction: choosing and using, reading environment, zone of proximal development

We respond to different kinds of reading – fiction, non-fiction, environmental print and so on – in different ways. Children are most likely to respond deeply to literary reading. We know children have enjoyed a work of fiction if they want to read the book again or seek another one by the same author. We can help children become thoughtful readers by creating opportunities for them to share their response to a book that has moved, excited or delighted them. The role of the adult as mature reader is also of great importance. Aidan Chambers considers that however helpful learners are to each other, in the end young readers 'depend on knowledgeable grown-ups because there are some things about every art and craft – that you only know from experience and can only be passed on by those who've learned them by experience' (Chambers, 1991: 15).

This has implications for how we educate primary teachers: children's literature should, I believe, be a core area of study. For ideas to help involve children with a wide range of reading together with classroom case studies, see Mallett, 2010.

Chambers, Aidan (1991) *The Reading Environment: How Adults Help Children Enjoy Books* Stroud: The Thimble Press (a new edition of this book came out in 2011, combined with Chambers' companion book *Tell Me*).

Mallett, Margaret (2010) *Choosing and Using Fiction and Non-fiction 3–11* London: Routledge.

RETRIEVAL DEVICES

See also: information books, library skills, non-fiction reading and writing

'Retrieval devices' are those parts of a text, the contents page and index, which help direct the reader to the exact information he or she needs. They also indicate the scope of a text. Publishers of children's information and reference books nearly always include satisfactory retrieval devices and teachers model retrieval

strategies in the shared reading part of Literacy Time.

RHYME

This is a literary term to refer to words that are the same or similar in sound.

RHYTHM

A poem's rhythm is its beat and gives it form and pattern. The rhythm of a poem contributes to its meaning by contributing to the mood and 'colour'.

RIDDLE

A riddle is a puzzle that we are invited to solve. Often it is in the form of a short rhyming poem on the lines of 'My first is in … ' (Mallett, 2010: 185). Riddles are linked with an oral tradition and they often turn up in nursery rhymes and playground rhymes (Opie and Opie, 1959). Poetry collections are a good source of riddles – see those of Pie Corbett (for example, *The Playground Treasury*). Riddles from different cultures are retold by Hugh Lupton and Sophie Fatus (illustrator) in Barefoot Books' *Riddle Me This! Riddles and Stories to Sharpen Your Wits*. Another lively collection is *Riddles for Children* collected by Armand Coallier, published by Virtual Bookworm.

Mallett, Margaret (2010) *Choosing and Using Fiction and Non-fiction 3–11* London: Routledge.

Opie, Peter and Opie, Iona (1959) *The Lore and Language of School Children* Oxford: Oxford University Press.

RIME

See: onset and rime

ROLE PLAY

See: drama and English

RUNNING READING RECORDS

See also: miscue analysis, reading, record keeping

Running records are a simple kind of miscue analysis which enable the teacher to observe how a young reader processes a text. There are different approaches and while some teachers choose an unfamiliar chunk of reading, others use a known but not known-by-heart text. The important thing is that the procedure shows how the child reconstructs meaning, uses available cues and integrates strategies.

This procedure is usually carried out with newly independent readers, who read out loud to the teacher from a book. Using a photocopy of the paragraphs to be read, the teacher marks each word read correctly with a stroke. Some of the symbols for miscue analysis are used to identify words read incorrectly. For example, missed-out words are circled, substituted words are written above, words supplied by the teacher are marked 'T' and 'SC' identifies parts of the text where the child self-corrected his or her reading. New Zealand's leading reading specialist, Marie Clay, gives detailed advice about every aspect of carrying out and interpreting running records (Clay, 1985). It is important to mark every miscue and to reflect on the child's strategies carefully to arrive at an accurate diagnosis. Do the child's miscues suggest he or she is cueing into the visual aspects of reading and not also searching for meaning? A child's comments during the reading are worth noting as they may confirm aspects of the diagnosis. There are interesting examples of filled-in running records in the appendix of Riley (1996).

Clay, Marie (1985, third edition) *The Early Detection of Reading Difficulties* Auckland: Heinemann.

Riley, Jeni (1996) *The Teaching of Reading: The Development of Literacy in the Early Years of School* London: Paul Chapman.

S

SACRED TEXTS

See also: Bible, parable, religious education and English

In a plural society we have to respect texts which are sacred to the different groups which make up our community. There are a number of books that explain the world's major religions including Christianity, Judaism, Islam, Hinduism, Sikhism, Buddhism, Shinto and Tao. *What I Believe* by Alan Brown and Andrew Langley (Five Mile Press) describes the main beliefs, practices and festivals for these eight religions, for children aged seven to ten years. It is difficult to explain the complexity of each different faith to children – scholars spend lifetimes studying just one of them. Perhaps, though, a book like this would provide some background for stories from different parts of the world where some understanding of a particular faith is helpful. A well-regarded book introducing younger children to some different religions is Emma Damon's *All Kinds of People*, a lift-the-flap book from Tango Books. For further consideration of these issues please see under 'religious education and English'.

SALFORD READING TEST (SENTENCES)

First published in 1976 by Hodder and Stoughton, this oral, individual, untimed reading test covers an age range from 6.10 to 11.9. The test assesses the young reader's ability to read progressively more difficult sentences.

SATS (STANDARD ASSESSMENT TASKS)

See also: assessment, attainment targets, Foundation Stage profile, reading, record keeping, running reading records, speaking and listening, writing

The UK National Curriculum Standard Assessment tasks/tests are criterion referenced using the National Curriculum Attainment Targets set out in the current orders. SATS are often reviewed and revised and details of changes are set out on the Government's Education website: www.education.gov.uk.

Key Stage 1

Assessment at Key Stage 1 (five to seven years) has been moving towards teacher-supported tests and tasks. In English, teachers administer those for reading and writing using the NC Attainment Target Levels during the children's last year in Key Stage 1. The tests and tasks are matched to a child's ability and their outcome informs the teacher's overall assessment of progress. Most children of about seven years will be working at National Curriculum Level 2 in their reading and writing.

The teacher observes each child's reading progress and makes a record. At some point towards the end of Key Stage 1 a reading test aims to show how well a child is using cue-systems. A 'running record' method is often used to judge a child's strategies. In the same way as a 'miscue analysis', a 'running record' identifies a child's degree of success in using 'phonic', 'graphic', 'syntactic' and 'contextual' cues to decode words. A child's accuracy is judged and the teacher also notes if the child can retell the story and comment on its meaning. Further tests may be given if a child seems likely to be approaching Level 3.

The assessment of writing at Key Stage 1 draws on the result of a timed account as well as other writing the child has done. The timed writing task is done on one occasion, takes about an hour and is based on the kind of writing the class are currently concentrating on, for example a recount, an invitation or a story. It should not seem very different from the everyday writing tasks the children are used to doing, but it is essentially 'first draft' writing. The teacher assesses the result using sample assessment sheets with guidelines. A check is made that the result of the timed writing task is in line with other assessments and records of the child's writing progress. Key Stage 1 teachers moderate each other's assessments and a proportion of the cohort's scores, together with evidence, are sent for outside moderation. Parents receive a letter informing them of the NC English Level which most accurately reflects their child's achievement at the end of Key Stage 1.

Key Stage 2

Year 6 children (at the end of the primary years), who are operating in the teacher's estimation at Level 3 or above take unseen timed tests over a week in May. The reading tests are in the form of a booklet of a set of readings of different genres, some of which are linked to a theme. Children read through the extracts and questions for fifteen minutes and then for the next forty-five minutes answer the comprehension questions in an answer booklet. Children judged to be working at Level 6 proceed to a sixty-minute extension test in the same sort of format, but which requires an extended written response in the last question. In his review of assessment at key stage 2, Lord Bew came to the view that while grammar, punctuation and handwriting might usefully be assessed by timed tests, other aspects of writing (not least creative kinds) were best assessed over a period of time (Bew, July 2011).

What are the issues raised by the SATs?

The tests make considerable demands when children have to cope with different kinds of reading material in a short space of time. This may prevent some children from giving of their best. It is also the case that where the results of an assessment are fed into published league tables, teachers, children and parents experience considerable anxiety and teachers might 'teach to the test', causing a narrowing of the curriculum. The possible bias of the tests towards gender or ethnicity are a concern too. Boys seem to achieve slightly higher scores with certain kinds of text, for example, those with cartoon illustrations.

Many teachers have reservations about the forty-five-minute story-writing task at Year 6. Sue Palmer, for example, fears coaching for the test may 'distract attention from real creative writing, an activity from which children really benefit, since it gives them the chance to explore and express their ideas' (Palmer, 2001: 12). Thus Lord Bew's review which favours assessment over a longer period of time is welcomed by many (Bew, 2011). A number of other teachers and educationists have considered the SATs in the context of wider assessment issues (see for example

Wyse and Jones, 2007; Graham and Kelly, 2007). We must remember that the SATs are a snapshot of a child's reading and writing competence and may not reflect his or her true achievement. This means that teachers' ongoing assessments have an important role in providing a fuller picture of a child's literacy as well as evidence of what has been accomplished, and information on which to base planning for the child's future needs (Graham and Kelly, 2007). Other ways of assessing and recording reading and writing are under entries on portfolios, reading, record keeping and writing.

Bew, Paul (2011) *Independent Review of Key Stage 2 testing, assessment and accountability* London: HMSO, July 2011.

DfEE/QCA (1999) *English: The National Curriculum for England* London DfEE.

Graham, Judith and Kelly, Alison (2007, third edition) *Reading Under Control* London: David Fulton.

Palmer, Sue (2001) 'Dear *English 4–11*' on 'Issues' page in *English 4–11*, Summer, 12.

Wyse, Dominic and Jones, Russell (2007) *English, Language and Literacy* London: RoutledgeFalmer.

SCAFFOLDING

See also: metaphor, zone of proximal development

This is a metaphor used by Jerome Bruner to indicate the support the older person gives to the younger person in a teaching situation. Like Vygotsky, but unlike Piaget, Bruner developed a theory of instruction alongside his developmental stages. Both Vygotsky and Bruner believed that intellectual development could be facilitated and that children could achieve more if supported by skilful practitioners.

Just as scaffolding on a building is a temporary support, so the help given by the adult is expected to be needed for a limited time; the aim is for the young learner to achieve independence as soon as possible.

Bruner, Jerome (1966) *Towards a Theory of Instruction* Cambridge, Mass.: Harvard University Press.

SCAN

To scan involves a kind of reading in which the eye travels down the page seeking out a particular item, such as name or a date.

SCHONELL GRADED WORD READING TEST

See also: Standardised Reading Tests

This widely used individual test, which was re-standardised in 1972 (Oliver and Boyd), requires the child to read out loud from a list of progressively demanding words. The test, which is untimed, gives reading ages from 6.06–12.06 years.

The test is easy to administer and inexpensive. However, more recent tests are often now preferred since they take a broader view of reading and tend to use sentences and paragraphs to be read and understood rather than merely providing single words to decode.

Schonell Graded Word Reading Test (1972) London: Oliver and Boyd.

SCHOOL DEVELOPMENT PLANS

See: English/Literacy Co-ordinator

SCHOOL LIBRARY ASSOCIATION (SLA)

See also: libraries in primary schools

This association is a registered charity, founded in 1937. It aims to promote and develop libraries and offers advice, training and information bulletins to support library staff. It also helps and encourages initiatives to ensure school children's literacy. It provides a network of information in the UK, Europe and beyond for all school library sectors.

The association publishes a journal, *The School Librarian*, a quarterly that includes articles and reviews on fiction and non-fiction, print and electronic texts.

The Association believes that the resources in school libraries play a crucial role in learning across the curriculum and therefore works at regional and national level to promote appropriate provision for school libraries and school library services.

The School Library Association: www.sla.org.uk

SCHOOL STORIES

See also: history of children's literature

School stories are an important category of children's fiction, popular throughout the twentieth century and beyond. There have been stories for boys about boys' schools – for example Anthony Buckeridge's Jennings series set in Linbury Court Preparatory School – but it is a genre that has appealed perhaps even more to girls from about eight to thirteen. The two-volume *Encyclopedia of School Stories*, one section on boys' stories and the other on girls' stories, is a helpful guide up to the end of the twentieth century (Auchmuty and Wotton, 2000). In 1925 the very successful *Chalet School* series of books by Elinor Brent-Dyer began and the books remain in print (Girls Gone By Publishers). In the 1940s and 1950s Enid Blyton's adventures of Malory Towers, a girls' school in Cornwall, dominated the reading choices of many girls. Blyton is also the author of the St Clare's school series. Both series of school stories have been published by Egmont Books in new editions. Why are these books, written so long ago, still enjoyed by so many girls today? I suspect, from talking to children

and looking at the customer reviews on Amazon, that one reason is that readers can enjoy boarding school life vicariously. In spite of school rules, in some ways the boarding school girls enjoy a lot of freedom and today's young readers savour their adventures – for example accompanying Darrell Rivers and her friends as they tiptoe to the beach for midnight feasts. Of course, as Judith Humphrey points out, schools like the one in the Chalet School series are idealised versions and some real boarding schools may offer a rather more mixed and less exciting experience (Humphrey, 2009).

School stories are often in series: this is not unconnected with their marketing success, as Victor Watson points out in *Reading Series Fiction*. He goes on to show us the development in the school story and other books in series as they made their way through the twentieth century. The effect of wider cultural change on the school story is also explored in Sheila Ray's analysis 'School stories' (Ray, 2004). Some appeal to both boys and girls – Gene Kemp's stories about Cricklepit Combined School, for example. The comic situations in *The Turbulent Term of Tyke Tiler*, first published in the late 1970s, continue to amuse each generation of children. Young readers seem to like Tyke's adventurous spirit combined with a genuine concern for the less bright Danny and the surprise at the end never fails to amaze the first-time reader of the book. Louis Sachar's *There's a Boy in the Girls' Bathroom* also seems to appeal widely. Bradley fights and bullies and is generally badly behaved. Can he be persuaded to change? Then there is R.L. Stine's Rotten School series, including *The Good, the Bad and the Very Ugly*, liked for its jokey comic book flavour.

The school story, whether of the traditional kind or in new modern versions, is likely to remain popular as it taps into a common experience – nearly all of us have experienced school and know that all schools have rules, customs and routines. It is attractive also because it describes friendships and events relatively distant from the demands and worries of the wider society. The culture of fair play can be attractive to children, particularly those who feel their world is less ordered. Perhaps the immense popularity of the Harry Potter stories can be partly explained because they are exciting fantasies set in the context of a school which, however unusual it may be in some ways, has its own structures and routines and its own moral code.

Auchmuty, Rosemary and Wotton, Joy (compilers) (2000 edition) *The Encyclopedia of School Stories* Aldershot: Ashgate (two volumes: one on girls' school stories, the other on boys' school stories).

Humphrey, Judith (2009) *The English Girls' School Story: Subversion and Challenge in a Traditional Conservative Literary Genres* London: Academic Press.

Ray, Sheila (2004) 'School stories' in Hunt, P. (ed.) *International Companion Encyclopaedia of Children's Literature Volume 1* London: Routledge.

Watson, Victor (2000) *Reading Series Fiction: From Arthur Ransome to Gene Kemp* London: RoutledgeFalmer.

SCHOOLS' RADIO PROGRAMMES

See also: audio resources, radio programmes for children: a history, schools' television programmes, television and literacy

Present practice has an important history and so this entry begins with a summary of the history of radio broadcasting for schools. Here I have drawn on the information set out in Asa Briggs' five-volume work (Briggs, 1961–95). Then there is a consideration of current radio programmes as a resource for schools.

Early days of radio broadcasting

The BBC has had a commitment to Schools Broadcasting from the time of its foundation in the 1920s. The first experimental radio programme for schools went out on 26 February 1924 from its Glasgow station. It was heard by the children of just one school on specially set up equipment. Schools broadcasting was well established by the end of 1926 and soon seven or eight hours of programmes, for all ages, were being transmitted each week (Briggs, vol. I). By 1939 nearly 10,000 schools could choose between thirty-nine weekly programmes and by 1947 around 40 per cent of schools were registered for listening. In these days of varied and plentiful resources it is salutary to reflect that at this time not every school could afford to buy a radio for classroom listening.

In these early days the challenge for the BBC was to learn how the education system was administered, the role of the teacher and the place of listening in the teaching programme. There was an emphasis on imparting knowledge, combined with the recognition that programmes had to interest children of all abilities and backgrounds. As with the best publishers of non-fiction today, the BBC wanted broadcasters who were expert in their fields. They published illustrated pamphlets to support the programmes, covering history, geography, nature study, storytelling and language study, and worked with manufacturers to get good reception and the quality of sound that would help children produce strong mental pictures. There was a realistic notion of the attention span of young children and producers believed it would be difficult to hold their attention for more than twenty minutes and that it was enough to get three points across. Today's schedules still reflect these principles. Responsibility for schools broadcasting was put in the hands of a body broadly representative of the best educational opinion. Through its subcommittees the Central Council for Schools Broadcasting (formed in 1929) and its successor, the Schools Broadcasting Council (formed in 1947) drew on the skills of teachers, teacher trainers and the universities. However, some of the problems with which they wrestled seem familiar today. In 1948 the Council considered: 'why all attempts to stimulate reading and writing among school children by broadcasts had failed' (Briggs, vol. IV).

Schools radio today

'All of the Schools Radio resources for English have this purpose in common: to exploit the magic of audio and stimulate the imagination of the listener'.

(English and Literacy link of the BBC website, March 2011)

Changes to the scope and nature of schools radio are partly driven by economic necessity. The details of schools radio scheduling are available on www.bbc.co.uk/schoolradio/schedule and it is clear that the days of schools tuning in several times a week to hear educational programmes are gone. Yet, as the quotation from the BBC site that begins this section says, there is still a commitment to audio media and a recognition of its distinctive contribution to learning. The other positive aspect of change is that there is now tremendous flexibility in how the programmes can be accessed. The BBC Radio website has been redesigned so that programmes can be heard online via the central BBC iPlayer site and many programmes are now available as podcasts. Episodes from some programmes, for example one presenting *A Christmas Carol*, aimed at nine to eleven year olds, are available on the School Radio website for streaming at any time. There is a rich menu of material for use by busy teachers; for example, programmes have included

'Tales of Hans Andersen' for five to nine year olds, read by David Jacobi and David Tennant and accompanied by music and sound effects; 'The Wind in the Willows', that classic story about the adventures of Ratty, Mole, Badger and Toad, read by Bernard Cribbins, for seven to nine year olds; and 'Meet the Authors', a programme for seven to eleven year olds in which children interview leading authors. Notes for teachers are added to the site to coincide with transmission times. Pre-recorded CDs of programmes are available too. Today's teachers have access to a wealth of material from a number of sources, many of them visual, and will use radio programmes and audio resources selectively and flexibly. So it is rather a different scenario to the days when radio was the main medium, apart from print materials, used in primary schools. The best radio programmes to support English work still follow the principles underlying that classic of an earlier time, *Living Language*. The producer, Joan Griffiths, understood the potential of the medium to release the imaginative power of young listeners and to help them picture scenes and characters and to empathise with feelings. The poetry readings at the centre of these programmes were inspirational because of the careful use of the human voice, intimate and confiding. I remember my first class, ten year olds, listening rapt to the poems of John Walsh about everyday experiences and to some of the early work of Michael Rosen. Just as is the case today, teachers were invited to send in children's writing to be read out and shared with the listening audience. Current programmes like 'Meet the Authors' are very much in the spirit of dynamic and interactive programmes like *Living Language*.

BBC Radio: www.bbc.co.uk/schoolradio/schedule

The Pearson website includes details of audio resources to use with interactive whiteboards: www.pearsoned.co.uk/Imprints/BBCActive

Briggs, Asa (1961–95) *History of Broadcasting in the United Kingdom, Vols. I–V* London: Oxford University Press.

SCHOOLS' TELEVISION PROGRAMMES

See also: radio programmes for children: a history, schools' radio programmes, television and literacy, television programmes for children, visual literacy

A visit to the BBC Schools and Independent Television websites reveals a rich variety of television programmes, substantially in DVD format, to support every lesson, especially English and mathematics lessons. You may want to look at what is available on the BBC2 Learning Zone, broadcasting between 4.00am and 6.00am for recording and subsequent use. Or you may prefer to look at the BBC website: bbc.co.uk/learningzone, which has class clips that can be streamed onto a whiteboard. This highly visual and dynamic resource needs to be evaluated in terms of its suitability for an age group or particular class and in terms of the quality of both its visual and verbal content. Also, of course, we need to keep in mind how all this links and integrates with the bigger shapes of the children's learning. Children growing up in a visual and electronic age can often be the teacher's partners in evaluating particular programmes. At best, a television programme on literacy and English will both encourage and inspire children to develop as speakers and listeners and as independent readers and writers. This entry begins with a selective history and then moves into a consideration of some current programmes.

Early years of schools' television

The principle that there should be schools broadcasting on television was discussed in 1946 as television transmissions began again after the Second World War. However, the very high cost of television sets was a problem for schools and early experimental programmes were not thought to be up to the standard of the educational films which had an established place in many schools. Regular programmes did not begin until 1957, the year after the newly formed independent television company, Associated-Rediffusion, announced that it was proposing a series of schools broadcasts. The commercial television companies agreed that the schools programmes should not contain advertising and set up advisory committees to help ensure some quality in the programmes, especially after a good deal of press and public hostility and doubts about whether they could be expected to comply with the nation's standard of taste! (Sendall, 1982–90: vol. 1, 270.) All this activity stimulated the BBC into action and by the end of 1957, when the independent channels were reaching a few hundred schools, the BBC were reaching a few thousand. The growth in viewing figures was affected by the high cost of television sets and unwillingness or inability of government and local education authorities to find the money to buy them. However, there was some, albeit limited, financial support from government: in 1957 a grant of 50 per cent of the cost of a television was available from the Ministry of Education on the basis of one set per 100,000 children (Sendall, 1982–90: vol. 1, 274). This will not have been a hardship for the Head of Manchester Grammar School, who said that 'television would enter his school over his dead body'. By 1963 there were 5,000 'viewing schools', around two-thirds of which were primary schools. Support came from Lady Plowden who took a positive view of the educational value of television (Plowden Report, 1967). By 1977 Independent Television Company schools' programmes were reaching over 20,000 primary schools. The use of these programmes had been helped and made more flexible from the early 1970s by the arrival of video recorders. However, at that time school inspectors noted that programmes were not always used effectively because of inadequate equipment and because teachers had not been trained to make the best use of what was available. Independent television programmes in the 1970s included *Seeing and Doing* for infant classes and programmes such as *Fun to Read* and *Primary Maths* which tried to address contemporary concerns about literacy and numeracy. Nothing changes it seems!

Schools' television in the 2000s

From these beginnings schools' television has continued to thrive as we see from the listings on the websites of the BBC and Channel 4. Television is a dynamic medium so we should not be surprised to find rapid changes in the names and content of programmes. Of course, programmes are dropped and others added. There is also constant expansion of kinds of media and methods of presentation and communication. Starting with the BBC website – www.bbc.co.uk – links to the latest information on schools television, DVD and video-film resources can be found. BBC Active (formerly known as BBC Worldwide Learning and including BBC Children's learning and BBC languages) is now part of Pearson Education (www.pearsoned.co.uk/Imprints/BBCActive). This website informs about a range of resources including videos and DVDs with content from BBC programmes, for example from CBeebies and David Attenborough's Natural World programmes.

Teachers will find two hours of educational programmes on the BBC2 Learning Zone, broadcast between 4.00am and 6.00am for recording and later use. Another source of material is at www.bbc.co.uk/learningzone, where there are broadband offerings and short 'class clips' to download and stream to the class onto a computer or interactive whiteboard. There are audio resources as well as visual ones. The same expansion and developments apply to Channel 4's learning programmes and resources. On their website – www.channel4learning.com – there is information about online resources to support and enhance classroom learning. Some link with Channel 4's morning schedule, others are purely online.

Some examples of current and recent programmes and resources

- *Foundations of Literacy* (BBC2 and also available on BBC Digital Radio 4) is a programme for the Foundation Stage (three to six years). This programme, which is part of CBeebies, broadcast from early morning, takes children through the key 'stepping stones' within the Foundation Curriculum strand for Communication, Language and Literacy and is supported by a video-film, a teacher's book and colourful posters. The print materials are written by Sue Palmer and Pie Corbett.
- *The Magic Key* is for five to six year olds who can enjoy and respond to the language play of the magic key characters (BBC2).
- *Words and Pictures* (BBC2) for five to seven year olds presents language games using an interactive whiteboard to help with phonic knowledge.
- *Spelling with the Spellits* (BBC2) is a programme for seven to eleven year olds to support National Literacy Strategy word-level objectives.
- *English Express – Language Knowledge* (BBC2) for nine to eleven year olds provides structured teaching covering nouns, adjectives, verbs and conjunctions.
- *English File – In Context* (BBC2) for ages seven to eleven provides the essential social and cultural background to six provocative classics of the twentieth

century. These television programmes are supported by materials of various kinds. Thus for the series 'Let's Write a Story' there are video-films for each unit and a teacher's activity book which includes teacher notes and lesson plans, activity sheets, writing frames and colourful posters.

- *The Illustrated Mum* (Channel 4) for ten to fourteen year olds is based on Jacqueline Wilson's book. This is one of Channel 4's occasional programmes to support English, and comes with videos/DVDs and programme notes.

While schools television has rich resources to offer teachers and children, decisions about which programmes to view, what resources to buy and how all this is integrated into the English programme will lie with English Co-ordinators and their teams. The reflective practitioner will look critically at the programmes and resources on offer and make sure they serve their purposes and priorities.

Briggs, Asa (1961–95) *History of Broadcasting in the United Kingdom Vols I–V* London: Oxford University Press.

The website www.broadcastforschools.co.uk gives details of BBC and independent radio and television programmes.

Sendall, Bernard (1982–90) *Independent Television in Britain Vols. 1–4* London: Macmillan.

Teachers' TV (www.teachers.tv) offers support with planning across the primary (and secondary) school curriculum. It provides lists of resources including DVDs and video-film which incorporate clips from television programmes.

SCIENCE AND ENGLISH

See also: CD-ROM, diagrams, factual genres, genre, information books, language across the curriculum, non-fiction reading and writing

In science, as in other lessons, children and their teachers use language – speaking, listening, reading and writing – to discuss, explain, question and understand concepts and to encode them in writing. We think of science involving diagrams, but even in these contexts language helps organise the learning achieved. Part of learning in science is to do with acquiring a technical vocabulary to clinch the concepts. This vocabulary is used and explained in the non-fiction texts children use in science lessons – work cards, reference books like science dictionaries and encyclopedias and in information books and software on topics like electricity, water and magnets. The internet is also a source of a great deal of information. So children's literacy is developed through their work in science; this link between science and literacy has been strengthened by the use of science texts in the shared reading and writing part of Literacy Time as an example of scientific genre. We need to look for certain qualities in the science materials we select for children of different ages, interests and abilities, and the criteria we might keep in mind for information books and CD-ROMs are discussed under the appropriate entries. Let me just say that I think a good science book, as well as scoring well on accuracy, clear format, quality of writing and illustration, needs to encourage an enquiring mind and a curiosity to find out more.

It is worth mentioning here some of those science books that have a lyrical quality, and use imagery in ways we associate more with arts subjects. For example, in *Think of an Eel* by Karen Wallace and Mike Bostock, the young elver is an 'eel-leaf' and the creature 'wriggles, slips and climbs'. These poetic images are precise enough to help children learn about the physical features of the creature and how it moves. The books of Mick Manning and Brita Granström on nature and wildlife, for example *Voices of the Rain Forest*, use language and illustration

389

in an imaginative and lyrical way (Mallett, 2006).

Perhaps we are less likely to think of fiction as a source of inspiration for science, but stories and poems can link science and English in a fruitful and sometimes exciting way. There is some evidence that girls in particular find a story approach to science humanises the subject for them and makes it more attractive (Frost, 1997). In her interesting book *Creativity in Primary Science* Jenny Frost describes how five and six year olds enjoyed hearing a Masai story called *Who's in Rabbit's House* told by Verna Aardema. The story tells how Rabbit returns to his house to hear some rather puzzling sounds inside. The tale was used as a starting point for making Rabbit's house out of cardboard and then developing a listening activity; some children made noises using shells, pencils and so on and asked the other children to guess which implement is making the sounds. Each child speaker held a large conch shell when it was their turn to guess. One outcome was a wonderful hard-backed book, made by the teacher and children, with charts showing the results of the listening activities. Ted Hughes' modern fairy tale *The Iron Man* can stimulate an interest in magnetism and, for younger children, Verna Aadema's *Bringing the Rain to Kapiti Plain* can reinforce the understanding that plants need water and light to grow.

Of course, there are many aspects of science where it will be hard to find a related fiction text. I think the most promising areas for poems and stories arise from environmental and animal welfare issues. There are many works of fiction that reach out to children's love of and interest in wildlife and the natural world. If we want scientists who care about the environment deeply and about wildlife we should not underestimate the role of fiction in awakening concern and interest. Younger children enjoy Beatrix Potter's *The Tale of Squirrel Nutkin* (Frederick Warne) and

reading this would be a good preliminary to reflecting on the fate of the red squirrel, once prolific but now rare in the British Isles. Since the turn of the century we have lost much of the woodland that was this creature's habitat. The same sort of problems have affected the animals introduced in fictional guise in the children's classic Kenneth Grahame's *Wind in the Willows* (Methuen). The book creates the riverbank environment before pollution wrought havoc. In *The Willows and Beyond*, William Horwood has created sequels to the original stories in which the Wild Wood has been cut down by housing developers. Texts like Ted Hughes' *The Iron Woman* and Barbara Jeffers' *Brother Eagle, Sister Sky* (a retelling of an American-Indian legend) are also used to bring home environmental issues, and manage to take on the complexity of these.

Poetry, too, can link science and English. *Nature Adventures* by Mick Manning and Brita Granström, dedicated to the Wildlife Trusts, is full of scientific information and careful drawings of plants and creatures, and demonstrates how children might create their own nature journals of pictures and observations. Interestingly, the book also brings the poet's eye, which can be precise in observing nature, to comment on the countryside with quotations, sometimes in speech bubbles from, for example, Blake, Wordsworth, Keats, Brontë and Walter de la Mare. The quotations are chosen to pinpoint the features and essence of natural phenomena: Yeats' powerful and telling image of a seabird in just two lines is a good choice: 'Lonely the seabird lies at her rest, Blown like a dawn-blenched parcel of spray'. Children aged about five to eight years would like the poems in the selection in *Bees and Trees*, published by Super Sandcastle. Adrian Henri's *H25* – a three-verse poem about hedgehogs and the poet's wish to save them and badgers, frogs and toads from death crossing the motorway, is one of the poems in Roger McGough's *Ring of Words*. Referring to this poem, Sian Hughes of The Poetry Society comments that the idea of a hedgehog motorway is not so far-fetched: there are underpasses built for animals under busy roads in some places and groups of people go out at night to carry toads across dual carriageways safely to their ponds (Hughes, 1999). The poem could be the start of lively discussion about how we can help as well as study animals, and might also lead to children's writing (there is food for thought and writing suggestions at www.britishhedgehogs. org.uk). Poems for older children that encourage the questioning of certain environmental strategies include Judith Nicholls' selection *Earthways: Poems on Conservation*. With older readers in mind I also recommend Andrew Fusek Peters' poetry books about the four elements, for example *Poems About Earth*, and there are amusing poems about the human anatomy in Alan Wolf and Greg Clark's *The Blood Hungry Spleen*.

Frost, Jenny (1997) *Creativity in Primary Science* Buckingham: Open University Press.

Hughes, Sian (1999) 'Hedgehogs' in *Child Education,* January.

Mallett, Margaret (2006) *The Lyrical Voice in Non-fiction* Leicester: English Association (bookmark 3).

SCRIBING

In a teaching context, this refers to the role of a teacher, parent or older child in writing down what a young child dictates, enabling them to 'compose' like a more mature writer. Seeing what they say written down can be a motivating experience.

Sometimes the teacher scribes in the shared writing part of Literacy Time, writing down the children's suggestions. In a group writing context one child may take up the role of scribe, either handwriting or using the computer.

SEMANTIC CUE-SYSTEM

See also: 'big shapes', critical discourse, cue-systems, miscue analysis, reading, 'top-down' approaches to reading

This is one of a number of cue-systems on which a reader draws. The others are explained under 'syntactic cue-system', 'grapho-phonic cue-system' and 'bibliographic cue-system'. When drawing on the semantic cue-system, the search for the meaning of a text is paramount, but not only does the reader draw on meaning in the text – he or she also draws on their knowledge from everyday life and the other reading they have done. In a miscue analysis, the teacher can check whether or not a child is using the semantic cue-system well. If a child says 'home' when the actual word is 'house' we know they understand the gist of the story even though the actual word read out is not correct. If they substituted 'hole' for house it would indicate they were not cueing into the meaning successfully.

SEMI-COLON

See also: punctuation

A semi-colon is a punctuation mark used in three main ways:

- Instead of two short sentences or a conjunction to link two parallel statements:

  'Children need to have some breakfast; it gives them the energy to concentrate during morning lessons'.

- To link two independent clauses[1] within a compound sentence[2] when a conjunctive adverb[3] connects them:

  'The teacher remarked that she had never taken a music lesson; however, she added that she had always

391

taught in schools where a specialist took responsibility for music'.

- To separate items in a list, often after a colon:

    'The basket contained: a story book for the lesson after break; some spare pencils; a cartridge for the printer; a carton of fruit juice'.

When thinking about punctuation points like semi-colons, we are reminded of the hierarchy of building blocks: the smallest building blocks are words, next come phrases, next clauses and finally sentences. Punctuation marks help to structure sentences in a way that makes for the clear communication of meaning in writing.

Notes

1 An independent clause is one that is sentence-like in its construction, having a subject and an object.
2 A compound sentence has two or more main clauses.
3 A conjunctive adverb has a connective role, as 'however' has in the example.

SEMI-PHONETIC STAGE IN SPELLING

According to Richard Gentry's stages, this is the second stage in a child's spelling development; it refers to the time when there is some evidence of making sound-symbol connections.

Gentry, Richard (1982) 'An analysis of developmental spelling in GNYS AT WRK' in *The Reading Teacher*, 36 (2) (for a helpful summary of the stages, see Graham and Kelly (2009) *Writing Under Control*).

SENCO

See: Special Educational Needs (SEN) in language and literacy

SENTENCE

See also: grammar

A sentence is a group of words which make sense. There are three main kinds of sentence:

- A simple sentence has only one clause with one subject and one verb: 'Anna loves fruit'.
- A complex sentence has one main clause and one or more subordinate clauses: 'Anna loves fruit, particularly the kind you can pick in the countryside in the autumn'.
- A compound sentence has two or more main clauses which could stand as short sentences: 'The rain fell and the wind blew'.

Within a sentence are smaller groups of words which also make sense and these are called clauses. Clauses are made up of phrases. A number of authors aim to strengthen teachers' knowledge about language so that they can help children understand and use the parts of speech that make up sentences. Two that I find helpful when thinking about sentences are *Primary English: Knowledge and Understanding* and *Language Knowledge for Primary Teachers*. The latter book uses interesting samples of text as examples, from fiction to Facebook (Medwell *et al.*, 2009; Wilson and Scanlon, 2011).

Medwell, Jane, Moore, George, Wray, David and Griffiths, Vivienne (2009) *Primary English: Knowledge and Understanding* Exeter: Learning Matters.
Wilson, Angela and Scanlon, Julie (2011, fourth edition) *Language Knowledge for Primary Teachers* London: David Fulton.

SENTENCE-LEVEL WORK

See: literacy hour

SHAKESPEARIAN DRAMA (IN THE PRIMARY YEARS)

See also: drama and English, playscript

Why do teachers use the work of Shakespeare in the primary years when many adults find the language and themes of the plays difficult? Probably there are two main reasons. First, many of the stories round which the plays are built are exceptionally engaging for any age group – a king giving away his kingdom, the confused adventures of jealous lovers in a wood where magic is at work, people shipwrecked on a strange, enchanted island. As we all know, Shakespeare often got the bare bones of his plots from other sources but he developed the characters and situations to produce works that come fully to life when they are performed. Second, we want children to enjoy, as early as possible, Shakespeare's unsurpassed use of language, both prose and poetry, to bring situations and the thoughts and feelings of characters alive for us.

Classic fiction is properly part of the English programme for older primary children. Reading and perhaps performing a complete Shakespeare play, even in considerably abridged form, would be a challenge for any Year 6 class. Many teachers and children prefer to work with single scenes or their own scripts drawing on the plays. In my experience, where children in Year 6 are to be able to take on the challenges of the study of a Shakespeare play, English Co-ordinators working with their colleagues have created a culture where the children have been exposed to his work from an early age. How is this achieved? Perhaps the first thing to say is that there are some implications for teachers' subject knowledge here. You might find helpful 'The qualities of drama', chapter 12 in Medwell *et al.* (2009), which includes sections about writing playscripts and about Shakespearian drama. Sedgwick's (1999)

Shakespeare and the Young Writer would also provide good background.

How then do we involve children with Shakespeare's work? A good way in for younger children is through stories based on Shakespeare's plays. There are a number of good collections including Garfield's *Shakespeare Stories* (1988). I have sometimes started with such a story and added some quotations from the play when I have read to a class. Having a grip on some of the stories will be very helpful to children later on, but the stories are enjoyable in their own right. When it comes to appreciating Shakespeare's language and particularly his poetry, introducing it as part of telling the story of one of the plays helps make it meaningful for the children – the fairies' chant to Titania in the context of the story of *A Midsummer Night's Dream*, for example. In Year 5, sonnets are often introduced as a poetic form and teachers use 'Shall I compare thee to a summer's day' as an introduction. Another way in which the school builds a tradition of work on classic drama is in the context of working with texts for drama. Children enjoy reading a scene from a Shakespeare play and then adapting the script for their own purposes. Colleen Johnson (2000) has provided a very helpful list of activities round Caliban's 'The isle is full of noises' speech from Act III, Scene ii, Shakespeare's *The Tempest*. Including the fruits of this kind of work in assemblies and on open days for parents makes Shakespeare's work accessible to children. It has an impact on the children presenting the work and on the younger children who see what will be expected of them when they are older. In some schools part of the expectation will be that when they get to Year 6 it will be their turn to work with a complete Shakespeare play and to perform part or all of it for others. Enjoying Shakespeare's work with children is explored in the section 'The qualities of drama' in Medwell *et al.* (2009). The authors discuss the challenges and pleasures of working with plays as distinctive text types. One inspiring case study known to me involved Years 5 and 6 (nine to eleven year olds) in work on Shakespeare's *Cymbeline*. The play was chosen because of its strong characters and compelling story. The teachers involved downloaded a text and edited, manipulated and copied it to suit their purposes. Almost all the plot was included but the play was reduced to 'a child and audience friendly one and a half hours running time' for performance to the school and visitors (Alexander, 2000: 8). Some modern speech narrative was used to help understanding of the plot through the device of two narrators dressed as Shakespeare who announced the locations of the different scenes and assembled the characters. You need to read this case study for yourself to appreciate the richness of the project – it was so much more than just the school play. It fed into National Curriculum English and also spread into extra-curricular activity and the daily life of the school. Fred Sedgwick, author of *Shakespeare and the Young Writer* (Sedgwick, 1999), worked with the children on the 'Fear no more' song from *Cymbeline* and one of the results was some moving writing by the children on a person they had lost. This was one of many examples of extension work which helped the children become fully involved in the themes and undercurrents in the play.

You might also like to read about another imaginative use of a Shakespeare play, this time *A Midsummer Night's Dream* with nine to eleven year olds, evaluated in chapter 3 of *The Prose and the Passion* (Styles, 1994). The many exciting lessons drew on their knowledge of popular culture in understanding the appeal of the play: the jealousy of the lovers, for example, was linked to the shenanigans of characters in television soap operas. Work on the rude mechanicals' scenes led to children telling tall stories to get 'under the

skin' of Bottom the Weaver. A huge amount of learning was involved – about Shakespearian times and particularly Shakespearian theatre, about comedy, the function of sub-plots and the use of magic in plays. After work on the character and motivation of Puck, the teacher heard the children playfully chanting some of his lines – 'I am that merry wanderer of the night' and 'I go, I go, look how I go/ swifter than an arrow from a tartar's bow'. The many activities and sustained work through drama involved the children imaginatively and emotionally. Yes, this is the point: if we truly involve children in work of this quality, as Styles remarks, children can rise to 'the difficulties involved – unfamiliar language, complicated plot, and challenging demands on acting and memory' (Styles, 1994: 51).

For workshops and events, a school visit to the Royal Shakespeare Company's education department is inspiring, but even if you cannot visit, the website provides interesting case studies of primary school work and some free online resources for developing classroom drama. It is also worth consulting journals about primary English for ideas about using Shakespeare's plays, for example NATE's *Classroom Magazine* and the English Association and UKLA'S *English 4–11*. The English Association's Special Interest Group on Children's Literature, set up in 2010, has online advice and classroom examples about approaches to all kinds of texts, including classic texts.

Alexander, Catherine (2000) 'The Cymbeline Project' *English 4–11*, No. 9, Winter 2001 (this project was carried out at St Andrew's Primary School, Stanstead Abbotts).

The English Association: www.le.ac.uk/eng assoc/links/shakespeare.html

Garfield, Leon (1988) *Shakespeare Stories* London: Heinemann.

Johnson, Colleen (2009 [2000]) 'What did I say?: speaking, listening and drama' in Fisher,

Robert and Williams, Mary (eds) *Unlocking Literacy* London: David Fulton.

Matthews, Andrew (2001) *The Orchard Book of Children's Stories* London: Orchard Books (retelling of eight plays with atmospheric illustrations by Angela Barrett).

Medwell, Jane, Moore, George, Wray, David and Griffiths, Vivienne (2009) *Primary English: Knowledge and Understanding* Exeter: Learning Matters.

National Association of English (NATE): www.nate.org.uk

Royal Shakespeare Company (RSC): www.rsc.org.uk/education

Sedgwick, Fred (1999) *Shakespeare and the Young Writer* London: Routledge.

Styles, Morag (1994) "'Am I that geezer, Hermia": children and "Great Literature"' in Styles, Morag, Bearne, Eve and Watson, Victor (eds) *The Prose and the Passion: Children and Their Reading* London: Cassell.

SHARED READING

See: class reader, fiction: choosing and using, literacy hour, novels, short stories, story time, text-level work

SHARED WRITING

See also: literacy hour, text-level work, writing

The term 'shared writing' refers to any collaborative writing task. For example, a group of children may write a story together with or without the teacher's help – on a whiteboard, flip chart, or on the computer or interactive whiteboard.

The term is also used to refer to the class-based shared writing activity taking place in Literacy Time and intended to move children towards becoming independent writers. Teachers draw on text, sentence and word-level objectives. Shared writing gives the teacher an opportunity to model the writing process, for example by encouraging the children to rehearse sentences orally before committing them to the page. The children reread what has been written to ensure a flow from one sentence to another and to put right errors. There can be valuable discussion on punctuation and on why one writing decision is better than another. As with any writing task, teacher and children need to be clear from the outset about to whom the writing is addressed and its purpose. The concept of 'audience' and 'purpose' was at the heart of the work of Jimmy Britton and his colleagues on the Schools Council Writing Projects of the 1970s. An issue for teachers is how to make shared writing tasks more than exercises – the 'dummy runs' Britton refers to. One way is to draw on work which has engaged and interested the children in other lessons to give real purpose to Literacy Time tasks. The children writing about Cocoa the Bear felt great commitment to their work (see the entry on 'short stories').

Britton, James (1970) *Language and Learning* London: Allen Lane, The Penguin Press.

SHORT STORIES

See also: creation stories, fairy tales, fiction: choosing and using, folk tales, narrative, realism (in children's fiction), traditional tales

Short stories are a genre in their own right and those specially written for children share many of the characteristics of those for adults. The setting and the characters have to be communicated swiftly and there is not normally space for the long descriptions of scenery and the introspection possible in a full-length work. Nevertheless, good short stories offer insights into the human condition and can awaken children's own wish to write.

Class writing project: The story of Cocoa the Brown Bear

Elaine Shiel, an Edinburgh primary teacher, wanted to create an exciting context for children's writing. While on holiday in London she bought a little brown bear from Hamley's and brought it to school to show her class of seven year olds. Her intention was to base storytelling and story writing round the bear's pretend adventures. The children's imaginations shifted into top gear as they reflected on what it must have been like for Cocoa when he was pushed to the back of the shelf when no-one wanted to buy him. Night time was worst as he could not see a thing.

The children and teacher began to construct stories about his adventures and his thoughts and feelings as he adjusted to life in Primary 3's hut. The scene was set for the teacher to direct the children's interest and enthusiasm towards different kinds of writing. There were stories about visiting the teacher's home and meeting Happeny the puppy, Posh Giraffe and One-eyed Duck and about going on holiday. One day when the class came into school Cocoa had disappeared. This led to a flurry of activity and meetings to decide how to track him down. Then the children made posters asking for his return and they put up notices, sent messages and wrote letters asking the school secretary and the caretaker to help find him.

On another occasion the children wrote about Cocoa going to a teddy bears' picnic at Corstorphine Fair with the children's teddy bears.

After a while the children wanted to make a book about Cocoa and the teacher took up the role of editor. Their joint work led to the children learning about chapters, how to engage the reader's interest and how to match illustrations to the narrative. This was the final structure of the book. Each chapter is a short story in its own right.

The adventures of Cocoa

Chapter 1. In the toyshop
Chapter 2. The journey to Scotland and Primary 3's hut
Chapter 3. A weekend at Miss Shiel's house
Chapter 4. Meeting Happeny, Posh Giraffe and One-eyed Duck
Chapter 5. Cocoa disappears
Chapter 6. Cocoa tells of his adventures
Chapter 7. Cocoa acquires a rug
Chapter 8. Cocoa's camping holiday
Chapter 9. A new friend
Chapter 10. The teddy bears' picnic

To give a flavour of this work, the first page of chapter 1 is displayed here. For a more detailed account of this interesting project, see E. Shiel's article in *English 4–11*, No. 9, 2000.

Short stories provide a bridge between the picture books for the very young and the novels enjoyed by older primary children. Their relative shortness allows teacher and children to look at global aspects of the text – the development of the characters and the situation, for example. A number of teachers of children aged eight or under have mentioned to me that the stories in *The Practical Princess and Other Liberating Fairy Tales* by Jay Williams seem to encourage discussion. Other favourites, about a range of human experience and feelings, are those in Philippa Pearce's entertaining collection *Lion at*

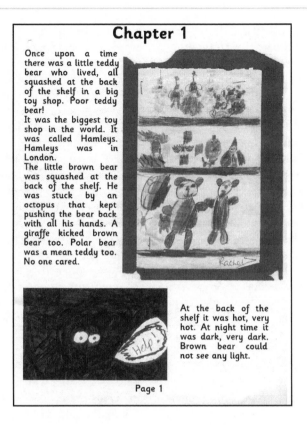

Chapter 1

Once upon a time there was a little teddy bear who lived, all squashed at the back of the shelf in a big toy shop. Poor teddy bear!

It was the biggest toy shop in the world. It was called Hamleys. Hamleys was in London.

The little brown bear was squashed at the back of the shelf. He was stuck by an octopus that kept pushing the bear back with all his hands. A giraffe kicked brown bear too. Polar bear was a mean teddy too. No one cared.

At the back of the shelf it was hot, very hot. At night time it was dark, very dark. Brown bear could not see any light.

Page 1

Figure 22

School and Other Stories, Dick King-Smith's animal stories, for example *Sophie's Snail*, Berlie Doherty's lively *Tilly Mint Tales* and Michael Broad's amusing stories in his Jake Cake series, for example *The Robot Dinner Lady*. Still thinking of younger readers and listeners, Usborne have brought out *Usborne Stories for Little Children* which has retellings of a range of short stories originally told or written by such tellers of tales as Aesop and Hans Andersen. This sort of resource is good to draw on when a space emerges in the school day, a space long enough to read one of the shorter short stories to the class. Andrew Lang's colour fairy story books – *The Blue Storybook* and so on – are timeless classics that stay in print and are good to read aloud. Young children enjoy short stories from around the world and it is worth looking through the lists of publishers like Frances Lincoln and TARA books, which both specialise here. By about age eight children would appreciate *The Ogress and the Snake and Other Stories from Somalia*, retold by Elizabeth Laird and illustrated by Shelley Fowles. The stories are not unlike those of Aesop as they have talking animals and they explore the relationship between animals and human beings. To ring the changes there are many audio and DVD versions of short stories for teachers to use. There are, for example, DVD collections of Lauren Child's Charlie and Lola stories, for example *Charlie and Lola: I Can't Stop Hiccupping and Other Stories*.

For older children there are some good 'fantasy' collections, for example Nicholas Fisk's *The Puffin Book of Science Fiction, Enchantment, Fairy Tales, Ghost Stories and Tales of Wonder* and Dennis Pepper's *Alien Stories*. The latter collection includes

397

some truly unsettling tales: 'The Star Beast' by Nicholas Stuart is a story about alien infiltration in which a creature 'hurt, hungry and afraid' comes to someone's door for help ...

If you are looking for an anthology of different genres of short stories by well-known children's writers, *The Turning Tide and Other Stories* edited by Gervase Phinn would be helpful. Of course, for all age groups traditional tales are very often short story length. By the time children reach the later primary years they will have enjoyed many folk and fairy tales from around the world and have become able to identify common themes that interest and 'speak to' human beings everywhere. Oxford University Press has reissued its well-known collections of folk tales in paperback, for example Kathleen Arnott's retelling of *Tales from Africa* and Philip Sherlock's retelling of *Tales from West Africa*.

Short-story collections come in different styles and formats – the character of a book becomes immediately apparent when we see the illustrations. As well as the traditionally illustrated book of short stories, there are those whose authors/illustrators use cartoon and comic strip – Leigh Hobbs' 'Old Tom' series and Marcia Williams' *Greek Myths*, and those with graphic or Manga-type illustrations, for example Steve Barlow, Steve Skidmore and Sonia Leong's *Pirate Gold*.

SHORT-TERM PLANS

See: English/Literacy Co-ordinator, planning

SIBLINGS (AND LITERACY)

See also: parents and families

Brothers and sisters are very much part of a child's life at home and there is evidence that they extend each other's literacy experiences in important and interesting ways. The impact of siblings on each other's literacy development was one of the aspects studied in the Elmswood research which Jo Weinberger has described and evaluated in her book *Literacy Goes to School*. She looked at children's literacy development from three to seven years and concentrated on the adult who provided the 'parent' as opposed to the 'school' perspective on children's literacy learning. Half of the sixty children in the study had an older brother or sister and during the interviews Weinberger found that there were a number of positive ways in which siblings enriched each other's literacy. Turning to reading first, younger children benefited from being with their older siblings when they were read to by adults and older siblings quite often enjoyed reading to their younger brothers and sisters. A child with older siblings was also likely to have access to a wider range of books and materials than 'only' or firstborn children. Younger children were also involved in writing activity earlier than they might otherwise have been as older children were effectively 'models' for writing behaviour. One mother commented that 'when we help Joanne to write, Sarah pretends to write too ... ' (Weinberger, 1996: 57). All that we know about early writing suggests that children who see the purposes of writing early are at a considerable advantage in learning to write.

Most of the children in the Elmswood study were monolingual. What might be the role of siblings when children are learning to read in a second or additional language? Eve Gregory illuminates the issues here in her book *Learning to Read in a Second Language*. In Gregory's research we see a culture of sibling support developing in some families: eleven year old Fatima remarks that she was teaching her little brother and sister to read in English just as her older brother had taught her. Gregory found that older siblings were excellent 'brokers' of a new language because they are able to link school and home reading practices (Gregory, 2008).

Gregory's work on the ESRC project 'Siblings as mediators of literacy in two East London communities (1998–2000)' provides further evidence of how successful siblings often are as 'teachers' of school literacy practices (Gregory *et al.*, 2004). In 'Invisible teachers of literacy', Gregory (2004) argues that an unspoken collusion sometimes takes place between teacher and older sibling in initiating younger children into literacy. She shares interesting case studies showing what was revealed during 'play school' sessions in Bangladeshi-British households in East London. For example, there is a transcript showing ten year old Farjana's poetry lesson at home for her younger sister Hana in which she seems to be imitating what she has learnt from her teacher at school. The older child takes up a teacherly role and form of language. For example she says: 'Now we are going to do a short poem and memorise it' and, on looking at Hana's poem, 'Good. But I'm sorry to say I didn't say it doesn't have to rhyme … '. Are there any disadvantages, from the literacy point of view, as a result of being a younger child? It is possible that some parents are not able to give younger children the quality and amount of time that they gave to their eldest child and that this may have had an effect on their literacy development. Older children may also encourage distractions away from literacy – like watching television and playing computer games. In the Elmwood study the positive aspects of the contribution of older siblings seemed to outweigh the possible negative ones. Perhaps the most enjoyable context in which help was given was when older children read out loud to younger ones.

Gregory, E. (2004) 'Invisible teachers of literacy' in *Literacy*, UKLA, 38 (2).

——(2008, second edition) *Learning to Read in a Second Language: Making Sense of Words and Worlds* London: Sage.

Gregory, E., Long, S. and Volk, D. (eds) (2004) *Many Pathways to Literacy: Early learning with siblings, grandparents, peers and communities* London: Routledge.

Weinberger, Jo (1996) *Literacy Goes to School* London: Paul Chapman.

SILENT LETTERS

Some letters are used to spell a word but they are not pronounced when the word is said. They may be at the beginning of a word like the 'k' in 'kneel', at the end like the 'e' in 'nose', or in the middle of a word, for example the silent 'l' in salmon. Silent 'e' at the end of a word often makes another vowel sound long.

SILENT READING

See: ERIC, independent reader, USSR

SIMILE

A simile is a figure of speech which makes a comparison nearly always using either 'like' or 'as'. Some similes have lost their power through constant use – 'as white as snow', 'as pleased as Punch'. The challenge for a young poet is to find new and startling ones. Learning to recognise and talk about similes and other figures of speech is helpful in the context of enjoying poetry but opinions differ about whether or not we should encourage children to contrive them in their own writing. If you want to read about an approach where children are encouraged to practise techniques to apply later in their writing you would find interesting Sandy Brownjohn's book *What Rhymes with Secret?* (Brownjohn, 1994). To help children with simile and metaphor, Brownjohn has developed 'The Furniture Game': children think of someone known to the others in the class and help them to guess who it is by comparing them to a piece of furniture, a plant or a type of food (ibid.: 19). Brownjohn takes up a playful approach to language, but believes that children need to control the techniques so that they are free to write the sort of poem they want to.

Similes can be used in everyday speech and in factual writing as well as poetry: nine year old Jarinder uses a simile in his account of the Spanish Armada. 'Then I saw the Spanish Armada scatter around us like a bunch of rats being chased by a cat' (Laycock, 2009).

Brownjohn, Sandy (1994) *What Rhymes with Secret?* London: Hodder & Stoughton.
Laycock, Liz (2009, third edition) 'Monitoring and assessing writing' in Graham, Judith and Kelly, Alison (eds) *Writing Under Control: Teaching Writing in the Primary School* London: David Fulton.

SINGULAR AND PLURAL

When a noun or verb refers to one thing, it is said to be 'singular'. Uncountable nouns like 'cotton' or 'envy' tend to be regarded as singular to match with the verbs with which they are used. 'Singular' contrasts with 'plural', the latter showing there is more than one thing. There are a number of exceptions in forming the plural of nouns in English which children are encouraged to learn. For example:

Table 6

child	children
salmon	salmon
mouse	mice

SKIMMING

Skimming refers to a reading strategy where we read quickly through a passage or article to get the gist of the argument

swiftly. Lunzer and Gardner (1979) contrast this kind of reading with the more reflective kind when we evaluate a set of facts or ideas. Flexible readers know when to apply each reading strategy.

Lunzer, Eric and Gardner, Kenneth (1979) *The Effective Use of Reading* London: Heinemann.

SLANG

See also: language change, language variety, standard English

Slang refers to informal words and expressions often thought to be inferior to standard forms of language. Perhaps, though, it is more to do with what is appropriate in a particular context. Slang is used to identify us with an age group or a social group. People who normally use standard English may use slang words and phrases if they are relaxing with a group of people with whom they share activities and attitudes.

Although some 'slang' words become accepted into language and even into dictionaries, the colloquial expressions in vogue change constantly.

SOCIO-ECONOMIC GROUPS AND LITERACY

See: elaborated and restricted codes

SOFTWARE

See: CD-ROM, Information and Communications Technology (ICT) and English

SONNET

This is a poem of fourteen lines with a regular rhythm and rhyming pattern. Two well-known types of sonnet are the Petrarchan or Italian sonnet and the Shakespearian sonnet. The Petrarchan sonnet has two parts, the first of eight lines and the second of six; each part has a separate rhyming pattern. The Shakespearian sonnet does not separate its fourteen lines into separate parts and has a different rhyming pattern to the Petrarchan sonnet: ababcdcdededgg – three quatrains and a rhyming couplet.

Older primary children often read sonnets as part of the English programme. Teachers usually find examples from Shakespeare's 154 sonnets – a favourite being 'Shall I compare thee to a summer's day?' – William Wordsworth and, more recently, W.H. Auden and Dylan Thomas, who are also writers of sonnets. There are some examples of children's sonnets in Sandy Brownjohn's book *Does it Have to Rhyme?*

Brownjohn, Sandy (1980) *Does it Have to Rhyme?* London: Hodder & Stoughton.

SPEAKING AND LISTENING

See also: accent, Bristol Language at Home and School Project, Bullock Report, collaborative learning, conferencing, dialect, dialogic teaching, discourse analysis, discussion, drama and English, language acquisition, language and thought, National Oracy Project, response partner, slang, speech act, storytelling

'All learning across the whole curriculum, could be said to begin and end with speaking and listening. It would be almost impossible to introduce any new topic or revise an old one without some form of questioning or discussion by the teacher or children'.

(Grugeon *et al.*, 2005: 64)

This entry concentrates on speaking and listening in the classroom. I have begun with a quotation from Grugeon *et al.* because they remind us of the central place of oracy in all learning. What is written here is best read in conjunction with the entries on 'language acquisition' and 'language and thought', where you will find some analysis of the theoretical contributions of the developmentalists Piaget, Vygotsky and Bruner and the socio-linguistic perspective of M.A.K. Halliday. In the classroom, it is helpful to keep in mind that speaking and listening each have three main elements: social, cognitive and linguistic. These elements are present in all episodes of speaking and listening, but often one dominates. A teacher may aim to stress the social aspect by encouraging children to take turns in putting their points and listening to each other. On another occasion the cognitive function of talk might be uppermost, if for example children are hypothesising, summarising points, inferring or referring back to previous points. The linguistic element is always present, but comes to the fore when teachers encourage children to rephrase to make their meaning clearer or to show flexibility in their language use according to context.

We must also remember that a teacher's own use of language is of great importance. Not only should instructions be clear and intervention helpful – sometimes the teacher has to sharpen the focus with a question or comment – but the teacher also provides a model of mature language use. It is the teacher's role to create contexts where children will feel comfortable and able to contribute. The teacher's own skill at telling anecdotes and stories is of great value.

Planning for speaking and listening

Children use their speaking and listening abilities in every lesson. In English much talk centres round children learning to read and write, responding to literature and creating roles and incidents in drama. Storytelling is an ability worth nurturing as it is a source of great enjoyment and satisfaction and helps children develop a sense

401

of characterisation, pace and sequencing of events. Evaluation of all that they do is achieved through discussion. Although teachers often work within official frameworks, including those to do with the latest national curriculum and the early learning goals, there are some general planning questions which will always be helpful. The following planning diagram is adapted from that in *Teaching Talking and Learning* by Kate Norman (1990).

---

1. What do you want the children to learn?
2. What are the stages in the activity and the time scale?
3. What is the role of speaking and listening in the learning?
4. Is the work to be done collaboratively?
5. What kinds of groupings (issues of special needs, gender and young learners of English as an additional language to be considered here)?
6. What resources are needed?
7. If the work is in groups how will the reporting back to an audience be organised?
8. How will the children's evaluation of what has been achieved be built into the work?
9. How will I record the work?

Gender issues

Although there are quiet boys and exuberant girls, teachers often find that boys are more dominant in discussion. Because boys seem more noisy and demanding – more of a threat to classroom order perhaps – teachers sometimes unwittingly reinforce such behaviour by giving boys more opportunities to participate in discussion. In a much-quoted research study, Swann and Graddol (1988) provide evidence for this.

We can use strategies in our planning to achieve more balance: girls can be encouraged to be more assertive by direct invitation of their views and boys can be praised when they interact with other children in a group discussion and listen to contributions. Some teachers set up non-stereotypical role play for younger children's interactions in the home corner and older children's role play in drama. It is a matter of making sure that some contexts encourage girls to be more forthcoming while boys are given the chance to 'engage in activities that will enable them to use the quiet, sensitive, caring aspects of their natures' (Browne, 2009: 182). The role of talk in helping boys reflect on their reading and writing has a strong emphasis in the book based on the research project *Raising Boys' Achievement* (Warrington *et al.*, 2006) and on the Safford *et al.* (2004) project *Boys on the Margin*.

Sometimes it is appropriate to make issues about boys' and girls' language development explicit by discussing them. Two books which I have used to encourage thoughtful conversation with older primary children are *The Turbulent Term of Tyke Tiler* by Gene Kemp and *The Tunnel* by Anthony Browne. Literature has a wonderful distancing effect, enabling children to talk about issues without making direct reference to themselves unless, of course, they want to.

Children learning English as a second or additional language

A young bilingual child's receptive English may be ahead of his/her productive English and this needs to be kept in mind when talk contexts are planned. Teachers also need to record information about the languages spoken in the child's home.

Special educational needs

Pupils who appear to lack concentration and involvement in small group talk may suffer from a physical disability, for example hearing loss or speech impairment. Visual disability may mean children miss facial expression and gesture which give meaning to what other pupils say. Such pupils need support, possibly by the sympathetic understanding of other pupils who can repeat instructions if necessary. Other children may be reluctant talkers because of lack of confidence. After raising the matter with the child and his or her parents, teachers may place a child with a sympathetic partner so that they feel confident to speak. Sometimes children who are shy are much more forthcoming when they use a puppet allowing them to talk 'in role'. A Year 6 girl who had literacy difficulties was encouraged to tell stories to younger children using a puppet. She greatly improved her skill and her general self-image as a learner was transformed (see *Teaching Talking and Learning in Key Stage 2* by Kate Norman, 1990).

Teaching and learning contexts

Suggestions for developing children's speaking and listening appear in a number of entries. 'Drama and English' introduces the powerful kinds of talk which can accompany improvisation. Entries that consider fiction as a starting point for talk include 'fiction: choosing and using', 'play and language and literacy', and 'storytelling'. Talk round the computer is discussed in the 'Information and Communications Technology (ICT) and English' entry. I recommend two inspirational books which, while first published decades ago, continue to illuminate examples of classroom talk. They are Gordon Wells' *The Meaning Makers* (Hodder and Stoughton, 1986) and Aidan Chambers' *Tell Me* (The Thimble Press, 1993). Another inspirational work, *Exploring Talk in School*, brings researchers and classroom teachers together in a celebration of the work of Douglas Barnes (Mercer and Hodgkinson,

2008). This book has chapters sharing the fruits of the research of teachers and scholars in Britain (for example Gordon Wells, Robin Alexander and the editors) and of that carried out in the USA (for example Courtney Cazden, Judith Green and Beth Yeager). While the classroom examples in Barnes' classic and groundbreaking study in *From Communication to Curriculum*, published some decades ago, are from secondary school classrooms, his belief in the power of 'dialogic teaching' has relevance to every teacher and learner. This approach favours a reciprocal building on each other's ideas so that learning is interactive and collaborative. The teacher's role as skilful guider of talk is recognised and explored. Taking Barnes' work as a starting point, the contributors to Mercer and Hodgkinson's book show how there has been a move from cognitive theories towards 'more social, culturally located interpretations of learning (Mercer and Hodgkinson, 2008: xi). Behind this is the acceptance that knowledge is socially constructed and talk is a vital tool to achieve this.

Teachers and their young learners are members of an increasingly technological society which constantly throws up new texts and new tools for learning – the interactive whiteboard seems well established now. However, the teachers and scholars in *Exploring Talk in School* claim classroom talk as still the most fundamental way of young learners striving to make sense of what their teachers and peers mean. Books and texts of all kinds are amongst the most important resources to encourage talk. In her book *Talking Beyond the Page*, Janet Evans shows how wordless picture books, postmodern, graphic and multimodal novels can all connect with children's preoccupations and encourage talk about complicated issues, sometimes in their own lives (Evans, 2009). Classroom based research carried out by Gill Robins shows the power of teacher guided talk as a way of improving writing.

403

In this study able young learners were helped through classroom talk and listening to develop their capacity to use more sophisticated sentence structure in their writing (Robins, 2011). This approach is compatible with Robin Alexander's view of the value of dialogic teaching which involves deep talk and careful listening as a way of learning and of reflecting on learning (Alexander, 2006).

Using talk to support writing

The role of talk in planning, reflecting on and evaluating children's writing has long been recognised. Research carried out by Ros Fisher and her colleagues on the Talk to Text Project, funded by the Esmée Fairbairn Foundation, has clarified our understanding of the ways in which talk can support children's writing. The team worked with teachers in first schools in West Sussex on a project which was truly collaborative between teachers and researchers. Analysis of lessons with five, six and seven year olds led to the identification of three main ways in which talk helps promote writing: talk to generate ideas, talk for oral rehearsal and talk for metacognitive purposes. The book usefully suggests sets of classroom activities to enrich each of these three kinds of support (Fisher *et al.*, 2010).

Assessing and recording progress in speaking and listening

Many otherwise good schools seem to have a problem with assessment. Yet once you have a good system working it becomes part of the teaching and learning cycle. A good approach in my view is systematic, economic of teachers' and children's time, and worked out and monitored collaboratively within the school. There are two main aspects when we turn to the assessment of speaking and listening: assessment *of* speaking and listening and assessment *through* speaking and listening.

Assessment *of speaking and listening*

This is to do with assessing pupils' capacity to use the spoken language and their listening skills for different audiences and a variety of purposes. Schools choose or create a format for summarising children's progress over a period of time. Such assessment is *formative* in that it helps the teacher give help where it is needed, but it can also provide the basis of a *summative* assessment as it is a record of achievement.

Let us look at the main stages in the learning and assessing cycle. We begin planning for a range of speaking and listening contexts across the whole curriculum. Then we introduce them into the teaching programme. We establish routines for observing and recording the progress of individuals in some different settings. Some teachers use a ring binder file for notes, allocating several pages to each child; others prefer a box file. These notes (and perhaps evidence from photographs, short transcripts or even occasional recordings) can then be summarised, perhaps twice a year, in a useful format. What is a useful format? One which a school constructs collaboratively and which communicates effectively the achievements of each child. Many schools use the speaking and listening part of the Centre for Primary Literacy in Education's primary language record or a similar system. One of the many strengths of this record is that there is space for the views and observations of the children's parents. There is also a slot for the child's own perception of his or her progress. The notes, and the record that summarises them, provide an evidence base which shows us what has been achieved so far and provide useful information about how we might help a particular child to progress further. Thus the assessment of progress feeds into our planning and the next round of teaching. Where a summative assessment is required, the information on the record can be matched with level requirements. In the United Kingdom, primary children's level of achievement is judged at seven and eleven years according to brief descriptions of six achievement levels in the statutory orders. Class teachers often work with the English/Literacy Co-ordinator or another colleague to establish common standards of comparison. The notes and observations and the summarising record provide rich material to share with parents on open evening.

So far, though, we have not considered exactly what we are looking for. When observing speaking and listening, the three overlapping categories mentioned earlier are helpful: social, cognitive and linguistic. Social aspects include the ability to listen to and value what others say as well as making a contribution to the discussion. In the cognitive area we look for a growing ability to use talking to think through and organise ideas and to build on what we have heard others say. Articulation of how children feel about important issues also fits here. Linguistic aspects are to do with becoming able to express ideas and thoughts clearly in appropriate language. Of course, all three aspects come into play in most discussions and conversations. If a group of ten year olds are arguing a case, perhaps about how we can preserve the environment, and from time to time summarising their viewpoints they need to draw on their intellectual or cognitive ability to organise the ideas, their social skills to respond to others as well as to attract and keep their attention and their communicative ability to clothe their ideas and feelings in appropriate language. From these three main headings, more detailed lists can be drawn up. For example, under 'cognitive' at Key Stage 1 (five to seven year olds) we might include 'listening to others' reactions' and 'taking different views into account'. At Key Stage 2 (seven to eleven year olds) we might include giving/responding to instructions, asking/answering questions, summarising an argument, planning a

group activity and responding to a story or poem. Teachers following the National Curriculum often organise the items listed in the orders under the main headings of social, cognitive and linguistic.

We will also need to make sure our observations of the children's speaking and listening cover different kinds of groupings – whole class, small groups and pairs. Some groupings will place the children in a more formal setting than others.

Assessment *through* speaking and listening

Here we are concerned with a pupil's progress in understanding skills and concepts in an area of study. Often we can judge their linguistic development at the same time. The focus of our assessment depends on our purpose at the time. We can judge children's degree of knowledge and understanding in every lesson by what they say. However, we have to keep in mind that children may know more than they are able to articulate. This is especially the case where children are very young, where the context is unfamiliar and where children are at an early stage in learning English as a second or additional language.

Teachers judge children's prior knowledge of a subject by helping them organise their ideas through talk before beginning new work. Work on amphibians might begin with the teacher asking if anyone has touched a frog or toad and what the skin felt like. These discussions show a teacher where the children are in relation to the topic and helps inform good planning of how to proceed. Of great importance is the talk that links first- and second-hand experience. You will find transcripts of children engaged in this kind of discussion in *Young Researchers*: for example in case study 2.2 'Ourselves', four year olds make links between what they observed when a young baby was brought into the nursery class and what the teacher is reading from an illustrated information book about the stages of a baby's development. Victoria and Edward talk about whether baby Mathew can sit up at the same age as the baby in the book. Edward uses a phrase from the book, saying 'The baby is propped up' (Mallett, 1999: 2:41).This process of listening to what children say as they go about their work contributes throughout the learning and assessing cycle. Both closed questions (those where there is a definite answer) and more open questions (those where several different answers or opinions are welcomed) often encourage children to reveal what they know and where some help is needed, perhaps with a particular concept. Where the emphasis is on sensitive intervention, assessment is of a formative kind and the teacher helps the children by improving their learning opportunities. At the end of a series of lessons teachers often seek evidence about what individual children have learnt by setting up class and group discussions. Here, children often find it satisfying to evaluate their own learning and the quality of the resources they have been using.

A final thought

Over-prescription – the sheer anxiety of meeting termly objectives – can risk sapping the vitality of teachers' planning and practice. However, as good teachers put the current statutory requirements into effect they take control and interpret what is set out flexibly and creatively. They insist on keeping talk in a central role in promoting reading and writing. They make time for the kind of discussions that generate excitement and energy, keeping alive what Chris Powling calls 'the rumour of magic' in the classroom (Powling, 1998: 1).

Alexander, Robin (2006) 'Towards Dialogic Teaching: Rethinking Classroom Talk' in *Dialogos*, Vol. 2, p. 57.

Barnes, D. (1969) *From Communication to Curriculum* Harmondsworth: Penguin.

Browne, Ann (2009, third edition) *Developing Language and Literacy 3–8* London: Paul Chapman.

Evans, Janet (2009) *Talking Beyond the Page: Reading and Responding to Picturebooks* London and New York: Routledge.

Fisher, Ros, Myhill, Debra, Jones, Susan and Larkin, Shirley (2010) *Using Talk to Support Writing* London: Sage.

Grugeon, Elisabeth, Hubbard, Lorraine, Smith, Carol and Dawes, Lyn (2005, third edition) *Teaching Speaking and Listening in the Primary School* London: David Fulton.

Mallett, Margaret (1999) *Young Researchers: Informational Reading and Writing in the Early and Primary Years* London: Routledge.

Mercer, Neil and Hodgkinson, Steve (2008) *Exploring Talk in School: Inspired by the Work of Douglas Barnes* London: Sage.

Norman, Kate (1990) *Teaching Talking and Learning in Key Stage One* and *Teaching Talking and Learning in Key Stage 2* London: National Curriculum Council and the National Oracy Project. (Although these works have been published some time, they include the insights of many excellent practitioners who took part in the National Oracy Project in Great Britain. They also make a valuable contribution to our understanding of how children can be helped to use spoken language effectively and imaginatively to communicate and learn.)

Powling, C. (1998) *Talkback: Antidote to the Worst Excesses of Educational Reform* Reading: University of Reading.

Robins, Gill (2011) 'The effect of exploratory talk on the development of sentence structure in able writers' in *Literacy*, Volume 45, Number 2, July 2011.

Safford, K., O'Sullivan, O. and Barrs, M. (2004) *Boys on the Margin: Promoting Boys' Literacy Learning at Key Stage 2* London: CLPE.

Scottish Committee on Language Arts (1982) *Mr Togs the Tailor* (although this was written a long time ago it is one of the most inspiring accounts ever written about situating children's talk, listening and learning in a strong human context).

Swann, J. (1992) *Girls, Boys and Language* London: Blackwell.

Swann, J. and Graddol, D. (1988) 'Gender inequalities in classroom talk' *English in Education*, 22(1): 48–65.

Warrington, M., Younger, M. and Bearne, E. (2006) *Raising Boys' Achievement in Primary Schools* Maidenhead: Open University.

SPEAKING AND LISTENING FRAMES

See also: collaborative learning, discussion, drama and English, response partner, speaking and listening

How do we give structured support to promote children's speaking and listening abilities? Sue Palmer's 'Speaking and listening frames' series shows how children can be helped to 'fill in' a speaking frame orally, working in small groups or pairs. There is advice on how to be a good listener as well as a good speaker (Palmer, 2004). *Speaking and Listening Games* is another resource on which teachers can draw to strengthen this aspect of their language teaching (Warren, 2004).

Role play is a strong context in which children's spoken language can be fostered. Dee Reid's series *Starting with Role Play* is based on classroom action research and makes many creative suggestions which teachers can adapt for their own lessons (Reid, 2004). Lindsay and Grogan cover group discussion and drama presentations round exciting themes such as toys in the past, *Six Dinner Sid* (Hodder Wayland) and seaside holidays (Lindsay and Grogan, 2004).

As with all published resources, these texts are a starting point for the teacher's creative interpretation and application in their own classroom.

Lindsay, Joyce, and Grogan, Deirdre (2004) *Speaking and Listening: Ages 5–7* London: Scholastic.

Palmer, Sue (2004) *Speaking Frames* (Year 4, Year 6) London: David Fulton.

Reid, Dee (2004) *Starting with Role Play* London: Hopscotch Books.

Warren, Celia (2004) *Speaking and Listening Games* London: Scholastic.

SPECIAL EDUCATIONAL NEEDS (SEN) IN LANGUAGE AND LITERACY

See also: autocorrect, Code of Practice, cue-systems, dyslexia, gifted and talented children, miscue analysis, parents and families, phonics, reading recovery, running reading records, Warnock Report, zone of proximal development

This entry considers Special Educational Needs in the area of literacy under two main headings. First, I consider the needs of children who struggle with learning to read and write, under the heading 'Struggling young readers and writers – how can we help?' Second, under the heading 'Able young readers and writers – what are their additional needs?' I turn to what might be the needs of children who are achieving well above what seems usual for their chronological age and discuss the kind of support and resources which will keep pace with their swift development. Communication is essential: meeting the needs of both struggling children and those growing especially fast intellectually requires liaison between the class teacher, the Special Educational Needs Co-ordinator (SENCo) and the English/Literacy Co-ordinator as well as the involvement of the children and their parents (Birkett, 2006). It is important, too, that the strategies the school adopts in this very important area of co-operation are written into the school's policy document. There are, of course, a number of issues here which never seem to be fully resolved. For example, at which point do we consider a child's intellectual abilities to be so impaired that the best option seems to place them in a special school? Where children with quite severe language difficulties are in an ordinary primary school, are they best withdrawn from the class for special help in reading and writing? The trend at the moment is to keep children together with their age group and offer support within the classroom.

Struggling young readers and writers – how can we help?

Difficulties with reading and writing can affect children's progress in all parts of the curriculum and over time can adversely affect their self-esteem. So it is important that those with this kind of special need are helped as soon as possible. This is very much the philosophy of Marie Clay whose intervention programme is explained under the 'reading recovery' entry. There is a vast literature about this important challenge for teachers. Before turning to recent books, one published some decades ago stands out. Tony Martin's book *The Strugglers* presents an unforgettable case study of how the author helped Leslie, a nine year old boy, break through to literacy. Martin explains simply how his version of an approach called 'paired reading' helped Leslie. In a 'paired reading' context an adult begins by reading a book to a child, next the adult reads it with the child joining in and then gradually withdraws support as the child gains confidence and competence. More than any other this book shows that the first challenge is to find how to help a struggling reader improve their attitude towards reading (Martin, 1989). *Special Educational Needs in the Primary School* (Gross, 2002) and *How to Support and Teach Children with Special Educational Needs* (Birkett, 2007) both give a general overview of special educational needs in the primary years. Chapter 8 in Ann Browne's *Developing Language and Literacy 3–8* provides an analysis of how to support young learners finding it difficult to break through to literacy (Browne, 2009). Support and insight is also available in the publications listed on the site of the National Association for Special Educational Needs (NASEN), for example *Language and Learning: A Practical Guide for Supporting Pupils with Language and Communication Difficulties across the Curriculum* (Hayden and Jordan, 2007).

The first task when faced with the challenge of helping a child with special literacy needs, who has just arrived in your class perhaps, is to diagnose the child's problems for yourself, even though there will already be reading records on file. A miscue analysis, perhaps in its simpler 'running record' form, will help show which of the cue-systems seems to be posing most difficulty. Is the child, for example, always guessing from the context or only using grapho-phonic correspondence, which will not work in the deciphering of all words? This guides us in planning a programme to help.

Anything we can do to improve a child's understanding of the purposes of reading and the pleasures it can bestow is helpful. Talking about books and discussing the illustrations can be a good starting point. Parents and family members can be encouraged to help at home, reinforcing the teacher's efforts. Good language recording systems like *The Primary Language Record* have space for reports based on regular discussions with parents about their child's reading progress.

Building on a sight vocabulary of commonly used words – a, and, be, I, in, is, it, of, that, the, to, was, and so on – helps confidence.

Teachers have to work within official frameworks and recent requirements from governments have moved towards privileging the phonic cue-system and synthetic phonics, which has had official backing as the preferred kind of phonics for the initial teaching of reading for a number of years. Long before these official requirements were made explicit teachers and researchers in reading have recognised that we need to give careful attention to the phonic cue-system and how we teach children to use it. Way back in 1991, Goswami and Bryant showed in their research that many struggling readers need to improve their phonic awareness (Goswami and Bryant, 1991). However, it is just one of several cue-systems which need to be used together in learning to read. Some children find it easier to make sound-symbol correspondences if they work with larger units like rhyming words rather than with letters, digraphs and blends alone. There is an analysis of the phonics debate under the 'phonics' and 'phonological awareness' entries. For the latest statutory requirements visit the government education site: www.education.gov.uk. The United Kingdom Literacy Association (UKLA), dedicated to the advancement of literacy at home and school, is one of a number of organisations with a huge concern for helping all children to read and write well, and their website details research into the best ways of doing this: www.ukla.org.

Whatever method or combination of methods of teaching reading is used, children's attitudes to reading affect their progress. Encouragement helps: Marie Clay recommends that we praise these young readers with difficulties, pointing out specific achievements, saying perhaps something like 'good, you looked at the beginning of the word' rather than a more general 'well done'. Good word-reading skills can be encouraged while, at the same time, supporting young readers' ability to extract the overall meaning of a text (Cain, 2010).

The quality of reading resources is of great importance; interesting and appropriate resources are important for all children but especially so for children with special literacy needs. It is not so much that the latter need different books, but rather that they need imaginative help to appreciate and respond to them. Younger children can be drawn into the excitement and pleasure that books can provide by the imaginative picture books now available. With their interesting stories and imaginative illustrations they help show that reading is worthwhile. A few favourites from a potentially enormous list include *Traction Man* and *Biscuit Bear* (Mini Grey), *Dirty Bertie* (David Roberts), *The Tiger That Came to Tea* (Judith Kerr) and *Pumpkin Soup* (Helen Cooper). Print books with digital art work and quick-moving plots are liked by most young learners, not least those who find reading difficult. So some of the books on these lines in the Oxford University's Press Project X, by Tony Bradman and others, are worth trying. Teachers of children who find reading difficult or have not yet become interested in books often find the Barrington Stoke titles worth considering. This publisher recognizes that the last thing that these struggling young readers need is boring books. They need the best they can get! They have managed to get good and often well-known authors to write ghost stories, adventure stories, science fiction and mysteries. The books look no different from any other book and, while there is no patronising sense of a restricted vocabulary, the stories are mostly fast-moving and gripping with powerful illustrations. Two examples for age nine and over are *Game Boy* by Alan Durant and *Fox Friend* by Michael Morpurgo. The books in their 4u2read series have plots and characters interesting enough to involve children whose reading age is less than their chronological age. Cartoon strip and quirky drawings can appeal too; older readers who need encouragement often like the scribbly drawings, notes and maps in Cressida Cowell's dragon books, for example *How to Train Your Dragon*. Multi-sensory approaches using drama, storyboard telling and music can awaken interest as well as listening to stories on CD and following them in a print book. The greater availability of multimedia texts with their music, sound and animations can provide the breakthrough to interest in reading some young learners need.

The usual sources of information about books and resources are helpful for less forward young readers. Print guides to resources include *The Core Booklist*, updated every two years, *The School Librarian* and *English 4–11*. Online help is available from Booktrust, which has booklists for young readers of different stages and different abilities (www.booktrust.org.uk). Other support online is available at, for example, the following websites: www. booksforkeeps.co.uk; www.justimaginestory centre.co.uk; www.nate.org.uk; www.love reading4kids.co.uk.

When it comes to supporting the efforts of children with special educational needs to write, the careful use of ICT and word processing have the potential to transform young learners' images of themselves as readers and writers. The opportunity to create text on the computer has been of enormous help to many, not least those who find handwriting challenging and laborious. We must not forget that it is above all through talk that a struggling young learner can be moved forward. I am thinking here both of the teacher's talk to explain and inspire and the encouragement they can give to the young learners to use powerful technology to help get their minds round ideas and to share their thoughts and feelings. Whether a child is handwriting their account or story or using the computer, teachers try to give help at the planning stage and support throughout the writing task, but no one pretends it is easy to enthuse the more reluctant young writers. Finding a topic that inspires a child is the first step and an exciting story can often awaken interest and provide a starting point. Writing frames, either adapted from Lewis and Wray's (1996) work or structured by child and teacher together for a particular task, can help provide a scaffold. Shared writing is another approach worth trying as struggling writers

often feel more supported in a collaborative context. *I know what to write now!* is an inspiring book for teachers of children with special writing needs: it recognises that children's experiences are shaped by the new media. Multimodal and multimedia texts can enliven children's reading and writing (Bhojwani *et al.*, 2010). Although it was first published some years ago, the chapter in *The Primary Language Record in Use* on using the Primary Language Record to record the achievements of children with special needs is still of great help to teachers (O'Sullivan, 1995).

Able young readers and writers – what are their additional needs?

Children who advance quickly as young readers and writers need to be challenged and supported if they are to make progress commensurate with their promise. This means building on the core programme of work in Literacy Time, and outside it, and agreeing with the SENCo and other colleagues on some differentiated activities appropriate for this group of learners. Bear in mind, however, that many of the activities that benefit all children are suitable for the gifted language user if we adapt them to make greater demands. There are publications to do with supporting forward young learners listed on the site of the National Association for Special Educational Needs (NASEN), for example *The Gifted and Talented Education A–Z* (Callander, 2004).

When it comes to reading, able children enjoy the challenge of more difficult fiction and non-fiction texts and more advanced activities responding to those texts. Forward readers from the Reception class upwards are able to understand the language features of different genres and benefit from talk with the teacher about these features. As well as enjoying the picture books liked by all young children – Raymond Briggs' *The Snowman*, Maurice

Sendak's *Where the Wild Things Are*, for example – able young children can also rise to the challenge of the layers of meaning and interesting illustrations in more complex works such as Anthony Browne's *The Tunnel* and *Voices in the Park*, and Neil Gaiman's *The Wolves in the Walls*. Some of these young readers, still at Key Stage 1, would be intrigued by books like Helen Ward's *Wonderful Life* which creates a sort of parallel world in which an engaging little character called Smutt, an Ift, has an extraordinary space adventure.

By Key Stage 2 all children, and particularly the more able, are ready for the challenge of an exciting range of fiction from classic novels and poetry to traditional tales. There are some excellent ideas for supporting a range of fiction reading and extending it into writing in Barrs and Cork's *The Reader in the Writer* and in the Centre for Literacy in Primary Education's Core Booklist, updated every two years. In *Choosing and Using Fiction and Non-fiction 3–11* there is an annotated list of books to challenge the older, abler primary school reader (Mallett, 2010: 136). Young Booktrust helps too, with reading suggestions on its website for abler readers of ten years and over. Teachers who keep up by reading reviews find that there are some exciting and innovative books on the market. *Varmints* by Helen Ward and Marc Craste is both linguistically and visually alive and makes young readers ponder on identity and change. The front cover illustration with the rabbit-like creature staring into space is rather unsettling and curiosity awakening. One of the more extraordinary is Brian Selznick's *The Invention of Hugo Cabret*, a huge 500-page tome which tells the story of an adventure in words and through groundbreaking visual effects. Young readers of stamina might also appreciate Ann Fine's *Flour Babies*, Philip Pullman's His Dark Materials series and Geraldine McCaughrean's *The Stones are Hatching*. For some

young readers it is not too soon to read the classics – Robert Ingpen's fine illustrations of a new edition of R.L. Stevenson's *Treasure Island* should add greatly to enjoyment and understanding.

There is also thought-provoking non-fiction to inspire able young readers. Imaginative illustrations and interesting text combine to raise environmental issues and ethical puzzles in Jeannie Baker's *Where the Forest Meets the Sea* and David Smith's *If the World was a Village*. Sometimes the profundity of the questions young children ask mean that we have to read aloud to them from texts intended for much older readers. This need for advanced texts is explained in Doyle and Mallett's case study about the work on whales by a Reception class. The interest of all the children was engaged by a visit to the Natural History Museum. What was interesting was that the questions of the more able children obliged the teacher to seek out, and read aloud, some much more advanced books than those written for the age group (Doyle and Mallett, 1994; Mallett, 1999). By the later primary years able readers are ready to tackle more advanced kinds of non-fiction themselves, for example full-length autobiographies, biographies and travel books intended for older readers. They are likely, too, to be able to understand and reflect on difficult arguments in more controversial areas to do with environmental, social and political issues. One way of supporting this reflection is to encourage them to read quality newspapers and magazines where there will be features and correspondence of interest and challenge.

Texts other than books can also nourish thinking and writing. In his exceptionally valuable book *Challenging the More Able Language User*, Geoff Dean argues that video-film and DVD texts can help all children, and particularly gifted children, to reflect more deeply on the themes of the books from which they have sprung. He refers to interesting work with able

411

children at Key Stage 1 who studied John Burningham's picture book *Granpa* alongside a video-film based on the book, made by TVS and Channel 4. The children first read the book and were then asked what a director would need to keep in mind when making the video. They enjoyed talking about music and sound effects and how the illustrations in the book might be built on in the animation process (Dean, 2001: chapter 7). Older children also benefit from this combined study of book and video-film or DVD. Sometimes more than one film version of a book exists so that children can consider the choices made by different directors, say for example by the directors of Frances Hodgson Burnett's *The Secret Garden*. Other media have potential for stretching able learners: planning and recording 'radio' programmes is one example.

Many of the texts mentioned above, and the reflection on them, can lead to writing tasks that enthuse and stretch the able. Forward writers control the genre features of different texts more quickly than other children. This ability to approach the same subject matter using different kinds of writing can be exploited both in Literacy Time and in other areas of the curriculum. Children might present the content of a factual account as a letter, diary entry, advertisement, email or newspaper article. Information technology develops language abilities in ways we are still discovering, but not least in the area of writing where children can use word processing and desk-top publishing systems to present work in interesting and novel ways. Children can now experience working with multimedia authoring programs which can help them integrate written text with sounds, pictures and video clips.

Teachers need to bear in mind that their abler pupils often have a particularly flexible 'zone of proximal development' and are likely to benefit from some quality one-to-one teaching. This is valuable at the planning stage of a piece of writing and at the various stages of drafting. Their work can be shared with peers either by being read aloud with invitations for questions or displayed in the literacy area of the classroom. We must remember that able children, like others, need to have their efforts recognised and praised.

Barrs, Myra and Cork, Valerie (2002) *The Reader in the Writer* London: CLPE.

Bhojwani, Petula, Lord, Bill and Wilkes, Cath (2010) *'I know what to write now!' Engaging Boys (and Girls) through a Multimodal Approach* Leicester: UKLA.

Birkett, Veronica (2006) *How to Survive and Succeed as a SENCO in the Primary School* London: LDA Publishers (practical advice given with a touch of humour).

——(2007) *How to Support and Teach Children with Special Educational Needs* London: LDA Publishers (reflects the increased emphasis on inclusion and suggests how schools can provide for diverse and complex needs of all children; checklists for assessment are useful).

Browne, Ann (2009, third edition) *Developing Language and Literacy 3–8* London: Sage (Chapter 8 'Special needs').

Cain, Kate (2010) *Reading Development and Difficulties* London: Wiley, Blackwell.

Callander, B. (2004) *The Gifted and Talented Education A–Z* London: David Fulton.

Dean, Geoff (2001, second edition) *Challenging the More Able Language User* London: David Fulton in association with the National Association for Able Children in Education (NACE).

Doyle, Kathleen and Mallett, Margaret (1994) 'Were dinosaurs bigger than whales?' TACTYC *Early Years Journal*, 14(2), Spring.

Goswami, U. and Bryant, P. (1991) *Phonological Skills and Learning to Read* Hillsdale, N.J.: Lawrence Erlbaum Associates.

Gross, Jean (2002, second edition) *Special Educational Needs in the Primary School* Milton Keynes: Open University Press (recommended as practical and on sound principles).

Hayden, S. and Jordan, E. (2007) *Language and Learning: A Practical Guide for Supporting Pupils with Language and Communication Difficulties across the Curriculum* London: David Fulton.

Lewis, Maureen and Wray, David (1996) *Writing Frames* Reading University: National Centre for Language and Literacy.

Mallett, Margaret (1999) *Young Researchers: Informational Reading and Writing in the Early and Primary Years* London: Routledge.

——(2010) *Choosing and Using Fiction and Non-fiction 3–11* London and New York: Routledge.

Martin, Tony (1989) *The Strugglers: Working with Children who Fail to Learn to Read* Milton Keynes: Open University Press.

Myers, Julia and Burnett, Cathy (2004) *Teaching English 3–13* London and New York: Continuum (Chapter 11 'Meeting diverse needs in English').

National Association for Special Educational Needs (NASEN), Tamworth: www.nasen.org.uk. See publication lists including books/leaflets about language development and special literacy needs. Journals include *Support for Learning, British Journal of Special Education* and *Special!*

O'Sullivan, Olivia (ed.) (1995) *The Primary Language Record in Use* Leicester: CLPE.

Tassoni, Penny (2003) *Supporting Special Needs: Understanding Inclusion in the Early Years* London: Heinemann.

SPECIAL EDUCATIONAL NEEDS CO-ORDINATOR (SENCO)

See: Code of Practice, Special Educational Needs (SEN) in language and literacy, Warnock Report

SPEECH

See: speaking and listening

SPEECH ACT

A 'speech act', according to philosophers of language, for example J.L. Austin, is an utterance that performs an act. So an apology 'I apologise for arriving late' performs the act of apologising and a promise 'I will send the letter tomorrow' performs the act of promising.

SPEECH MARKS

See also: inverted commas, quotation marks

Speech marks are punctuation marks used in written texts to show when we are indicating direct speech or a quotation from another source. For a longer explanation with examples, please see under 'quotation marks'.

SPELLING

See also: transcriptional aspects of writing, writing

How do children gain the knowledge to become good spellers? We now have quite a lot of research to help us support children at each stage in their development. Much information is available about how spelling and reading are linked and the most promising kinds of teacher intervention are suggested in O'Sullivan and Thomas' (2007) *Understanding Spelling*. Another book which gives practical help for spelling at Key Stages 1 and 2 is Norma Mudd's (1994) *Effective Spelling*. Tony Martin considers that children's attitudes to spelling are an important factor in their success and suggests we can create enthusiasm and understanding by the way we talk to children about it. Words are interesting (Martin, 2010)!

The research of Margaret Peters, set out in her book *Spelling: Caught or Taught*, was one of the first systematic accounts of children's spelling development. The book was first published in 1967; she wrote another edition in 1985 which contains a similar message to the first: that teachers need to intervene to help individual children develop their spelling competence and that

413

visual strategies are needed as well as those based on sound. Phonics helps us with regular words but we need visual strategies to help us learn the exceptions. For many years teachers have referred to the 'magic e', the split digraph which lengthens the vowel. Some children have a strongly developed visual memory and remember the 'look' of words easily and this helps them benefit from their reading when it comes to spelling. We have to help children whose visual memory is less developed to acquire useful strategies. There has been a recent trend towards linking spelling to phonics work as well as developing visual strategies.

Richard Gentry's work and that of others indicates that spelling develops in stages. Children begin by writing something that creates the flow of adult-type writing. Then they realise there are different letter shapes – in the pre-communicative stage. When they begin, for example, to use 'r' for 'are' we know they have arrived at the pre-phonetic stage. The next stage is the phonetic stage where there is better control over sound-symbol relationships. Visual strategies strengthen at the 'transitional' stage. Individuals may not go neatly through the stages.

If we want children to use their minds to explore the spelling system we have to allow them to risk sometimes being wrong. As Wyse and Jones point out, the true test of learning a spelling is 'whether it is written correctly in the course of normal writing' (Wyse & Jones, 2007: 144).

Gentry, Richard (1982) 'An analysis of developmental spelling in GNYS AT WRK' *Reading Teacher*, 36: 192–200.

Martin, Tony (2010) *Talk for Spelling* Leicester: UKLA, Minibook 31.

Mudd, Norma (1994) *Effective Spelling: a Practical Guide for Teachers* London: Hodder & Stoughton.

O'Sullivan, Olivia and Thomas, Anne (2007) *Understanding Spelling* London: The Centre for Literacy in Primary Education.

Peters, Margaret (1985 edition) *Spelling: Caught or Taught: A New Look* London: Routledge and Kegan Paul

Wyse, Dominic and Jones, Richard (2007) *Teaching English, Language and Literacy* London: Sage (see pp. 140–6).

SPIRAL CURRICULUM

See also: prior knowledge, spontaneous and scientific concepts

This concept is associated with the work of Jerome Bruner who challenged the view that learning is in a simple sequence (Bruner, 1975). Rather, we get a foothold in an idea or piece of information when we are first introduced to it and then refine our understanding, perhaps relating it to a structured set of relationships, when we revisit it on possibly several later occasions. Two things are useful to keep in mind, particularly when we help children get a first grounding in an area. First, incorporating first-hand and practical experience into the lessons encourages an intuitive sense of what is involved. So in science children might work with simple series circuits using batteries, wires and bulbs and get a 'sense' of how electricity behaves. As older pupils they will build on this when they learn about the laws and sophisticated application of electric power. Second, language can be used by teacher and pupils to support understanding about objects, processes and concepts each time a topic or idea is visited. Children's talk and writing about real experiences and purposes takes their understanding forward at each stage. Talk about ideas and information helps children share and organise developing knowledge.

Bruner, Jerome (1975) *Entry into Early Language: Spiral Curriculum* Swansea: University College of Swansea.

SPOKEN LANGUAGE

See: speaking and listening

SPONTANEOUS AND SCIENTIFIC CONCEPTS

See also: prior knowledge

The difference between 'spontaneous' concepts which are acquired through everyday experience – cup, pleased, dog – and 'scientific' concepts which are formally taught – feudal, solution, igneous – was first pointed out by the developmentalist Jean Piaget and later used by Vygotsky. In *Thought and Language* Vygotsky explains how part of the role of the adult is to help children make helpful connections between the two kinds of concept. Mallett and Newsome (1977) apply Vygotsky's theory to an analysis of a primary school science lesson on igneous and sedimentary rocks. When introducing a new topic it is helpful for a teacher to keep in mind that children will have some common sense or spontaneous concepts about it. This is often referred to as 'prior knowledge'. School learning connects this prior learning or spontaneous concepts with related 'scientific' concepts. So in a study of frogs, children might bring prior knowledge – frogs live in or near ponds, can live on land and in water, and start life as frog-spawn – which can be developed into scientific concepts like habitat, belonging to a class of creatures called amphibians, and life cycle.

Mallett, Margaret and Newsome, Bernard (1977) *Talking, Writing and Learning 8–13* London: Evans/Methuen.
Vygotsky, L.S. (1986 edition) *Thought and Language*, ed. A. Kozusin, Cambridge, Mass.: MIT Press.

STANDARD ENGLISH

See also: dialect, language variety

Standard English enjoys a high social status and is the form of English usually used in writing. It is not linguistically superior to non-standard dialects but for historical and cultural reasons it became the form used in speech and writing by people of high social and educational status. It is associated with BBC voices, royalty and is the form of English learnt by people abroad.

It is important to realise that, like other dialects, it has a distinctive grammar and vocabulary but need not be expressed in 'received pronunciation'. Standard English can be spoken in any accent.

As Medwell *et al.* point out, the English language changes constantly in both its oral and written forms, and therefore 'There can never be an absolute statement of correct standard English – the aim is appropriate use of English' (Medwell *et al.*, 2009). This 'appropriateness' is constantly negotiated by the speakers of the language.

The notion of 'appropriateness' is helpful in the sensitive area of helping children to use standard English in speech and writing. Many teachers feel concern that if they correct children's regional dialect the implication is that their family and community speak an inferior form of language; however, if the emphasis is on appropriateness rather than correctness, a much more positive approach can be taken. We can agree that in writing and in formal situations like interviews and lessons, the standard form is most appropriate, not least because it has become the dialect most people can understand most easily.

Among the useful and interesting contexts for teachers and children to explore dialect forms in a constructive way are improvised drama, traditional dialect songs and poems, and direct speech in stories.

Medwell, Jane, Moore, George, Wray, David and Griffiths, Vivienne (2009) *Primary English: Knowledge and Understanding* Exeter: Learning Matters.

STANDARDISED READING TESTS

See also: assessment, reading, reading age, and under names of particular tests

Standardised Reading Tests provide a summative picture of aspects of children's reading progress. The reading activities in the test booklets aim to identify particular skills like decoding, word recognition, accuracy, comprehension and fluency. From the results, the teacher or educational psychologist work out the child's reading age which enables comparisons to be made between children and with national norms. Some tests, for example the very well known *Schonell Graded Word Reading Test* (restandardised in 1972), require the child to read a list of separate words which become progressively more difficult. Others present sentences – like the *Salford Sentence Reading Test* (Bookbinder, 1976). More recent tests – *Group Reading Test* (Young, 1980 version) for example – tend to assess understanding as well as decoding skills. There is a growing recognition on the part of test constructors that no one test can assess all aspects of reading progress. *The Edinburgh Reading Test* (Godfrey Thompson Unit, 1977–81) and the *Effective Reading Tests* (Vincent & De La Mare, 1986) both aim to tap into a number of aspects of reading including comprehension. We think of 'miscue analysis' as a diagnostic test but the revised Neale Analysis (1988) uses the approach to produce a summative measure. This test has been used by researchers, for example Riley (1996), to make comparisons of the progress of children in different early years classrooms since it produces reading ages from six years. The past assumption that these tests, even the most recent and sophisticated, are more objective than a teacher's judgement of progress has often been challenged. We now accept that a number of different ways of assessing progress, both summative and formative, are needed to gain a full and balanced profile of a child's developing reading abilities. The other issue we need to keep in mind is that the cultural and linguistic bias of any test, particularly those that have not been revised for some time, may disadvantage children from minority groups.

Graham, Judith and Kelly, Alison (2007, third edition) *Reading Under Control* London: David Fulton.

Riley, Jeni (1996) *The Teaching of Reading: The Development of Literacy in the Early Years of School* London: Paul Chapman (see 104–5 for details about the use of Neale Analysis).

STANZA

This is a verse in a poem usually consisting of at least four rhymed lines. A cinquain is a stanza of five lines.

STORY BOOKS

See: fiction: choosing and using, narrative, short stories

STORY BOX

See: storyboxes

STORY CHEST

See also: reading, reading schemes

This set of reading resources was first published by Kingscourt in 1981 and revised in 1996 for the three to eleven year old age range. It was organised into stages: stages 1–7 for Key Stage 1 (five to seven year olds) and stages 8–11 for Key Stage 2 (seven to eleven year olds). This publisher was one of the first to produce quality big books with clear text and attractive and helpful illustrations. Favourites are the humorous and rhythmic stories *Mrs Wishy Washy* and *The Hungry Giant* by Joy Cowley. There was a pleasing range of different formats and genres for older children, including non-fiction, poetry, plays and traditional tales. Both big and small format versions of the stories are still available from McGraw Hill Education.

STORY GRAMMARS

See: narrative

STORY PROPS

See also: speaking and listening, storytelling

These are pictures of characters and scenery from story books mounted on small magnets so that they can be placed on a magnetic board. Alternatively Blu-Tack can be used on a non-magnetic storyboard. The teacher or one of the children tells or reads the story and the items are placed on the board at appropriate points in the narrative.

STORY SACKS

See also: family literacy projects, parents and families

These are a development of the 'bookbag' strategy to encourage home-school links. Bookbags are robust bags containing books to read with a parent or older sibling at home. The adult writes the name of the book, the date it was read and, if they wish, a brief comment about progress in a reading diary, to which the teacher may also contribute. The Basic Skills Agency helped set up a National Support Project to promote special storybags called 'story sacks'. As well as the books and reading diary of the typical storybag, the story sack includes supporting materials like a magazine linking with the theme of the book in some way and a game or soft toy. Sometimes an audio recording and a card with suggested activities are added. Parents and children often help make the sack and assemble the items within. Story sacks are distributed by libraries and schools and many parents and children find them helpful in making reading at home enjoyable and collaborative. Another development from the 'bookbag' strategy is the 'curiosity kit' which is one outcome of the Exeter University Extending Literacy (EXEL) Project and is very like a 'story sack' except that it emphasises non-fiction and aims to support the reading activity of reluctant boy readers (Lewis and Fisher, 2003).

Lewis, M. and Fisher, R. (2003) *Curiosity Kits* Reading: National Centre for Language and Literacy.

STORY TIME

See also: fiction: choosing and using, reading, response to reading, storytelling

This is a designated time, often at the end of the day in nursery and Reception classes, for telling or reading stories to the whole class. The advantage of choosing an earlier time is that other activities like role play and drawing can follow during the day (Browne, 2009). Teachers seek quality stories – there are so many wonderful ones in picture book form – and try to ensure that over a period of time the stories cover a range of types and present different experiences. Fortunate are the children whose teacher is able to tell or read stories in a spellbinding way with pace and enthusiasm, a feel for mood and atmosphere and with different voices for the direct speech. In the Reception class stories are read during the Literacy Hour but it would be sad if stories were not read for sheer pleasure at story time as well. Last time I joined a Reception class at story time the children were enthralled by one of the books in the Mr Men series – *Mr Small*. They asked the teacher to read it again. They laughed in all the same places and there was an atmosphere of complete harmony and shared enjoyment in a class of children that had had their fair share of squabbles during the day. Reading and telling stories out loud is not just an activity for the very young. Older primary children greatly enjoy hearing the teacher read a novel over several weeks. It provides a valuable shared experience for all the children and helps make the class a community of listeners and readers. I remember the profound discussion which accompanied a Year 5 teacher's reading of *The Midnight Fox* by Betsy Byars. Tom had just confessed to Aunt Millie and Uncle Fred that it was he who let the baby fox escape after the chickens had been killed. The class talked about the conflicting interests of the farmers and the fox and Tom's difficult combination of loyalties. I hope reading out loud to the whole class, whatever their age, will always be part of good practice in primary English.

Browne, Ann (2009, third edition) *Developing Language and Literacy 3–8* London: Sage.
Wilson, J. (2006) *Great Stories to Read Aloud* London: Corgi.

STORYBOXES

See also: creativity in English, drama and English, speaking and listening, storytelling

These are containers for a collection of items round a theme to inspire children's improvisation and storytelling. A storybox might be a decorated shoebox containing some toys and objects round the theme of a fairy story like *Red Riding Hood* or some pictures and playthings to do with a creature like a cat or horse. Children sometimes paint the inside of the box to suggest a scene for their story or play. These decorative boxes can be a good focus for story work in groups. The children use the objects and scenery in the box to create characters and a story. Children seem to enjoy the playful, creative nature of the work and often seem to be inspired to use 'story language'. Listening abilities are also encouraged as children like to hear each others' tales.

The involvement and excitement generated can have a pay-off in children's writing. In an interesting article, 'The story's in the bag', Andrew Lambirth *et al.* show how children drew on storybox oral work in very successful independent writing (Lambirth *et al.*, 2004). Helen Bromley, one of the first teachers to develop the use of storyboxes, also finds the boxes help inspire writing and book making (Bromley, 2003).

Bromley, Helen (2003) *50 Exciting Ideas for Storyboxes* Birmingham: Laurence Educational Publications.
Lambirth, Andrew, Darchez, Louise, Nokes, Helen and Wood, Chris (2004) 'The story's in the bag' in *The Primary English Magazine*, 9 (5), June.

STORYTELLING

See also: anecdotes, drama and English, fiction: choosing and using, historical novel, history and English, narrative, picture books, short stories

Storytelling by both teacher and children can be a most enjoyable part of English work and plays a significant role in the development of children's oral language. It contributes particularly to children's ability to use narrative as a way of organising ideas and experiences. 'Storytelling' covers a range of activities from the short anecdotes children share to the performance of a gifted adult storyteller. Listening to stories can develop a certain quality of engaged and reflective listening too (Harrett, 2009).

We have a rich treasure house to draw on: not only have we our own store of United Kingdom traditional tales, riddles, sayings and nursery rhymes which can be told as well as read, but we can also draw on stories from oral cultures across the world. The arrival of children in our schools whose roots are in cultures rich in storytelling has heightened our interest (Graham and Kelly, 2007). Teachers often model storytelling, sometimes using story props – characters and scenery – on a felt storyboard. Some children are eager to take a turn at telling stories to the group. As well as retellings from stories they have heard others tell or those based on book stories, children with some encouragement tell anecdotes about their lives both inside and outside the classroom. With a new class or group I have found telling my own anecdotes – the day I lost three guinea pigs – often encourages the children to share their tales. Children also come to school with stories about their family's history – when they lived in another country or another part of the country or when Grandad or Grandma went to a Beatles concert in the 1960s. Student teachers I have worked with have, once they tried storytelling activities in the classroom, often been surprised at the rich resources on which children are able to draw. Medical emergencies including true tales of being admitted to casualty wards after accidents seem to be told with particular relish. Of course, with practice, children develop over the primary years in their control over a narrative, how they select and sequence the events, what they decide to emphasise in the characters to enhance the tale and how they bring the tale to a satisfying resolution.

In their book *Reading Under Control* Graham and Kelly set out one approach to first using storytelling in the classroom. They cover the preparation you will have to do if you begin by telling a story to the class yourself and suggest you might base it on a written-down story with lots of humour and action. How you tell the story depends on the age of the children but you need to keep the pace up and include direct speech to keep it lively.

It is hoped that the children will comment at the end without you asking them a question. Then, they could be invited to retell the story, perhaps several children telling part of it each (Graham and Kelly, 2007).

One very strong context for group storytelling is drama and role play. An interesting book on drama and traditional tales shows how events in stories are given new meaning and significance when children take on the roles and 'voices' of the characters. For example, the linguistic resources of a group of very young children were extended when they took on the role of the staff of building suppliers selling materials to the three little pigs to construct their houses (Toye and Prendiville, 2000). In early years settings in particular, the teacher needs to help the children develop the narrative, often by taking a central role.

The storybox approach is a way of drawing children into a fictional world which has considerable appeal to the very young. Developed, used and evaluated by Helen Bromley, it involves early years teachers in placing some objects in a shoebox which provide the bare bones of a story (Bromley, 2000). The children can build on miniature settings for the objects, choosing all or just some of the objects to tell a story. One box much favoured by the girls in the class with which Helen Bromley worked, presented a vet's surgery and had Playmobil people and some animals ready to be patients. Three boys chose a 'science fiction' box which, when the lid was lifted, looked like the inside of a moon crater and included spaceships and moon rocks. The children, with a little encouragement, involved themselves in imaginative play and spoke in the roles of the people and animals, using language appropriate for the various situations. This proved to be a window into children's thinking and therefore indicated what they knew and understood.

DVDs and television films can add helpfully to classroom storytelling resources. Story Spinners have brought out DVDs with each story told by an internationally acclaimed storyteller to the camera. Teachers find listening to the stories leads to children's lively discussion, drama and writing (Story Spinners, 2010).

Storytelling links with the development of literacy in several important ways. An introduction to the features of stories in oral form helps children understand the same features when they occur in written form and in other media like film and television. All stories have a setting, characters and a sequence of events or plot. Usually there is a conflict to be resolved. Being exposed to these features in a told story helps children bring a set of expectations about form, structure and events when they read from books. Older primary children can be helped to consider how told and written-down stories differ. What, for example, replaces tone, pitch, pace, gesture and facial expression in a written-down story?

Certainly a knowledge of traditional stories gained through oral tellings helps children enjoy fully books like Hoffman and Binch's *Amazing Grace* and *Grace and her Family* published by Frances Lincoln. These written-down stories draw on the ancient tales in all sorts of subtle ways: in the latter book Grace is shown reading a book about fairy tales when her stepmother offers her food. Other examples of intertextual stories are *I Like Books* (a book about genre for very young children) and *The Tunnel* both by Anthony Browne and *The Jolly Postman* by Allan and Janet Ahlberg.

Storytelling is not only for very young children. A Year 5 class told their own stories to the class about the pictures. The stories could be 'true' or from the world of the imagination. Later some of them adapted their stories into written form. So this series of lessons moved naturally from listening, to reading, to telling and then back to writing again. Another powerful example of how hearing a text read aloud encouraged children's desire to read involved nine to eleven year olds who had heard gifted storytellers tell stories from the *Iliad*. The classroom researchers found that an oral resource telling of great and dramatic adventures achieved a deep engagement on the part of the pupils (Reedy and Lister, 2007).

Storytelling can stretch out across a number of subjects – dance and drama, of course, but also history, geography, science and even mathematics – but in English lessons it is a valuable activity in its own right from the earliest years onwards.

Bromley, Helen (2000) 'The gift of transformation: children's talk and story boxes' in *Language Matters* Journal of the Centre for Literacy in Primary Education, Winter.

Graham, Judith and Kelly, Alison (2007, third edition) *Reading Under Control* London: David Fulton.

Grainger, Teresa (1997) *Traditional Storytelling in the Primary Classroom* Leamington Spa: Scholastic.

Grugeon, E. and Gardner, P. (2000) *The Art of Storytelling in the Primary Classroom* London: David Fulton.

Harrett, Jacqueline (2009, second edition) *Tell Me Another Story ... Speaking, Listening, Learning through Storytelling* Leicester: UKLA Minibook.

Howe, A. and Johnson, J. (1992) *Common Bonds: Storytelling in the Classroom* Sevenoaks: Hodder & Stoughton.

Reedy, D. and Lister, B. (2007) '"Bursting with blood and passion": the impact of an oral retelling of the *Iliad* in the primary classroom' *Literacy* 41(1).

Story Spinners (2010) *Stories from Around the World: A Cultural Treasure Trove* DVDs of stories told for the early years, Key Stage 1 and Key Stage 2, published by Story Spinners.

Toye, Nigel and Prendiville, Francis (2000) *Drama and the Traditional Story* London: RoutledgeFalmer.

STRUCTURAL GUIDERS

These are the headings and sub-headings that sometimes organise an information book. For more about structural guiders and other global aspects of non-fiction, see Bobbie Neate, 1992.

Neate, Bobbie (1992) *Finding Out About Finding Out* London: Hodder & Stoughton.

STRUCTURALIST MODEL OF LANGUAGE

Those linguists taking up a structuralist approach see language as a sort of web in which every part is related to the whole. The US structuralist, Leonard Bloomfield, aimed to set down a catalogue of elements in a language and the positions in which they can occur. The structuralist position was challenged by Noam Chomsky who developed 'generative linguistics' which went far beyond a description of elements (see under 'communicative competence/ competence and performance' and 'trans-formational grammar').

STUDY SKILLS

See also: CD-ROM, copying, encyclope-dia, Dewey system, dictionary, Directed Activities Round Texts, factual genres, information books, Information and Communications Technology (ICT) and English, internet, library skills, non-fiction reading and writing, retrieval devices, structural guiders, summary

'Study skills' is a term referring to all the strategies researchers of any age use when finding out about a topic. As well as learning how to use the library, and usually the Dewey system of cataloguing, children need to be taught how to find the information they want by using the retrieval devices – the contents pages and indexes of books – and how to access material from databases and sites on the internet. Children need also to learn to make useful notes and summaries of key passages. These will be the basis of their own writing. The acquisition of study skills is part of teaching non-fiction kinds of literacy (Mallett, 1999, 2007). In shared reading and writing teachers 'model' for example how to find one's way round a reference book or CD-ROM. Acquiring study skills helps make a young learner independent. We need to teach them, but too many decontextualised exercises can risk making the 'finding out' process seem dull. Learning to research is satisfying if it is linked to finding out what we need and if we want to take our knowledge and understanding of a topic further (Mallett, 1999, 2007).

If you seek detailed guidance on researching for essays and dissertations and on referencing, you would find chapters 6 and 7 in Herne *et al.* (2000) helpful.

Herne, Steve, Jessel, John and Griffiths, Jenny (2000) *Study to Teach: A Guide to Studying in Teacher Education* London: Routledge.
Mallett, Margaret (1999) *Young Researchers: Informational Reading in the Early and Primary Years* London: Routledge.
——(2007) *Active Encounters: Inspiring Young Readers and Writers of Non-fiction* UKLA minibook.

SUBJECT KNOWLEDGE

See also: adverb, adverbial clause, alliteration, cohesion, digraph, ellipsis, factual genres, fiction: choosing and using, first person writing, genre, grammar, grapheme, history of children's literature, metaphor, morpheme, narrative, noun, onomato-poeia, onset and rime, parts of speech, persuasive genre, phoneme, poetry, prefix, punctuation, sentence, Shakespearian drama, simile, spelling, suffix, syllable, verbs

Teachers have always needed a background of knowledge in language and literature to teach English in the primary school. The requirements for teachers' knowledge and understanding of English in its own right as well as in relation to children's learning were formalised in 1998 in DfEE Circular 4/98 entitled *Teaching: High Status, High Standards*. This document specified the essential core knowledge, skills and

421

understanding about subject knowledge required for qualified teacher status at that time. (Visit the government education website for the latest requirements: www. education.gov.uk.) Whatever the requirements of a particular time may be, though, primary teachers need to have some knowledge about language in order to teach English well (Cox, 2011). This study can be organised under three headings: lexical, grammatical and textual. Lexical study includes phonology (the sound system), graphology (the writing system) and morphology (word structure and derivations). Grammatical study consists of the grammar of spoken and written English and punctuation. Textual study takes in cohesion, layout and the organisation of different kinds of text. Part of the task is to learn the meanings of the technical terms for all three areas of study and to be able to use them appropriately. If you are a student teacher you may find the following suggestions help you feel more confident about your knowledge of language:

- Identify the areas where you feel you need to strengthen.
- Use a self-study aid or book to take forward your knowledge (for example Wilson and Scanlon, 2011, which is both scholarly and entertaining).
- Talk about your studies with a colleague or colleagues in college and school – collaborative study can be more enjoyable for something like this.
- Be pro-active in seeking advice from colleagues, teachers in school and your tutors.
- Research aspects of subject knowledge before working with children in school.

So, developing the idea in this last bullet point, if you are about to have some lessons telling and reading traditional tales with children it is helpful to research the features of this genre. In preparation for a study of poetry with older pupils you could check through different types of form like haiku, ballad and free verse, and secure your grasp of terminology like alliteration, metaphor and personification.

A huge pile of books, articles and CD-ROMs, including a good number on language study and grammar, have been my companions as I have worked on this encyclopedia. I find Tom McArthur's well-known book *The Oxford Companion to the English Language* comprehensive and clear. It is particularly helpful on literary terms and text types. There is a shorter version of the book (McArthur & McArthur, 2005). Angela Wilson and Julie Scanlon's *Language Knowledge for Primary Teachers* is written with a welcome touch of humour and covers all three important areas in language study – the lexical, the grammatical and the textual – thoroughly. Their insights about ways into understanding the genre features of both fiction and non-fiction are particularly valuable and, in my experience, enjoyed by students and teacher (Wilson and Scanlon, 2011).

For those who would like to learn more about linguistics, I recommend David Crystal's *Cambridge Encyclopedia of Language* and John Seely's *Grammar for Teachers* and *A–Z Grammar and Punctuation Guide*. There is also helpful information online and you may find a visit to the following websites helpful in clarifying points: www.bbc.co.uk/skillswise/words/grammar and correctpunctuation.explicatus.info.

Cox, Robyn (ed.) (2011) *Primary English Teaching* London: Sage/UKLA.

Crystal, D. (2010, revised edition) *The Cambridge Encyclopedia of Language* Cambridge: Cambridge University Press.

DfEE (1998) 'Teaching: high status, high standards' *Circular*, 4/98.

McArthur, Tom (1992) *The Oxford Companion to the English Language* Oxford: Oxford University Press.

McArthur, Tom and McArthur, Roshan (2005, revised shorter edition) *Concise Oxford*

Companion to the English Language Oxford: Oxford University Press.

Seely, John (2006) *Grammar for Teachers* London: Heinemann.

——(2009) *A–Z Grammar and Punctuation Guide* Oxford: Oxford University Press (this book helps make its points with examples of real usage and manages to make accessible such things as participles, split infinitives and use of 'may' and 'might').

Wilson, Angela and Scanlon, Julie (2011, fourth edition) *Language Knowledge for Primary Teachers* London: David Fulton.

SUFFIX

A suffix is an affix which ends a word, such as 'ful' in 'useful' or 'ed' in 'acted'.

SUMMARY (OR PRÉCIS)

See also: Directed Activities Round Texts, non-fiction reading and writing

This is a shortened version of a longer text containing the most important points. Children can be helped to practise activities which prepare them for summary writing – for example, underlining main points in a text and then developing the underlined points into notes in shared writing (Mallett, 2007).

Mallett suggests another promising strategy: read a section from an information book that is being currently used for work in any lesson and ask the children to write down five key points – about 'the diet of the Ancient Greeks' or about 'young and old rivers'. Children usually enjoy the opportunity to read out their list for constructive criticism. They learn to reflect on the status of particular pieces of information and from skeleton notes they can write summaries (Mallett, 1999: 108).

N.B. A summary at the beginning of a dissertation or academic article is called an abstract.

Mallett, M. (1999) *Young Researchers: Informational Reading in the Early and Primary Years* London: Routledge.

——(2007) *Active Encounters: Inspiring Young Readers and Writers of Non-fiction* UKLA minibook.

SUMMATIVE ASSESSMENT

See: assessment, SATs, standardised reading tests

SUSTAINED SILENT READING (SSR)

See: ERIC and USSR

SYLLABLE

See also: phoneme, phonological awareness

A syllable is part of a word that is pronounced as one beat. In the word 'subject' there are two syllables: 'sub' and 'ject'.

SYNONYM

See also: thesaurus

A synonym of a word means the same thing as that word. There is some doubt about whether any two words can ever have an identical meaning. McArthur, for example, writes that some linguists consider 'no two words have the same distribution, frequency, connotation or language level'. Nevertheless, a thesaurus works on the principle that it is useful for a speaker or writer to know synonyms for as many words as possible. *Chambers School Thesaurus*, for children over ten years, includes panels of important words for extended treatment such as anger, difficulty, money, health and happiness. Many dictionaries also include lists of synonyms at the end of definitions. Help with synonyms is to be found in *Dictosaurus*, a combined electronic dictionary and thesaurus from Oxford University Press (2006).

Children increase their knowledge of synonyms through listening and reading from an early age.

McArthur, Tom (1992) *The Oxford Companion to the English Language* London and Oxford: QPD Paperbacks and Oxford University Press.

SYNTACTIC CUE-SYSTEM

See also: cue-systems, grammar, miscue analysis, reading

When using this cue-system, readers draw on their knowledge of grammar and language to get a sense of what is coming next. Young readers know for instance that if they read at the beginning of a sentence 'the teachers' the next verb will be plural, and an adjective like 'beautiful' will often be followed soon by a noun, such as 'horse'.

The other cue-systems are semantic, grapho-phonic and bibliographic.

SYNTAX

See: grammar

SYNTHETIC PHONICS

See also: phoneme, phonics

This approach to teaching phonics involves young readers in first separating out the phonemes in a word and then blending them together to read the word. This way of perceiving phonics contrasts with 'analytic' approaches in which larger segments of words are analysed and patterns across words detected.

T

TALK

See: speaking and listening

TALKING BOOKS

'Talking books' are interactive reading aids. Children focus on the written text and pictures as the words are read aloud. Teachers also use software in shared writing sessions to produce their own talking books in collaboration with the children. Some of the books used in Literacy Time can provide a framework for children's first efforts at making their own talking book.

TAPED BOOKS

See: audio resources

TARGET SETTING

See also: assessment, portfolios, SATs

Often the statutory assessments (SATs) at the end of key stages are a stimulus and guide to teachers' target setting. The senior management team and the governors compare their school's results in reading and writing with the national figures, especially those for schools that are similar in intake and facilities. Targets are set to raise attainment gradually. Once realistic targets are agreed, everyone concerned should have a clear understanding of the action needed to achieve them. All this needs to be built into any target-setting chart. So we might have column headings as follows, which are based on the diagram in Tyrrell and Gill (2000: 159): Standard at (date); projected target; success criteria; action to be taken; standard at (date). The success criteria will be drawn from the National Curriculum objectives.

The challenge of increasing a child's attainment over time and measuring progress against projected targets is now built into educational culture. However, there are some issues that the English/Literacy Co-ordinator and class teachers need to bear in mind. First, there is the problem of pupil mobility. Tyrrell and Gill estimate that for some schools there may be inwards and outwards transfers of 50 per cent, making target setting somewhat imprecise. They conclude that too much reliance on figures risks misunderstanding the nature of schooling 'and shows a lack of awareness of anything other than the stereotypical childhood where a little boy or girl sets off to Reception and stays in the school until they leave at the end of Year 6' (Tyrrell and Gill, 2000: 158).

Another difficulty arises if we think schools are like businesses which can improve performance by higher sales or by putting economies in place. After a couple of years of considerable effort, schools may reach a plateau and in spite of excellent teaching, performance levels according to fairly crude measures are unlikely to show large rises. It is also the case that cohorts of children can vary in their levels of motivation and ability so that 'dips' in performance may occur.

As Graham and Kelly point out, in a target-setting climate teachers need to have some richer evidence than just test scores of a child's progress. They are very much in favour of building up portfolios with annotated samples of writing and other evidence and of involving children in setting targets. Where a number of key targets are identified each term or half term these can be shared with the children, 'who then decide ... how far the targets have been achieved, before moving on to set new targets' (Graham and Kelly, 2007). So an eight year old might for half a term be working on some particular letter strings to improve reading and spelling and on strengthening the use of dialogue in stories. Teacher and child would talk about progress, focused on the child's reading and writing samples at the end of the half term.

Graham, Judith and Kelly, Alison (2007) *Reading Under Control* London: David Fulton.
Tyrrell, Jenny and Gill, Narinderjit (2000) *Coordinating English at Key Stage 1* London: David Fulton.

TEACHER TRAINING AGENCY (TTA)

The Teacher Training Agency was a government body which set standards for all aspects of teaching. They set up national standards for subject leadership stressing that co-ordinators need to work towards high-quality teaching in every classroom, effective use of resources and the improvement of standards of achievement for all pupils. This work became the responsibility of the Training and Development Agency for Schools.

www.education.gov.uk

426

TEACHING ASSISTANTS

Teaching assistants (TAs) support the work of teachers right across the curriculum. Their contribution includes: helping to prepare materials and displays and to organise resources; joining in team planning discussions; supporting the activities of individual children and small groups; and recording children's progress. In Literacy Time they may, for example, fill in information grids during the 'shared reading' period which are then used by the class teacher in the plenary.

Teaching assistants (and other support staff like librarians, technicians and nursery nurses) can raise their status to that of Higher Level Teaching Assistant (HLTA), a qualification which recognises the levels of knowledge, skill and understanding many support staff have. There is information about HLTA assessment and training programmes and details of the HLTA standards on www.hlta.gov.uk. The qualification is awarded to those candidates who have reached the agreed national professional standards.

The contribution of support staff releases teachers to carry out duties in which they have expertise and helps schools meet the contractual changes introduced in September 2004 and in 2005 which help reduce teacher workloads. Schools and LEAs decide how individual TAs and HLTAs are deployed. An HLTA with expertise in ICT might contribute to lesson planning and delivery and work with groups of children across a number of age ranges in the school under the supervision of class teachers. While recognising the valuable contribution support staff make and welcoming the new opportunities available for their development through training, schools seek reassurance that support staff and teachers are not interchangeable. The guidance explains that each class or group timetabled for the primary school subjects and for religious education must be assigned a teacher and of course the teacher is accountable for overall learning outcomes. It also gives head teachers discretion over allowing some staff who 'have the appropriate skills, expertise and experience' to work with whole classes. This is where there is some concern that conceivably we might be heading towards a system where qualified teachers take on a mainly supervisory role. It should be stressed that this is not the case in current guidance.

Finally, what are the implications of the teaching assistant role for children's English and literacy work? Burnham and Jones (2008) cover this well in their book which has strong sections on developing the language and literacy skills and abilities of all children, supporting language progress of children with communication and interaction difficulties and those children learning English as an additional language. The National Association for Language Development in the Curriculum has a helpful website – www.naldic.org.uk.

Burnham, Louise and Jones, Helen (2008, second edition) *The Teaching Assistant's Handbook* London: Heinemann.
Teaching Assistant Centre: www.teachingassistant centre.com

TEACHING ENGLISH

See: history of English teaching (in the primary school)

TELEVISION AND LITERACY

See also: advertisements, CD-ROM, film making, internet, television programmes for children, video-film and DVDs, visual literacy

Watching television (unless it was educational television) was, until relatively recently, thought to be a much more passive activity than reading print. Apart from concerns about the possible effect on children of watching 'unsuitable' programmes intended for adults, there have long been suspicions that watching a lot of television could make children less likely to spend time reading. Research, for example that carried out by Brown (1999), tends to show that children's perceptions are that both parents and teachers are against 'watching too much television'. However, opinion is now swinging towards the positive contribution that viewing film, DVDs and television can make to children's developing literacy (Marsh and Millard, 2001; Palmer, 2008). Indeed, dramatic technological changes have expanded the ways in which meanings can be carried. So there are exciting new literacies to develop and support, not least visual literacy. It is these new literacies that we need to develop in the primary classroom alongside print literacy if we want children to be imaginative and flexible thinkers in a technological culture. Teachers have to know how to use the medium effectively, however. I consider the role of video-film, and particularly videos and DVDs of children's stories, in developing children's literary competence under the 'video-film and DVDs' entry. This entry looks more specifically at the educative role of television programmes first in the home and then in the school context.

The home context

If you watch very young children while they are viewing their favourite programmes – *Teletubbies, Sesame Street, The Tweenies* or *In the Night Garden* – you are likely to be struck at how active their response is. They jump up, sing, dance and ask questions. In her qualitative study of the role of televisual texts in children's development, Naima Brown (1999) observed that children did not always respond to adult presenters' explicit invitation to 'join in and sing along' but made their own decisions about how to participate. Often they insisted on seeing a favourite video over and over again. Brown believes the lively response of such young children shows the potential of television, or as Brown terms them 'televisual texts', as a starting point for role play, storytelling and, later on, writing.

Perhaps because of time constraints, parents do not often seem to watch television with their children, so opportunities to answer questions and generally mediate between child and programme are limited. Brown did find some families who watched programmes together. For example five year old India told the researcher that she and her seven year old brother and their parents watched *Coronation Street* before the children went to bed (Brown, 1999: 63).

There has been concern about children who spend long periods in front of the television without any talk or interaction with others. Some studies suggest children's listening skills are unlikely to develop under such circumstances. Sue Palmer points out that family rituals of singing nursery rhymes may be a causality of a television-dominated home (Palmer, 2008), but it does seem to be the lack of interaction which is the problem here. Not surprisingly, Brown found that in contexts where there was lively talk about programmes, children were more likely to extend the experience through storytelling and play. There are many examples of the creative response of her own child, see for example her retelling of *Pollyanna* at age 5.6 years (Brown, 1999: appendix F). Rehana sings a made-up tune at the beginning of her story – as she has heard introductory music on the many story and videotapes she has heard.

The new emphasis on televisual texts from mainstream television in school may change parents' perceptions of television to more positive ones.

The school context

A teacher's television resources fall into two main categories. First, there are the school programmes on every subject which may be watched live or pre-recorded for greater flexibility. Second, there are the pre-recorded programmes from mainstream television in DVD form. The latter may be factual programmes on wildlife or geographical themes, for example, but the 'English' collection is more likely to be of television serials of children's stories. (Teachers also use television advertisements for analysis of persuasive texts and this is covered in the 'advertisements' entry.) The second of these is discussed in the 'video-film and DVDs' entry, so I turn mainly to the first in the discussion below.

Over the years there have been a large number of educational programmes to support the teaching of English, some of them of high quality like *Storyworld* and *Words and Pictures* for younger children and *Living Language* and *The English Programme* for older ones. Many of today's television programmes help develop children's literacy and can be recorded to use at the most appropriate point in the teaching programme. In his study for the Independent Television Commission, Paul Kelley found that teachers preferred to use pre-recorded programmes so that they could stop the video machine to highlight points or invite discussion (Kelley, 1998). The programmes are usually interactive, inviting children to call out the names of letters, to predict and sometimes to join in other ways like singing. Very often there are programme notes for the teacher and booklets for the children and, increasingly, software packages. The linking of the different media through which teaching is planned and carried out makes demands on the practitioner, but the careful use of television programmes can prove an enjoyable whole-class activity and link home and school.

For older children there are programmes about the use of English and to promote reading and writing; sometimes such programmes are presented by children's writers and poets like Michael Rosen. There is no doubt that many programmes provide inspiration for literacy work as they provide whole works or extracts from literature ranging from Shakespeare and Aesop, to classic poetry and ballads, traditional tales from different cultures and modern fairy tales and popular fiction. (Visit www.bbc.co.uk/schools for details about Learning Zone Broadband – clips of texts to promote literacy can be streamed into home or classroom.) In the 'video-film and DVDs' entry I suggest that children can be helped to compare how aspects of the same narrative can be stressed in different media. In her chapter in Jon Callow's book *Image Matters*, Annemaree O'Brien suggests that we help children to discuss the features of a televisual text, including the acting, settings, lighting, use of sound and music and the angle of camera shots (O'Brien, 1999: 48). As well as televised stories specifically for children, teachers are now including for older primary children examples of popular television including carefully selected episodes of soap serials, cartoons and sports commentaries and, as mentioned above, advertisements. With help from the teacher, children can develop their thinking about important issues and expand their understanding of how a particular medium carries its meanings.

Film Education: www.filmeducation.org

Brown, Naima (1999) *Young Children's Literacy Development and the Role of Televisual Texts* London: RoutledgeFalmer.

Kelley, P. (1998) *The Future of Schools' Television* London: Independent Television Commission.

Marsh, Jackie and Millard, Elaine (2001) *Literacy and Popular Culture* London: Paul Chapman.

O'Brien, Annemaree (1999) 'Reading TV: a basic visual literacy' in Callow, Jon (ed.) *Image Matters: Visual Texts in the Classroom* Marrickville, Australia: PETA (Primary English Teaching Association).

Palmer, Sue (2008) *Detoxing Childhood: What Parents Need to Know to Raise Bright, Balanced Children* London: Orion (sets out a constructive approach to children's TV viewing).

TELEVISION PROGRAMMES FOR CHILDREN

See also: film making, radio programmes for children, schools' radio programmes, schools' television programmes, television and literacy, video-film and DVDs, visual literacy

Watching television takes up a significant part of the leisure time of most children and contributes hugely to their experience of popular culture. By the early twenty-first century one in three children under five in the United Kingdom had a television set in their bedroom (Strank, 2003). On average, school aged children read books for fifteen minutes each day but spend 200 minutes watching TV, video-film and DVD, seventy-five minutes on audio media and eighty minutes on the computer, often in combination and while also doing their homework (Buckingham, 2004). This entry concentrates on television programmes for children's entertainment. For a consideration of educational programmes see 'schools' television programmes' and for the implications of television for literacy see 'television and literacy'.

A little history

The first television programme for children was transmitted by the BBC in 1946 and by October *Muffin the Mule* had made his first appearance. Although very few people in post-war Britain could afford to buy a television set, the BBC debated whether there should be television programming to mirror radio's hugely popular *Children's Hour*. This debate was at a time when there was some concern that television

429

might lure children away from Sunday school and about whether it was discouraging children from reading.

The first children's television producers were appointed by the BBC in 1950 and worked at the Lime Grove studios. It was recognised from the start that they were making programmes for entertainment and that they should not stray into the area of educational broadcasting. In the 1950s two things happened that raised the profile of television, making it a serious alternative to listening to the wireless (as radio was called then). The first was the televising of the coronation of Queen Elizabeth II in 1953. The second was the launching of commercial television in 1955. Early BBC children's programmes such as *Billy Bunter*, *The Appleyards* (an early soap) and *Zoo Quest* (with David Attenborough) had then to compete with programmes on commercial television, many from the USA, such as *Roy Rogers*, *Hopalong Cassidy* and *Lassie*, and the British-made *Robin Hood*. Where BBC and commercial television were in competition, the BBC's audience share fell to 30 per cent (Home, 1993).

The additional air time provided by the launch of BBC2 in 1964 gave room for new children's programmes including the daily preschool programme, *Playschool*. The BBC fought for audience share with programmes like *Blue Peter*, *The Magic Roundabout* and *Jackanory* – the latter being a long-running storytelling programme in which actors read quality children's literature (Buckingham *et al.*, 1999).

Over the succeeding decades successful programmes like *Grange Hill*, *Magpie*, *Worzel Gummidge* and *Multicoloured Swap Shop* were launched. Some have become nostalgic memories while others, like the relaunched *Dr Who* and *Grange Hill*, continued into a new century (Sheridan, 2004). For information on children's television drama see *The Hill and Beyond* (Docherty and McGown, 2003).

Into the 2000s

The past decade has brought the sale of licences to new broadcasters and growth in the number of terrestrial and digital channels. On the one hand this trend has put pressure on costs and audience share targets, while on the other hand it has led to the opening up of opportunities for dedicated children's channels and space for children's programmes. However, despite these new opportunities, broadcasters have to compete for children's attention against other forces in popular culture – computer games, the internet, DVDs, text messaging and digital music players.

No doubt it is this competition that has caused new energy to flow into making children's programmes of great diversity and interest. So what are some of these new channels and programmes?

- *CBeebies*: a Freeview/Freesat channel broadcast from 6am to 7pm (and also at different times on BBC1 and BBC2 during the morning) is for preschool children and blurs the boundaries between television for entertainment and television with an educational purpose. The programmes are play- and activity-based and some use puppets to stimulate thinking and problem solving. They include cartoons, activities and stories and familiar series such as *The Fimbles*, *The Tweenies* and *The Koala Brothers*. The principles behind the programmes are made explicit in print and online articles by literacy specialists, for example Sue Palmer (www.bbc.co.uk/cbeebies). The research evidence on the effect of television on the very young suggests that two factors are very important in ensuring television viewing is a positive experience: the quality of the content of the programmes and the input of the adult co-viewer (Palmer, 2008).
- CBBC (Children's BBC): another Freeview/Freesat channel, the programmes

of which also appear on BBC1 and BBC2. CBBC on BBC1 includes such programmes as *Grange Hill*, *Blue Peter* and *Newsround*, programmes the parents of today's children would have watched.

- CITV: ITV's channel, which runs between 3.15pm and 5.50pm, includes programmes such as *Thomas the Tank Engine*, nursery rhymes from the *Fun Song Factory* and *The Worst Witch* for older children.
- Channel 4 has programmes for older children in the early morning, for example *The Hoobs*.
- Channel 5 shows old favourites like *Bagpuss*, *The Clangers*, *Noddy* and *Pooh*, also in the early morning.

Children can visit interactive websites to find out more about their favourite programmes. By accessing the Children's BBC website (www.bbc.co.uk/cbbc) children can find information and suggestions for exciting activities on programmes like the *Tracy Beaker* series, *Blue Peter*, *Byker Grove* and *Planet Cook*.

Since the 1980s, Saturday morning programmes have also been an important part of the scheduling and this continues today on terrestrial, digital and cable television.

The Disney and other digital and cable channels have films that might appeal to children in the primary years, but they might equally find something which builds on school work they have enjoyed on UKTV Documentary, Animal Planet, National Geographic or UKTV History.

Of course, children also watch programmes not intended for their age group and teachers and parents worry about this. Nor are all television programmes for children of outstanding quality. However, on the whole, rather than proclaim that many children 'watch too much television', it is more useful to 'accentuate the positive' and to do all we can to make children reflective, critical viewers (Buckingham, 2004: 329). Certainly, at the very least, it is

very much in the interests of teachers to be aware of the programmes that are favourites with the children in their classes. Not only are these programmes likely to be mentioned in conversation and class discussion, but they are likely to be brought into role play in the home corner and into older children's improvised drama. They also find their way into children's writing and may influence the books children choose. Teachers may want to actively direct children to programmes which link with learning in the curriculum and, in English lessons, we want children to reflect critically on media texts and consider how we learn and enjoy in different ways from a television programme than we do from print sources. Teachers find *Look Again!* a source of inspiration when teaching about the moving image (Cameron & Al-Saleh, 2003). *English Express* is a schools programme with an educational purpose, but it looks at different kinds of writing, including how to make a script for a soap. As it has much humour and originality, a programme like this can be both entertaining and help get the critical, reflective juices flowing. Perhaps we should not overdo this, though. Children have the right to enjoy their leisure activities for their own sake and look for 'spaces' that are their own for relaxation and amusement (Lewis, 2002).

BBC: www.bbc.co.uk

Buckingham, David (2004) 'Television' in Hunt, P. (ed.) *International Companion Encyclopaedia of Children's Literature, Vol. II* London and New York: Routledge.

Buckingham, David, Davies, Hannah, Jones, Ken and Kelley, Peter (1999) *Children's Television in Britain: History, Discourse and Policy* London BFI publishing (based on a research programme, this book looks critically at the changing nature of children's programming).

Cameron, Alex and Al-Saleh (designers) (2003) *Look Again! A Teaching Guide to Using*

Television with Three- to Eleven-Year Olds London: DfES with bfi, www.bfi.org.uk/education/teaching (this is a guide to help teachers to use and teach about the moving image; there is a wealth of teaching ideas and a good glossary helps discussion of the different aspects).

CBeebies: www.bbc.co.uk/cbeebies

Children's BBC (CBBC): www.bbc.co.uk/cbbc

Docherty, Mark and McGown, Alistair (2003) *The Hill and Beyond: Children's Television Drama – an Encyclopedia* London: British Film Institute (covers BBC and ITV programmes from 1950 onwards including adaptations of the classics such as The Railway Children, The Chronicles of Narnia and Stig of the Dump, and newer fantasy and science films. Readers are directed to online reviews).

Home, Anna (1993) *Into the Box of Delights: A History of Children's Television* London: BBC Books.

Lewis, Richard (2002) *The Encyclopedia of Cult Children's TV* London: Alison and Bushby (a light-hearted and essentially individual view of *Jackanory, Hector's House* and other programmes).

Palmer, Sue (2008) *Detoxing Childhood: What Parents Need to Know to Raise Bright, Balanced Children* London: Orion.

Sheridan, Simon (2004) *The A–Z of Classic Children's Television* London: Reynolds and Hearn (includes contributions from David McKee (Mr Benn), Jane Tucker (Rainbow) and Gay Soper (The Flumps) and detailed analysis of series such as The Moomins).

Strank, L. (2003) 'Listen to radio' *Times Educational Supplement*, 24 October: 24.

TENOR

See also: register

To understand what 'tenor' means we first have to consider the concept of 'register' of which 'tenor' is an aspect.

'Register' is an abstract linguistic concept that refers to the way in which language varies according to the situation in which it is spoken and written. 'Tenor' is to do with the way in which the message is given. An informal use of tenor might include the active voice and the use of the pronouns 'I' and 'you' while the passive voice indicates a more formal expression of the message.

TENSE

See also: verbs

The tense of a verb is a grammatical feature that situates in time the events, feelings, conditions and so on expressed in a sentence. All finite verbs have a tense. See examples under 'verbs'.

TERMINOLOGY (OF PRIMARY ENGLISH)

See also: Cox Report, Kingman Report, LINC materials, metalanguage, phonics, reading, speaking and listening, subject knowledge, writing

Primary school teachers have always needed a vocabulary to enable them to talk to children, colleagues and parents about the aspects of language and literature they have covered in the English programme. To understand how we have arrived at the more formal requirement for teachers' knowledge about language or 'subject knowledge', which includes an ability to use a technical vocabulary, we need to take a brief look at recent history. As part of the move towards a National Curriculum during the late 1980s, a committee, chaired by Sir John Kingman, was set up to explore models of how language works and to consider what pupils needed to be taught. After the Kingman Report (DES, 1988) was published, another committee, chaired by Brian Cox, was set up to build on the work of Kingman and to devise programmes for study and attainment targets to use in the National Curriculum. The first report of this committee was published in 1988 (DES, 1988) and concentrated on Key Stages 1 and 2. A whole chapter on linguistic terminology was included. The second version, sometimes referred to as Cox 2, included proposals for the teaching of pupils at Key Stages 3 and 4 in addition to primary aged children. There was an even more detailed chapter on 'knowledge about language' and reference to the fact that the government had set up a project to produce training materials to support the teaching of language in the National Curriculum. These were known as the LINC materials and the story of how these were received by the government of the day is told under the LINC and Cox Report entries. The work of the two committees and their reports gave rise to an explosion of interest in what children should be taught about language and many people took up entrenched positions on the teaching of grammar.

These debates about issues like whether a knowledge of grammatical structures transfers into children's writing still simmer away but what primary teachers in the United Kingdom must cover in English is now formalised. Statutory requirements and guidance change as new governments bring new perspectives and views to issues affecting practice. It was decided in the 1990s that intending teachers needed to achieve a high level of subject knowledge to enable them to cover the official requirements. *Circular 4/98, Teaching: High Status, High Standards* (DfEE, 1998) set down the statutory requirements for courses of initial teacher training and specified the subject knowledge teachers needed at their own level. This subject knowledge is set out under three categories: lexical, grammatical and textual. The technical vocabulary required to cover this is made fully explicit. As well as the better-known terms to refer to reading and writing – 'consonant', 'vowel' and 'letter' – teachers were also required to control terms like 'onset and rime', 'split digraph'

and 'affix'. In addition, there is a vocabulary to talk about texts, for example to refer to the different kinds like 'fable', 'sonnet' and 'fantasy' or, in the non-fiction categories, texts like 'recount', 'report' and 'instruction' (Graham and Kelly, 2007; Medwell *et al.*, 2009).

Knowing these terms and the concepts they express is helpful for teachers. Angela Wilson and Julie Scanlon have a light touch in their book on subject knowledge and cover the essentials well (Wilson and Scanlon, 2011). Judging when and if particular terms are used with children is more of an issue. Too technical an approach too early might inhibit the spontaneous enjoyment of learning about language and enjoying stories and poems. Still unresolved is that question about whether knowing about grammatical constructions and what they are called is likely to transfer to children's writing.

Of course, UK teachers need to read the current official documentation but there are also a number of publications that help them become secure in their knowledge of terminology. In addition to the texts mentioned so far, teachers find the work of the linguist David Crystal helpful, for example his analysis in *Rediscover Grammar* (Crystal, 2004).

Crystal, David (2004) *Rediscover Grammar* London: Longman.

Graham, Judith and Kelly, Alison (2007 edition) *Reading Under Control* London: David Fulton.

Medwell, Jane, Moore, George, Wray, David and Griffiths, Vivienne (2009) *Primary English: Knowledge and Understanding* Exeter: Learning Matters.

Wilson, Angela and Scanlon, Julie (2011, fourth edition) *Language Knowledge for Primary Teachers* London: David Fulton.

TEXTING

Texting or text messaging, which involves the sending and receiving of short amounts of abbreviated written text, has become a familiar means of communication for many people including young children. Messages can be sent by mobile and other portable devices over a network. Whatever the device, it should be possible to use all twenty six letters of the alphabet and ten numerals.

The economy of language typical of texting shares something with poetry and there have been a number of text poetry competitions including one organised by The Guardian. Andrew Wilson, the poet, advises that successful text messaging poems have 'a truthful moment and describe it'. It is about finding the 'luminous detail' that another poet, Ezra Pound, refers to. Things that happen in everyday lives can prove to be good material. Andrew Wilson mentions the following: seeing the red moon during a lunar eclipse, a child asleep in the car and everyone standing up at a key point in a football match.

In school, children not normally interested in writing are often enthusiastic and competent texters. Texting is perceived as innovative and socially interactive-attractive attributes to young people. And so teachers are finding that working on a text messaging poem or other short texts can unleash their pupils' creativity in interesting ways. Success in texting can lead to children becoming more confident in using traditional kinds of writing. Thus texting can be a stepping stone in writing development.

TEXT-LEVEL WORK

See also: fiction: choosing and using, genre, information books, literacy hour, National Curriculum, non-fiction reading and writing, subject knowledge

Text-level work helps develop children's understanding of and response to the global features of different texts (see Mallett, 2010: 298; Wilson and Scanlon, 2011: Chapters 9–10). In the case of a story or a novel, text-level aspects would include the plot, characterisation, setting and language style. The features of a typical children's information book, according to Christine Pappas, includes topic representation, representation of attributes and characteristic events (Pappas, 1986). So, according to this analysis, a book on mammals would begin with an explanation of the different kinds of mammal and where they live, then go on to explaining their characteristics and, after that, trace their life cycle.

Mallett, Margaret (2010) *Choosing and Using Fiction and Non-fiction 3–11* London and New York: Routledge.

Pappas, Christine (1986) 'Exploring the Global Structure of Children's Information Books' paper presented to the Annual Meeting of the National Reading Conference, Austin, Texas.

Wilson, Angela and Scanlon, Julie (2011, fourth edition) *Language Knowledge for Primary Teachers* London: David Fulton.

TEXTS

See also: CD-ROM, fiction: choosing and using, genre, history of children's literature, illustrations: finding a vocabulary, information books, multimodal texts, non-fiction reading and writing, television and literacy, video-film and DVDs, visual literacy

Text is a term used to refer to a continuous piece of writing such as a poem, a playscript or a novel. The term is now used more widely to refer to spoken as well as written language so that a conversation, for example, could be regarded as an oral text. Linguists examining everyday utterances record speech in a context and refer to it as a 'text' for the purpose of study. The coming of new technology has brought into the sphere of texts electronic and multimedia texts, which have visual, auditory and spatial features as well as visual ones.

TGAT REPORT

See also: assessment, reading, record keeping, speaking and listening, writing

This report was an outcome of the work of a group appointed to consider how the National Curriculum programmes should be assessed. Their recommendation that attainment in each subject was to be measured against a ten-level scale proved unmanageable and a slimmed-down Dearing version was introduced in 1995.

Many teachers found the most positive aspect of the TGAT Report was its view that assessment should not only occur at the end of phases of work. Rather, it should be an integral part of the educational process and be incorporated into planning and teaching strategies. This attitude to assessment was in line with assessment and record-keeping approaches like the Primary Language Record of the Centre for Literacy in Primary Education.

Centre for Literacy in Primary Education (1988) *Primary Language Record (PLR)* London: Centre for Literacy in Primary Education.

DES (1987) *Report of the Task Group on Assessment and Testing* London: HMSO.

THEME

See: cross-curricular projects, English projects

THESAURUS

See also: dictionary, genre

A thesaurus provides key words with lists of their antonyms and synonyms, arranged either alphabetically or thematically. The best ones, whether in print or built into a word processing package, reinforce a belief that language is essentially creative and help add to the range of options from which a speaker or writer can select.

Publishers of children's dictionaries – Chambers, Usborne, Oxford University Press, Collins – nearly always also include thesauri (note that 'thesauruses' is also an accepted plural) on their title lists. Most of these publishers produce a series of thesauri for children at different stages. In his introduction to his *Oxford Children's Thesaurus*, Alan Spooner – a distinguished compiler of thesauri for different age groups – expresses his view that a good thesaurus at any age should have a wide enough vocabulary to make it interesting and thought-provoking. *Oxford First Thesaurus*, for younger children from about age five, has a spacious, uncluttered format and entertaining illustrations. Under 'sound', synonyms – 'bang', 'bleep' and 'buzz' through to 'whirr' and 'whistle' – are arranged alphabetically along an imaginary machine. The encouragement to be an 'active word explorer' continues with the *Oxford Primary Thesaurus* for children of about age eight upwards; it offers 50,000 words and a clear, inviting design with bright blue headwords and sentence meanings in black. The *Usborne Illustrated Thesaurus*, for children of ten and over, has 60,000 words and fully labelled illustrations which make it a good browse. *Chambers School Thesaurus* is for the over tens and offers panels giving extended treatment to words where synonyms and antonyms are particularly important – for example 'get', 'happy', 'nice'. Strong help with such synonyms is also provided in *Dictosaurus*, a combined electronic dictionary and thesaurus from Oxford University Press. If you are looking for a thesaurus to interest and challenge older primary school children, there is a children's version of *Roget's Thesaurus*.

THINKING

See: critical discourse, language and thought, metacognition, philosophy and literacy, reflective reading

435

THRASS (TEACHING HANDWRITING, READING AND SPELLING SKILLS)

See also: phonics, phonological awareness, spelling

This organisation produces resources in print, audio, video and software formats to help teach children and adults (including teachers and parents) about what they term 'the building blocks' of reading and spelling: that is, the forty-four phonemes (speech sounds) of spoken English and the graphemes (spelling choices) of written English. The products are used in 8,000 institutions worldwide.

Davies, Alan (2000) 'The phoneme test: should all teachers pass it?' *Dyslexia Review*, the Journal of the Dyslexia Institute Guild, 11 (4), Summer: 9–12.
Davies, Alan and Ritchie, Denyse (1998) *THRASS Teacher's Manual*, www.thrass.co.uk

TICK SHEETS

See also: assessment, marking, portfolios

Tick sheets, in print or on screen, might show children's names down the left-hand side and detail tasks across the top. Lines are drawn so that boxes can be ticked when tasks are completed. So a tick sheet on writing might tell us that Scott has made a plan, written a list and drafted a story. An individual child's reading tick list might have a column with the names of books written on the left-hand side with ticks against those the child has read. Another kind of tick list for reading might indicate a child's progress in reading strategies with categories like 'uses semantic cues', 'sounds out words' and 'looks for letter strings'. These check lists are useful as quick reminders of a child's achievements for busy teachers. However, if too much reliance is placed on them they can lead to a superficial view of a child's pro-

gress, to a 'board game mentality' (Tyrrell and Gill, 2000: 142). Tick lists can give the impression that assessment is something that happens at the end of learning rather than, as the TAGT report (1987) suggested, a process that threads through planning and teaching.

We need to know what was good about Scott's story and how we might intervene to help him. By involving him in the process of evaluation we make it much more likely that he will have pride in his best work and an idea about how to improve further. Over-use of a tick list of books read could lead to a child thinking progress was a matter of rushing through as many books as possible when we really want to show we are in favour of talking about books and sometimes revisiting favourite ones for sheer enjoyment. Tick lists or sheets have a role as a quick way of checking what a young reader or writer has covered, but even brief annotation helps give a fuller picture.

DES (1987) *Report of the Task Group on Assessment and Testing* London: HMSO.
Tyrrell, Jenny and Gill, Narinderjit (2000) *Co-ordinating English at Key Stage 1* London: RoutledgeFalmer.

TIMELINES

See also: diagrams, history and English

Timelines are vertical or horizontal representations of a journey through time. They can cover a thousand years or the events of a day or even an hour. They always involve careful selection of what to include and what to leave out. Events can be denoted by words, by pictures or both.

In English lessons we often chart a journey of a character or characters through time, for example the journey through war-torn Europe to find their parents of the children in Ian Serraillier's *The Silver Sword*.

436

Children enjoy making timelines of fantasy characters like the Jumblies (see Edward Lear's *A Book of Nonsense*, Dragon's World Publishers) using words and perhaps some illustrations, bringing English and art together.

Timelines are most often used in history lessons to show the events of a monarch's reign or the movement of a people through the centuries across the globe. Now for an example from recent history. In preparation for the millennium, many UK teachers and children constructed their own timelines of the past 1,000 years, covering events like the coming of the Normans to Britain, the building of Notre Dame Cathedral, the arrival of the Renaissance, the Industrial Revolution, Art Deco images of the 1920s and 1930s, and the technology revolution of the present day. However, children did not echo adult views of history and some of the liveliest, most interesting timelines showed an emphasis on their own regional, ethnic and religious communities. Some children concentrated on music, sport or environmental issues and developments.

Choices had to be made from all the possibilities and children learnt that for a project like this you have to select, as all historians do, when telling the story of the past. In one school I visit often, children in each year group were responsible for a particular period of time or aspect, the youngest children taking up aspects of the present or recent past. The talk, discussion and writing involved linked history, English and art in fruitful ways.

'TOP-DOWN' APPROACHES TO READING

See also: 'big shapes', 'bottom-up' reading approaches, cue-systems, 'interactive' reading model, reading

Top-down approaches to reading emphasise the role of searching for 'meaning'

rather than the role of 'code-breaking' in the initial teaching of reading. Frank Smith (1978) and Goodman and Goodman (1979) are associated with the theoretical underpinning to approaches favouring top-down strategies for decoding based on prediction and guessing. Jeni Riley defines the strong point of these approaches as follows: 'Meaning provides the dynamo for the whole activity of reading, giving it purpose' (Riley, 1996: 23). However, she joins other critics of extreme forms of the model in pointing out that 'whole reading' or top-down approaches do not help teachers with the systematic teaching needed at the initial stages. This opinion was embodied in the Rose Report (2006), which recommended that beginning readers should be taught initially by an exclusively synthetic phonic method. Later there needs to be carefully planned work at letter and word level (a bottom-up approach) as well as attention to context and whole-text aspects (a top-down approach).

The entry under 'interactive reading model' explains how important aspects of top-down and bottom-up approaches can be combined. There is a careful explanation of how the combined approach can be achieved in Browne, 2009.

Browne, Ann (2009) *A Practical Guide to Teaching Reading in the Early Years* London: Sage.

Goodman, K.S. and Goodman, Y.M. (1979) 'To read is natural' in Resnick, L.B. and Weaver, P.A. (eds) *Theory and Practice of Early Reading Vol. 1* Hillside, N.J.: Lawrence Erlbaum Associates.

Riley, Jeni (1996) *The Teaching of Reading* London: Paul Chapman (Chapter 2).

Smith, Frank (1978, second edition) *Understanding Reading* New York: Holt, Rinehart & Winston.

TOPICS

See: cross-curricular projects, English projects

TRADITIONAL TALES

See also: creation stories, fable, fairy tales, folk tales, legend, myths

'Traditional tales' is an umbrella term for all the kinds of story discussed under the entries in the 'see also' list above. These ancient stories were told many times and passed down the generations. Some of the same universal themes are found in traditional stories from all over the world. Such stories are an important part of the fiction collection in the primary school and thread through the English programme. They impart much of importance about human nature in general and are an excellent way of understanding what is valued in cultures different from our own. Here it may be helpful to explain the emphasis of the main categories of traditional tale, although there is much overlapping.

- Creation stories are tales in a cultural context which try to explain how the Earth and all its objects, people and creatures came about.
- Fables are stories ending with a moral principle. They often involve animal characters, as in *Aesop's Fables.*
- Fairy tales always include an element of magic and often magical folk like elves, gnomes, sprites and fairies (see Carpenter and Prichard, 1984 for a substantial account of the history of the fairy tale).
- Folk tales are mainly about the lives, trials and tribulations of ordinary people from every part of the world. Some contain fairy tale elements such as characters being granted three wishes or people being transformed by magic.
- Legends are usually about heroic characters, for example King Arthur and his knights. They may be based on historical characters and events that actually happened, but they tend to be embroidered with detail and supernatural elements.

- Myths are ancient stories of gods and heroes, often about the origins of life and issues of deep human concern. (Creation stories are often thought of as a category of myth because of their emphasis on how things began.) Greek myths concentrate on stories about the gods, for example the story of Persephone, the daughter of Zeus, who spent half the year on Earth and half in the underworld. There are myths from all over the world and there are many excellent collections of retellings.

Tales for Telling and *The Ordinary and the Fabulous* are classic books on traditional tales in spite of their vintage (Steele, 1989; Cook, 1976). More recent annotated lists of the different kinds of traditional tale are

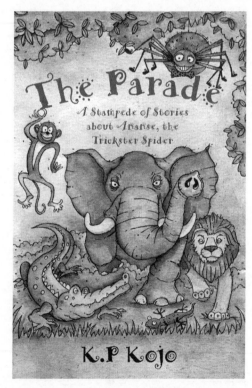

Figure 23 Front cover of *The Parade: A Stampede of Stories about Ananse, the Trickster Spider* by K.P. Kojo and Karen Lilje. Reproduced with the permission of the publisher, © Frances Lincoln.

found in Hallford and Zaghini (2004) and Mallett (2010: Chapter 5).

Carpenter, Humphrey and Prichard, Mari (1984) *The Oxford Companion to Children's Literature* Oxford: Oxford University Press.

Cook, Elizabeth (1976) *The Ordinary and the Fabulous: An Introduction to Myths, Legends and Fairy Tales* Cambridge: Cambridge University Press.

Hallford, D.P. and Zaghini, E. (2004) *Folk & Fairy Tales: A Book Guide* London: Booktrust.

Mallett, Margaret (2010) *Choosing and Using Fiction and Non-fiction 3–11* London and New York: Routledge.

Phinn, Gervase (2000) *Young Readers and Their Books* London: David Fulton.

Steele, Mary (1989) *Traditional Tales: A Signal Bookguide* Stroud: The Thimble Press.

TRANSACTIONAL WRITING

See also: factual genres, non-fiction reading and writing

The term 'transactional writing' was used by James Britton and his team on the Schools Council Writing Project (carried out in the 1970s) to refer to factual kinds of writing. Britton suggested that we relate to our experience in two ways: either as participants seeking to act directly in the world or as spectators, reflecting on and reorganising all that happens to us. Transactional kinds of language are the outcome of relating to our experience as a participant.

Britton, James N. (1970) *Language and Learning* London: Allen Lane, The Penguin Press (Chapter 3, 'Participant and spectator').

TRANSCRIPTIONAL ASPECTS OF WRITING

See also: handwriting, paragraphing, punctuation, spelling

These include spelling, punctuation, capitalisation, legibility and paragraphing. The distinction between compositional and transcriptional (or secretarial) aspects of writing was made by Frank Smith (1982). Noting the physical effort young children put into spelling and handwriting, Smith suggested teachers encourage them to concentrate first on what they wanted to communicate (the composition of the content of their writing) and second on bringing the transcriptional aspects to a good standard. This approach was intended to prevent the inhibiting of the content of the writing by premature worry about the secretarial matters. The distinction is recognised in the National Curriculum English programmes where transcriptional aspects are referred to as 'presentation'.

Smith, Frank (1982) *Writing and the Writer* London: Heinemann.

TRANSFORMATIONAL GRAMMAR

See also: communicative competence/ competence and performance, language acquisition, nativist approach to language acquisition

Transformational grammar refers to the way in which language structures can be changed (or transformed) while keeping their essential meaning. The concept is associated with the influential linguist Noam Chomsky, when based at the Massachusetts Institute of Technology, who revolutionised thinking about language and how we acquire it.

To come closer to understanding Chomsky's view we need to know about certain universal and fundamental properties of language – of all known languages – and their link with how human beings think. The proposal that there are language universals adds weight to Chomsky's theory that human beings have a genetic predisposition to language. First, every sentence has a subject-predicate relationship – the predicate tells us something about the subject. In 'The teacher read the picture book with the scarlet cover', 'the teacher' is the subject and the rest of the sentence is the predicate. Second, every sentence has a verb-object relationship which gives a logical relation between cause and effect. In the same example, 'picture book' is the object of the verb 'read'. Third, there are elements in a sentence that add to the meaning called 'modification'. In the sentence above, 'with the scarlet cover' is the modification.

Chomsky observed that the basic sentence could be expressed in different ways. One obvious alternative would be to put the sentence in the passive tense. So our sample sentence could be expressed as 'The picture book with the scarlet cover was read by the teacher'. Here what Chomsky refers to as the 'surface structure' has changed, but he contrasts this transformation of the 'surface structure' with the stability of the 'deep structure' – the profound meaning.

Chomsky made a clear distinction between what he called 'competence', a language user's knowledge of the rules and potential structures of their language, and 'performance' by which he meant the actual utterances made by particular speakers. If you would like to read a clear introduction to the work of Chomsky I recommend either 'Language and learning' in David Wood's book *How Children Think and Learn* or Chapter 65 'Linguistics' in David Crystal's *Cambridge Encyclopedia of Language*.

Crystal, David (2003, revised edition) *The Cambridge Encyclopedia of Language* Cambridge: Cambridge University Press.

Wood, David (1998) *How Children Think and Learn* London: Blackwell.

TRANSITIONAL GENRE

See also: faction, information stories

This term refers to texts in which some of the features of more mature forms have been modified for the benefit of young children (Baker and Freebody, 1989). For example, non-narrative texts may have a more conversational tone and a more appealing format than those for older children. Other transitional texts are organised, like stories, in a narrative form and sometimes called 'faction' because they use some devices more typical of fiction (Mallett, 1999). They may, for example, like *The Drop Goes Plop*, have characters that seem to have escaped from a fairy story – in this case a talking mother and baby seagull who nevertheless cover some basic concepts about the water cycle by following the journey of a drop of water. Structured round a sort of adult–child conversation, the mother's utterances are quite a good introduction to information book language: 'When the cloud gets heavy, the drops fall out as rain. If it's really cold, the drops freeze and fall as snow or hail'. The concept of how the water cycle works and the dynamic nature of the process comes through well. A sense of movement is achieved by some of the text waving along the page echoing the flow of the water.

Figure 24 'Every living thing takes its own time.' Scientific information for five to seven year olds is communicated through an appealing story and bright, clear illustrations. Cover illustration © 2006 Geoff Waring. From *Oscar and the Frog* by Geoff Waring. Reproduced by permission of Walker Books Ltd, London SE11 5HJ. www.walker.co.uk

Illustrations in some science books for young children are stylised and witty as in *Oscar the Frog* (see image of front cover). A group of seven year olds told me that this kind of text was 'an information story'.

Baker, C.D. and Freebody, P. (1989) *Children's First School Books* Oxford: Basil Blackwell.
Godwin, S. and Abel, S. (1998) *The Drop Goes Plop* London: Macdonald Young Books.
Mallett, Margaret (1999) *Young Researchers: Informational Reading and Writing in the Early and Primary Years* London: Routledge.

TRANSITIVE/INTRANSITIVE VERB

See also: verbs

Transitive verbs have objects as in, for example, 'He enjoyed the holiday', or 'Which one do you want?' Intransitive verbs lack objects as in, for example, 'She's tripped over' or 'They gesticulated'.

A verb may be transitive or intransitive according to its function in a sentence. So while the verb in 'The girl is playing' lacks an object and is therefore intransitive, if we add the object 'netball' the same verb structure becomes transitive in the sentence 'The girl is playing netball'.

TRIGRAPH

See also: digraph, reading

A trigraph is made up of three letters which make one sound, for example 'tch' in 'batch'.

U

UNITED KINGDOM LITERACY ASSOCIATION (UKLA)

See also: reading

UKLA is the professional association for teachers of language and literacy and aims to promote research, innovative practice and debate about current issues in its field of interest. Publications include *Literacy*, a refereed journal published three times a year and containing articles on all aspects of literacy including the description and evaluation of classroom work. It is read by practitioners, teacher educators and student teachers. *Journal of Research in Reading*, also refereed, provides a forum for researchers into reading in Britain and Europe. The articles report on empirical studies in reading and related fields. UKLA publishes *English 4–11* jointly with The English Association. This journal includes classroom case studies, information about recent developments in the area of language, literacy and learning, and reviews of professional and children's books.

The website provides accessible information about UKLA research projects, publications, awards and conferences: www.ukla.org.

USAGE

See also: accent, dialect, grammar, parts of speech, punctuation, received pronunciation, spelling, standard English

The term 'usage' when applied to use of English issues is to do with customary practice. So we might speak of 'standard usage' in spelling, grammar, pronunciation and punctuation, and all the 'see also' entries above include a consideration of this.

Primary school teachers in the United Kingdom are, more than ever, expected to know about conventional usage so that they can help children acquire standard forms in speaking and reading, but what is acceptable adapts to changes in society. As pointed out many times in this encyclopedia, language is dynamic and 'correct' usage at a particular period in history depends on a social consensus of educated people. There are a large number of books on usage in English, but the best known is still Fowler's dictionary which McArthur describes as 'a blend of prescription, tolerance and idiosyncrasy' (McArthur, 1992: 1076).

At one time split infinitives and ending sentences with prepositions were avoided, but both are now accepted in informal usage. The double negative, on the other hand, while being part of some non-standard dialects – 'I don't never go there' – is still not acceptable in standard English. Purists also keep an eye on word meanings and many struggled to keep the original meaning of 'nice' which is 'precise' rather than submitting to its contemporary meaning – 'affable' or 'pleasant'.

There are interesting social and moral factors in usage, for example the use of

'Ms' instead of 'Miss' or 'Mrs' is an attempt to avoid language-driven continuance of gender prejudice. We still lack a generally accepted third person, gender-neutral pronoun. In spoken language there has been an interesting change in what is grammatically acceptable: many people disobey the normal rules of concord (agreement between parts of speech), using a plural form to avoid saying 'he or she' or 'him or her'. For example we might say 'If any child arrives late, please ask them to report to the school secretary'. For a thorough discussion of this and many other issues see McArthur's entries on 'Usage' and 'Usage guidance and criticism'.

Fowler, H.W. (1965 edition) *A Dictionary of Modern English Usage* Oxford: Oxford University Press.

McArthur, Tom (1992) *The Oxford Companion to the English Language* London and Oxford: QPD and Oxford University Press.

USSR (UNINTERRUPTED SUSTAINED SILENT READING)

See also: ERIC, independent reader, reading, reading environment, response to reading

Silent, quiet or independent reading helps children extend the range and variety of their reading. Because they choose the books they develop their own tastes and critical standards. To achieve these things they need to read a lot and to respond directly and independently to the books. At home, the time spent at the computer and on other hobbies and activities may lessen the sustained reading a child does. All the more reason then for teachers to insist on quiet reading time in the classroom even though we face increasing demands on the curriculum. In an assessment-based school culture how do we convince others of the value of an activity that has no immediate physical end product?

Stuart Marriott asserts that 'books work in mysterious and subtle ways ... and reading the book of one's choice for a prolonged period is of just as much, if not more, value than other classroom activities that appear to be more immediately productive' (Marriott, 1995: 71).

Those of us who believe passionately in the value of reading time insist that it is *uninterrupted* because we are trying to help the children to achieve a special kind of engrossment, *sustained* so that there is time to achieve intense concentration and *silent* to avoid anyone being disturbed. Very young children may not achieve the last of these.

Aidan Chambers has good advice about encouraging newly independent readers, reluctant or inexperienced readers to enjoy reading time: ' ... read aloud for part of each session, because this draws everyone together and tunes their minds into story. For the rest of the session the children read their own books for a period of time that is gradually lengthened as they get used to the activity and their stamina grows' (Chambers, 1991: 38).

Chambers, Aidan (1991) *The Reading Environment: How Adults Help Children Enjoy Books* Stroud: The Thimble Press (Chapter 8, 'Reading Time'; available with the companion book *Tell Me* in a new edition, 2011).

Marriott, Stuart (1995) *Read On: Using Fiction in the Primary School* London: Paul Chapman (O/P; Chapter 4, section on silent reading).

UTTERANCE

See also: discourse analysis, speaking and listening

An utterance refers to something said, whether word, phrase or sentence. Used in linguistics, 'utterance' tends to mean something said which has more or less the syntax of a written-down sentence.

V

VERBS

See also: clause, parts of speech, sentence

A verb expresses an action, a process or a state. Often thought of as a 'doing' word – 'The boy *runs* to the playground each day – a verb may also indicate 'being' – 'The head teacher *was relieved* to learn of the successful results'.

Sometimes two or more words make up a verb phrase, for example 'had been hoping', 'did not think' and 'will be running'.

Verbs (except modal verbs like 'can' or 'will') have four or, in some cases five, different forms:

> Infinitive: to ride
> Continuous present: rides/am riding
> Present participle: riding
> Simple past: rode
> Past participle: ridden

In their finite forms, verbs can be active or passive, they have a tense and a person, have agreement with their subject, and may be main or auxiliary verbs. I look at each of these aspects in turn.

Active or passive

Verbs may be active ('Anna *made* a cake') or passive ('The cake *was made* by Anna').

The sentences seem to be saying the same thing, but in the first one the attention is on Anna, and in the second on the cake. When we use the passive tense we use the verb 'to be' together with a past participle. In the second sentence above 'was' is a form of the verb 'to be' and 'made' is the past participle of the verb 'make'. Another thing to note is that in a passive sentence, the 'doer' or 'agent' is often indicated by the use of the word 'by', as in the second sentence above which tells us the cake was made 'by Anna'. At other times the agent is not identified as in 'The house has been renovated'.

When we teach children about different levels of formality in writing, we draw attention to the passive as a formal and impersonal style often used in scientific, official or legal documents.

Verbs have a tense

I now set out the main tenses in English using the verb 'to run':

> Present: I run/I am running (continuous present)
> Present Perfect: I have run/I have been running (perfect continuous)
> Past: I ran/I was running (past continuous)
> Past Perfect: I had run (perfect)/I had been running (perfect continuous)
> Future: I will run/I run

445

Verbs have a 'person'

Verbs must have 'agreement' with their subject, so the pattern changes in the verb 'to be' as follows:

> I am happy/I was happy
> You are happy/You were happy
> She is happy/She was happy
> They are happy/They were happy

Main or auxiliary

There are some forms of verbs the definitions of which most of us need to check from time to time – auxiliary verbs, modal verbs, present and past participles, transitive and intransitive verbs – and I consider these below.

Auxiliary verb

An auxiliary verb is used together with other verbs in a verb phrase. So in 'Tom has departed', the main verb is 'departed' and the auxiliary verb 'has' supports this main verb. The most common auxiliary verbs are 'be', 'have' and 'do', but they can also sometimes be main verbs. I find it helpful to ask myself which is the main verb, and then I know that the other verbs in the verb string are supporting it as auxiliaries.

Modal verbs

A 'modal' verb is a special kind of auxiliary verb that modifies the meaning of a sentence or clause by expressing possibility, speculation and necessity. The modal verbs are can/could, will/would, shall/should, may/might and must/ought. They are followed by the infinitive form of the verb as in 'I shall stay', or by 'to' plus the infinitive as in 'I ought to go'.

Participles

Verbs have a present participle and a past participle. The present participle ends in 'ing' (playing, seeing, making) and is used in present continuous forms (she is bringing) and past continuous forms (she was bringing, she would have been bringing). The past participle often ends in 'ed', as in 'gambled' and 'moved', but there are many irregular forms like 'shown' and 'kept'. Past participles are used after 'have' (he has waited) to make the perfect form and after 'be' to make passive forms (it has been taken).

Transitive and intransitive verbs

Transitive verbs are verbs followed by an object – 'She enjoyed the outing' – or preceded by their object – 'What are you doing?' Intransitive verbs are verbs without objects – 'He ran home'.

Sources

In my analysis I have drawn on some of the definitions in McArthur (1992: see under Verb for further explanation). As Angela Wilson remarked, when she kindly cast her eye over this entry, it is sometimes difficult to know whose terminology to use. What used to be 'parts of speech' is now often termed 'word classes', and 'verb phrases' are now sometimes termed 'letter strings'. The linguist David Crystal prefers to refer to the 'ing' and 'ed' participles, while others refers to past and present participles. For interesting discussion of this last issue, see Crystal's (2004) book *Rediscover Grammar*. Angela Wilson's book *Language Knowledge for Primary Teachers*, now in a fourth edition with co-author Julie Scanlon, covers verbs and other parts of speech in a sound and entertaining way (Wilson and Scanlon, 2011).

In her article 'Finding your feet in the grammar minefield', Sue Palmer (who has written and lectured extensively to teachers about teaching grammar in an interesting way to primary children) argues that an understanding of verbs may be helpful in a number of ways. For example, we can help children become aware of the rich range of verbs so that commonly used ones like 'went' and 'got' can be less overworked. Teaching about verbs can also reinforce spelling rules like the endings 'ed' and 'ing' and the spelling patterns of irregular words. Knowing about verbs also helps us decide whether a group of words is a clause – it is if it has a subject and a verb (Palmer, 1999: 20).

For an activity-based approach to verbs see the appropriate sections in *The Primary Grammar Book* by Richard Bain and Marion Bridgewood. For example, there are cards on which sentences with different verb tenses are written and children are invited to sort these and to explain to each other how verbs change to form past, present and future. It is this invitation to make their understanding explicit that is particularly beneficial.

Bain, Richard and Bridgewood, Marion (1998) *The Primary Grammar Book: Finding Patterns – Making Sense* Sheffield: NATE.

Crystal, David (2004) *Rediscover Grammar* London: Longman.

McArthur, Tom (1992) *The Oxford Companion to the English Language* London and Oxford: QPD and Oxford University Press.

Palmer, Sue (1999) 'Finding your feet in the grammar minefield' *TES*, 22 January, English Curriculum Supplement.

Wilson, Angela and Scanlon, Julie (2011, fourth edition) *Language Knowledge for Primary Teachers* London: David Fulton.

VERSE

See also: ballad, nursery rhyme, poetry

In everyday usage 'poetry' and 'verse' may be used interchangeably. Verse describes a stanza of a poem and a distinctive metrical structure like 'iambic' verse. However, in traditional literary criticism 'verse' tends to apply to technique and can be used as a pejorative term implying that some forms are not worthy of being called 'poetry'.

Verse is a familiar form in the modern world and the tradition of nursery rhymes and ballads continues in the rhymes children repeat and those they make up in the playground, and in the jingles used in radio and television advertising.

VIDEO-FILM AND DVDS

See also: television and literacy, visual literacy

Video-film and DVDs, films at the cinema and television are important cultural media and likely to have a considerable effect on children's developing literacy. One obvious link between books and screen are the films of children's picture books (Raymond Briggs' *The Snowman*) and serials of children's stories (E. Nesbit's *The Phoenix and the Carpet*, Clive King's *Stig of the Dump* and Jacqueline Wilson's *Tracy Beaker*) on mainstream television. Good resource collections for English work now include a range of films and DVDs, some featuring advertisements and extracts from factual programmes and others based on children's novels and picture books. For more about the use of advertisements please see the appropriate entry and see, too, the entry on television and literacy. Here I want to reflect on the reasons many teachers have for helping children enjoy and evaluate films and DVDs of stories, often alongside reading the print versions in the English lesson. First, it is a motivating experience for most children to study a medium that is so central in our culture. Seeing a film of a story on television or DVD links the sitting room with the classroom in a life-enhancing way.

Second, the visual image can sometimes awaken powerful emotions that can lead to enthusiastic storytelling, role play and writing (Brown, 1999). A study carried out for Film Education suggests that boys particularly enjoy writing on themes from film. Such a highly visual medium is also likely to be helpful to children learning English as an additional language.

Third, there are useful 'tie-ups' between books and film: children may see a film version of a story and be drawn into reading the book or vice versa. Brown found in her study, *Young Children's Literacy Development and the Role of Televisual Texts*, that generally girls have a more wide-ranging viewing pattern in terms of genre and types of narrative than boys. Girls favoured books and films that had a strong emotional impact – Hans Andersen's *The Little Mermaid* and E. Nesbit's *The Railway Children* – or those with an intriguing or unusual set of events like Frances Hodgson Burnett's *The Secret Garden* or Mary Norton's *The Borrowers*. Boys had far fewer 'tie-ups', the most mentioned in Brown's research being Roald Dahl's *The BFG*, Rev. W. Awdry's *Thomas the Tank Engine* and Rudyard Kipling's *The Jungle Book* (Brown, 1999). Imaginative teaching, using a wide range of narratives in video-film and print form, might help boys appreciate some of the narratives they would not choose to view or read independently.

It is clearly worth persevering with these 'tie-ups' as evidence is building that experiencing a story in more than one medium leads to more refined understandings of both forms. In his research for the British Film Institute and King's College London, David Parker found that seven year olds who had worked with both the book and the film version of Roald Dahl's *Fantastic Mr Fox* were able to answer more insightfully in written tests than those who had only read the book. Teachers can show how, in a print version of a narrative, the written word carries the full weight of plot and characterisation. This can be compared through careful observation and discussion with how in film features – the nature of the acting, the camera angles, the lighting, the settings,

the sound and the music – all contribute to the impact.

For all these reasons we need to recognise the potential of English work round DVDs and film. The work does need sensitive handing and Richard Hoggart in *The Way We Are Now* urges us to keep in mind that reading a book and watching a film are distinct experiences and one cannot replace the other.

For teachers just starting to work in this way, particularly with older primary children, I recommend *Reel Lives* (British Video Association, 1999), a helpful resource which includes video-film based on stories. It shows clips from many well-known children's films and television programmes including adaptations of the classics – *The Borrowers*, *The Wind in the Willows* and *The Animals of Farthing Wood*.

British Video Association (1999) *Reel Lives* London: British Video Association, www.bva.org.uk (video extracts are used to explore issues like bullying and care of the environment).

Brown, Naima (1999) *Young Children's Literacy Development and the Role of Televisual Texts* London: Falmer Press (ebook, 2006).

Film Education's website: www.filmeducation.org

VIRTUAL LEARNING ENVIRONMENTS (VLES)

See also: Information Communication Technology

The classroom book corner is a traditional and physical environment to encourage children's reading. Now teachers and children can, in addition, use web pages providing virtual learning environments, including virtual reading environments. The advantage of VLEs is that they have great potential to use images and sound as well as writing to enthuse young learners. As Cremin *et al.* point out, VLEs by integrating video and other multimodal texts, often help make readers of even reluctant young learners (Cremin *et al.*). By their nature they can also provide a huge amount of information. Glen Stone gives the example of young readers who have enjoyed reading Kensuke's Kingdom being able to use the links on a VLE to find other books by this author, books by other authors on desert islands and on a friendship theme (Stone, 2011).

Cremin, Teresa, Mottram, Marilyn, Bearne, Eave and Goodwin, Prue (2008) 'Exploring Teachers' Knowledge of Children's Literature' in *Cambridge Journal of Education*, Vol. 38, No. 4, p. 449–465.

Stone, Glen (2011) 'Virtual Learning Environments as an Extension to the Classroom Reading Environment' in *English 4–11*, Autumn 2011, No. 14, pp. 14–16.

VISUAL LITERACY

See also: advertisements, art and English, CD-ROM, chart, comics, diagrams, illustrations: finding a vocabulary, multimodal texts, photographs, picture books, television and literacy, video-film and DVDs

Visual literacy is to do with 'reading' images of all kinds and seeing the connections between picture and print. Today's children live in a society where images – in entertainment, advertising and information sources – are a very important part of the culture. So becoming literate is no longer a matter of just learning to read and write, but is also to do with interpreting and evaluating both static and moving images in different contexts. Children bring to school considerable knowledge and experience about visual images since they are likely to have watched television, viewed video-films and have been surrounded by print images. However, if they are to develop their capacity to use and evaluate the visual and see how it complements and extends the verbal, this kind of literacy

needs to be brought explicitly into the curriculum.

The cultural context of images

In many ways reading a visual text is similar to reading a written text; in his introduction to *Image Matters* the Australian academic Jon Callow observes that both kinds of reading are dynamic processes involving 'not only a text (verbal or written) but the person reading/viewing, the authors, and the wider cultural context of all three' (Callow, 1999: 2). Visual images can pass us by, remaining implicit and unevaluated: this is why it is so helpful to explore with children the meaning of images in advertisements and other mass media where they can be used to manipulate. They can lead us to assume certain interpretations of the world are universal or 'the norm', while in reality they represent the favoured

Figure 25 This visually exciting encyclopedia for the over tens shows the positive impact of electronic technologies on print texts. The front cover of *Pick Me Up, Put Me Down* edited by David Roberts and Jeremy Leslie (Dorling Kindersley, 2006), is reproduced with the permission of the publishers. © 2006 Dorling Kindersley Ltd.

view of one group. Getting behind images to intentions helps put the young viewer in control. The increasingly 'multimodal' nature of classroom texts, drawing as many of them do on spoken, written, visual, spatial and musical modes, is exciting but can also be overwhelming. Even print texts for young children sometimes assume they are familiar with the typical icons on the computer screen. We can help children by making time to explore and evaluate the different strands of such rich input together. (These issues are discussed by Kress and van Leeuwen, 2006.)

Ways of representing experience

In order to explore how we make sense of a visual world I want to look briefly at the work of the developmental psychologist, Jerome Bruner. He identified three main ways in which the growing child represents the world: enactive, iconic and symbolic. The baby knows the world through doing and through experience and this is termed 'enactive representation'. The roots of many later activities are here, including acquiring the skills to operate all the technology to be found in a typical home or classroom or by using dramatic improvisation to explore how people lived in another historical period. As infants grow older they begin to have mental images of familiar objects and places, even if they are not present, for example 'teddy in the bedroom' or 'Peter Rabbit plate in the kitchen'. This Bruner termed the 'iconic' mode: from early beginnings this is the way of representing the world that develops into all kinds of visual literacy – how we make sense of maps, photographs and paintings and of moving images. The last mode of representing experience to develop is the 'symbolic' – this includes the ability to use language to express ideas and information. By the age of about five years a child is using all three modes of representation in making sense of and acting in the world. So when we think about visual literacy, we also need to consider how Bruner's three ways of representing experience interrelate in the child's learning.

A framework for teaching visual literacy

One of the most helpful frameworks in which to plan the teaching of visual literacy is suggested in *Image Matters*, edited by Jon Callow. There are chapters by teachers and academics on different image contexts in the classroom, including information books, picture books, television programmes and CD-ROMs. The framework for teaching visual literacy described in his introduction is a good starting point for classroom work with any age group. It suggests that learning about images parallels learning about language. We learn language from early childhood and refine and develop our verbal ability; we use language to learn about all manner of subjects both in and out of the classroom; and we learn about language as a system with structures and functions. Let us see how becoming visually literate links with this analysis.

- Learning images – here the child learns to recognise symbols and patterns that represent the things they come across in everyday life and tries to make his or her own representations. So a sort of visual vocabulary is acquired.
- Learning through images – these help children learn in every part of the curriculum – in science, the humanities and the arts and about every aspect of our culture. Children's own productions – electronic and print books, models and diagrams – help make learning active.
- Learning about images – this involves knowing how to comment on and evaluate their cultural and contextual aspects and also (following the arguments of Kress & van Leeuwen, 2006) coming to understand the 'grammar' inherent in images. For many of us this

450

is a new area of understanding and we need to learn alongside our pupils how images work and what they 'mean'.

Explaining how the three aspects of this framework for organising visual literacy relate to print pictures and information texts, to the moving image in video, DVDs and CD-ROMs and in television, would take a whole book to explore thoroughly. The books in the reference section of this entry will help build your understanding. You might like to take to your reading some thoughts about the different kinds of visual image children encounter.

Print images

A major art form in many countries is the children's picture book where text and pictures can relate in exciting ways – sometimes to illustrate the action in a story, sometimes to extend the written text and occasionally to contradict it in a tantalising way (Arizpe and Styles, 2002). Some picture books like Raymond Briggs' *The Snowman* and Shirley Hughes' *Up and Up* – a cartoon about a little girl's flying fantasy – are wordless and rely on quite young children's cultural knowledge to gain meaning. Both these books yield their meaning through action. The sophistication of the best picture books make them valuable contributors to children's literacy, both verbal and visual (see 'picture books' entry).

Pictures have always provided powerful ways into bodies of information. Visual media can convey concepts that might be difficult to explain in writing. Harnett (1998: 72) reminds us that medieval paintings showed the mysteries of heaven and hell, with beautiful angels and terrifying demons, to non-literate people. Even in our more literate society, advertisers exploit the power of pictures to move, persuade and excite. The money spent shows how much advertisers believe in the power of the visual image to affect people's views and actions. How teachers might approach a study of advertisements to put children in control of their viewing is discussed further under the 'advertisements' entry.

Children's information books make considerable demands on children's visual literacy as they feature a rich variety of illustrations including photographs, drawings, diagrams, maps and portraits. These need to integrate well with the written text so that they are illuminating and not obscuring or misleading. Children themselves enjoy discussing how useful the illustrations are in particular books they have been using. The increase in variety of illustrations has come about since the end of the Second World War. Those of us of a certain age well remember the distinctive black and white line drawings in Unstead's history series along with a few coloured pictures. Artists' drawings continued to dominate in the 1960s and 1970s. Since then there have been vast improvements in reprographic techniques and, while artists' illustrations are still used a great deal, photographs are equally favoured. Books and CD-ROMs show animals in their environments and wonderful close-ups of creatures. In the United Kingdom the National Curriculum programmes have included visual literacy. For example, in history the role of photographs of objects and buildings as a valuable source of historical information has been stressed. The potential role of diagrams in 'explanation' texts is also recognised.

There is interesting research on children's use of pictures in history. Blyth (1988) found that children by about the age of nine could be helped to understand abstract concepts like change and power with the help of pictures. Seeing a number of pictures of people and objects from a particular period helps children make generalisations about, for example, what people wore and the objects they used. Harnett (1998) found a development in children's competence in using pictures as information

451

sources. Around five years old children talked about all the details in a picture, while as they neared eleven years they were able to look more broadly at a series of pictures and draw specific conclusions. Sequencing abilities in both history and in English can be developed by looking at a series of pictures and ordering them.

What comes through particularly powerfully in Harnett's study is the way in which children supported each other in making sense of visual input. Some children were looking at a portrait of Elizabeth I and a child said that the Queen had a 'heart-shaped frill' on her back. Another child explained that it was not really a heart shape, 'it just goes round like a semicircle'. The social, collaborative side of history work links it with English. A study of portraits through the ages helps children understand how image is constructed and puts them in a position to question the way today's media images manipulate us.

There has been recent research and interest in print multimodal texts. These combine in different ways design, illustration and words and may use speech balloons, different type faces, print colours and sizes to add meaning. Teachers are also more aware that children's writing can be combined with drawing, and that this combination is motivating to many young learners (Bearne and Wolstencroft, 2007).

Creators of contemporary picture books use multimodality in groundbreaking and interesting ways. You may know Emily Gravett's books – for example *Little Mouse's Big Book of Fears* in which each page is a medley of newspaper cuttings, handwritten notes, pictures and pop-ups as well as holes in the pages and chewed edges. This is an area of research of The United Kingdom Literacy Association (see their website for more information, www.ukla.org). Eve Bearne has analysed children's multimodal texts and noted that eight and nine year olds are capable of combining words and pictures in sophisticated ways (Bearne, 2004, 2009).

Moving images

We encounter the moving image in CD-ROM texts, televisual texts and on film. CD-ROM versions of information texts have the advantage of being able to show function as well as structure. A print version of a diagram of the blood system could indicate the direction in which the blood is flowing using devices like arrows, but the electronic version could show the system and the blood flows in action. Concepts like the water cycle, migration, earthquake and so on can be brought to virtual reality. These dynamic texts are discussed further under the 'CD-ROM' entry.

Turning to watching television and film, while many people of all ages are frequent viewers of serials and other narratives, they tend not to have a profound understanding of the medium. There is, however, an evolving language to talk about the moving image. Annemaree O'Brien (1999) in her chapter 'Reading TV: a basic visual literacy' argues that learning to 'read' television texts can start early and can help develop visual literacy and analytical and critical thinking abilities.

O'Brien identifies two key aspects to reading television. First, we need to understand how visual and sound techniques create meaning in television and film stories and how they influence how we interpret them. Second, it is important that we help our pupils to understand that television programmes are created to affect the viewers in particular ways. Programme makers make choices about scripts, locations, dialogues, the order in which events are shown, colours used and sounds. Like other texts there may be multiple layers of meaning and bias. There is more about this under the 'advertisements' entry.

For more about the benefits of children experiencing the same story in both print and film formats, see 'video-film and DVDs'.

Arizpe, Evelyn and Styles, Morag (2002) (eds) *Children Reading Pictures: Interpreting Visual Texts* London: Routledge.

Bearne, Eve (2009) 'Multimodality, literacy and texts: developing a discourse' in *Journal of Early Years Literacy*, Summer: 2–65.

Bearne, E., Ellis, S., Graham, L., Hulme, P., Merchant, G. and Mills, C. (2004) *More Than Words: Multimodal Texts in the Classroom* London: UKLA.

Bearne, Eve and Wolstencroft, Helen (2007) *Visual Approaches to Teaching Writing: Multimodal Literacy 5–11* London, Leicester: Sage/UKLA.

Blyth, Joan (1988) *History 5–9* London: Hodder & Stoughton.

Callow, on (Ed.) (1999) *Image Matters: Visual Texts in the Classroom.* Marrickville, Australia: PETA (Primary English Teaching Association).

Harnett, Penelope (1998) 'Children working with pictures' in Hoodless, Pat (ed.) *History and English: Exploring the Links* London: Routledge.

Kress, G. and van Leeuwen, T. (2006, second edition) *Reading Images: The Grammar of Visual Design* London: Routledge.

Morris, Susan (1989) *A Teacher's Guide to Using Portraits* London: English Heritage.

National Portrait Gallery: www.npg.org.uk. Runs courses for teachers and children on decoding period and contemporary portraits.

O'Brien, Annemaree (1999) 'Reading TV: a basic visual literacy' in Callow, Jon (ed.) *Image Matters: Visual Texts in the Classroom* Marrickville, Australia: PETA (Primary English Teaching Association).

VOCABULARY

See: word-level work

VOICE

In ordinary usage we may describe someone as having, for example, a cultured voice or a shrill voice. There are three more technical aspects. First, the notion of 'voice' in phonetics where the 'voiced' sounds are 'b', 'd', 'g' and 'z', and the 'voiceless' sounds are 'p', 't', 'k' and 's'. Second, in grammar we speak of the 'active' or 'passive' voice. Third, the 'narrative voice' is a literary term for the narrator or the character who 'speaks' in a story.

VOWEL

See also: digraph, diphthong, phoneme, phonics

The vowels are a, e, i, o, u with 'y' functioning as a vowel as in 'ay', 'ey' and 'oy'. Vowel sounds are produced with a steady flow of air from throat, tongue and lips.

When children begin to learn to read using the phonic approach they are taught to hear individual vowel and consonant speech sounds – phonemes. Then they learn the written symbols for these sounds – graphemes. The grapho-phonic system is not regular and children need to understand that while words can usually be sounded out, sometimes there are exceptions to the usual rules.

Useful terms to understand when teaching about vowels include:

- the short vowel sound, for example 'rag', 'peg', 'fig', 'dog' and 'tug';
- the long vowel sound, which is the name of an alphabet letter – 'A', 'E', 'I', 'O', 'U';
- the diphthong, which is a single sound made of two vowels, for example 'ee', 'oa' and 'au'; and
- the split digraph, which is a 'vowel digraph' where there is a consonant between the two vowels that make the phoneme but it keeps its sound, as in 'pine' (ie) and 'complete' (ee). Some teachers explain split digraphs to children by referring to the 'magic e' rule which makes the preceding vowel sound its name – as 'i' in 'line'.

W

WARNOCK REPORT

See also: Code of Practice, Special Educational Needs (SEN) in language and literacy

The Warnock Report of 1978 recommended that children with learning difficulties have a statement of 'special need' which set out what was required to help them benefit from the curriculum. *The Code of Practice* (1994) developed further the recommended strategies requiring that school-based assessments should lead to an Individual Education Plan (IEP).

Another important recommendation of the Warnock Report was that children with special needs should, whenever possible, be educated in mainstream schools. The report was also the beginning of a trend in the United Kingdom towards providing extra support to children within the classroom rather than withdrawing them for their special help.

Teachers vary in their views on this. Some feel that many struggling young learners benefit from the quietness of a separate special needs room, particularly when they are receiving help with their reading. On the other hand, many consider that there are advantages in not being singled out as 'special' and yet often still receiving help from an extra teacher in the classroom who is in tune with what the class teacher is doing. In 2005 there was debate about whether the Warnock recommendations had proved entirely successful in practice, and Lady Warnock herself has called for a review.

WEBSITES AND PRIMARY ENGLISH

See also: internet

There is a rich and ever-growing field of websites to do with primary English. Reference is made to these in the individual entries. Practitioners know that websites are constantly updated, added to and removed. The addresses of new websites are available in professional journals and through search engines. The websites mentioned throughout this encyclopedia fall into three main categories:

- Government sites: these, for example www.education.gov.uk, provide access to the latest requirements.
- Professional sites: sites like the National Association for the Teaching of English (www.nate.org.uk), The English Association (www.le.ac.uk/engassoc) and the Centre for Literacy in Primary Education (www.clpe.co.uk) support the teachers' professional role with advice, news and reviews.
- Sites for children: these provide classroom resources, and many, like that of the Children's Laureate (www.childrens laureate.org.uk), encourage reading.

455

WHITEBOARD

See: interactive whiteboard

WHOLE CLASS TEACHING

See also: discussion, shared writing

When teachers plan for and organise English work they decide when to teach the whole class and when to help the children to learn in groups or on an individual basis. Teachers have always tended to work with the whole class when introducing new topics, reading the class novel, short story or a series of poems out loud, and when bringing children together for class discussion. In the United Kingdom there was new emphasis on class teaching in the 1900s and up to the mid 2000s, in line with National Literacy Strategy requirements. The establishment of the Literacy Hour led to shared reading and shared writing sessions and this policy arose partly from a belief that children learn more in class-based contexts. The Literacy Framework was dropped in 2008, but some elements continue to influence practice. The idea of using texts, often enlarged texts, with a group or class is in the spirit of Don Holdaway's belief that the teacher could demonstrate reading strategies while also emphasising the enjoyment and satisfaction reading can bring (Holdaway, 1979). In current practice in the United Kingdom, sometimes the teacher and at other times the children read aloud from enlarged texts. Not only can the teacher give support to word recognition skills and sentence structure, he or she can also encourage children's comments on and response to textual features. Valuable experience of speaking and listening in the relatively formal context of the whole class setting is gained. Many teachers believe that children's individual reading is enriched by their application of what they have learnt in the class reading context. Similarly, the practice of shared writing helps children learn useful strategies to take to their individual writing assignments.

While reading, writing, listening and speaking in class-based contexts has an important place in the English programme, certain kinds of learning are best supported in individual and group settings. For example, children benefit from learning to express a view or ask a question in a small group before speaking out in front of the class. Indeed, many of the National Curriculum Speaking and Listening objectives are best achieved in the small group context. For more about these other settings, see the entries on 'collaborative learning', 'ERIC', 'speaking and listening', and 'writing'.

Holdaway, Don (1979) *The Foundations of Literacy* London: Ashton Scholastic.

WORD – AS A UNIT OF MEANING

One of the first things the beginning reader has to acquire is an understanding of that most fundamental of language units – the word. When we speak, spaces between words are not always evident but in writing the spaces separating words from one another are fundamental. One of the most interesting analyses of a young child's efforts to make sense of the reading and writing systems is *GNYS AT WRK* by Glenda Bissex. Bissex noted that her young son Paul at just over five years of age tended to concentrate on whole words when he was reading but on sounds when he was writing.

For a detailed and challenging account of concepts of 'word' for your own background knowledge, I recommend McArthur, 1992, and Wilson and Scanlon's book *Language Knowledge for Primary Teachers* (Wilson and Scanlon, 2011).

Bissex, Glenda (1980) *GNYS AT WRK: A Child Learns to Write and Read* Cambridge, Mass.: Harvard University Press.

McArthur, Tom (1992) *The Oxford Companion to the English Language* London and Oxford: QPD and Oxford University Press.

Wilson, Angela and Scanlon, Julie (2011, fourth edition) *Language Knowledge for Primary Teachers* London: David Fulton.

WORD BANKS

Word banks are a feature of children's word processors, for example Textease (Softease) or Clicker (Cricksoft). The feature allows a teacher to enter words or phrases into the word bank which the child may then select to write a phrase or sentence into a piece of writing they are word processing. Word banks may contain all the words needed to construct a sentence or just keywords. Picture clues can be added. Drop down menus can be made in Microsoft Word using the Form menu to give multiple choices of words.

WORD BOOKS

See: alphabet, dictionary

WORD CLASSES

See also: adjective, adverb, conjunction, noun, parts of speech, preposition, pronoun, verbs

The main word classes are discussed in detail under the entries mentioned above under 'see also'. Words can belong to more than one class. 'Play' can be either a verb – I play, or a noun – a play; 'that' can be a determiner – that book, a pronoun – who did that?, or a conjunction – she said that she …

WORD-LEVEL WORK

See also: antonym, 'bottom-up' reading approaches, cue-systems, dictionary, homonyms, language change, onomatopoeia, parts of speech, phonics, poetry, reading, slang, synonym, thesaurus, writing

Word-level work involves helping children to understand about words, as readers and writers, and helps children extend their vocabulary. There are links between word-level and sentence-level work, for example the terms for parts of speech have grammatical implications as well as being the names of units. Indeed, the careful selection and placing of individual words can have a cumulative effect on a whole text, creating atmosphere, mood and making a contribution to its identification with a particular genre.

While phonics is to do with how a word or phoneme sounds, graphics is the study of the recognition of written forms of words and letter strings. In the United Kingdom, teachers are required to follow prescribed programmes when teaching about the grapho-phonic cue-system. There is more about this under 'phonics' and 'grapho-phonic cue-system'. You would also find useful, before turning to the official publications, the sections on 'Phonics and phonological awareness' and 'Teaching phonic and graphic knowledge' in Graham and Kelly (2007). These authors are amongst those who feel strongly that, while following the requirements, teachers should be allowed some flexibility, for example in the order in which they teach phonemes.

There is considerable discussion amongst teachers about when it is appropriate to help children to use terms like phoneme, vowel and consonant. The teacher is best placed to know how to introduce these terms to the children in his or her class.

Other vocabulary to clinch concepts includes antonyms, synonyms and onomatopoeia. A good way of introducing these is by sharing examples from literature and encouraging children to write down their own examples. The use of dictionaries and thesauri, print and on screen, can be modelled here.

Another aspect of work at word level involves children in making collections of words with particular origins. In a very helpful video-film made by the Centre of Literacy in Primary Education we see eight to nine year olds tracking down words with Greek roots. As well as helping children grapple with word meanings, this kind of research makes them more conscious of word structures and spellings (CLPE, 1999).

An excellent context for learning about words in a playful way is poetry and verse. The youngest children enjoy nursery rhymes and we know from the work of Goswami and Bryant that attention can be drawn to grapho-phonic patterns (Goswami and Bryant, 1991). Older children go on to experiment with riddles, haiku and rhymes which highlight poetic devices in an enjoyable way. Children enjoy constructing 'shape' poems, making the words follow an appropriate pattern to match themes like fireworks, climbing a hill or the dance of a bee. I have often seen good results when poems have started from subjects like feeling hot or cold or chasing an escaping hamster. These are more than word games as children can be helped to a more sensitive use of vocabulary. I remember an eight year old girl being very pleased to discover and use in her poem the word 'tepid' to describe water that was neither very hot nor very cold. Another memory from the classroom presses on me when I think about language play and activities with words. A class of eight year olds made a wonderful 'language thermometer' which was made of silver paper and stretched along a whole wall. They started by placing 'cold' words at one end and then created a continuum with increasingly 'warm' words ending up with sizzling. The most striking thing was the quality of the discussion of the order of words according to intensity of heat and cold. For example, is 'tepid' hotter than 'warm', and is 'frozen' colder than 'icy'? A powerful context for refining and extending vocabulary will always be the reading of literature – novels and poetry. If we want motivated and

enthusiastic young learners we need to find ways of making language learning interesting and relevant.

CLPE (1999) *Communities of Writers: Writing at Key Stage 2* a video-film in the Learning to be Literate series of the Centre for Literacy in Primary Education (see 29.35 for work on word roots).

Goswami, Ursula and Bryant, Peter (1991) *Phonological Skills and Learning to Read* Hillsdale, NJ: Lawrence Erlbaum Associates.

Graham, Judith and Kelly, Alison (2007) *Reading Under Control: Teaching Reading in the Primary School* London: David Fulton.

McArthur, Tom (1992) *The Oxford Companion to the English Language* London and Oxford: QPD and Oxford University Press.

WORD PROCESSING

See: Information and Communications Technology (ICT) and English

WORKSHEETS

See also: constructivism, non-fiction reading and writing

Worksheets: are they manacles or wings? The answer is – it all depends on what you mean by 'worksheet'. It is one of those umbrella terms under which quite a collection of different resources are gathered. It is usually a sheet, card or small, stapled booklet with headings and subheadings, numbered tasks and illustrations. Whatever form the worksheet takes and whatever subject it supports, the following criteria may be helpful:

- does it fit into current work or extend it in a coherent way?
- is the language at an appropriate level for the children and are any new terms explained or evident from the context?
- are diagrams carefully drawn and labelled?

- do at least some of the activities require thought rather than just a 'right' answer?
- is there some opportunity for collaborative work?

In science and mathematics work cards or sheets (either commercially produced or made by the teacher) usually meet the first of these criteria. They guide children through the stages of an experiment or practical activity that is linked to the theme of a series of lessons. In science it might be 'grouping and classifying materials' and in mathematics 'using and applying shape, space and measures'. Often laminated to make them sufficiently robust to stand up to constant use, if worksheets meet the other criteria of clear language and helpful diagrams they can be good models of procedural writing.

In subjects like English, history, religious education and geography, teachers have often structured some of the work by using worksheets that guide the children's independent or group research. When a lot of content has to be covered, particularly with older primary classes, the worksheet has a role so it is unfortunate that worksheets, particularly in the humanities, have acquired a negative connotation. What are some of the criticisms? Used too often for independent learning, they can cut children off from the energising effect of interaction with the teacher and the other children. Questions can be rather dull and require 'right' answers rather than stimulating thinking – thus assuming a transmission model of learning where children respond to stimuli rather than a constructivist approach where children are active learners. The same worksheet is unlikely to challenge the ablest children and be at the right reading level for the less forward readers. All these criticisms can be met if worksheets are carefully constructed, not used too often and the same core of work be adjusted for the different ability levels in the class.

A glimpse of an actual example of good practice might help here. A Year 6 class teacher had covered core history work on the Tudors using pictures and video-film to accompany her own account over a number of lessons. She wanted to give the children the opportunity to carry out some work in groups to go a little deeper into some of the topics. Groups of four children each had a worksheet with suggested activities: some groups chose 'Tudor buildings', others chose 'the *Mary Rose*' or topics like 'crime and punishment'. There was a space at the bottom of each worksheet for the group's own ideas for tasks or modifications to one of the suggested tasks. The other interesting thing about these worksheets was the request to 'make some notes on any issues you think your study has raised'. Each group had some folders of pictures, contemporary documents and access to information books in the library and to the internet. Judging by the lively work and the group presentations that followed, these worksheets were 'wings' rather than 'manacles'.

In English, worksheets can provide a starting point for interesting research into language change, dialect and traditional tales. I have also seen work cards used imaginatively to develop drama and to focus discussion on a text or on a topic. There are, however, less interesting examples – passages taken from longer texts with rather dull comprehension, like questions to answer or uncontextualised dictionary work. Children may, for example, be asked to look up the meanings of words and to put them in sentences.

In short, a worksheet is as good as the tasks and activities it invites and its relevance to children's learning.

WORLD WIDE WEB

See: Information and Communications Technology (ICT) and English, internet, websites and primary English

WRITERS FOR CHILDREN

See: history of children's literature

WRITING

See also: composition, copying, creative writing, critical discourse, diary, Early Learning Goals, editing, emergent writing, EXEL Project, expressive talk and writing, factual genres, fiction: choosing and using, first person writing, gender and language development, genre, grammar, handwriting, independent group work, Information and Communications Technology (ICT) and English, interactive whiteboard, letters, marking, multimodal texts, National Curriculum, persuasive genre, poetry, proof reading, punctuation, reading on screen, scribing, shared writing, spelling, transactional writing, transcriptional aspects of writing, worksheets, writing corner/area, writing frames

Writing is one of the four language processes, the other three being speaking, listening and reading. It is a powerful organiser of thinking and reasoning and enables us to communicate meaning through written text in a relatively permanent form to an absent audience across space and time. In an increasingly complex society people need to be able to write effectively for many different purposes. Today children encounter written text in many forms and will learn to use keyboards as well as handwriting, so it is not surprising that learning to write is a major component of the primary curriculum. However, the journey towards becoming a competent and enthusiastic writer is a demanding one and children need skilled and imaginative support on that journey. Many books have been written about helping children to write; some are referred to in the further reading for this entry and others are mentioned in the many other related entries listed above. This entry serves as an introduction to

what has always been a very challenging task for teachers. I raise what, for me, are some of the most pertinent issues and show where to find further help, support and insight. I have taken a developmental approach because this allows me to focus on what is significant at different stages in the primary years, looking first at what is important for beginning writers and second at what is important for developing writers.

Beginning writers (three to seven years)

Early representation

Young children in literate cultures are surrounded by print in their environment – print on signs, notices and shop fronts outside the home and on food packets, instructions on household machines and toys inside. They soon try to 'write' themselves – we have all seen the wavy lines which are the first attempts of very young children at writing – and to mimic the use of keyboards on home computers and mobile phones. Then they start to make links between letters and sounds, as they do in reading. Most importantly they grasp that the names of objects – and these names are arbitrary – are symbols of the real things for which they stand. To emphasise the symbolic nature of writing, early years teachers encourage children to write their own names for all sorts of purposes – on their work, their pegs and their belongings. Children come to realise that their name symbolises them – who they are in all their complexity (see 'emergent writing' for a more detailed account).

There are a number of books on these early stages of writing and I particularly recommend chapter 8 'Early representation and emerging writing' in Marian Whitehead's (2010) book *Language and Literacy in the Early Years*. This sets out important principles to guide our support of very young writers, drawing on research findings and including interesting examples of early writing. Another particularly helpful book is Temple *et al.*'s *The Beginnings of Writing* which was first published in 1982. The third edition, which appeared in 1992, has a particularly detailed account of children's progress from making scribbles, to invented spelling and then to understanding of the conventions. The fourth edition continues to investigate the key question: what are children trying to do when they write? (Temple *et al.*, 2012).

Writing from five to seven years (Key Stage 1): purpose and audience

In many books about writing, and in statutory and guidance material, you will find your attention drawn to two major dimensions. First, children need to have real purposes, and second, they need a sense of the audience for which they are writing. This raises some important issues. It certainly suggests that children should not be obliged to carry out mere exercises – what James Britton (1970) referred to as 'dummy runs' – but from the earliest stages should have reasons or purposes for their writing. Skilled practitioners create contexts strong enough to nourish the urge to write. Inviting children to write lists for a real use can be an interesting and not too difficult task for young children just acquiring some confidence as writers. This is what the teacher of a Reception class had in mind when she asked the children to help her write a shopping list for food for the classroom snails. The children's suggestions – apples, green beans and lettuce – were written on a flip chart. Labelling some of the things in the classroom is another strong purpose for writing. I remember visiting a student in a Year 1 class in which children studying the classroom tadpoles wrote about their development on labels and placed these on the side of the tank.

The second aspect mentioned above is 'audience' – for whom is the writing? The teacher and the other children can provide a strong audience and children often like to be invited to read their work out loud. There are also wider audiences for children's work – letters to museum guides, parents and writing for the school magazine.

The enabling adult

As children try to gain control over their writing teachers need to make sensitive interventions. They talk about the writing task in hand, and sometimes demonstrate a piece of writing taking shape. They might do this round a computer with one or two children or, with the help of a flip chart or an interactive whiteboard, to a group or the whole class.

When considering how we can intervene it is helpful to make a distinction between two different aspects of the writing process, the 'compositional' and 'transcriptional' aspects – a distinction made by several authors, perhaps most memorably by Frank Smith (1982) in his book *Writing and the Writer*. 'Compositional aspects' have to do with content and with being a writer creating for a purpose and an audience. Our purpose and audience affect how we organise what we are composing, whether it is a story to share with others or a notice for the classroom asking people not to disturb the tadpoles. At this stage we search for ideas, select a vocabulary to convey our thoughts, feelings and those ideas, and use the syntactic constructions available to us. 'Transcriptional' or 'secretarial' aspects have to do with spelling, capitalisation, paragraphs and with handwriting or word processing. Shared writing is a context where the teacher models writing for the children, folding in their contributions and suggestions to the developing account on the whiteboard or flip chart. Here the teacher

461

supports both the compositional and the transcriptional aspects during these shared sessions.

Inspiration for composition – stories as a starting point for writing

When helping children write fiction, the stories read to them can be an excellent 'scaffold' or support. In exciting classroom work shown on the video-film *Gaining Control* (CLPE), we hear that one of the snails in a Year 1 classroom had climbed out of its tank and had started to eat a book about snails on the display table. This was a wonderful example of life imitating art. When the teacher asked the children if this reminded them of a book they had enjoyed they all shouted out – *The Very Hungry Caterpillar*. Using the structure of Eric Carle's book, the children wrote their own stories about the very hungry snail.

Another book which seems to inspire lively writing is Jeannie Baker's picture book *Where the Forest Meets the Sea*, now in big book format. It appeals to children of different age groups and of different abilities. The book tells of a young boy's visit to the Australian rainforest. After showing him enjoying the natural beauty of the forest, the final picture shows the ghost of the future where hotels and service stations replace the trees, plants, animals and birds of a unique environment. Children usually enjoy taking on the issues in the book in discussion and writing. Sensitive intervention and encouragement from the teacher help children to shape their ideas into satisfying stories.

Encouraging informational kinds of writing: first-hand observation and experience

There are a number of ways in which teachers can support children's informational writing. For example, when children hear an information text read out loud it helps them become accustomed to the flow of the language and familiar with the way such a text is structured. This helps them begin to control this kind of writing. Another important way of moving children forward is to demonstrate the features of non-fiction texts in shared writing contexts. However, children need not only knowledge about the form of the writing, they also need some inspiration to provide the content (Mallett, 2003, 2010). The things children see and do – practical experiences of all kinds – provide an excellent starting point for talk and writing. The children learning about the classroom snails mentioned above commented on their 'delicate shells and tiny eyestalks' and on 'the tininess of the babies' shells' when they hatched out of their eggs. Jane Bunting, the teacher, understood that these careful observations were worth writing down. So the children saw their contributions written down on the flip chart as the first stage in making a joint book. Whether we use an interactive whiteboard or a flip-chart, we need to provide this sort of sensitive help which allows children to explore and take risks without fearing criticism (*Gaining Control* CLPE video-film). Please see more about this aspect of writing under the extended entry 'non-fiction reading and writing'.

Supporting transcriptional aspects

I have already mentioned that shared writing contexts help teachers demonstrate both compositional and transcriptional aspects of writing. Beginning writers need help to develop their understanding of spelling, punctuation and handwriting. In becoming able to spell, the child explores the system and many teachers and educationists have identified stages through which each young learner moves. Gentry's model is particularly well known and includes pre-communicative, pre-phonetic and phonetic stages. By the phonetic stage a child has a better grasp of the sound-symbol relationship. Spelling is partly to do with sound, but visual aspects – getting to know the look of words – are also important. Teachers both combine teaching of spelling and phonics and draw attention to visual patterns in words. Using dictionaries and their own word books also helps reinforce visual aspects. In some classrooms part of the wall becomes a huge dictionary so that the children can track down the words they want to spell. For further discussion of the issues in the teaching of spelling, punctuation and handwriting see under the appropriate entries. In recent years there have been a number of statutory requirements set out in the National Curriculum as well as government publications for guidance on the teaching of writing to young children. Readers can find out about the latest changes and details of the 2013 National Curriculum on the government education website, but wider reading makes for more reflective practitioners. Out of a large number of good books covering writing for children up to about seven or eight, I find chapters 4 and 5 in Ann Browne's book *Developing Language and Literacy 3–8* (Browne, 2009) clear and practical. Chapter 6 on bilingual learners and the input on gender and writing is insightful too. Although written some time ago, Pam Czerniewska's (1992) book *Learning About Writing* explains some of the differences between spoken and written forms and how this informs good practice. *Developing Writing for Different Purposes* by Jeni Riley and David Reedy (Riley & Reedy, 2000) has strong examples of children's writing across the curriculum and shows how we can help young children think through an argument. *Writing Under Control* contains articles by different authors and covers most aspects of developing writing abilities in a lucid and interesting way (Graham & Kelly, 2009).

Developing writers (seven to eleven years)

Audience and purpose are still important

By about seven most children are developing some confidence as writers. Nevertheless, writing continues to be one of the most challenging activities in school. What can we do to support children's writing development over these later primary years? Just as in the case of younger children, it is a strong sense of 'purpose' – why am I writing this – and of 'audience' – for whom am I writing this – that makes all the effort seem worthwhile. Being in control of purpose and audience helps decide the text type (the type or 'genre' of the writing) and the sort of language features that are appropriate. The writer's self-image is strengthened if the teacher responds first to the content or 'composition' of the writing. Then help can be given with the transcriptional aspects – spelling, punctuation and paragraphing – so that the writing communicates clearly to others. In the later primary years above all we are trying to help children develop a distinctive authorial 'voice'. Donald Graves writes, memorably, that: 'Voice is the imprint of ourselves in our writing ... the dynamo in the process' (Graves, 1983: 227).

Helpful intervention

Planning

Everyone has their own idea about what is a helpful plan and, while we can make suggestions, I do not think imposing a particular format for planning is always appropriate. I have come across children who prefer to have a plan 'in their head' and this works well for them. Others like to make their planning visible – either in a list of ideas with main points underlined or in the form of webs to sort out the different elements.

Teachers help with planning in shared writing contexts where children can collaborate by sharing developing ideas and information. There is nothing like talk for helping children organise their ideas and feel some enthusiasm for the writing task. In this way some of the valuable aspects of what Donald Graves termed 'conferencing' can be included.

Drafting and composing

Writing is a complicated process in which planning, composing and drafting can intermingle. Thinking about your writing as you draft involves throwing bits away and putting bits in – all of us who struggle to write well know how complicated a process it is. Often it is only when we start to struggle with a topic that we find out what we actually think and feel about it. Drafting becomes more demanding as children move through the primary years for the simple reason that they are learning to control more genres each with particular features. One of the most challenging genres children work with from about Year 4 onwards are the genres known as 'persuasion' and 'discussion'. Under the entries on these subjects I look at how focused discussion and writing frames can help children develop a standpoint from which to structure their accounts.

As I pointed out in the first paragraph of this entry, one important function of writing is to organise our thinking. We need to convince children that the grammatical structures they select help structure their thoughts and belong to the compositional aspect of the writing task. Think, for example, how syntax can help put the emphasis where it is needed. Children can be shown how a point in the form of a question can alert the reader and add variety to the page. A short sentence with an exclamation mark can add to the energy that inhabits a dialogue. Making a sentence active rather than passive often infuses life into writing. Once the first draft is written older children can be encouraged to work further on the content and how it is ordered and expressed. Particularly when it comes to informational kinds of writing we will want to help children to find the clearest ways of expressing information and their ideas about the issues the information raises. Children seek something that excites them and seems worth sharing with an audience. Purpose is bound up with a sense of audience: part of becoming a mature writer involves having the imaginative insight to have the readers' needs in mind. Children need help in dispensing with parts of their accounts which seem repetitive or of little interest, while adding to and developing the parts that seem successful and likely to appeal to readers. Let us not underestimate the challenge of this task. Children find it difficult to make more than superficial changes to their writing without a great deal of help.

Back in 2000 DfEE's guidance material *Grammar for Writing* examined sentence-level aspects of writing and how we can support children's developing control over different genres. There is an issue here: too much stress on grammatical construction might stifle fluency. It is a matter of finding a balance between technical and creative aspects. Many teachers like the playful approach to grammatical constructions taken in Bain and Bridgewood's (1998) materials in *The Primary Grammar Book*.

Transcriptional aspects

There is a full account of how to support children's developing control over transcriptional aspects of writing under the entry of that name and under 'spelling', 'punctuation', 'handwriting' and 'proof reading'. In the 'Information and Communications Technology (ICT) and English' entry, I point out that word processing with its spellcheck system makes these drafting processes much easier. So there is everything to be gained by helping children have confidence on the keyboard.

When children start to bring a piece of writing to final draft we need also to draw their attention to punctuation and help them understand how this can enhance the communication of meaning. Teachers can help here as model writers in shared writing contexts showing for example how colons and semi-colons are used by thinking aloud as they make notes on the flip chart or whiteboard.

Learning about genre

As they get older, with the teacher's help children will develop an understanding of the features of different texts as they move through the primary years. This was formalised in the National Curriculum English programmes and in some now abandoned guidance material. In Literacy Time children move systematically through a range of texts, but this sensitivity to different texts, not only print but across a range of media, begins very early as children begin to have an intuitive and often quite sophisticated grasp of texts in different media. During time spent watching television and DVDs they may see cartoons, cooking programmes and science fiction, and while they might not be able to articulate the differences, they are aware of them. It is on all this intuitive knowledge, which includes the beginnings of visual literacy, that the teacher can draw when promoting children's writing as well as their reading. Multimodality – combining different modes in the texts children read and those they create themselves – is a theme in many professional books. I recommend *Visual Approaches to Teaching Writing* (Bearne and Wolstencroft, 2007), which gives practical guidance on a multimodal approach to writing in the classroom. There are interesting examples of children's work in which paper texts combine writing, images and design, and of

electronic texts which often add animation, speech and music. We need to reinforce children's understanding that genres are not static – new forms of writing emerge to reflect social need – email and text messaging, for example – and they soon grasp that different genres enjoy different statuses. As they move towards the end of the primary years children develop sensitivity to the different levels of formality required in writing.

Next I want to make some observations first on fiction and then on non-fiction kinds of writing.

Enjoying writing fiction

Children need the opportunity to try out some different kinds of writing and often a story, comic strip, poem or factual account can be a starting point. Teachers of older primary children would find inspirational *The Reader in the Writer* (Barrs and Cork, 2001), a book about how we can use the links between reading literature and writing to help children make writing progress. It describes and evaluates the literacy work over a year of some Year 5 classes. The examples of writing 'in role' are particularly interesting. Nine year old Yossif wrote a letter as one of the characters after hearing the teacher read aloud Kevin Crossley-Holland's book *The Green Children*. There is no doubt that this writing task helped him reflect profoundly on the themes of the book. A major finding from this research was how important it is to select texts of emotional power to awaken the desire to write as well as reflect and discuss; among the many books used were *The Midnight Fox* by Betsy Byars, Shirley Hughes' *The Lion and the Unicorn* and *Goodnight Mister Tom* by Michelle Magorian (Barrs and Cork, 2001). Interestingly, a report published by the Basic Skills Agency found that in schools where children's writing achievements were particularly good, time was found to read

465

whole texts, not just the extracts to which the now abandoned Literacy Hour format seemed to lead. The nourishing of writing with reading was another practice linked with success. You will find suggestions for encouraging children's writing of stories and poems under the entries for 'fiction: choosing and using', 'novels' and 'poetry'.

Supporting non-fiction kinds of writing

When it comes to non-fiction writing there are a number of ways of helping children plan, draft, edit and present their work. One outcome of Wray and Lewis' Extending Literacy project was the EXIT model, which shows how support can be given at each stage. Entries in this encyclopedia which aim to advise on this important aspect of literacy include 'prior knowledge', 'process approach to writing', 'editing', 'summary', 'proof reading', 'writing frames', 'non-fiction reading and writing' and the entries on kinds of texts like 'recount', 'report', 'explanation text' and 'persuasive genre'. A main challenge is to teach about study, research and presentational skills while keeping up high levels of involvement and interest. In chapters 4 and 5 of *Young Researchers* (Mallett, 1999) and in chapters 33 and 34 of *Choosing and Using Fiction and Non-fiction 3–11* (Mallett, 2010) there are suggestions for helping place note taking and study skills within the broader framework of children's intentions and purposes.

First-hand experience continues to be a strong context for writing across the curriculum – experiments in science, work with artefacts in history and outings to see rivers and valleys in geography. Writing about what has been seen or done, however, often needs to be enriched by information from secondary sources (Mallett, 2007). Uniting input from first-hand and second-hand sources coherently stretches most of us. This is where a strong urge to make sense of issues and information helps greatly. Let

me give one example: Year 6 children saw a Tudor sailor's shoe found when the *Mary Rose* wreck was raised. The effect of seeing this artefact with evidence, as one child remarked, that 'the little toe might have had a corn that pushed the leather out of shape' was considerable. Committed research into Tudor shoes followed to enrich the children's writing.

Just as reading and writing fiction are connected, so reading and writing non-fiction are linked activities. Sometimes it is an inspirational book that is not only the spur to children's research and writing but which also shows new and exciting ways of presenting information. Nel Marshall's *Letters to Henrietta* about a young girl's letters to and from her brothers at the front in the Second World War indicates how social history can be presented in a powerful and involving way. There are interesting collages of writing and pictures to bring alive the story of a young boy's experiences during the First World War in Marcia Williams' information picture book *Archie's War*. I know of several classrooms where this book has been the starting point for children's own writing and drawing. Response can be in different media to ring the changes. Email is often used now as an alternative to letter writing. There is more about the role of texts in developing children's interest and control over informational writing under 'information books', 'factual genres', 'first person writing' and 'persuasive genre'.

Turning now to further reading on all aspects of writing, in addition to those already mentioned in the body of this entry, there are a number of other helpful books, some of which cover writing development across age phases, including the older primary children discussed in the last few sections. *Writing Under Control* has already been mentioned as it has much of relevance to younger children. It is a well-regarded text which serves as a very good introduction to teaching all aspects of writing across the primary school years including composition and transcription, writing on screen, meeting individual needs and assessment (Graham and Kelly, 2009). Most of us welcome a little inspiration now and again to energise ideas for children's writing. Jacqueline Harrett's (2006) *Exciting Writing* offers suggestions for writing across the curriculum and includes advice about writing approaches like visualisation and using paintings, film and television. She also suggests we encourage the writing of cartoon strip and other kinds of multi-modal text. This might be a good way of helping some young writers and illustrators to find a 'voice'. There are also strong sections on writing in *Teaching English, Language and Literacy* (Wyse and Jones, 2007). Those wishing to do some advanced reading about writing development across age ranges would find *The SAGE Handbook of Writing Development* a comprehensive and authoritative guide. This huge work is in thirty-eight chapters divided into four sections: theoretical perspectives; the development of writing; conceptual and empirical issues in writing development; and challenges in writing development. It is an outcome of a seminar series attended by international scholars and researchers into writing development, funded by the United Kingdom Economic and Social Research Council. When approaching writing development, researchers have traditionally worked in particular disciplines and a major contribution this book makes is to bring together different perspectives, for example linguistic, psychological and socio-cultural. This is a significant move towards a coherent picture of writing development. There is no doubt that this is a large and demanding book and one which will tend to be consulted in a library and dipped into. It addresses many issues of current importance and current interest; for example, there is insight on bilingual writing development, on semiotic-based investigation including multimodality and

that area of continuing concern – motivation. How do teachers help inspire young writers (Beard *et al.*, 2009)?

Assessing writing and recording progress

There are two purposes in assessing children's writing. We may wish to use children's writing, as indeed we do with their speaking, to assess their progress in lessons across the curriculum. In this case we are using writing to monitor their grasp of historical, geographical or scientific information and concepts or their powers of observation during an educational visit. In this entry, though, we are concerned mainly with the assessment of writing more generally as a means of organising, making sense of and communicating experience and information. There are a number of ways of doing this, each of which tells us something different about a young writer's development. Ways of assessing writing and keeping records need to be economic of the time of both teachers and children. Too complicated a system risks taking the pleasure out of children's writing and teachers' support.

The writing SATs (see separate entry) that children take at seven and eleven years (that is at the end of Key Stage 1 and Key Stage 2) give us a summative assessment – a snapshot of what a child has achieved at a particular time. Writing for the SATs is awarded a grade on the National Curriculum levels of achievement. Evidence from teacher-assessed sampling of children's writing can also contribute to a summative judgement. In his review of assessment at Key stage 2, Lord Bew agreed with those who considered that creative kinds of writing are best assessed by looking at writing over a period of time and not by a timed test (Bew, 2011).

Sampling also helps us make a formative assessment, highlighting what a young learner is doing well and where they need some intervention to make progress.

Formative assessments of writing, using a sampling strategy, are diagnostic and we are interested not just in the products but also in the processes – how the child goes about the writing process, making plans, drafts and perhaps notes. Most teachers either make a comment orally to the child or write down some constructive comments – see 'marking'. Sampling, if carried out thoughtfully, helps us chart a child's progression as a writer both in terms of increasing the range of genres they control and their increasing skill within a genre. The English Co-ordinator usually takes the lead in producing sampling sheets to help teachers make their sampling systematic. Sampling sheets usually have space to give the date the writing was done and the context in which it arose. There is usually a heading to do with how the young writer goes about their task – the process of writing – and nearly always sections to comment on compositional (expressing and communicating meaning) and transcriptional or secretarial aspects, including spelling, punctuation and presentation. Often the child will be invited to give their own comment on their progress. One of the most valuable parts of the sampling sheet will be to do with the 'next step' or target. Teachers make notes on their observations of children's writing progress during shared, guided and independent writing sessions. They also select, often together with the child, a range of dated and annotated writing samples to include in the child's English portfolio. The children's progress using the National Curriculum English levels of achievement (perhaps enriched and extended by using the CLPE's Writing Scales which are more detailed), evidence from the samples in the portfolios, together with SATs results, can be recorded in a system like the Primary Language Record of the Centre for Literacy in Primary Education (Barrs *et al.*, 1998) – see the 'record keeping' entry. The samples and summaries of progress

help the English Co-ordinator discuss any strengths or weaknesses in a class teacher's approach to writing. It also helps the Co-ordinator have background knowledge for meetings about the school's success in supporting writing.

In the United Kingdom there is a culture of target setting. Some schools adopted statements, for example 'We can plan our writing carefully by thinking up and collecting ideas and using charts and story boards'. Progress towards targets can sometimes be a focus for discussion with children and with parents and could inform records of achievement as the child moves through the school years.

Final thoughts

What I want to leave you with at the end of this entry is first, that although writing is one of the most challenging things we ask children to do, we should encourage them to see it as useful, creative and satisfying. The second is that the teacher can be a powerful enabling force. In her preface to *The Reader in the Writer* Margaret Meek writes: 'When young writers believe that teachers are interested, really interested, in what they want to communicate they will do all they can to get their meaning across … ' (Barrs and Cork, 2001: 10). It is the quality of the encouragement they receive and the chance to write about something important to them that helps young writers find a distinctive 'voice'.

Bain, Elspeth and Bain, Richard (1996) *The Grammar Book: Finding Patterns, Making Sense* Sheffield: NATE.

Bain, Richard and Bridgewood, Marion (1998) *The Primary Grammar Book: Finding Patterns – Making Sense* Sheffield: NATE.

Barrs, Myra *et al.* (1998) *Gaining Control: Writing at Key Stage 1* Centre for Literacy in Primary Education with Southwark Education.

Barrs, Myra and Cork, Valerie (2001) *The Reader in the Writer: the Links between the*

Study of Literature and Writing Development at Key Stage 2 London: CLPE.

Beard, Roger, Myhill, Debra, Riley, Jeni and Nystrand, Martin (eds) (2009) *The Sage Handbook of Writing Development* London: Sage.

Bearne, E. and Wolstencroft, H. (2007) *'Visual Literacy': Visual Approaches to Teaching Writing: Multimodal Literacy 5–11* London: Paul Chapman Publishing (book and CD-ROM).

Bew, P. (2011) *Independent Review of Key Stage 2 testing, assessment and accountability* London: HMSO, July 2011.

Britton, James (1970) *Language and Learning* Harmondsworth: Allen Lane, The Penguin Press.

Browne, Ann (2009, third edition) *Developing Language and Literacy 3–8* London: Sage.

Czerniewska, Pamela (1992) *Learning About Writing* Oxford: Blackwell.

Frater, Graham (2001) *Key Stage 2 Writing* survey for the former Basic Skills Agency.

Graham, Judith and Kelly, Alison (eds) (2009, third edition) *Writing Under Control: Teaching Writing in the Primary School* London: David Fulton.

Graves, Donald (1983) *Writing: Teachers and Children at Work* London and New York: Heinemann (O/P).

Harrett, Jacqueline (2006) *Exciting Writing: Activities for 5–11 Year Olds* London: Sage.

Mallett, Margaret (1999) *Young Researchers: Informational Reading and Writing in the Early and Primary Years* London: Routledge.

——(2003) *Early Years Non-fiction* London and New York: Routledge.

——(2007) *Active Encounters: Inspiring Young Readers and Writers of Non-fiction, 4–11* UKLA minibook.

——(2010) *Choosing and Using Fiction and Non-fiction 3–11* London and New York: Routledge.

Riley, J. and Reedy, D. (2000) Writing for Different Purposes London: Paul Chapman.

Smith, Frank (1982) *Writing and the Writer* London: Heinemann.

Temple, C.A., Nathan, R.G., Burris, N.A. and Temple, F. (1992, third edition) *The Beginnings of Writing* Boston, Mass.: Allyn & Bacon.

Temple, C.A., Nathan, R.G. and Temple, C. (2012, fourth edition) *The Beginnings of Writing* Boston, Mass.: Allyn & Bacon.

Whitehead, Marian (2010, fourth edition [1982]) *Language and Literacy in the Early Years* London: Paul Chapman (Chapter 8, 'Early representation and emerging writing').

Wray, David and Lewis, Maureen (1997) *Extending Literacy: Children Reading and Writing Non-fiction* London: Routledge.

Writing Scales (information available from CLPE, www.clpe.co.uk).

Wyse, Dominic and Jones, Richard (2007) *Teaching English, Language and Literacy* London and New York: Routledge.

WRITING CORNER/AREA

See also: displays, reading corner/area, writing

Reading and writing are complementary and mutually enriching activities, so the classroom writing area is nearly always part of the reading area or next to it. A special area for writing in relative privacy, whether alone or as part of a small group, is appropriate and desirable for every year group from nursery to the final year, although naturally the emphasis in resources and activities changes. Space may be limited but the area must look attractive. One Reception teacher known to me displays enlarged pictures of the children at work on their writing: this helps their self-image as writers and is a good talking point. Displays help make the area inviting and are likely to include, for every age group, examples of the children's best work, clearly labelled and annotated. Children's reviews of both fiction and non-fiction are often shown, and posters showing writing routines, advice about note making and the principles of paragraphing are helpful reminders.

Examples of different kinds of writing can be displayed for reference. For example, children in Year 4 and above will need to learn about the format of some journalistic and persuasive writing, such as newspaper reports and advertisements.

When it comes to writing implements, young children like to have pens, pencils, crayons, chalks and writing brushes, while older children will appreciate the addition of biros, felt tips, pastels and calligraphy pens. Materials to write on include paper and card of different sizes, shapes, colours and textures, an assortment of envelopes, some ready-made sewn books of different proportions, concertina books and bookmaking materials like hard covers and book spines. Other items to have to hand are sellotape, display folders, staplers, paperclips, rulers, rubbers and glue. Word books, dictionaries and thesauri at the right level of difficulty for the children are necessary and, of course, a word processor, a printer and access to the internet.

To be effective a writing area must go beyond just looking good: it needs to both reflect the work of the class and be referred to in everyday work. Children's input to the planning and setting up of displays is important. Some teachers have a rota of helpers to put up displays and to keep the writing corner tidy. A developing display – one that is constantly modified and extended – reflects the dynamic nature of children's learning. The Teaching Ideas site has examples of lively learning walls and displays (www.teachingideas.co.uk). The best displays include work that is a genuine outcome of current work. Experienced teachers make time for children's writing to be read out loud and discussed as well as displayed.

Good organisation and sensitivity ensures fair access to the relative privacy of the area for individuals and groups. The good writing area provides a space where children can experiment, take initiative and enjoy their writing.

WRITING FRAMES

See also: EXEL Project, genre, non-fiction reading and writing, scaffolding, writing

Writing frames are frameworks provided by the teacher to help children structure their writing. The children are launched into their writing by 'sentence starts' like 'I want to explain why … ' and supported by 'connectives' such as 'moreover', 'next' and 'then'. This strategy became widely known through the work of Wray and Lewis on the Exeter University Extending Literacy (EXEL) Project in the 1990s. They have published several books on writing frames, including *Writing Frames: Scaffolding Children's Non-fiction Writing in a Range of Genres*, 1996. The frames arose out of classroom-based research during which, drawing also on the work of the Australian genre theorists, they identified six different kinds of informational writing. These six genres are: recount, report, instruction, explanation, discussion and persuasion. They were used in the now abandoned literacy *Framework* but have survived in practice as ways of classifying non-fiction. One of the persuasive frames has the following headings: 'I think that', 'because', 'another reason is', 'moreover', 'these facts/arguments/ideas show that'.

Writing frames have been put forward as one answer to the challenge of a genre-based National Curriculum. Even older primary children find it challenging not only to have to wrestle with new hierarchies of facts and ideas but also to control a particular format. The researchers consider that when it comes to a new genre, having a skeleton structure, often with a vocabulary that drives the writing on, leaves the children free to concentrate on the content. It is not recommended that the frames are used to teach children about the different genres in decontextualised exercises. They should be used in the context of meaningful writing tasks where there is an understanding of purpose and audience. There is no doubt that some children benefit from the organisational and linguistic support a frame can provide. Young learners who struggle with the writing process are particularly likely to find the prop useful to get started, but of course we want children to learn to organise their own written accounts and Wray and Lewis would be the first to say that the frames are a temporary aid not to be used too long or too mechanistically. Nevertheless, there is still some concern that too enthusiastic a use of the frames might jeopardise a young writer's spontaneity and delay their effort to structure their own writing. Even before the work of Lewis and Wray in this area, Myra Barrs was concerned about too genre-based an approach particularly where young children are concerned. She was not making her point in relation to writing frames but rather was arguing that children need to be encouraged to use 'provisional and informal genres' – lists, memos, logs and journals. These more accessible kinds of writing are likely to help young learners use language as a tool for thinking (Barrs, 1987: 2).

So while the frames have a role to play, it is hoped that their use will not be prescribed and teachers will use their professional judgement to decide if and when to use them.

Barrs, M. (1987) 'Mapping the world' *English in Education*, 21(3), NATE.

Lewis, Maureen and Wray, David (1996) *Writing Frames: Scaffolding Children's Non-fiction Writing in a Range of Genres* Reading: Reading University Reading and Language Information Centre.

WRITING RESOURCES

See: writing corner/area

471

Y

YOUNG'S GROUP READING TEST

See also: assessment, Standardised Reading Tests

This is a timed, written attainment test given to groups of children. First published by Hodder and Stoughton in 1968, it covers an age range from six and a half to just over twelve years. The later versions, including that published in 1980, include sentences in which the children fill gaps to indicate some understanding of what they are reading.

Graham, Judith and Kelly, Alison (2009, third edition) *Reading Under Control: Teaching Reading in the Primary School* London: David Fulton (gives a clear account of the different reading tests, and the issues they raise, in Chapter 4, 'Monitoring and assessing reading).

Z

ZONE OF PROXIMAL DEVELOPMENT

See also: collaborative learning, language acquisition

This is the area of a child's emerging abilities. A standardised test gives a summative score but with help from an adult or older pupil, a child's level of working may be raised. The gap between what a child can achieve on their own and what they can achieve with help was termed the 'zone of proximal development' by the great Russian developmentalist and psychologist L.S. Vygotsky in *Thought and Language* (1987). The zone of proximal development can vary considerably in children of the same age who have a similar set of standardised scores: one child may have a much more elastic potential and be able to benefit from a level of teaching for which the other child is not yet ready. One child needs to be challenged while for the other teaching may be best aimed just beyond present achievements.

The theory supports a social interactionist view of learning since it suggests that interaction with others – both peers and adults – can further children's progress. The right kind of teacher intervention, carefully adjusted for individual learners, can provide vital support in a child's journey towards competence, not least in language and thinking but also in other areas of development.

Vygotsky, L.S. (1987) *Thought and Language*, revised and edited by A. Kozulin, Cambridge, Mass.: MIT Press.

Wood, David (1998) *How Children Think and Learn* London: Blackwell.

A who's who in primary English

ADAMS, MARILYN J.

A US specialist in cognition and education, she has published a number of books and journal articles on learning to read, including *Beginning to Read: Thinking and Learning about Print* (Cambridge, Mass.: MIT Press, 1990, 1994). Adams makes a clear distinction between graphic and phonic cue-systems in learning to read. She is often cited to support phonic approaches, but she believes reading skills should be situated in a programme of good quality and interesting reading materials.

ALEXANDER, ROBIN

Professor Alexander, a Fellow of Wolfson College and University Director of Research at Cambridge University, is the Director of the Cambridge Primary Review. This independent study of all aspects of children's experience of primary school was launched in October 2006. The findings are too considerable to summarise here, but interim reports and the final report are available on www.primaryreview.org.uk. One of Professor Alexander's main research interests is what he terms 'dialogic teaching'. This special kind of classroom interaction is explained under the entry entitled 'dialogic teaching'.

ARNOLD, HELEN

During her career Arnold was a teacher, lecturer, adviser and researcher into children's literacy development. She is known best for her books *Listening to Children Reading* (1982, Hodder and Stoughton) and, with Vera Southgate and Susan Johnson, *Extending Beginning Reading* (London: Heinemann, 1980). Her work on non-fiction reading and writing is wise and useful, not least her chapter 'Do the blackbirds sing all day? Literature and information texts' in *After Alice* (M. Styles, E. Bearne and V. Watson (eds), London: Cassell, 1992). She believed children deserved the very best quality non-fiction texts and that these relate to their own questions and their own experience.

BAIN, RICHARD

With co-author M. Bridgewood, Bain wrote *The Primary Grammar Book: Finding Patterns, Making Sense* (Sheffield: NATE, 1998), which contains many suggestions for language games and activities to help children enjoy learning about syntax and parts of speech.

BARNES, CLIVE

Former Principal Children's Librarian at Southampton City, Barnes has contributed articles and reviews on children's books to *Books for Keeps* for many years. What he has to say is perceptive and helpful and often entertaining. He combines reviewing with research and writer as a freelance.

BARNES, DOUGLAS

Although his main experience was in secondary schools, Barnes' work on the role of talk in classroom learning, particularly in small groups, made an impact on primary practice. The ideas from *Language, the Learner and the School* (1969, Harmondsworth: Penguin), written with co-authors James Britton and Harold Rosen, influenced the Bullock Report which reached a wide audience of primary practitioners and researchers and still supports best practice. Look out for *Exploring Talk in School: Inspired by the work of Douglas Barnes* by Neil Mercer and Steve Hodgkinson (Sage, 2008).

BARRS, MYRA

From 1986 until 2004, Myra Barrs was Director and then Co-Director of the Centre for Literacy in Primary Education. She has been a major influence on best practice in primary English. Myra's work has covered every aspect of English, language and literacy in the primary years. The resource centre she and her colleagues built up has texts of every kind, in print and electronic media. Online digital resources can be accessed from the CLPE library. Teachers and parents have been drawn to the Centre to explore the resources and to attend the excellent courses and workshops. Her many books and articles are both scholarly and rooted in the classroom and she led the development of a strong research tradition at the Centre. She and her colleagues all stressed that they worked as a team and some of those who made a considerable contribution to the Centre's research and publications include Valerie Cork, Sue Ellis, Hilary Hester, Clare Kelly, Ann Lazim, Deborah Nicholson, Anne Thomas and Olivia O'Sullivan.

Myra's most notable contributions were in the areas of assessment, writing, creativity and gender.

An early project was the development of the *Primary Language Record* (PLR, 1988), which linked planning, teaching and learning and has become the basis of assessment models used in education systems across the world. Her interest in children's writing is to be seen in articles in journals in the UK and the USA and the formulation of the Centre's Writing Scales. These give a more detailed picture of progress than the National Curriculum English levels of achievement.

With her colleagues she contributed strongly to the debate on gender issues and most recently on boys' literacy, producing publications like *Reading the Difference* (1993), *Boys and Writing* (2002) and *Boys on the Margin* (2004). In 2005 Myra edited *The Best of Language Matters*, which included forty-eight articles from the Centre's journal. This provides a window into the history of English teaching at the primary stage from the 1970s until the first years of the twenty-first century.

BEARD, ROGER

Known by primary teachers for his work on the development of literacy, Professor Roger Beard communicates the issues clearly in books like *Children's Writing in the Primary School* (1984, London: Hodder & Stoughton) and *Developing Reading 3–13* (1990, second edition, London: Hodder & Stoughton). He has also produced in-service packages and edited a large number of books, for example *Teaching Literacy, Balancing Perspectives* (1993, London: Hodder & Stoughton) and *Rhyme, Reading and Writing* (1996, London: Hodder & Stoughton). He is a critic of extreme interpretations of 'apprenticeship' approaches to reading and 'process' approaches to writing. Now Professor of Primary Education at the London Institute of Education, Professor Beard is one of the editors, with Debra Myhill, Jeni Riley and Martin Nystrand, of *The SAGE Handbook of Writing Development*. The book was the outcome of a series of international seminars with researchers and teachers at the forefront of the field.

BEARNE, EVE

Bearne has taught and researched in all the main areas of language and literacy and has brought to her considerable volume of written work a rare insight valuable to teachers in both primary and secondary schools. In the world of children's literature she is known particularly for two books edited with her colleagues Morag Styles and Victor Watson: *After Alice* (1992) and *The Prose and the Passion* (1994). *Making Progress in Writing* (2002) won her the UKLA Teachers' Book Award for 2003. Following an international conference in Cambridge she wrote *Art, Narrative and Childhood* (2003) with her colleague Morag Styles. This goes beyond contemplating contemporary concepts of visual texts to thinking about 'visual literacy in the future'. Formerly a senior researcher of the University of Cambridge Faculty of Education, she now writes and researches on a freelance basis. She is interested in how children can be helped to make meaning through different modes and media. With her colleagues at the United Kingdom Literacy Association, she has researched into multimodality, digital resources and what is involved in reading on screen.

BENTLEY, DIANA

A well known-specialist in children's literacy, Bentley's book with Dee Reid *Supporting Struggling Readers* (Widnes: UKRA, 1995) provides an excellent analysis of reading difficulty with clear practical advice for classroom strategies. The book was published in a revised form in 2007.

BEREITER, CARL AND SCARDAMALIA, MARLENE

These US educationists are best known for their research into the development of children's writing. They believe the challenge is to encourage young writers to transform information rather than just recall it. See their main arguments set out in *The Psychology of Written Composition* (1987, Hillside, N.J.: Lawrence Erlbaum Associates).

BERNSTEIN, BASIL

Bernstein was an international figure in the world of sociology and education from the early 1960s. Based at the London Institute of Education, where he became professor in 1967, he influenced large numbers of teachers on postgraduate courses. In an obituary in *The Times Educational Supplement* (6 October 2000: 27), his first PhD student, Dennis Lawton, commented that: 'His major contribution was to demonstrate how nearly every aspect of a child's life was affected by the language used by its parents.' He was interested in the role of language in all kinds of social interaction and as a means of social control, but he is best known for his work on the distinction between elaborated and restricted codes. In his earlier work he seemed to be saying (although he modified this later) that while middle-class children had control over elaborated forms of language, including academic discourse, as well as over more personal speech forms, working-class children only had access to the latter, more restricted code. It is not difficult to see how this led in some cases to a deficit model which linked working-class underachievement at school to inadequate use of language. Many found this model determinist and abhorrent, although it did lead to much discussion, research and argument.

BIELBY, NICHOLAS

Bielby has written about the theoretical aspects of literacy and has explained the underpinning to 'the new phonics' in his book *Making Sense of Reading: The New*

Phonics and its Practical Implications (1994, Leamington Spa: Scholastic Publications).

BISSEX, GLENDA

Bissex is known for *GNYS AT WRK* [Genius at Work]: *A Child Learns to Write and Read* (1980, Cambridge, Mass.: Harvard University Press). This is a seminal work named after a sign the author's young child, Paul, hangs on his door. The case study of a child's writing and reading behaviour at home from age five years shows the importance of motivation in a child's progress and has implications for how we support children's writing in school.

BLAKE, QUENTIN

Blake began as a cartoonist and worked in advertising before turning his attention, with enormous success, to writing and illustrating children's picture books, poetry anthologies and story books. His economical style is both distinctive and versatile and he is considered to be one of the foremost and best-loved illustrators of children's books of the twentieth century and the first decades of the twenty-first century. His output is huge and the books he has both written and illustrated include many that have become classics – *Mister Magnolia, Clown* and *Mrs Armitage* for example. He has also illustrated the writings of others, most notably Roald Dahl's stories and Michael Rosen's poetry, and has published books about the art of the illustrator, for example *Words and Pictures* (Jonathan Cape, 2000).

BRICE-HEATH, SHIRLEY

A US educationist, anthropologist and linguist whose study of children's language development in different cultural and social contexts is clearly explained in *Ways with Words: Language, Life and Work in Communities and Classrooms* (1983, Cambridge University Press). Her research into ethnography continues and is the subject of her book with Brian Street *Ethnography: Approaches to Language and Literacy Research* (2008, Routledge).

BRITTON, JAMES

Best known for emphasising the role of talk in learning and for his classification of writing modes, James Britton helped draft the Bullock Report. A secondary teacher of English, a publisher and then an academic at the London University Institute of Education, he was also Director of a Schools Council Project on Writing, 11–18. Later, he was appointed Professor of Education at University of London Goldsmiths College. He had a deep concern for and interest in children's language development at the primary stage. His book *Language and Learning* (Allen Lane, 1970) has much to contribute to our understanding of language development in the primary school years and remains a seminal work.

BROADHEAD, PAT

A respected specialist in the early years, Pat Broadhead is the author of a number of books for teachers and students, including *Play and Learning in the Early Years* with Justine Howard and Elizabeth Wood. This book explains how we can enhance all aspects of play and explains its contribution to development.

BROWNJOHN, SANDY

Author of a number of books on the teaching of poetry including *Does it Have to Rhyme?* (1980), *What Rhymes with Secret?* (1982) and *To Rhyme or Not to Rhyme, Teaching Children to Write Poetry* (1994) (all published in London by Hodder & Stoughton), Brownjohn believes that children need to be taught the techniques to write different kinds of poem.

These strategies, which can be learnt through play and games, will encourage children to play with language and to control what they say. An inflexible interpretation might risk contrived lessons, but many teachers have found her work helps both them and the children they teach enjoy and feel confident about reading and writing poetry.

BRUCE, TINA

Professor of Playful Learning at Leeds Metropolitan University, Tina Bruce is a distinguished specialist in the area of children's development in the early years. Her many books include *Early Childhood: A Guide for Students* (Sage).

BRUNER, JEROME

Bruner is a US educationist and developmentalist known for his research into very early human communication and the language and thought of school aged children. He argues that the young child first knows the world through sensation (enactive stage), then becomes able also to make sense of experience through images (the iconic stage) and finally through symbols, including language (the symbolic stage). A good book to start with is *Making Sense: the Child's Construction of the World* (1987, Methuen, written with co-author Helen Haste), moving on to *Actual Minds, Possible Worlds* (1986, Harvard University Press). The first of these texts was brought out in a new edition in 2010 in the Routledge Revivals series.

In his early work he tends to concentrate on cognitive development, but his later books recognise the importance of developing an inner world of the imagination – not least through story.

BRYANT, PETER

An educational researcher with a special interest in how children make inferences,

Peter Bryant has also turned his attention, with his colleague Ursula Goswami, to phonological aspects of learning to read. See, for example, *Phonological Skills and Learning to Read* (1990, Lawrence Erlbaum Associates). His book with co-author Terezinhu Nunes, *Children's Reading and Spelling: Beyond the First Steps* (Wiley-Blackwell, 2009), explores how spelling and reading develop over the school years.

BUCKINGHAM, DAVID

This international expert on media education sets out his views in books like *Media Education: Literacy, Learning and Contemporary Culture* (2003, Polity Press). His book examining computer games as an exciting and rapidly developing media – *Computer Games: Text, Narrative and Play* (2006) with Diana Carr, Andrew Burn and Gareth Schott – is published by Polity Press. In *Beyond Technology: Children's Learning in the Age of Digital Culture* he explores the gap between the home experience of digital technology many children have and what is offered in school (2007, Polity Press).

BUTLER, DOROTHY

Author of *Babies Need Books* (1995, Harmondsworth: Penguin), Dorothy Butler drew in her writing on her experience as a New Zealand bookseller and a mother of a large family of children and grandchildren. This is a very human book which offers practical insight and help. There are many more children's books to choose from now, but Dorothy Butler sets out some principles for selecting – albeit with a light touch.

CARTER, RONALD

Ronald Carter is Professor of English Studies at the University of Nottingham. Known for his work on knowledge about language for teachers and school age children, one of his best-known books

481

is *Knowledge about Language and the National Curriculum: The LINC Reader* (London: Hodder & Stoughton, 1990). For an analysis of the controversy over the publication of the materials see the 'LINC materials' entry. His book *Language and Creativity: the Art of Common Talk* (Routledge, 2010) celebrates the creativity of the everyday mind as shown through spontaneous conversation.

CHAMBERS, AIDAN

Co-founder with his American wife, Nancy Chambers, of The Thimble Press, Aidan Chambers has published a large number of excellent novels for older children and young adults. He has also published books for teachers drawing on his work as a teacher and a lecturer. Two particularly inspiring books are *Tell Me: Children, Reading and Talk* (1993) and *The Reading Environment* (1991). These books are about the pleasure reading can provide and how teachers can help children become enthusiastic readers. They have been published together in a new edition by The Thimble Press (2011). The National Association for the Teaching of English (NATE) presented him in 2010 with a lifetime achievement award.

CHAMBERS, NANCY

Editor and founder in 1969 of The Thimble Press together with her husband, Aidan Chambers, Nancy has published many well-regarded publications on all aspects of children's books and reading as well as the journal *Signal*. The final *Signal* volume came out in September 2003.

CLARK, MARGARET

Clark drew attention to the role of the adult and of the library in supporting children's attitudes to reading before they receive formal instruction. Her book *Young Fluent Readers: what can they teach us?* (1976,

London: Heinemann Educational) examines the case studies of thirty-two children who read at an early age.

CLAY, MARIE

Clay was a leading reading specialist in New Zealand, well known for her successful approach to helping young struggling readers. Her programme, termed 'Reading Recovery', involved planning an intensive set of lessons and activities for each child in need of special help. The quality of interaction between teacher and child was crucial to the success of the intervention. She wrote a large number of books on reading and literacy, such as *What Did I Write?* (1975, Heinemann). Her work has been adapted for reading recovery programmes in the UK. The European Centre for Reading Recovery is based at the London Institute of Education.

CLEGG, ALEX

Creative writing flourished in the 1960s and one of the outstanding books celebrating children's work was Clegg's *The Excitement of Writing* (1964, London: Chatto & Windus). The book is based on the belief that children write powerfully and imaginatively out of their own experiences and using their own choice of language.

The creative writing approach has had many critics and it can lead to children keeping to a rather narrow range of writing. Nevertheless, Clegg's work is still an inspiration and a reminder that some of the writing children do should arise from their own lives and wishes.

CLIPSON-BOYLES, SUZI

A major contributor to our understanding of educational drama and its potential role in children's developing literacy, Clipson-Boyles directed the Catch Up Project, a literacy intervention programme for struggling readers in Year 3, at Oxford Brookes University. As well as teaching and lecturing she has published a number of inspiring books and articles on drama including *Teaching Primary English Through Drama* and 'The role of drama in the literate classroom' in *The Literate Classroom*, edited by Prue Goodwin, both books published by David Fulton.

CORBETT, PIE

How many of us can say we have written 250 books? Pie Corbett – a poet and writer as well as a former head teacher and Inspector of English – can. His particular contribution is to help teachers meet statutory requirements in a creative manner. Examples of his work include the *Writing Models* series for David Fulton, *Black's Rhyming Spelling Dictionary* and, with Sue Palmer, *Literacy: What Works?* for Nelson Thornes.

COX, BRIAN

Chair of the Cox Committee which produced the two Cox Reports on primary English and laid the foundation for the first National Curriculum English orders, Cox has been a critic of the more prescriptive revisions of the English orders – see, for example, his book *Cox on Cox: An English Curriculum for the 1990s* (1991, Hodder & Stoughton).

CREMIN, TERESA

A former editor of UKLA journal *Literacy*, Professor Cremin is a major figure in teacher education through her lecturing, conference organisation and many publications. She has written on all aspects of primary English and is known particularly for her books on drama, creativity and storytelling, for example *Traditional Storytelling in the Classroom* (Scholastic, 1997). Her book *The RoutledgeFalmer Reader in*

Literacy (2003) brings together twenty-five articles to show the world of language and literacy in 'a constant state of transition and transformation'.

CRYSTAL, DAVID

Honorary Professor of Linguistics at Bangor University in Wales, David Crystal is a leading linguist and author of a large number of books and educational materials on language for different age groups. Amongst his best-known books are *Child Language, Learning and Linguistics* (Penguin), *The English Language* (Penguin) and *The Cambridge Encyclopedia of Language* brought out in a third edition in 2010 by Cambridge University Press. Teachers of all age groups find his books interesting and useful for reference as well as a means of refining their knowledge about language.

CZERNIEWSKA, PAMELA

Director of the *National Writing Project* and author of many books and articles on children's writing development including *Learning About Writing* (1992, Oxford: Blackwell).

DOMBEY, HENRIETTA

Professor of Education, more recently Emeritus Professor, at the University of Brighton, Henrietta Dombey has taught, lectured and researched in the area of children's reading. She is a widely respected expert in the field and is never afraid to appraise new initiatives in literacy with a critical eye. Her book with co-author H. Moustafa, *Whole to Part Phonics: How Children Learn to Read and Spell* (1998, CLPE), argues we should encourage phonological understanding in the context of whole texts. Her book with Eve Bearne and Teresa Grainger, *Classroom Interactions in Literacy* (2003), takes up a social and cultural perspective towards classroom discourse.

DONALDSON, MARGARET

An educational researcher and developmentalist based for a number of years at Edinburgh University, Donaldson has lectured and written about children's intellectual development. Just a very few education books are truly exciting and ground-breaking and, for many teachers and students, this is true of *Children's Minds* (1978, Fontana). Here she argued that children under eleven coped best when learning made 'human sense'. She suggests a number of strategies to help the successful teaching of reading and writing and shows how becoming literate can bring about a special kind of intellectual growth.

ECCLESHARE, JULIA

Julia Eccleshare, writer, broadcaster and children's book editor at *The Guardian*, succeeded Myra Barrs as a Co-Director (with Sue Ellis) of the Centre for Literacy in Primary Education in 2004. Her edited book *1001 Children's Books You Must Read Before You Grow Up* (Cassell) is full of wisdom, information and enhanced by a treasure store of illustrations.

EDWARDS, VIV

Viv Edwards has made a major contribution through books like *The Power of Babel, Teaching and Learning in Multilingual Classrooms* (1998, Stoke-on-Trent: Trentham Books) to our understanding of how we best support young learners who speak two or more languages. Her colleagues on the Multilingual Resources project include Urmi Chana and Sue Walker. She worked with Sue Walker on dual-language texts and this work is described and evaluated in their book *Building Bridges: Multilingual*

Resources for Children (1995, The Multilingual Resources for Children Project, University of Reading: Multilingual Matters). One of her most recent publications is *Learning to be Literate: Multilingual Perspectives* (2009, Multilingual Matters).

She is a Professor of Language in Education at Reading University and the Director of The National Centre for Language and Literacy (www.ncll.org.uk) formerly known as the Reading University Reading and Language Information Centre. Her colleagues and members of her research team have included Sue Abbas, Angela Redfern, Pam Brown, Prue Goodwin, Chris Routh, Barbara Shaw and Judy Tallet.

EGAN, KIERAN

Like Jerome Bruner, Egan sees children as active meaning-makers rather than storers of symbols in the mind for later retrieval. His books, such as *Imagination in Teaching and Learning* (1992, Chicago University Press), emphasise the creativity at the centre of all learning and share exciting examples of children's work in science and history. His research into and writing about creativity continues and one outcome is *An Imaginative Approach to Teaching*, Jossey Bass publishers, 2010. He shows how teachers use story, play and rhythm to bring lessons alive.

EVANS, JANET

Evans is a senior lecturer in education at Liverpool Hope University whose research interest is in critical reader response. Out of her publications let me choose two on which to comment. *Beyond the Page* (2009, Routledge) is a most interesting exploration of how children respond to a rich range of picture books and includes an illuminating interview with the Children's Laureate in 2009–11, Anthony Browne. Her edited book *Literacy Moves On* (David

Fulton, 2004) is on my 'most used' book-shelf, as the chapters on popular culture and new technologists are by leading experts.

FISHER, MARGERY

An expert on children's books of all genres and author of *Intent upon Reading* (1964, Brockhampton), which was one of the first surveys to view children's books as part of mainstream literature, Fisher was also one of the first to recognise the importance of offering children quality non-fiction – see *Matters of Fact* (1972, Brockhampton Press).

FOX, CAROL

Carol Fox has shown us the influence of experiences of the real world and of the world of books on young children's narra-tives. Her analysis in *At the Very Edge of the Forest: The Influence of Literature on Story-telling by Children* (1993, Longman) sug-gests that we see young children's stories as forms of verbal symbolic play. Children use 'story language' from books for retelling their own stories. (Those interested in cul-tural influences on young children's literacy would also find interesting Naima Brown's *Young Children's Literacy Development and the Role of Televisual Texts* (Falmer Press, 1999), in which she illuminates how young children's literacy is enriched by watching video-film and television.)

FOX, GEOFF

Fox is Honorary Fellow of Exeter Uni-versity and Editor Emeritus of the journal *Children's Literature in Education*. Co-author (with M. Benton) of one of the most inspirational books ever written on English teaching, *Teaching Literature 9–13* (Oxford University Press, 1987), Geoff Fox has shared his ideas on books, illustra-tion and reading fiction over many years. He shares a love of children's books in *Celebrating Children's Literature in Edu-cation* (1995, London: Hodder & Stoughton). His book *Dear Mr Morpingo: Inside the World of Michael Morpurgo* (2003) shares with children the ideas behind Morpurgo's stories and how he goes about writing them. With co-author Kate Agnew, he wrote *Children At War* – an analysis and appreciation of books showing children's experience of war (Continuum, 2004).

FROEBEL, FRIEDRICH

An educator who had great influence on child-centred approaches to educating young children, Froebel recognises the importance of stories in a child's develop-ment – not least as a way of understanding the circumstances of others in different times and places – in his book *The Education of Man* (1887, Appleton Century Croft).

GAMBLE, NIKKI

Founder and Director of Just Imagine, a specialist independent children's books and story centre in Chelmsford, Nikki arranges high-profile conferences and has published several important books. She is the author, with Sally Yates, of one of the best books on Children's Literature for intending tea-chers – *Exploring Children's Literature* (Sage, 2010). This book shows us what it means to be a reader and supports the knowledge that a practitioner needs to teach about literature well.

GENTRY, RICHARD

Gentry is best known for setting out a model of developmental stages in spel-ling – see 'An analysis of developmental spelling' in GNYS AT WRK, *Reading Teacher*, 36: 192–200, 1982. The stages are included in N. Mudd's comprehensive book on spelling *Effective Spelling: A Practical Guide for Teachers* (1994, Lon-don: Hodder & Stoughton).

GIPPS, CAROLINE

Gipps has examined the theoretical underpinning to good primary practice and many teachers will know her *What Makes a Good Primary Teacher?* (Routledge). Her special interest in the issues raised in assessment resulted in several publications – see for example her book with P. Murphy *A Fair Test? Assessment, Achievement and Equity* (1994, Buckingham: Open Books). She is the Vice-Chancellor of Wolverhampton University.

GOODMAN, KENNETH

Kenneth Goodman argued over many years that learning to read is a natural development and not essentially different from learning to speak. In fact, he saw spoken language as a key tool in deciphering new words. Children were helped to make out an unfamiliar word by the meaning of the rest of the sentence and other contextual clues. His views had enormous influence and his references to reading as 'a psycholinguistic guessing game' and miscue analysis as 'a window onto the reading process' are familiar to many (see K. Goodman (1973) 'Miscues: windows on the reading process' in K. Goodman (ed.) *Miscue Analysis: Application to Reading Instruction* Urbana, Ill.: ERIC Clearing House on Reading and Communication, NCTE). There are several revised versions of Goodman's original miscue analysis procedure which are easier to use in the classroom, for example Cliff Moon, 1984, Helen Arnold, 1982 and Robin Campbell, 2007. See under the miscue analysis entry for more detail.

The opposite view of reading to Goodman's requires that children be taught letter-sound relationships as a basis for learning to read and write. In practice, most people who favour the latter approach also understand there is more to reading than decoding. Similarly, Good-man accepted that there is a phonological cue-system playing its part alongside the contextual, semantic and syntactic systems. It is a matter of emphasis. While teaching phonics assumed a greater role in the National Curriculum following the Rose Report (2006), Goodman's influence is still evident in the recognition of the importance of all the cue-systems beyond the earliest stage of learning to read.

GOODWIN, PRUE

Author of *The Literate Classroom* (third edition, 2010, David Fulton), she researches and teaches about all aspects of literacy including reluctant readers in the primary years. Prue Goodwin has a special interest in picture books as works of art in their own right and as a powerful push into children's literacy. *Understanding Children's Books: A Guide for Professionals* (David Fulton, 2008), which she edited and contributed to, brought together the insights of some of the foremost teachers and scholars in the field.

GOSWAMI, USHA

Author of *Rhyme and Analogy, Teacher's Guide* (1996, Oxford University Press), Usha Goswami has worked with Peter Bryant on how children develop phonemic awareness and has made a considerable contribution to the reading debate. She argues that children use their awareness of rhyme to make rime analogies which draw attention to phonemes. From this perspective, what are known as 'organic phonics' using onset and rime would be preferred to, or at least go alongside, the use of synthetic phonics in the initial teaching of reading. Her books about children's general intellectual development include *Cognitive Development: The Learning Brain*, (Psychology Press, 2007).

GRAHAM, JUDITH

Now a freelance researcher and writer, Judith Graham was a principal lecturer at Roehampton University for many years. She has expertise in all aspects of children's literacy and is the author of many influential books. With co-author Alison Kelly, she wrote the well-regarded and successful books *Reading Under Control* and *Writing Under Control* (David Fulton). She has helped students and teachers interpret government requirements in a flexible and creative way. For many years she has had a special interest in children's picture books and in what is learnt from illustrations as well as text. Her chapter 'Reading contemporary picturebooks' in *Modern Children's Literature*, edited by Kimberley Reynolds, and her two chapters on picture books in *Understanding Children's Books*, edited by Prue Goodwin, are inspirational. Look out for her work on illustration of Aesop's Fables.

GRAINGER, TERESA

See: Cremin, Teresa

GRAVES, DONALD

A researcher and author who has made a considerable contribution to our understanding of writing as a process, Donald Graves drew attention to the importance of 'conference' (talking to children about the content and organisation of their writing before and during the task) and of 'publishing' (presenting children's writing in books to make their work attractive and permanent). See his classic book *Writing: Teachers and Children at Work* (1983, Heinemann).

GREGORY, EVE

A former teacher of young children, now Professor of Language and Culture at Goldsmiths College, University of London and Head of Goldsmiths Centre for Language, Culture and Learning, Eve Gregory has carried out major research projects on the literacy practices of ethnic minorities and the effect of these literacy practices on their children.

Her research drew teachers' attention to the fact that young bilingual children do not bring certain culturally acquired knowledge (for example, words that go together like 'fish and chips' and 'bread and butter') to their reading in a second language. This has implications for how the teaching of reading and writing is best approached with young bilingual children. These issues are explored in her book *Learning to Read in a New Language: Making Sense of Words and Worlds* (Sage, 2008).

She has extended her research to 'city literacies' – to the literacy practices of several different communities in inner London – and to the role of siblings in children's developing literacy.

GRUGEON, ELIZABETH

A specialist in primary English, she has written a number of valuable books including, with P. Gardner, *The Art of Storytelling for Teachers and Pupils* (2000) and, with Lorraine Hubbard, Carol Smith and Lyn Dawes, *Teaching Speaking and Listening in the Primary School* (2006), both published by David Fulton.

HALL, KATHY

Professor Kathy Hall was Head of the Centre for Educational Research at Leeds Metropolitan University before taking up a post as Professor of Education at the Open University. She has published widely in the area of literacy and assessment and directed the United Kingdom Literacy Association's funded research on effective literacy teaching. She was editor for some years of UKLA's journal *Literacy*. Her book *Listening to Ste-*

487

phen Read: Multiple Perspectives on Literacy (2002) analyses the responses of leading literacy scholars to the question: how would you advise the teacher to support Stephen who is underachieving in reading? She concludes that rather than always adopting one single approach, we should have 'multiple perspectives' guided by the needs of a particular young learner. With co-author Winnifred Burke she has written *Making Formative Assessment Work* (Open University Press, 2004), a book which provides strong case studies of teachers using formative approaches to assessment in different curriculum areas. The authors show how formative assessment and learning can be powerfully linked in good practice. She addresses wide issues to do with education policy in *Literacy, Schooling and Society: Towards Renewal in Primary Education Policy* (Ashgate Publishing, 2004).

HALL, NIGEL

Hall is known both for his work on the literacy of young children and for his role as Co-Director (with Anne Robinson) of The Punctuation Project, Manchester Metropolitan University.

Hall and Robinson set out the first attempt to offer a comprehensive account of the issues involved in learning and teaching punctuation in their book *Learning About Punctuation* (1996, Clevedon, Philadelphia and Adelaide: Multilingual Matters). His analysis 'Developing understanding of spelling' is a chapter in *The SAGE Handbook of Writing*, edited by Roger Beard *et al.*, 2009.

HALLIDAY, M.A.K.

Halliday is a systemic-functional linguist who has investigated how language changes according to a particular social context. In his book *Language as Social Semiotic* (1978, London: Arnold) he shows how, as we express meaning through language, we

recreate social reality. For teachers of young children, Halliday's most relevant book is *Learning How to Mean* (1975, London: Arnold), in which he presents a case study of his own child as he manages to 'mean' before he has verbal language. So Halliday sees the human infant as essentially a meaning-maker who communicates before he or she has words. The social impetus into speech is stressed – 'to take on a language is to take on a culture'.

Functional linguists are more interested in the functions or uses to which we put language than the structure of the system. Halliday's functions of language model (see under the functions of language entry) has had great influence on how we construe the young child's language development.

HEATHCOTE, DOROTHY

Dorothy Heathcote, who died in 2011, has made an outstanding contribution to the development of educational drama with many different age groups. A mill worker who left school at fourteen, she rose through sheer brilliance and hard work to become a lecturer and researcher in drama at the universities of Newcastle and Durham. Her work with primary aged children has often been connected with history. Children are invited to 'put themselves in somebody else's shoes', whether they are a Saxon villager coping with a failing harvest or a Viking about to invade. In her many articles, lectures and demonstrations she has pointed to the potential of the teacher-in-role. By adopting this position the teacher can comment, question and help inform and shape the children's improvisation in a natural way. Gradually some of the responsibility can be shifted to the children and they then take over what Heathcote terms 'the mantle of the expert'.

The potential of drama as a tool for learning and imagining across the curriculum, explored by Heathcote with Gavin Bolton, who is also distinguished in the field of educational drama, is set out in *Drama for Learning: Dorothy Heathcote's Mantle of the Expert Approach to Education* (1995, Portsmouth, NH: Heinemann).

If you want to read a case study carried out by Tom Stabler, a former student of Heathcote at Newcastle University, see Margaret Mallett and Bernard Newsome (1977) *Talking, Writing and Learning 8–13* Evans/Methuen for the Schools Council: 52–61. The range of writing encouraged by participation in the improvisation on conflict in a Saxon village is impressive. The story of this inspirational teacher's life and work can be read and savoured in Gavin Bolton's biography, *Dorothy Heathcote's Story: The Biography of a Remarkable Drama Teacher*, Trentham Books, 2003.

HOLDAWAY, DON

Holdaway is known for his books both about the parent's role in encouraging literacy and the use of enlarged texts to demonstrate aspects of the reading process to children in the classroom. Much of his wisdom is contained in his book *The Foundations of Literacy* (1979, London: Ashton Scholastic). We must remember that Holdaway's aim in using large texts was to make available to a group or even a class the special benefits of individualised reading. He was very much in favour of teacher and children making some of their own reading materials, including big books. Shared reading in English lessons, when done well, is a realisation of Holdaway's principles.

HUGHES, TED

As well as producing many books of stories and poetry for children, including *The Iron Man* – a modern fairy tale – Ted Hughes wrote books and articles for teachers, for example *Poetry in the Making*, first published in 1967 and now in a new edition from Faber & Faber, 2008. This inspira-

tional book explores how we can help young writers to acquire that special concentration needed to write poetry. His writing for teachers includes articles about teaching poetry and about the power of traditional tales, for example 'Myth and education', in *Children's Literature in Education*, 1, March 1970, about the cultural importance of myth.

HYNDS, GEOFF

A specialist in children's reading development across the key stages, Geoff Hynds is known for his belief that children should have quality books and resources. One of his initiatives was the Geoff Hynds Bookshop.

JONES, RICHARD

Jones is the author of an exciting book, *Fantasy and Feeling in Education* (1972, Penguin), which gives a central place to play, dreams and storytelling in the educational process and is inspiring to teachers of any age group.

KELLY, CLARE

Dr Clare Kelly has been a primary school teacher, a lecturer and researcher at the Centre for Literacy in Primary Education and is now Head of Language and Literacy in Initial Teacher Training at Goldsmiths College. She specialises in all aspects of English teaching in the early and primary years. Her book *Hidden Worlds: Young Children Learning in Multicultural Contexts* (Trentham Books, 2010) presents case studies of six young children all attending the same nursery but from different cultural backgrounds. The book illuminates how teachers' understanding of home experience and adult together with peer support can help children make the link with the world of literacy.

LAMBIRTH, ANDREW

Lambirth is Professor of Education at the University of Greenwich and has lectured and written on the primary school curriculum and all aspects of children's language and literacy development. With Judith Roden he wrote *The Primary Curriculum: A Creative Approach* (2011, London: Sage).

LATHEY, GILLIAN

Dr Gillian Lathey was an early years teacher before joining the education faculty of Roehampton University. Her research area is in children's books in translation and she is the author of *The Role of Translation in Children's Literature: Invisible Storytellers* (Routledge, 2010). Now Director of the National Centre for Research in Children's Literature, she teaches on postgraduate courses on children's literature.

LAZIM, ANN

Ann Lazim is the Specialist Librarian at the Centre for Literacy in Primary Education, which has an outstandingly comprehensive collection of books and resources. It has many books, CDs and DVDs for children and a collection of professional books for teachers and online access to digital resources for visitors to the library. She plays a major role in the activities of the Centre, including organisation of the poetry competition. She is editor (with contributions from Elaine Moss and Deborah Nicholson) of the well-regarded *Core Booklist*, which is updated every two years. She contributed a chapter, 'Traditional tales: the bedrock of storytelling', to *Understanding Children's Books* (Goodwin, ed.). Ann has been IBBYUK (International Board on Books for Young People) Chair and was appointed Co-Director of IBBY World Congress in 2012.

LEWIS, DAVID

David Lewis was a primary school teacher before taking up posts at Goldsmiths College and then Exeter University to teach all aspects of primary English. He is a leading scholar on the nature and importance of children's picture books. His insights on studying and understanding picture books are shared in a number of articles and in his groundbreaking book *Reading Contemporary Picturebooks: Picturing Text* (2001, RoutledgeFalmer).

LEWIS, MAUREEN

After many years teaching in primary schools, Maureen Lewis became Research Fellow for the Exeter University Extending Literacy (EXEL) Project. With David Wray and a team of classroom teachers, she produced a framework for reading non-fiction which had considerable influence on the *National Literacy Strategy Frameworks*. Although these were abandoned in 2008, they shaped teachers' attitudes towards texts, not least non-fiction texts. The work of the EXEL Project is explained in a number of books including *Extending Literacy: Children Reading and Writing Nonfiction* (1997, Routledge), which Maureen wrote with co-author David Wray. Maureen has worked on many initiatives, including the compiling of 'curiosity kits' to encourage reluctant boys to read. She also advised on the creation of Project X, a modern reading scheme using multimodal and multimedia texts (Oxford University Press).

LITTLEFAIR, ALISON

Littlefair is the author of *Reading All Types of Writing* (1991, Open University Press). The book provides a useful taxonomy of the kinds of writing children learn to control as they move through the school years. It is compatible with the genre-based approach of the National Curriculum English orders and is a particularly clear account.

MACKAY, DAVID

Mackay is best known as one of the authors of the book and materials known as *Breakthrough to Literacy* (1970, Longman), which showed an approach that based children's early reading on their own sentences made in plastic sentence makers from folders of letters and syllables.

MARSHALL, BETHAN

Director of MA courses at King's College London, Marshall has a distinctive 'voice' on many important issues – setting homework and the danger of over-prescriptive frameworks for literacy and English lessons; see for example her chapter 'English teachers and the third way', in B. Cox (ed.) (1998) *Literacy is Not Enough: Essays on the Importance of Reading* Manchester University Press and Booktrust. Her critical approach to English teaching continues with her book written with Dylan Wiliam, *English Inside the Black Box* (2006, NFER-Nelson) and in *Testing English: Formative and Summative Approaches to English Assessment* (2011, Continuum).

MARSHALL, SYBIL

Sybil Marshall taught in a village primary school during and after the Second World War. She found that children produced writing of great vitality when it was linked with music and art. One of her books – *An Experiment in Education* (1963, Cambridge: Cambridge University Press) – described and evaluated the truly creative teaching that is possible when cross-curricular connections are forged by an imaginative practitioner. Times change and so do priorities, but Marshall's account is still inspirational.

MARTIN, JOHN R., CHRISTIE, FRANCES AND ROTHERY, JOAN

These three university teachers and researchers are the main figures in the Australian 'genre theory' school. They had reservations about 'process' approaches to writing, associated with Donald Graves and Frank Smith, and believed that different kinds of writing have distinctive global structures and linguistic features about which children needed to be directly taught. Their research in Australian schools showed that children wrote more fiction than non-fiction and that there tended not to be any direct teaching of how to write in the different genres. There have been opposing voices. Myra Barrs (1994), for instance, considers that the genre approach does not fit with what we know about children's development as writers. Children seem to learn through using 'transitional' genres including lists and 'expressive' kinds of writing.

In their paper, 'Social processes in education: a reply to Sawyer and Watson and others' (1987, Centre for Studies in Literary Education, Deakin University, Victoria) Martin, Christie and Rothery replied to their critics.

The Australian genre theorists have influence in and outside Australia and their work continues to stimulate heated discussion. Wray and Lewis adapted some of the writing categories in their EXEL Project and the National Curriculum and National Literacy Strategy have a genre-based emphasis.

MARTIN, TONY

A former president of the United Kingdom Literacy Association, Tony Martin has written and researched widely in the area of language and literacy. Many were impressed by his excellent book on reading and special needs, *The Strugglers* (1989, Open University). In a powerful case study about Leslie, a young learner with reading difficulties, Martin shows how he was able to help by a strategy of paired reading. His recent publications include, with co-authors Chira Lovat and Glynis Purnell, *The Really Useful Literacy Book* (Routledge, 2007) and *Talk for Spelling* (UKLA, 2011).

MEDWELL, JANE

Jane Medwell, Associate Professor in Education at the University of Warwick, teaches on PGCE and early years courses. Her research interests span the effective teaching of literacy, ICT and literacy, children's writing development, speaking and listening and teacher education. She has written books in Learning Matters' Achieving QTS series including, with colleagues George Moore, Viv Griffiths and David Wray, *Primary English: Knowledge and Understanding* setting out the subject knowledge that underpins successful English teaching. One outcome of her research into children's handwriting development is her article with David Wray 'Handwriting – a forgotten art?' in *Language and Education*, 22 (1), 2008: 34–47.

MEEK-SPENCER, MARGARET

Margaret Meek-Spencer is a leading scholar in the area of the links between literature and literacy. She has written extensively about becoming literate, children's literature and the power of fiction in children's learning and development. Her books include *On Being Literate* (London: The Bodley Head, 1991) and *How Texts Teach What Readers Learn* (Stroud: The Thimble Press, 1988) – which must be one of the most influential books on literacy ever written. With Aidan Warlow and Griselda Barton she edited *The Cool Web: The Pattern of Children's Reading* (1977, The Bodley Head), which is a collection of fifty chapters by distinguished authors who are bound by their belief that stories are a major way of making sense of our experience. Her book on information texts –

Information and Book Learning (1996, The Thimble Press) – has contributed considerably to our understanding of this difficult aspect of literacy.

MILLARD, ELAINE

Millard has written about several aspects of primary English, including reading in the middle years, but is particularly known for her book on gender and literacy in which she argues that the very act of reading is often seen as 'gendered' – *Differently Literate: Boys, Girls and the Schooling of Literacy* (1997, London: Routledge-Falmer). Her interest in teachers' use of strategies that build on children's engagement with popular culture, media and new technologies is explored in *Popular Literacies, Childhood and Schooling* (2005) with Jackie Marsh (Routledge).

MILLER, LINDA

Based at the Open University's Centre for Curriculum and Teaching Studies, Linda Miller has written and researched extensively on the literacy experiences of very young children. She is concerned that early years practitioners feel able to interpret the Foundation Stage curriculum in creative ways rather than feeling pressurised into preparing children for practice characteristic of Key Stage 1 classrooms. Her book with R. Drury and R. Campbell, *Exploring Early Years Education and Care* (David Fulton, 2002), reveals her interest in different kinds of early childhood setting in both the UK and in other countries. Her book with Linda Pound, *Theories and Approaches to Learning in the Early Years* (Sage, 2010), communicates the opportunities and challenges for the early years teacher today.

MINNS, HILARY

Now based at the University of Warwick, Minns has researched and written on all aspects of language and learning and is particularly well known for her study of the emergent literacy of five four year olds – *Read it to Me Now! Learning at Home and at School* (Buckingham: Open University Press, 1997 edition).

MISKIN, RUTH

Author of books setting out phonic teaching programmes, she believes in the systematic teaching of the alphabet to children in reception and Year 1, and of phonics, both 'synthetic' and 'analytic'. Her forceful views have brought critics as well as admirers and are expressed in 'Fast track to reading', *The Times Educational Supplement Primary Magazine* and in a 'good practice' video from OFSTED, 22 January 1999.

MOON, CLIFF

Author of many publications on reading, Cliff Moon is known particularly for *Individualised Reading* published by the National Centre for Language and Literacy. This useful book used to be updated yearly, but the last edition was published in 2007. Moon placed books in twelve colour-coded categories based on their 'readability', but was cautious about assigning ages to stages. He offered the lists to teachers as a rough guide and believed that a child's interests are a factor in selecting a book.

MORRIS, JOYCE

Joyce Morris is known for her belief in phonics as the basis of learning to read. She describes the phonics work in her reading programme as 'linguistically informed' (see, for example, her chapter entitled 'New phonics for old' in D.V. Thackray (ed.) *Growth in Reading* (London: Ward Lock, 1979). Morris took issue with the Goodman-Smith notion that learning to read is 'natural'. When thinking about Joyce

Morris' position on whether or not learning to read is 'natural' I am always reminded of Keith Gains' entertaining analogy that learning to read is about as natural as 'a vegetarian hedgehog-flavoured pot noodle' (chapter on special literacy needs in Beard, 1993, *Teaching Literacy, Balancing Perspectives*).

NEATE, BOBBIE

Author of *Finding Out About Finding Out* (London: Hodder & Stoughton, 1992), Bobbie Neate is a writer of children's information books, editor and reviewer. She has written about the structures and registers of children's information texts and has firm views on what 'good' non-fiction texts should be like and how children are best helped to acquire study skills.

OPIE, IONA AND OPIE, PETER

The Opies are compilers of anthologies of poetry and nursery rhymes (*The Oxford Dictionary of Nursery Rhymes*, 1951) and fairy stories (*The Classic Fairy Tales*, 1974, Oxford University Press), and researchers of children's playground rhymes (*The Language and Lore of School Children*, 1959, Oxford University Press).

The Opie Collection of Children's Literature is housed in the Bodleian Library, Oxford.

O'SULLIVAN, OLIVIA

Co-Director of the Power of Reading Project at the Centre for Literacy in Primary Education, O'Sullivan has expertise in all aspects of primary English including using ICT texts and reading on screen. She engaged in research into children's spelling development at the Centre and one outcome was *Understanding Spelling* (Routledge, 2007) written with Anne Thomas. She is also, with colleagues Kimberley Safford and Myra Barrs, author of *Boys in the Margin* (CLPE, 2004), in which drama, discussion and interactive ICT were found to be successful ways of helping reluctant readers and writers to become more successful.

PAINE, JOHN

John edited the English Association and UKLA's primary journal *English 4–11* since it began publication in 1991 until 2010 and organised the Association's annual picture book awards. His enthusiasm for quality children's books of all kinds continues to inspire teachers. For a number of years he was Treasurer of the United Kingdom Literacy Association (UKLA).

PALMER, SUE

A former teacher and head teacher, Sue Palmer is a leading independent literacy consultant. She is known for her creative and flexible approach to interpreting current requirements in primary English. She lectures, reviews books for teachers and children and writes books and articles on educational topics, including grammar and spelling.

She has written, with co-author Pie Corbett in 2003, *Literacy: What Works?* and with Ros Bayley *Foundations of Literacy: a Balanced Approach to Language, Listening and Literacy Skills in the Early Years* (2004). *Toxic Childhood* (2007, second edition) attracted worldwide interest and alerted educators and parents to the importance of children having exercise, a good diet and plenty of sleep as a defence against certain troubling aspects of life in the modern world. This book was followed up by *Detoxing Childhood: What Parents Need to Know to Raise Bright, Balanced Children* (Orion, 2008). In *21st Century Boys* (Orion, 2010) she offers practical suggestions to keep up boys' interest and nurture their progress at school.

Sue Palmer holds to clear principles and speaks out when she feels new proposals or new developments threaten the well-being and learning of children. She is always concerned about mechanistic approaches to assessment and the sort of unrealistic expectations of young children that hinder creative teaching.

PERERA, KATHARINE

Now Professor Emeritus, she has worked as a teacher, journal editor and as Professor of Educational Linguistics at Manchester University. A member of the Cox Committee, she has written many books and articles on aspects of primary language and literacy, for example *Children's Writing and Reading: Analysing Classroom Language* (1984, Oxford: Basil Blackwell) and was for some years the editor of the *Journal of Child Language*.

PERKINS, MARGARET

An experienced teacher of young children and respected early years specialist, Perkins runs the primary graduate programme at the University of Reading. She is the author, with Diana Godwin, of *Teaching Language and Literacy in the Early Years* (David Fulton, 2002).

PETERS, MARGARET

Peters is author of one of the most influential books on an aspect of children's language – *Spelling: Caught or Taught?* (1967, Routledge). It was published in a second edition as *Spelling: Caught or Taught – A New Look* (1985). Peters believed that good verbal ability, interest in words, good visual perception and careful handwriting all seemed to be linked with good spelling.

PIAGET, JEAN

A developmentalist and psychologist who described stages of development but did not write directly about classroom matters, Piaget nevertheless exerted considerable influence on teaching approaches. His view on language – in a nutshell – was that it is only one important way of dealing with experience alongside other kinds of mental functioning. After about age eleven years, when children hypothesise about phenomena not actually present, Piaget considered language took on a more important role.

In stressing the importance of a stimulating environment in which a young child can learn by using objects, the role of interaction with adults and peers was sometimes undervalued by educators influenced by his work. The work of both Bruner and Vygotsky restored language to a central position in children's learning. One of Piaget's clearest considerations of his view of the role of language is in Chapter 5, 'Language', in *Six Psychological Studies* (1968, Random House, New York: Vintage Books).

His adaptive model of learning remains useful. The metaphor is of the digestive system: we *assimilate* any item of new learning (by altering it to fit with existing frameworks just as gastric juices prepare food intake) and *accommodate* our existing knowledge base to take in the new (just as the organs of digestion reshape to accept food). For me, this is one of the most powerful models of how we learn. We must also remember that the distinction between 'spontaneous' concepts – those that we learn through everyday living (mother, cup, happy) and 'non-spontaneous' or 'scientific' concepts – those usually acquired through formal education (solution, feudal, igneous) was made by Piaget although the ideas were usefully extended by Vygotsky.

Piaget has also contributed to our understanding of children's play as an essentially assimilatory activity. In his book *Play, Dreams and Imitation in Childhood* (Routledge & Kegan Paul edition, 1962) he links the satisfactions children get from telling stories and reading fiction with play and daydream. There are links here between Piaget's thinking and the work of Freud, 1908, Winnicott, 1972 and Britton, 1971. New editions of some of Piaget's books have been published in the Routledge Classics series.

PLOWDEN, BRIDGET

Bridget Plowden chaired the committee which, in 1967, produced the 1,100-page report on primary education known as the Plowden Report. The proposals included setting up 'educational priority areas', the expansion of part-time nursery education, greater parental involvement in school and the abolition of corporal punishment. However, Lady Plowden is remembered most for the child-centred approach to teaching and learning she recommended. She believed learning should be active and that while direction by teachers and the practice of skills should be included in the programme, too much formal work was inappropriate for children under eleven. Her views had a major influence on primary practice and the creators of the first National Curriculum orders reacted to what some felt was too unstructured an approach by imposing a subject-centred curriculum. Her critics have felt that she tended to project infant practice into the later primary years encouraging teachers to plan work round projects and themes. While the best project work awakened children's interest and produced lively talk and writing, the less successful work lacked a clear content and focus. Classroom organisation for children's activities in English and other lessons has also been a contentious issue. The Plowden Report praised individual and group work and this has attracted criticism that some learning is best achieved in class-based teaching. This concern has led to requirements for some class teaching in both the National Curriculum, in all its editions, and the National

495

Literacy Strategy (the latter was abandoned in 2008).

The educational climate has changed considerably since The Plowden Report was published and a much more systematic model of teaching primary English is now in place. Nevertheless, the notion that children should be active in their learning and that school activities should be enjoyable is one that we would do well to hang on to.

POWLING, CHRIS

A former teacher, head teacher, college lecturer and broadcaster, Chris Powling continues to write inspiring books for children (for example stories in A&C Black's White Wolves series and books for Oxford University's Project X). *The Book About Books* (A&C Black) which he created with Scoular Anderson informs in an entertaining way and asks questions like 'What is a classic?' This would be very helpful to teachers guiding children's author studies. Chris Powling is a former editor of *Books for Keeps* and author of professional books. With co-author Morag Styles he edited *A Guide to Poetry 0–16* (1996, London and Reading: Books for Keeps).

REEDY, DAVID

For some years Senior Adviser in Primary Language and Communication for the London Borough of Barking, David Reedy has researched and published in the area of literacy in the early and primary years. His books include, with Jeni Riley, *Writing for Different Purposes* (Paul Chapman). He was President of the United Kingdom Reading Association (2009–11) and has engaged his members in the ever-present debate about the initial teaching of reading.

REID, DEE

An educational consultant and author, Dee Reid has written about a number of language and literacy topics including special literacy needs and how to meet them, for example in her book with Diana Bentley *Supporting Struggling Readers* (2007). One outcome of her classroom-based project on role play in the early years was *Starting with Role Play* published by Hopscotch Books.

REYNOLDS, KIMBERLEY

Reynolds founded the Centre for Research in Children's Literature at the University of Surrey, Roehampton, before becoming Professor of Children's Literature at the University of Newcastle upon Tyne. She runs postgraduate courses and supervises doctorates on children's literature at Newcastle; the resources of Seven Stories, Centre for Children's Books, including considerable archive material, are available to students. Professor Reynolds has published a large number of books and articles including her edited book *Modern Children's Literature* (Palgrave Macmillan, 2005).

RILEY, JENI

Jeni Riley is a leading specialist in the literacy development of young children, based at the London Institute of Education. Two of her best-known books are *The Teaching of Reading* (1996, London: Paul Chapman) based on her research into reading in reception classrooms and, with David Reedy, *Developing Writing for Different Purposes* (2000, London: Paul Chapman). She is one of the editors of the *SAGE Handbook of Writing Development* (Beard *et al.*, 2009).

ROSE, JIM

Professor Rose is best known for his report, *Review of the Teaching of Early Reading* (Nottingham: DfES Publications, 2006). This report, commissioned by the then Secretary of State for Education in England, argues the case for making synthetic phonics the preferred method for the teaching of early reading. However, in all fairness one should point out that Professor Rose recommended that the teaching of phonics were embedded in a reading programme that acknowledged the role of the other cue-systems and the availability of quality books. It was what he wrote about phonics that was seized on and this has had a considerable impact on national educational policy in the UK. For a critical appraisal of Professor Rose's recommendations, see Wyse and Styles in *Literacy*, 41 (1), April 2007. The Rose Curriculum, setting out a plan for a more integrated primary curriculum, rather than one that was subject centred, was never put into practice as the government changed to a coalition in May 2010.

ROSEN, CONNIE

Connie and Harold Rosen were directors of the Schools Council Project 'Language in the primary school', one outcome of which was *The Language of Primary School Children* (1974, Penguin). This book, full of examples of lively, creative language work showing the links between language and learning, inspired many students and teachers. It belongs to a time when we spoke about primary language work rather than English work.

ROSEN, MICHAEL

Rosen is the author of many books of poetry with the rhythms of natural speech and about the everyday concerns of children, including *Wouldn't You Like to Know* and *You Can't Catch Me*, and picture books such as *We're Going on a Bear Hunt* (Walker Books) illustrated by Helen Oxenbury. He is also known for his broadcasting – he is presenter of 'Treasure Islands' on Radio 4 – and speaks and writes about wider aspects of literacy, see for example his book for teachers and parents

Did I Hear You Write? He visits schools and works with children of all age groups throughout this country and overseas. He made children's enjoyment of reading and writing poetry the centrepiece of his Children's Laureateship, 2007–09.

SASSOON, ROSEMARY

A specialist in educational and medical aspects of handwriting, Rosemary Sassoon has made a major contribution to our understanding of the factors that affect children's handwriting. She has lectured all over the world and produced many publications including *Handwriting: A New Perspective* and *Handwriting: A Way to Teach It*, both published in 1990 by Stanley Thornes. Her work has continued with her reflections on the future predicament of our descendents now that society relies on electronic resources for much communication. This issue is explored in *Keeping Chronicles: Preserving History Through Written Memorabilia* (A&C Black, 2010).

SMITH, FRANK

Smith, together with Kenneth and Yetta Goodman, is associated with the psycholinguistic approaches to the teaching of reading influential in the 1970s and 1980s. The starting point for this model is the young reader's expectations about the text. Then he or she is encouraged to test out these expectations or predictions. Mistakes are regarded as 'miscues' and systematic attention to these – 'miscue analysis' – helps teachers give appropriate support. Thus the reading process is seen as essentially interactive, predictive and to do with getting meaning from text. Among his many publications are *Understanding Reading* (1971) and *Psycholinguistics and Reading* (1972), both published by Holt, Rinehart & Winston. Smith fell out of favour because of his unwillingness to recognise the role of phonics in teaching reading. His argument was that a phonics approach does not provide an entirely reliable word decoding system and meaning tends to be marginalised. Smith's positive legacy is twofold. First, he has helped keep in our minds the importance of quality materials to make children feel reading is worthwhile. The term 'real books approach' has often been used pejoratively, but there is no doubt that it has encouraged the publication of excellent books and resources both inside and outside structured reading approaches. More recently, the gap between quality books and reading scheme books has narrowed. Second, Smith is one of those who has emphasised the crucial role of the adult as expert reader to model the reading process. He will always be associated with the 'apprenticeship' metaphor. The importance of the adult's role continues in current approaches to the teaching of reading.

When it comes to writing, Smith will be remembered for drawing attention to 'composition' and 'transcription' as two different elements in the process (see Smith, 1982, *Writing and the Writer*). These terms are still used frequently by teachers and educational writers and used in assessment and record keeping materials. Smith recommended that children concentrated first on 'composition' – the organisation of what they want to say – and then on 'transcription' – the secretarial aspects including spelling, punctuation and presentation. The practice of encouraging children to plan their writing and to write first and second drafts has been encouraged in the National Curriculum, Key Stages 1 and 2; however, some of the writing required first draft response.

STYLES, MORAG

Known for her work on poetry (*The Books for Keeps Guide to Poetry 0–16*), Styles was editor of two books on children's literature – *After Alice* and *The Prose and the Passion* (1992, London: Cassell) with her colleagues at Homerton College, Eve Bearne and Victor Watson. She has turned her attention to the importance of visual texts. Her wide-ranging scholarship is evident in *Reading Lessons from the Eighteenth Century: Mothers, Children and Texts* (2006, Pied Piper Publishing Ltd) with Evelyn Arizpe and Shirley Brice-Heath.

SWANN, JOAN

A sociolinguist with an interest in children's cultural worlds, Swann is known for her work on gender and race issues: see for example her book *Girls, Boys and Language* (Blackwell, 1992). Recently, emphasis in the UK has changed from a concern for girls' possible disadvantage in talk contexts, very evident in Swann's work, to worry about boys' achievements in literacy. Her book with Rajend Mesthrie, *Sociolinguistics and Education* (Edinburgh University Press, 2009) covers topics and issues of concern and interest to teachers of all age groups: multilingualism, gender and dialect in the classroom.

TIZARD, JACK AND HUGHES, MAUREEN

The work of Tizard and Hughes on the important contribution to learning made by the home environment, see *Young Children Learning: Talking and Thinking at Home and at School* (1994, London: Fontana Press), has been most influential. They contrasted the lively demeanour of children in their research when they were in the home environment compared with a less linguistically active one in the nursery.

In his later work, with Greenhough, Hughes has studied how schools can encourage quality conversations at home, see in 'Parents' and teachers' interventions in children's reading', *British Educational Research Journal*, 1998, 24(4): 283–398.

TOWNSEND, JOHN ROWE

Townsend is a writer for both children and adults. The definitive edition of *Written for Children: an Outline of English-Language Children's Literature* was published in 1995 by The Bodley Head. It is a scholarly, perceptive and often amusing contribution to the study of children's literature.

TUCKER, NICHOLAS

Honorary Senior Lecturer in Cultural and Community Studies at Sussex University, Nicholas Tucker is a major contributor to our understanding of children's response to books and to concepts of childhood at different times in history. He reviews books for journals and newspapers, is a frequent broadcaster and lectures at conferences throughout the world. In one of his most influential books – *The Child and the Book* (1981, Cambridge University Press) – he relates children's response to reading to their intellectual and affective development. An educational psychologist by training, he writes from careful observation of how children approach books rather than how adults think they should. He has written a number of books analysing the work of authors of children's books, for example *Darkness Made Visible: Inside the World of Philip Pullman* (Wizard Books, 2002) and, with co-author Nikki Gamble, *Family Fictions* (Continuum, 2001).

UNSTEAD, SUE

For many years a publisher of children's books, Sue Unstead is now a freelance editor, reviewer and writer. She has written insightful articles and book reviews for journals like *Books for Keeps*. She has written particularly perceptively about children's non-fiction; her articles for *Books for Keeps* include those on subjects like books on green issues and on choosing diction-aries for children. Her work is contained in the *Books for Keeps* online archive at www.booksforkeeps.co.uk.

VYGOTSKY, L.S.

Vygotsky's best-known book, *Thought and Language* (1986, Kozulin edition, Cambridge, Mass.: MIT), is about concept development but has relevance to all aspects of language and thinking, including those pertinent to reading and writing.

Primary practice benefits particularly from the following aspects of Vygotsky's work.

First, he stresses the social nature of learning – interaction with other human beings accompanies all aspects of development including, of course, language development. This supports practice which includes much collaboration, co-operation and discussion between pupils. Second, he recognises that it is verbal communication through talk and writing that makes possible the higher order kinds of thinking and meaning making. Control over the word 'meaning' helps a child clinch understanding of a concept. Language is needed to make links between the 'spontaneous' concepts children bring to school and the 'scientific' concepts that are part of formal learning. A child might bring to school the spontaneous concepts 'frog' and 'pond' where he or she might, in the science lesson, add the related scientific concepts 'amphibian' and 'habitat'. Third, he recognises the importance of adult intervention in children's learning. The adult's skilfully judged comments and questions can extend a child's thinking. Part of successful teaching is to do with estimating a child's 'zone of proximal development' – the space between where he or she is intellectually at present and where they could be with the right sort of adult help. Bruner extends Vygotsky's 'zone of proximal development' theory by using the metaphor of 'scaffolding' to describe the enabling role of the teacher or parent.

WADE, BARRY

Wade is the author of many books on reading including the influential *Reading for Real* (ed.) (1990, Open University Press) and a director of a project on books for babies which led to the publication of *Baby Power*.

WATERLAND, LIZ

Liz Waterland was an infant teacher who found inspiration in the Goodman-Smith model of reading. In her book *Read With Me* (1985, Stroud: The Thimble Press) she promoted an approach to reading that regarded the young learner as an apprentice who would read alongside the teacher who modelled the process. She was also in favour of 'real' books rather than those written for a reading scheme. Since her book was written the climate has changed. Publishers use respected authors to write books for their programmes so the social stereotypes and the linguistic impoverishment of reading schemes is largely a thing of the past. Research into phonological aspects of learning to read (for example by Bryant and Bradley, 1985; Goswami and Bryant, 1991) indicates that children need to be helped to acquire phonemic knowledge and understanding as well as the 'big shapes' of reading.

Nevertheless, Waterland drew attention to the importance of quality books and the search for meaning as an important basis for learning to read.

WATSON, VICTOR

A Director of Research at Homerton College, Cambridge, Victor Watson was editor, with his colleagues Morag Styles and Eve Bearne, of *After Alice* (Cassell, 1992) and its companion book *The Prose and the Passion*. He is also a specialist in books for children in the eighteenth and nineteenth centuries and reviews for the *TES* and for *Signal*. He is editor of *The Cambridge Guide to Children's Books in English* (2001).

WELLS, GORDON

Formerly Director of the 'Bristol Language at Home and School' longitudinal research study, Wells is now Professor of Education at the University of California. During his time on the Bristol project he studied the spontaneous speech of children and caregivers. In his books, for example *The Meaning Makers* (Hodder & Stoughton, 1987, now in a revised edition 2009), he identifies talk as a major means of making sense of experience and school learning. Story and talk about stories were shown in his research to be linked to success at reading and writing at school. One of his clearest accounts of the role of talk is his essay 'The centrality of talk in education' in *Thinking Voices*, a book about the National Oracy Project, edited by Kate Norman and published in 1992 by Hodder & Stoughton.

WHITE, DOROTHY

The 'message' of some books survives through time and this is true of children's librarian Dorothy White's fascinating diary of her daughter's early book experiences – *Books Before Five* (1956, New Zealand Council for Educational Research). The account emphasises the interplay between characters and incidents in the books read and real-life incidents. For example, when Carol has been given a little smack, she and her mother find it helpful to read about Beatrix Potter's *Tom Kitten* whose mother also loses patience. The comforting message is that parents still love their children even when they make them, temporarily, cross. (A more recent example of a single case study is R. Campbell's (1999) *Literacy from Home to School: Reading with Alice*.)

500

WHITEHEAD, MARIAN R.

Whitehead has made a major contribution to our understanding of early years language, literacy and literature. After some years of teaching young children she took up a role at Goldsmiths College as Lecturer and then Senior Lecturer teaching Early Years students on BA (Ed.) courses and co-ordinating the MA in Language and Literature. Her publications are constantly revised into new editions. *Language and Literacy in the Early Years* is now in its fourth edition (Sage, 2010), covers new research and has excellent input on young learners with mother tongues other than English. *Supporting Children's Language and Literacy Development in the Early Years* (2009) stresses the enjoyment involved in supporting young children's development as speakers, listeners, writers and readers. Marian Whitehead's belief in the role of picture books, nursery rhymes and stories as crucial, imagination-developing resources in the early years classroom comes through strongly in her books and articles. There are, of course, a number of others who have written illuminatingly about early years language and literacy – Ann Browne, Robin Campbell, Diane Godwin, Cathy Nutbrown, Peter Hannon and Margaret Perkins, to name a few – but Marian Whitehead was one of the first to do so and brings her own experience as an avid reader of fiction to her analyses.

WILKINSON, ANDREW

Wilkinson is known particularly for his research into children's writing development and the assessment of progress. The study produced what has become known as the Crediton Model of writing assessment and the findings are set out in his book with authors G. Barnsley, P. Hanna and M. Swann in *Assessing Language Development* (1980, Oxford: Oxford University Press). Writing was assessed mainly in terms of its meaning and analysed in terms of categories like thought, feeling and social awareness. However, the growth of syntax from the simple and literal to more elaborate syntax and cohesion was included.

WILSON, ANGELA

After some years as a classroom teacher and as a Schools Inspector, Angela Wilson joined the North-East Wales Institute of Higher Education in Wrexham as a Senior Lecturer in Education. Her interests and writing are to do with all aspects of language, literacy and literature, but perhaps she is known to many primary teachers and students especially for her work on subject knowledge. Her book *Language Knowledge for Primary Teachers: A Guide to Textual, Grammatical and Lexical Study*, now in a fourth edition with co-author Julia Scanlon (David Fulton, 2011), is both sound and entertaining and refers to modern means of communication like Facebook, texting and emailing.

WRAY, DAVID

A university professor and researcher, David Wray has written many books and articles on all aspects of English teaching and language and literacy. He has lectured widely, directed research projects and organised conferences.

He was Co-Director of the Exeter Extending Literacy (EXEL) Project funded by the Nuffield Foundation. This 'grass roots' research was school based and the findings were the basis of the National Literacy Strategy's non-fiction programmes. Building on research in Australia (for example that of Martin and Rothery, 1986), Wray and his team proposed six non-fiction writing types – recount, report, instruction, explanation, persuasive and discussion – each with distinctive features and purpose. He has also suggested how teachers can use writing frames (structured writing plans) and genre exchange (writing in one genre following reading in another) to develop children's writing. One outcome of the EXEL Project was his book with co-researcher Maureen Lewis – *Extending Literacy: Children Reading and Writing Non-fiction* (Routledge, 1997). The use of writing frames has caused some controversy. Wray and Lewis never intended the frames to be used to teach genre and they would be the first to advise against mechanistic or too frequent use.

Now Professor of Education at the University of Warwick, David Wray has continued to carry out research and to write books and articles on different kinds of texts, on ebooks and on handwriting. With Jane Medwell, and other colleagues at Warwick University, he wrote the series of books for Learning Matters, for example *Primary English: Knowledge and Understanding* (Continuum Books, 2009).

WYSE, DOMINIC

Now involved in university teaching and research, Dominic Wyse has a background in the classroom where, for some time, he was an English Co-ordinator. He teaches and writes on all aspects of primary English but has a particular interest in writing development. His book, with Russell Jones, *Teaching English, Language and Literacy* (London and New York: RoutledgeFalmer, 2007, third edition), indicates the issues the reflective practitioner should keep in mind. His book with Russell Jones entitled *Creativity in the Primary Classroom* (2004) aims to support teachers who disdain the photocopied worksheet and seek to put in place an exciting approach to teaching that will 'spark a flame in young children's minds' and shape their time in school.

My ten top texts

Some professional books in the area of English, language and literacy have timeless qualities which mean that they will always have something of real worth to say to teachers and student teachers. Here is a list of books that I value.

Barrs, Myra and Cork, Valerie (2001) *The Reader in the Writer: The Links Between the Study of Literature and Writing Development at Key Stage 2* London: CLPE/London Borough of Southwark.

Drawing on a year's research in Year 5 classrooms, this book helps teachers reflect on the links between reading quality literature and children's own writing. The research team found that children engaged most strongly with books that had an emotional appeal and significance for them. They also found that reading aloud can help develop an understanding of the features of different kinds of text because it gives children the chance to hear and to talk about their distinctive rhythms and styles. This is the most coherent and exciting analysis so far of how reading and writing connect.

Britton, James (1970) *Language and Learning* London: Allen Lane: The Penguin Press.

What is the impact of language acquisition on how young children think and operate in the world? In answering this question the author draws on the work of philosophers, psychologists, linguists and psychiatrists as well as of teachers and educationists. James Britton also makes an original contribution to theory: we use language as a means of organising a representation of the world and use this 'world picture' to steer the course of our lives. All this is brought to a practical level when he turns to language use in school, giving lively examples of primary school drama and interesting writing from across the age ranges. The author claims to have learnt as much about children's language by being a parent as by being a teacher and this is, perhaps, the reason why the book has such a human feel to it.

Chambers, Aidan (1993) *Tell Me: Children, Reading and Talk* Stroud: The Thimble Press (there is a new edition, combined with the companion book *The Reading Environment*, 2011).

How can we help children deepen their response to the books they read? This is the timeless challenge of the English lesson. Building on a wealth of classroom experience, his own and that of others, Chambers pinpoints 'book talk' as the crucial factor in encouraging reflective reading. My students and I have found the 'three sharings' recommended – sharing enthusiasms, sharing puzzles and sharing connections – of great practical help and inspiration in the classroom.

Hughes, Ted (1967) *Poetry in the Making: An Anthology of Poems and Programmes from 'Listening and Writing'* London: Faber and Faber (a revised edition was published in 2008).

Arising from Hughes' talks for a radio programme (way back in the 1960s) for children of about ten to fourteen years, this book aims to inspire young learners to lift their own pens and find a writing 'voice'. However, he does not do this by offering models of writing for children to emulate. For Ted Hughes it is not a matter of showing children how to write but rather of explaining 'how to say what you really mean'. He claims point and value for poetry in such chapters as 'Capturing animals', 'Wind and weather' and 'Writing about people'. Writing a poem involves settling your mind very intensely on something. Hughes found his boyhood experience of fishing a helpful 'mental exercise in concentration' on which he drew years later as a poet. Watching a float on the water demands the same sort of intense concentration as that involved in writing a poem. Would it help if we asked children to choose an object in the classroom and write about it intensely? Among the many reasons for treasuring this book are Hughes' insights about his own poems, particularly *The Thought Fox* and *View of a Pig*.

Hunt, Peter (1995) *The Illustrated History of Children's Books* Oxford: Oxford University Press.

There is something very attractive about a large tome with copious colour illustrations which include a page from William Crane's *The Baby's Own Aesop* (1887), a decorated endpaper of *Little Red Riding Hood* (1804) by Benjamin Tabart, and Peter Farmer's cover for the 1970 paperback of *Tom's Midnight Garden*. This celebration of books written for and adopted by children over the centuries takes us from the medieval horn book to picture books, pop-ups and multimedia comics. Organised as twelve fine essays, the book covers children's literature in the USA, Canada, Australia and New Zealand as well as the British Isles.

Meek, Margaret (1996) *Information and Book Learning* Stroud: The Thimble Press.

For me, this is the most insightful exploration we have of the issues that surround helping children to read to learn. It is scholarly, speculative and extremely thought provoking. The author's main problem with children's non-fiction texts, whether print or electronic, is that they present 'the facts' as a given rather than encouraging speculation and further research. There is helpful comment on individual books to support learning in particular parts of the curriculum. We get glimpses of what information texts could be like: a good information text would share an author's experience and enthusiasm and encourage a young reader's further thought and research. You may be wondering why a book on informational kinds of reading is included in a list of top texts about English. The reason is that we can never predict when children might need to unlock information – perhaps about the history of a place or custom – to enrich their understanding of and enjoyment of a novel or poem. Of course the English class is the home of discussions about human, and perhaps controversial, issues where children need to have an informed view to argue their case with conviction.

Meek, Margaret, Warlow, Aidan and Barton, Griselda (eds) (1977) *The Cool Web: The Pattern of Children's Reading* London: The Bodley Head.

We have a large, rich palette here. Arranged in five sections, the fifty essays in this book are by authors and critics across the whole world of children's literature. Each author is concerned in their own way with the nature and growth of children's literary understandings. There are children's writers (Joan Aiken, Maurice Sendak), psychologists (D.W. Harding, Richard Gregory) and literary critics (Barbara Hardy). A well-thumbed part of my own copy is Barbara Hardy's essay on narrative. At first, essays from so many different perspectives can seem overwhelming, but the editors' section introductions are of considerable help.

Styles, Morag, Bearne, Eve and Watson, Victor (1992) *After Alice: Exploring Children's Literature* London: Cassell.

These lively essays by distinguished contributors, including Helen Arnold, Jan Ormerod, Chris Powling and Michael Rosen, cover such important areas as media literacy, storytelling and children as authors and poets. The book provides a challenging but interesting and thought-provoking introduction to issues in the world of children's literature.

Townsend, John Rowe (1995, sixth edition) *Written For Children* London: The Bodley Head.

If you believe that nursery and primary teachers need to be knowledgeable about children's books and understand something of their history, this book is extremely helpful as a resource. What makes it stand out from other texts on this huge theme is the author's willingness to share his own strong feelings about what he thinks is admirable and what less so – with style, humour and courage.

Whitehead, Marian (2010, fourth edition) *Language and Literacy in the Early Years* London: Paul Chapman.

All the important issues about language and literacy from birth to eight years are covered here. Insights from a wide range of research in the fields of linguistics, psycholinguistics and sociolinguistics are carefully applied to the early years. So this is a scholarly book that sets out a theoretical underpinning for those working with very young children. The author rejects 'quick-fix' approaches to language and narrow prescriptive rules for teaching it. The many examples of young children learning to talk and write and the photographs of children using language in different settings make this a creative and life-enhancing text. Above all, it shows the imagination-expanding power of picture books and stories.

My top fifteen children's books published since 2000

Almond, David (2010) *My Name is Mina* London: Hodder Children's Books. 9+

Mina is Michael's friend in David Almond's book *Skellig*. She does not cope well with school routines and requirements, but she has an extraordinary imagination and this is evident in the hugely original and insightful writing in her journal. 'Words should wander and meander. They should fly like owls and flicker like bats and slip like cats. They should murmur or scream or sing.' The typography in the book varies to enhance the meaning, and so we have print that gives the impression of handwriting and which varies at times in size and print strength.

Browne, Anthony (2003) *The Shape Game* London: Doubleday. 8+

A family visit to the gallery starts out without much enthusiasm, but the children's experiences help them appreciate the paintings. This picture book showing Browne's distinctive surrealist images arose out of the 'Visual Paths', London Tate Britain's visual literacy project for primary age children.

Duffy, Carol Ann and Hyde, Catherine (illustrator) (2009) *The Princess Blankets* London: Templar. 9+

'There was once a princess who was always cold … ' So the king and queen ordered fires to be lit and the warmest blankets and heaviest fleeces to be brought to the palace. Nothing seemed to work, so the king offered a reward to anyone who could help solve the problem. First an unsuitable person comes forward, but then a musician arrives and plays on his flute and all is well. This modern fairy story is engrossing and illustrated with pictures that shimmer and glow.

French, Vivian and Bartlett, Alison (illustrator) (2004) *T-Rex* London: Walker. 6+

A young boy is taken to a dinosaur museum by his grandfather. He finds out what we know from fossil evidence about this huge prehistoric creature. However, there are some things that 'We don't really know, it was millions and millions of years ago!' With arresting pictures and a lively rhyming text, this book helps young readers understand that knowledge is sometimes provisional.

McCaughrean, Geraldine and Williams, Sophy (illustrator) (2003) *Oxford Treasury of Fairy Tales* Oxford: Oxford University Press. 5+

These twenty stories from the European tradition are ideal for reading aloud. There are classic favourites like Cinderella and Snow White and Andersen's The Little Mermaid, and some lesser-known ones like Cap-of-Rushes on a Cinderella type theme. The illustrations range from full-page paintings to tiny sketches of objects and animals.

McGough, Roger and Monks, Lydia (illustrator) (2003) *All the Best* London: Puffin. 8+

Winner of the CLPE Award for Poetry in 2004, this anthology selects poems from McGough's other anthologies. The black and white illustrations match the poet's inventiveness and humour.

Manning, Mick and Granström, Brita (2009) *Woolley Mammoth* London: Frances Lincoln. 7+

This book gives a tremendous sense of the fight for survival these animals endured during the Ice Age. It has a lyrical rhyming text, fact panels and illustrations that live on the page. With a light touch it shows young readers how fossil evidence can tell us a certain amount and then we add informed speculation. Did senior female mammoths lead the herd in migration between feeding grounds? We know that large animals like elephants and reindeer do today, so possibly mammoths did the same.

Paver, Michelle (2004) *Wolf Brother* London: Orion Children's Books. 10+

How did northern Europeans live 6,000 years ago? This first novel in the Chronicles of Ancient Darkness series tells of hunter-gathering, clans, superstitions and harsh environments. Torak, aged twelve, and his wolf ally battle against evil to save their world.

Pullman, Philip (2003) *Lyra's Oxford* London: David Fickling. 10+

This book takes young readers into an extraordinary parallel world. It includes wonderful illustrations such as John Lawrence's map of landmarks in the Dark Materials trilogy.

Queneau, Raymond (2002) *Exercices de Style* France: Gallimard Jeunesse. 10+

A young man on a bus accuses another passenger of jostling him: this event is repeated with illustrations by ninety-nine artists, including Quentin Blake and Satoshi Kitamura. The writing ranges from book blurb, reported speech and an official letter. Much to fascinate children here.

Voake, Charlotte (2004) *A Little Guide to Wild Flowers* London: Eden Project. 8+

This is a botanical reference book full of proverbs and anecdotes which will be appreciated by children living in both urban and rural settings.

Williams, Marcia (2007) *Archie's War* London: Walker Books. 8+

The scrapbook format of this picture book, written from the point of view of young Archie during the First World War, works extremely well. Cartoon characters, doodles, mementos, drawings, snippets of writing and letters are combined in wonderful collages on each double spread. This book is about growing up, albeit in exceptionally difficult circumstances, and has a timeless quality.

Willis, Jean and Ross, Tony (2003) *Tadpole's Promise* London: Andersen Press. 6+

'Promise me you'll never change' said the caterpillar to her tadpole lover. So there's no 'happy ever after' ending here, but it is an intriguing way to learn about the life cycles of frogs and butterflies.

Wilson, Jacqueline (2004) *Secrets* London: Corgi Yearling. 10+

The author explores the struggle of two children to cope with difficult families. An aim of Wilson's laureateship has been to encourage children to read the classics: this book helps by having one girl hide in the attic in the manner of her heroine, Anne Frank.

Yamamoto, Lani (2005) *Albert 2* London: Frances Lincoln. 4+

This second book in the 'Albert' series shows the little boy grappling with notions of time and a world that seems to be moving too fast.

List of entries in the Encyclopedia

Extended entries are highlighted in **bold**.

Abbreviation
Abstract noun
Accent
Acronym
Acrostic
Adjectival clause
Adjective
Adventure stories
Adverb
Adverbial clause
Adverbial phrase
Advertisements
Affix
Agreement (or concord)
Alliteration
Alphabet
Analogy
Anaphoric reference
Anecdotes
Animals (in children's stories and information texts)
Anthology
Antithesis
Antonym
Apostrophe
Apposition
Apprenticeship approach to reading
Appropriateness in language
Argument
Art and English
Article
Assessment
Assimilation and accommodation

Assonance
Atlas
Attainment Targets
Audio resources
Audit (of primary English)
Author studies
Autobiography
Autocorrect
Auxiliary verb
Ballad
Bias (in children's books)
Bible (The)
Bibliographic cue-system
Big books
'Big shapes'
Bilingualism
Biography
Blank verse
Blend
Blurb
Book making
Book review
Books for Keeps online
Bookstart
Booktrust
'Bottom-up' reading approaches
Boys' literacy
Breakthrough to Literacy
Bristol Language at Home and School Project
British Film Institute (bfi)
British Library (The)
Bullet point

Discussion text
Displays
Domestic and family novels
Drafting
Drama and English
Dual-language texts
Dyslexia
Early Learning Goals
Early years language and literacy
Ebooks
Edinburgh Reading Tests
Editing
Effective Reading Tests
Elaborated and restricted codes
Elementary schools
Elision
Ellipsis
Email
Emergent writing
Emotional literacy
Enabling adult
Encyclopedia
English 21
English Association (The)
English development plan
English/Literacy Co-ordinator (The)
English/literacy policy
English projects (themes, topics)
Environmental print
Epic poetry
Epiphany
Equal opportunities
ERIC (everyone reading in class)
Exclamation
EXEL Project
EXIT model
Explanation text
Expository text
Expressive talk and writing
Fable
Faction
Factual genres
Fairy tales
Family literacy projects
Fantasy
Fiction: choosing and using
Fiction as a source of information
Field of discourse

Figurative language
Film making
First person writing
Flash cards
Flow chart
Folk tales
Formative assessment
Foundation Stage (The)
Foundation Stage profile
Free verse
Full stop
Functional literacy
Functions of language
Gender and language development
Genre
Genre exchange
Geography and English
Gifted and talented children
Girls' literacy
Glossary
Grammar
Grapheme
Graphology
Grapho-phonic cue-system
Group reading scales
Guided reading/writing
Haiku
Handwriting
Hearing impairment
Historical novel
History and English
History of children's literature
History of children's non-fiction literature
History of the English language
**History of English teaching (in the
  primary school)**
Hobbies and English
Homographs
Homonyms
Homophones
Horn book
Horror stories
Hot seating
Hyperbole
Hypermedia
Hyperstudio
Hypertext
Hyphen

513

515

Index

Browne, Anthony 10, 62–63, 97, 107, 116, 150, 153, 163, 206, 221, 224, 244, 311, 323, 324, 336, 402, 411, 507
Browning, Robert 15, 28, 69, 179, 279
Brownjohn, Sandy 331, 399–400, 401, 480–81
Bruce, Lisa 25, 368
Bruce, Tina 94, 95, 481
Bruna, Dick 9
Bruner, Jerome 19, 93, 221, 230, 248, 250, 257, 261, 281, 383, 414, 450, 481, 500
Bryant, Peter 246, 306, 309, 319–20, 409, 458, 481, 486
Buchanan, George 196
Buckeridge, Anthony 203, 384
Buckingham, David 333, 334, 481
bullet point 50, 303
Bullock Report (1975) 50, 216, 258, 372, 478, 480
Bunting, Jane 70
Bunting, Rebecca 123, 174, 262, 263
Bunyan, John 199–200
Burnett, Frances Hodgson 72, 116, 127, 201, 412, 448
Burnham, Louise 427
Burningham, John 9, 122, 172, 206, 222, 223, 323, 412
Bussis, A. 108, 282
Butler, Dorothy 481
Byars, Betsy 11, 24, 70, 249, 266, 418, 465

Caldecott, Randolph 202, 206
Callow, Jon 429, 449, 450
Cambridge Reading 51
capitalisation 51
caption 51
Carey, Joanna 221, 223
Carle, Eric 42, 273, 360, 462
Carnegie Medal 67
carnival 15, 51–52, 288; Notting Hill Carnival 52
Carpenter, Humphrey 55–56
Carroll, Lewis 72, 162, 200, 201
Carter, Ronald 90, 269–70, 481–82
cartography 19
catalogue 52
cataphoric reference 52
Catt, Robert 28
Causley, Charles 28, 47, 99
Cave, Kathryn 9, 180
CBeebies 388, 430
CD-ROM 52–53
CDs (compact discs) 53–54
Centre for the Children's Book (Seven Stories) 66
Centre for Children's Literature, University of Cambridge 54
Centre for Literacy in Primary Education (CLPE) 17, 46, 47, 54–55, 89, 99–100, 161,

302, 313, 339, 357–58, 370, 374, 376, 435, 455, 468
Chambers, Aidan 97–98, 104–5, 124, 125, 142, 151, 204, 250, 363, 378, 444, 482
Chambers, Catherine 341
Chambers, Nancy 204, 482
Channel 4 39, 388
chapbooks 55–56, 199, 200
chart 56
Child, Lauren 221, 222, 223, 244
child-centred learning 56–57, 216, 354
children as authors 57–60
Children's Hour 351
Children's Laureate 60–63
children's literature 63–67
children's literature awards 67–68
children's literature in translation 68–69, 109, 133, 200
Childs, Rob 38
Chomsky, Noam 82, 173, 255, 256, 298–99, 421, 439–40
choosing books and resources 69
chorus 69
Christie, Frances 178, 260, 491
chronological non-fiction 69
circle time 69
Clark, Margaret 482
class discussion 69
class reader 70
classic texts 70–72
classics 72–73
clause 73, 85; adjectival 2; adverbial 4
Clay, Marie 84, 108, 123, 365, 379, 408, 482
Cleary, Beverly 3, 25
Clegg, Alex 482
cliché 73–74
Clipson-Boyles, Suzi 482–83
cloze procedure 74, 234
cluster 74
code of practice 74–75, 455
cognitive skills 401
cognitive theories 255, 256, 257, 261
cohesion 75–76; lexical cohesion 75
Cole, Babette 160
Coleridge, Samuel Taylor 27
collaborative learning 76–78
collective noun 78
colloquialism 78
colon 78
colour coding 78
Colwell, Eileen 204
comics 78–81; *Eagle* 79; *Girl* 79
comma 81
command 82
'common knowledge' between teachers and children 123
common noun 82